Encyclopedia of Business and Finance

SECOND EDITION

Editorial Board

II

Encyclopedia of Business and Finance

SECOND EDITION

VOLUME 1
A–I

Burton S. Kaliski

EDITOR IN CHIEF

MACMILLAN REFERENCE USA

An imprint of Thomson Gale, a part of The Thomson Corporation

THOMSON

GALE

Detroit • New York • San Francisco • New Haven, Conn. • Waterville, Maine • London • Munich

Encyclopedia of Business and Finance, Second Edition
Burton S. Kaliski, Editor in Chief

LIBRARY OF CONGRESS CATALOGING-IN-PUBLICATION DATA

Encyclopedia of business and finance / Burton S. Kaliski, editor-in-chief.— 2nd ed.
  p. cm.
  Includes bibliographical references and index.
  ISBN 0-02-866061-7 (set hardcover : alk. paper) — ISBN 0-02-866062-5 (volume 1 : alk. paper) — ISBN 0-02-866063-3 (volume 2 : alk. paper)
  1. Business—Encyclopedias. 2. Commerce—Encyclopedias. 3. Finance—Encyclopedias. 4. North America—Commerce—Encyclopedias. 5. Finance—North America—Encyclopedias. I. Kaliski, Burton S. II. Macmillan Reference USA.

  HF1001.E466 2007
  650.03—dc22   2006005185

This title is also available as an e-book.
ISBN 0-02-866081-1
Contact your Thomson Gale representative for ordering information.

Printed in the United States of America
10 9 8 7 6 5 4 3 2 1

Contents

V

Editorial and Production Staff

Preface

Business is the backbone of American society and is one of the keys to making our system work as well as it has for over two hundred years. Yet as a body of knowledge, business is much younger, and in its brief history, there have been few attempts to present the discipline of business in a single place. The major purpose of the *Encyclopedia of Business and Finance, Second Edition* is to summarize the body of knowledge that we know as business in one place and in language appropriate to the layperson.

This two-volume collection of over 315 articles presents a wealth of information about the major functional areas of business: accounting, economics, finance, information systems, law, management, and marketing. Articles vary in length and depth, in bibliographic support, and in writing style. Thus, the reader will encounter a variety of approaches to and perspectives about business. Some articles are quantitative, since some aspects of business are numerically based. Other articles tend more toward the qualitative to accommodate the more descriptive aspects of business. Some of the articles present an historical perspective, incorporating long-validated knowledge, while other articles focus on current concepts and more recent data. Other articles provide "how-to" advice. Regardless of the approach, available data are accurate to the best of each writer's knowledge as of 2006. All articles have the same goal: to provide useful knowledge about the business and financial world.

Because of their importance, special treatment has been given to two subject areas: careers and ethics. In each area, an overview article is followed by an article about that topic in each functional area of business. Thus, there are articles about careers in accounting, careers in economics, and so forth. There is a similiar series of articles about ethics.

There is also a strong emphasis on organizations in the fields of business and government. Wherever an organization is discussed, the article provides contact information about it, including a Web site.

Relevant business-related federal legislation is included in this work. Articles on all acts that have had a major impact on business and the government agencies that regulate them are included in the *Encyclopedia*.

Encyclopedia of Business and Finance, Second Edition includes 32 new articles. The major areas of these new contributions are in the applications of technology to business (such as cyber crime, e-marketing, identity theft, and online education), new areas of business knowledge (including agency theory, earnings management, forensic accounting, green marketing, intellectual capital, and social marketing), international topics (such as international business and international marketing), and new organizations and legislation. Further, all articles in the *Encyclopedia* have been thoroughly reviewed and updated in content and references to 2006.

Entries are arranged in alphabetical order. The *Encyclopedia* includes extensive cross-referencing of two types: "See" and "See Also" references. "See" references fall within the body of the work and refer the reader to articles disucussing that topic. For example, if one wanted to find information about bait-and-switch advertising and looked under "Bait and Switch," there would not be an article, but rather the instruction to "SEE *Ethics in Marketing; Ethics in Law for Business; Government Role in Business.*" "See Also" cross-references fall at the end of articles and direct the reader to one or more other articles that may shed more light on the topic. At the conclusion of the article on Insurance, for example, you will find "**SEE ALSO** *Investments; Personal Financial Planning.*" At the end of Volume 2, there is an extensive Index to terms and concept in the articles.

Is the knowledge contained in this work the definitive and final word on each topic? The answer is "most certainly not!" In this day and age of dynamic and rapidly growing knowledge, a positive answer would be quite inappropriate. However, this is not necessarily a negative. The information contained in this edition of *Encyclopedia of Business and Finance* is valid and reliable and enables readers to do further research by going to easily accessible sources. Today's technology offers a unique opportunity to extend one's knowledge of every topic presented, an opportunity not available so easily to previous generations.

This work was designed for different types of users. The middle school student may be looking for a starting point for a paper on careers. The high school student may be seeking background information on a major research topic, such as international trade. The businessperson may be seeking a summary of antitrust laws. The business teacher may be preparing a lesson on the history of computing. The interested layperson may simply want to learn something new about such topics as the No Child Left Behind legislation or investments.

Encyclopedia of Business and Finance, Second Edition can serve as a survey document for the many aspects of business or as a guide to those aspects. It can be the starting point for a lengthy secondary research project, or the ending point for a specific item covered within its pages. It can be used to help ask questions or to find answers. It can be used as a summary of existing knowledge or the basis for acquiring new knowledge.

A number of individuals deserve special mention for their contributions to this project. First I must thank the four associate editors: Dorothy Maxwell, Jim Maxwell, Mary Ellen Oliverio, and Allen Truell. Without their tireless efforts at securing quality writers, we would have a very small work. Second, great appreciation goes to Miranda Ferrara, the editor at Macmillan Reference USA/Thomson Gale in charge of this project, for her organization, efficiency, and human kindness throughout this entire project. In addition special thanks go to Mike Weaver and Luann Brennan also at Thomson Gale, who handled many of the technical details of the *Encyclopedia*. Lastly, I must thank all of the contributors for the best effort that each put forth to codify and record knowledge in each article. Writing for an encyclopedia is hardly a financially rewarding activity; however, it is a contribution to posterity, so what each contributor has written is of great value to current and future scholars. And, speaking for all of us, thanks to our families for their encouragement and support.

Burton S. Kaliski

List of Articles

Contributors

Mohammad J. Abdolmohammadi
Bentley College
AUDITING

Michael Alles
Rutgers University
ELECTRONIC COMMERCE

Connie Anderson
PROFESSIONAL EDUCATION

Marcia Anderson
Southern Illinois University,
Carbondale
BEHAVIORAL SCIENCE MOVEMENT
EMPLOYEE DISCIPLINE
SCIENTIFIC MANAGEMENT

Carolyn H. Ashe
University of Houston Downtown
OUTSOURCING IN THE BUSINESS
ENVIRONMENT
RECORDS MANAGEMENT

Thomas Baird
Ball State University
BUSINESS MARKETING
CONSUMER AND BUSINESS PROD-
UCTS
CUSTOMER SERVICE
DISCOUNT STORES
MARKETING CONCEPT
PACKAGING
PRODUCT LABELING
TELEMARKETING

C. Richard Baker
Adelphi University
INDEPENDENCE STANDARDS BOARD
RISK MANAGEMENT

Laurie Barfitt
Delta State University
CONSUMER PRODUCT SAFETY ACT
OF 1972
FAIR PACKAGING AND LABELING
ACT OF 1966
FEDERAL TRADE COMMISSION ACT
OF 1914
FOOD, DRUG, AND COSMETIC ACT
OF 1938
ROBINSON-PATMAN ACT OF 1936
STAGGERS RAIL AND MOTOR CAR-
RIER ACTS OF 1980

Lloyd W. Bartholome
Utah State University
MANAGEMENT INFORMATION SYS-
TEMS

Marsha L. Bayless
Stephen A. Austin State University
ELECTRONIC MAIL

Jean C. Bedard
Bentley College
ANALYTICAL PROCEDURES

Dennis R. Beresford
University of Georgia
FINANCIAL ACCOUNTING STAN-
DARDS BOARD

Robert G. Berns
Bowling Green State University
DECA
ENTREPRENEURSHIP

Craig A. Bestwick
San Francisco, California
CAREERS IN LAW FOR BUSINESS

Keith A. Bice
Bingham McHale LLP
CONTRACTS

Heather Bigley
University of Houston
COMMUNICATIONS IN BUSINESS

Lauren G. Block
Baruch College
CONSUMER BEHAVIOR

Charlotte J. Boling
University of Western Florida
INFORMATION TECHNOLOGY

Shaheen Borna
Ball State University
INTERNATIONAL MARKETING

Richard F. Bortz
Southern Illinois University,
Carbondale
JOB ANALYSIS AND DESIGN

David A. Bowers
Case Western Reserve University
BUSINESS CYCLE

Louis Braiotta, Jr.
SUNY, Binghampton
AUDIT COMMITTEES

Clarice P. Brantley
Pensacola, Florida
SEXUAL HARASSMENT

Betty J. Brown
Ball State University
FINANCIAL LITERACY
SPREADSHEETS
TRANSPORTATION

Clifford Brown
Bentley College
ACTIVITY-BASED MANAGEMENT
COST ALLOCATION

Michael Brun
Illinois State University
FACTORS OF PRODUCTION

Phyllis Bunn
Delta State University
CONSUMER PRODUCT SAFETY ACT
OF 1972
FAIR PACKAGING AND LABELING
ACT OF 1966
FEDERAL TRADE COMMISSION ACT
OF 1914
FOOD, DRUG, AND COSMETIC ACT
OF 1938
ROBINSON-PATMAN ACT OF 1936
SHERMAN ANTITRUST ACT OF 1890
STAGGERS RAIL AND MOTOR CAR-
RIER ACTS OF 1980

Charles H. Calhoun
Englewood, Colorado
CERTIFIED INTERNAL AUDITOR
FOREIGN CORRUPT PRACTICES ACT
OF 1977

Patrick Casabona
St. John's University
DERIVATIVES

Joseph D. Chapman
Ball State University
PERSONAL SELLING

Judith Chiri
Colorado Springs, Colorado
CAREERS: AN OVERVIEW

Frederick D.S. Choi
New York University
INTERNATIONAL FEDERATION OF
ACCOUNTANTS

Diane M. Clevesy
CORPORATE EDUCATION

B. Douglas Clinton
Northern Illinois University
STATEMENTS ON MANAGEMENT
ACCOUNTING

John L. Conant
Indiana State University
SUPPLY AND DEMAND

Tena B. Crews
University of South Carolina
WORK GROUPS (TEAMS)

Lori A. Dailey
MASS MARKETING

Henry H. Davis
Eastern Illinois University
INTEREST RATES

Amy Lynn DeVault
Roosevelt University
SERVICE INDUSTRIES

Ian Domowitz
Investment Technology Group, Inc.,
STOCK EXCHANGES

Roger K. Doost
Clemson University
BUDGETS AND BUDGETING

Douglas R. Emery
University of Miami
CAPITAL INVESTMENTS

Jerry S. Evans
University of Houston
COMMUNICATIONS IN BUSINESS

Samir Fahmy
St. John's University
SECURITIES ACTS: REQUIREMENTS
FOR ACCOUNTING

John D. Finnerty
Fordham University
CAPITAL INVESTMENTS

Mary L. Fischer
University of Texas at Tyler
GOVERNMENT ACCOUNTING
SINGLE AUDIT ACT OF 1984

Marie E. Flatley
San Diego State University
COMMUNICATION CHANNELS
POLICY DEVELOPMENT

Carrie Foley
Baldwin School, Hiram, Maine
TIME MANAGEMENT

Nashwa George
Montclair State University
PUBLIC OVERSIGHT BOARD
REENGINEERING
WORK MEASUREMENT

Roy J. Girasa
Pace University
BANKRUPTCY

Rajeev K. Goel
Illinois State University
OLIGOPOLY

Keith Goree
St. Petersburg College
ETHICS: AN OVERVIEW

Patrick M. Graham
MARKET SEGMENTATION

Audrey A. Gramling
Georgia State University
INTERNAL CONTROL SYSTEMS

Patricia R. Graves
Eastern Illinois University
ERGONOMICS
MOTIVATION

Winifred L. Green
DISCOUNT STORES
MARKETING CONCEPT
TELEMARKETING
TRADE SHOWS

Mary Brady Greenawalt
Greensboro, North Carolina
FINANCIAL STATEMENT ANALYSIS

Janet S. Greenlee
University of Dayton
NOT-FOR-PROFIT ACCOUNTING

Lisa E. Gueldenzoph
North Carolina A&T State University
ARTIFICIAL INTELLIGENCE
CAREERS IN INFORMATION PRO-
CESSING
CORPORATE EDUCATION
INTERNET
PRIVACY AND SECURITY

Mahendra Gujarathi
Bentley College
INTERNATIONAL ACCOUNTING
STANDARDS

Louise Dratler Haberman
NASBA
    NATIONAL ASSOCIATION OF STATE
       BOARDS OF ACCOUNTANCY

Jewel E. Hairston
Virginia State University
    BUSINESS PROFESSIONALS OF AMER-
       ICA
    DECA
    ENTREPRENEURSHIP

Gary Hansen
Brigham Young University
    DATABASES

John W. Hansen
    PRODUCTIVITY

Richard O. Hanson
Southern New Hampshire University
    FORENSIC ACCOUNTING

Jan Hargrave
Jan Hargrave & Associates
    LISTENING SKILLS IN BUSINESS
    SPEAKING SKILLS IN BUSINESS

Jean E. Harris
Pennsylvania State University,
Harrisburg
    CHIEF FINANCIAL OFFICERS ACT OF
       1990 AND FEDERAL FINANCIAL
       MANAGEMENT ACT OF 1994
    INCOME TAX: HISTORICAL PERSPEC-
       TIVES
    UNITED STATES GOVERNMENT
       ACCOUNTABILITY OFFICE

Trish W. Harris
The Institute of Internal Auditors
    INSTITUTE OF INTERNAL AUDITORS

Thomas Haynes
Illinois State University
    ETHICS IN MANAGEMENT
    MANAGEMENT/LEADERSHIP STYLES
    MANUFACTURING
    SOCIAL RESPONSIBILITY AND ORGA-
       NIZATIONAL ETHICS

Matthew F. Hazzard
    GOODS AND SERVICES

K. Virginia Hemby-Grubb
Middle Tennessee State University
    DOCUMENT PROCESSING

Ronda B. Henderson
North Carolina A&T State University
    INFORMATION PROCESSING: HIS-
       TORICAL PERSPECTIVES
    PROGRAMMING

Harvey S. Hendrickson
Florida International University
    ACCOUNTING

Patrick J. Highland
Iowa City Community School District
    DIVERSITY IN THE WORKPLACE
    EMPLOYEE ASSISTANCE PROGRAMS
    HUMAN RELATIONS

Laurie Collier Hillstrom
Northern Lights Writers Group
    CONSUMER ADVOCACY AND PRO-
       TECTION

Val Hinton
Delta State University
    AMERICAN MARKETING ASSOCIA-
       TION
    CONSUMER BILL OF RIGHTS
    ENVIRONMENTAL PROTECTION
       AGENCY
    FOOD AND DRUG ADMINISTRATION
    INTERSTATE COMMERCE COMMIS-
       SION
    NATIONAL RETAIL FEDERATION
    NATIONAL TRANSPORTATION
       SAFETY BOARD
    OCCUPATIONAL SAFETY AND
       HEALTH ADMINISTRATION
       (OSHA)
    SECURITIES AND EXCHANGE COM-
       MISSION
    SMALL BUSINESS ADMINISTRATION
    STANDARD METROPOLITAN STATIS-
       TICAL AREAS

Vicky B. Hoffman
University of Pittsburgh
    COMPILATION AND REVIEW SERV-
       ICES

Edward Wei-Te Hsieh
California State University, Los
Angeles
    MONETARY POLICY

Lisa S. Huddlestun
    MACROECONOMICS/MICROECO-
       NOMICS

Jesse W. Hughes
Old Dominion University, emeritus
    GOVERNMENTAL ACCOUNTING
       STANDARDS BOARD

David J. Hyslop
Bowling Green State University
    TRAINING AND DEVELOPMENT

Christine M. Irvine
    VOICE MESSAGING

Jeffrey L. Jacobs
Quinnipiac University
    TAXATION

Christine Jahn
University of Bamberg
    HUMAN RESOURCE MANAGEMENT
    ORGANIZATIONAL STRUCTURE

Edmund L. Jenkins
Norwalk, Connecticut
    GENERALLY ACCEPTED ACCOUNT-
       ING PRINCIPLES

Carol Larson Jones
California State Polytechnic
University, Pomona
    ONLINE EDUCATION
    TELECOMMUTING

Randy L. Joyner
Wilkesboro, North Carolina
    CAREERS IN MARKETING
    CERTIFICATIONS, LICENSURES, AND
       DESIGNATIONS
    COPYRIGHTS
    PATENTS
    TRADEMARKS

Burton S. Kaliski
Southern New Hampshire University
    CREDIT/DEBIT/TRAVEL CARDS

Surendra K. Kaushik
Pace University
    CAPITAL MARKETS
    FINANCE
    FINANCIAL INSTITUTIONS

Edward J. Keller, Jr.
    INSURANCE

Lawrence A. Klein
Bentley College
    ACTIVITY-BASED MANAGEMENT
    COST ALLOCATION

Masaaki Kotabe
Temple University
    INTERNATIONAL INVESTMENT
    TRADING BLOCS

Alan G. Krabbenhoft
Roosevelt University
SERVICE INDUSTRIES

Lawrence M. Krackov
FINANCE

Tatum Krause
University of Hartford
TARGET MARKETING

Janel Kupferschmid
Bloomington, Illinois
ANTITRUST LEGISLATION
OPERATIONS MANAGEMENT

Dennis J. LaBonty
Utah State University
NETWORKING

Gerard A. Lange
St. John's University
FRAUDULENT FINANCIAL REPORT-
ING

Audrey E. Langill
SHOPPING

Christine F. Latino
Atkinson, New Hampshire
MARKETING RESEARCH

Lee Wonsick Lee
Central Connecticut State University
EMPLOYEE COMPENSATION
LEADERSHIP
PERFORMANCE APPRAISAL

Mark Lefebvre
INVENTORY CONTROL

Joel Lerner
Monticello, New York
INVESTMENTS
PERSONAL FINANCIAL PLANNING
STOCK INDEXES
STOCKS

Paula Lee Luft
Black Hawk College-East Campus
COLLECTIVE BARGAINING

Roger L. Luft
Eastern Illinois University, retired
CIRCULAR FLOW
ECONOMICS
ECONOMICS: HISTORICAL PERSPEC-
TIVES
ETHICS IN ECONOMICS
FORECASTING IN BUSINESS

MANAGEMENT
MANAGEMENT: HISTORICAL PER-
SPECTIVES
QUALITY MANAGEMENT

Mary Jean Lush
Delta State University
AMERICAN MARKETING ASSOCIA-
TION
CONSUMER BILL OF RIGHTS
CONSUMER PROTEST
ENVIRONMENTAL PROTECTION
AGENCY
FOOD AND DRUG ADMINISTRATION
INTERSTATE COMMERCE COMMIS-
SION
NATIONAL RETAIL FEDERATION
NATIONAL TRANSPORTATION
SAFETY BOARD
OCCUPATIONAL SAFETY AND
HEALTH ADMINISTRATION
(OSHA)
SECURITIES AND EXCHANGE COM-
MISSION
SMALL BUSINESS ADMINISTRATION
STANDARD METROPOLITAN STATIS-
TICAL AREAS

James J. Maroney
Northeastern University
ANALYTICAL PROCEDURES

Laurence Mauer
St. John's University
SECURITIES ACTS: REQUIREMENTS
FOR ACCOUNTING

Dorothy A. Maxwell
Sacopee Valley High School, Hiram,
Maine
DATABASES
DIGITAL DIVIDE
FACSIMILE REPRODUCTION
INTERNATIONAL ASSOCIATION OF
ADMINISTRATIVE PROFESSIONALS
INTERNATIONAL BUSINESS
NATIONAL BUSINESS EDUCATION
ASSOCIATION
NO CHILD LEFT BEHIND LEGISLA-
TION
SKILLSUSA
TELEPHONE SKILLS
TEMPORARY EMPLOYMENT
WORKERS' COMPENSATION

G. W. Maxwell
San Jose State University, retired
CAREERS IN LAW FOR BUSINESS
CONSUMER PRICE INDEX
CORPORATIONS
FISCAL POLICY

GLOBAL ECONOMY
JOB SATISFACTION
LABOR UNIONS
MONOPOLY
SOLE PROPRIETORSHIP
WRITING SKILLS IN BUSINESS

Marty Maxwell
Creative Composition, Inc.
COMPUTER GRAPHICS

Cheri Reither Mazza
Fordham University
GENERALLY ACCEPTED ACCOUNT-
ING PRINCIPLES

Donna L. McAlister-Kizzier
Morehead State University
DIVISION OF LABOR
NEGOTIATION

Thaddeus McEwen
North Carolina A&T State University
CAREERS IN MANAGEMENT

Melanie A. Meche
University of Louisiana, Lafayette
ETHICS IN INFORMATION PROCESS-
ING

Barry C. Melancon
American Institute of CPAs
AMERICAN INSTITUTE OF CERTI-
FIED PUBLIC ACCOUNTANTS

Earl C. Meyer
Eastern Michigan University, retired
CONSUMER AND BUSINESS PROD-
UCTS
DISCOUNT STORES
GOODS AND SERVICES
MARKET SEGMENTATION
MARKETING CONCEPT
MASS MARKETING
TELEMARKETING
TRADE SHOWS

Mary Michel
Manhattan College
COST-BENEFIT ANALYSIS
NORTH AMERICAN INDUSTRY CLAS-
SIFICATION SYSTEM

Michael Milbier
San Jose, California
ADVERTISING
CRIME AND FRAUD
GOVERNMENT ROLE IN BUSINESS
INTERNATIONAL TRADE
PRICING
PRODUCT LABELING

PRODUCT LINES
PRODUCT MIX
PROMOTION

James E. Miles
VIDEOCONFERENCING

Allie F. Miller
Drexel University
ACCOUNTING CYCLE
BONDS

Theodore J. Mock
University of Southern California
ACCOUNTING INFORMATION SYSTEMS

Hassan Mohammadi
Illinois State University
MONEY SUPPLY

Melvin Morgenstein
Plainview, New York
FEDERAL RESERVE SYSTEM

George A. Mundrake
Ball State University
MULTIMEDIA SYSTEMS

Robert J. Muretta, Jr.
Touro University International
GOVERNMENT FINANCIAL REPORTING

Michael Nelson
TRANSFER PAYMENTS

Anna Nemesh
University of Maryland
OFFICE TECHNOLOGY
PARTNERSHIPS

Mary Nemesh
Anne Arundel County Public Schools
INFORMATION PROCESSING
TELECOMMUNICATIONS

Bernard H. Newman
Pace University
ASSOCIATION OF CERTIFIED FRAUD
EXAMINERS
BUREAU OF LABOR STATISTICS
CAREERS IN ACCOUNTING
FINANCIAL FORECASTS AND PROJECTIONS
GOVERNMENT AUDITING STANDARDS
INTELLECTUAL CAPITAL
INTERNATIONAL MONETARY FUND
MERGERS AND ACQUISITIONS

PUBLIC COMPANY ACCOUNTING
OVERSIGHT BOARD
STANDARD COSTING
UNIFORM CERTIFIED PUBLIC
ACCOUNTANT EXAMINATION

Cheryl L. Noll
Eastern Illinois University
CHANGE PROCESS
MANAGEMENT: AUTHORITY AND
RESPONSIBILITY
ORGANIZATIONAL BEHAVIOR AND
DEVELOPMENT

Carol J. Normand
University of Wisconsin–Whitewater
ACCOUNTING: HISTORICAL PERSPECTIVES

Mary Ellen Oliverio
Pace University
AGENCY THEORY
BONDS
CAREERS IN ACCOUNTING
COST-BENEFIT ANALYSIS
FINANCE: HISTORICAL PERSPECTIVES
GOVERNMENT AUDITING STANDARDS
MERGERS AND ACQUISITIONS
PERFORMANCE AUDITS
STANDARD COSTING
UNIFORM CERTIFIED PUBLIC
ACCOUNTANT EXAMINATION

Sharon Lund O'Neil
Univeristy of Houston
COMMUNICATIONS IN BUSINESS
PRODUCTIVITY

Don M. Pallais
Richmond, Virginia
ASSURANCE SERVICES

Priscilla Payne
Institute of Management Accountants
CERTIFIED MANAGEMENT
ACCOUNTANT (CMA)/CERTIFIED
IN FINANCIAL MANAGEMENT
(CFM)

Louis E. Pelton
University of North Texas
CHANNELS OF DISTRIBUTION

Lawrence F. Peters, Jr.
Sacopee Valley High School, Hiram,
Maine
CIVIL RIGHTS ACT OF 1964
EQUAL EMPLOYMENT OPPORTUNITY
ACT OF 1972

EQUAL PAY ACT OF 1963
EUROPEAN UNION

Nikole M. Pogeman
AMERICAN MANAGEMENT ASSOCIATION
AMERICANS WITH DISABILITIES ACT
OF 1990

Jeffrey J. Pompe
Francis Marion University
DEREGULATION

Karen J. Puglisi
CLASSIC BRANDS

Zane K. Quible
Oklahoma State University
OFFICE LAYOUT

Robert F. Randall
IMA
INSTITUTE OF MANAGEMENT
ACCOUNTANTS

Barry L. Reece
CUSTOMER SERVICE

Brenda J. Reinsborough
Yarmouth, Maine
HEALTH ISSUES IN BUSINESS
MEETING MANAGEMENT

Tod W. Rejholec
NATIONAL LABOR RELATIONS
BOARD

James R. Rinehart
Francis Marion University, emeritus
DEREGULATION

Wendy Rinholen
Black Hawk College, East Campus
CAREERS IN ECONOMICS

Rita Shaw Rone
Gulf Breeze, Florida
SEXUAL HARASSMENT

Jim D. Rucker
Fort Hays State University
STRESS

Robert J. Sack
University of Virginia
EARNINGS MANAGEMENT

Massimo Santicchia
Standard & Poor's
FINANCE

Marcy Satterwhite
Lake Land College
COMPETITION
COOPERATIVE
DECISION MAKING
EMPLOYEE BENEFITS
JOB ENRICHMENT

Jennifer L. Scheffer
Manchester, New Hampshire
FADS
PUBLICITY

B. June Schmidt
READING SKILLS IN BUSINESS

Armand Seguin
Emporia State University
HARDWARE
INTRANET/EXTRANET

Cynthia Shelton (Anast) Seguin
Emporia State University
HARDWARE
INTRANET/EXTRANET

Anand G. Shetty
Iona College
BUSINESS CYCLE
ETHICS IN FINANCE
INSURANCE
MUTUAL FUNDS
STOCK EXCHANGES

Victoria Shoaf
St. John's University
FINANCIAL STATEMENTS

Kathleen Simons
Bryant College
STATE SOCIETIES OF CPAS

Sharon K. Slick
CONSUMER AND BUSINESS PROD-
UCTS

Douglas C. Smith
University of Kentucky
INFORMATION SYSTEMS
SOFTWARE

G. Stevenson Smith
West Virginia University
COST-VOLUME-PROFIT ANALYSIS
NOT-FOR-PROFIT ACCOUNTING

Mark J. Snyder
MSA Consulting Group
ARTIFICIAL INTELLIGENCE
CAREERS IN INFORMATION PRO-
CESSING

CORPORATE EDUCATION
INTERNET
PRIVACY AND SECURITY

Patricia A. Spirou
Southern New Hampshire University
FRANCHISING
INTERSTATE COMMERCE
PRICE FIXING
RETAILERS
WHOLESALERS

Wanda L. Stitt-Gohdes
University of Georgia
STANDARD-BASED WORK PERFORM-
ANCE

James E. Stoddard
Appalachian State University
MARKETING: HISTORICAL PERSPEC-
TIVES

David Strutton
University of North Texas
CHANNELS OF DISTRIBUTION

Jan Sweeney
Baruch College
ETHICS IN ACCOUNTING

John A. Swope
East Carolina University
ADVERTISING AGENCIES
ETHICS IN MARKETING

Ellen Jean Szarleta
Indiana University Northwest
ECONOMIC DEVELOPMENT

Philip D. Taylor
Wesleyan College
INTERACTIVE TECHNOLOGY

Jay C. Thibodeau
Bentley College
AUDITING

Gary P. Tripp
Southern New Hampshire University
BALANCE OF TRADE

Allen D. Truell
Ball State University
ADVERTISING
CHANNELS OF DISTRIBUTION
CRIME AND FRAUD
GOVERNMENT ROLE IN BUSINESS
GREEN MARKETING

INTERNATIONAL TRADE
MARKETING
MARKETING MIX
PRICING
PROMOTION
SOCIAL MARKETING

Gregory P. Valentine
University of Southern Indiana
GROSS DOMESTIC PRODUCT (GDP)
INCOME

John Vann
Ball State University
TRIPLE BOTTOM LINE REPORTING

Carson Varner
Illinois State University
ETHICS IN LAW FOR BUSINESS
LAW IN BUSINESS

Miklos A. Vaserhelyi
Rutgers University
ELECTRONIC COMMERCE

Annette Vincent
University of Louisiana, Lafayette
ETHICS IN INFORMATION PROCESS-
ING

Michelle Voto
Hesser College
LIFESTYLES

Julie A. Watkins
Brownfield, Maine
COTTAGE INDUSTRIES

Roman L. Weil
University of Chicago
COSTS
TIME VALUE OF MONEY

Jill T. White
University of West Florida
FUTURE BUSINESS LEADERS OF
AMERICA
SCHOOL TO CAREER MOVEMENT

Kathy Williams
IMA
INSTITUTE OF MANAGEMENT
ACCOUNTANTS

Patricia Williams
University of Pennsylvania
CONSUMER BEHAVIOR

Scott Williams
Burlington, NC
ADVERTISING AGENCIES

Mark D. Wilson
Ohio State University
CAREERS IN FINANCE

Denise Woodbury
Southern Utah University
CURRENCY EXCHANGE
ECONOMIC SYSTEMS
MONEY
OPPORTUNITY COST

Charles W. Wootton
Eastern Illinois University
ACCOUNTING: HISTORICAL PER-
SPECTIVES

Ralph D. Wray
Bloomington, Indiana
ECONOMIC ANALYSIS

Norman S. Wright
Brigham Young University
STRATEGIC MANAGEMENT

Ray L. Young
Brigham Young University
DESKTOP PUBLISHING
WORD PROCESSING

Jensen J. Zhao
Ball State University
CYBER CRIME
E-MARKETING
IDENTITY THEFT
PUBLIC RELATIONS
RESEARCH IN BUSINESS

A

ACCOUNTING

Accounting is a field of specialization critical to the functioning of all types of organizations. Accounting often is referred to as "the language of business" because of its role in maintaining and processing all relevant financial information that an entity requires for its managing and reporting purposes.

Accountants often have a specific subspecialization and function at one of several levels. Preparation for the field is provided by secondary schools, postsecondary business schools, community colleges, and four-year colleges and universities.

WHAT IS ACCOUNTING?

Accounting is a body of principles and conventions as well as an established general process for capturing financial information related to an entity's resources and their use in meeting the entity's goals. Accounting is a service function that provides information of value to all operating units and to other service functions, such as the headquarters offices of a large corporation.

Origin of Accounting. Modern accounting is traced to the work of an Italian monk, Luca Pacioli, whose publication in 1494 C.E. described the double-entry system, which continues to be the fundamental structure for contemporary accounting systems in all types of entities. When double-entry accounting is used, the balance sheet identifies both the resources controlled by the entity and those parties who have claims to those assets.

Early histories of business identify the bookkeeper as a valuable staff member. As businesses became more complex, the need for more astute review and interpretation of financial information was met with the development of a new profession—public accounting. In the United States, public accounting began in the latter part of the nineteenth century. The first organization was established in 1887; the first professional examination was administered in December 1896.

In the early days of the twentieth century, numerous states established licensing requirements and began to administer examinations. During the first century of public accounting in the United States, the American Institute of Certified Public Accountants (and its predecessor organizations) provided strong leadership to meet the changing needs of business, not-for-profit, and governmental entities.

Generally Accepted Accounting Principles (GAAP). No single source provides principles for handling all transactions and events. Over time, conventional rules have developed that continue to be relevant. Additionally, groups have been authorized to establish accounting standards. The Financial Accounting Standards Board (FASB) assumed responsibility for accounting standards and principles in 1973. It is authorized to amend existing rules and establish new ones. In 1992, the Auditing Standards Board established the GAAP hierarchy. At the highest level of the hierarchy are FASB statements and interpretations; APB opinions were issued from 1959 to 1973 by the Accounting Principles Board (APB), and Accounting Research Bulletins, issued until 1959 by the Committee

Luca Bartolomes Pacioli (ca. 1445–ca. 1517). *Fra Luca Pacioli's 1494 publication described the double-entry system of accounting.* © **ARCHIVO ICONOGRAFICO, S.A./CORBIS**

on Accounting Procedure (CAP); both the APB and CAP were committees of the American Institute of Certified Public Accountants (AICPA).

What type of unit is served by accounting? Probably no concept or idea is more basic to accounting than the accounting unit or *entity*, a term used to identify the organization for which the accounting service is to be provided and whose accounting or other information is to be analyzed, accumulated, and reported. The entity can be any area, activity, responsibility, or function for which information would be useful. Thus, an entity is established to provide the needed focus of attention. The information about one entity can be consolidated with that of a part or all of another, and this combination process can be continued until the combined entity reaches the unit that is useful for the desired purpose.

Accounting activities may occur within or outside the organization. Although accounting is usually identified with privately owned, profit-seeking entities, its services also are provided to not-for-profit organizations such as universities or hospitals, to governmental organizations, and to other types of units. The organizations may be small, owner-operated enterprises offering a single product or service, or huge multi-enterprise, international conglomerates with thousands of different products and services. The not-for-profit, governmental, or other units may be local, national, or international; they may be small or very large; they may even be entire nations, as in national income accounting. Since not-for-profit and governmental accounting are covered elsewhere in this encyclopedia, the balance of this article will focus on accounting for privately owned, profit-seeking entities.

What is the work of accountants? Accountants help entities be successful, ethical, responsible participants in society. Their major activities include observation, measurement, and communication. These activities are analytical in nature and draw on several other disciplines (e.g., economics, mathematics, statistics, behavioral science, law, history, and language/communication).

Accountants identify, analyze, record, and accumulate facts, estimates, forecasts, and other data about the unit's activities; then they translate these data into information that can be useful for a specific purpose.

The data accumulation and recording phase traditionally has been largely clerical; typically and appropriately, this has been called bookkeeping, which is still a common and largely manual activity, especially in smaller firms that have not adopted state-of-the-art technology. But with advances in information technology and user-friendly software, the clerical aspect has become largely electronically performed, with internal checks and controls to assure that the input and output are factual and valid.

Accountants design and maintain accounting systems, an entity's central information system, to help control and provide a record of the entity's activities, resources, and obligations. Such systems also facilitate reporting on all or part of the entity's accomplishments for a period of time and on its status at a given point in time.

An organization's accounting system provides information that (1) helps managers make decisions about assembling resources, controlling, and organizing financing and operating activities; and (2) aids other users (employees, investors, creditors, and others—usually called stakeholders) in making investment, credit, and other decisions.

The accounting system must also provide internal controls to ensure that (1) laws and enterprise policies are properly implemented; (2) accounting records are accurate; (3) enterprise assets are used effectively (e.g., that idle cash balances are being invested to earn returns); and (4) steps be taken to reduce chances of losing assets or incurring liabilities from fraudulent or similar activities, such as the carelessness or dishonesty of employees, customers, or suppliers. Many of these controls are simple (e.g., the prenumbering of documents and accounting for all numbers); others require division of duties among employees to separate record keeping and custodial tasks in order to reduce opportunities for falsification of records and thefts or misappropriation of assets.

An enterprise's system of internal controls usually includes an internal auditing function and personnel to ensure that prescribed data handling and asset/liability protection procedures are being followed. The internal auditor uses a variety of approaches, including observation of current activities, examination of past transactions, and simulation—often using sample or fictitious transactions—to test the accuracy and reliability of the system.

Accountants may also be responsible for preparing several types of documents. Many of these (e.g., employees' salary and wage records) also serve as inputs for the accounting system, but many are needed to satisfy other reporting requirements (e.g., employee salary records may be needed to support employee claims for pensions). Accountants also provide data for completing income tax returns.

What is the accountant's role in decision making? Accountants have a major role in providing information for making economic and financial decisions. Rational decisions are usually based on analyses and comparisons of estimates, which in turn, are based on accounting and other data that project future results from alternative courses of action.

External or financial accounting, reporting, and auditing are directly involved in providing information for the decisions of investors and creditors that help the capital markets to efficiently and effectively allocate resources to enterprises; internal, managerial, or management accounting is responsible for providing information and input to help managers make decisions on the efficient and effective use of enterprise resources.

The accounting information used in making decisions within an enterprise is not subject to governmental or other external regulation, so any rules and constraints are largely self-imposed. As a result, in developing the data and information that are relevant for decisions within the enterprise, managerial accountants are constrained largely by cost-benefit considerations and their own ingenuity and ability to predict future conditions and events.

But accounting to external users (financial accounting, reporting, and auditing) has many regulatory constraints—especially if the enterprise is a "public" corporation whose securities are registered (under the United States Securities Acts of 1933 and 1934) with the Securities and Exchange Commission (SEC) and traded publicly over-the-counter or on a stock exchange. Public companies are subject to regulations and reporting requirements imposed and enforced by the SEC; to rules and standards established for its financial reports by the FASB and enforced by the SEC; to regulations of the organization where its securities are traded; and to the regulations of the AICPA, which establishes requirements and standards for its members (who may be either internal or external accountants or auditors).

If the entity is a state or local governmental unit, it is subject to the reporting standards and requirements of the Government Accounting Standards Board. If the entity is private and not a profit-seeking unit, it is subject to various reporting and other regulations, including those of the Internal Revenue Service, which approves its tax status and with which it must file reports.

Largely as a result of the governmental regulation of private profit-seeking businesses that began in 1933, an increasingly clear distinction has been made between managerial or internal accounting and financial accounting that is largely for external users. One important exception to this trend, however, was the change adopted in the 1970s in the objectives of financial reporting such that both managerial and financial accounting now have the same objective: to provide information that is useful for making economic decisions.

But it must be recognized that although the financial accounting information reported to stakeholders comes from the organization's accounting system, its usefulness for decision making is limited. This is because it is largely historical—it reflects events and activities that occurred in the past, not what is expected in the future. Even estimated data such as budgets and standard costs must be examined regularly to determine whether these past estimates continue to be indicative of current conditions and expectations and thus are useful for making decisions. Thus historical accounting information must be examined carefully, modified, and supplemented to make certain that what is used is relevant to expectations about the future.

But it also must be recognized that accounting can and does provide information that is current and useful in making estimates about future events. For example, accounting provides current-value information about selected items, such as readily marketable investments in debt and equity securities and inventories, and it provides reports on what the organization plans to accomplish and its expectations about the future in budgets and earnings forecasts.

Who uses accounting information for decision making?
The information developed by the accountant's information system can be useful to:

- Managers in planning, controlling, and evaluating their organization's activities

- Owners, directors, and others in evaluating the performance of the organization and determining operating, compensation, and other policies

- Union, governmental, regulatory, taxing, environmental, and other entities in evaluating whether the organization is conforming with applicable contracts, rules, laws, and public policies and/or whether changes are needed;

- Existing and potential owners, lenders, employees, customers, and suppliers in evaluating their current and future commitments to the organization

- Accounting researchers, security analysts, security brokers and dealers, mutual-fund managers, and others in their analyses and evaluations of enterprises, capital markets, and/or investors

The services that accounting and the accountant can provide have been enhanced in many ways since the 1970s by advances in computers and other information technology. The impact of these changes is revolutionizing accounting and the accounting profession. But the changes have yet to reach their ultimate potential. For example, accounting in the 1990s began to provide current-value information and estimates about the future that an investor or other user would find useful for decision making. The availability of computer software and the Internet greatly enhanced the potential for data and information services. Such changes create opportunities for accounting and accountants and also will require substantial modifications in the traditional financial accounting and reporting model.

What is the profession of accounting? At the core of the profession of accounting is the certified public accountant (CPA) who has passed the national CPA examination, been licensed in at least one state or territory, and engages in the practice of public accounting/auditing in a public accounting or CPA firm. The CPA firm provides some combination of two or more of four types of services: accounting, auditing, income tax planning and reporting, and management advising/consulting. Analysis of trends indicates that the demand for auditing services has peaked and that most of the growth experienced by public accounting firms is in the consulting area.

Accounting career paths, specializations, or subprofessions for CPAs who join profit-seeking enterprises include being controllers, chief financial officers, or internal auditors. Other career paths include being controllers or chief financial officers in not-for-profit or government organizations and teaching in colleges and universities. Students should note that non-CPAs also could enter these subprofessions and that certificates, but not licenses, could be earned by passing examinations in several areas, including internal auditing, management accounting, and bank auditing.

How do environmental changes impact the accounting profession? Numerous changes in the environment make the practice of accounting and auditing much different in the new century than it was in the 1970s. For example, professional accounting firms now actively compete for clients by advertising extensively in various media, a practice that at one time was forbidden by their code of professional conduct. Mergers of clients have led CPA firms into mergers as well, such that the Big Eight is now the Big Five and the second-tier group has been reduced from twelve firms to about five. Another result of competition and other changes has been that some of the largest employers of CPAs now include income tax and accounting services firms such as H&R Block and an American Express subsidiary.

Competition among CPAs also has led the SEC to expand its regulatory and enforcement activities to ensure that financial reports are relevant and reliable. From its inception, the SEC has had legal authority to prescribe the accounting principles and standards used in the financial reports of enterprises whose securities are publicly traded, but it has delegated this responsibility to the accounting profession. Since 1973, that organization has been the FASB, with which the SEC works closely. But because the FASB is limited to performing what is essentially a legislative function, the SEC has substantially increased its enforcement activities to ensure that the FASB's standards are appropriately applied in financial reports and that accountants/auditors act in the public interest in performing their independent audits—for which the Securities Acts have given the CPA profession a monopoly.

How does a student prepare for the accounting profession? Persons considering entering the accounting profession should begin by doing some self-analysis to determine whether they enjoy mathematical, problem- or puzzle-solving, or other analytical activities; by taking some aptitude tests; or by talking with accounting teachers or practitioners about their work.

Anyone interested in becoming an accounting professional should expect to enter a rigorous five-year education program and to earn a master's degree in order to qualify to enter the profession and to sit for the CPA examination. To build a base for rising to the top of the profession, students should select courses that help them learn how to think and to define and solve problems. The courses should help them to develop analytical (logical, mathematical, statistical), communication (oral, reading, writing), computer, and interpersonal skills. The early part of the program should emphasize arts and sciences courses in these skill-development areas.

The person should begin to develop word-processing, data-processing, and Internet skills long before entering

college and should expect to maintain competence in them throughout his or her professional career. These skills greatly enhance and facilitate all phases and aspects of what accounting and accountants attempt to do. What can be done is limited only by technology and by the sophistication of the system, its operators, and users.

SEE ALSO *Accounting Cycle; Accounting: Historical Perspectives; Careers in Accounting; Ethics in Accounting*

BIBLIOGRAPHY

Hansen, Don R., and Mowen, Maryanne M. (2000). *Management Accounting* (5th ed.). Cincinnati, OH: Southwestern College Publishing.

Kimmel, Paul D., Weygandt, Jerry J., and Kieso, Donald E. (2000). *Financial Accounting* (2nd ed.). New York: Wiley.

Harvey S. Hendrickson

ACCOUNTING CYCLE

The primary objectives of the accounting function in an organization are to process financial information and to prepare financial statements at the end of the accounting period. Companies must systematically process financial information and must have staff who prepare financial statements on a monthly, quarterly, and/or annual basis. To meet these primary objectives, a series of steps is required. Collectively these steps are known as the accounting cycle.

THE STEPS OF THE CYCLE

1. *Collect and analyze data from transactions and events:* As transactions and events related to financial resources occur, they are analyzed with respect to their effect on the financial position of the company. As an example, the sales for a day in a retail establishment are collected on a cash register tape. These sales become inputs into the accounting system. Every organization establishes a chart of accounts that identifies the categories for recording transactions and events. The chart of accounts for the retail establishment includes Cash and Sales.

2. *Journalize transactions:* After collecting and analyzing the information obtained in the first step, the information is entered in the general journal, which is called the book of original entry. Journalizing transactions may be done continually, but this step can be done in a batch at the end of the day if data from similar transactions are being sorted and collected, on a cash register tape, for example. At the end of

the day, the sales of $4,000 for cash would be recorded in the general journal in this form:

Cash 4000

Sales 4000

3. *Post to general ledger:* The general journal entries are posted to the general ledger, which is organized by account. All transactions for the same account are collected and summarized; for example, the account titled Sales will accumulate the total value of the sales for the period. If posting were done daily, the Sales account in the ledger would show the total sales for each day as well as the cumulative sales for the period to date. Posting to ledger accounts may be less frequent, perhaps at the end of each day, at the end of the week, or possibly even at the end of the month.

4. *Prepare an unadjusted trial balance:* At the end of the period, double-entry accounting requires that debits and credits recorded in the general ledger be equal. Debit and credit merely signify position—left and right, respectively. Some accounts normally have debit balances (e.g., assets and expenses) and other accounts have credit balances (e.g., liabilities, owners' equity, and revenues). As transactions are recorded in the general journal and subsequently posted to the ledger, all amounts recorded on the debit side of accounts (i.e., recorded on the left side) must equal all amounts recorded on the credit side of accounts (i.e., recorded on the right side). Preparing an unadjusted trial balance tests the equality of debits and credits as recorded in the general ledger. If unequal amounts of debits and credits are found in this step, the reason for the inequality is investigated and corrected before proceeding to the next step. Additionally, this unadjusted trial balance provides the balances of all the accounts that may require adjustment in the next step.

5. *Prepare adjustments:* Period-end adjustments are required to bring accounts to their proper balances after considering transactions and/or events not yet recorded. Under accrual accounting, revenue is recorded when earned and expenses when incurred. Thus, an entry may be required at the end of the period to record revenue that has been earned but not yet recorded on the books. Similarly, an adjustment may be required to record an expense that may have been incurred but not yet recorded.

6. *Prepare an adjusted trial balance:* As with an unadjusted trial balance, this step tests the equality of debits and credits. However, assets, liabilities, owners' equity, revenues, and expenses will reflect the adjustments that have been made in the previous step. If there should be unequal amounts of debits and credits or if an account appears to be incorrect, the discrepancy or error is investigated and corrected.

7. *Prepare financial statements:* Financial statements are prepared using the corrected balances from the adjusted trial balance. These are one of the primary outputs of the financial accounting system.

8. *Close the accounts:* Revenues and expenses are accumulated and reported by period, either a monthly, quarterly, or yearly. To prevent their not being added to or commingled with revenues and expenses of another period, they need to be closed out—that is, given zero balances—at the end of each period. Their net balances, which represent the income or loss for the period, are transferred into owners' equity. Once revenue and expense accounts are closed, the only accounts that have balances are the asset, liability, and owners' equity accounts. Their balances are carried forward to the next period.

9. *Prepare a post-closing trial balance:* The purpose of this final step is two-fold: to determine that all revenue and expense accounts have been closed properly and to test the equality of debit and credit balances of all the balance sheet accounts, that is, assets, liabilities and owners' equity.

COMPUTERIZED ACCOUNTING SYSTEM

A computerized accounting system saves a great deal of time and effort, considerably reduces (if not eliminates) mathematical errors, and allows for much more timely information than does a manual system. In a real-time environment, accounts are accessed and updated immediately to reflect activity, thus combining steps 2 and 3. The need to test for equality of debits and credits through trial balances is usually not required in a computerized system accounting since most systems test for equality of debit and credit amounts as they are entered. If someone were to attempt to input data containing an inequality, the system would not accept the input. Since the computer is programmed to post amounts to the various accounts and calculate the new balances as new entries are made, the possibility of mathematical error is markedly reduced.

Computers may also be programmed to record some adjustments automatically at the end of the period. Most software programs are also able to prepare the financial statement once it has been determined the account balances are correct. The closing process at the end of the period can also be done automatically by the computer.

Human judgment is still required to analyze the data for entry into the computer system correctly. Additionally, the accountant's knowledge and judgment are frequently required to determine the adjustments that are needed at the end of the reporting period. The mechanics of the system, however, can easily be handled by the computer.

SEE ALSO *Accounting*

BIBLIOGRAPHY

Dansby, Robert, Kaliski, Burton, and Lawrence, Michael (2004). *Paradigm College Accounting* (5th ed.). St. Paul, MN: EMC-Paradigm.

Ingram, Robert W., Baldwin, Bruce A., and Albright, Thomas L. (2004). *Financial Accounting: A Bridge to Decision Making* (5th ed.). Cincinnati, OH: South-Western College Publishing.

Larson, Kermit D. (1997). *Essentials of Financial Accounting: Information for Business Decisions*. Chicago: Irwin/McGraw-Hill.

Meigs, Robert F., Meigs, Mary A., Bettner, Mark, and Whittington, Ray (1998). *Financial Accounting*. Boston: Irwin.

Needles, Belverd E., Jr., and Powers, Marian (2005). *Financial Accounting* (8th ed.). Boston: Houghton Mifflin.

Porter, Gary A., and Norton, Curtis L. (2004). *Financial Accounting: The Impact on Decision Makers* (4th ed.). Mason, OH: Thomson/South-Western.

Allie F. Miller

ACCOUNTING: HISTORICAL PERSPECTIVES

With the establishment of the first English colonies in America, accounting, or bookkeeping, as the discipline was referred to then, quickly assumed an important role in the development of American commerce. Two hundred years, however, would pass before accounting would separate from bookkeeping, and nearly three hundred years would pass before the profession of accounting as it is practiced in the twenty-first century would emerge.

For individuals and businesses, accounting records in Colonial America often were very elementary. Most records of this period relied on the single-entry method or were simply narrative accounts of transactions. As rudimentary as they were, these records were important because the colonial economy was largely a barter and credit system with substantial time passing before payments were made. Accounting records were often the only reliable records of such historical transactions.

THE EMERGENCE OF ACCOUNTING

Prior to the late 1800s, the terms *bookkeeping* and *accounting* were often used interchangeably because the recording/posting process was central to both activities. There was little need for financial statements (e.g., income statements) because most owners had direct knowledge of their businesses and, therefore, could rely on elementary bookkeeping procedures for information.

Although corporations (e.g., banks, canal companies) were present in the United States prior to the early 1800s, their numbers were few. Beginning in the late 1820s, however, the number of corporations rapidly increased with the creation and expansion of the railroads. To operate successfully, the railroads needed cost reports, production reports, financial statements, and operating ratios that were more complex than simple recording procedures could provide. Alfred D. Chandler, Jr. (1977) noted the impact of the railroads on the development of accounting in his classic work, *The Visible Hand*, when he stated "after 1850, the railroad was central in the development of the accounting profession in the United States" (p. 110).

With the increase in the number of corporations, there also arose a demand for additional financial information that A.C. Littleton (1933) in his landmark book, *The Rise of the Accounting Profession*, called "figure" knowledge. With no direct knowledge of a business, investors had to rely on financial statements for information, and to create those statements more complex accounting methods were required. The accountant's responsibility, therefore, expanded beyond simply recording entries to include the preparation, classification, and analysis of financial statements. As John L. Carey (1969) wrote in *The Rise of the Accounting Profession*, "the nineteenth century saw bookkeeping expanded into accounting" (p. 15).

Additionally, as the development of the corporation created a greater need for the services of accountants, the study of commerce and accounting became more important. Although there had been trade business schools and published texts on accounting and bookkeeping, traditional colleges had largely ignored the study of business and accounting. In 1881, however, the Wharton School of Finance and Economy was founded, and two years later the school added accounting to its curriculum. As other major universities created schools of commerce, accounting secured a significant place in the curriculum.

With a separation of management and ownership in corporations, there also arose a need for an independent party to review the financial statements. Someone was needed to represent the owners' interest and to verify that the statements accurately presented the financial conditions of the company. Moreover, there was often an expectation that an independent review would discover whether managers were violating their fiduciary duties to the owners. Additionally, because the late nineteenth century was a period of major industrial mergers, someone was needed to verify the reported values of the companies. The independent public accountant, a person whose obligation was not to the managers of a company but to its shareholders and potential investors, provided the knowledge and skills to meet these needs.

In 1913, the responsibilities of and job opportunities for accountants again expanded with the ratification of the sixteenth amendment to the U.S. Constitution, which allowed a federal income tax. Accountants had become somewhat familiar with implementing a national tax with the earlier passage of the Corporation Excise Tax Law. Despite the earlier law, however, many companies had not set up proper systems to determine taxable income and few were familiar with concepts such as depreciation and accrual accounting.

As tax rates increased, tax services became even more important to accounting firms and often opened the door to providing other services to a client. Accounting firms, therefore, were often engaged to establish a proper accounting system and audit financial statements as well as prepare the required tax return.

Thus, in contrast to bookkeeping, which often had been considered a trade, the responsibilities of accounting had expanded by the early twentieth century to such an extent that it now sought professional status. One foundation of the established professions (e.g., medicine, law) was professional certification, which accounting did not have. In 1896, with the support of several accounting organizations, the state of New York passed a law restricting the title certified public accountant (CPA) to those who had passed a state examination and had acquired at least three years of accounting experience. Similar laws were soon passed in several other states.

PROFESSIONAL ORGANIZATIONS

Throughout the history of accounting, professional organizations have made major contributions to the development of the profession. For example, in 1882, the Institute of Accountants and Bookkeepers of New York (IABNY) was organized with the primary aim of increasing the level of educational resources available for accountants. In 1886, the IABNY became the Institute of Accounts, and it continued to be active in promoting accounting education for nearly twenty years. Meanwhile, the first national organization for accounting educators, the American Association of University Instructors in Accounting (AAUIP), was organized in 1916. In 1935, the AAUIP was reorganized as the American Accounting Association.

The national public accounting organization, the American Association of Public Accountants (AAPA), was incorporated in 1887. Reflecting the need of most professions for a code of ethics, the AAPA added a professional ethics section to its bylaws in 1907. The AAPA was reorganized as the American Institute of Accountants (AIA). In 1921, the American Society of Certified Public Accountants (ASCPA) was established and became a rival to the AIA for leadership in the public accounting area. The rivalry continued until 1937, when the ASCPA merged with the AIA. In 1957, the AIA became the American Institute of Certified Public Accountants (AICPA).

In contrast to the public accounting emphasis of the AIA and ASCPA, the National Association of Cost Accountants (NACA) was founded in 1919. The NACA placed an emphasis on the development of cost controls and proper reporting within companies. In 1957, the NACA changed its name to the National Association of Accountants (NAA) in recognition of the expansion of managerial accounting beyond traditional cost accounting. Then, in 1991, recognizing its emphasis on the managerial aspects of accounting, the NAA became the Institute of Management Accountants.

EXTERNAL AND INTERNAL REGULATION

During the nineteenth century, the federal government generally allowed accounting to regulate itself. Then, in 1913, Congress established the Federal Reserve System and, one year later, the Federal Trade Commission (FTC). From this date forward, federal agencies have had an increasing impact on the profession of accounting.

The government's first major attempt at the formalization of authoritative reporting standards was in 1917 with the Federal Reserve Board's publication of *Uniform Accounting*. In 1918, the bulletin was reissued as *Approved Methods for the Preparation of Balance Sheet Statements*. Although directed toward auditing the balance sheet, the report presented model income and balance sheet statements. Because the proposal was only a recommendation, however, its acceptance was limited.

The impetus for stricter financial reporting was provided by the collapse of the securities market in 1929 and the revelation of massive fraud in a company listed on the New York Stock Exchange (NYSE). In 1933, the NYSE announced that companies applying for a listing on the exchange must have their financial statements audited by an independent public accountant. The scope of these audits had to follow the revised guidelines set forth by the Federal Reserve in 1929.

Another major innovation in the regulation of accounting was the passage of the Securities Act of 1933 and the Securities and Exchange Act of 1934. The 1933 act conferred upon the FTC the authority to prescribe the accounting methods for companies to follow. Under this act, accountants could be held liable for losses that resulted from material omissions or misstatements in registration statements they had certified. The 1934 act transferred the authority to prescribe accounting methods to the newly established Securities and Exchange Commission (SEC) and required that financial statements filed with the SEC be certified by an independent public accountant.

With the creation of the SEC and the passage of new securities laws, the federal government assumed a central role in the establishment of basic requirements for the issuance and auditing of financial reports. Additionally, these acts increased the importance of accountants and enlarged the accountant's responsibility to the general public. Under these acts, not only did accountants have a responsibility to the public, they were now potentially liable for their actions.

In 1938, the SEC delegated much of its authority to prescribe accounting practices to the AIA and its Committee on Accounting Procedures (CAP). In 1939, CAP issued its first of fifty-one Accounting Research Bulletins. Responding to criticism of CAP, the AICPA (formerly the AIA) in 1959 replaced the CAP with the Accounting Principles Board (APB). The APB was designed to issue accounting opinions after it had considered previous research studies, and in 1962, the APB issued its first of thirty-one opinions. Although the SEC had delegated much of its standard-setting authority to the AICPA, the commission exercised its right to approve all standards when it declared that companies did not have to follow the rules set forth in APB No. 2, The Investment Credit.

Responding to criticism of the APB, a study group chaired by Francis M. Wheat was established to review the board structure and the rule-making process. The committee recommended that an independent, full time, more diverse standards board replace the APB. Following the recommendations, the Financial Accounting Standards Board (FASB) was established in 1973. This board is independent of the AICPA and issued its first statement in 1973.

THE CHANGING GENDERIZATION OF THE WORK FORCE

With the separation of bookkeeping from accounting, the demand for women bookkeepers dramatically increased, and by 1930, over 60 percent of all bookkeepers were women. A similar increase in the demand for women accountants, however, did not occur. Although World War II created some opportunities for women in accounting, at the start of the second half of the twentieth century

accounting still was not considered an appropriate career for most women. In fact, in 1950, only 15 percent of the more than 300,000 accountants in the United States were women. Moreover, less than 4 percent of college students majoring in accounting then were women.

In the 1960s, social and legal events began that ultimately provided opportunities for women in the profession of accounting. As these events occurred, the overall demand for accounting services and accountants also greatly increased. This demand became so large that the traditional labor pool of men was not sufficient to maintain the accounting work force. Concurrently, women majoring in accounting increased dramatically from less than 5 percent of all accounting majors in 1960 to more than 50 percent in 1985.

Given the increase of women accounting majors and the inability of the traditional labor pool to meet the work force demand, accounting (especially public accounting) increased the hiring of women. By 1990, women comprised a majority of the accounting work force. It would be the beginning of the twenty-first century, however, before women began to obtain a significant number of upper-level management positions in accounting.

THE TWENTY-FIRST CENTURY

The accountant, the accounting firm, and the accounting profession of the twenty-first century are quite different from what existed at the beginning of the twentieth century. In contrast to a bookkeeper manually recording entries in a large bound volume, an accountant is now responsible for information concerning all facets of a business and is dependent on the latest technology for processing that information. In contrast to small local firms, accounting firms now can be large international organizations with reported revenues of billions of dollars. In addition to the traditional audit/attest information, accounting firms provide their clients with tax services, financial planning, system analysis, consulting, and legal services. At the beginning of the twentieth century, the accounting profession was just emerging. Today, the profession is comprised of thousands of men and women working in public and private firms as well as profit and nonprofit organizations as members of management teams or as valued consultants.

SEE ALSO *Accounting*

BIBLIOGRAPHY
Carey, John L. (1970). *The Rise of the Accounting Profession to Responsibility and Authority 1937–1969.* New York: American Institute of Certified Public Accountants.
Chandler, Alfred D., Jr. (1977). *The Visible Hand: The Managerial Revolution in American Business.* Cambridge, MA: Harvard University Press.

Chatfield, Michael, and Vangermeersch, Richard, eds. (1996). *The History of Accounting: An International Encyclopedia.* New York: Garland.

Edwards, James Don (1988). *History of Public Accounting in the United States.* New York: Garland.

Hills, George H. (1982). *The Law of Accounting and Financial Statements* (2nd ed.). New York: Garland.

Johnson, H. Thomas, and Kaplan, Robert S. (1987). *Relevance Lost: The Rise and Fall of Management Accounting.* Boston: Harvard Business School Press.

Littleton, A.C. (1988). *Accounting Evolution to 1900* (2nd ed.). New York: Garland.

Lockwood, Jeremiah (1938). "Early University Education in Accountancy." *Accounting Review* 38(2): 131-143.

Miranti, Paul J., Jr. (1990). *Accountancy Comes of Age: The Development of an American Profession.* Chapel Hill: University of North Carolina Press.

Previts, Gary John, and Merino, Barbara Dubis (1998). *A History of Accountancy in the United States: The Cultural Significance of Accounting.* Columbus: Ohio State University Press.

Reid, Glenda E., Acken, Brenda T., and Jancura, Elise G. (1987). "An Historical Perspective on Women in Accounting." *The Journal of Accountancy* 163(5) (May): 338-355.

Study on Establishment of Accounting Principles. (1972) "Recommendation on the Study on Establishment of Accounting Principles." *The Journal of Accountancy* 133(5) (May): 66-71.

Wootton, Charles W., and Kemmerer, Barbara E. (1996). "The Changing Genderization of Bookkeeping in the United States, 1870–1930." *Business History Review* 70(4) (Winter): 541-586.

Wootton, Charles W., and Kemmerer, Barbara E. (2000). "The Changing Genderization of the Accounting Workforce in the US, 1930–1990." *Accounting, Business & Financial History* 10(2) (July): 303-324.

Carol J. Normand
Charles W. Wootton

ACCOUNTING INFORMATION SYSTEMS

An accounting information system (AIS) combines the study and practice of accounting with the design, implementation, and monitoring of an information system. Such a system involves applying modern information technology resources to traditional accounting controls and methods to provide users the financial information necessary to manage their organizations. This system is often a component of an entity's management information system.

TECHNOLOGY

Contemporary technological capabilities permit a range of possible designs for an AIS. Yet, the basic structure of a system continues to include essentially the same three components: input, processing, and output.

Input. The input devices commonly associated with an AIS include standard personal computers (PCs) or workstations running applications, scanning devices for standardized data entry, and electronic communication devices for electronic data interchange (EDI) and electronic commerce (e-commerce). In addition, many financial systems come "Web enabled" to allow devices that connect to the World Wide Web AIS access.

Processing. Basic processing is achieved through computer systems ranging from individual PCs to large-scale enterprise servers. Conceptually, however, the underlying processing model is still the double-entry accounting system invented many centuries ago.

Output. The output devices used include computer displays, impact and nonimpact printers, and electronic communication devices for EDI and e-commerce. The output content may encompass almost any type of financial report, from budgets and tax reports to multinational financial statements and sustainability reports.

MANAGEMENT INFORMATION SYSTEMS

Management information systems (MISs) are interactive human/machine systems that support decision making for users both in and out of traditional organizational boundaries. These systems are used to support an organization's daily operational activities, current and future tactical decisions, and overall strategic direction. MISs are made up of several major applications, including the financial information and human resources systems.

Financial Information Applications. Financial information applications make up the heart of AIS in practice. Modules commonly implemented include: general ledger, payables, procurement/purchasing, receivables, billing, inventory, assets, projects, and budgeting.

Human Resource Applications. Human resource applications make up another major part of modern information systems. Modules commonly integrated with the AIS include: human resources, benefits administration, pension administration, payroll, and time and labor reporting.

INFORMATION SYSTEMS IN CONTEXT

AISs cover all business functions from backbone accounting transaction processing systems to sophisticated financial management planning and processing systems.

Financial Reporting. Financial reporting starts at the operational levels of the organization where the transaction processing systems capture important business events such as normal production, purchasing, and selling activities. These events (transactions) are classified and summarized for internal decision making and for external financial reporting.

Cost Accounting Systems. Cost accounting systems such as activity-based costing (ABC) systems are used primarily in manufacturing environments, but increasingly are being applied to service companies, such as banks, real estate firms, and insurance companies. These allow organizations to track the costs associated with production of goods and performance of services.

Management Accounting Systems. Management accounting systems such as master budgets are used to facilitate organizational planning, monitoring, and control for a variety of activities. Such systems allow all managerial levels to have access to prompt reporting and statistical analysis. The systems are used to gather information to consider alternative scenarios, and to identify an optimal answer among the hypothetical scenarios.

DEVELOPMENT OF AN AIS

The development of all AISs includes the basic phrases of planning, analysis, design, reporting, implementation, and support. The time associated with each of these phrases can be as short as a few weeks or as long as several years.

Planning. The first phase of systems development is the planning of the project. This entails determination of the scope and objectives of the project, the definition of project responsibilities, control requirements, project phases, project budgets, and project deliverables.

Analysis. The analysis phase requires a thorough evaluation and documentation of the accounting and business processes in use by the organization. This phase may include reengineering to take advantage of modern best practices and the operating characteristics of modern system solutions.

Data analysis involves a thorough review of the accounting information that is being collected by an organization. Such data are often compared to budgeted data prepared for financial management and for external financial reporting.

Decision analysis is a through review of the decisions a manager is responsible for making. The primary decisions that managers are responsible for are identified on an individual basis. Then models are created to support the manager in gathering financial and related information, developing and designing alternatives, and making actionable choices. This method is used when decision support is the system's primary objective.

Process analysis is a thorough review of the organization's business processes. Organizational processes often are identified and segmented into a series of events that either add or change data. These processes can then be modified or reengineered to improve the organization's operations in terms of lowering cost, improving service, improving quality, and improving management information.

Design. The design phase takes the results of the analysis phase and turns them into detailed specific designs that can be implemented in a subsequent phase. It involves the detailed design of all inputs, processing, storage, and outputs of the proposed accounting system. Inputs may be defined using screen layout tools and application generators. Processing can be shown through the use of flowcharts or business process maps that define the system logic, operations, and work flow. Logical data storage designs are shown by modeling the relationships between the organization's resources, events, and agents in diagrams. Also, entity relationship diagram modeling is used to document large-scale database relationships. Output designs are documented through the use of a variety of reporting tools such as report writers, data extractions tools, query tools, and online analytical processing tools.

Data capture and storage. Screen designs and system interfaces are the primary data capture devices of AISs and are developed through a variety of tools. Storage is achieved through the use of normalized databases that increase functionality and flexibility.

Processing. Business process maps and flowcharts are used to document the operations of the systems. Modern AISs use specialized databases and processing designed specifically for accounting operations. This means that much of the base processing capabilities come delivered with the accounting or enterprise software.

Reporting. Reporting is the driving force behind AIS development. If the system analysis and design are successful, the reporting process provides the information that helps drive management decision making and external financial reporting. Accounting systems make use of a variety of scheduled and on-demand reports. The reports can be tabular, showing data in a table or tables; graphic, using images to convey information in a picture format; or matrices, to show complex relationships in multiple dimensions.

There are numerous characteristics to consider when defining reporting requirements: The reports must be accessible through the system's interface. They should convey information in a proactive manner. They must be relevant. Accuracy and reliability must be considered. Lastly, reports must meet the information processing (cognitive) style of the audience they were meant to inform and meet applicable reporting standards.

Management reports come in three basic types:

- *Filter reports*—separate selected data from a database, such as a monthly check register

- *Responsibility reports*—such as a weekly sales report for a regional sales manager

- *Comparative reports*—created to show period differences, percentage breakdowns and differences (variances) between actual and budgeted expenditures, such as a report showing the expenses from the current year and the prior year as a percentage of sales

Implementation. The implementation phase consists of two primary parts, construction and delivery. Construction includes the selection of hardware, software, and vendors for the implementation; building and testing the network communication systems; building and testing the databases; writing and testing the new program modifications; and installing and testing the total system from a technical standpoint. Delivery is the process of conducting final system and user acceptance testing, preparing the conversion plan, installing the production database, training the users, and converting all operations to the new system.

Tool sets. Tool sets are a variety of application development aids that are vendor specific and used for customization of delivered systems. They allow the addition of fields and tables to the database along with ability to create screen and other interfaces for data capture. In addition, they help set accessibility and security levels for adequate internal control within the accounting applications.

Security. Security exists in several forms, including physical security. In typical AISs the equipment is located in a locked room with access granted only to technicians. Software access controls are set at several levels, depending on the size of AIS. The first level of security occurs at the network level, which protects the organization's communication systems. Next is the operating system level security, which protects the computing environment. Then

database security is enabled to protect the organizational data from theft, corruption, and other threats. Lastly, application security is used to keep unauthorized persons from performing operations within the AIS.

Testing. Testing is performed at four levels. Stub or unit testing is used to ensure the proper operation of individual modifications. Program testing involves the interaction between the individual modification and the program it enhances. System testing is used to determine that the program modifications work within the AIS as a whole. Acceptance testing ensures that the modifications meet user expectations and that the entire AIS performs as designed.

Conversion. Conversion entails the method used to change from an old to a new AIS. Several methods are available to achieve this goal. One is to run the new and old systems in parallel for a specified period. A second method is to directly cut over to the new system at a specified time. A third method is to phase in the system, either by location or system function. A fourth method is to pilot the new system at a specific site before converting the rest of the organization.

Support. The support phase has two objectives. The first is to update and maintain the AIS. This includes fixing problems and updating the system for business and environmental changes. For example, changes in generally accepted accounting principles (GAAP) or new regulations such as the Sarbanes-Oxley Act of 2002 might necessitate changes to the AIS. The second objective of support is to continue development by continuously improving the business through adjustments to business and environmental changes. These changes might result in future problems, new opportunities, or management or governmental directives requiring additional system modifications.

ASSURANCE, AUDIT, AND ATTESTATION

Quality control of AISs involves many activities, including the services of both external auditors (public accountants) and internal auditors. External auditors can provide a variety of services, including providing assurance that the controls over external financial reporting are adequate and attestations that the external financial statement are "fairly presented" in accordance with GAAP. Internal auditors focus on providing assurance that AISs are effective and efficient in providing information to assist managerial decision making.

Continuous improvement of AISs change the way internal controls are implemented and the types of audit trails that exist within a modern organization. The lack of traditional forensic evidence, such as paper, necessitates the involvement of accounting and auditing professionals in the design of such systems. Periodic involvement of public auditing firms can be used to make sure the AIS is in compliance with current internal control requirements, such as the Section 404 requirements of the Sarbanes-Oxley Act and revised financial reporting standards.

After the implementation, the focus of attestation is the review and verification of system operation. This requires adherence to such standards as ISO 9000 for software design and development, as well as standards for control of information technology.

Periodic functional business reviews should be conducted to make sure the AIS remains in compliance with the intended business functions. Quality standards dictate this review should be done according to a periodic schedule.

TRADITIONAL AIS AND MODERN ENTERPRISE RESOURCE PLANNING SYSTEMS

Enterprise resource planning (ERP) systems are large-scale information systems that affect an organization's AIS. These systems permeate all aspects of the organization and require such technologies as client/server and relational databases. Other system types that affect AISs are supply chain management and customer relationship management.

Traditional AISs recorded financial information and produced financial statements on a periodic basis according to GAAP pronouncements. Modern ERP systems provide a broader view of organizational information, enabling the use of advanced accounting techniques such as ABC and improved managerial and financial reporting using a variety of analytical techniques.

SEE ALSO *Accounting; Information Systems; Management Information Systems*

BIBLIOGRAPHY
Hall, James A. (2007). *Accounting information systems* (5th ed.). Cincinnati: Thomson South-Western.

Jones, F., and Rama, D. (2006). *Accounting information systems: A business process.* Cincinnati: Thomson South-Western.

O'Brien, J. A., and Marakas, G. (2006). *Management information systems* (7th ed.). New York: McGraw-Hill.

Theodore J. Mock

ACFE
SEE *Association of Certified Fraud Examiners*

ACQUIRED-NEEDS THEORY
SEE *Motivation*

ACQUISITIONS
SEE *Mergers and Acquisitions*

ACTIVITY-BASED MANAGEMENT

Activity-based management (ABM) is an approach to management in which process managers are given the responsibility and authority to continuously improve the planning and control of operations by focusing on key operational activities. ABM strategically incorporates activity analysis, activity-based costing (ABC), activity-based budgeting, life cycle and target costing, process value analysis, and value-chain analysis. Enhanced effectiveness and efficiencies are expected for both revenue generation and cost incurrences. Since the focus is on activities, improved cost management is achieved through better managing those activities that consume resources and drive costs. The focus for control is shifted away from the financial measurement of resources to activities that cause costs to be incurred.

As an overall framework, ABM relies on ABC information. ABC deals with the analysis and assignment of costs. In order to complete cost analyses, activities need to be identified and classified. An activity dictionary can be developed, listing and describing all activities within an organization, including information on each activity's location, performance measure(s), and key value-added and non-value-added attributes. ABC information is extremely helpful in the strategic analysis of areas such as process and plant layout redesign, pricing, customer values, sourcing, evaluation of competitive position, and product strategy.

ACTIVITY AND ACTIVITY ANALYSIS

An activity is a business task, or an aggregation of closely related purposeful actions, with clear beginning and ending points, that consumes resources and produces outputs. An activity could be a single task or a simple process.

Resources are inputs, such as materials, labor, equipment, and other economic elements consumed by an activity in the production of an output. Outputs are products, services, and accompanying information flowing from an activity. In seeking continuous business improvement, an overall examination of variations in performances of key organizational activities and their causes is referred to as activity analysis. Performance is measured by a financial or nonfinancial indicator that is causally related to the performance (adding value to a product or service) of an activity and can be used to manage and improve the performance of that activity.

The level of an activity within an organization depends on the level of operations supported by that activity. For instance, a unit-level activity is one that is performed directly on each unit of output of an organizational process. A batch-level activity is one performed on a small group, or batch, of output units at the same time. For example, the setup activity to run a batch job in a production process and the associated cost for completing such a setup is a batch-level activity. A customer-sustaining activity supports an individual or a particular grouping of customers, such as mailings or customer service. A product-sustaining activity supports an individual product or product line, such as product (re)design or (re)engineering. These last two types of activities are sometimes referred to as service-sustaining activities. Last, a facility-sustaining activity supports an entire facility, such as the actions of the manager of an entire plant, with an associated cost equal to the manager's compensation package. Not every activity within an organization is significant enough to isolate in an activity analysis.

A process is a set of logically related activities performed in order to achieve a particular objective, such as the production of a unit of product or service. Identification of all such processes within an organization along with a specification of the relationships among them provides a value chain. Value chains are often presented in terms of functional areas (a function provides the organization with a particular type of service or product, such as finance, distribution, or purchasing). Within each of these key processes, activities can be classified as primary activities, secondary activities, and other activities. Primary activities contribute directly to the providing of the final product or service. Secondary activities directly support primary activities. The "other activities" category is comprised of those actions too far removed from the intended output to be individually noted. They should be examined to determine if they are necessary and should be continued.

VALUE-ADDED AND NON-VALUE-ADDED

Each of the key (primary and secondary) activities noted from this analysis must be categorized as either value-added or non-value-added. This analysis is referred to as value analysis. An activity is value-added to the extent that its performance contributes to the completion of the product or service for consumers. While value-added activities are necessary, the efficiency with which they are performed often can be improved through best practice analysis and benchmarking. This process of improvement is referred to as business process redesign or reengineering.

Because many activities may not fit neatly into a value-added/non-value-added dichotomy, weightings may be assigned to indicate the extent to which an activity is value-added, such as a scale ranging from one to eight, with an eight representing total value-additivity and a zero representing none. A non-value-added activity transforms a product or service in a way that adds no usefulness to the product or service. Non-value-added activities should be minimized or eliminated. An overall value-chain analysis would examine all the activities and associated processes in an attempt to provide greater value at the same cost, the same value at less cost, or both.

ACTIVITY-BASED COSTING

Because costs are initially assigned from resource cost pools to activity cost pools and from there to final cost objects, activity-based costing is viewed as a two-stage allocation process. Once activities have been identified, an activity-based costing analysis can be completed. Activity-based costing is a form of cost refinement, designed to obtain greater accuracy than traditional allocations in cost assignments for product costing and decision-making purposes. Costs are assigned to activities from resource cost pools. Costs are first accumulated according to the type of resource, such as materials or labor, with which they are associated. Then resource (cost) drivers, which measure the consumption of a resource by an activity, are identified and used to assign the costs of resource consumptions to each activity. The result of this assignment is an activity cost pool for each activity.

From the activity cost pool, the focus shifts to one or more activity drivers. An activity driver measures the frequency or intensity with which a cost object requires the use of an activity, thereby relating the performance of an activity's tasks to the needs of one or more cost objects. A cost object is why activities are performed; it is a unit of product or service, an operating segment of the organization, or even another activity for which management desires an assignment of costs for unit costing or decision-making purposes. The activity cost pools are then reassigned to the final cost objects according to the intensity with which each cost object used the respective activity drivers.

A cost driver may be defined to be "any factor that has the effect of changing the level of total cost for a cost object" (Blocher et al., 1999, p. 8). In general, four types of cost drivers can be identified: volume-based, activity-based, structural, and executional (Blocher, et al., 1999, p. 61). Activity-based management focuses on activity-based cost drivers. In investigating and specifying cost drivers, many methods are used, such as cause-and-effect diagrams, cost simulations, and Pareto analysis.

Traditional cost assignment systems typically would assign directly to the cost objects the costs of those resource consumptions that can be economically traced directly to units of output requiring the resources. The remaining costs, referred to as indirect costs, would be accumulated into one or more cost pools, which would subsequently be allocated to the cost objects according to volume-related bases of allocation. When different products consume resources at rates that are not accurately reflected in their relative numbers (volumes), a traditional cost allocation approach will result in product cost cross-subsidization. That is, a high-volume, relatively simple product will end up overcosted and subsidizing a subsequently undercosted, low-volume, relatively complex product, resulting in inaccurate unit costing and suboptimal product-line pricing decisions and performance evaluations. Activity-based costing tries to take the nonuniformity of resource consumption across products into account in the assignment of costs.

SEE ALSO *Management*

BIBLIOGRAPHY
Blocher, Edward J., Chen, Jung H., and Lin, Thomas W. (2002). *Cost Management: A Strategic Emphasis* (2nd ed.). New York: Irwin/McGraw-Hill.

Cooper, Robin, Kaplan, Robert S., Maisel, Lawrence S., Morrissey, Eileen, and Oehm, Ronald M. (1992). *Implementing Activity-Based Cost Management: Moving from Analysis to Action.* Montvale, NJ: Institute of Management Accountants.

Hilton, Ronald W., Maher, Michael W., and Selto, Frank H. (2003). *Cost Management: Strategies for Business Decisions* (2nd ed.). Boston: McGraw-Hill.

Clifford Brown
Lawrence A. Klein

ADVERTISING

Advertising is often thought of as the paid, nonpersonal promotion of a cause, idea, product, or service by an identified sponsor attempting to inform or persuade a partic-

ular target audience. Advertising has taken many different forms since the beginning of time. For instance, archaeologists have uncovered walls painted in Rome announcing gladiator fights as well as rock paintings along Phoenician trade routes used to advertise wares. From this early beginning, advertising has evolved to take a variety of forms and to permeate nearly every aspect of modern society.

The various delivery mechanisms for advertising include banners at sporting events, billboards, Internet Web sites, logos on clothing, magazines, newspapers, radio spots, and television commercials. Advertising has so permeated everyday life that individuals can expect to be exposed to 1,500 to 3,000 different messages each day. While advertising may seem like the perfect way to get a message out, it does have several limitations, the most commonly noted ones being its inability to focus on an individual consumer's specific needs, provide in-depth information about a product, and be cost-effective for small companies.

FORMS OF ADVERTISING

Advertising can take a number of forms, including advocacy, comparative, cooperative, direct mail, informational, institutional, outdoor, persuasive, product, reminder, point-of-purchase, and specialty advertising.

Advocacy Advertising. Advocacy advertising is normally thought of as any advertisement, message, or public communication regarding economic, political, or social issues. The advertising campaign is designed to persuade public opinion regarding a specific issue important in the public arena. The ultimate goal of advocacy advertising usually relates to the passage of pending state or federal legislation. Almost all nonprofit groups use some form of advocacy advertising to influence the public's attitude toward a particular issue.

One of the largest and most powerful nonprofit advocacy groups is the American Association of Retired Persons (AARP). The AARP fights to protect social programs such as Medicare and Social Security for senior citizens by encouraging its members to write their legislators, using television advertisements to appeal to emotions, and publishing a monthly newsletter describing recent state and federal legislative action. Other major nonprofit advocacy groups include the environmental organization Greenpeace, Mothers against Drunk Driving, and the National Rifle Association.

Comparative Advertising. Comparative advertising compares one brand directly or indirectly with one or more competing brands. This advertising technique is very common and is used by nearly every major industry,

Billboards, such as these along the Palmetto Expressway in Miami, Florida, are a popular form of advertising. AP IMAGES

including airlines and automobile manufacturers. One drawback of comparative advertising is that customers have become more skeptical about claims made by a company about its competitors because accurate information has not always been provided, thus making the effectiveness of comparison advertising questionable. In addition, companies that engage in comparative advertising must be careful not to misinform the public about a competitor's product. Incorrect or misleading information may trigger a lawsuit by the aggrieved company or regulatory action by a governmental agency such as the Federal Trade Commission (FTC; see the FTC's statement of policy regarding comparative advertising at http://www.ftc.gov/bcp/policystmt/ad-compare.htm).

Cooperative Advertising. Cooperative advertising is a system that allows two parties to share advertising costs. Manufacturers and distributors, because of their shared interest in selling the product, usually use this cooperative advertising technique. An example might be when a soft-drink manufacturer and a local grocery store split the cost of advertising the manufacturer's soft drinks; both the manufacturer and the store benefit from increased store traffic and its associated sales. Cooperative advertising is

especially appealing to small-store owners who, on their own, could not afford to advertise the product adequately. For examples of cooperative advertising programs, see the John Wiley & Sons, Inc. (http://www.wiley.com/WileyCDA/Section/id-10671.html) and the New Mexico Department of Tourism (http://www.newmexico.org/go/loc/department/page/dept-coop-advertising.html) Web sites.

Direct Mail. Brochures, catalogs, flyers, letters, and post-cards are just a few of the direct-mail advertising options. Direct-mail advertising has several advantages, including detail of information, personalization, selectivity, and speed. But while direct mail has advantages, it carries an expensive per-head price, is dependent on the appropriateness of the mailing list, and is resented by some customers, who consider it junk mail.

Informational Advertising. In informational advertising, which is used when a new product is first being introduced, the emphasis is on promoting the product name, benefits, and possible uses. Thus, informational advertising is used early in the product life cycle. Car manufacturers used this strategy when sport-utility vehicles were first introduced.

Institutional Advertising. Institutional advertising takes a broad approach to advertising, concentrating on the benefits, concept, idea, or philosophy of a particular industry. Companies often use it to promote image-building activities, such an environmentally friendly business practices or new community-based programs that it sponsors. Institutional advertising is closely related to public relations, since both are interested in promoting a positive image of the company to the public. As an example, a large lumber company may develop an advertising theme around its practice of planting trees in areas where they have just been harvested. A theme of this nature keeps the company's name in a positive light with the general public because the replanting of trees is viewed positively by most people. For example, the idea that "The Future Is Growing," is noted on the Weyerhaeuser (http://www.weyerhaeuser.com) Web site.

Outdoor Advertising. Billboards and messages painted on the sides of buildings are common forms of outdoor advertising, which is often used when quick, simple ideas are being promoted. Since repetition is the key to successful promotion, outdoor advertising is most effective when located along heavily traveled city streets and when the product being promoted can be purchased locally. Only about 1 percent of advertising is conducted in this manner. For more information on outdoor advertising, see the Lamar Advertising Company Web site at http://www.lamaroutdoor.com/main/home/default.cfm. Lamar Advertising Company is among the largest in the United States.

Persuasive Advertising. Persuasive advertising is used after a product has been introduced to customers. The primary goal is for a company to build selective demand for its product. For example, automobile manufacturers often produce special advertisements promoting the safety features of their vehicles. This type of advertisement could allow automobile manufacturers to charge more for their products because of the perceived higher quality the safety features afford. Both Ford Motor Company (http://www.ford.com) and General Motors Corporation (http://www.gm.com) provide extensive information regarding product safety on their Web sites.

Product Advertising. Product advertising pertains to nonpersonal selling of a specific product. An example is a regular television commercial promoting a soft drink. The primary purpose of the advertisement is to promote the specific soft drink, not the entire soft-drink line of a company.

Reminder Advertising. Reminder advertising is used for products that have entered the mature stage of the product life cycle. The advertisements are simply designed to remind customers about the product and to maintain awareness. For example, detergent producers spend a considerable amount of money each year promoting their products to remind customers that their products are still available and for sale. Reminder advertising is often used during the maturity stage of the product life cycle.

Point-of-Purchase Advertising. Point-of-purchase advertising uses displays or other promotional items near the product that is being sold. The primary motivation is to attract customers to the display so that they will purchase the product. Stores are more likely to use point-of-purchase displays if they have help from the manufacturer in setting them up or if the manufacturer provides easy instructions on how to use the displays. Thus, promotional items from manufacturers who provide the best instructions or help are more likely to be used by the retail stores. For more information regarding point-of-purchase advertising, see the Point-of-Purchase Advertising International Web site (http://www.popai.com//AM/Template.cfm?Section=Home).

Specialty Advertising. Specialty advertising is a form of sales promotion designed to increase public recognition of a company's name. A company can have its name put on a variety of items, such as caps, glassware, gym bags, jackets, key chains, and pens. The value of specialty advertising varies depending on how long the items used in the effort last. Most companies are successful in achieving their goals for increasing public recognition and sales through these efforts. For more information about specialty advertising, see the Specialty Advertising Association of California Web site (http://www.SAAC.net).

ADVERTISING OBJECTIVES

The objectives of advertising are to reach specific customers during a particular time frame and get them to buy a particular product. A company that advertises usually strives to achieve one of four types of advertising objectives: trial, continuity, brand switching, and switchback. Which of the four advertising objectives is selected usually depends on where the product is in its life cycle.

Trial. The purpose of the trial objective is to encourage customers to make an initial purchase of a new product. Companies will typically employ creative advertising strategies in order to cut through other competing advertisements. The reason is simple—without that first trial of a product by customers, there will not be any repeat purchases.

Continuity. Continuity advertising is a strategy to keep current customers using a particular product. Existing customers are targeted and are usually provided new and different information about a product that is designed to build consumer loyalty.

Brand Switching. Companies adopt brand switching as an objective when they want customers to switch from competitors' brands to their brands. A common strategy is for a company to compare product price or quality in order to persuade customers to switch to its product brand.

Switchback. Companies subscribe to this advertising objective when they want to get back former users of their product brand. A company might highlight new product features, price reductions, or other important product information in order to get former customers of its product to switch back.

ADVERTISING BUDGET

Once an advertising objective has been selected, companies must then set an advertising budget for each product. Developing such a budget can be a difficult process because brand managers want to receive a large resource allocation to promote their products. Overall, the advertising budget should be established so as to be congruent with overall company objectives. Before establishing an advertising budget, companies must take into consideration other market factors, such as advertising frequency, competition and clutter, market share, product differentiation, and stage in the product life cycle.

Advertising Frequency. Advertising frequency refers to the number of times an advertisement is repeated during a given period to promote a product's name, message, and other important information. A larger advertising budget is required in order to achieve a high advertising frequency. Estimates have been put forward that a consumer needs to come in contact with an advertising message three times before it will be remembered.

Competition and Clutter. Highly competitive product markets, such as the soft-drink industry, require higher advertising budgets just to stay even with competitors. If a company wants to be a leader in an industry, then a substantial advertising budget must be earmarked every year. Examples abound of companies that spend billions of dollars on advertising in the United States alone in order to be key players in their respective industries (e.g., Ford Motor Company, Johnson & Johnson, and McDonald's Corporation).

Market Share. Desired market share is also an important factor in establishing an advertising budget. Increasing market share normally requires a large advertising budget because a company's competitors frequently counterattack with their own advertising blitz. For example, when General Motors Corporation initiated an employee pricing for everyone campaign, both DaimlerChrysler and Ford Motor Corporation established similar offers. Successfully increasing market share depends on advertisement quality, competitor responses, and product demand and quality.

Product Differentiation. How customers perceive products is also important to the budget-setting process. Product differentiation is often necessary in competitive markets where customers have a hard time differentiating between products. For example, product differentiation might be necessary when a new laundry detergent is advertised. Since so many brands of detergent already exist, an aggressive advertising campaign would be required. Without this aggressive advertising, customers would not be aware of the product's availability and how it differs from other products on the market. The advertising budget is higher in order to pay for the additional advertising.

Stage in the Product Life Cycle. New product offerings require considerably more advertising to make customers aware of their existence. As a product moves through the product life cycle, fewer and fewer advertising resources are needed because the product has become known and has developed an established buyer base. Advertising budgets are typically highest for a particular product during the introduction stage and gradually decline as the product matures.

SELECTING THE RIGHT
ADVERTISING APPROACH

Once a company decides what type of specific advertising campaign it wants to use, it must decide what approach should carry the message. A company must decide on such items as frequency, media impact, media timing, and reach.

Frequency. Frequency refers to the average number of times that an average consumer is exposed to the advertising campaign. A company usually establishes frequency goals, which can vary for each advertising campaign. For example, a company might want to have the average consumer exposed to the message at least six times during the advertising campaign. This number may seem high, but in a crowded and competitive market, repetition is one of the best methods to increase the product's visibility and to increase company sales. The more exposure a company desires for its product, the more expensive the advertising campaign. Thus, often only large companies can afford to have high-frequency advertisements during a campaign.

Media Impact. Media impact generally refers to how effective advertising will be through the various media outlets (e.g., television, Internet, print). A company must decide, based on its product, the best method to maximize consumer interest and awareness. For example, a company promoting a new laundry detergent might fare better with television commercials rather than simple print ads because more consumers are likely to see the television commercial. Similarly, a company such as Mercedes-Benz, which markets expensive products, might advertise in specialty car magazines to reach a high percentage of its potential customers. Before any money is spent on any advertising media, a thorough analysis is done for each one's strengths and weaknesses in comparison to the cost. Once the analysis is done, the company will decide which media outlet is best to use and will embark on its advertising campaign.

Timing. Another major consideration for any company engaging in an advertising campaign is when to run the advertisements. For example, some companies run ads during the holidays to promote season-specific products. The other major consideration for a company is whether it wants to employ a continuous or pulsing pattern of advertisements. Continuous refers to advertisements that are run on a scheduled basis for a given period. The advantage of this tactic is that an advertising campaign can run longer and might provide more exposure over time. For example, a company could run an advertising campaign for a particular product that lasts years with the hope of keeping the product in the minds of customers.

Pulsing indicates that advertisements will be scheduled in a disproportionate manner within a given time frame. Thus, a company could run thirty-two television commercials over a three- or six-month period to promote the specific product is wants to sell. The advantage with the pulsing strategy is twofold. The company could spend less money on advertising over a shorter period but still gain the same recognition because the advertising campaign is more intense.

Reach. Reach refers to the percentage of customers in the target market who are exposed to the advertising campaign for a given period. A company might have a goal of reaching at least 80 percent of its target audience during a given time frame. The goal is to be as close to 100 percent as possible, because the more the target audience is exposed to the message, the higher the chance of future sales.

ADVERTISING EVALUATION

Once the advertising campaign is over, companies normally evaluate it compared to the established goals. An effective tactic in measuring the usefulness of the advertising campaign is to measure the pre- and post-sales of the company's product. In order to make this more effective, some companies divide up the country into regions and run the advertising campaigns only in some areas. The different geographic areas are then compared (advertising versus nonadvertising), and a detailed analysis is performed to provide an evaluation of the campaign's effectiveness. Depending on the results, a company will modify future advertising efforts in order to maximize effectiveness.

SUMMARY

Advertising is the paid, nonpersonal promotion of a cause, idea, product, or service by an identified sponsor attempting to inform or persuade a particular target audience. Advertising has evolved to take a variety of forms and has permeated nearly every aspect of modern society. The various delivery mechanisms for advertising include banners at sporting events, billboards, the Internet, logos on clothing, magazines, newspapers, radio spots, and television commercials. While advertising can be successful at getting the message out, it does have several limitations, including its inability to focus on an individual consumer's specific needs, provide in-depth information about a product, and be cost-effective for small companies. Other factors, such as objectives, budgets, approaches, and evaluation methods must all be considered.

SEE ALSO *Advertising Agencies; Promotion*

BIBLIOGRAPHY

Adams, R. (2003). *WWW.advertising: Advertising and marketing on the World Wide Web.* New York: Watson-Guptill.

Boone, Louis E., and Kurtz, David L. (2005). *Contemporary marketing 2006* (12th ed.). Eagan, MN: Thomson South-Western.

Brierley, S. (2002). *The advertising handbook* (2nd ed.). New York: Routledge.

Churchill, Gilbert A., Jr., and Peter, Paul J. (1998). *Marketing: Creating value for customers* (2nd ed.). New York: Irwin McGraw-Hill.

Farese, Lois, Kimbrell, Grady, and Woloszyk, Carl (2002). *Marketing essentials* (3rd ed.). Mission Hills, CA: Glencoe/McGraw-Hill.

Kotler, Philip, and Armstrong, Gary (2006). *Principles of marketing* (11th ed.). Upper Saddle River, NJ: Pearson Prentice-Hall.

Pride, William M., and Ferrell, O. C. (2006). *Marketing concepts and strategies.* New York: Houghton Mifflin.

Richards, Barry, MacRury, Iain, and Botterill, Jackie (2000). *The dynamics of advertising.* Amsterdam: Harwood Academic.

Semenik, Richard J., and Bamossy, Gary J. (1995). *Principles of marketing: A global perspective* (2nd ed.). Cincinnati: South-Western.

Special report: Leading national advertisers. (2002, June 24). *Advertising Age.*

Tellis, G. J. (2004). *Effective advertising: Understanding when, how, and why advertising works.* Thousand Oaks, CA: Sage.

Allen D. Truell
Michael Milbier

ADVERTISING AGENCIES

Advertising agencies are independent businesses that evolved to develop, prepare, and place advertising in advertising media for sellers seeking to find customers for their goods, services, and ideas (American Association of Advertising Agencies, 2000). Advertisers use agents when they believe the agency will be more expert than they are at planning and creating advertisements or at developing an advertising campaign. As businesses have become more complex and diversified, many of them have consulted agencies to help them carry out their marketing communication efforts.

The modern advertising agency provides a variety of important services to clients, including media planning and buying, research, market information, sales promotion assistance, campaign development and creation of advertisements, plus a range of services designed to help the advertiser achieve marketing objectives. The first advertising agency in the United States was opened in Philadelphia by Volney Palmer in 1841 (John Hartman Center, 2000). At this time, advertising agents were largely space brokers agents who solicited ads from businesses and then sold them to newspapers that had difficulty getting out-of-town advertising (Lane, King, & Russell, 2005).

EVOLUTION OF THE ADVERTISING AGENCY FROM THE 1870S TO THE EARLY 1900S

While the invention of printing paved the way for the development of modern advertising, the influence of salesmanship began to influence the evolution of advertising toward more like what we recognize today. The advertising agency, working on a commission basis, has been chiefly responsible for this evolution. During the late nineteenth century, most advertising appeared in newspapers, on posters, and in handbills (Wells, Burnett, & Moriarty, 2000). Because it was difficult to reproduce illustrations, most of these ads were simple text-based items.

By 1900, the first specialized magazines had begun to appear in the United States. Magazines such as *Field & Stream* (in 1895) and *Good Housekeeping* (in 1900) established niche markets, which allowed for mass marketing to consumers with varied interests. Also, print technology had evolved considerably, making full-color illustrations possible. Advertising agencies began to use the new technology to create more attractive advertisements for the new niche markets, thus becoming creative centers rather than merely space brokerages.

The late nineteenth and early twentieth centuries were also times of public concern about unethical business practices. Many professions formed their own organizations to create ethical standards of operation. The American Association for Advertising Agencies (AAAA) was founded in 1917 to represent the agencies, partially in response to these ethical concerns.

Newspapers also set their own ethical standards concerning rates charged for advertisements. By 1917, publishers had agreed to set a flat rate of 15 percent as the standard commission an advertising agency would receive with the exception of local advertising, for which there was generally no predetermined commission (Lane et al., 2005).

In addition, two laws were passed to alleviate concerns about unethical advertising practices. The Federal Trade Commission Act of 1914 was originally designed to make all unfair methods of competition unlawful. It was not until 1922 that advertising was legally regulated under this act. The case that set this legal precedent was *FTC v. Winsted Hosiery Company* (1922) (Lane et al., 2005). The Pure Food and Drug Act of 1906 was the first act that limited the advertising of patent medicines—drugs that were advertised using exaggerated claims of effectiveness—for use by children.

EVOLUTION OF THE ADVERTISING AGENCY FROM 1920 TO THE EARLY 1950S

During the first part of the twentieth century, agencies expanded their role from one largely comprised of selling space to one of "full service" to clients—involvement in all advertising functions, from market research to ad production, to space buying (Jones, 2004). Agency development was stimulated after World War I when consumers were demanding more goods and services (Wells et al, 2000).

By the 1920s, market research suggested the role of women in making many family purchasing decisions.

Thus, advertising agencies created full-color magazine advertisements for goods such as automobiles, refrigerators, and radios. Newspapers continued to use simple advertisements. In the 1920s and 30s, radio also became popular for home and family use as an inexpensive form of entertainment (Wells et al., 2000). Advertising agencies produced radio programs for the sole purpose of attracting consumers for popular national products. For example, the term "soap opera" was coined by the American press in the 1930s to denote these popular serialized domestic radio dramas. The "soap" in soap opera alluded to their sponsorship largely by manufacturers of household cleaning products (Museum of Broadcast Communications, 2005).

The 1930s were a time of renewed public interest in legislation concerning unfair and deceptive business practices. The Robinson-Patman Act of 1936 prevented manufacturers from providing promotional allowances to a retail customer unless it also offered promotional allowances to that customer's competitors. The 1938 Wheeler-Lea Amendments to the Federal Trade Commission Act enabled the Federal Trade Commission (FTC) to protect consumers from deceptive advertising in the food, drug, therapeutic device, and cosmetic industries (Lane et al., 2005).

Although World War II suspended production of many peacetime goods and services, many advertising agents found employment working for the War Advertising Council, which was responsible for mobilizing public support for the war effort. This organization later became the Ad Council.

EVOLUTION OF THE ADVERTISING AGENCY FROM THE 1950S TO THE EARLY 1990S

The end of World War II saw a culmination of more than a decade of unsatisfied consumer demand as a result of the Great Depression and war. Most markets for goods and services found a willing consumer base for new products—including television sets. Because television is a medium that combines the visual element available in print ads with sound and motion, this created a change in the structure of advertising agencies. For example, prior to the 1950s, the main source of creativity was the person writing the advertising message—referred to as the copywriter. As television became more popular, the art director and artist became more important (Wells et al., 2000).

Between 1945 and 1960, large numbers of returning veterans began to marry and have children—the generation of children known as baby-boomers. For the first time in the United States, advertising agencies found it profitable to market certain goods and services directly to the youth market. Ads for blue jeans and stereo equipment appeared in newspaper inserts, in youth-oriented niche market magazines, and on television.

Advances in product design during the 1960s and 1970s forced advertising agencies to become more creative in order to differentiate their client's product from competitors' equally good products. The resulting newer, more creative advertisements proved both popular and profitable, allowing agencies to spend more money on advertising research—often employing behavioral psychologists to design elaborate studies of consumer buying behavior. All of this creativity had a cost: it became very expensive to produce lengthy TV advertisements. Advertising agencies addressed the cost issue by designing thirty-second television commercials with memorable advertising slogans short phrases designed to keep a consumer's attention and maintain recognition of a particular brand of good or service.

As the cost of advertising rose, agency clients began to demand results for increasingly expensive ad efforts—in the form of consumer research. During the 1980s and 1990s, many advertising agencies merged in order to remain financially competitive in this period of consolidation and rising costs. Some agencies moved toward providing a range of marketing services options to clients, including direct marketing, sales promotion, and public relations (Lane et al., 2005). Some advertising agencies moved from traditional radio and TV advertising toward sales promotion techniques such as rebates, coupons, and sweepstakes that offered measurable proof of increased sales (Wells et al., 2000).

Evolution of the Advertising Agency from 1995 to the Present. The traditional advertising agency is now facing competition from many different directions. In recent years, a number of advertising media companies have consolidated their businesses. These large organizations have sought to blend media, such as television, print, cable, and Internet to be able to better design messages to meet individual consumer needs (Lane et al., 2005). Some large advertisers are directly employing branding specialists, media specialists and CRM specialists and dissolving their longstanding relationships with agencies in an effort to increase the effectiveness of their marketing dollars. Marketing, branding and research consultancy firms have developed, with each claiming to provide the strategic planning offered by agencies. In addition, media firms and production houses are now delving into concept development (Williams, 2004).

Present-day agencies employ many of the techniques that were popular in the early years of advertising. Newspapers continue to advertise primarily in text format, although color inserts are becoming popular. Advertising agencies continue to be able to advertise in smaller and smaller niche-market magazines. Radio remains a popular advertising medium in local markets. The widespread availability of cable TV and satellite transmission has fragmented television advertising into niche markets. However, new and enhanced technologies plus continuing innovation in product development are adding an interactive flavor to advertising. With the development of new media channels new marketing opportunities will arise. These developments in the advertising industry continue to influence how agencies operate. The changes are discussed next.

Globalization and International Marketing. Advertising agencies are under increasing pressure to create ads for products distributed in a global market. Costs for producing and executing advertising campaigns across international markets can be very high. Success often depends on a brand maintaining a uniform position across the markets in different countries. Agencies must often consider culture, language, and customs when designing an advertisement tailored to the international market. In order to meet the demands of a global market, advertisers are forming large multinational agencies and continuing to debate whether to standardize advertising globally or to segment advertisements by culture or nationality (Wells et al., 2000).

Interactive Marketing and the Internet. Since 2000, interactive marketing has been the fastest growing area within marketing. Interactive marketing includes Internet advertising, permission e-mail, marketing web sites, mobile media (including digital mobile communication devices) and other new media (Stafford & Faber, 2005). These media are distinctive among the mass media in that they permit people the chance to communicate outside the traditional medium limitations of time and space.

The Internet allows advertising agencies to target consumers worldwide and to conduct market research inexpensively. The easy access to market research information may permit advertising agencies to continue developing ads to reach smaller and smaller niche markets worldwide. At the same time, certain forces are reducing the availability and use of information gathered over the Internet. For example, the Children's Online Protection Act (1998), or COPA, is a U.S. law that affects business transactions by children using the Internet. COPA requires Web sites soliciting personal information from children under the age of 13 to prominently post a privacy policy and require parental consent for the release of personal information provided by those children before any business can be transacted. Many countries are developing laws similar to COPA, and it remains to be seen how

COPA and other impending legislation will affect advertising agencies that conduct business globally.

The Role of Government in Advertising. Very few industries have been more thoroughly regulated than advertising. Advertising's visibility in society sometimes makes it a target for criticism. Consumers often believe that many advertisements are untruthful and manipulative, which draws attention from citizens, the media, government, and competitors (Wells et al., 2000). At these times, government often has taken steps to regulate advertising practices and content.

The Ad Council is a private, non-profit organization that marshals volunteers from advertising and communications, media facilities, and the resources of the business and non-profit communities to deliver messages to the American public. Since its founding in 1942 as the War Advertising Council, the Ad Council has produced public service ads and acted as an agency that addresses social issues such as improving the quality of life for children, preventative health, education, community well being, environmental preservation and strengthening families (The Ad Council, 2005).

Changing Incentives. Advertising agencies produce revenue and profits by charging commissions and fees for their services. The 15-percent commission has remained a common practice, with the rate sometimes negotiated downward are account budgets become large. In recent years, fees have become the largest source of revenue for agencies. Increasingly, agency revenues are based on sales or market distribution goals (Lane et al., 2005).

Evolving Career Fields in Advertising. Today's advertising agencies include a vast array of specialists who work together to create a complete and thorough advertising campaign. Account managers allocate agency resources, including time, money, and personnel for individual projects. An account manager often assembles a team of individuals, each bringing a particular advertising specialty to the project. The team includes an art director, creative director, artist(s), copywriters, and designers. The team may also include other specialists such as media analysts, product testers, researchers, and public relations consultants.

SEE ALSO *Advertising*

BIBLIOGRAPHY

The Ad Council (2005). Retrieved March 21, 2006, from http://www.adcouncil.org.

American Association of Advertising Agencies (2005). Retrieved March 24, 2006, from http://www.aaaa.org.

Balachandran, M.E., & Smith, M.O. (2000). "E-Commerce: The new frontier in marketing." *Business Education Forum,* 54(4), 37-39.

Jones, J. P. (2004). *Fables, fantasies, and facts about advertising.* Thousand Oaks, CA: Sage Publications.

Lane, W.R., King, K.W., & Russell, J.T. (2005). *Kleppner's advertising procedure* (16th ed.). Upper Saddle River, NJ: Pearson/Prentice-Hall.

Museum of Broadcast Communications (2005). Retrieved from http://museum.tv.

Stafford, M. R., & Faber, R. J. (2005). *Advertising, promotion, and new media.* London: M. E. Sharpe.

Wells, W., Burnett, J., & Moriarty, S. (2000). *Advertising: principles & practice.* Upper Saddle River, NJ: Prentice-Hall.

Williams, T. (2004). "Evolve or die: The changing model of the advertising agency." Retrieved from http://www.marketingprofs.com.

John A. Swope
Scott Williams

AGENCY THEORY

Agency theory pertains to the relationship between two parties; the first is the principal (or principals) and the second, the agent (or agents), who are engaged as employees or independent contractors. Considered a subunit of the theory of contracts, agency theory deals with the determination of the general structure of such contractual relationships and factors that influence behavior of the parties involved.

While the principal/agent relationship was recognized in the writing of early economists, including Adam Smith, the identification of this special aspect of contracts dates to the 1970s. A significant paper published in 1976 by Michael Jensen and William Meckling identified elements from the theory of agency in their consideration of the theory of the firm. They commented:

> The firm is a "black box" operated so as to meet the relevant marginal conditions with respect to inputs and outputs, thereby maximizing profits.... Except for a few recent and tentative steps, however, we have no theory which explains how the conflicting objectives of the individual participants are brought into equilibrium so as to yield this results.

The theory has continued to evolve since the Jensen-Meckling paper was written. In noting the basic analyses still to be undertaken, J. Gregory Dees stated in 1992, "principal-agent analysis is a diverse and rapidly developing field.... While commonly referred to as 'agency theory,' ... I ... believe the label is misleading. It is more

accurate to describe it as a modeling approach within which there are some common structure and assumptions with wide variations" (p. 27). Yet, in 2002 Eric Brousseau hinted at the incompleteness of the theory in considering the future economic analysis of this type of contract and in stating that this would require the "collaboration with professionals and scholars in other disciplines" (p. 27).

SOME PROBLEMS IDENTIFIED

Some problem areas that have been highlighted in studies are: agency costs, adverse selection, and moral hazard. Each of these aspects is briefly defined and explained below.

Agency Costs. Expenditures for monitoring, perceived to be necessary, are critical costs in a principal/agency relationship. Since the principal is delegating authority and responsibility, prudent management undertakes some type of monitoring to have assurance that decisions are optimal from the point of view of the principal. Reports, observational visits, and supervision are common types of monitoring, none of which is cost-free.

Adverse Selection. The incompleteness of information that is generally available to the principal and to the agent is the core concept of adverse selection. Agents present their credentials in résumés; they discuss their qualifications in interviews. Based on such information, the principals conclude whether such agents are qualified or not for positions to be filled. In some instances, such résumés are later found to contain inaccurate information, or representations made in interviews are later recognized as not the same as what is learned about actual performance.

Principals, too, may misrepresent information or provide incomplete information. Principals in interviewing prospective accountants, for example, may state that high ethical standards are to be maintained in processing and reporting financial information to shareholders. Agents accept such representations as in line with their beliefs. After accepting positions as accounting managers, though, agents are informed that the company figures must reflect a specified level of profit for the end of the fiscal year, regardless of what the actual accounting records reflect. The words of the principal during the initial interview are not supported by the demand to manipulate the figures.

Moral Hazard. The possibility that agents will not choose to optimize the wishes of principals is the essence of this problem. For example, a company executive hires a manager for a manufacturing plant for which standards of output have been established. The manager agrees to a fixed income with no bonus. The manager soon learns that the standards of output are not demanding; it would be possible to readily achieve higher levels of output—which seems a good idea because the demand for the product is greater than current production. The manager, however, perceives no incentive to increase the level of activity, since just meeting the standards is the critical basis for evaluation and determination of the next year's salary for the manager. The manager has decided to keep "the job easy," rather than inform a supervisor that a higher level of productivity is reasonable and would aid in meeting the unmet demand for the product.

THE REALITY OF CONTEMPORARY PRINCIPAL/AGENT EFFECTIVENESS

Financial accounting scandals in U.S. companies reflect the ineffectiveness of principal/agent relationships and the insufficiency of current agency theoretical efforts. As a result of the cascade of scandals in the decade prior to 2002, the U.S. Congress enacted the Sarbanes-Oxley Act of 2002, which imposed new regulations on public companies and their auditors. Such rules are assumed to be effective in ensuring that executives fulfill their obligations. Such rules affect a hierarchy of principal/agent relationships: Shareholders are principals of public companies and their immediate agents are boards of directors. Boards of directors are principals; their agents are the executives selected to carry out policies and the independent auditors they engage to audit the financial statements of the company. The principal/agent relationships continue to lower levels of organizations.

Many opportunities exist within publicly owned companies for less than optimum effectiveness in principal/agent relationships. Such opportunities are predicted to decline with successful implementation of the new rules and regulations. Even with new rules and regulations, however, there is an awareness that the knowledge of how equilibrium (where both the principal and agent are optimally behaving for both the interests of the entity and of the personal executive or employee) can be predicted continues to be insufficient.

SUMMARY

The need for increasing understanding of the principal/agent relationship continues. While attention to agency theory began in the field of economics—including the practical fields of finance and accounting—interest in the subject has developed among some political scientists, historians, sociologists, psychologists, and ethicists. Considerable empirical investigations, as well as refinements at the theoretical level, are needed. Studying and thinking are continuing.

SEE ALSO *Contracts*

BIBLIOGRAPHY

Bowie, Norman E., and Freeman, R. Edward (Eds.) (1992). *Ethics and agency theory: An introduction.* New York: Oxford University Press.

Brousseau, Eric, and Glachant, Jean-Michel (Eds.) (2002). *The economics of contracts: Theories and applications.* New York: Cambridge University Press.

Dees, J. Gregory (1992). Principals, agents, and ethics. In Norman E. Bowie and R. Edward Freeman (Eds.), *Ethics and agency theory: An introduction* (p. 25). New York: Oxford University Press.

Gutner, Tamar L. (2005, May). *Explaining the gaps between mandate and performance: agency theory and world bank environmental reform.* Cambridge: The Center for Strategic and International Studies and the Massachusetts Institute of Technology. Retrieved July 25, 2005 from LexisNexis.

Jensen, M., and Meckling, W. (1976, October). Theory of the firm: managerial behavior, agency costs and ownership structure. *Journal of Financial Economics. (3)4,* pp. 305–360.

Karake-Shalhoub, Zeinab (2002). *Trust and loyalty in electronic commerce: An agency theory perspective.* Westport, CT: Quorum Books.

Mary Ellen Oliverio

AGGREGATE INCOME

SEE *Income*

AMERICAN INSTITUTE OF CERTIFIED PUBLIC ACCOUNTANTS

The American Institute of Certified Public Accountants (AICPA) is a leading national organization for certified public accountants (CPAs) in the United States. It traces its origin to a meeting of accountants in 1887. The AICPA's Web site (http://www.aicpa.org), offers the public a comprehensive source of information about the profession.

MEMBERSHIP

As of 2005, AICPA membership included more than 327,000 CPAs. Approximately 43 percent worked in business and industry, nearly 40 percent worked in public accounting firms, and others were employed by government bodies and agencies and educational and other not-for-profit institutions. In addition, some members worked in the legal profession, offering consulting services. Some were retired. The membership includes associates (those who have passed the Uniform CPA Exam and are fulfilling other requirements to become CPAs in their states), accounting students, and international affiliates. In total, membership in 2005 was approximately 350,000.

PRIMARY ACTIVITIES

The AICPA's primary mission is providing leadership, resources, and information to enable CPAs to perform services in a professional manner for the benefit of the public as well as for employers and clients. Activities are broadly characterized as advocacy, communication, recruitment and education, and standards and performance. To carry out its mission, the AICPA works with local CPA societies in fifty-five accountancy jurisdictions (the 50 states plus Washington, D.C., Puerto Rico, the U.S. Virgin Islands, Guam, and the Northern Marianas Islands).

The AICPA represents CPAs before governments, regulatory bodies, and other organizations in protecting and promoting members' interests while preserving public confidence in the financial reporting system. It also promotes public awareness of and confidence in the integrity, objectivity, competence, and professionalism of CPAs. As part of its efforts to enhance the public's understanding of the skills, knowledge, and character of CPAs, the AICPA launched the CPA Ambassador Program, which has provided public speaking and media training to more than 600 CPAs across the nation.

As individuals, CPAs take their public interest responsibilities seriously. The profession, with the leadership of the AICPA, has taken many steps to uphold the faith of investors in U.S. financial markets. Those efforts have focused on detecting and preventing fraud, improving audit quality, contributing to more-effective corporate governance, and enhancing the value of business financial reporting.

The CPA profession has enhanced fraud-related standard setting and related education and training activities. The AICPA has collaborated with the Association of Certified Fraud Examiners to establish an Institute for Fraud Studies at the University of Texas at Austin. The AICPA has also established a relationship with the Federal Bureau of Investigation (which employs many CPAs) and developed several antifraud training programs.

The financial statement audit is a key service of public accountants. To maintain quality of this service, the AICPA has three centers, each focused on audit quality in different environments:

1. audits of publicly held companies
2. governmental, or *Yellow Book,* audits
3. audits of employee benefit plans

Firm membership in these centers is voluntary. Member firms demonstrate their commitment to quality by signing on and complying with membership requirements.

The AICPA's Audit Committee Effectiveness Center, a Web-based resource center of best practices, guidance, and tools, was launched in early December 2003 to support the corporate governance process of company audit committees. The components of the center are the Audit Committee Toolkits (corporate, not-for-profit, and government), Audit Committee Matching System, Audit Committee e-Alerts, and a bank of materials containing information for and about audit committees.

The CPA profession's commitment to the public good extends beyond financial reporting. In 2003 the AICPA, working with state CPA societies, launched the award-winning 360 Degrees of Financial Literacy program, which takes a broad leadership role in volunteering to educate the American public, from schoolchildren to retirees. In 2005 the AICPA published objective guides on two public policy issues—Social Security reform and tax reform. Through its volunteer member committees and professional staff, the AICPA also establishes, monitors, and enforces professional standards, as well as assists members in continually improving their professional conduct and performance. The AICPA develops the Uniform CPA Examination, which is administered to all candidates for the CPA designation in all states and U.S. licensing jurisdictions. A computerized CPA exam was launched in April 2004. The new examination is more closely aligned with the real-world environment of entry-level CPAs and allows for a better evaluation of their qualifications.

A weekly e-newsletter and the monthly *CPA Letter* and *Journal of Accountancy* are among many periodicals distributed and available online. The AICPA houses the nation's most extensive accounting library and publishes numerous volumes of technical standards and topical publications. The AICPA is a major provider of educational courses and materials for continuing professional education, a requirement of most jurisdictions for the continued licensing of CPAs and membership in the AICPA.

In 2001 the AICPA launched a comprehensive effort to recruit late high school and early college students into the accounting profession. The flagship of this program is the interactive Web site (http://www.startheregoplaces.com). Through connection to the collegiate academic community, cooperative curriculum development, and the distribution of promotional materials, the AICPA aids in encouraging qualified accounting students to sit for the Uniform CPA Examination.

Focused information and tools for members working in specialized areas led to the establishment of seven Web-based communities: personal financial planning, business valuation and forensic and litigation services, information technology, taxation, firm practice management, financial management, and accounting education. Each center is accessible from the home page of the AICPA Web site.

ORGANIZATIONAL STRUCTURE

Organizationally, the AICPA is member-driven and -managed. It carries out its mission and objectives through the volunteer work of approximately 2,000 members who serve on a governing council, board of directors, boards, committees, subcommittees, and task forces. The governing council, the nearly 300-member governing body of the AICPA, meets twice a year. There is representation from each of the fifty-five accountancy jurisdictions. In addition, the board of directors, past chairs, and twenty-one members-at-large serve on the council.

The board of directors, which is the executive committee of the council, provides leadership in meeting objectives established. There are twenty-three members, including the president of the AICPA, who is also a member of the AICPA staff.

In 2005 the AICPA had a staff of approximately 600 in five offices, with the headquarters located at 1211 Avenue of the Americas, New York, NY 10036-8775. Other locations were in Washington, D.C.; Jersey City, New Jersey; Ewing, New Jersey, and Lewisville, Texas. The Jersey City office was scheduled for closing as of July 2006, with 400 positions moving to Durham, North Carolina.

SEE ALSO *Accounting; State Societies of CPAs*

Barry C. Melancon

AMERICAN MANAGEMENT ASSOCIATION

The American Management Association (AMA) is the world's leading membership-based management development organization. The business education and management development programs offered by the AMA provide its members and customers the opportunity to learn superior business skills and the best management practices available. The AMA fulfills this goal through a variety of seminars, conferences, assessments, customized learning solutions, books, and online resources. The range of programs offered by the AMA includes finance, human resources, sales and marketing, manufacturing, and international management, as well as numerous others.

The philosophy of the AMA is to be a nonprofit, membership-based educational organization that assists individuals and enterprises in the development of organizational effectiveness, which is the primary sustainable competitive advantage in a global economy. A major goal of the AMA is to identify the best management practices worldwide to provide assessment, design, development, self-development, and instruction services. The AMA meets this goal with an abundance of print and electronic media and learning methodologies, which are designed for the sole purpose of enhancing the growth of individuals and organizations.

The origins of the AMA can be traced back to 1913, when the National Association of Corporation Schools was founded. Around 1922, the National Association of Corporation Schools merged with the Industrial Relations Association of America, which had been founded in 1918. The result of the merger was the National Personnel Association. Shortly after the merger, in 1923, the National Personnel Association's board of directors chose the new name of the American Management Association. The modern AMA, as it is known in the early twenty-first century, began with a consolidation of five closely related national associations, which were all dedicated to management education. The consolidation of the organizations into one organization prompted the regents of the State University of New York to grant the AMA the title of an educational organization.

The AMA offers numerous beneficial programs aimed at a variety of people. In addition to its traditional programs, the AMA also provides programs for high school and college students and has special partnerships with local management training organizations. More information is available from the American Management Association at 1601 Broadway, New York, NY 10019; (212) 586-8100 (phone), (212) 903-8168 (fax), (800) 262-9699 (customer service); or www.amanet.org.

SEE ALSO *Management*

Nikole M. Pogeman

AMERICAN MARKETING ASSOCIATION

During the mid-1930s, the American Marketing Society (organized in 1931) and the National Association of Teachers of Marketing (founded in 1915) arrived at two realizations: both organizations held common interests in marketing, and many of their publications and memberships overlapped. Following such realizations, the idea of merging the groups became a reality in 1937 with the inception of the American Marketing Association (AMA).

The AMA is a professional, nonprofit organization for marketers with more than 500 North American professional chapters and worldwide membership (in ninety-two countries) in excess of 45,000. AMA also furthers students' professional development through approximately 400 collegiate chapters globally.

AMA was organized to advance marketing science and has always emphasized improving marketing management through marketing knowledge gained through researching, recording, and disseminating information. Today, AMA strives to encourage greater interest in and concern for education, to assist marketing professionals in their efforts toward personal and career development, and to promote integration of ethical considerations and general marketing practices.

In 1938, the AMA agreed to work with the U.S. Bureau of the Census to unify government agency marketing definitions. The AMA board debated appropriate definitions and, in 1985, approved definitions for marketing and marketing research. In August 2004, marketing was redefined as "… an organizational function and a set of processes for creating, communicating, and delivering value to customers and for managing customer relationships in ways that benefit the organization and its stakeholders." Marketing research also was redefined as "the function that links the consumer, customer, and public to the marketer through information—information used to identify and define marketing opportunities and problems; generate, refine, and evaluate marketing actions; monitor marketing performance; and improve understanding of marketing as a process. Marketing research specifies the information required to address these issues, designs the method for collecting information, manages and implements the data collection process, analyzes the results, and communicates the findings and their implications" (MarketingPower, Inc., *Marketing Definitions*, 2005).

The AMA disseminates information through four scholarly journals, which provide forums for sharing marketing research efforts; three business magazines, which provide discussions on emerging marketing issues for senior-level marketing executives; and one newsletter, which addresses all aspects of marketing, including insights on ethics, new products, and more. Online versions of these publications are available at www.ama.org/pub. More information is available from the AMA at 311 South Wacker Dr., Suite 5800, Chicago, Illinois 60606; (312) 542-9000 or (800) AMA-1150; or online at http://www.marketingpower.com.

SEE ALSO *Marketing*

BIBLIOGRAPHY

MarketingPower, Inc. (2005). "About AMA." Retrieved September 8, 2005, from http://www.marketingpower.com/content407.php.

MarketingPower, Inc. (2005). "Marketing Definitions." Retrieved September 8, 2005, from http://www.marketingpower.com/content4620.php.

MarketingPower, Inc. (2005). "Key Events in AMA History." Retrieved September 8, 2005, from http://www.marketingpower.com/content1591.php.

Val Hinton
Mary Jean Lush

AMERICANS WITH DISABILITIES ACT OF 1990

The Americans with Disabilities Act of 1990 (ADA) is a comprehensive civil rights act for people with disabilities. On July 26, 1990, President George H.W. Bush signed the ADA into law as wide-ranging legislation intended to make American society more accessible to people with disabilities and to prohibit discrimination on the basis of disability. The act is divided into five titles:

1. Employment. Businesses must provide reasonable accommodations in all aspects of employment to protect the rights of individuals with disabilities.

2. Public services. People with disabilities cannot be denied participation in public service programs or activities that are available to people without disabilities.

3. Public accommodations. All new construction must be accessible to individuals with disabilities.

4. Telecommunications. Telecommunication companies must have a telephone relay service for individuals who use telecommunications devices for the deaf (TTYs) or similar devices.

5. Miscellaneous. This title includes a provision prohibiting coercing, threatening, or retaliating against individuals with disabilities or those assisting them in asserting their rights under the ADA.

The protection of the ADA applies primarily, but not exclusively, to individuals with physical and mental disabilities.

Built on a foundation of statutory, legal, and programmatic experience, the ADA was modeled after the Civil Rights Act of 1964 and the Rehabilitation Act of 1973. In order to understand the basis for the enactment

President George H. W. Bush signs the Americans with Disabilities Act during a ceremony on the South Lawn of the White House July 26, 1990. With the president are Rev. Harold Wilke, rear left, Evan Kemp, chairman of the Equal Opportunity Employment Commission, left, Sandra Parrino, chairman of the National Council on Disability and Justin Dart, chairman of The President's Council on Disabilities. **AP IMAGES**

of the ADA, one must look at certain historical events of the 1970s and the disability rights movement. First and foremost has been the desire of individuals with disabilities to work toward their goal of full participation in American society, which led to the Rehabilitation Act of 1973 and the Individuals with Disabilities Education Act of 1974 that so strongly influenced the ADA.

Effects the ADA may have on businesses include restructuring or altering the layout of a building, modifying equipment, and removing barriers. For example, in September 1999, Greyhound Bus Lines of Dallas, Texas, removed architectural barriers and began to provide assistance to passengers with disabilities by means of lift-equipped buses. Another example of the effects of the ADA occurred in February 1997, when Harrison County, Mississippi, gave people who are deaf or hard of hearing an equal opportunity to serve as jurors.

The Americans with Disabilities Act of 1990 has been regarded as the most sweeping piece of legislation since the Civil Rights Act of 1964. More information on the ADA is available at (800)514-0301 (voice) or (800)514-0383 (TDD).

BIBLIOGRAPHY

The Consumer Law Page; Retrieved August 30, 2005, from http://consumerlawpage.com

Department of Rehabilitation Web Site. Retrieved August 30, 2005, from http://www.rehab.cahwnet.gov

Indiana University/Purdue University Web Site; Retrieved August 30, 2005, from http://www.iupui.edu/~aao/legis.html

Job Accommodation Network; Retrieved August 30, 2005, from http://www.jan.wvu.edu/links/adasummary.htm

U.S. Department of Justice Web Site; Retrieved August 30, 2005, from http://www.usdoj.gov/crt/ada/adahom1.htm

Nikole M. Pogeman

ANALYTICAL PROCEDURES

Analytical procedures have become increasingly important to audit firms and are considered to be an integral part of the audit process. The importance of analytical procedures is demonstrated by the fact that the Auditing Standards Board, which establishes the standards for conducting financial statement audits, has required that analytical procedures be performed during all audits of financial statements. The Auditing Standards Board did so through the issuance of Statement on Auditing Standards (SAS) No. 56 in 1988, which requires that analytical procedures be used by auditors as they plan the audit and also in the final review of the financial statements. In addition, SAS No. 56 encourages auditors to use analytical procedures as one of the procedures they use to gather evidence related to account balances (referred to in auditing as a substantive test). The purpose of this article is to provide the reader with a general understanding of analytical procedures and to describe the process that auditors use in applying analytical procedures.

SAS No. 56 describes analytical procedures as the "evaluation of financial information made by a study of plausible relationships among both financial and non-

financial data" (AICPA, 1998, 56 p. 1). Accounting researchers have helped to clarify the process that auditors use to perform analytical procedures by developing models that describe the various stages of the process. One such model developed by Hirst and Koonce (1996) describes the performance of analytical procedures as consisting of five components: expectation development, explanation generation, information search and explanation evaluation, decision making, and documentation.

The first step in the analytical procedures process is the development of an expected account balance. SAS No. 56 and auditing textbooks (e.g., O'Reilly et al., 1998) provide some guidance as to the sources of information an auditor can use to develop these expectations. Examples of such sources include the following:

- Financial information from comparable prior periods adjusted for any changes expected to affect the balances of the current period. For example, an expectation of sales revenues for the current year might be based on the prior year's sales, adjusted for factors such as price increases or the known addition or loss of major customers.

- Expected results based on budgets or forecasts prepared by the client or projections of expected results prepared by the auditor from interim periods or prior comparable periods.

- Available information from the company's industry. For example, changes in sales revenue or gross margin percentages might be based on available data from industrywide statistics.

- Nonfinancial information. For example, sales revenue for a client from the hotel industry might be based on available data as to room occupancy rates.

After an auditor has developed an expectation for a particular account balance (e.g., sales revenue), the next step in the analytical procedures process is to compare the expected balance to the actual balance. If there is no significant difference (referred to by auditors as a material difference) between the expected and actual balance, this conclusion provides audit evidence in support of the account balance being examined. However, if there is a material difference between the expected and actual balance, the auditor will investigate this difference further. At this point the auditor will develop an explanation for the difference. Hirst and Koonce (1996) interviewed auditors from each of the six largest accounting firms and found that the source of the explanation usually depends on what types of analytical procedures are being performed. If analytical procedures are being performed during the planning phase of the audit, the auditor usually asks the client the reason for the unexpected difference. However, if the analytical procedures are being performed as a substantive test (method of obtaining corroborating evidence) or during the final review phase of the audit, in addition to asking the client, auditors will often generate their own explanation or ask other members of the audit team for an explanation.

When developing an explanation for an unexpected change in account balances, an auditor considers both error and nonerror explanations. Nonerror explanations are sometimes referred to as environmental explanations, since they refer to changes in the business environment in which the client operates. For example, an environmental explanation for an unexpected decline in gross profit (sales revenue less cost of sales) may be that the client faces increasing foreign competition and has been forced to reduce selling prices. An error explanation, on the other hand, might be that the client has failed to record a profitable sale to a major customer. If this mistake is unintentional, then auditors refer to the mistake as an error. However, if this mistake was intentional (i.e., the client failed to record the sale on purpose), auditors refer to the mistake as a fraud. Auditors are much more concerned about errors and fraud than changes resulting from environmental factors. In fact, auditors are most concerned about fraud, since this raises doubts about the integrity of the client as well as about the process of recording transactions affecting other account balances.

Once an auditor has a potential explanation, whether self-generated or obtained from the client, the next step in the analytical procedures process is to search for information that can be used to evaluate the adequacy of the explanation. Similar to the explanation generation phase of the process, the extent of information search and explanation evaluation depends on the type of analytical procedures being performed. Hirst and Koonce (1996) found that during the planning phase of analytical procedures, auditors do little if any follow-up work to evaluate an explanation. Instead, consistent with SAS No. 56, auditors typically use analytical procedures at the planning stage to improve their understanding of the client's business and to develop the audit plan for the engagement. For example, if analytical procedures performed on inventory during audit planning indicated the inventory balance was higher than expected, the auditor would most likely adjust the audit plan by increasing the number of audit tests performed on inventory or assigning more experienced personnel to the audit of inventory. Thus, if an error or fraud has occurred with inventory, the revised audit plan for obtaining corroborating evidence will lead to detection of the error or fraud.

If analytical procedures are being performed as a substantive test, the auditor will need to gather information to evaluate the explanation being considered, since the primary purpose of substantive analytical procedures is to provide evidence as to the validity of an account balance. The type and amount of corroboration for the explanation will vary based on factors such as the size of the unexpected difference, the significance of the difference to the overall financial statements, and the risks (e.g., internal control and inherent) associated with the account balance(s) affected. As any of these factors increase, the reliability of the information obtained in support of the explanation should also increase. SAS No. 56 provides guidance for auditors in the evaluation of the reliability of data. Some of the factors to be considered by the auditors include the following:

- Data obtained from independent sources outside the entity are more reliable than data obtained from sources within the entity.

- If data are obtained from within the entity, data obtained from sources independent from the amount being audited are more reliable.

- Data developed under a system with adequate controls are more reliable than data from a system with poor controls.

After an auditor gathers information for purposes of evaluating an analytical procedures explanation, it is a matter of professional judgment in determining whether the evidence adequately supports the explanation. This is one of the most important steps of the analytical procedures process and is referred to as the decision phase of the process. Factors the auditor should consider in evaluating the acceptability of an explanation include the materiality of the unexpected difference, reliability of the evidence obtained to support the explanation, and whether the explanation is sufficient to explain a material, or significant, portion of the unexpected difference. If, after evaluating the evidence, the auditor finds that the explanation being considered does not adequately explain the unexpected difference, the auditor should return to the "explanation generation" phase of the process. If the auditor believes that the audit evidence obtained adequately supports the explanation, the auditor may proceed to the final step of the process, which is documentation. While the extent of written documentation will vary depending on the materiality of the unexpected difference, the audit work papers will generally include a written description of material unexpected differences, an explanation for the difference, evidence that corroborates the explanation, and the judgment of the auditor as to the adequacy of the explanation.

The purpose of this article has been to provide the reader with a basic understanding of analytical procedures. For more detailed information, refer to the Statement on

Auditing Standards No. 56 (AICPA, 1988) or to *Montgomery's Auditing* (O'Reilly et al., 1998) for a more in-depth discussion. Further, while the focus of this article has been on the use of analytical procedures during financial statement audits, portions of analytical procedures can also be helpful to both management and investors. For example, managers of a business may develop certain key ratios and statistics, which can be used to monitor the progress of the business. For example, a manager may use data such as the number of new customers, number of customer complaints, and other customer satisfaction measures to monitor the sales revenue and profitability of the company. An investor might also use analytical procedures to evaluate his or her investment portfolio. For example, an investor may try to forecast the future sales of a company based on knowledge of the industry in which the company operates and the prior sales history of the company. The sales forecast could then be used to develop an earnings forecast for that company, which is a critical component in developing an investment decision. Thus, while analytical procedures are an integral part of the audit process, they can also be a useful tool for managers and investors.

SEE ALSO *Accounting; Auditing; Financial Statement Analysis*

BIBLIOGRAPHY

American Institute of Certified Public Accountants (1988). *Statement on Auditing Standards No. 56: Analytical Procedures.* New York: Author.

Hirst, Eric D., and Koonce, Lisa (Fall 1996). "Audit Analytical Procedures: A Field Investigation." *Contemporary Accounting Research* 13(2), 457-486.

O'Reilly, Vincent M., McDonnell, Patrick J., Winograd, Barry N., Gerson, James S., and Jaenicke, Henry R. (1998). *Montgomery's Auditing* (12th ed.). New York: J. Wiley & Sons.

Jean C. Bedard
James J. Maroney

ANTITRUST LEGISLATION

In the United States, at the end of the nineteenth century, widespread business combinations known as trust agreements existed. These agreements usually involved two or more companies that combined with the purpose of raising prices and lowering output, giving the trustees the power to control competition and maximize profits at the public's expense. These trust agreements would result in a monopoly. To combat this sort of business behavior, Congress passed antitrust legislation.

In 1890 Congress passed the Sherman Antitrust Act, which forbade all combinations or conspiracies in restraint of trade. The act contained two substantive provisions. Section 1 declared illegal contracts and conspiracies in restraint of trade, and Section 2 prohibited monopolization and attempts to monopolize. When an injured party or the government filed suits, the courts could order the guilty firms to stop their illegal behavior or the firms could be dissolved. The Sherman Antitrust Act pertained only to trade within the states, and monopolies still flourished as companies found ways around the law.

In 1914 Congress passed the Clayton Act as an amendment to the Sherman Act. The Clayton Act made certain practices illegal when their effect was to lessen competition or to create a monopoly. The main provisions of this act included (1) forbidding discrimination in price, services, or facilities between customers; (2) determining that antitrust laws were not applicable to labor organizations; (3) prohibiting requirements that customers buy additional items in order to obtain products desired; and (4) making it illegal for one corporation to acquire the stock of another with intention of creating a monopoly. Because loopholes were also present in the Clayton Act, the Federal Trade Commission (FTC) was established to enforce the antitrust legislation.

Passed in 1914, the Federal Trade Commission Act provided that "unfair methods of competition in or affecting commerce are hereby declared unlawful." The FTC consists of five members appointed by the president and has the power to investigate persons, partnerships, or corporations in relation to antitrust acts. Examples of unlawful trade practices include misbranding goods quality, origin, or durability; using false advertising; mislabeling to mislead consumer about product size; and advertising or selling rebuilt goods as new. The act also gave the FTC the power to institute court proceedings against alleged violators and provided the penalties if found guilty.

The Robinson-Patman Act of 1936 strengthened the price discrimination provisions of the Clayton Act. One amendment involved the discrimination in rebates, discounts, or advertising service charges; underselling and penalties. Another provided for the exemption of non-profit institutions from price-discrimination provisions. The main purpose of this act was to justify the differences in product costs between customers and clarify the Robinson-Patman Act.

The Celler-Kefauver Antimerger Act, passed in 1950, extended the Clayton Act's injunction against mergers. Because the purpose of this act was to forbid mergers that prevented competition, corporations that were major

Political cartoon depicts the Sherman Antitrust law being resurrected to attack monopolies.

competitors were prohibited from merging in any manner. This amendment extended the FTC's jurisdiction to all corporations. This act, however, was not intended to stop the merger of two smaller companies or the sale of one in a failing condition. Due to court decisions that had weakened the Clayton Act, the Celler-Kefauver Antimerger Act was necessary to restrict mergers.

Although antitrust laws have contributed enormously to improving the degree of competition in the U.S. economic system, they have not been a complete success. A sizable number of citizens would like to see these laws broadened to cover professional baseball teams, labor unions, and professional organizations. Without the antitrust legislation that now exists, however, the national economy would be worse off in the end.

SEE ALSO *Federal Trade Commission Act of 1914; Robinson-Patman Act of 1936; Sherman Antitrust Act of 1890*

BIBLIOGRAPHY

Antitrust statutes. Retrieved September 6, 2005, from http://www.stolaf.edu/people/becker/antitrust/statutes/sherman.html.

"The Clayton Antitrust Act (1914)." Retrieved September 7, 2005, from http://www.stolaf.edu/people/becker/antitrust/statutes/clayton.html.

"The Federal Trade Commission Act (1914)." Retrieved September 7, 2005, from http://www.stolaf.edu/people/becker/antitrust/statutes/ftc.html.

Mueller, Charles E. (1997). "Antitrust Law and Economics Review." Retrieved September 7, 2005, from http://www.metrolink.net/~cmueller/i-overvw.html?

Janel Kupferschmid

ARTIFICIAL INTELLIGENCE

In simplest terms, artificial intelligence (AI) is manufactured thinking. It is a machine's ability to think. This process is deemed "artificial" because once it is programmed it occurs without human intervention. AI is generally applied to the theory and practical application of a computer's ability to think like humans do. AI capability is designated as either strong AI or weak AI. Strong AI is a computer system that actively employs consciousness, a machine that can truly reason and solve problems independently. Critics of AI systems argue that such a machine is unrealistic, and even if it were possible, a true artificially intelligent machine is unwanted.

Popular perceptions of AI have been dramatized in movies such as *2001: A Space Odyssey* (1968), in which a starship computer named HAL 9000 is capable of speech and facial recognition, natural language processing, interpreting emotions, and expressing reason. Another famous make-believe computer was the star of *WarGames* (1983). In this movie, the line, "Do you want to play a game?" allows the teenage hero to persuade the computer to play a game rather than start World War III. In both examples, the computers undertook independent actions that were potentially harmful to their human creators. This is the reason most often given for not creating strong AI machines.

Modern working applications of AI are examples of weak AI. Current AI research focuses on developing computers that use intelligent programming to automate routine human tasks. For example, many customer service telephone banks are automated by AI. When a recorded voice asks for a "yes" or "no" response or for the caller to choose a menu item by saying specific words, the computer on the other end of the telephone is using weak AI to make a decision and select the appropriate response based on caller input. These computers are trained to recognize speech patterns, dialects, accents, and replacement words such as "oh"—rather than "zero"—for the number 0.

Long before the development of computers, the notion that thinking was a form of computation motivated the formalization of logic as a type of rational thought. These efforts continue today. Graph theory provided the architecture for searching a solution space for a problem. Operations research, with its focus on optimization algorithms, uses graph theory to solve complex decision-making problems.

PIONEERS OF AI

AI uses syllogistic logic, which was first postulated by Aristotle. This logic is based on deductive reasoning. For example, if A equals B, and B equals C, then A must also equal C. Throughout history, the nature of syllogistic logic and deductive reasoning was shaped by grammarians, mathematicians, and philosophers. When computers were developed, programming languages used similar logical patterns to support software applications. Terms such as *cybernetics* and *robotics* were used to describe collective intelligence approaches and led to the development of AI as an experimental field in the 1950s.

Allen Newell and Herbert Simon pioneered the first AI laboratory at Carnegie Mellon University in the 1950s. John McCarthy and Marvin Minsky of the Massachusetts Institute of Technology opened their original AI lab in 1959 to write AI decision-making software. The best-known name in the AI community, however, is Alan Turing (1912–1954). Alan Turing was a mathematician, philosophy, and cryptographer and is often credited as the founder of computer science as a discipline separate from mathematics. He contributed to the debate of whether a machine could think by developing the Turing test. The Turing test uses a human judge engaged in remote conversation with two parties: another human and a machine. If the judge cannot tell which party is the human, the machine passes the test.

Originally, teletype machines were used to maintain the anonymity of the parties; today, IRC (Internet relay chat) is used to test the linguistic capability of AI engines. Linguistic robots called Chatterbots (such as Jabberwacky) are very popular programs that allow an individual to converse with a machine and demonstrate machine intelligence and reasoning.

The Defense Advanced Research Projects Agency, which played a significant role in the birth of the Internet by funding ARPANET, also funded AI research in the early 1980s. Nevertheless, when results were not immediately useful for military application, funding was cut.

Robby the Robotic Pharmacist, Hackensack University Medical Center. *Following data entered in the hospital's computer system, Robby uses his "arms" to find prescriptions to be given to patients among the sorted medicine packets on the wall.* © ED KASHI/CORBIS

Since then, AI research has moved to other areas including robotics, computer vision, and other practical engineering tasks.

AN EVOLUTION OF APPLICATIONS

One of the early milestones in AI was Newell and Simon's General Problem Solver (GPS). The program was designed to imitate human problem-solving methods. This and other developments such as Logic Theorist and the Geometry Theorem Prover generated enthusiasm for the future of AI. Simon went so far as to assert that in the near-term future the problems that computers could solve would be coextensive with the range of problems to which the human mind has been applied.

Difficulties in achieving this objective soon began to manifest themselves. New research based on earlier successes encountered problems of intractability. A search for alternative approaches led to attempts to solve typically occurring cases in narrow areas of expertise. This prompted the development of expert systems, which reach conclusions by applying reasoning techniques based on sets of rules. A seminal model was MYCIN, developed to diagnose blood infections. Having about 450 rules, MYCIN was able to outperform many experts. This and other expert systems research led to the first commercial expert system, R1, implemented at Digital Equipment Corporation (DEC) to help configure client orders for new mainframe and minicomputer systems. R1's implementation was estimated to save DEC about $40 million per year.

Other classic systems include the PROSPECTOR program for determining the probable location and type of ore deposits and the INTERNIST program for performing patient diagnosis in internal medicine.

THE ROLE OF AI IN COMPUTER SCIENCE

While precise definitions are still the subject of debate, AI may be usefully thought of as the branch of computer science that is concerned with the automation of intelligent behavior. The intent of AI is to develop systems that have the ability to perceive and to learn, to accomplish physical tasks, and to emulate human decision making. AI seeks to design and develop intelligent agents as well as to understand them.

AI research has proven to be the breeding ground for computer science subdisciplines such as pattern recognition, image processing, neural networks, natural language processing, and game theory. For example, optical character recognition software that transcribes handwritten characters into typed text (notably with tablet personal computers and personal digital assistants) was initially a focus of AI research.

Additionally, expert systems used in business applications owe their existence to AI. Manufacturing companies use inventory applications that track both production levels and sales to determine when and how much of specific supplies are needed to produce orders in the pipeline. Genetic algorithms are employed by financial planners to assess the best combination of investment opportunities for their clients. Other examples include data mining applications, surveillance programs, and facial recognition applications.

Multiagent systems are also based on AI research. Use of these systems has been driven by the recognition that intelligence may be reflected by the collective behaviors of large numbers of very simple interacting members of a community of agents. These agents can be computers, software modules, or virtually any object that can perceive aspects of its environment and proceed in a rational way toward accomplishing a goal.

Four types of systems will have a substantial impact on applications: intelligent simulation, information-resource specialists, intelligent project coaches, and robot teams.

Intelligent simulations generate realistic simulated worlds that enable extensive affordable training and education which can be made available any time and anywhere. Examples might be hurricane crisis management, exploration of the impacts of different economic theories, tests of products on simulated customers, and technological design testing features through simulation that would cost millions of dollars to test using an actual prototype.

Information-resource specialist systems (IRSS) will enable easy access to information related to a specific problem. For instance, a rural doctor whose patient presents with a rare condition might use IRSS to assess competing treatments or identify new ones. An educator might find relevant background materials, including information about similar courses taught elsewhere.

Intelligent project coaches (IPCs) could function as coworkers, assisting and collaborating with design or operations teams for complex systems. Such systems could recall the rationale of previous decisions and, in times of crisis, explain the methods and reasoning previously used to handle that situation. An IPC for aircraft design could enhance collaboration by keeping communication flowing among the large, distributed design staff, the program managers, the customer, and the subcontractors.

Robot teams could contribute to manufacturing by operating in a dynamic environment with minimal instrumentation, thus providing the benefits of economies of scale. They could also participate in automating sophisticated laboratory procedures that require sensing, manipulation, planning, and transport. The AI robots could work in dangerous environments with no threat to their human builders.

SUMMARY

A variety of disciplines have influenced the development of AI. These include philosophy (logic), mathematics (computability, algorithms), psychology (cognition), engineering (computer hardware and software), and linguistics (knowledge representation and natural-language processing). As AI continues to redefine itself, the practical application of the field will change.

AI supports national competitiveness as it depends increasingly on capacities for accessing, processing, and analyzing information. The computer systems used for such purposes must also be intelligent. Health-care providers require easy access to information systems so they can track health-care delivery and identify the most effective medical treatments for their patients' conditions. Crisis management teams must be able to explore alternative courses of action and make critical decisions. Educators need systems that adapt to a student's individual needs and abilities. Businesses require flexible manufacturing and software design aids to maintain their leadership position in information technology, and to regain it in manufacturing. AI will continue to evolve toward a rational, logical machine presence that will support and enhance human endeavors.

SEE ALSO *Information Processing; Interactive Technology*

Mark J. Snyder
Lisa E. Gueldenzoph

ASSETS

SEE *Financial Statements*

ASSOCIATION OF CERTIFIED FRAUD EXAMINERS

The Association of Certified Fraud Examiners (ACFE) was established in 1988. Its founder, Joseph T. Wells, was previously a public accountant and also a special agent of the Federal Bureau of Investigation, with experience in public accounting and in heading his own consulting firm. He continues to be active in the ACFE and serves as chairman of the board of the association. As of mid-2005, there were more than 34,000 members worldwide, with approximately 120 local chapters. Over forty states in the United States have at least one local chapter.

The ACFE's mission, as stated in its official materials, is to reduce the incidence of fraud and white-collar crime and to assist the membership in its detection and deterrence. The primary means of achieving this mission are through a certification program, continuing education and training of members, and publications and a range of research activities. Local chapters provide activities to enhance professional knowledge and skills while the national office offers seminars, conferences, custom training, and antifraud materials to universities and other entities. Activities are provided at locations throughout the world.

Publications are available for those preparing for the examination for professional certification, as well as for members and others interested in extending their knowledge of fraud detection and prevention. Additionally, the ACFE provides leadership, through speeches, newsletters, and other means, in maintaining public confidence in the integrity and objectivity of its members.

Of the 34,000 members of the ACFE, more than 15,000 are certified fraud examiners. Certification requires prior experience related to detection or deterrence of fraud. Those who are certified participate in continuing educational programs.

Those seeking certification must first be associate members of the ACFE. Requirements for membership include a 10-hour computer-based examination that includes topics related to criminology and ethics, financial transactions, fraud investigation, and legal elements of fraud.

More information is available from the ACFE at its world headquarters: The Gregor Building, 716 West Avenue, Austin, TX 78701-2727; (800) 245-3321 (USA & Canada only), +1 (512) 478-9000 (phone numbers); +1 (512) 478-9297 (fax); or, http://www.cfenet.com.

SEE ALSO *Forensic Accounting; Fraudulent Financial Reporting*

Bernard H. Newman

ASSURANCE SERVICES

Assurance services are a class of services provided by certified public accountants (CPAs) in public practice. While the term is sometimes used inconsistently among individual CPA firms, the American Institute of Certified Public Accountants (AICPA) Special Committee on Assurance Services defined assurance services as "independent professional services that improve the quality of information, or its context, for decision-makers."

Assurance services are rooted in the CPA's tradition of independent verification of data prepared by others. They differ from many services historically provided by CPAs in that they represent an expansion of the information and forms of reports provided. Indeed, they represent an evolution in the nature of services provided by CPAs, as CPAs have begun to provide services not just on accounting information but on many other types of information that people need in order to make decisions.

THE EVOLUTION OF CPA SERVICES

Since the early part of the twentieth century, CPAs have audited financial statements. The audit is the CPA's defining service and, aside from preparation of income taxes, the service most closely associated with the CPA profession. In an audit of financial statements, the CPA examines the transactions that underlie an entity's financial statements and reports whether the financial statements are fairly stated in conformity with generally accepted accounting principles. Such an opinion is required by the Securities and Exchange Commission (SEC) for companies whose stock is publicly traded and is often demanded by others, such as lenders, for entities that are not subject to the SEC.

Figure 1 is a pictorial depiction of the relationship among CPA services.

Beginning in the 1970s, financial statement users requested that CPAs provide some of the benefits of audits at a lower cost. As a result, CPAs began providing a lower-level service, called a review, on financial statements. Reviews are based on inquiry and analytical procedures applied to financial statement amounts, rather than on the more rigorous procedures required in an audit, such as physical inspection and confirmation with third parties. The review culminates in a report that provides limited assurance, that is, that the CPA is not aware of any material modifications that should be made to the accompanying financial statements in order for them to be in conformity with generally accepted accounting principles. Reviews are used for quarterly financial statements of publicly held companies. Reviews are performed for privately owned companies when the financial statement user wants some assurance about the statements but do not require the level of assurance provided in an audit.

CPAs also provide a third level of service on financial statements, the compilation. This service, provided only to privately owned companies, is usually done in connection with helping the company record its transactions and transform its records into financial statements. The accountant does not do any tests of the underlying data, but helps put the data into financial statement form and reads the statements for material misstatements. The compilation report expresses no assurance, but if the accountant discovers material misstatements, they must be corrected or described in the CPA's report.

The 1980s brought additional expansion of the CPA's role. Users wanted CPAs to use the audit and review services to report on subjects in addition to financial statements, such as the effectiveness of internal control and the company's compliance with laws, regulations, or contracts. The profession's response was the creation of standards for attestation engagements. In an attestation

engagement, the CPA applies the tools used in audits and reviews to provide assurance on whether the subject matter of the engagement (such as internal control or management's discussion and analysis of operations) complies with applicable criteria for measurement and disclosure. The result is a report much like an audit (reasonable assurance) or review (limited assurance) of financial statements. In addition, CPAs can apply procedures specifically designed by the expected users of the report to financial or nonfinancial items. This service is neither an audit nor a review. These engagements, called agreed-upon procedures engagements, result in a report in which the CPA describes the procedures applied and their results but provides no overall conclusion.

By the 1990s CPAs were being asked to expand still further into additional services, including those that involve subjects far removed from financial reporting and that do not involve an explicit report or conclusion. This area of service—assurance services—is an extension of the audit/attest tradition. It is generally distinct from common consulting services, which generally either provide advice to clients or create internal systems. Probably the most famous assurance service is that provided in controlling and counting the ballots for the annual Oscars ceremony. Another common assurance service involves CPAs observing the drawing of numbers in state lotteries.

Assurance services might involve the type of reports provided in more traditional attestation engagements or they might provide less structured communications, such

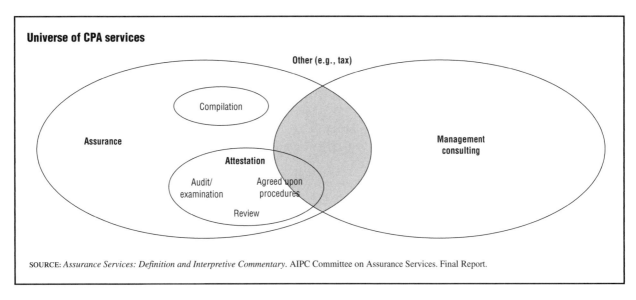

Universe of CPA services

Other (e.g., tax)

Compilation

Assurance

Attestation

Audit/ examination

Agreed upon procedures

Review

Management consulting

SOURCE: *Assurance Services: Definition and Interpretive Commentary.* AIPC Committee on Assurance Services. Final Report.

Figure 1

as reports without explicit conclusions or reports that are issued only when there are problems. Assurance services are often desired to be more customized to information needs of decision makers in specific circumstances. To be responsive to those needs, the form of CPA communication is expected to be more flexible. Thus, a significant difference between assurance and attestation engagements is that assurance engagements do not necessarily result in a standard form of report, whereas attestation engagements (and more familiar audits and reviews) do. Yet assurance services require adherence to key professional qualities by practitioners.

ELEMENTS OF AN ASSURANCE ENGAGEMENT

The important elements involved in assurance engagement are:

- Independence
- Professionalism
- Information or context improvement
- Decision makers

The CPA should be independent in order to provide an assurance service; that is, he or she should have no vested interest in the information reported on. The CPA's only interest should be the accuracy of the information, not whether the information portrays results favorable or unfavorable to either the entity that prepares the information or the one that uses it.

An assurance service is a professional service, meaning it draws on the CPA's experience, expertise, and judgment. It is based on the skills brought to bear in more traditional services, such as measurement, analysis, testing, and reporting.

Information in an assurance service can be financial or nonfinancial, historical or forward-looking, discrete data or information about systems, internal or external to the decision maker. The information's context relates to how it is presented. An assurance service improves the information or its context by providing assurance about its reliability, increasing its relevance, or making it easier to use and understand.

Decision makers are the users of the information and immediate beneficiaries of the assurance service. They might be internal to an entity, such as the board of directors, or a trading partner, such as a creditor or customer. The goal of an assurance service is to improve the information or its context so that decision makers can make more informed—presumably better—decisions. The decision maker need not be the party engaging the CPA or paying for the service.

The needs of decision makers are evolving. For decades their needs were generally met by periodic cost-based financial statements. As information technology advances and needs become more decision-specific, decision makers are likely to:

Replace their need for . . .	With a need for . . .
periodic information	real-time or continuous data
historical data	forward-looking data
cost-based information	value-based information
financial information	comprehensive data that includes nonfinancial information
static statements	searchable databases

Assurance services, how they are delivered, and the types of information they deal with are evolving to meet these changing needs.

Although the needs of each decision maker are unique, in research done by the Special Committee on Assurance Services, decision makers expressed keen interest in better information about topics such as:

- Business risks
- Product quality
- Performance measures
- Quality of processes and systems
- Strategic plan execution
- Government performance

TYPES OF ASSURANCE SERVICES

The Special Committee on Assurance Services identified hundreds of assurance services that CPAs provide. It also identified several services that it believed would be of particular appeal to decision makers in the near future. They included the following.

Comprehensive risk assessments. The CPA identifies and assesses the various risks facing an organization, such as the operating environment, operating systems, or information systems. The risks might be internal, external, or regulatory. The CPA can help prioritize the risks and assess the entity's efforts to control or mitigate risks faced.

Business performance measurement. Many organizations use, or should use, data to run their businesses other than that emanating from the financial reporting system. The service deals with identifying or providing explicit assurance on the financial or nonfinancial measures used to evaluate the effectiveness or efficiency of the organization's activities. While CPAs have historically been involved in the development of financial statement information, their skills and knowledge can add similar value to the creation of other information that can monitor the organization's results and its effectiveness in implementing strategic plans.

Electronic commerce. As more business is conducted electronically (via the Internet or in business-to-business electronic data interchange systems) participants have concerns about the integrity and security of data transmitted in furtherance of those transactions. An assurance service can help to address the risks and promote the integrity and security of electronic transmissions, electronic documents, and the supporting systems. One such service, CPA WebTrust, provides explicit assurance about the disclosure of an entity's business policies and about the controls over privacy and information integrity in consumer purchases over the Internet.

Systems reliability. As information technology advances, it becomes increasingly common for critical information to be produced and acted on electronically. Accordingly, decision makers need confidence that the information is continuously reliable. There is an increased need for assurance that systems are designed and operated to produce reliable data in such areas as information about customers, suppliers, and employees, project costing, rights and obligations related to contractual agreements, and competitors and market conditions. In systems reliability engagements, CPAs provide assurance about the design and operation of such systems.

Elder care services. The CPA assists the increasing population of older adults with a wide range of services such as bill paying, providing assurance that health care providers are delivering services in conformity with the client's criteria, and consulting on care alternatives and how to pay for them. The CPA provides independent, objective information to protect vulnerable clients from potentially unethical individuals and businesses as well as more traditional services (such as financial control) for nontraditional clients.

Policy compliance. The CPA provides assurance that a company complies with its own policies. The policies—such as ones involving treatment of women or minorities, conflicts of interest, animal testing, environmental matters, or customer service—might be based on internal concerns, calls for social accountability, or laws and regulations.

Trading partner accountability. The CPA provides assurance that the client's trading partners—such as suppliers, customers, or joint venture partners—have appropriately fulfilled their responsibilities. Common situations involve collecting rents or royalties based on sales made by another entity or agreements regarding use of lowest prices or specific billing practices.

Mergers and acquisitions. The CPA applies the types of services done on a client's records and practices to a potential acquisition. He or she can, for example, provide insights into the acquisition target's business risks, appropriateness of accounting methods, the value of its assets, or the adequacy of its systems and controls.

SEE ALSO *Auditing*

BIBLIOGRAPHY

Elliott, Robert K., and Pallais, Don M. (1997). "Are You Ready For New Assurance Services?" *Journal of Accountancy* June: 47-51.

Pallais, Don M., Spradling, L. Scott, and Ecklund, Kathy J. (2004). *Guide to Nontraditional Engagements*. Fort Worth, TX: Practitioners Publishing Company

Don M. Pallais

ATTESTATION ENGAGEMENTS
SEE *Assurance Services*

AUDIT COMMITTEES

Audit committees are a key institution in the context of corporate governance. They ensure that boards of directors fulfill their financial and fiduciary responsibilities to shareholders. Through their audit committees, boards of directors establish a direct line of communication with internal and external auditors as well as with the chief financial officer of the entity. Such an organizational structure combined with reporting responsibility in an environment of free and unrestricted access enables full boards of directors not only to gain assurance about the quality of financial reporting and audit processes, but also to approve significant accounting policy decisions. Moreover, strong and effective audit committees, through their planning, reviewing, and monitoring activities, can recognize potential problem areas and take corrective action before problems that affect companies' financial statements and other financial disclosures arise. Thus, audit committees have an important role in helping boards of directors avoid litigation risk because such committees provide due diligence related to financial reporting.

REQUIREMENT FOR AUDIT COMMITTEES

Audit committees have long been seen as an important group in ensuring greater corporate accountability in the United States. The value of such committees has been noted by the U.S. Congress, the U.S. Securities and Exchange Commission (SEC), the New York Stock Exchange (NYSE), and the American Institute of Certified Public Accountants. Audit committees are required by the NYSE, American Stock Exchange (AMEX), and National Association of Securities Dealers (NASDAQ/National Market System issuers).

Prior to changes imposed by the passage of the Sarbanes-Oxley Act of 2002, other major efforts were directed at the betterment of audit committees. One such effort was the publication of the *Report and Recommendations of the Blue Ribbon Committee on Improving the Effectiveness of Corporate Audit Committees* in 1999. There followed, in the same year, new rules and disclosures related to audit committees by the NYSE, NASDAQ, and AMEX.

Notwithstanding earlier events, in 2001 with the disclosure of a number of major accounting scandals (e.g., Enron and WorldCom), questions were raised about the effectiveness of audit committees. As a result, the U.S. Congress passed the Sarbanes-Oxley Act and the SEC adopted final rules amending the securities laws. Such actions have had an impact on audit committees. In response, the self-regulatory organizations (such as NYSE, AMEX, and NASDAQ) enacted amendments to their listing standards with respect to the role and responsibilities of audit committees within the corporate governance framework. Hence, the major thrust of these reforms is to create a new legal and regulatory environment and corporate governance framework. The goal is to restore investor confidence through an efficient securities market system.

The events noted have led to a number of audit committee best practices becoming federal statutes. Audit committees, as a result of the changes, must adhere to higher standards in corporate accountability to ensure the quality of financial information and investor protection against accounting scandals. The Sarbanes-Oxley Act has mandated significant changes in how boards and their audit committees can meet their oversight responsibilities in both the auditing and financial reporting areas.

In addition to the presence of audit committees in companies listed on U.S. stock exchanges, a number of stock exchanges in Canada, Europe, Africa, the Middle East, and the Asia/Pacific region have adopted requirements for audit committees for their listed companies. As worldwide financial markets expand and more companies are listed on major stock exchanges in different countries, the international investing public's demand for consistent and equal oversight protection through the use of audit committees will continue. In addition, international investors are concerned about the quality of corporate governance because of the impact of financial collapses and alleged frauds on securities markets. In response, to more effectively attract foreign equity investment, a number of stock exchanges around the world have adopted audit committees to increase transparency and competence in the management of their listed member companies.

ORGANIZATION AND STRUCTURE OF AUDIT COMMITTEES

The Sarbanes-Oxley Act of 2002 explained that the term *audit committee* means:

(A) a committee (or equivalent body) established by and amongst the board of directors of an issuer for the purpose of overseeing the accounting and financial reporting processes of the issuer and audits of the financial statements of the issuer; and

(B) if no such committee exists with respect to an issuer, the entire board of directors of the issuer.

Section 301 of the act contains an amendment to Section 10A of the Securities Exchange Act of 1934, which relates to independence of audit committee members. The requirement is stated in these words:

INDEPENDENCE—

(A) IN GENERAL—Each member of the audit committee of the issuer shall be a member of the board of directors of the issuer, and shall otherwise be independent.

(B) CRITERIA—In order to be considered to be independent for purposes of this paragraph, a member of an audit committee of an issuer may not, other than in his or her capacity as a member of the audit committee, the board of directors, or any other board committee—

(i) accept any consulting, advisory, or other compensatory fee from the issuer; or

(ii) be an affiliated person of the issuer or any subsidiary thereof.

Boards of directors form their audit committees by passing a board resolution or by amending corporate bylaws. Audit committees' responsibilities should be clearly defined and documented in their charter. Although the scope of the audit committees' responsibilities is predetermined by boards, the committees should be allowed to expand their charge with board approval and investigate significant matters that affect financial reporting disclosures.

Boards of directors should carefully give consideration to the following points with respect to their appointments of directors to audit committees:

1. *Number of directors*. The number of independent directors appointed to audit committees depends on the nature of the business and industry dynamics, the size of the company, and the size of the board of directors. The general consensus seems to be that three to five members are adequate.

2. *Composition*. Because members of audit committees have varied backgrounds and occupations, they provide a mix of skills and experience. Although the members have different levels of expertise, it is strongly advisable to have at least one individual who has a financial accounting background.

3. *Meetings*. Audit committees meet one to four times each year, with three or four meetings being the most common.

NATURE OF AUDIT COMMITTEES' RESPONSIBILITIES

Boards of directors define the role and responsibilities of their audit committees. This jurisdictional charge is usually disclosed in the audit committees' written charter, which includes the terms of reference, such as mission statement, membership (size and composition), term of service, frequency of meetings, scope of responsibilities, and reporting responsibilities. Audit committees are primarily responsible for the quality related to such matters as:

- External auditing process
- Internal auditing process
- Internal controls
- Conflicts of interest (code of corporate conduct, fraud presentation)
- Financial reporting process
- Regulatory and legal matters
- Other matters (interim reporting, information technology, officers' expense accounts)

Although boards of directors have defined the responsibilities of audit committees, boards may expand the scope of the audit committees' charter; boards should, however, avoid diluting the committees' charge with information overload. Recognizing that audit committees operate on a part-time basis and serve in an advisory capacity to boards, it is essential that boards place limitations on the scope of the committees' charge. Such a scope limitation enables boards to evaluate the committees' performance as well as protect the committees against legal claims for their inactions that are outside their charge. Roles and responsibilities of audit committees are disclosed in the annual proxy statements of publicly owned companies.

SUMMARY

Since the Enron and WorldCom fallout, a number of public and private sector institutions have issued reforms with respect to audit committees in the corporate governance context. Presumably these reforms and the new legal and regulatory framework will provide guidance and assistance to boards of directors and their audit committees in effectively discharging their fiduciary responsibilities to shareholders. Likewise, these reforms will enable audit committees to maintain quality in their oversight of both the internal and external audit processes as well as the financial reporting process to restore investor confidence in the financial reporting system.

Finally, it is evident that the scope for the responsibilities of audit committees will significantly increase. Therefore, it is essential that audit committees engage in an active, continuous educational improvement program to help their boards discharge their fiduciary responsibilities to shareholders. Contemporary corporate governance imposes serious responsibility on audit committees. Failure to assume such responsibility may require different organizational structures for corporate governance.

SEE ALSO *Auditing*

BIBLIOGRAPHY
American Institute of Certified Public Accountants. http://www.aicpa.org

American Institute of Certified Public Accountants. (1978). *Audit committees, answers to typical questions about their organization and operations.* New York: Author.

American Institute of Certified Public Accountants. (2005). *Professional standards, U.S. auditing standards/attestation standards* (Vol. 1). New York: Author.

Blue Ribbon Committee on Improving the Effectiveness of Corporate Audit Committees. (1999). *Report and recommendations of the Blue Ribbon Committee on improving the effectiveness of corporate audit committees.* New York: New York Stock Exchange; Washington, DC: National Association of Securities Dealers.

Braiotta, Louis (2004). *The audit committee handbook* (4th ed.). New York: Wiley.

The Business Roundtable (2002). *Principles of Corporate Governance.* Washington, DC: Author.

Director & Boards. http://www.directorsandboards.com

Levitt, Arthur (2001, January 5). Letter to audit committees chairman of the top 5000 public companies. Washington, DC: Security and Exchange Commission.

National Association of Corporate Directors. http://www.nacdonline.org

Sarbanes-Oxley Act of 2002, H.R. Rep. No. 107-610, July 25, 2002. Title 1 of Public Law No. 107-204.

U.S. Securities and Exchange Commission. http://www.sec.gov

Louis Braiotta, Jr.

AUDITING

The objective of an audit is to provide reasonable assurance that an assertion corresponds with a set of specified and established criteria. An audit involves gathering and evaluating sufficient evidence to determine whether the assertion does correspond with the criteria. The auditors then prepare a communication indicating the work they have performed and their opinion regarding the degree of correspondence between the assertions and the established criteria.

TYPES OF AUDITS

The three primary types of audits are financial, operational, and compliance audits. In a financial audit, the management of an organization asserts that the financial statements are prepared in accordance with generally accepted accounting principles (GAAP), the applicable criteria. After gathering and evaluating relevant and reliable evidence, the financial statement auditor then attests to the degree of correspondence between the audited financial statements and GAAP.

In an operational audit, the management of an organization asserts that the operations of the organization are being conducted in accordance with management's established policies and procedures. Typically, the policies and procedures of the organization are designed by management to ensure effective and/or efficient operations. After gathering and evaluating relevant and reliable evidence, the operational auditor then attests to the degree of correspondence between the actual operations and the specified policies and procedures of the organization. Operational audits can result in recommended changes to increase the effectiveness and/or efficiency of operations.

In a compliance audit, an organization's management asserts that the organization or individual is complying with specific laws and/or regulations. After gathering and evaluating relevant and reliable evidence, the compliance auditor then attests to the degree of correspondence between the subject matter identified and the specific law and/or regulation. As such, the compliance auditor provides assurance that the organization or the individual is complying with the applicable laws and/or regulations.

Audits of governmental agencies are typically both financial and compliance audits. Standards to be used when auditing federal government agencies and recipients of federal funds are found in *Government Auditing Standards,* issued by the comptroller general of the United States. This publication, which is referred to as the *Yellow Book,* specifies that the auditor must evaluate compliance with laws and regulations when completing a governmental audit.

TYPES OF AUDITORS

The three broad groups of auditors are external, internal, and governmental. External auditors are certified public accountants (CPAs) licensed by their states to provide auditing services. The CPA profession has played an active role in developing and providing attestation, assurance, and auditing services. The American Institute of Certified Public Accountants (AICPA), a voluntary national professional organization, represents the accounting profession in the United States, in general, and the public accounting profession, in particular. The AICPA publishes books, journals, and other materials, manages a Web site (http://www.aicpa.org), lobbies legislators, and sets professional standards in a number of areas. State professional societies (e.g., the New York State Society of CPAs) provide a range of professional support at the state level.

The AICPA Code of Professional Conduct guides the CPA in the performance of professional services, including audits. The code consists of principles, rules, interpretations, and rulings, going from the very broad to the very specific. There are six ethical principles of professional conduct (e.g., integrity) that provide the basis for the rest of the code. The rules address more specific ethical concerns (e.g., independence). The interpretations provide more details regarding the rules (e.g., conflicts of interest). Rulings are answers to specific questions (e.g., may a CPA accept a gift from a client?). In addition, the AICPA has an elaborate enforcement mechanism in place to ensure compliance with the Code of Professional Conduct.

One of the most important provisions of the code is that external auditors must be independent of their clients when performing financial audits. According to Article IV of the AICPA's Code of Professional Conduct, "a member in public practice should be independent in fact and appearance when providing auditing and other attestation services" (http://www.aicpa.org). To be independent in fact, an auditor must have integrity; a character of intellectual honesty and candor; and objectivity, a state of mind of judicial impartiality that recognizes an obligation of fairness to management and owners of a client, creditors, prospective owners or creditors, and other stakeholders. To be independent in appearance, the auditor must not have any obligations or interests (in the client, its management, or its owners) that could cause others to believe the auditor is biased with respect to the client, its management, or its owners.

Internal auditors are employees of individual organizations. To increase internal auditors' objectivity, typically, internal auditors report to the audit committee of the board of directors, rather than to the management. Internal auditors are primarily involved in completing operational and compliance audits, although some perform financial audits of segments of their companies. The Institute of Internal Auditors (IIA) is an international professional organization representing the internal auditing profession. The IIA publishes materials, encourages local chapter activities, offers certification as a certified internal auditor, and provides general support for practicing internal auditors.

Government auditors are employed by a particular agency of local, state, or federal government. Government auditors are primarily involved in performing compliance audits. Internal Revenue Service (IRS) auditors and Government Accountability Office (GAO) auditors are the most visible government auditors. IRS auditors examine tax returns to ensure that organizations and individuals report their information in compliance with the Internal Revenue Code. The GAO is an arm of the U.S. Congress that responds to Congressional requests for oversight, review, and evaluation of federal agencies and recipients of federal funds. Thus, GAO auditors often determine whether the agency being audited has spent the money in a manner that is consistent with Congressional mandates.

MANAGEMENT AND AUDITOR RESPONSIBILITY

When preparing the financial statements, management must follow GAAP, which are the principles and practices that govern financial reporting. Formal statements on financial accounting standards are issued by the Financial Accounting Standards Board, an independent standards-setting organization in the United States. When financial statements of an entity are presented to the external auditor for a financial audit, the entity's management asserts that the financial statements are prepared in accordance with GAAP. Based on their audit, the auditors are responsible for rendering an opinion on whether the financial statements have been presented in accordance with GAAP in all material respects. To promote independence and objectivity, the audit committee of the company's board of

directors is responsible for selecting and hiring the external auditors. In this role, the audit committee also acts as a liaison with the auditors who are performing the financial statement audit.

THE SECURITIES AND EXCHANGE COMMISSION

The Securities and Exchange Commission (SEC) was established by Congress in 1934 to enforce the Securities Exchange Act of 1934. The act requires publicly held companies to file annual audited financial statements (on Form 10-K) with the SEC. While not required by the act, nonpublic companies may also have their financial statements audited for several reasons. For example, the company may be planning to go public in the near future for which it will need audited financial statements for several previous years. Banks or other creditors may also require audited financial statements annually. Finally, a business may voluntarily hire an auditor to provide the owners with some assurance that its financial statements are reliable.

SARBANES-OXLEY ACT OF 2002

A significant number of high-profile business scandals (e.g., Enron, Tyco, and WorldCom in the United States, and Parmalat and Royal Ahold in Europe) that resulted in the restatement of previously issued financial statements early in the twenty-first century eroded investor confidence worldwide. Consequently the U.S. Congress responded by passing the Sarbanes-Oxley Act (SOX) of 2002 in an attempt to restore investor confidence.

An important aspect of SOX is that it increases the regulation of the external auditors at publicly traded companies. In addition, SOX has designated the SEC as the body to enforce the provisions of the act. The SEC has delegated the oversight of external auditors to the newly created Public Company Accounting Oversight Board (PCAOB). According to Section 103 of SOX, the PCAOB shall:

> (1) register public accounting firms; (2) establish, or adopt, by rule, "auditing, quality control, ethics, independence, and other standards relating to the preparation of audit reports for issuers;" (3) conduct inspections of accounting firms; (4) conduct investigations and disciplinary proceedings, and impose appropriate sanctions; (5) perform such other duties or functions as necessary or appropriate; (6) enforce compliance with the Act, the rules of the Board, professional standards, and the securities laws relating to the preparation and issuance of audit reports and the obligations and liabilities of accountants with respect thereto; (7) set the budget and manage the

operations of the Board and the staff of the Board. (http://www.aicpa.org/info/sarbanes_oxley_summary.htm)

In essence, this section of SOX provides for government regulation of the audit profession and it represents one of most dramatic changes mandated by the new law.

Other changes mandated by SOX have significantly affected external auditors. For example, Section 404 of SOX mandates that all publicly traded companies include in their annual report an assessment made by management about the effectiveness of their internal controls and procedures for financial reporting purposes. SOX also requires that the company's independent auditors attest to and report on management's evaluation of their internal controls and procedures.

Section 302 of SOX mandates that the chief executive officer (CEO) and chief financial officer (CFO) of each publicly traded company prepare a statement to certify the "appropriateness of the financial statements and disclosures contained in the periodic report, and that those financial statements and disclosures fairly present, in all material respects, the operations and financial condition of the issuer" (http://www.aicpa.org/info/sarbanes_oxley_summary.htm). If CEOs or CFOs knowingly and intentionally violate Section 302, they can be held criminally liable. And, under Title IX of SOX, the penalty for filing false financial statements with the SEC "for willful and knowing violations" are "a fine of not more than $5,000,000 and/or imprisonment of up to 20 years" (http://www.aicpa.org/info/sarbanes_oxley_summary. htm). For external auditors, this section of SOX has dramatically increased the attention being focused on the financial statement reporting process.

CPA FIRMS

Audited financial statements submitted to the SEC or to other stakeholders are audited by CPAs. These CPAs practice in public accounting firms, many of which are referred to as professional services firms. The largest firms are commonly referred to as "The Big Four." These four firms are: Deloitte & Touche, Ernst & Young, KPMG, and PricewaterhouseCoopers. These companies, and many other public accounting firms, typically operate as limited liability partnerships (LLPs) and thus carry the LLP designation in their names. In addition to accounting and auditing services, many CPA firms offer tax and consulting services. These consulting services include systems design, litigation support, pension and benefits consulting, and financial planning.

To ensure independence, CPA firms are not allowed to complete most consulting services for their publicly traded audit clients. Under Section 201 of SOX, it is unlawful for a CPA firm to provide any nonaudit service to an audit client,

> including: (1) bookkeeping or other services related to the accounting records or financial statements of the audit client; (2) financial information systems design and implementation; (3) appraisal or valuation services, fairness opinions, or contribution-in-kind reports; (4) actuarial services; (5) internal audit outsourcing services; (6) management functions or human resources; (7) broker or dealer, investment adviser, or investment banking services; (8) legal services and expert services unrelated to the audit; (9) any other service that the Board determines, by regulation, is impermissible. (http://www.aicpa.org/info/sarbanes_oxley_summary.htm)

GENERALLY ACCEPTED AUDITING STANDARDS

External auditors must follow generally accepted auditing standards (GAAS) when performing financial statement audits. These ten broad standards include three general requirements for the individual CPA, three standards for fieldwork, and four reporting standards. Authoritative guidance regarding the application of these ten general standards is provided in Statements on Auditing Standards, which are issued by the AICPA's Auditing Standards Board.

The general standards require CPAs to be proficient in accounting and auditing, to be independent from their clients, and to exercise due professional care. Before accepting an audit client, auditors must determine if they will be able to provide the necessary services on a timely basis and must have no financial or managerial relationship with the company whose financial statements are being audited.

The fieldwork standards address what is required when actually performing the audit work. The auditor must plan the engagement and supervise assistants. The auditor must obtain an understanding of the company's internal controls. The auditor must obtain sufficient competent evidence to support the financial statement assertions.

The reporting standards set requirements for the auditor's report. The report must explicitly refer to GAAP and must state an opinion on the financial statements as a whole. If there has been a change in accounting principles used by the company or inadequate disclosure of significant information, the auditor's report should address those issues.

For audits of publicly traded companies, the external auditor must also follow the auditing standards issued by the PCAOB. The first standard essentially adopts GAAS for publicly traded company audits and specifies the intention of the PCAOB to consider changes to GAAS on a go-forward basis. The second standard specifies the audit requirements for the internal control audits completed by external auditors, and the third standard specifies documentation requirements related to the evidential matter gathered on an audit of publicly traded companies.

TYPES OF AUDITORS' REPORTS

The auditor can issue five types of reports on financial statements: unqualified opinion, unqualified opinion with modified wording, qualified opinion, adverse opinion, or disclaimer of opinion. Importantly, SOX has brought about dramatic changes to the audit process followed by auditors at publicly traded companies. As a result, the auditors' reports for publicly traded and privately held companies are different. For privately held companies, if the financial statements present fairly, in all material respects, an entity's financial position (i.e., the balance sheet), results of operations (the income statement), and cash flows (the statement of cash flows) in conformity with GAAP, and if the audit is performed in accordance with GAAS, then a standard unqualified report can be issued.

The auditor would issue an unqualified report with modified wording in situations such as a change in accounting principle made by the client, when more than one auditor participated in the audit, where there is a question about the client continuing as a going concern for a year from the date of the balance sheet, or when the auditor wishes to highlight a specific matter. The modification does not affect the opinion.

Auditors would issue a qualified opinion in situations where they view a departure from GAAP as being material, but not pervasive or highly material relative to the entire set of financial statements; or when the auditors have not been able to obtain sufficient competent evidence pertaining to a material, but not pervasive or highly material, part of the financial statements. The auditors must add an explanatory paragraph before the opinion paragraph describing the reason for the qualification and then qualify the opinion paragraph. In the case of inadequate evidence, which is referred to as a scope limitation, the second paragraph of the report would also be modified.

If in the auditor's judgment, pervasive or highly material deviation(s) from GAAP exist and the auditee fails to adjust the financial statements to the satisfaction of the auditor, then the auditor must express an adverse opinion. In this condition, the auditor expresses an opinion that the financial statements taken as a whole do not present fairly the financial position, results of operations, and cash flows of the company in accordance with GAAP. Adverse opinions are rarely, if ever seen in practice.

A disclaimer of opinion, which means that the auditor provides no opinion, is issued when the scope limitation (typically lack of evidence regarding financial statement assertions) is so pervasive or highly material that the auditor cannot conclude as to the fairness of the financial statements, taken as a whole. A disclaimer is also issued when the auditor lacks independence from the company being audited. Disclaiming an opinion is also permitted, but not required, in conditions of major uncertainty about the company's ability to continue as a going concern for a year following the date of the financial statements.

For publicly traded companies that report to the SEC, the guidelines issued by the PCAOB must be followed by auditors. Under Section 404 of the law, the audit firms are required to audit both the internal control system and the financial statements on an annual basis. As a result, the auditor report for publicly traded companies has changed.

SEE ALSO *Accounting; Audit Committees; Government Auditing Standards; Performance Audits*

BIBLIOGRAPHY

American Institute of Certified Public Accountants Web site: http://www.aicpa.org retrieved February 2, 2006.

Internal Revenue Service Web Site: http://www.irs.gov retrieved February 2, 2006.

Messier, William F., Jr., Glover, Steven M., and Prawitt, Douglas F. (2006). *Auditing & Assurance Services* (4th ed.). Boston: McGraw-Hill/Irwin.

Mohammad J. Abdolmohammadi
Jay C. Thibodeau

AUDITOR REPORTS
SEE *Auditing*

AUTHORITY
SEE *Management: Authority and Responsibility*

B

BAIT AND SWITCH

SEE *Ethics in Marketing; Ethics in Law for Business; Government Role in Business*

BALANCE OF TRADE

Even though the United States is well endowed with both human and natural resources, as well as the ways and means to use them in the production and distribution of goods and services, it cannot provide its people with all that they want or need. For this reason, the United States engages in international trade, which is the exchange of goods and services with other nations. Without international trade, goods would either cost more, not be available, or, if available, be of unreliable supply.

On a broader level, the world's endowment of natural resources is both uneven and capricious. For example, Canada, with its huge forests, is a major producer of lumber and paper products; the Middle East has rich oil reserves; and the coastal regions of the world are leaders in the fishing industry. Ironically, however, each of these nations (or regions) may lack resources (or goods) that are abundant elsewhere.

Without international trade, each country would have to be totally self-sufficient. Each would have to make do only with what it could produce on its own. This would be the same as an individual being totally self-sufficient, providing all goods and services, such as clothing and food, that would fulfill all wants and needs. International trade allows each nation to specialize in the production of those goods it can produce most efficiently. Specialization, in turn, allows total production to be

---

Four largest U.S. trading partners: 2004
(Merchandise exports and imports, in millions)

Rank	Country	Exports	Imports	Trade Balance	Percent of Total Trade
1	Canada	190	256	-66	19.5%
2	Mexico	111	156	-45	11.6%
3	China	35	197	-162	10.1%
4	Japan	54	130	-76	8%

Note: Trade Balance = Exports − Imports

SOURCE: U.S. Bureau of the Census, Foreign Trade Division, 2004.

Table 1

greater than would be true if each nation attempted to be completely autonomous.

EXPORTS AND IMPORTS

Goods and services sold to other countries are called exports; goods and services bought from other countries are called imports. The Foreign Trade Division of the U.S. Bureau of the Census states that U.S. exports include such goods as corn, wheat, soybeans, plastics, iron and steel products, chemicals, and machinery, while imports include such goods as chemicals, crude oil, machinery, diamonds, and coffee.

The balance of trade, also known as net exports, is the difference between the dollar amount of merchandise exports and the dollar amount of merchandise imports. The United States has many trade partners. Table 1 shows the U.S. balance of trade with its four largest trading partners.

In order to have a trade surplus, a country must export (sell) more tangible goods than it imports (buys). If the opposite were true, a trade deficit would exist. On an individual nation-to-nation basis, a country can have a trade surplus with one country, yet a trade deficit with another. The Bureau of the Census records indicated that in 2004, the United States had a trade deficit with each of its four largest trading partners. Table 1 also reveals the total percentage of trade accounted for by the four largest trading partners of the United States (this percentage is derived by adding total exports to, and total imports from, a particular country and expressing this sum over the sum of aggregate exports and imports with all nations in a particular year).

The Bureau of the Census also reported that the United States experienced its first trade deficit (total of all exports minus total of all imports) of the twentieth century in 1971, with a trade deficit of approximately $1.5 billion. For the most part, this condition continued throughout the 1980s, 1990s, and into the twenty-first century when, by 2004, the United States realized a record trade deficit of nearly $651 billion. Table 2 shows the U.S. balance of trade for 1960 through 2004. As may be noted, while the volume of total exports and imports increased in dollar terms over the period, the disparity between merchandise imports and exports widened in the later years.

ABSOLUTE ADVANTAGES

As stated earlier, total production increases when a nation specializes in the production of those goods it can produce most efficiently instead of attempting to be totally self-sufficient. Allen Smith stated that "a country that can produce a product more efficiently than another country is said to have an absolute advantage in the production of

Trade balance, goods on a census basis

VALUE IN MILLIONS OF DOLLARS
1960 – 2004

Year	Balance	Total Exports	Total Imports
1960	4,609	19,626	15,018
1961	5,476	20,190	14,714
1962	4,583	20,973	16,390
1963	5,289	22,427	17,138
1964	7,006	25,690	18,684
1965	5,333	26,699	21,366
1966	3,830	29,372	25,542
1967	4,122	30,934	26,812
1968	837	34,063	33,226
1969	1,290	37,332	36,042
1970	3,225	43,176	39,951
1971	-1,476	44,087	45,563
1972	-5,729	49,854	55,583
1973	2,389	71,865	69,476
1974	-3,884	99,437	103,321
1975	9,551	106,856	99,305
1976	-7,820	116,794	124,614
1977	-28,353	123,182	151,534
1978	-30,205	145,847	176,052
1979	-23,922	186,363	210,285
1980	-19,696	225,566	245,262
1981	-22,267	238,715	260,982
1982	-27,510	216,442	243,952
1983	-52,409	205,639	258,048
1984	-106,702	223,976	330,678
1985	-117,711	218,815	336,526
1986	-138,280	227,159	365,438
1987	-152,119	254,122	406,241
1988	-118,526	322,426	440,952
1989	-109,400	363,812	473,211
1990	-101,719	393,592	495,311
1991	-66,723	421,730	488,453
1992	-84,501	448,164	532,665
1993	-115,568	465,091	580,659
1994	-150,630	512,626	663,256
1995	-158,801	584,742	743,543
1996	-170,214	625,075	795,289
1997	-181,488	689,182	870,671
1998	-230,852	682,977	913,828
1999	-328,820	695,798	1,024,618
2000	-436,103	781,918	1,218,021
2001	-411,899	729,100	1,140,999
2002	-468,262	693,104	1,161,366
2003	-532,351	724,769	1,257,120
2004	-650,929	818,776	1,469,705

Note: Balances are rounded

SOURCE: U.S. Bureau of the Census, Foreign Trade Division, 2004.

Table 2

that product" (1986, p. 315). When a nation can use fewer resources to produce the same amount of a product, it has an absolute advantage in the production of that product. For example, Brazil has an absolute advantage over the United States in the production of coffee; the nations of the Middle East have an absolute advantage over the United States in the production of crude oil.

Because of its ideal climate, Ecuador can produce bananas more efficiently than can the United States; therefore, Ecuador has an absolute advantage over the United States in the production of bananas. In contrast, however, the United States has an absolute advantage over Ecuador in the production of most other products. Given these absolute production possibilities, both the United States and Ecuador stand to benefit by engaging in the production (and subsequent trade) of those products which each can produce most efficiently. Since exchange is voluntary, nations will (most typically) not trade with one another unless the outcome is mutually beneficial. Nevertheless, the gains realized by each of the trading partners may not necessarily be equal.

Smith also stated that "any time a nation has an absolute advantage in the production of two goods or services, the nation has a comparative advantage in the production of that good or service where the absolute advantage is greater" (p. 315). In other words, if a nation has a two-to-one absolute advantage in the production of one product and a three-to-one absolute advantage in the production of another product, the comparative advantage lies with the product with the larger (three-to-one) ratio. Smith went on to add that "even though a nation has an absolute disadvantage in the production of two products, it has a comparative advantage in the production of that product in which the absolute disadvantage is less" (p. 316). For example, even though a nation has a disadvantage in the production of a certain product, if that disadvantage is small compared to its disadvantage in the production of other products, it still has a comparative advantage with the former product.

MONETARY TRANSACTIONS

When the United States buys goods from another country, it will usually pay for those goods in the currency of the exporting country. Many international transactions involve the exchange of money between nations. The balance of payments is an accounting record of the difference between the amount of money that a country receives (known as inpayments) and the amount of money that it pays out (known as outpayments). A positive overall balance of payments means that a country has realized more aggregate inpayments than outpayments over a period (typically one year). In contrast, a negative balance of payments exists when a country pays out more money than it takes in.

Any transaction that involves a flow of funds between countries is recorded in one of several accounts within a nation's balance of payments. The largest single account in the overall balance of payments is, for most countries, the current account. The balance of trade, as noted above, records the flow of merchandise exports and imports and is a component of the current account. When adding the net flow of funds arising from services to a nation's balance of trade, one obtains the balance on goods and services (also recorded in the current account). Finally, net unilateral transfers (one-way flows by individuals, governments, and businesses) are included in a nation's current account as well.

Across global markets, it is not uncommon to observe the buying and selling of both real assets (plant and equipment, land) and financial assets (stocks, bonds). Such transactions are recorded in the capital account of a nation's balance of payments. One last category of international transactions involves those arising among governments and central banks. These transactions are recorded in the official reserve account of a nation's balance of payments.

While unimpeded free trade tends to promote the greatest benefits arising from international specialization, the importing and exporting of some goods and services is controlled by the U.S. government (and the governments of other nations as well). Three of the most common impediments to trade are tariffs, quotas, and embargoes. A tariff is a tax levied by the government on the importation of goods. An import quota sets a physical limit on the amount of goods that may be imported during a given period. An export quota does the same for a nation's exports. Finally, an embargo (import or export) is employed when a government wishes to completely halt all imports or exports of a specific product.

SEE ALSO *International Trade*

BIBLIOGRAPHY

Gottheil, Fred M. (2005). *Principles of economics* (4th ed). Mason, OH: Thomson Pub.

Smith, Allen W. (1986). *Understanding economics*. New York: Random House.

U.S. Bureau of the Census. Foreign Trade Division. http://www.census.gov/foreign-trade/statistics

Gary P. Tripp

BANKRUPTCY

In 2005 the U.S. Congress enacted profound changes to the Bankruptcy Reform Act of 1978. Known as the Bankruptcy Abuse Prevention and Consumer Protection Act of 2005, the amendments were designed to correct perceived abuses by debtors who allegedly took advantage of the pro-debtor tone and provisions of the 1978 statute. The emphasis has been shifted from a pro-debtor enactment to one favoring creditors.

The basic premise for enabling debtors to file for bankruptcy is to have a "fresh start" by permitting them to end their overwhelming debt and begin anew to rebuild their credit and engage in day-to-day activities without fear of creditors seizing their assets and imposing liens on their salaries. Congress had concluded that a sizable percentage of debtors had taken advantage of liberal Bankruptcy Code provisions and grossly abused their credit access. Thus, Congress imposed a number of roadblocks to the discharge of indebtedness while refraining from limiting creditors' persistent inundation of offers of credit to consumers—especially by credit card companies.

The Bankruptcy Code contains a number of chapters, including preliminary sections concerning procedural and administrative requirements and substantive chapters that detail requirements for debtors regarding liquidation, reorganization, or adjustment of debts. The most relevant chapters are 7, 11, and 13.

CHAPTER 7 LIQUIDATION PROVISIONS

The most significant change to the 1978 statute concerns consumer bankruptcy under the Chapter 7 liquidation provisions. Previously, debtors had the choice of filing for liquidation—which means that debtors are completely discharged from all indebtedness except for certain nondischargeable debts, after their assets have been reduced to cash and distributed to creditors—or filing a plan under Chapter 13 with the court for the payment of all or part of the indebtedness.

The act continues the choice but now requires consumer debtors electing to file under the act to initially secure credit counseling within 180 days preceding the filing and to provide a certificate from an approved nonprofit budget and credit counseling agency concerning services provided to the debtors, including a copy of the repayment plan, if any. The act also continues to permit debtors to have their debts discharged, after compliance with the statute, and to possess a not-insignificant amount of assets upon termination of the proceeding.

Exemptions. Contrary to what many persons believe, the debtor being discharged in bankruptcy is able to retain a substantial amount of property (which would be double the sum if there is a joint filing). This is a further inducement to seek bankruptcy protection before being reduced to an impoverished condition. The assets that a bankrupt person may retain are:

- Interest in property held jointly or as tenants by the entirety if the tenant is exempt from the process under nonbankruptcy law

- Retirement funds pursuant to statute

- Debtor's aggregate interest up to $18,450 in value in real or personal property used as a residence, cooperative, or burial plot

- Debtor's interest in one motor vehicle up to $2,950 in value

- Debtor's interest up to $475 in any particular item or $9,850 in total value in household furnishings and goods, and various personal items, such as clothing

- $1,225 in value for jewelry for personal, family, or dependent use

- Any property up to $975 plus up to $9,250 of any unused amount of exemption

- $1,850 in any implements, professional books, tools of trade

- Unmatured life insurance

- Prescribed health aids

- Various other benefits and payments, such as Social security

Priority of Distributions. Not all creditors are treated alike with respect to the distribution of net assets that remain after the deduction of costs, expenses, and other indebtedness. The order of distribution of assets remaining is as follows:

1. Secured creditors to the extent of their security on specific property (e.g., mortgage interest on real property)

2. Unsecured domestic support obligations

3. Administrative expenses

4. Claims up to $10,000 earned by the creditor within 180 days of filing or cessation of business for wages, sales, or commissions

5. Contributions to an employee benefit plan arising within 180 days of filing or cessation of business up to $10,000 per employee

6. Claims of persons engaged in farming or fishing up to $4,925 each

7. Other claims for rental, sale, or use of property or services rendered up to $2,225

8. Certain claims by governmental entities including income and property taxes

9. Claims for death or personal injuries arising from use of an automobile or vessel while debtor was intoxicated

10. All other indebtedness

Nondischargeable Debts. The act provides that certain debts may not be discharged since Congress has determined that bankrupt persons should continue to be responsible for such debts even if they cannot currently make payment. The reasons for the nondischargability of such debts include: the nature of the debt, policy reasons to protect the creditors (e.g., support obligations for one's family), and debts arising because of the debtor's misconduct. They are as follows:

- Taxes, including state and local taxes, and customs duty
- Money or other financial benefit received by reason of false pretenses
- Consumer debts incurred within ninety days before filing totaling more than $500 owed to a single creditor for luxury goods and services; cash advances of $750 from a single creditor within seventy days of filing
- Debts not listed
- Debt for fraud, embezzlement, and larceny
- Domestic support obligation
- Willful or malicious injury to another person or property
- Fines, penalties, forfeitures payable to a governmental entity, including for state and local taxes, that is not compensation for actual money loss, other than a tax penalty imposed before three years before date of filing of petition
- Educational benefit funded by government unless undue hardship; also, student loans payable to for-profit and nongovernmental entities
- For death or injury by auto, vessel, or an aircraft while intoxicated from drugs, alcohol, or other substance
- To a spouse or former spouse
- Fee or assessment due to condominium or coop
- Fee imposed on a prisoner
- Debts owed to a pension, profit-sharing, or stock bonus plan
- Violation of the federal securities laws

Dismissal of Petition for Abuse—The Means Test. The revised act mandates the dismissal of a Chapter 7 filing if the grant of relief would constitute an "abuse" of the act by individual consumer debtors. The tests that may be used by the Bankruptcy Court in dismissing a petition for abuse include a median income test and a means test. If the debtor's current monthly income exceeds the state's medium income for a family of equivalent size or if the debtor's monthly income less allowable expenses exceeds an amount allowed under the act for a family of equivalent size, then there is a presumption of abuse; otherwise, no such presumption may be inferred.

The court may also use noneconomic factors in determining if abuse does exist. The formulas presented are quite complex and may necessitate the services of professionals. Thus, the act seeks to require debtors able to pay their debts over time to adopt the provisions of Chapter 13 and pay all or a portion of the debt over a period of years rather than expeditiously having a clean slate to start anew. The debtor thus has extensive filing requirements, including the credit counseling certificate, pay stubs, and statements of pre- and postpetition income and expenses.

A previous source of abuse was that debtors could use either the act's exemptions or the exemptions provided in the state in which they resided, whichever was greater. Thus, certain states had homestead exemptions that permitted multimillion-dollar homes to be exempt from claims of creditors. The act now limits the exemption to $125,000 if there is an abuse in the filing or other defined bases.

The revised statute makes use of attorneys potentially very costly or otherwise inaccessible. The signature by an attorney on the bankruptcy petition is a certification that he or she has no knowledge, after a diligent inquiry, that the information on the schedules is incorrect. The effect of this provision is that an attorney has to make a detailed investigation of the debtor's finances and be ready to be subject to expenses of a trustee in making a motion to dismiss as well as to incur potential fines. Thus, many attorneys may refrain from representing debtors or significantly increase the fees they charge for services rendered because of the additional time required in assisting debtors, as well as the heightened potential liability for the attorneys.

Discharge. After the assets are distributed, then the unpaid claims are discharged. Partnerships and corporations must liquidate under state law before or on completion of the proceeding. The debtor cannot file another Chapter 7 proceeding until the expiration of eight (formerly six) years.

Other Liquidation Provisions. There are separate liquidation provisions for stockbrokers, commodity brokers, and clearing bank liquidations. Also, municipal governmental bankruptcies are treated under Chapter 9 of the act.

CHAPTER 11 REORGANIZATION

The Bankruptcy Code recognizes that liquidating a company may entail the loss of jobs as well as other disruptive events. Accordingly, Chapter 11 seeks to permit companies to become solvent again by reorganizing themselves in such a way as to permit them to continue functioning as viable entities. Chapter 11 applies to individuals, partnerships, corporations, unincorporated associations, and railroads, although corporations are almost always the petitioners. It does not apply to companies that are regulated by other statutes, such as banks, savings and loan associations, unions, insurance companies, and brokerage firms.

The advantage to a Chapter 11 filing is that the debtor is permitted to remain in possession of the entity, which is especially important in business filings since the debtor may continue to operate the business. If the court believes there may be adverse circumstances, such as possible fraud or other dishonesty or gross mismanagement, then it may appoint a trustee or examiner to review the debtor's finances.

Once an order of relief is granted, the court will appoint a creditors' committee, which generally consists of the seven largest unsecured creditors. Their function includes appearances at court hearings, participation in the plan of reorganization, and asserting possible objections to the plan. As in Chapter 7, there is an automatic stay that prevents creditors from pursuing other judicial proceedings or collecting debts.

Chapter 11 permits the debtor to accept or reject executory contracts (contracts whose completion is to be accomplished in the future). The plan of reorganization is to be filed within 120 days after date of the order of relief. The plan sets forth the debtor's proposed new capital structure, designates the different classes of claims and interests, and proposes possible alteration of the rights of creditors, conversion of unsecured creditors to equity holders, sale of assets, and other items. The creditors are to receive a disclosure statement containing necessary information concerning the plan of reorganization. The creditors and interests are to accept or reject the plan before confirmation by the court. Confirmation requires that the plan be in the best interests of each class of claims and interests, and be feasible. If creditors object, the court is empowered to compel acceptance and participation.

CHAPTER 13 CONSUMER DEBT ADJUSTMENT

Chapter 13 applies to natural persons and is intended to allow the debtors to file a petition with the Bankruptcy Court in an endeavor to permit the debtors to become solvent by either extending the time to pay their debts or by a composition that permits the debtors to pay a sum less than the full amount to each of the creditors. Eligible persons are natural persons who have regular income and who possess noncontingent, liquidated, unsecured debts of less than $250,000 and secured debts of less than $750,000.

The plan of payment must be filed within fifteen days after the filing of the Chapter 13 petition. The plan must recite the debtors' finances, estimated income, and expenses with a payout over a three-year period (5 years if approved by the court). The advantages to debtors include continuation of possession of their property. The planned installment, which is made to the trustee, is to commence within thirty days of filing. The trustee is responsible for paying the creditors.

Objections to the plan may be filed by the creditors, which are then determined at a hearing. The court examines whether the plan was made in good faith, whether it is feasible (if the debtor will be able to make the proposed payments), and be in the interests of the creditors, that is, the creditors must receive at least what they would have received under a Chapter 7 liquidation proceeding.

BIBLIOGRAPHY

Borges, W., and Nathan, B. C. (2005, April 15). Bankruptcy abuse and consumer protection act of 2005: Significant business bankruptcy changes in store for trade creditors. Retrieved September 7, 2005, from http://www.nacm.org/resource/Bankruptcy-Act apr15-05.html

Davis Polk & Wardwell. (2005, June 2). Bankruptcy code and selected other provisions of the United States code. Retrieved November 28, 2005, from http://www.dpw.com/practice/code.blackline.pdf

Houlden, L., and Morawetz, G. (2004). *The 2005 annotated bankruptcy and insolvency act.* Toronto, Ontario, Canada: Carswell.

Jeweler, Robin (2005, March 14). The Bankruptcy Abuse Prevention and Consumer Protection Act of 2005 in the 109th Congress. *Congressional Research Service.* Retrieved November 28, 2005, from http://www.bna.com/webwatch/bankruptcycrs4.pdf

Resnick, A., and Sommer, H. (2005). *The Bankruptcy Abuse Prevention and Consumer Protection Act of 2005: With analysis.* New York: LexisNexis/Matthew Bender.

Reynolds, J. (2005, August). Debtor relief or grief? The bankruptcy act of 2005. Retrieved September 8, 2005, from http://www.dcbar.org/for_lawyers/washington_lawyer/august_2005/bankruptcy.cfm

Roy J. Girasa

BANKS AND BANKING
SEE *Financial Institutions*

BARTER
SEE *Currency Exchange; Economic Systems; Marketing; Money*

BEHAVIORAL MANAGEMENT THOUGHTS
SEE *Management*

BEHAVIORAL SCIENCE MOVEMENT

The exact date of when the behavioral science, or human relations, movement came into being is difficult to identify. However, it was not until the second half of the nineteenth century that much attention was paid to workers' needs, because there was little understanding of how those needs affect total worker productivity. Prior to that time, most managers viewed workers as a device that could be bought and sold like any other possession. Long hours, low wages, and miserable working conditions were the realities of the average worker's life.

Then, at the beginning of the twentieth century, Frederick Winslow Taylor (1856–1915), one of the most widely read theorists on management, introduced and developed the theory of scientific management. The basis for scientific management was technological in nature, emphasizing that the best way to increase output was to improve the methods used by workers. According to this perspective, the main focus of a leader should be on the needs of the organization, not the needs of the individual worker. Taylor and his followers were criticized on the grounds that scientific management tended to exploit workers more than it benefited them.

In the 1920s and early 1930s the trend started by Taylor was gradually replaced by the behavioral science movement, initiated by Elton Mayo and his associates through the famous Hawthorne studies. Efficiency experts at the Hawthorne, Illinois, plant of Western Electric designed research to study the effects of illumination on worker productivity. At first, nothing about this research seemed exceptional enough to arouse any unusual interest, since efficiency experts had long tried to find the ideal mix

Abraham Harold Maslow (1908–1970). *Psychologist Abraham Maslow proposed his motivation theory in 1943.* © BETTMANN/CORBIS

of physical conditions, working hours, and working methods that would stimulate workers to produce at maximum capacity. Yet by the time the Hawthorne studies were completed ten years later, there was little doubt that they were one of the most important organizational studies, causing the behavioral science movement to gather momentum. The major conclusion of the Hawthorne Studies was that attention to workers, not illumination, affected productivity. Essentially, then, the scientific management movement emphasized a concern for output, while the behavioral science movement stressed a concern for relationships among workers.

Various individuals have made important contributions to the behavioral science movement. In 1943 psychologist Abraham Maslow (1908–1970) proposed a theory of motivation according to which workers' behavior is determined by a wide variety of needs. Motivation starts when an individual experiences a need; the individual then formulates a goal, which, upon achievement, will satisfy the need. Maslow (1954) identified these needs and arranged them in a hierarchy, positing that lower-level needs must be satisfied, at least in part, before an individual begins to strive to satisfy needs at a higher level.

Douglas McGregor (1960–1964), Maslow's student, studied worker attitudes. According to McGregor (1960), traditional organizations are based on either of two sets of assumptions about human nature and human motivation, which he called Theory X and Theory Y. Theory X assumes that most people prefer to be directed; are not interested in assuming responsibility; and are motivated by money, fringe benefits, and the threat of punishment. Theory Y assumes that people are not, by nature, lazy and unreliable; it suggests that people can be basically self-directed and creative at work if properly motivated.

Management is often suspicious of strong informal work groups because of their potential power to control the behavior of their members, and as a result, the level of productivity. In 1950 George C. Homans (1910–1989) developed a model of social systems that may be useful in identifying where these groups get their power to control behavior.

In 1959 another psychologist, Frederick Herzberg (1923–2000), examined sources of worker satisfaction and dissatisfaction. Herzberg cited achievement, responsibility, advancement, and growth as job satisfiers—factors that motivate workers. He also proposed that other aspects of the job environment called job maintenance factors—company policy, supervision, working conditions, interpersonal relations, salary and benefits—contribute to the desired level of worker satisfaction, although these factors rarely motivate workers.

Also in the 1960s, another behavioral science researcher, Chris Argyris (1923–), presented his immaturity-maturity theory (1964). He said that keeping workers immature is built into the very nature of formal organizations. These concepts of formal organizations lead to assumptions about human nature that are incompatible with the proper development of maturity in the human personality. He saw a definite incongruity between the needs of a mature personality and the structure of formal organizations.

More and more leaders in both for-profit and non-profit organizations recognize the importance of the goals of the behavioral science (human relations) movement. Those goals consist of fitting people into work situations in such a manner as to motivate them to work together harmoniously and to achieve a high level of productivity, while also providing economic, psychological, and social satisfaction.

SEE ALSO *Management; Motivation*

BIBLIOGRAPHY
Argyris, Chris (1990). *Integrating the Individual and the Organization*. New Brunswick, NJ: Transaction Publishers.

Benton, Douglas A. (1998). *Applied Human Relations*. Upper Saddle River, NJ: Prentice-Hall.

Greenberg, Jerald (1999). *Managing Behavior in Organizations: Science in Service to Practice*. Upper Saddle River, NJ: Prentice-Hall.

Hersey, Paul, Blanchard, Kenneth H., and Johnson, Dewey E. (1996). *Management of Organizational Behavior*. Upper Saddle River, NJ: Prentice-Hall.

Herzberg, Frederick, Mausner, Bernard, and Snyderman, Barbara Bloch. (1993). *The Motivation to Work*. New Brunswick, NJ: Transaction Publishers.

Homans, George C. (1992). *The Human Group*. New Brunswick, NJ: Transaction Publishers.

Maslow, Abraham H. (1987). *Motivation and Personality* (3rd ed.). New York: Harper & Row.

McGregor, Douglas (2006). *The Human Side of Enterprise* (annotated ed.). New York: McGraw-Hill.

Rue, Leslie W., and Byars, Lloyd L. (1990). *Supervision: Key Link to Productivity*. Boston: McGraw-Hill.

Whetten, David A., & Cameron, Kim S. (2005). *Developing Management Skills* (6th ed.). Upper Saddle River, NJ: Pearson/Prentice Hall.

Wray, Ralph D., Luft, Roger L., and Highland, Patrick J. (1996). *Fundamentals of Human Relations*. Cincinnati, OH: South-Western Educational Publishing.

Yukl, Gary (1994). *Leadership in Organizations*. Upper Saddle River, NJ: Pearson/Prentice-Hall.

Marcia Anderson

BENCHMARKING
SEE *Standard-Based Work Performance*

BENEFITS
SEE *Employee Benefits*

BONDS

Bonds are debts to the issuers, whereas they are investments to buyers. Such debts appear on balance sheets of the issuing entities as long-term liabilities. Bonds provide a source of funds for the issuer and a payment to the buyer in the form of interest. Both bonds and stocks are referred to as securities, yet the two are different types of investments.

BONDS: LONG-TERM AND VARIED

Bonds are generally considered long-term obligations. Nevertheless, since there is trading in the secondary market for some types of bonds, it is possible to buy and sell such bonds at any time. Bonds are issued by entities seeking funds for a variety of reasons.

Corporations issue bonds often for expansion purposes, when they have determined that extension of their long-term debt obligations is a better strategy than to expand their ownership base through the issuance of additional stock. Corporations are frequently motivated to choose bonds over expansion of stock owners for two basic reasons: The cost of interest is deductible as a yearly expense, and there is no dilution of ownership through the extension of the company's liabilities.

The federal government issues bonds, along with short-term notes, for the expenditures required to operate the federal government and to pay off debt that is maturing. Municipalities and states issue bonds for capital expenditures that are perceived necessary to maintain the infrastructure of the entity. Such bonds provide funds to build local roads, stadiums, schools, and other public buildings.

Investors can choose from a wide variety of bonds. Among them are: corporate bonds, federal government bonds, municipal bonds, asset-backed bonds, mortgage-based bonds, and foreign government bonds. For each of these categories, there are variations. Additionally, there are bond funds related to government bonds, corporate bonds, and foreign government bonds. It is possible to buy bonds that are convertible into stock. The bond market is indeed complex and varied. For purposes of the discussion here, the focus will be on basic bond types: corporate, federal government, and municipal. There will follow a discussion of bonds as an investment for an individual.

CORPORATE BONDS

In a corporation, the board of directors is responsible for making the decisions related to a bond issue including determining how much money is to be raised, what type of bond will be sold, what the maturity date will be, and what the interest rate will be. Corporations with sound credit standing are able to issue bonds without pledging assets. Such bonds are called debenture bonds, or unsecured bonds. Companies with low credit standing often issue secured bonds, for which specified assets have been pledged as collateral.

Issuance Process. Corporations generally do not sell directly to the public; rather, they sell their entire issues to an underwriter, often an investment bank, which acts as

"middleman" for the corporation and the bondholders. (Sometimes more than one underwriter participates in the sell of an issue, especially if the value of the issue is high.) The issuing company also engages a trustee, generally a bank or trust company, to monitor the sale to ensure that all the details of the bond indenture are honored by the underwriters.

The contract for a purchase of bonds is called a bond indenture, which provides a description of the bond issue as well as the rights of both the buyer and seller. The buyer, for example, may have the right to convert a bond into stock. Sellers often state options, which modify the basic agreement. For example, a common option is the right to retire a bond before its maturity date. Such bonds are called callable bonds. Before the possibility of paperless transactions, bond certificates were issued, but now transactions tend to be book entries only.

Bonds have a predetermined rate of interest called the stated or contract rate, which is established by the board of directors. The actual interest rate, however, determined at auction, is referred to as the market rate. The market rate may equal the stated rate, or it may be higher or lower. The bond that sells at the stated rate is considered to have sold at par value. If the market rate is higher, the bond is sold at discount, which means that the buyer will pay less than the face value of the bond, therefore earning interest at a rate higher than the stated rate. If the market rate is lower, the bond is sold at a premium, which means that the buyer is paying more than the face value of the bond, and earning less than the stated rate. Although there may be a difference between stated and market rates, the actual interest paid is based on the stated rate and the face value of the bond. Interest is usually paid semiannually.

Bonds are registered in the name of the person who purchased them. The registered owner receives the interest on the interest payment date. If a $1,000 bond carried interest at a contract rate of 6 percent, the registered owner would received a check for $30 semiannually. Since electronic processing began, the book entry means that the bonder holds a virtual bond. The corporation's computer files merely contain the names and addresses of those to whom interest checks will be sent on the appropriate dates. Additionally, with the ability to transfer funds electronically, corporations are able to deposit interest payments directly into their bondholders' bank accounts.

The Nature of the Bond Market. The bond market is dominated by institutional investors, such as insurance companies, mutual funds, and pension funds, but bonds can be purchased by individual investors as well. Bonds are traded both in the primary market, which is the initial sale of the bonds, and in the secondary market, which is the sale of bonds subsequent to the initial sale by the issuer or underwriter. While the stated rate is the same throughout the life of the bond, the effective rate varies with the buying and selling of corporate bonds in the secondary market.

An investor who wishes to buy or sell corporate bonds must contact a broker or dealer who might carry that particular bond in inventory. A dealer who does not have that bond would contact another dealer who did. Many major newspapers report information about bonds, both corporate and U.S. government bonds.

Rating of Corporate Bonds. There are three organizations that rate corporate bonds: Fitch Investors Service, Moody's Investors Service, and Standard & Poor's Corporation (S&P). Each has a ranking system. For example, S&P uses AAA as the highest ranking, meaning in general that bonds so ranked are issued by corporations that are judged to have extremely strong capacity to pay interest and to repay the principal. S&P's lowest ranking is D, which indicates that the corporation's bonds are in default, and payments are in arrears. Between the two are AA, A, BBB (all indicating levels of adequate assessments), with AA being higher than A, and A higher than BBB. Bonds rated BB, B, CCC, and CC are predominately speculative, with the lower ratings often referred to as junk bonds or high-yield bonds. C is reserved for bonds no longer paying interest.

FEDERAL GOVERNMENT BONDS

The U.S. federal government borrows large amounts of money in order to meet its obligations. The U.S. Treasury issues a number of debt obligations in addition to bonds. Securities with maturity dates of less than a year are called Treasury bills (or T-bills); those with maturities from one to ten years are called notes; those with maturities exceeding ten years are generally called bonds. There are I bonds and EE bonds, however, that may be redeemed at any time after a twelve-month-minimum holding period. Collectively, the issues of the U.S. Treasury are referred to as Treasuries.

Federal government bonds are auctioned according to a schedule that is posted at the Treasury's Web site (http://publicdebt.treas.gov), after announcements at press conferences. The bonds available are varied. A description of a limited number of what is available follows:

Thirty-Year Treasury Bonds. The U.S. Treasury sells thirty-year bonds twice a year. These bonds pay interest every six months until maturity. The bondholder receives

face value at maturity. Price and yield are determined at auction. Both noncompetitive and competitive bids are accepted. Choosing a noncompetitive bid means that the buyer accepts the interest rate determined at auction and the buyer is guaranteed to receive the bond in the full amount requested. Such a bid may be made through TreasuryDirect (http://www.savingsbonds.gov), a government Web site that is run by the Bureau of the Public Debt, part of the U.S. Department of the Treasury. A competitive bid requires that the buyer use a bank, broker, or dealer. With a competitive bid there is uncertainty of about whether the buyer will be accepted or, if accepted, will get the number of bonds requested. These bonds are available only in electronic entries in accounts.

I Bonds and EE Bonds. I bonds and EE bonds are not typical bonds. They are available in small denominations. They can be purchased at local banks and other financial institutions, as well as through TreasuryDirect, and sometimes through payroll deductions.

I bonds, whose rate of return is tied to the inflation rate, may be purchased in denominations of as little as $50. I bonds are a low-risk, liquid savings product. They are available through TreasuryDirect or payroll deduction, as well as at most local banks and other financial institutions. These bonds earn interest from the first day of their issue month. They are an accrual-type security, which means they increase in value monthly and the interest is paid when they are cashed. They can earn interest for up to thirty years. The I bond's interest is based on a composite rate that is a fixed rate for the life of the bond and an inflation rate that changes twice a year.

EE bonds are popular, low-risk savings products with interest rates based on a fixed rate of return. EE bonds are available at the TreasuryDirect Web site. If purchased electronically, EE bonds are sold at face value, which means the buyer pays $50 for a $50 bond. Purchases in amounts of $25 or more, to the penny, are possible.

Paper EE bonds are also available. The price is 50 percent of face value, that is, $25 for a $50 EE bond. Buyers are issued bond certificates. Paper EE bonds are purchased through local banks, other financial institutions, or through an employer's payroll deduction plan, if available.

MUNICIPAL BONDS

State, county, and local governments also borrow money by selling municipal bonds (frequently referred to as "munis"). Municipal bonds are either general obligation or revenue bonds. The principal of general obligation bonds (also known as "GOs") is paid from tax payments from citizens and from user fees for services provided by the political unit. The costs of building schools and sewers, for example, are paid for through general obligation bonds. A revenue bond is one that is issued by an enterprise for a public purpose that is expected to generate revenues, such as the building of airports, utility company infrastructure, toll roads, universities, and hospitals. The money to pay bond interest and principal at maturity will be paid by successful enterprises' revenue-generating activities.

Municipal bonds are ranked by financial information rating services. For example, the same ranking used by S&P for corporate bonds is used for municipal bonds.

BONDS AS AN INVESTMENT

Bonds are purchased by Americans for investment. Bonds are considered to be a less-risky type of investment. Bonds of the U.S. government are perceived to be the safest of all investments. Among the considerations for an investment are the following:

Risk Involved. There are several risks associated with bonds, even though there is a general belief that they are safer than, for example, investments in stocks and real estate. Among the risks are these:

Market risk: the risk an investor faces should interest rates rise after the bonds have been purchased. As market interest rates rise, the price of bonds falls (and vice versa). All bonds—corporate, Treasury, and municipal—are subject to market risk.

Credit risk: the risk associated with investments in corporate and municipal bonds (but not Treasuries). This risk relates to the actual creditworthiness of the issuer of the bonds. Since a bond is a loan, a bondholder has to assess the likelihood that the issuer will be able to pay the periodic interest payments and the bond's par value at maturity.

With Treasury bonds, there is virtually no credit risk since most investors see them as having the full faith of the U.S. government behind them. Because of this perceived absence of default, investors typically use the rate offered on Treasuries as the benchmark against which other investments are evaluated.

Call risk: the risk that issuers may call back, or retire, the bonds. Such bonds may be retired when interest rates are declining. The bondholder is paid par value (and usually a small "call premium" as well) and any accrued interest since the last interest payment date. At such a time, the investor may want to replace the earlier bonds, but finds that the interest earned will be less than was the case earlier. Furthermore, if the investor had originally purchased the bonds at a premium, it is likely that the original purchase price would not be realized when the bond is called.

Corporate and municipal bonds may be callable. U.S. Treasuries are not.

Tax Effects of Bond Holdings. While interest on corporate bonds is fully taxable to the bondholder, interest on Treasuries is exempt from state (but not federal) income tax. Interest on municipal bonds is exempt from federal income tax. If the municipal bond is issued by the jurisdiction in which the bondholder resides, the interest is tax-exempt from both the federal government and the state government. If there is a local income tax, the interest is tax-exempt at this level, too. Thus in some instances the bondholder has a triple exemption. Because of the tax-exempt nature of municipal bonds, their rates are usually one- to two-percentage points lower than that of a comparable taxable corporate bond, for which there is no tax exemption.

SOME GENERAL CONSIDERATIONS.

Bonds typically earn a return greater than that offered by a bank on its savings account or certificates of deposit. Bonds provide certainty about the interest payments that will be received. Prices of bonds are much less volatile when compared to prices of stocks. Defaults on bonds are not common. It is also possible to buy bond funds, similar to those provided for stocks.

Much information is available at Web sites. Using such keywords terms as *asset-backed bonds, bond fund, foreign government bonds,* or *zero bonds* at a comprehensive search engine will provide descriptions and characteristics of each.

SEE ALSO *Capital Markets; Finance; Investments*

BIBLIOGRAPHY

Bond Market Association (2001). *The fundamentals of municipal bonds* (5th ed.). New York: Wiley.

Brigham, E. F., and Horeston, J. F. (2004). *Fundamentals of financial management* (10th ed.). Cincinnati: Thomson South-Western.

Fabozzi, F. J. (2003). *Bond markets: Analyses and strategies* (5th ed.). New York: Prentice Hall.

Thau, A. (2001). *The bond book: Everything investors need to know....* New York: McGraw-Hill.

Mary Ellen Oliverio
Allie F. Miller

BRANDING

SEE *Advertising Agencies; Mass Marketing; Product Labeling; Product Lines*

BREAK-EVEN ANALYSIS
SEE *Cost-Volume-Profit Analysis*

BROKERS AND DEALERS
SEE *Financial Institutions*

BUDGETS AND BUDGETING

A budget is a financial plan for the upcoming period. A capital budget, on the other hand, involves an organization's proposed long-range major projects. The focus of this section is on budget. Public and private entities both engage in the budgetary process. A government budget starts with the projection of sources and amounts of revenue and allocates the potential receipts among projects and legislatively mandated programs based on projected needs and public pressure. Government entities actually record budgets in the accounting records against which expenditures can be made.

A budget is a quantitative plan of operations that identifies the resources needed to fulfill the organization's goals and objectives. It includes both financial and nonfinancial aspects. Budgeting is the process of preparing a plan, commonly called a budget. A master budget is comprised of operating budgets and financial budgets. Operating budgets identify the use of resources in operating activities. They include production budgets, purchase budgets, human resources budgets, and sales budgets. Financial budgets identify sources and outflows of funds for the budgeted operations and the expected operating results for the period. Some variations of budgets are continuous budgets and continuously updated budgets. Rather than preparing one budget for the upcoming year, in a continuous budget one updates the budget for the following twelve months at the end of each month or each quarter. Such a budget remains more current and relevant. A good budget uses historical data as a base and for reference but at the same time incorporates anticipated costs and volumes based on a comprehensive knowledge and understanding of both internal and external factors that affect the business.

COMPONENTS OF THE MASTER BUDGET
The master budget includes a sales budget, which shows expected sales in units and in dollars. A merchandising firm needs to budget for the goods it needs to purchase for resale; these purchases become its cost of sales. A manu-facturing organization's master budget includes a production budget, which uses the sales budget and inventory levels anticipated at the beginning and end of the period to determine how much to produce.

The production budget needs to be exploded into budgets for direct material, direct labor, and manufacturing overhead. Direct material and direct labor are items clearly identifiable in the finished product. Manufacturing overhead includes all costs of manufacturing *except* direct material and direct labor, such as machine depreciation, utilities, and supervision. The direct material budget explodes the production into basic ingredients; quantities to be purchased are anticipated based on expected inventory levels at the beginning and end of the period. With the help of the purchasing department, the prices for the needed materials are computed to arrive at the material purchases budget. The direct labor budget uses industrial engineering guidelines and production needs to estimate labor requirements. The human resources department provides the labor rates for the skill levels required. Overhead costs are estimated based on production level and appropriate cost drivers (i.e., the factors that cause costs to vary). Some overhead costs are considered variable because they vary with the level of output. Others are considered fixed because the level of output does not affect the amount of those costs. For example, the production supervision cost is assumed to be the same regardless of how much is produced within a shift in a plant. One can, then, estimate production costs and cost per unit for goods to be produced. Cost of goods sold can be determined based on the inventory levels of finished goods. Selling and general administration costs are then estimated, taking into consideration those costs that vary with sales, such as sales commission, as well as fixed costs that remain the same regardless of the level of sales, such as office rent. The information put together so far gives one all one needs to prepare a forecasted income statement.

At this point, the cash budget is developed. This item starts with cash at the beginning of the period plus cash that will be generated through collection of receivables, cash sales, and other sources minus anticipated minus cash disbursements, which include payroll disbursements, payment for taxes, and accounts payable depending on the terms for payment. The resulting cash balance may be negative if there are more disbursements than receipts, in which case borrowing needs are determined. A positive cash balance may be more than needed for operating expense. Such excess cash may be deposited in a temporary investment account. The final part of master budget preparation is the forecasted balance sheet, where the anticipated cash balance, investments, accounts receivable, inventory, fixed assets, accounts payable, wages payable, taxes payable, long-term liabilities, and equity accounts are recorded to assure that the two sides of the equation balance; that is, assets = liabilities + equity.

THE BUDGETING PROCESS

Budgeting is, or should be, the result of teamwork. A top-down budget is a budget that is essentially imposed on the organization by top management. This may be an efficient way to prepare a budget but because of lack of participation by the employees, such budgets often bring with them a level of employee resentment and resistance that leads to problems in implementation of what is proposed. Employees do not feel a sense of ownership in a budget in which they have not been participants. A participatory, or bottom-up budget, on the other hand, starts with the employees in each department determining their needs and requirements in order to achieve the company goals. Because employees feel a sense of ownership in such budgets, they attempt to meet or exceed those expectations. A balance between the two extremes can often be achieved. Top management should be involved in setting the tone and providing the guidelines and parameters within which the budget will be set. Incentives should be put into place so that those who achieve or exceed the budgetary expectations will receive suitable rewards for their efforts.

There must also be guidelines to discourage budgetary *slacks* and abuses whereby the requested budget amounts are in excess of anticipated needs in order for the department to look better and reap some rewards. A very tight budget, on the other hand, may prove discouraging and unattainable. No matter what approach is taken, it is important to realize that the budget should serve as a map and guideline in anticipating the future. Top management must take it seriously in order for the employees to take it seriously as well. At the same time, the budget should not be seen as a strict and unchangeable document. If opportunities arise, circumstances change, and unforeseen situations develop, there is no reason why the budget should be an impediment to exploring and taking advantage of such opportunities. Many companies form a budget committee to oversee the preparation and execution of the budget. The budget can also be seen as a tool that helps in bridging the communications gap between various parts of the organization. Sales, production, purchasing, receiving, industrial relations, sales promotion, warehousing, computing, treasury, quality control, and all other departments see their roles and understand the roles of the other players in achieving the goals of the organization. Such participation also necessitates budget negotiation among the various parties to the budgetary process until the budget is finalized. Goal congruence occurs when the goals of the employees and the goals of the company become intertwined and meshed together. A budget that does not consider the goals of the employees often fails. The finalization of the budget requires acceptance by the affected departments and approval and sign-off by top management. If circumstances change due to factors such as change in product mix, costs, selling prices, negotiated labor rates, or engineering specifications, there may be a need for budget revision.

OTHER BUDGETING TECHNIQUES

An incremental budget is a budget that is prepared based on prior-year figures, allowing for factors such as inflation. Although such an approach is used by some government entities, most people frown upon such a practice because it is contrary to the whole notion of a budget, which is supposed to be a calculated and wise anticipation of the future course of events with due consideration of all potential factors. A zero-based budget, on the other hand, is a budget that does not take anything for granted. It starts from point zero for each budgetary element and department each year and attempts to justify every dollar of expenditure. Although some industries had implemented such a method earlier, it was first used in preparing the state of Georgia's budget in the early 1970s and was later used to prepare the federal budget in late 1970s during President Carter's administration. However, it was soon abandoned because the paperwork generated and timeframe necessary to do this task proved to be too cumbersome for the federal government. *Kaisen* budgeting, a term borrowed from Japanese, is a budgeting approach that explicitly demands continuous improvement and incorporates all the expected improvements in the budget that results from such a process. Activity-based budgeting is a technique that focuses on costs of activities or cost drivers necessary for production and sales. Such an approach facilitates continuous improvement. An easily attainable budget often fails to bring out the employees' best efforts. A budget target that is very difficult to achieve can discourage managers from even trying to attain it. So budget targets should be challenging and at the same time attainable.

MONITORING THE BUDGET

A flexible budget modifies the budget to the actual level of performance. Obviously, if the original budget is prepared for say, 1,000 units of a product, but 2,000 units are produced, comparing the original budget to the actual volume of output does not provide meaningful information. Accordingly, the budgeted costs per unit for all variable costs can be used and multiplied by the actual volume of output to arrive at the flexible change proportionately to the level of output for the former and to the level of sales for the latter cost. Fixed costs, such as rent, however, do not normally change with the level of production or sales.

These budgeted costs, therefore, are not adjusted and left intact even though the volume of sales and output may be different from the originally budgeted levels.

Ultimately, a good budget is one that not only uses good budgeting techniques but is also based on a sound knowledge of the business as well as the external factors that affect it. The budget serves as a planning tool for the organization as a whole as well as its subunits. It provides a frame of reference against which actual performance can be compared. It provides a means to determine and investigate variances. It also assists the company in planning again based on the feedback received considering the changing conditions. An attainable, fair, and participatory budget is also a good tool for communication, employee involvement, and motivation.

SEE ALSO *Financial Forecasts and Projections*

BIBLIOGRAPHY

Blocher, Edward J. et al. (2005). *Cost Management: A Strategic Emphasis* (3rd ed.). Boston, MA: McGraw-Hill/Irwin.

Horngren, Charles T., Foster, Datar, and Foster, George (2005). *Cost Accounting: A Managerial Emphasis* (12th ed.). Upper Saddle River, NJ: Prentice Hall.

Raiborn, Cecily A., Barfield, Jesse T., and Kinney, Michael R. (1999). *Managerial Accounting*, (3rd ed.) Cincinnati: South-Western College Pub.

Schick, Allen, ed. (1980). *Perspectives on Budgeting*. Washington, DC: American Society for Public Administration.

Willson, James D. (1995). *Budgeting and Profit Planning Manual*. Boston, MA: Warren, Gorham, Lamont.

Young, S. Mark (1997). *Readings in Management Accounting* (2nd ed.). Upper Saddle River, NJ: Prentice Hall.

Roger K. Doost

BUREAU OF LABOR STATISTICS

"Is employment below or above the level of last month?" "What has happened to prices during the past month?" Such questions—and thousands of others about a wide range of labor-related topics—are answered by personnel of the Bureau of Labor Statistics (BLS). When the BLS was established by Congress on June 27, 1884, its mission was stated in these words: "The general design and duties of the Bureau of Labor shall be to acquire and diffuse among the people of the United States useful information on subjects connected with labor, in the more general and comprehensive sense of that word, and especially upon its relation to capital, the hours of labor, social, intellectual, and moral prosperity." The BLS is an independent national statistical agency that collects, processes, analyzes, and disseminates essential statistical data to the citizens of the United States, the U.S. Congress, other federal agencies, state and local governments, businesses, and labor. The president appoints the head of the BLS, the commissioner, with approval by the Senate for a specific term that does not coincide with that of his administration.

The BLS is distinct from the policy-making and enforcement activities of the Department of Labor. The BLS is impartial, with a strong commitment to integrity and objectivity; its data have credibility because of the standards maintained throughout the agency. The major areas of BLS activity are:

- Employment and unemployment
- Prices and living conditions
- Compensation and working conditions
- Productivity and technology
- Employment projections
- Safety and health statistics

Employment and unemployment. In addition to monthly figures on employment and unemployment, the BLS does a comprehensive breakdown of the age, sex, and racial and ethnic composition of the work force as well as of industries and occupations in which the workers are employed. Other characteristics are also tracked, including patterns of regional employment and the extent of participation in work by teenagers, blacks, Hispanics, women, and older Americans.

Price and living conditions. Each month the Consumer Price Index (CPI) and the Producers Price Index (PPI) are prepared. The BLS also reports how households spend their incomes.

Compensation and working conditions. Comprehensive studies of employee compensation—wages and benefits—are undertaken that relate to occupations, industries, and areas of the country. An initiative begun in 2000 produces national employment cost indexes, employment cost levels, and employee benefit incidence.

Productivity and technology. This office produces productivity measures for industries and for major sectors of the U.S. economy. Additionally, it provides comparisons for key BLS labor statistics series as well as training and technical assistance in labor statistics to people from other countries.

Employment projections. There is much interest in the projections provided by this unit of the BLS. Information about future employment growth—and the nature of that growth—is of critical importance to public officials, businesses, young people preparing for careers, and those who design educational programs at all levels.

Safety and health statistics. The extent of workplace injuries and illnesses is the concern of the office that compiles safety and health statistics. Information analyzed and summarized includes job-related injuries and illnesses by industry, nature of the injury or illness, and the workers involved. There is also a compilation of work-related deaths. The statistics provided are useful in developing safety and health standards, in controlling work hazards, and in the allocation of resources for workplace inspection, training, and consultation services.

THE MANNER OF WORK AND SOURCES OF INFORMATION

The BLS, as is the case for all federal agencies, functions in an open environment. As changes are contemplated, they are discussed with users and advisory committees and described in published materials. Fair information practices are used; maintaining confidentiality of individual responses is assured. The BLS promises the public that users will be provided assistance in understanding the uses and limitations of data provided.

The BLS gathers its information from business and labor groups throughout the country through voluntary advisory councils. The councils were established in 1947; current members meet with BLS staff for discussions related to such matters as planned programs and day-to-day problems the BLS faces in collecting, recording, and analyzing statistics as well as in the publishing of reports.

KEY PUBLICATIONS

The most widely distributed publications, which are available in public as well as other libraries, include: *Monthly Labor Review, Employment and Earnings*, and *Occupational Outlook Quarterly*. Additionally, a variety of surveys, including those related to the Consumer Price Index and the Producer Price Index, are published.

RESPONSE TO CHANGE IN THE WORKPLACE

Rapid technological changes, globalization of world markets, and demographic shifts are all forces that are reshaping the U.S. workplace in relation to the nature and types of jobs, the composition of the work force, and workers' education, skills, and experiences. The BLS in its Revised Strategic Plan 1997–2002 stated that it "has been and will continue to be responsive to users' need to understand changes."

The BLS has undertaken efforts to improve its programs so that they capture workplace and work-force changes. The *Current Population Survey*, which provides monthly data on the demographic and educational characteristics of the work force, includes supplemental surveys on workplace issues such as contingent employment, worker displacement, and work schedules. A new monthly survey of job openings and labor turnover for the country and major industry sectors will provide information that had not been available earlier.

EMPLOYMENT OPPORTUNITIES

As of the end of 2005, there were approximately 2,600 BLS employees working in Washington, D.C., and in the regional offices in seven cities: Boston, New York, Philadelphia, Atlanta, Chicago, Dallas, and San Francisco. The BLS reports that there is a continuing need for economists, mathematical statisticians, and computer specialists. There is a more limited need for administrative and financial specialists as well as for many types of technicians and assistants. Employment is restricted by law to U.S. citizens. Most professional jobs require a bachelor's degree or its equivalent in experience. Specific qualifications and educational requirements are described in BLS pamphlets available from the agency and also on the Internet (http://www.bls.gov/).

BIBLIOGRAPHY

Goldberg, Joseph P., and Moye, William J. (1985). *The First Hundred Years of the Bureau of Labor Statistics*. Washington, DC: U.S. Government Printing Office.

Bernard H. Newman

BUSINESS CYCLE

A business cycle refers to the ups and downs of the general level of economic activity for a country. Such changes are normally visible in key macroeconomic measures such as gross domestic product (GDP), real income, employment, industrial output, and wholesale-retail sales. The upward movement in economic activity is referred to as the expansion phase and the downward movement as the contraction phase of the cycle. The turning points of the cycle are called the peak, which is at the end of the expansion phase, and the trough, which is at the end of the contraction phase.

Much attention is paid to the timing of these turning points and the duration of the phases. The expansion phase of the business cycle starts with a short period of recovery before becoming a full-blown expansion. Similarly, a period of recession occurs at the start of the contraction phase. Thus the cycle is generally referred to as

Business cycle expansions and contractions

Business cycle reference dates		Duration in months			
		Contraction (trough from previous peak)	Expansion (trough to peak)	Cycle	
Trough	Peak			Trough from previous trough	Peak from previous peak
December 1854	June 1857	—	30	—	—
December 1858	October 1860	18	22	48	40
June 1861	April 1865	8	*46*	30	*54*
December 1867	June 1869	*32*	18	*78*	50
December 1870	October 1873	18	34	36	52
March 1879	March 1882	65	36	99	101
May 1885	March 1887	38	22	74	60
April 1888	July 1890	13	27	35	40
May 1891	January 1893	10	20	37	30
June 1894	December 1895	17	18	37	35
June 1897	June 1899	18	24	36	42
December 1900	September 1902	18	21	42	39
August 1904	May 1907	23	33	44	56
June 1908	January 1910	13	19	46	32
January 1912	January 1913	24	12	43	36
December 1914	August 1918	23	*44*	35	*67*
March 1919	January 1920	*7*	10	*51*	17
July 1921	May 1923	18	22	28	40
July 1924	October 1926	14	27	36	41
November 1927	August 1929	13	21	40	34
March 1933	May 1937	43	50	64	93
June 1938	February 1945	13	*80*	63	*93*
October 1945	November 1948	*8*	37	*88*	45
October 1949	July 1953	11	*45*	48	*56*
May 1954	August 1957	*10*	39	*55*	49
April 1958	April 1960	8	24	47	32
February 1961	December 1969	10	*106*	34	*116*
November 1970	November 1973	*11*	36	*117*	47
March 1975	January 1980	16	58	52	74
July 1980	July 1981	6	12	64	18
November 1982	July 1990	16	92	28	108
March 1991	March 2001	8	120	100	128
November 2001		8	—	—	—
Average, all cycles:					
1854–2001 (32 cycles)		17	38	55	[1]56
1854–1919 (16 cycles)		22	27	48	[2]49
1919–1945 (6 cycles)		18	35	53	53
1945–2001 (10 cycles)		10	57	67	67
Average, peacetime cycles:					
1854–2001 (27 cycles)		18	33	51	[3]52
1954–1919 (14 cycles)		22	24	46	[4]47
1919–1945 (5 cycles)		20	26	46	45
1945–2001 (8 cycles)		10	52	63	63

[1] 31 cycles
[2] 15 cycles
[3] 26 cycles
[4] 13 cycles

Notes:
1) Figures printed in bold italic are the wartime expansions (Civil War, World Wars I and II, Korean war and Vietnam war), the postwar contractors, and the full cycles that induce the wartime expansions.
2) The determination that the last contraction ended in November 2001 is the most recent decision of the Business Cycle Dating Committee of the National Bureau of Economic Research.

SOURCE: National Bureau of Economic Research, Inc., 1050 Massachusetts Avenue, Cambridge MA 02133.

Table 1

consisting of four phases: recovery, expansion, recession, and contraction.

THE PHASES OF A CYCLE

The transition from phase to phase is described in terms of the rate of growth of the economy. During the recovery phase, the economy turns into a positive growth period with an increasing rate of growth. During the expansion period, the economy continues to grow, but gradually at a decreasing rate. After the peak is reached, the rate of growth will turn negative, causing the economic activity to decline and the economy to slip into recession. The recession phase is marked by a rapidly declining economy from its peak. The rate of decline slows down as the cycle approaches its trough and the economy passes through the contraction phase. A severe contraction is referred to as a depression, the type that occurred in 1930s. During the Great Depression, the output fell by almost 50 percent and employment by 22 percent. All the recessions since then have been shorter in duration and less severe.

LENGTH OF BUSINESS CYCLES

The time taken to complete a cycle can vary from cycle to cycle, with the time usually measured from peak to peak or trough to trough. Considerable variability of the duration of business cycles has been observed in the past. Between 1854 and 1982, there were 30 business cycles with an average length from trough to trough of 46 months and standard deviation of 16 months. The average length of the expansion in these cycles was 27 months with a standard deviation of 11 months, and the average contraction was 19 months with a standard deviation of 13. Though they varied greatly in duration and scope, all of them had some common features. They were national or international in scope; they affected output, employment, retail sales, construction, and other macroeconomic variables; and they lasted for years, with upward movement longer than downward movement.

SPECIFIC CYCLES

It is sometimes useful to speak of the cycles of specific time series; that is, the interest rate cycle, the inventory cycle, the construction cycle, and so forth. Given the diversity of general economic cycles, one can find turns in the general level of economic activity in which individual sectors of the economy do, at least for a time, appear to be independent of the rest of the economy. The most frequently mentioned individual cycles are the inventory cycle, the building or construction cycle, and the agricultural cycle. The standard business cycle is sometimes referred to as the inventory cycle, and some business cycle theorists explain the severity of turns in the economy by the coincidence of timing in the individual cycles.

DATING OF BUSINESS CYCLES

The idea of the timing of individual time series relative to the general level of business implies specific dates for the business cycle. How does one establish the peaks and troughs for the business cycle? To say whether something leads or lags the business cycle, one must have some frame of reference; hence, the business cycle is referred to as the reference cycle and its peaks and troughs as reference turning points. (See Table 1.)

For the United States, the reference turning points are established by the National Bureau of Economic Research (NBER), a nonprofit research organization. This organization, originally under the guidance of Wesley Clair Mitchell (1874–1948), pioneered business cycle research in the late 1920s. In the early twenty-first century the NBER's decisions regarding the reference cycle are often viewed as infallible, although they are actually quite subjective. No single time series or group of time series is decreed to be "the" reference cycle. A committee of professional business cycle analysts convened by the NBER establishes the official peaks and troughs in accordance with the following definition:

> Business cycles are a type of fluctuation found in the aggregate economic activity of nations that organize their work mainly in business enterprises: a cycle consists of expansions occurring at about the same time in many economic activities, followed by similarly general recessions, contractions, and revivals which merge in the expansion phase of the next cycle; this sequence of changes is recurrent but not periodic; in duration business cycles vary from more than one year to ten or twelve years; they are not divisible into shorter cycles of similar character with amplitudes approximately their own. (Burns and Mitchell, 1946, p. 3)

With slight modification, this definition has been used since 1927. Although most of the definition is self-explanatory, it is not all that rigorous. It does not say something like, for example, if the total output of the economy (real GDP) falls at an annual rate of 1 percent for two consecutive quarters, a recession has begun. The definition does say unambiguously that business cycles are "recurrent but not periodic." The only real constraint in the definition is that if a business cycle is defined as, say, from peak to peak, one should not be able to find another cycle of equal amplitude between those two peaks. If so, one did it wrong.

The NBER's business cycle dating committee follows standard procedures by using economy-wide measures of economic activity. The primary measure it looks at is the real GDP, which it considers to be the single best measure of aggregate economic activity. It also looks at other measures such as real personal-transfer payments, employment, and industrial production. According to the dating committee, the decline of real GDP for two or more consecutive quarters is the criterion for determining the beginning of a recession. Table 1 provides the NBER's chronology of U.S. business cycles since 1854.

The most recent turning point identified by the NBER was November 2001, marking the end of the recession that started in March 2001 and inaugurating an expansion. As of December 2005, the U.S. economy continued to expand. The expansion that began in March 1991 and ended in March 2001, lasting exactly ten years, was the longest in the NBER's chronology. Notice from the table that all that is established with regard to "the" business cycle is the peak and trough of each cycle. This determination tells readers absolutely nothing about the rate of rise or fall in the general level of economic activity, nothing about the magnitude of the boom or the severity of the recession.

THEORIES OF THE BUSINESS CYCLE

The first lecture in an introductory economics course usually makes the point that the expenditures of one economic unit are the incomes of other economic units. This provides a fairly firm basis for expecting sympathetic movements in many sectors of the economy. A good theoretical basis and substantial empirical support exist for cumulative upward and downward movement in the economy. One sector's expansion is the basis for another sector's expansion, general prosperity lowers risk and makes credit more readily available, and so on; but the weakest part of business cycle theory and the toughest problem in forecasting is turning points. Why does the general upward or downward movement end? Sometimes it is obvious. When, for example, a war begins or ends with a commensurate and dramatic change in military expenditures, the cause of the beginning or end of an economic boom is fairly unambiguous.

Historically, however, only a small minority of the turning points are the result of specific, identifiable events such as wars, changes in population, and advances in technology. Even when exogenous events initiate a business cycle, what generates cumulative up-and-down movements in the economy is the internal mechanism of the economy responding to the external stimuli. A satisfactory theory of business cycle, therefore, must explain how cyclical movements are generated by the internal mechanism of the economy when affected by outside shocks. Many theories have been advanced over the years to explain these cumulative up-and-down movements.

One set of theories developed around the turn of the twentieth century focused on such factors as innovations, variations in funds flow, and overinvestment as the initiating causes of cyclical movements in the economy. Internal dynamics of the economy also played a key role in the various phases of the cycle in these theories. Theories developed during the interwar and immediate postwar period focused more on internal instability to explain how cyclical fluctuations in economic activity are created and sustained.

In 1917 an eminent American economist, J. M. Clark (1884–1963), published an article titled "Business Acceleration and the Law of Demand: A Technical Factor in Economic Cycles." His technical factor was the observation that with a fixed capital-output ratio, a small percentage change in final sales would give rise to a large percentage change in investment. Each innovation generates a temporary demand for the required investment goods. Once the initial investment has been made, the replacement market requires a lower rate of investment. This is referred to as the principle of acceleration. If it takes $10 worth of steel mills to produce $1 worth of steel per year, growth in demand for steel by $1 will temporarily generate $10 worth of demand for steel mills.

Another early business cycle theorist, Joseph Schumpeter (1883–1950), noted that nothing is constant over the business cycle and nothing ever really returns to its starting place. That is what makes each business cycle unique. The economy grows and changes with each cycle—new products, new firms, new consumers. As Schumpeter observed in 1939, "As a matter of history, it is to physiology and zoology, not to mechanics, that our science is indebted for an analogous distinction which is at the threshold of all clear thinking about economic matters" (p. 37). The economy grows and changes. He referred to this as the process of "creative destruction."

Schumpeter concluded that what most people consider "progress" is at the source of the problem. He believed that as entrepreneurs come up with new ways of doing things, this disturbs the equilibrium and creates fluctuations. Schumpeter distinguished between inventions, which may gather dust for years, and innovations, which are commercial applications of previous inventions. Inventions occur randomly through time. Innovations tend to be bunched, thereby creating cycles of economic activity.

Many business cycle theorists give a prominent role to the monetary system and interest rates. Early in the twentieth century, a Swedish economist, Knut Wicksell (1851–1926), argued that if the "natural" rate of interest rose above the "bank" rate of interest, the level of economic activity would begin to increase. In contemporary terms, the natural rate of interest is what businesses expect to earn on real investment. The bank rate is the return on financial assets in general and commercial bank loans in particular. The boom begins when, for whatever reason, the cost of borrowing falls significantly below expected returns on investment. This difference between the rate of return on real and financial assets generates a demand for bank loans by investors seeking to exploit the opportunity for profit. The economy booms.

At some point the bank rate will start to rise and/or the real rate will start to fall. When the expected rate of return on investment falls below the rate at which funds can be borrowed, the process will begin to reverse itself and the recession is on. As bank loans are paid off (or defaulted on), bank credit is reduced, and the economy slows accordingly.

Since the late twentieth century, business cycle theory has centered on the argument about the source of cyclical instability. The question of the root causes of ups and downs in the level of economic activity received a lot of attention in the 1980s and 1990s.

Figure 1 shows how the parties to the debate are divided up. First, there is the question of whether the private sector of the economy is inherently stable or unstable—which is to say, do the observed fluctuations originate in the government or private sector? On one side are what might be called classical economists, who are convinced that the economy is inherently stable. They contend that, historically, government policy has destabilized it in a perverse fashion. On the other side are what might be called Keynesians, named after the British economist John Maynard Keynes (1883–1946). Keynesians believe that psychological shifts in consumers' purchasing

and savings preferences and in businesses' confidence are a substantial source of instability.

There is a whole body of literature on political business cycles. As economist William D. Nordhaus noted: "The theory of the political business cycle, which analyzes the interaction of political and economic systems, arose from the obvious facts of life that voters care about the economy while politicians care about power" (1989, p. 1). The idea is that politicians in power will tend to follow policies to promote short-term prosperity around election time and allow recessions to occur at other times. The evidence that the state of the economy influences voting patterns is strong, as is the apparent desire of incumbent politicians to influence the economy; but it is difficult to make a case that the overwhelming determinant of the level and timing of business fluctuations is politically determined. At some points in modern history, politically determined policies were apparently a determining factor and at other times not.

With respect to the impact of governmental policies, there is a dispute as to the relative importance of monetary policy (controlling the money supply) and fiscal policy (government expenditures and taxes). Those who believe that monetary policies have had a generally destabilizing effect on the economy are known as monetarists. Most economists accept that fiscal policy, especially in wartime, has been a source of cyclical instability.

As noted above, it is the so-called Keynesian economists who believe that the private sector is inherently unstable. While noting the historical instability of investment in tangible assets, they have also emphasized shifts in liquidity preference (demand for money) as an independent source of instability. As a counter to the standard Keynesian position, there has arisen a school of thought emphasizing real business cycles. This school contends that nonmonetary variables in the private sector are a

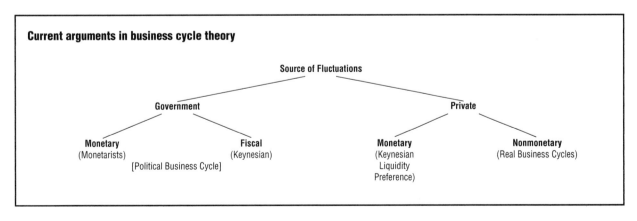

Current arguments in business cycle theory

Source of Fluctuations

Government   Private

Monetary (Monetarists)   Fiscal (Keynesian)   Monetary (Keynesian Liquidity Preference)   Nonmonetary (Real Business Cycles)

[Political Business Cycle]

Figure 1

major source of cyclical instability and that the observed sympathetic movements between monetary variables and the level of economic activity result from a flow of causation from the latter to the former. The changes in real factors cause the monetary factors to change, not vice versa. In this way they are somewhat like Wicksell.

BUSINESS CYCLE INDICATORS

Changes in the magnitudes of certain economic series provide clues to the direction of changes in the cyclical behavior of economy. These series are identified, measured, and used for forecasting the turning points of the business cycle. Called economic indictors, they are divided into three groups—leading, lagging, and roughly coincidental. The leading indicators are those economic series that change direction in advance of the business cycle. The lagging indicators change direction after the overall economy has moved, while coincident indicators move in tandem with the aggregate economic activity. Basic economic indicators consist of 10 leading, 7 lagging, and 4 coincident series.

In order to smooth out the volatility of individual series in each group and to provide a single measure to represent the entire group, a composite index for each group (composite indicator) is constructed. The measures of basic indicators and the composites are calculated and published by the Conference Board, a not-for-profit organization.

SEE ALSO *Economics*

BIBLIOGRAPHY

Achuthan, Lakshman, and Banerji, Anirvan (2004). *Beating the business cycle.* New York: Currency Doubleday.

Blanchard, Olivier (2000). *What do we know about macroeconomics that Fisher and Wicksell did not?* (National Bureau of Economic Research Working Paper No. W7550). New York: National Bureau of Economic Research.

Burns, Arthur, and Mitchell, Wesley C. (1946). *Measuring business cycles.* New York: National Bureau of Economic Research.

Clark, J. M. (1917). Business acceleration and the law of demand: A technical factor in economic cycles. *Journal of Political Economy, 25,* 217–235.

Conference Board. (2001). *Business cycle indicators handbook.* New York: Author.

Hicks, J. R. (1958). *The trade cycle.* London: Oxford University Press.

King, Robert, and Plosser, Charles (1984). Money, credit and prices in a real business cycle. *American Economic Review, 74*(3), 363–380.

King, Robert, and Rebelo, Sergio (2000). *Resuscitating real business cycles* (National Bureau of Economic Research Working Paper No. W7534). New York: National Bureau of Economic Research.

Long, John B., Jr., and Plosser, Charles I. (1983). Real business cycles. *Journal of Political Economy, 91*(1) 39–69.

Lucas, Robert E. (1981). *Studies in business cycle theory.* Cambridge, MA: MIT Press.

Lucas, Robert E., and Sargent, Thomas J. (Eds.) (1981). *Rational expectations and econometric practice.* Minneapolis: University of Minnesota Press.

Mankiw, N. Gregory (1989). Real business cycles: A new Keynesian perspective. *The Journal of Economic Perspectives, 3*(3), 79–90.

Mitchell, Wesley Clair (1952). *The economic scientist.* New York: National Bureau of Economic Research.

Nordhaus, William D. (1989). Alternative approaches to the political business cycle. *Brookings Papers on Economic Activity, 2,* 1–50.

Rotemberg, Julio J., and Woodford, Michael (1996). Real-business-cycle models and the forecastable movements in output, hours, and consumption. *The American Economic Review, 86*(1), 71–89.

Schumpeter, Joseph (1939). *Business cycles.* New York: McGraw-Hill.

Schumpeter, Joseph (1961). *The theory of economic development.* New York: Oxford University Press.

Wicksell, Knut (1901). *Lectures on political economy.* New York: Augustus M. Kelly.

Willet, Thomas D. (Ed.) (1988). *Political business cycles: The political economy of money, inflation, and unemployment.* Durham, NC: Duke University Press.

Zarnowitz, Victor (1985). Recent work on business cycles in historical perspective: A review of theories and evidence. *Journal of Economic Literature, 23*(2), 523–580.

Zarnowitz, Victor (1996). *Business cycles, theory, history, indicators, and forecasting.* Chicago: University of Chicago Press.

Anand Shetty
David A. Bowers

BUSINESS MARKETING

Business marketing is the marketing of products to organizations for the direct use of the product in the production of another product, for use in the general daily operations of the organization, or for reselling the product to other businesses or the final consumer. Marketing goods and services to businesses and organizations, while sharing some similarities with consumer markets, is different in many ways. The nature and characteristics of the business market, the types of consumers, the different buying situations that occur in businesses and organizations, who is involved in the decision-making process and the business-to-business buying process all differ significantly from the consumer market. These differences often make the normal purchasing process more involved and complex.

NATURE AND CHARACTERISTICS OF THE BUSINESS MARKET

The first obvious difference is that there are significantly fewer customers in the business market than in the consumer market. These customers also buy in significantly larger quantities (e.g., tires by the thousands) and the prices of some of their single item purchases far exceed those of an individual consumer (e.g., millions of dollars for a new bridge). Finally, business customers in the same industry often tend to be located in a concentrated geographic region. For example, the Silicon Valley in California has a high concentration of firms in the high-tech industry.

The nature of the demand for products differs from consumer demand because it is often derived from consumer demand. A derived demand means that the demand for original equipment leather seat covers installed in new cars depends on the demand for the models of automobiles that use those seat covers. They have a more inelastic demand curve because the demand for the seat covers depends on the consumer demand for the automobiles, not on the price of the seat covers. Another factor influenced by derived demand is that it may cause large fluctuations in the demand for the seat covers. If the demand for the automobiles drops, it may have a small effect on the sales figures of the auto manufacturer, but if this particular contract represents a large share of the seat cover vendor's production, that vendor could suffer a significant loss of revenue.

Finally, the products and the buying process may differ from the consumer market to varying degrees. While some products purchased in the business market are the same or very similar to the products bought by consumers (e.g., office supplies), the buying process may be much more involved because of negotiated contract and unique or customized needs. Product specifications, price, quantity, service requirements, length of the contract, and delivery schedules are just a few of the terms that may need to be negotiated. On the other hand, many of the products are very complex and often custom-made to agreed-upon specifications. The complexity of the buying process is further complicated because a given purchase will need to satisfy a number of different individuals and departments within the company. Because of these factors, the buying decisions in businesses and organizations are often determined by a group of individuals known as the buying center, which is discussed later in this entry.

TYPES OF CONSUMERS

The business market consists of many different organizations involved in many different primary activities, but they generally fall into four major types:

1. *Manufacturers*—Manufacturers produce products to be sold at a profit. They buy products and services that are directly used in the products they produce or are consumed in the general operations of the firm.

2. *Trade*—Trade includes organizations that purchase finished goods and resell them at a profit or use products and services for the general operations of the firm. Wholesalers and retailers are included in this type of business customer.

3. *Government*—Federal, state, and local governments represent the largest single business or organizational market. Collectively they spend trillions of dollars for services and products needed for governmental operations and to provide citizens with the products and services needed for their general welfare.

4. *Institutions*—Institutions are those organizations whose primary activities and goals are charitable, educational, community, or nonbusiness in nature. They include both public (such as libraries) and private (some hospitals) institutions, which may be nonprofit (charitable organizations) or profit (some nursing homes) oriented.

TYPES OF BUYING SITUATIONS

There are three major types of buying situations, each requiring a different buying approach. The straight rebuys are routine purchases of standard products from an existing vendor without modifying specifications or without renegotiating new terms. Little effort, beyond a short performance review, is necessary.

On the other hand, modified rebuys occur when the product is not purchased on a regular basis, when there is a change in the specification of the product, when there is dissatisfaction with the current vendor, or if a new vendor offers better terms. Modified rebuys may involve new product specifications, additional evaluation of vendors, or renegotiation of contracts.

The third buying situation is a new task buy. This situation normally involves purchases made by a business for the first time The buying process needs to start from scratch and will probably be an extended problem-solving endeavor. One of the early decisions will be whether the firm wants to purchase the product from a vendor, lease the product, or produce the product in-house. These decisions and the actual purchase decisions are often the responsibility of a buying center.

THE BUYING CENTER

Because of the size, importance, complexity, and commitment involved in a business buying decision, often a committee called the buying center is formed. The buying center is responsible for deciding how best to acquire the products and services needed to operate the business. The individuals included in the buying center can differ from one buying decision to another, but may involve representatives from the purchasing, finance/accounting, and engineering departments, as well as the departments that will use the product, and an executive from management. The members of any given buying center committee could play one or more of the following roles:

- *Gatekeeper*—The individual responsible for the flow of information to the other members of the buying center

- *User(s)*—The member(s) most likely to use or be responsible for the use of the product

- *Influencer(s)*—The individual(s) who will influence(s) the decision but may not necessarily use the product

- *Decider(s)*—The member(s) who make(s) the final decision

- *Purchaser*—The member who negotiates the actual purchase

BUSINESS-TO-BUSINESS BUYING PROCESS

The typical process that is followed by the buying center to analyze the needs and develop solutions to meet those is:

1. Recognize or anticipate and clearly define a need

2. Determine and evaluate alternative solutions
   a. Straight rebuy
   b. Modified rebuy
   c. New task buy

3. Select a course of action and develop product specification

4. Select a vendor
   a. Identification of potential vendors
   b. Evaluation of vendors—solicitation and analysis of proposals
   c. Select a vendor

5. Negotiate a contract

6. Review performance

SEE ALSO *Careers in Marketing; Consumer and Business Goods; Marketing*

BIBLIOGRAPHY

Boone, Louis E., and Kurtz, David L. (2004). *Contemporary marketing* (11th ed.). Mason, OH: Thomson South-Western.

Hoffman, K. Douglass (2006). *Marketing principles and best practices* (3rd ed.). Mason, OH: Thomson South-Western.

Kotler, Philip, and Armstrong, Gary (2006). *Principles of marketing* (11th ed.). Upper Saddle River, NJ: Pearson Prentice Hall.

Lascu, Dana-Nicoleta, and Clow, Kenneth E. (2004). *Marketing frontiers: Concepts and tools.* Cincinnati: Atomic Dog.

Pride, William M., and Ferrell, O. C. (2006). *Marketing concepts and strategies.* Boston: Houghton Mifflin.

Solomon, Michael R., Marshall, Greg W., and Stuart, Elnora W. (2006). *Marketing: Real people, real choices* (4th ed.). Upper Saddle River, NJ: Pearson Prentice Hall.

Thomas Baird

BUSINESS PROFESSIONALS OF AMERICA

Business Professionals of America (BPA) is a national vocational student organization for individuals preparing for careers in business and/or office occupations. With nineteen state associations and 45,000 members in middle, secondary, and post-secondary schools throughout North America, the BPA strives to contribute to the preparation of a world-class work force by advancing leadership, citizenship, and academic and technological skills. Using a co-curricular focus, the BPA integrates local programs and services into a business classroom curriculum and focuses on real-world teaching and learning strategies. Additionally, the BPA develops professionalism in students and teachers through unique programs and services.

Historically, the need for a student organization serving individuals in vocational office programs was recognized shortly after the passage of the Vocational Education Act of 1963. The articles of incorporation for the Office Education Association, the original name of the BPA, were officially filed in 1966. The name was changed to Business Professionals of America on July 1, 1988.

Business Professionals of America offers its student, teacher, and alumni members a variety of programs and services. The National Leadership Conference annually hosts national officer elections and competitive events that allow students to demonstrate workplace skills obtained through the business classroom curriculum and Industry Certification and Behavioral Skills Assessment ("Workplace Skills Assessment Program," 1998). Awards programs also recognize successes of members and chapters.

Various written materials and the official quarterly journal, *Communique*, provide members with services, updates, and promotional opportunities. Additionally, scholarship programs are sought at universities to encourage participation in business education at the postsecondary level. More information is available from Business Professionals of America, 5454 Cleveland Ave., Columbus, Ohio 43231-4021, (800) 334-2007, or http://www.bpa.org/.

SEE ALSO *DECA; Future Business Leaders of America; SkillsUSA*

BIBLIOGRAPHY

Business Professionals of America (2004). "History of Business Professionals of America." Retrieved September 26, 2005, from http://www.bpa.org/history.htm.

Jewel Evans Hairston

C

CAPITAL

SEE *Factors of Production*

CAPITAL BUDGETING

SEE *Budgets and Budgeting; Finance; Government Accounting*

CAPITAL INVESTMENTS

Companies make capital investments to earn a return. This is like individuals wanting to make money when they invest in stocks and bonds. The amount of money made or lost is measured as the investment's rate of return. When making an investment, the expected rate of return is determined by the amount, timing, and riskiness of the funds expected from the investment.

RATE OF RETURN

Amount. An investment's rate of return is expressed as a percentage. For example, if a company invests $1,000 and expects to get back $1,100 one year from today, it expects to earn 10 percent (= (1,100 – 1,000)/1,000). If the company expects $1,200, it expects to earn 20 percent. So a rate of return depends first on the amount of money expected back from the investment.

Timing. Just as getting more money produces a higher rate of return, getting the money sooner also produces a

higher rate of return. If a company earns 10 percent in six months, that is a higher rate of return than 10 percent earned in one year. So an investment's rate of return also depends on when the company expects to get the money back.

Risk. For most capital investments, the amount of money and/or the time at which the company expects to get it back are uncertain. What are the chances it will get exactly what it expects? What are the chances it will get more or less? What are the chances it will get a lot more or a lot less—or even lose all the money invested and get nothing back? The risk of the investment depends on these chances, and, in turn, how the investment's rate of return is calculated depends on this risk. So the third important dimension of an investment's rate of return is the risk connected with the amount of money a company expects to get back from the investment.

Time value of money. When a company evaluates a capital investment, the amount of money expected back from the investment is adjusted for its timing and risk. For example, suppose a company expects to get $100 one year from today. If it had that $100 now, it could invest the money—for example, earn interest from a bank—and have more than $100 next year. If the money earned 5 percent, the company would have $105 next year. If the process is reversed, the $100 the company expects to get next year is worth less than $100 today. At 5 percent interest, next year's $100 is worth only $95.24 (=$100/1.05) today. (This is because if the company had $95.24 now and earned 5 percent on the money, it would have $100 next year.) Similarly, if there is risk connected with the expected money—the company expects $100, but could get more or less—its value today is less than $95.24. Furthermore, the riskier it is, the lower its value today.

Typically, in order to make fair comparisons, the value of all of the amounts of money expected back from capital investments are converted into what are called present values. The rate of return used to calculate the present value for a capital investment is called the cost of capital. The cost of capital is the minimum rate of return the company must earn to be willing to make the investment. It is the rate of return the company could earn if, rather than making the capital investment, it invested the money in an alternative, but comparable, investment. The cost of capital exactly reflects the riskiness of the money expected back from the capital investment. The mathematical methods used to calculate present values are called the time value of money and are explained in more detail in the books in the bibliography.

Net present value (NPV). A capital investment's net present value (NPV) is the amount of value the company expects the investment to create. The NPV equals the sum of the present values of all of the money expected back from the investment minus the investment's cost.

MAKING CAPITAL INVESTMENTS

The capital investment process includes the following:

1. Generating ideas for capital investments
2. Classifying capital investments
3. Evaluating and choosing proposed capital investments

Generating Ideas. The first, and most important, part of the capital investment process is generating new ideas. Ideas for capital investments can originate anywhere in a company. Often plant managers are responsible for identifying potential projects that will enable their plants to operate on a different scale or on a more efficient basis. For instance, a plant manager might suggest adding 10,000 square feet of production space to a plant or replacing a piece of equipment with a newer, more efficient machine. Ideas for better types of equipment that can help the company operate more efficiently may come from individuals on the plant floor. After screening out undesirable ideas, managers send the ones that appear to be attractive to the divisional level, with supporting documentation.

Division management not only reviews such proposals but also adds ideas of its own. For example, division management may propose the introduction of a new product line. Alternatively, management may want to combine two plants and eliminate the less efficient one. Such ideas are less likely to come from the plant managers!

This bottom-up process results in ideas percolating upward through the organization. At each level, ideas submitted by lower-level managers are screened, and attractive ones are forwarded to the next level. In addition, managers at successively higher levels, who are in a position to take a broader view of the company's business, add ideas that may not be visible, or desirable, to lower-level managers.

At the same time, there is also a top-down process at work in most companies. Strategic planners will generate ideas regarding new businesses the company should enter, other companies it might acquire, and ways to modify its existing businesses to achieve greater profitability. Strategic planning is a critical element in the capital investment process. The processes complement one another. The top-down process generates ideas of a broader, more strategic nature, whereas the bottom-up process generates ideas of a more project-specific nature.

In addition, many companies have a research and development (R&D) group, either within a production division or as a separate department. An R&D group often provides new ideas for products that can be sent on to a marketing research department.

Classifying Capital Investments. Analysis costs money. Therefore, certain types of investments receive only cursory checks before approval, whereas others are subjected to extensive analysis. Generally, less costly and more routine investments are subjected to less extensive evaluation. As a result, companies typically categorize investments and analyze them at the level judged appropriate to their category. Potential investments in each category may have a lot in common and are able to be analyzed similarly. A useful set of investment classifications is:

Maintenance projects

Cost-saving/revenue-enhancement projects

Capacity expansions in current businesses

New products and new businesses

Projects required by government regulation or company policy

Maintenance expenditures. At the most basic level, a company must make certain investments to continue to be a healthy, profitable business. Replacing worn-out or damaged equipment is necessary to continue in business. Therefore, the major questions concerning such investments are "Should we continue in this business?" and if so, "Should we continue to use the same production process?" Since the answers to these questions are so frequently yes, an elaborate decision-making process is not needed, and typically such decisions are approved with only routine review.

Cost savings/revenue enhancement. Projects in this class include improvements in production technology to realize cost savings and marketing campaigns to achieve revenue enhancement. The central issue is increasing the difference between revenue and cost; the result must be sufficient to justify the investment.

Capacity expansion in current businesses. Deciding to expand the current business is inherently more difficult than approving maintenance or cost-saving proposals. Firms have to consider the economics of expanding or adding new facilities. They must also prepare demand forecasts, keeping in mind competitors' likely strategies. Marketing consultants may help, but this class of projects naturally has more uncertain return projections than do maintenance or replacement projects.

New products and new businesses. Projects in this category, which include R&D activities, are among the most difficult to evaluate. Their newness and long lead times make it very difficult to forecast product demand accurately. In many cases, the project may be of special interest because it would give the company an option to break into a new market. For example, a company that has a proprietary technology might spend additional R&D funds trying to develop new products based on this technology. If successful, these new products could pave the way for future profitable investment opportunities. Access to such opportunities represents valuable options for the company.

Meeting regulatory and policy requirements. Government regulations and/or company policies concerning such things as pollution control and health or safety factors are viewed as costs. Often, the critical issue in such projects is meeting the standards in the most efficient manner and at the minimum cost.

Evaluating Proposals. The typical stages for the development and approval of a capital investment proposal are:

1. Approve funds for research that may result in a product *idea*.

2. Approve funds for market research that may result in a product *proposal*.

3. Approve funds for product development that may result in a usable *product*.

4. Approve funds for plant and/or equipment for the *production* and sale of the new product.

Each stage involves an investment decision at one or more levels of the company. At each stage, the company re-estimates the value expected to be created—the NPV—of going ahead. With this kind of sequential appropriation of funds, an automatic progress review is enforced, enabling early cancellation of unsuccessful projects. At each stage there are options to abandon, postpone, change, or continue.

Proposed expenditures that are larger than certain company-set limits generally require a written proposal from the initiator. Typically, such limits are higher in smaller privately owned companies, which tend to have relatively informal organizational structures. Most companies use standard forms, and these are often supplemented by written memoranda for larger, more complex projects. Also, there may be consulting or other studies prepared by outside experts; for example, economic forecasts from economic consultants.

For a successful company, a maintenance project might require only limited supporting information. In contrast, a new product would require extensive information gathering and analysis. At the same time, within a category, managers at each level usually have upper limits on their authority regarding both expenditures on individual assets and the total expenditure for a budgeting period. In this way, larger projects require the approval of higher authority.

For example, at the lowest level, a department head may have the authority to approve $50,000 in total equipment purchases for the year. However, that same person might have to obtain specific approval from higher authority to spend more than $10,000 for any single piece of equipment. A plant manager might have authorization limits of $500,000 per year and $100,000 per piece of equipment, for example.

A system of authorization, such as illustrated in the preceding paragraph, requires more extensive review and a greater number of inputs to approve larger expenditures. The hierarchical review structure reflects the obvious fact that misjudging a larger project is potentially more costly than misjudging a smaller one.

CAPITAL INVESTMENT IN OTHER COMPANIES

Sometimes companies make capital investments in other companies. In concept, these are just like any other capital investment. They range from the simple, such as buying stock in another company in a passive investment, to acquiring, or purchasing, another company outright or merging with another company. With an acquisition or merger, the details connected with such things as taxes, corporate cultures, distribution of responsibilities, and logistics, among others, can be exceedingly complex.

Companies give many different reasons for acquisition or merger. In most cases, they want to achieve operating efficiencies and/or economies of scale. For example, in a merger the companies may be able to save money marketing, producing, and delivering their products by combining their operations and eliminating duplication. Combining may also allow greater efficiency in coordinating activities across the companies' units.

A company may be able to expand more cheaply and more quickly through an acquisition or merger. There are also other possible reasons, such as realizing tax benefits and capturing surplus cash. The essence of all the possible reasons is a belief that the merger or acquisition is a good capital investment. Therefore, the analytical tools and basic decision rules are the same for mergers and acquisitions as they are for other capital investments. However, particular care must be taken in applying these tools because of the enormous size and complexity of the investment.

Beyond the basic investment considerations, there can also be important legal considerations connected with a merger or acquisition. These include aspects such as compliance with federal antitrust laws, state anti-takeover statutes, financial securities laws, and the charters of the corporations involved.

SEE ALSO *Finance; Time Value of Money*

BIBLIOGRAPHY

Brealey, Richard A., Meyers, Stewart C., and Marcus, Alan J. (2007). *Fundamentals of Corporate Finance* (5th ed.). Boston: McGraw-Hill/Irwin.

Emery, Douglas R., Finnerty, John D., and Stowe, John D. (1998). *Principles of Financial Management*. Upper Saddle River, NJ: Prentice-Hall.

Ross, Stephen A., Westerfield, Randolph W., and Jordan, Bradford D. (2006). *Fundamentals of Corporate Finance*. Boston: McGraw-Hill/Irwin.

Douglas R. Emery
John D. Finnerty

CAPITAL MARKETS

The capital market provides financing to meet the denomination, liquidity, maturity, risk (with respect to credit, interest rate, and market), and other characteristics desired by those who have a surplus of funds and those who have a deficit of funds. The capital market as a whole consists of overnight to long-term funding. The short to medium end of the maturity spectrum is called the money market proper, and the long end is identified as the capital market. The financial instruments range from money market instruments to thirty-year or longer bonds in credit markets, equity instruments, insurance instruments, foreign-exchange instruments, hybrid instruments, and derivative instruments. Since about 1960 an explosion of innovation in the creation and development of instruments in the money and capital markets has occurred in both debt and equity instruments.

Some of the important (by volume) money market instruments are Treasury bills and bonds, federal agency securities, federal funds, negotiable certificates of deposits, commercial paper, bankers' acceptances, repurchase agreements, eurocurrency deposits, eurocurrency loans, futures instruments, and options instruments. Similarly, some of the key capital market instruments are U.S. securities; U.S. agency securities; corporate bonds; state and local government bonds; mortgage instruments; financial guarantees; securitized instruments; broker-dealer loans; foreign, international, and global bonds; and eurobonds.

THE CAPITAL MARKET IN THE UNITED STATES

The capital market in the United States is highly developed, marked by sophisticated technology, specialized financing institutions and functions, wide-ranging geographic locations, and continuous innovation in financial products and services to meet the needs of financial investors and those seeking to acquire funds. There are both direct and indirect markets. Corporations, for example, engage in direct finance when they invest in one another's paper directly without the services of brokers and other specialized intermediaries, similar to the proverbial entrepreneur getting funds from an uncle. Most of the financing in the United States, however, is done indirectly through financial intermediaries who substitute their credit for the credit of the borrower (user) of funds. The total amount of credit for 2005 in the United States was projected to reach approximately $3,000 billion, of which debt instruments accounted for $2,700 billion and equity instruments (net) for $300 billion.

Money and capital market instruments are traded directly among participants, in the over-the-counter markets and in organized exchanges. Many of the exchanges specialize in the type of securities traded, thus giving focus and depth to that instrument or market. The major U.S. exchanges are the New York Stock Exchange (NYSE), Philadelphia Stock Exchange, Pacific Stock Exchange, Boston Stock Exchange, Cincinnati Stock Exchange, Midwest Stock Exchange, Chicago Board of Trade (CBT), Chicago Mercantile Exchange (CME), International Money Market, National Association of Securities Dealers

Automated Quotations System–American Exchange (NASDAQ-AMEX), Globex, Archipelago, and DMA & NYFI.

The regional exchanges—such as Boston, Cincinnati, the Midwest, the Pacific, and Philadelphia—each list a small number of regional companies to facilitate their raising of capital in the market. The national/international markets are the NYSE, NASDAQ-AMEX, CBT, CME, Archipelago, and DMA & NYFI.

The NYSE, organized by twenty-four brokers in 1792, is the oldest exchange in the U.S. capital market. The first traded company on the NYSE was the Bank of New York. It is still traded today, but has not been continuously listed on the NYSE. The NYSE states its mission as:

> To add value to the capital-raising and asset management process by providing the highest-quality and most cost-effective self-regulated marketplace for the trading of financial instruments, promote confidence in and understanding of that process, and serve as a forum for discussion of relevant national and international policy issues. (http://www.nyse.com/about/theorganization/1088623922144.html)

According to the NYSE, it is "the largest equities marketplace in the world." The NYSE is home to some 2,800 world-class companies with a total global market value of $20 trillion as of late 2005. It had a daily average of over 1.5 billion shares traded in 2005. In late 2005 the NYSE had 401.6 billion shares listed. These companies include a cross-section of leading U.S. companies, midsize and small capitalization companies. Non-U.S. issuers play an increasingly important role on the NYSE. As of October 31, 2005, 460 non-U.S. companies worth $7.1 trillion were listed on the NYSE.

Organized in 1971, NASDAQ was the world's first electronic stock market. According to its mission statement, NASDAQ-AMEX's purpose is "to facilitate capital formation in the public and private sector by developing) operating and regulating the most liquid, efficient and fair securities market for the ultimate benefit and protection of the investor." Its vision is:

> to build the world's first truly global securities market … a worldwide market of markets built on a worldwide network of networks … linking pools of liquidity and connecting investors from all over the world … assuring the best possible price for securities at the lowest possible cost. (http://www.nasdaq.com/about/overview.stm)

In 2005 NASDAQ was the largest electronic screen-based equity securities market in the United States. With

The New York Stock Exchange, April 25, 2005. AP IMAGES

approximately 3,250 companies, it listed more companies and, on average, traded more shares per day than any other U.S. market.

INITIAL PUBLIC OFFERINGS AND ROLE OF VENTURE CAPITAL

The appeal of being a public company, which requires a filing with the U.S. Securities and Exchange Commission (SEC), in accordance with the requirements of the Securities Act of 1933, is closely related to the liquidity of issued securities provided through the stock markets. Companies seeking to "go public" engage an investment bank that will serve as underwriter for an initial issue of stock. Generally, for large offerings, an underwriter will form a syndicate of other investment bankers and brokers who will participate in the initial selling of the issue. Shortly after the sale of the initial offering the stock will be listed on a stock exchange.

Venture capital, which consists of funds raised on the capital market by specialized operators, is one of the most relevant sources of financing for innovative companies. Venture capitalists buy shares or convertible bonds in a company. They do not invest in order to receive an immediate dividend, but rather to allow the company to expand and ultimately increase the value of their investment. Hence, they are interested in innovative small companies with very rapid growth rates. Some venture capitalists specialize in certain business sectors (e.g., biotechnology, information technology). Others may invest only at certain stages in the development of a project or company.

FINANCIAL INNOVATION AND THE MARKETS IN DERIVATIVE INSTRUMENTS

Financial innovation has been one of the most influential trends in international financial markets since the early 1980s. A large number of new financial products and instruments have been created as the traditional barriers among types of financial institutions have increasingly eroded. Banks, for example, are increasingly competing with markets for what was once considered to be traditional intermediated credits. Markets are becoming more global, and competition among financial institutions has intensified. This increase in financial innovation has taken place in an environment of steady deregulation coupled with significant advances in information and communication technologies.

Securitization, perhaps the most important trend in international financial markets in the 1980s and early 1990s, continues to redefine the operations of banks and has important regulatory implications. Both bank and nonbank financial institutions are relying more on income from off-balance-sheet activities. A greater share of credit now flows through capital market channels, which are characterized by less supervision in comparison to banks. Deregulation, improved technology, growing competition, and volatile exchange and interest rates are the main stimulus for financial innovation. Innovation can improve the efficiency of international financial markets by offering a broader and more flexible range of instruments for borrowing. It also provides hedging instruments that can help banks, borrowers, and investors to manage the risks associated with volatile exchange and interest rates.

The derivatives market took a major step forward with the formation of the CBT in 1848. It developed standardized agreements as to the quality, quantity, delivery time, and location, and called futures contracts for trading of grains in 1865. The development of financial futures resulted from a changing world economy following World War II (1939–1945). Futures contracts provide for efficient forward pricing and risk management.

The CME (also known as the Merc) is another major futures exchange in the United States. The Merc's diverse product line consists of futures and options on futures in agricultural commodities, foreign currencies, interest rates, and stock indexes. In the mid-1960s it introduced a futures contract on a nonstorable commodity—live cattle. In 1972 it launched a contract in foreign currency futures.

The U.S. futures industry operates under an extensive regulatory umbrella. Federal legislation governing the industry has existed since 1924. The Commodity Futures Trading Commission, established under the 1974 amendments to the Commodity Exchange Act, has far-reaching authority over a wide variety of commodity industry activities.

ROLE OF THE SECURITIES AND EXCHANGE COMMISSION

The SEC was organized under the Securities Exchange Act of 1934 to create fair market conditions in the securities markets by setting standards for and requirements of information from the issuer of the security to the general public. The SEC has overall responsibility for this process that creates competitive and fair pricing and trading of securities, and it prevents abuse and fraud by issuers, brokers, and dealers. Issuers are required to file detailed information with the SEC on all publicly traded securities, which becomes available to the public on an equal basis. Privately traded securities and investments by wealthy individuals are exempt from registration, based on the assumptions that these investors understand the risks involved in a given security and that they are able to tolerate the consequences of those risks if they materialize.

ROLE OF THE FEDERAL RESERVE SYSTEM

The Federal Reserve (the Fed) plays a key role in the functioning of the capital market in the U.S. economy and, by extension, in the world economy. It manages the overall liquidity and credit conditions in the U.S. financial system. The Fed strives to maintain a noninflationary level of liquidity in the economy, on an ongoing basis, in order to foster conditions for maximum sustainable growth of the economy. It does so by regulating the money supply through the banking system and its interaction with the public.

The Fed pays similar attention to availability of credit; in that regard it is authorized to set the margin rate on stock purchases, thus exercising a direct role in the use of credit in equity market transactions. The Fed is also the commercial and investment banker to the federal government; in this capacity, it conducts the U.S. Treasury's operations in the Treasury securities bond market through the securities dealers recognized by it and so authorized to be dealers in Treasury bills, notes, and bonds.

ROLE OF THE U.S. TREASURY

The U.S. Treasury is the biggest player in the U.S. credit markets. Because the market in U.S. government securities is the largest, most active, and most liquid market, it creates a base for conditions in the U.S. credit markets. The Treasury operations bridge the timing of the cash inflows and outflows of the government. The extent of activity is related to whether the federal budget is in deficit or surplus. As anticipated, federal debt is expanded when a deficit is faced and is retired when a surplus arises.

REGULATORY REQUIREMENTS

Regulation plays an important role in a fair and orderly functioning of the capital market. Parts of the market are more heavily regulated than other parts. Commercial banking, for example, is one of the most regulated parts of the financial services industries. This heavy regulation came about because large bank failures, due to either fraud or mismanagement, can destabilize banking markets and lead to loss of faith in the banking system—and therefore in the currency and money (as the liability of commercial banks).

The Gramm-Leach-Bliley Financial Services Modernization Act of 1999 has reduced or eliminated the need for many of the regulations on commercial banks and their activities and affiliations with investment banks and insurance companies by allowing competition for the same or similar products offered by the three. This act provided for an eighteen-month period for the SEC to implement the provisions related to rule making. A number of new regulations have been issued since 2001 by the SEC.

KEY CAPITAL MARKETS OUTSIDE THE UNITED STATES

The increasing integration of the world economy and the growth of other economies have led to the emergence of several key financial centers, the prime examples of which are London, Tokyo, Frankfurt, Zürich, Paris, Hong Kong, and Singapore. Efforts at cross-border exchanges have been successful, too.

Euronext N.V. was the leading cross-border exchange organization in Europe in 2005. It began in 2000, headed by a Dutch holding company. By 2004 this cross-border exchange was providing services for regulated stock and derivatives markets in Belgium, France, the Netherlands, and Portugal, as well as in the United Kingdom (derivatives only). In late 2005 Euronext was the leading derivative exchange in the world and Europe's leading stock exchange, based on trading volumes on the central order book. The euro area capital market, the U.S. capital market, and the Asian capital market were predicted to be the three key markets in the global financial world of the twenty-first century.

SEE ALSO *Finance*

BIBLIOGRAPHY

Board of Governors of the Federal Reserve System. (1999). *The Federal Reserve system: Purposes and functions.* Retrieved December 16, 2005, from http://www.federalreserve.gov/pf/pf.htm

Burch, John C., and Forester, Bruce S. (2005). *Capital markets handbook* (6th ed.). New York: Aspen Law & Business.

Kidwell, D. S., Blackwell, D. W., Whidbee, D. A., and Peterson, R. L. (2005). *Financial institutions, markets, and money* (9th ed.). New York: Wiley.

Kohn, M. (2003). *Financial institutions and markets* (2nd ed.). New York: Oxford University Press.

Madura, Jeff (2006). *Financial markets and institutions* (7th ed.). Cincinnati: Thomson South-Western.

Mayo, Herbert B. (2004). *Financial institutions, investments, and management: An introduction* (8th ed.). Cincinnati: Thomson South-Western.

Mishkin, F. S., and Eakins, S. G. (2004). *The economics of money, banking and financial markets* (7th ed.). Reading, MA: Addison-Wesley.

Molyneux, P., and Shamroukh, N. (1999). *Financial innovation.* New York: Wiley.

NASDAQ. http://www.nasdaq.com retrieved February 2, 2006.

New York Stock Exchange. http://www.nyse.com retrieved February 2, 2006.

Rose, Peter S. (2005). *Money and capital markets* (8th ed.). New York: Irwin McGraw-Hill.

Securities and Exchange Commission. http://www.sec.gov retrieved February 24, 2006.

Seifert, Werner G., Mattern, G. F., and Streit, C. C. (2000). *European capital markets.* New York: St. Martin's.

Stulz, René M., and Karolyi, G. Andrew (Eds.). (2003). *International capital markets.* Northampton, MA: Edward Elgar.

Tobin, James (1989). Financial intermediaries. In John Eatwell, Murray Milgate, and Peter Newman (Eds.), *The New Palgrave: Finance* (pp. 35–52). New York: Macmillan.

Surendra K. Kaushik

CAPITALISM

SEE *Economic Systems*

CAREERS: AN OVERVIEW

The concept of careers ranges from descriptions of jobs, occupations, or vocations to the pattern of work and work-related activities that develop through a lifetime. Career is defined in the *Merriam-Webster Collegiate Dictionary* (1999) as "a field for or pursuit of consecutive progressive achievement especially in public, professional, or business life."

The perception of a career has various connotations. A career could be a job. A job, as defined in the *Merriam-Webster Collegiate Dictionary* (1999), is "a regular remunerative position; something that has to be done: task." A job might be washing dishes or typing reports. In other works, a job is a task.

An occupation, as defined in the *Merriam-Webster Collegiate Dictionary* (1999), is "an activity in which one engages; the principal business of one's life: vocation." An occupation may mean practicing law, teaching school, and so forth. In other words, an occupation is a vocation.

Careers are the patterns of work and work-related activities that develop through a lifetime. Having several careers during a lifetime is not uncommon. One may train to become a business teacher—a satisfying occupation (vocation) for years. After that, one may leave teaching and train to become a financial planner (a second vocation).

Also, having more than one job within a career is common. A business teacher might begin teaching middle school general business subjects (a first job), then progress to teaching secondary-level business subjects (another job). While teaching secondary business subjects, the same person might supervise the publication of the school's yearbook (still within the career field of education).

CHOOSING A CAREER

To be successful in a vocation, it is first necessary to obtain knowledge about choosing a career and then to acquire the education needed to grow in that career and in the job(s) pursued within that career.

The Myers-Briggs Personality Test, available at employment offices, at school career/college centers, or on the Internet, could be a first step in choosing a career. Based on the work of Karl Jung, the test was developed by Katherine Briggs and her daughter Isabel Briggs Myers, to determine whether someone was primarily extroverted or introverted, sensing or intuitive, thinking or feeling, judging or perceiving. Combining these traits, they formed sixteen distinct personality types, known as the Myers-Briggs Personality Types. Understanding one's own personality type, as well as that of other people, can help in

finding the "perfect" job and make it easier to manage personal and professional relationships.

Along with the Myers-Briggs Personality Test, a person should consider the following when choosing a career:

1. Skills you currently possess and need to acquire
2. Education you have or will need
3. Salary you are willing to accept
4. Working conditions in which you would be comfortable
5. Working schedule preferred (day or night shift, part-time, or full-time work, etc.)

Anyone searching for a position, whether this is a first job or the next step up the career ladder, needs to go through the following steps.

Know which jobs are suitable. The information from the Myers-Briggs Personality Test will provide an idea of your abilities and interests. However, this is not the sole source of information for determining the perfect job(s). School or public libraries, job counselors, and employment agencies all have information and testing facilities to assist in finding the perfect job.

Prepare a flawless resume. Sales representatives know that when calling on a potential customer, displaying their product in the most favorable way enhances the prospect of a sale. The same principles apply when searching for a job. You are selling yourself based largely on your resume—education, experience, abilities, and talents that apply to their company or organization.

There are two primary resume formats. One is the traditional hard-copy format. The second is the scanner ready format meaning that the resume is ready to be posted on the Internet, distributed via e-mail, or submitted to employers with scannable databases. Because a computer software program will probably read the resume initially, a keyword paragraph must be included in the resume. Keywords are critical words matching the applicant with the required job qualifications. For instance, in an application for a job as a programmer, the keyword paragraph might look like this:

Keywords: Programmer, Unix, C, C++, Cobol, Java, Systems Engineer, and Solaris

The keywords are critical if an employer has resume-tracking software. They should fit the positions for which you are applying. It is also important that experience and background match the job.

The resume and cover letter are the first documents that the potential employer or resume-tracking system sees or scans. Even if the company has resume-tracking software, when a resume pops up from a search, a human resources professional will read it. A resume creates an all-important excellent first impression.

Search for jobs. Acquire knowledge about various career choices. The following is a list of the most popular careers for the twenty-first century (*Occupational Outlook Handbook, 2000*): (1) air transportation-related occupations, (2) engineering and engineering technicians, (3) architects and surveyors, (4) computer, mathematical, and operations research, (5) scientists and science technicians, (6) legal, (7) social scientists, (8) social and recreation workers, (9) teachers and instructors, counselors, and library occupations, (10) health diagnosticians, (11) health assessment and treating, (12) health technologists and technicians, (13) communications-related, (14) visual arts and design, (15) performing arts.

Determine what education is needed. Research the qualifications necessary. Use the Internet to begin gathering facts on a particular career. Firm-specific data can be found in books such as *Hoover's Handbook of American Business*, *Dunn's Regional Business Directory*, and other business directories available online or in library reference sections. Judy Kaplan Baron, a nationally certified career counselor in San Diego, recommends reading about a target occupation in resources such as the *Occupational Outlook Handbook* published by the U.S. Department of Labor.

Baron believes that it does not occur to most people to use friends, co-workers, and neighbors as referral sources: "You may have what you need as a referral living right next door."

Research the company and/or industry. The task of business research has gotten easier, since the Internet contains information on almost every business. Use search engines to gather information on public and private companies or use information gleaned from the local library.

Prepare for an interview. Knowledge is power, especially in an interview. The more known about the company and what is going to occur in an interview, the more likely you are to be an intelligent candidate. If you are familiar with the interview procedure, you can talk confidently to a potential employer. Rather than worrying about the upcoming interview, time can be spent rehearsing and preparing for the interview.

Be aware of implicit rules during the interview. Never ask for a job and respect the interview's time limits. When time is up, offer to end the meeting. Maintain the conversation only if urged by the interviewer to do so.

The interview should be ended by asking the interviewer to suggest other people with whom it would profitable to talk. Then ask permission to mention the interviewer's name when contacting those recommended.

Within twenty-four hours of the interview, send a thank-you note. John Klube, site manager for the Army Career and Alumni Program at Fort Carson, Colorado (1998), also recommends additional follow-up, stating that never hearing from a candidate again makes interviewers feel used. He recommends contacting interviewers again four or five weeks after the initial interview to thank them again and to let them know how any referrals worked out.

Figure the Level of Salary. Check with employment agencies, read the want ads in local papers, and talk with others to find out what an expected salary should be. There are Internet sites, such as salary.com or homefair.com, that will calculate and compare the cost of living in cities worldwide, based on selected origin and destination sites. For example, if a job-seeker currently live in Denver, Colorado, and wants to move to Boston, Massachusetts, that information should be entered. The online calculator would calculate if $100,000 in Denver would be equal to a salary of $154,621 in Boston.

SEARCH STRATEGIES

The Myers-Briggs Personality Test, discussed earlier, is useful in helping determine interests and capabilities. The figures published by Bernard Haldane Associates (Vincent, 1998), a nationwide career search firm, show that nearly 70 percent of all jobs are acquired by those who mix personal initiative with a compelling search strategy: building professional contacts and making themselves known to employers. A job seeker does this through brief, data-gathering dialogues with corporate managers and referrals by those managers to other knowledgeable sources; candidates can gather real-world tips for career success and gain valuable professional contacts.

Roles of colleges and universities. Most of the careers listed earlier require education beyond high school. The length and type of education varies from technical training to a doctoral degree.

Advances in technology have changed the traditional role of the college and university. The Internet, computer-assisted training (enhanced by video technology and courseware authoring tools), interactive CD-ROMs, and distance learning can provide education beyond high school. Training for a career involves competencies consistent with the demands of business and industry. Computer skills, subject-matter skills, and the soft skills of human relations and workplace ethics are central to the curriculum.

SEE ALSO *Certifications, Licensures, and Designations*

BIBLIOGRAPHY

http://www.acap.army.mil/default.cfm. Retrieved September 26, 2005.

http://www.careermag.com. Retrieved September 26, 2005.

Merriam-Webster Online (2005). http://www.m-w.com/.

"The Myers & Briggs Foundation" (2005). Retrieved September 26, 2005, from http://www.myersbriggs.org.

"NBEA Online" (2001). Retrieved September 26, 2005, from http://www.nbea.org.

Judith Chiri

CAREERS IN ACCOUNTING

Many career opportunities are available in accounting. The importance of the accounting function continues to be enhanced in a complex, global business community. Increased scrutiny of company financial reporting and new regulations, such as those implemented with the passage of the Sarbanes-Oxley Act of 2002, have resulted in intense need for qualified, highly technical accounting staffs in corporations, accounting firms, and governmental agencies.

Accounting positions range from bookkeeping clerks who maintain financial data in computer and paper form to chief financial officers who are responsible for providing leadership in the design and operations of a total accounting information system and the financial statements it produces. Opportunities for employment are present for those with basic accounting/computer skills acquired in secondary schools or community colleges as well as for those with college degrees and postgraduate degrees.

OVERVIEW OF ACCOUNTING AS AN OCCUPATIONAL FIELD

The U.S. Department of Labor identifies accounting essentially at two levels. At the "executive, administrative, and managerial" occupational level, accountants and auditors are included. Under "bookkeeping, accounting, and auditing clerks," positions are available to those who have completed secondary school or community college programs and have some training and interest in working with financial records.

Persons employed in accounting are generally expected to have strong computer, analytical, interpersonal, and communications skills in addition to sound knowledge in accounting related to the level of the position.

In general, according to Department of Labor projection, the rate of growth of employment for accountants with college degrees or master's degrees was expected to be about the same as the average for all other occupations through the year 2012.

The impact of computer technology will continue to change the nature of demand for employees in accounting who have less than college preparation. The projection of the Department of Labor for this category of accounting and bookkeeping workers was that growth would be slower than average in overall employment, but job opportunities were expected to be numerous because of high turnover of individuals in this category.

Accounting is a field that is appealing to individuals who enjoy working with figures and who appreciate the need for impeccable accuracy and careful adherence to policies and schedules. Accountants must be computer-savvy. Thus, individuals who enjoy the challenge of the continuing need to learn new software and new work procedures find the field of interest. Those who become certified must continue to be learners, since renewal of licenses requires continuing professional education. Accountants who are not certified also enroll in a range of in-company and other types of programs to upgrade their skills and knowledge to be able to handle emerging responsibilities.

Accountants must be individuals of high integrity so that the financial information they prepare is viewed as trustworthy by the users of the information. Accountants who are certified are expected to adhere to professional codes of ethics. These codes impose rules and regulations that are meant to encourage behavior in relation to their work that maintains the credibility of financial reporting, both within and outside the organization.

CAREERS FOR CERTIFIED ACCOUNTANTS

Professional accounting positions that require at least an undergraduate college degree and certification are certified public accountant (CPA), certified management accountant, certified internal auditor, and the certified government financial manager.

Accountants in Public Accounting Firms. Accountants who plan to complete the CPA examination and meet certification requirements, as well as those who hold the CPA certificate, are likely to begin employment in a public accounting firm as a staff accountant. Some states in the United States require experience in auditing for certification. While public accounting firms hire recent graduates of college programs for beginning positions, such firms expect new employees to have taken the examination or be planning to sit for it. While many CPAs leave public accounting to enter other positions in all types of organizations, some remain in public accounting.

The promotional opportunities in public accounting for CPAs are related to level of responsibility. Successful staff accountants become seniors; seniors become managers; a limited number of managers become partners. In many public accounting firms, there are additional levels for all of these categories.

In addition to accounting and auditing, public accounting firms provide other services, such as tax advisement and management consulting. Some CPAs choose to move to other services after they gain experience in accounting and auditing. Others decide to establish their own firms; in 2002, for example, 10 percent of accountants were self-employed. Many choose to work in other types of positions after gaining certification and experience. Many accept positions in corporations, not-for-profit entities, and government agencies, where promotional opportunities include both accounting and nonaccounting responsibilities. Some accountants become chief executive officers in corporations or other types of organizations.

Accountants in Organizations. The range of positions for accountants in organizations is extensive. Accountants are employed in corporate reporting, in controllers' offices, and in budget and strategic planning departments. Certification is provided for management accountants through the Institute of Management Accountants. To be a certified management accountant (CMA), a candidate must successfully complete a comprehensive examination that includes accounting and related topics relevant to the broad responsibilities assumed by management accountants. Work experience in some aspect of management accounting before a candidate is certified is required. CMAs have many promotional opportunities in organizations. They are identified for leadership positions, in much the same way as CPAs, at executive levels of their own and other organizations.

Accountants as Internal Auditors. Some accountants choose to work as internal auditors. The Institute of Internal Auditors provides a certification program for candidates who seek to be certified internal auditors (CIA). Certification requires experience as an internal auditor. In many organizations, especially large ones, there is a separate department of internal audit that provides valuable

oversight of the total organization. Internal auditors who are certified are expected to adhere to the professional standards as they perform their responsibilities. CIAs have promotional opportunities in internal auditing through moving into managerial positions within the department or moving to operational units where they assume supervisory and executive responsibilities.

Government Accountants. The most common certification for government accountants is that provided by the Association of Government Accountants. An examination and relevant experience are required. The designation achieved by a successful candidate is certified government financial manager. Government accountants are employed throughout the public sector, at federal, state, and local levels.

CAREERS FOR ACCOUNTANTS WITHOUT CERTIFICATION

There are more accountants in the United States who are not certified than there are those who are certified. Of the 1.1 million workers classified as accountants and auditors in the United States in 2002, it was estimated that fewer than half were certified. Individuals who have studied accounting at the community college, business college, or university level are employed in beginning accounting positions. Through on-the-job training and experience, many of these individuals move into higher-level positions.

Many individuals who study in accounting programs in universities choose not to be certified. Others study some accounting as an elective program and then enter a beginning accounting position, such as staff accountant.

Many promotional opportunities are available to accountants. Technical skills and managerial skills are both important if an individual aspires to higher-level positions. Employees who are knowledgeable about accounting and continue to learn as new accounting rules and interpretations are introduced by professional bodies are invaluable to employers. Such knowledge, however, must be accompanied by strong organizational and interpersonal skills if promotional opportunities are to be realized. Some commonly identified positions for persons who have studied accounting at the college level are listed in Table 1.

CHANGING REQUIREMENTS FOR ACCOUNTANTS AND AUDITORS

The basic education requirements for those who aspire to be CPAs have been increased in most U.S. jurisdictions (the 50 states, Guam, the District of Columbia, Puerto Rico, and Virgin Islands). As of the end of 2003, there

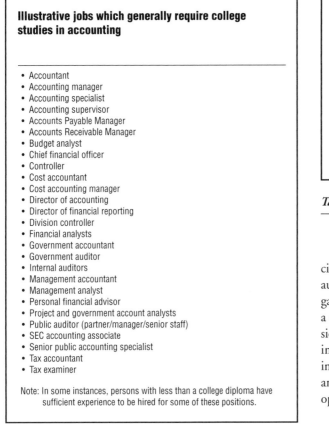

Illustrative jobs which generally require college studies in accounting

- Accountant
- Accounting manager
- Accounting specialist
- Accounting supervisor
- Accounts Payable Manager
- Accounts Receivable Manager
- Budget analyst
- Chief financial officer
- Controller
- Cost accountant
- Cost accounting manager
- Director of accounting
- Director of financial reporting
- Division controller
- Financial analysts
- Government accountant
- Government auditor
- Internal auditors
- Management accountant
- Management analyst
- Personal financial advisor
- Project and government account analysts
- Public auditor (partner/manager/senior staff)
- SEC accounting associate
- Senior public accounting specialist
- Tax accountant
- Tax examiner

Note: In some instances, persons with less than a college diploma have sufficient experience to be hired for some of these positions.

Table 1

Jobs which generally do not require college studies in accounting

- Accounting assistant
- Accounting clerk
- Accounts Payable assistant
- Accounts Payable clerk
- Accounts Receivable assistant
- Accounts Receivabel clerk
- Bookkeeper
- Cost Accounting clerk
- Payroll clerk

Table 2

were forty-four states and the District of Columbia that required CPA candidates to complete 150 semester credits of college coursework. This requirement adds thirty credits to the usual four-year college program in accounting. Many of the remaining jurisdictions were considering adopting legislation requiring 150 credits, to be effective no later than August 2009. There are many significant differences among the jurisdictions related to both education and experience. The Web sites of the accountancy boards of each jurisdiction provide useful information about requirements.

Knowledge of accounting and auditing continues to be critical to handling job responsibilities. Such knowledge alone, however, is not sufficient. Accountants are expected to have advanced competencies in handling a variety of accounting and auditing software and in designing accounting information systems. Furthermore, accountants and auditors are expected to strategically analyze, interpret, and assess the information from the systems they develop and implement.

Because of the growing complexity of business, specializations have been established within accounting and auditing. For example, auditors who have studied and gained considerable experience in financial services, or in a critical aspect, such as acquisitions and mergers or pensions, are in demand in service firms that provide consulting services. Specializations in the accounting for industries, such as retailing, entertainment, insurance, gas and oil, or consumer products, often provide promotional opportunities.

CAREERS IN ACCOUNTING THAT DO NOT REQUIRE A COLLEGE DEGREE

As noted before, there are positions in accounting that are identified by the U.S. Department of Labor as requiring less than a college degree. A variety of positions identified by the Labor Department as financial clerks, including those classified as bookkeeping, accounting, and auditing clerks, are needed in all types of organizations; in 2002 there were 3.7 million such clerks. The outlook for employment (to 2012) is that virtually all job openings will be related to replacement of individuals who have left positions. There is high turnover in this category of workers as workers move to other types of positions, including ones that represent promotions. Therefore, there are opportunities for those wishing to enter such positions.

Most positions require a high school diploma and exist in virtually every industry in the United States. Such workers are expected to know basic computer software programs. Most U.S. comprehensive and career-technical high schools offer courses in accounting and in computer software applications. Also, proprietary business colleges as well as junior and community colleges have programs that prepare students with the basic knowledge and skills needed in many beginning accounting positions. Many employers provide training on the job for the specific applications that new employees need to understand and use. Many employers provide training when there are software or system changes in the accounting information system. All levels of government, from local to federal, have many opportunities in the field of accounting for individuals who have earned a secondary education diploma.

The key task of accounting-related clerks is to maintain financial records. Such workers compute, classify, process, and verify numerical data. In large as well as midsize businesses, for example, there are departments that handle accounts payable, accounts receivable, and cash. For such departments, companies seek employees who have a basic understanding of accounting principles, possess an organized style of work, and can handle communications with vendors (in accounts payable), customers (in accounts receivable), or personnel in human resources (benefits, pensions). Ability to work under pressure and meet deadlines is also important in some positions. Entry-level workers are generally responsible for handling the details of transactions and for preparing schedules that show the results of processing transactions. The activities for which entry-level employees are responsible, if done with thought and attention, provide a means of learning a great deal about the organization's activities and about proper work habits.

Promotional opportunities are available in many organizations. Individuals who continue their education on a part-time basis and who display maturity and wisdom in their associations with coworkers are considered good candidates for supervisory positions. Responsible, dependable managers often began as clerks but were willing to continue to learn not only all aspects of their jobs but also the total work of the organization in relation to the accounting function. Some common job titles for positions available to persons without college study of accounting are shown in Table 2.

CAREERS IN ACCOUNTING RELATED TO DOCTORAL DEGREES

University programs that lead to doctoral degrees in accounting produce graduates who find employment in college teaching and in technical positions in public accounting firms, professional standard-setting organizations, and other organizations in which high-level expertise is in demand. Some such specializations in this area include accounting theory, accounting systems design, and accounting policy.

Opportunities for accountants with doctorates reflect the need for accountants to have leading-edge vision in a rapidly changing global business environment. Advanced studies leading to a doctorate will provide individuals with theoretical understanding so that they can devise new principles to ensure the relevance of financial information

that is reported to shareholders and others. Advanced studies will also train individuals who will be able to design the effective and efficient accounting information systems needed in business and government.

SPECIALIZATIONS IDENTIFIED BY ORGANIZATIONS

The American Institute of Certified Public Accountants provides specialized certificates in accredited in business valuation and for the positions of information technology professional and personal financial specialist. These certificate programs require that individuals have CPA certificates.

Other initiatives in the United States relate to environmental accounting, forensic accounting, international accounting, and fraud accounting. Organizations with missions related to a specialization are active in establishing standards to guide practitioners who choose to participate in the field.

RELATED FIELDS

Accounting is often referred to as "the language of business." That language has wide application. Many occupations are open to those who have both a background in accounting and analytical skills. Among occupations in which accounting training is perceived to be valuable are budget officers, lending officials in banks, securities advisers, financial analysts, Federal Bureau of Investigation agents, and financial managers in not-for-profit entities.

SEE ALSO *Accounting*

BIBLIOGRAPHY

American Institute of Certified Public Accountants. http://www.aicpa.org

Association of Government Accountants. http://www.agacgfm.org

Institute of Internal Auditors. http://www.theiia.org

Institute of Management Accountants. http://www.imanet.org

National Association of State Boards of Accountancy. http://www.nasba.org

U.S. Department of Labor. Bureau of Labor Statistics. *Occupational outlook handbook, 2004–05.*

Bernard H. Newman
Mary Ellen Oliverio

CAREERS IN ADVERTISING

SEE *Advertising Agencies*

CAREERS IN ECONOMICS

Economists study how society uses, regulates, and distributes its natural and human-made resources such as land, labor, raw materials, and machinery to produce goods and services (*Horizons*, 2000). In simpler terms, they study how effectively society meets its human and material needs. Economists also study how economic systems address three basic questions: What shall we produce?; How shall we produce it?; For whom shall we produce it? They then compile, process, and interpret the answers to these questions (Economists, 2005). Economists may analyze the relationship between supply and demand and develop theories and models to help predict these future relationships. They help provide a logical, ordered way of looking at various problems. They attempt to explain social concerns such as unemployment, inflation, economic growth, business cycles, tax policy, or farm prices. Most economists apply their skills to solve problems in specific areas, such as transportation, labor, heath, finance, marketing, corporate planning, energy, or agriculture. Business firms, banks, insurance companies, labor unions, governmental agencies, and others seek advice from economists to use in their decision making.

TYPES OF ECONOMISTS

Theoretical economists, employing mathematical models, develop theories to examine major economic phenomena, such as the causes of business cycles or inflation or the effects of unemployment, energy prices, or tax laws. Most economists, however, concern themselves with the practical application of economic policy to such areas as finance, labor, agriculture, health, and transportation (Harkavy, 1999). Although there is a wide range of careers open to economists, there are three main career paths: business, government, and academia. Each type of economist applies the economic approach to decision-making in a different setting.

Business economists work in such areas as manufacturing, mining, transportation, communications, banking, insurance, retailing, private industry, securities and investment firms, management consulting firms, and economic and market research firms, as well as trade associations and consulting organizations (*Careers*, 2001). Many private firms, both large and small, recruit undergraduate economics majors for jobs. These jobs are general-purpose ones for which employers seek bright, highly-motivated students who can learn a specific business through on-the-job training. To become a professional business economist requires graduate training. Business economists perform such tasks as forecasting the business environment, inter-

preting the impact of public/governmental policy on the firm, and collecting and processing data. They also supply information to management that affects decisions on the marketing and pricing of company products, as well as providing long- and short-term economic forecasts ("Economics," 1997). For example, a business firm's managers might ask its marketing analysts to provide specific information on which to base marketing and pricing policies. Using econometric modeling techniques, the analysts develop projections of market reactions to various price levels throughout the industry. On the basis of these projections, the mangers can make informed pricing decisions. Informed, rational decision making on economic matters is what economics is all about.

Government economists work for federal, state, and local governments in a wide variety of positions involving analysis and policy making. The federal government is a major source of employment for economists with an undergraduate degree; information about job openings in various agencies is available from the Federal Employment Information Center. A bachelor's degree in economics is a good qualification for an entry-level position; a person can advance to higher positions by obtaining a graduate degree or by promotion from within. There are jobs for labor, international, development, and population economists, as well as micro- and macroeconomists (*Careers*, 2001). Economists who work for government or private research agencies assess economic trends in order to formulate policy in such areas as agriculture, forestry, business, finance, labor, transportation, urban economics, or international trade and development (*Horizons*, 2000). Working for Congress is a relatively new area for economists. Legislation and the issues facing Congress are becoming more complex and economic in nature, and as a result, members of Congress are turning to economists for advice on these issues.

Academics is another major area in which economists are found. Economics professors teach basic macro- and microeconomics courses (the "big picture" versus individual companies/persons) as well as courses on advanced topics, such as economic history and labor economics. They also do research, write papers and books, and give lectures, contributing their knowledge to the advancement of the discipline (Economists, 2005). In order to teach at a four-year college, it is essential to have a Ph.D. in economics. Faculty members usually divide their time among teaching, research, and administrative responsibilities. Many academic economists also have the opportunity to consult either for business or government.

Administration degree, and many graduate business schools encourage students to take at least some economics courses. Studying economics is also excellent preparation for becoming a lawyer; many believe that economics is one of the best backgrounds for success in law school because of its emphasis on a logical approach to problems, logical reasoning, and analytical skills. Publishing companies and trade associations also employ economists. Newspapers provide economics majors with opportunities to write about economic and business events. The demand for economics teachers in secondary schools is growing as economics becomes an increasingly important and popular course (*Careers*, 2001).

WORK CONDITIONS

Economists generally work in offices or classrooms. The average work week for government economists is forty hours, but the schedules of academic and business economists are less predictable. Regular travel may be necessary to collect data or attend conferences or meetings. International economists may spend as much as 30 percent of their time traveling and 40 percent of their time on the telephone or the Internet researching current trends in foreign economic systems (for this subgroup, language skills are important).

Economists in nonteaching positions often work alone writing reports, preparing statistical charts, and using computers, but they may also be part of a research team. Faculty economists have flexible work schedules, dividing their time among teaching, research, consulting, and administrative duties. High levels of satisfaction are found throughout this field, which encourages discussion, detailed examination, and lively disagreement.

DESIRABLE PERSONAL QUALITIES

The field of economics rewards creative, curious, analytical, and logical thinkers. Helpful qualities for an economist include the following:

- The ability to work accurately with details

- The ability to work well independently as well as with others

- The ability to be objective and systematic in one's work

- Patience and persistence (since economists and marketing research analysts must spend long hours on independent study and problem solving)

- Effective communication skills

- Intellectual curiosity

- The ability to collect, organize, interpret, and analyze data

---

Career opportunities for which an economics background is well suited

- Economist
- Business Manager
- Property Manager
- Labor Relations Specialist
- Market Research Analyst
- Securities Broker
- Urban/Regional Planner
- Public Administrator
- Government Economist
- Industrial Traffic Manager
- Technical Writer
- International Trade Specialist
- Farm and Land Appraiser
- Food Store Manager
- Marketing Advisor
- Professional Farm Manager
- Sales Representative
- Statistician
- Journalist (especially business reporting)
- Actuary
- Researcher
- Agricultural Economist
- Tax Economist
- Tax Examiner/Collector/Revenue Agent
- Political Scientist
- Stockbroker
- Commodities Trader/Broker
- Financial Analyst
- Financial Investment Analyst
- Population Studies Analyst
- Bank Administrator
- Business Administrator
- Investor Relations Manager
- Chamber of Commerce Analyst
- Transportation Planner
- Commodity Analyst
- Data Analyst
- Cost Analyst
- Credit Analyst
- Rate Analyst
- Bank Research Analyst
- Compensation/Benefits Coordinator
- Financial Researcher
- Investment Banking Analyst
- Compensation Analyst
- Cost Estimator
- Demographer
- Regional Planner
- Underwriter
- Management Consultant

Table 1

RELATED USES FOR AN ECONOMICS DEGREE

Economics is widely recognized as a solid background for many jobs and professions in business, government, and the law. Economics majors have a wide range of choices and a great deal of flexibility when deciding on a profession (see Table 1).

An undergraduate major in economics can be an ideal preparation for work on a Master of Business

- Leadership ability
- The ability to present findings clearly, both orally and in writing
- The ability to make decisions based on experience and using data
- Enjoyment of the research process

Especially for advancement purposes, it is helpful to continue pursuing education and to take graduate-level courses. It is also important to be able to work successfully under the pressure of deadlines and tight schedules and to be able to bear the responsibility of knowing that the information provided will affect the future policies of current employers.

EDUCATION AND TRAINING

People who are interested in this field should be able to work accurately and precisely, because economics entails careful analysis of data. Good communications skills are also necessary. One should also take as many mathematics and computer science courses as possible in high school (Economics, 2005).

A college major in economics is the basic preparation for a career in economics. Students should also study political science, psychology, sociology, finance, business law, international relations, statistics, regression analysis, and econometrics. Those who are comfortable with the written and spoken word have a significantly higher rate of advancement and overall job satisfaction than those who are not.

Although most professional economists hold a master's degree or a doctorate, a bachelor's degree often suffices for an entry-level position in business or government, perhaps in an economics-related area such as sales or marketing, beginning research, or administrative and management training (Economics, 2005). The primary responsibilities in entry-level positions are the collection, adaptation, and preparation of data. In the federal government, applicants for entry-level economist positions must have a bachelor's degree with a minimum of twenty-one semester hours of economics and three hours of statistics, accounting, or calculus. However, additional courses and/or superior academic performance are likely to be required. The importance of quantitative analysis makes it highly desirable for those planning a career in economics to take courses in mathematics, statistics, sampling theory and survey design, and computer science (Harkavy, 1999).

Postgraduate degrees in economics, with concentration in areas such as economic theory, econometrics, comparative economic systems, economic planning, labor economics, and international economics, are generally required for advancement in government or private industry (Harkavy, 1999). Business economists with a graduate degree and experience may advance to management or executive positions in banks, industry, or other organizations, where they determine business and administrative policy. A master's degree is usually the minimum requirement for a job as an instructor in junior and community colleges. For a faculty position in most colleges and universities, however, a Ph.D. is normally required. A Ph.D. plus extensive publications in academic journals are required for a professorship, tenure, and promotion. Economists in education may advance to be department heads or to administrative or research positions (Economists and Marketing, 2000).

Overall, good mathematical and analytical skills are essential; persistence, objectivity, and creativity in problem solving are important; and computer skills and excellent communication skills are invaluable. No special licensing or certification is required for economists (Harkavy, 1999).

LOCATION OF JOBS

Generally economists who are not in academia work in large cities, where there is the highest concentration of major financial and government power; New York City and Washington, DC, are main centers of employment, along with Chicago and Los Angeles. Academic positions are spread throughout the country. American economists are also employed in foreign countries by international companies and organizations and by U.S. government agencies (Economists, 2005).

EARNINGS AND PROSPECTIVE JOB OUTLOOK

Economists are the highest-paid social scientists. The highest-paid economists in business are in securities and investment, insurance, and retail and wholesale trade. The lowest-paid economists work in education, nonprofit research institutions, and real estate (Harkavy, 1999).

Job opportunities for economists should be best in manufacturing, financial services, advertising, and consulting firms. The complexity of modern national and international markets will continue to spur a demand for those skilled in quantitative analysis. In addition, lawyers, accountants, engineers, and urban and regional planners, among others, will continue to need economic analysis. The majority of openings will come about as the result of replacement needs for those retiring or leaving the profession for some other reason (Harkavy, 1999).

Demand for qualified marketing research analysts should be strong because of the increasingly competitive economy. Marketing research provides organizations with valuable feedback from purchasers that enables companies to evaluate consumer satisfaction and plan more effectively for the future. As companies seek to expand their market and consumers become better informed, the need for marketing professionals will increase (Economists and Marketing, 2000).

Economists with a bachelor's degree will face strong competition in securing jobs in business or industry; some may find positions as management or sales trainees or as research or administrative assistants. Those with master's degrees and a strong background in marketing and finance will have the best prospects in business, banking, advertising, and management consulting (Harkavy, 1999). Those holding doctoral degrees in economics and marketing are likely to face strong competition for teaching positions in colleges and universities. However, opportunities should be good in other areas, such as industry and consulting firms.

CONCLUSION

Economics is the only social science for which a Nobel Prize is awarded—an indication of its importance. Economic concepts have been applied in the natural sciences; both the theory of natural selection and the study of ecology, for example, have drawn extensively on economic concepts. Economics is both a theoretical and an applied discipline. It analyzes the way an economy can be changed and improved through learning how the various parts of society affect each other and studying the relationships between government, business, and the individual (Basta, 1991). Economic concepts are so powerful and versatile that they have been applied to attempts to understand nearly every aspect of human activity. Economics provides important insights in areas from government fiscal and monetary policy, to business, to law and property rights, to poverty and health issues, to environmental and natural resource issues, to the choice of marriage partners.

SEE ALSO *Economics*

BIBLIOGRAPHY

Basta, Nicolas. (1991). "Economics." *Major Options: The Student's Guide to Linking College Majors and Career Opportunities During and After College.* New York: Stonesong Press.

Careers in Economics. (2001). McGraw-Hill Higher Education: The McGraw-Hill Companies. Retrieved September 7, 2005, from http://www.mhhe.com/economics/sharp/student/careers.mhtml.

"Economics," (1997). *VGM's Careers Encyclopedia* (4th ed.). Lincolnwood, IL: VGM Career Horizons.

"Economists." (2005). *Encyclopedia of Careers and Vocational Guidance,* vol. 2. New York: J.G. Ferguson Publishing.

"Economists and Marketing Research Analysts." (2000). *Occupational Outlook Handbook.* Washington, DC: U.S. Department of Labor, Bureau of Labor Statistics.

Harkavy, Michael. (1999). "Economists." *101 Careers: A Guide to the Fastest-Growing Opportunities.* New York: J. Wiley.

"Why Major in Economics?" *Questions and Answers.* (2000). Retrieved September 7, 2005, from http://www.wiu.edu/users/miecon/wiu/whymajor/questions_answers.html.

Wendy Rinholen

CAREERS IN FINANCE

In exploring careers in finance, one quickly begins to realize that there are a variety of jobs, with several types of organizations, requiring varying levels of education and training. Unfortunately, the word finance reveals few details about what one actually does as work in a finance career. The *Career Guide to Industries 2004–05*, produced by the Bureau of Labor Statistics, organizes finance careers according to three broad categories: banking, insurance, and securities and commodities. Careers in the banking industry focus on providing loans, credit, and payment services to individual and large institutional customers. Insurance industry jobs focus on providing clients with protection against financial losses and hardships due to such things as fire. Finally, securities and commodities careers are typically what most people think of when considering a career in finance. These jobs focus on advising and assisting individual and institutional investors with purchasing and selling stocks, bonds, and commodities.

BANKING CAREERS

The majority of jobs in the banking industry are clerical and administrative support positions. Bank tellers make up the bulk of the clerical positions in banking institutions. Tellers work directly with customers, assisting them with basic banking services such as depositing funds and cashing checks. New accounts clerks, also called customer service representatives, assist customers with opening and closing bank accounts and with applying for loans or credit cards. As a result, bank tellers and new accounts clerks need to be knowledgeable about a wide range of banking services and be able educate customers about these services.

There are several other entry-level administrative positions in the banking industry. Bookkeeping, auditing, and accounting clerks are needed to help maintain and update financial records, process deposit slips and checks, and enter data. Credit or loan clerks are responsible for organizing the paperwork needed to complete the required records for approved loans or lines of credit. Banks also need secretaries, receptionists, and computer operators to assist with the many administrative support duties.

According to the *Career Guide to Industries*, 25 percent of the positions in the banking industry are comprised of executive, administrative, and managerial occupations. Examples of these occupations include loan officers, trust officers, and financial managers. Loan officers are responsible for determining whether or not a customer can pay back a loan and then approving or declining the customer's loan application. They also help to bring in new business by developing relationships with customers who will need bank loans in the future. Loan officers and counselors also tend to specialize in either commercial, consumer, or mortgage lending. Trust officers are responsible for managing the finances of customers or organizations that have been placed in trust with the bank. Very often they are called upon to be the executor of an individual's estate upon that person's death. Last, financial managers supervise operations at branch offices or departments to make sure customers receive quality service.

Education and training requirements for finance careers in banking vary according to the special skills required for success and the level of responsibility. Bank tellers and clerks typically need, at minimum, a high school education. Some basic skills and interests needed for success as a teller or clerk are math skills, interpersonal communication skills, and comfort in handling large amounts of money. Typically banks provide tellers and clerks with additional training on the organization's procedures and regulations. The American Institute of Banking, American Bankers Association, and the Institute of Financial Education all offer accredited courses for advanced training. Bank tellers and clerks take these educational courses to prepare for more responsibilities and to assist with career advancement. However, most banks have their own training programs.

Financial managers, loan officers, and trust officers usually have a college degree if not a more advanced professional or graduate degree. Most study business administration or earn a degree with a major in business administration. Any college degree plus a master of business administration or a law degree are excellent preparation for one of these financial management positions. Managers who also sell securities need to be licensed by the National Association of Securities Dealers.

Earnings in the banking industry reflect the amount of responsibility and education required of the position. As a result, the more responsibility and education a job requires, the higher the salary, as can be seen in the salary ranges of commercial loan officers, trust officers, and top

executives. Other factors that influence salary are experience, length of time with the bank, and location and size of the bank.

Employment in the banking industry is expected to grow at 3 percent, which is much lower than the growth rate of the overall economy, which is expected to increase 15 percent between 1998 and 2008. The downsizing and cost cutting that occurred in this industry in the early to mid-1990s is expected to decline. Most of the growth in the banking industry is expected to occur in small regional credit unions and banks. As banks become more automated and ATMs are able to provide more services, fewer bank tellers and clerks will be needed. Areas of growth can be found in customer service representatives for staffing call centers and trust officers to administer the estates of an aging population.

INSURANCE INDUSTRY CAREERS

The *Career Guide to Industries* states that more than 40 percent of the positions in the insurance industry are administrative support positions such as secretaries, bookkeepers, word processors, and clerks. These support positions often require skills and knowledge that are specific to the insurance industry. For example, because insurance policy clerks focus on processing insurance policy applications, changes to policies, and cancellations, they need to have a strong understanding of insurance policies. They often verify both the completeness of an application and the accuracy of the insurance company's records. Insurance claims examiners and investigators often investigate questionable claims or claims that exceed the amount the insurance company is willing to pay. Investigators and examiners spend most of their time checking claim applications for accuracy, obtaining information needed for decisions from experts, and consulting current policy about claims.

Executive, managerial, and administrative jobs make up about 30 percent of the positions in the insurance field. Three examples of job titles found at this level of employment in the insurance industry are risk manager, sales manager, and underwriter. Risk managers develop the policies the insurance company follows when making decisions regarding claims. These policies are developed by analyzing historical data about natural disasters, car accidents, and other situations that may result in physical or financial loss. Sales managers sell insurance products, assist clients with questions about policies, and supervise staff. They make up the majority of managers in local sales offices. Finally, underwriters review applications for insurance and the level of risk involved in agreeing to issue an insurance policy. Essentially, the underwriter determines whether to accept or reject the application and how much a client should pay in premiums.

A smaller percentage, about 15 percent, of salaried employees in the insurance industry is made up of salespeople, often called insurance brokers or insurance agents, who focus on selling insurance policies to businesses and individual customers. Insurance agents can sell insurance exclusively for one insurance company or insurance policies issued by several different insurance companies. Some of the typical types of insurance polices an agent or broker may sell include health, life, annuities, property, casualty, and disability. In addition to these services, some agents are now licensed to sell mutual funds, annuities, and securities.

An even smaller career field in the insurance industry is the area of actuary science. Although there may not be as many actuaries as there are salespeople in insurance, they are very important to the industry. Actuaries set rates paid by customers at a level where the premiums that are collected will generate enough money to cover the claims that are paid out. Yet the premiums cannot be too expensive or customers will switch to other insurance companies. Actuaries accomplish this by studying the probability of an insured loss and the premium rates of other insurance companies.

Education requirements for jobs in the insurance industry vary, depending on the position and its responsibilities. Many of the entry-level clerical positions in the insurance industry require only a high school diploma. Higher-level executive, managerial, and sales positions require more education, with employers usually preferring to hire college graduates. Most managerial positions are filled by promoting people from within the organization. Such employees usually have a college education, some special training in the insurance industry, and experience with the company. Actuaries typically have a college degree in actuary science, math, or statistics. After completing college, actuaries must pass a series of exams over a period of five to ten years to become fully qualified. Overall, advancement opportunities are good in the insurance industry.

Earnings for insurance clerks and clerical staff are below those of insurance examiners, adjusters, and investigators. Higher annual salaries are typical for higher-level general managers and top executives. Salaries for sales agents are difficult to pinpoint because many are paid a salary, plus commissions and plus bonuses for reaching sales goals. In addition, an agent's earnings will rapidly increase as he or she gains experience and develops a client base.

The employment rate for the insurance industry is projected to increase more slowly than the average for all industries combined. Job growth in the insurance field is expected to be limited by the downsizing of large insurance companies, computerization, and a trend that points toward direct-mail and telephone sales campaigns. One area of growth in this industry is that of financial services and products sales. Another growth area stems from the need to cover large liability awards resulting from lawsuits. Finally, the number of claims professionals will grow faster than any other position in the industry because of the need for better customer service and actual inspection of damaged property or consultation with doctors.

SECURITIES AND COMMODITIES CAREERS

There are large numbers of workers in this area of the finance industry. The national brokerage companies have extensive systems of branch offices throughout the country; as a result, these brokerage firms employ the majority of the workers in this industry. Headquarters for these firms are located in New York City, where most of the executives and support personnel work. Mutual fund management companies and regional brokerages also employ many people. Although it is very well known, the New York Stock Exchange actually employs a small number of people compared to the rest of the industry.

A great deal of attention is focused on tracking performance, transactions, and the value of investments. Brokerage clerks are responsible for the majority of the daily operations and for processing much of the paperwork that is generated. These positions are often considered entry-level jobs with the potential for promotion into securities sales and even into higher positions. For example, a sales assistant takes calls from clients, writes up the order, processes the paperwork, and keeps clients updated on their portfolio's performance. With experience and a license to buy and sell securities, brokerage clerks can be promoted into higher-level sales positions.

The largest number of people employed in the securities and commodities industry can be found in three occupations: securities, commodities, and financial services sales. These careers involve buying and selling shares of stocks, mutual funds, and other financial services. The majority of these workers are sales representatives who work directly with individual investors. They are known as brokers, account executives, or financial consultants. Securities and commodities brokers differ in the investments they buy and sell. Securities brokers typically buy and sell stocks, bonds, and mutual funds. Commodities brokers buy and sell futures contracts for metals, energy supplies such as oil, and agricultural products. In addition to buying and selling securities, brokers can advise and educate their clients on investments, saving for retirement, and tolerance for risk. Overall, brokers spend a great deal of time marketing their services and products in order to establish a strong customer following.

Financial planners go a step further in advising and educating their clients. They often provide advice on investments, investing for retirement, tax planning, and employee benefits. Their strategy tends to be more of a comprehensive approach to advising clients on financial matters when compared to brokers. These planners can also buy and sell stock, mutual funds, bonds, and annuities.

Investment bankers and financial analysts make recommendations about potential profits from investments in specific companies by reviewing the companies' financial records and evaluating market trends. They also play a very important role in determining the market value for stocks that are traded publicly or stocks being purchased when a company is merging with or acquiring another company. Financial analysts often specialize in a specific industry sector, such as technology stocks.

Another career in the securities and commodities area of the finance industry is that of portfolio manager. These finance professionals are responsible for investing large amounts of money. The portfolios they manage are often mutual funds, pension funds, trust funds, and funds for individuals who are investing very large amounts of money. Most importantly, portfolio managers must have a clear understanding of a mutual fund's or a client's investment goals in order to ensure that the investment decisions they make meet the financial goals and guidelines set by the mutual fund or client.

As a whole, the workers in this area of the finance industry are well educated and highly trained. Even entry-level brokerage clerk positions often require a college degree. Also, to sell securities professionals are required to pass an examination testing their knowledge of investments. The National Association of Securities Dealers (NASD) conducts this testing and licenses professionals to sell a variety of investment products. Most brokers and sales assistants obtain the Series 7 license from the NASD by passing the General Securities Registered Representative Exam. In addition to passing the exam, these professionals are required to take classes on regulatory issues and new investment products in order to keep their licenses. Currently, there is no special licensing requirement to become a financial planner. However, many financial planners earn a certified financial planning (CFP) or chartered financial consultant (ChFC) designation. The CFP is issued through the CFP Board of Standards and the ChFC is offered by the American College. A series of exams on investments, taxes, insurance, retirement, and estate planning must be passed in order to receive one of these designates. In addition, the CFP must follow the rules and regulations set forth by the CFP Board of Standards.

Most of the workers in the entry-level analyst and managerial positions have a college degree and studied finance, general business administration, economics, accounting, or marketing. In order to advance, many take part in management trainee programs where they briefly work and learn about different departments. To advance further and gain access to higher salaries and more prestigious positions, many people obtain a master's degree in business administration.

For many brokers and commodities dealers, income is based on a salary and on commissions from the sale or purchase of stocks, bonds, or futures contracts. When the economy is strong these commissions and bonuses are much higher than they are when the economy is in a slump. Another factor in determining earnings in this area of finance is the amount of assets the manager is responsible for managing.

Yearly earnings for entry-level brokerage clerks are at the start of the scale. Further up the scale are financial analysts and sales agents. At the next level are the financial managers. The highest-paid professionals in the securities and commodities industry are general managers and top executives. Many firms also offer their employees profit sharing and stock options. In addition, most salaried employees receive health benefits, paid vacation, and sick leave.

Job growth in this industry is being fueled by several factors. First, more than ever, people are investing in securities as a way to save money and plan for retirement, resulting in a large influx of money into the stock market. Second, although online trading is reducing the need for direct contact with brokers, there is still a need for investment advice. Finally, the increased demands of investing in a complex global market have created a need for skilled investment managers. According to the *Occupational Outlook Handbook*, these factors have contributed to an employment growth projection of 40 percent for this segment of finance careers, which is much greater than the 15 percent projected for all other industries combined.

SEE ALSO *Finance*

BIBLIOGRAPHY

Career Guide to Industries, 2004–05 Edition (2004). U.S. Department of Labor, Bureau of Labor Statistics. Washington, DC: The Bureau.

Careers in Focus: Financial Services (2006). New York: Ferguson Publishing Company

Occupational Outlook Handbook, 2004–05 Edition (2004). U.S. Department of Labor, Bureau of Labor Statistics. Washington, DC: The Bureau.

Pandy, Anil, and Okusanya, Omotayo T. (2001). *The Harvard Business School Guide to Careers In Finance 2001 Edition.* Boston: Harvard Business School Press.

Mark D. Wilson

CAREERS IN INFORMATION PROCESSING

Information processing is defined as the collection of data into an organized and readable format. It is the process of changing raw data into information that can be used to make decisions and solve problems. Careers that process information are referred to as information technology (IT) positions. IT uses computer hardware and software to collect, maintain, protect, process, and distribute information. Careers include positions that fall within three broad categories: hardware, software, and management.

IT HARDWARE CAREERS

Careers in the IT hardware area include product design, development, manufacturing, service, and repair. Engineering degrees, particularly those of electrical engineers, are the basis for product development teams in all hardware areas. The development of motherboards, random-access memory chips, networking products, graphics and sound cards, and disk drives define modern computer development. Ergonomics engineers provide expertise on design, look and feel, physical interface, and usability for all new products in IT.

Individuals who are interested in assembly, service, and repair of IT hardware components may be able to obtain nondegree jobs. These jobs normally require industry certification that includes A+, Net+, Comptia, or on-the-job training from specific vendors as well as specific industry certifications offered by Oracle, Cisco, Sun Microsystems, and Microsoft. Skills required for hardware careers include hands-on capability, being comfortable with test and evaluation equipment, and the ability to troubleshoot a problem to successful conclusion. The ability to write clear and concise engineering evaluations and trouble reports separates the most successful hardware engineers from their peers.

IT SOFTWARE CAREERS

Careers in software design and development fall into two categories: programmers and analysts. Programmers work in one or many programming languages each of which has specific software applications. These languages may work only on mainframes, only on personal computers, or only on networks. The more languages programmers are fluent in, the more valuable they are to their employer, but every programmer must be exceptional in at least one language. Languages in vogue in the first decade of the twenty-first century included .Net, C# (C sharp), Java, Visual J++, XML, Perl, and Ada. Programmers usually have a degree in computer science or advanced mathematics, but it is

Careers in information processing

- Computer Programmers
- Computer Systems Administrators
- Computer Consultant
- Data Communications Analysts
- Database Administrators
- Design and Development
- Ergonomics Engineers
- Help Desk
- Implementation and Evaluation
- Information Security Specialists
- IT Manufacturing
- Medical Record/Health Information Technicians
- Network Managers/Administrators
- Product Design and Development
- Computer Sales
- Security Managers/Administrators
- Computer Service and Repair
- Software Analysts
- Software Sales
- Software/Computer Support Specialists
- Support Managers/Administrators
- System Analysts
- Web Design Specialists

Table 1

not unusual to see exceptionally gifted teenage programmers who have not completed high school. Programming ability, more than education, is the requisite for employment. Most organizations that hire younger programmers will pay for their collegiate education and advanced degrees.

Programming requires specific skills to be successful. Programmers must be precise and detail oriented. They must have the patience to find one bad line of code among millions and recognize the error and how to fix it in the most expedient manner possible. The very best programmers are both creative and logical, using both sides of the brain to accomplish their tasks. All programmers must have exceptional time management skills since they are always under a deadline. Finally, programmers must be able to operate in teams. Programming teams are the de facto standard in twenty-first century IT.

Software analysts are programmers who advance to the point of analyzing new customer needs or product requirements and define specifications for new software or software upgrades. They develop needs analysis documents that specify software tools or features that will improve or enhance existing software. When completely new software is needed, a client request is often ill-defined. It is up to the software analyst to interpret this request and develop a strategy to create software that meets the needs of the client. Software analysts must be able to think outside the box, see possibilities that do not exist in available software, and create a development plan that programmers can use in the creation of the new software.

IT MANAGEMENT CAREERS

Management positions in IT departments include jobs at all levels of the design, development, implementation, evaluation, and sales cycles. Product and process managers are responsible for design, development, and production of IT hardware and software components. Once the components are available for sale, sales managers are responsible for placing the product with customers. Once the customer has the product, network managers, support managers, and security managers become responsible for usability, upkeep, and safety.

Managers and team leaders with extensive experience may choose to work independently as consultants. Consultants may work for specific consulting organizations, such as Deloitte & Touche, Gartner, and EDS, or develop their own contacts and work on specific projects as independent contractors. In an era of IT layoffs, with jobs being outsourced to foreign workers, more and more skilled IT personnel are choosing the consultant role. This provides them independence, increased salary, increased responsibility, and the opportunity to showcase their skills. The downside of independent consulting is the lack of guaranteed work, no corporate-paid benefits, and the uncertainty associated with getting the next contract.

OUTSOURCING AND OFFSHORING

A significant trend in the new millennium is the outsourcing of programming, help desk, software support, and related services. Workers in such countries as India, China, Taiwan, and Pakistan are receiving multiyear contracts to take over these functions for large- and medium-sized organizations. The impact of these job losses directly affects low- and midlevel programmers and support personnel whose jobs have been sent overseas. Two reasons are routinely given for these job losses: first, significantly lower employee salaries and second, the availability of highly skilled and available workforces. Organizations who outsource these primary functions report mixed results. While costs for employees and management are substantially reduced, response time, customer satisfaction, and the ability to directly oversee projects appear to be lacking. Outsourcing as a management decision will undoubtedly continue at least until foreign workers begin to demand comparable salary, benefits, and lifestyle.

SUMMARY

The U.S. Bureau of Labor Statistics predicted that between 2002 and 2012 the following occupations would show the most growth in new jobs:

- Network systems and data communications analysts
- Network and computer systems administrators
- Medical records and health information technicians
- Computer software engineers
- Database administrators
- Computer support specialists and systems analysts
- Computer programmers
- Information security specialists

Even in an era of outsourcing and offshoring, the IT industry still provides lucrative, challenging, and interesting career opportunities. Students who acquire the requisite education, skills, and industry training can find rewarding careers in all areas of information technology.

SEE ALSO *Information Processing*

Mark J. Snyder
Lisa E. Gueldenzoph

CAREERS IN LAW FOR BUSINESS

A wide variety of choices are available for a career in law. However, work and determination are required to complete law school and pass a state bar examination.

To be admitted to law school, students must have completed a bachelor's degree, although generally without restriction concerning the choice of undergraduate major. Law students have bachelor's degrees in business, engineering, science, history, politics, and many other disciplines.

ENGAGING IN LAW PRACTICE

The individual states administer the licensing of lawyers. Requirements for attorneys to enter the law field vary from state to state. Generally, a prospective lawyer must pass a state bar examination following graduation from law school. In a very few states, a person is automatically admitted to practice upon graduation from law school. It is possible for a person to sit for bar examinations and become licensed to practice in more than one state.

The states also control discipline once lawyers are admitted to practice. Complaints from clients or others may be made to the state bar, which reviews them and imposes discipline, if necessary. Discipline may range from fines or suspensions up to disbarment. In many states, the state supreme court reviews disciplinary actions imposed upon lawyers.

AREAS OF LEGAL PRACTICE

Lawyers deal with business organizations, individuals, international business, labor relations, educational law, poverty law, legal research and writing, and other areas.

Legal Practice With Domestic Business Organizations. In the United States, attorneys engage directly with business organizations in many fields in which they practice.

Publicly held corporations. Many areas of law involve publicly held corporations (stock available for purchase by any investor). For example, control and management have legal ramifications, as do capital procurement and maintenance. Attorneys are called upon to settle a wide range of disputes, such as those developing between stockholder and corporation.

Antitrust legislation. Antitrust laws prohibit price fixing, which could result when businesses gain monopoly power in their field. Major legislation in this realm includes the Sherman Act of the 1890s, the Clayton Act of 1914, and the Cellar-Kefauver Act of 1950. The Robinson-Patman Act prohibits manufacturers from discriminating against small retailers in favor of large chains. These acts are enforced by the Federal Trade Commission and the Antitrust Division of the Department of Justice.

Unfair trade practices. These laws involve various types of business competition, especially with reference to trademarks, price maintenance, and price discrimination.

Patents. Patents are issued by the Patent and Trademark Office of the U.S. government. They grant inventors exclusive rights to make, sell, and use inventions in the United States for a given period of time. Patents often require an attorney's counsel.

Copyrights. Copyrights provide protection for original works of literary, dramatic, musical, or artistic expression. The Copyright Office of the Library of Congress administers these laws.

Trademarks. Trademarks are used to distinguish one business firm's products from another. Their symbols may be a word or words, name, design, picture, or sound. Trademark rights have an indefinite life. A company may register its trademark with the U.S. Patent and Trademark Office in Arlington, Virginia, or with the trademark office in its state.

Accounting. Accounting statements provide financial details concerning the operation of a business or other form of organization. Balance sheets list assets (things that are owned), liabilities (debts), and net worth (assets minus liabilities). Income statements show net income for a period of time (income minus expenses). Business firms, particularly those with stockholders, must prepare honest and conservative financial statements. Very stringent laws have been passed dealing with accounting practices.

Negotiations. Attorneys orchestrate a variety of negotiations, including those involving injury claims, criminal charges, family disputes, and commercial disputes.

Business organizations. Business organizations become involved with the law of employment, agency, partnership, limited partnership, and other types of unincorporated associations.

Regulated industries. Price, supply, and services are a part of Regulation C control in various industries, such as transportation agencies and public utilities. Regulatory policy can involve interaction among legislatures, administrative agencies, and the courts. Advanced legal work may be required for business planning and counseling concerning corporate and tax issues. Clients often need representation before regulatory bodies and at administrative hearings.

Contracts. Attorneys become involved in the creation of promissory liability, the interpretation of words and conduct as well as the nature of obligations assumed by entering into contracts. They also solve problems relating to breach of contract, unfairness as a reason for avoiding contractual liability, and the rights of those not a party to the contract.

The Uniform Commercial Code. Articles 3, 4, and 5 concern negotiable instruments, bank collection systems, and letters of credit. Article 9 deals with secured transactions; Article 7 deals with documents of title.

Creditors' and debtors' rights. Attorneys deal with consumer credit regulation, including attachments, garnishments, assignments for the benefit of creditors, judgments, and bankruptcy.

Insurance law. This branch as law deals with property, life, and liability insurance; fire and automobile insurance forms; and the regulation of insurance companies' policies and practices.

Remedies. Remedies of quasi-contract, constructive trust, equitable lien, and reformation must be applied to redress enrichment secured by tort, part performance of contract, duress, or mistake.

Government contracts. Laws and regulations apply to contracts with governmental bodies and agencies.

Legal Practice for Individuals. Individuals need a wide range of legal services in the area of business. Some services are provided for investors or owners in business situations; others, for persons finding themselves in difficulty.

Trust and estates. Legal consideration must be given to community property systems, federal gift and estate taxes on property transfers, estate planning not involving property, living wills, delegation of health care decision-making, and gifts to as well as guardianship of minor children. Related legal forms involve living trusts and gift strategies.

Family law. Family law can involve relationships of married couples, unmarried couples, or couples undergoing divorce. Additional family relationships that may involve lawyers include parent and child. unmarried parents, neglected children, foster care, and adoption.

Taxes. Attorneys can assist in tax planning for individuals. especially where issues arise between the taxpayer and the Internal Revenue Service or state taxing authorities. They also deal with taxation implications for corporate organization, reorganization, and liquidation. Some attorneys deal with international tax problems, such as jurisdictional rules, tax situations between industrialized countries and developing countries, and host country taxation of foreign persons.

Real estate transactions. In this field, lawyers deal with options, binder contracts, and rights and duties between vendor and vendee among other things. Lawyers also practice in basic land contract and mortgage law as well as real estate recording systems. They work with both land-use controls and water-rights laws. They may also deal with environmental law and institutions.

Legal Practice for International Business. International trade in the world is becoming more prevalent and increasingly legally complex. This increases openings for interested attorneys.

International legal practice may involve issues of recognition and nonrecognition of governments and nations, interpretation of treaties and other international agreements, the effect of peace and war, and international claims.

Lawyers may advise on the risks, assumptions, and benefits of doing business in a foreign country. Questions may arise concerning international commercial transactions and investments, the impact of U.S. securities and antitrust laws, and trade laws of the United States and other countries.

Labor Relations Law. State and federal laws deal with employee representation, collective bargaining, and employer-union practices. These laws, the National Labor Relations Act, and related federal and state labor laws often make legal counsel necessary.

Attorneys provide counsel in collective bargaining and with the negotiation and arbitration processes.

Statutes such as those involving fair employment practices, workers' compensation, fair labor standards, unemployment compensation, and Social Security protect workers against insecurity, discrimination, economic exploitation, and physical damage. Their purpose is to guard against unequal opportunity linked to race, sex, religion, age, physical disability, and other factors.

Legal questions linked to public policy arise from representation questions, limitations on the right to strike, grievance arbitration, impasse procedures, and the scope of bargaining.

Educational Law Practice. Legal issues arise from educational financing, integration and segregation, punishment methods applied to children, and alternatives to public school education.

Poverty Law. Although often unable to pay, the poor frequently require legal services. Some indigents make contact with public-interest law firms or offices that provide legal services for the poor. In this area, lawyers deal with issues such as welfare rights, health, education, public assistance, or housing.

Legal Research and Writing. Some lawyers engage in legal research and writing. This work involves library and computerized research, brief and memorandum writing, organization of legal material, and prediction of rules of law. Much of this activity takes place in law schools or at the appellate court level.

Other Areas of Law Practice. There are a number of additional areas of law practice. These include legal problems related to technology and society, bioethics, science, psychiatry, and attempts to achieve progress in developing countries.

U.S. COURT SYSTEM

The court system also offers career opportunities. An understanding of the court system is relevant to a career discussion. The courts in the United States fall within two classifications: the federal court system and the state court systems.

Federal Court System. The federal court system is comprised of the Supreme Court, circuit courts of appeal, and district courts. There are also specialized federal courts.

The U.S. Supreme Court is the final court of appeal for both civil and criminal law. It was created by Section 1, Article III of the U.S. Constitution. Title 28 of the U.S. Code establishes its jurisdiction. The Court's organization is specified by legislation, although the rules governing case presentations are formulated by the Court itself.

Judicial review is an important power given to the U.S. Supreme Court. This refers to (1) declaring invalid laws that violate the U.S. Constitution, (2) asserting the supremacy of federal laws or treaties if they differ from state and local laws, and (3) serving as the final authority on the interpretation of the U.S. Constitution.

The U.S. Supreme Court includes a chief justice and eight associate justices. Appointed by the president with the approval of the Senate, they serve for life or until they retire, resign, or are impeached.

The U.S. Supreme Court has original jurisdiction in some cases, particularly where a state is a party or diplomatic personnel are involved. The remaining cases come from lower courts. Requests for review number approximately 4,500 annually; less than 200 cases are selected for decision by the U.S. Supreme Court.

Some appeals to the U.S. Supreme Court come from any of the twelve federal courts of appeal or the ninety-four federal district courts. These cases involve the U.S. Constitution, federal laws or cases in which the U.S. government is a party, disputes between residents of different states ("diversity" jurisdiction), or matters assigned by federal legislation.

Appeals also come from specialized federal courts. The Court of Military Appeals reviews courts-martial cases appealed from military courts. These cases concern offenses committed by members of the armed forces and are sometimes brought before the U.S. Supreme Court.

The U.S. Court of Claims hears cases dealing with claims against the federal government. Its decisions may also be appealed to the U.S. Supreme Court. In addition, the U.S. Supreme Court may rule on cases involving decisions of U.S. Custom offices, such as import duties.

State Court Systems. Each state has its own court system. These courts are created by state statute or constitution to enforce state civil and criminal laws. Most of the states have trial courts, intermediate courts of appeal, and a supreme court.

Most states have local trial courts—municipal, county, district, and small-claims courts. Millions of civil and criminal cases are tried at this level. Other state courts may include police courts, magistrate's courts, justices of the peace, and probate or surrogate courts that handle wills and inheritances. There are also traffic courts, juvenile courts, and domestic relations courts.

State appeals courts (sometimes called error-correcting courts) review trial court cases to determine if errors caused an incorrect decision. Their decisions may be appealed to the federal courts, including the U.S. Supreme Court in certain instances.

Supreme courts in each state, like the U.S. Supreme Court at the federal level, interpret their state constitutions, statutes enacted by their state legislatures, and the body of state common law.

SEE ALSO *Law in Business*

BIBLIOGRAPHY

Margolis, Wendy, Gordon, Bonnie, Puskarz, Joe, and Rosenlieb, David, eds. (2005). *The ABA-Official Guide to ABA-Approved Law Schools*, American Bar Association and Law School Admission Council.

Martindale-Hubbell Law Directory, (2001). Martindale-Hubbell.

"U.S. Courts," Retrieved October 15, 2005, from http://www.uscourts.gov/.

Craig A. Bestwick
G. W. Maxwell

CAREERS IN MANAGEMENT

Management is a very exciting and rewarding career. A career in management offers status, interesting work, and the satisfaction of working closely with other people. People are considered the most important resource in organizations. If they perform effectively, the organizations will succeed. Managers work closely with people, ranging from top managers to clerical workers, to ensure that organizations achieve their objectives.

A management career also offers the opportunity to make the world a better place. Managers help organizations succeed. When organizations are successful, there is better utilization of resources, less stress among employees, less chaos in society, and a better quality of life for all. Effective managers play an important role in shaping the world in which we live. Certo and Certo (2006) emphasized this point when they stated that our society would not be as developed as it is today without effective managers to guide its organizations.

WHAT DO MANAGERS DO?

Management is a people job. The manager coordinates the work of other people to ensure that the unit is run efficiently and profitably. A manager may have direct responsibility for a group of people in one department or a team of people from several different departments. For some managers, it could mean supervising one person.

Managers provide overall direction and leadership for the organization. The manager sets clear objectives for the team and makes sure they know what the focus is, assigns duties to team members, and encourages them to perform those duties. The manager also evaluates the team's actual performance against organizational objectives and decides on promotions and salary increases where appropriate. When team members are not performing satisfactorily, the manger makes the changes necessary to ensure that they reach the company's objectives. Managers use their people skills and business skills, such as marketing and cost controls, to achieve the company's objectives while at the same time making sure to stay within budget.

The manager's job is varied. Managers are involved with planned and unplanned activities. These activities include scheduled and unscheduled meetings, inspection tours, report writing, new product launches, disagreements among employees, customer grievances, and changes in business trends. According to Miller and associates (1996), a manager should be able to shift continually from person to person and from one subject or problem to another. A manager who is also the business owner makes all the daily decisions involved in the business.

Managers make things happen in organizations. They decide what will be done, who will do it, when will it be done, and what resources will be used. They hire and train new employees, and they coordinate their departments' activities with other departments. Managers are the heart of organizations, the force that unites everything in the organization to ensure optimum efficiency and profitability.

TYPES OF MANAGEMENT CAREERS

In large organizations, managers work in a variety of areas, including operations, human resources, finance, and marketing:

- Operations managers see that the company's products and/or services meet quality standards and satisfy the needs of customers and clients. They plan production schedules to ensure the most efficient

use of plant, manpower, and materials. The operations manager is responsible for production control, inventory control, quality control, plant layout, and site selection. New graduates will start as management trainees. After successfully completing the program they will be promoted to production supervisor, then to plant manager. The top management position is vice president for operations.

- Human resources managers provide the organization with competent and productive employees. The duties of the human resources manager include human resource planning, recruiting and selecting employees, training and development, designing compensation and benefits systems, and formulating performance appraisal systems. In small firms one person may be responsible for all the human resource activities, while in large firms separate departments deal with each function.

- Financial managers deal with the financial resources of the organizations. They are responsible for such activities as accounting, cash management, and investments. They also keep up-to-date records for the use of funds, prepare financial reports, and gather information to assess the financial status of the organization.

- Marketing managers are responsible for getting customers and clients to buy the organization's products or services. They develop the business marketing strategy, set prices, and work closely with advertising and publicity personnel to see that products are promoted adequately.

Apart from the career opportunities in the specialized areas of management, management careers are also available in government agencies, hospitals, not-for-profit agencies, museums, educational institutions, and even political organizations. Good managers are also needed in foreign and multinational companies. All organizations exist for certain purposes and need good managers to guide their operations to achieve the best possible results. Regardless of the type of organization, managers are obviously one of its most important resources.

There are many specific management positions, including the following:

Management trainees work under the supervision of an experienced manager while learning. They receive formal training in a variety of management areas. The management trainee position is designed to prepare trainees for work as administrators or managers. Their duties include providing customer service, preparing work schedules, and assisting with coordination of support services.

Labor relations managers have an interest in labor law and are good communicators. They negotiate collective bargaining agreements and develop grievance procedures to handle complaints. When problems arise between management and labor, they interpret and administer the labor contract and resolve the disputes according to the terms of the contract. They also work closely with the human resources director on issues such as wages, benefits, pensions, and work practices.

Administrative services managers coordinate and direct supportive services of larger businesses and government agencies. They are responsible for services such as clerical support, records management, payroll, conference planning, information processing, and materials distribution and scheduling. However, corporate restructuring has resulted in many organizations outsourcing their administrative services. This means that the demand for administrative services managers will greatly increase in companies providing management consulting, management services, and facilities support services.

Food service managers have very similar duties to restaurant managers, catering managers, and fast-food restaurant managers. In fact, the food service manager works in a variety of facilities, including fast-food restaurants, hospitals, and school cafeterias. Food service managers coordinate all aspects of the food and beverage activities for the organization. They set the standard for quality food service, hire and assign employees, and plan menus. They also perform some clerical duties, such as payroll and inventory.

Building managers, also called real estate managers, administer rental properties, such as apartment buildings and office buildings, for the owners. As the agents of the owners, they market vacant space, negotiate leases, set and collect rents, and arrange for security and maintenance of the properties. They also handle all the bookkeeping and accounting records and provide periodic reports to the owners.

Fitness center managers are physically fit and interested in exercise science. Companies, government agencies, and cruise ships with fitness facilities are looking for managers who can develop programs that satisfy customers' health and fitness needs. The fitness center manger conducts research to identify customer needs, develops and manages programs for the center and its clients, and monitors health and safety requirements. In small centers, the manager is also responsible for delivering fitness training and maintaining center equipment.

City managers, also called town managers, are responsible for the day-to-day operations of various departments of city government. A main responsibility of city managers is to prepare budgets for the city council's approval.

The city manager must also provide reports to the council members on ongoing and completed projects.

Health services managers work in clinics, hospitals, and health maintenance organizations (HMOs). They make most of the business or operational decisions in the health care facility. The health services manager establishes billing procedures, handles budgets, supervises staff, and interacts with the public. Health services managers start as management trainees or assistant administrators.

Hotel and motel managers are responsible for the full range of activities in a lodging establishment. These include guest registration and checkout, housekeeping, accounting, maintenance and security, and food service. The manager is also responsible for coordinating activities, such as meetings and other special events. In large hotels, assistant managers are responsible for the operations of various departments. Hotel managers begin as department heads and, after gaining experience, are promoted to manager.

Retail managers supervise employees and deal with customer complaints. In addition, they are responsible for managing the store inventory. They keep up-to-date records of merchandise, make pricing decisions, and decide on advertising and promotions. The retail manager works long hours and may be employed in a wide variety of stores, including department stores, discount stores, or specialty stores. Retail managers often begin as assistant managers responsible for a department in a large store. They are then promoted to merchandising manager or to store manager.

Sales managers exist in almost every firm and perform one of the most important functions in the organization. They find customers for the company's products and/or services and therefore provide revenues for the company. They recruit, hire, train, and supervise the company's sales force. Sales managers begin as sales representatives. Being a successful sales representative leads to promotion to senior sales representative or sales supervisor, then to a sales manager.

Procurement managers, sometimes called purchasing agents or industrial buyers, buy the supplies and materials needed by a company. They must be knowledgeable about the various vendors and their offerings. They must acquire the best possible deals for their company in terms of price, quality, delivery, and payment schedules. Managers in large companies sometimes specialize in specific types of purchases.

EDUCATIONAL REQUIREMENTS

Educational requirements for a career in management vary. However, most employers require a college degree in either the liberal arts, social sciences, or business administration. A master's degree in business administration (MBA) is also a common requirement. For students interested in getting into management trainee programs in major corporations, an MBA gives the best opportunity for these top programs. An MBA or the master's degree in health services administration is generally required for a career in health service management.

Apart from major corporations, many other organizations have management trainee programs that college graduates can enter. Such programs are advertised at college fairs or through college job placement services. These programs include classroom instruction and might last one week or as long as one year. Training for a department store manager, for example, might include working as a salesperson in several departments, in order to learn about the store's business, before being promoted to assistant manager.

In small organizations, depending on the type of industry, experience may be the only requirement needed to obtain a position as manager. When an opening in management occurs, the assistant manager is often promoted to the position, based on past performance. In large organizations a more formal process exists. The management position to be filled is advertised with very specific requirements concerning education and experience.

Persons interested in a career in management should have good communication skills and be able to work well with a variety of people, ranging from other managers, supervisors, and professionals, to clerks and blue-collar workers. They should be analytical, flexible, and decisive. They should also be able to coordinate several activities simultaneously and be able to solve problems quickly. Ability to work under pressure and cope with deadlines is also important.

Recruiters look for self-starters who can use their initiative, recognize what needs to be done, like responsibility, and have high ethical standards. Self-starters and team players are the types of people corporations are looking for.

CAREER OPPORTUNITIES IN MANAGEMENT

According to the U.S. Bureau of Labor Statistics (1996), the number of managerial jobs was expected to increase by 17 percent by 2005. The greatest increase in management positions is projected to be in health services, management consulting, marketing, advertising, and public relations fields. Opportunities for management careers in financial services, restaurant and food service, and real estate industries will also grow at a faster than average rate through 2005. Educational institutions, industrial production, and administrative services were expected to grow about as fast as the average for all occupations through 2005.

The outlook for management careers is good, despite the headlines about downsizing and corporate restructuring. As the economy continues to grow, many businesses are expanding, and this creates additional opportunities for management jobs. Also, as the economy becomes more global, an increasing number of American firms are expanding overseas, and an equally large number of foreign companies are doing business in the United States. This means that despite the layoffs of some middle-level managers, there continues to be a worldwide need for good managers.

The future is bright for women and minorities interested in management. Title VII of the Civil Rights Act 1964 bans discrimination in employment on the basis of race, color, religion, sex, or national origin. Many companies, because of affirmative action rules, are actively seeking out women and minorities to fill management positions.

As a result, women are well represented at the lower levels of management; however, the number of top executive positions remains low. Only about 10 percent of the top jobs in the 500 largest U.S. companies are held by women. However, companies are taking steps to attract and promote women executives.

Minority groups remain underrepresented at all levels of management. A Rutgers University study (cited in Certo and Certo, 2006) found that in 400 *Fortune* 1000 companies, less than 9 percent of all managers were members of a minority group (p. 16). Since more and more new entrants into the labor market are members of various minority groups, it is becoming essential for business to recruit talented minority managers.

There are numerous opportunities for management careers available in all types of organizations, especially small and medium-sized companies. Every organization is looking for competent managers who can increase employee performance and help the company to be successful. Mosley and associates (1996) put it best when they said: "Managers in organizations of all sizes, in all industries, and at all levels have an impact on performance … they make the difference between success and failure for their companies" (p. 7).

SOURCES OF ADDITIONAL INFORMATION

For further information, readers are encouraged to contact any of the following organizations:

American Hotel and Lodging Association, 1201 New York Avenue, NW, #600, Washington, DC 20005-3931, www.ahma.com

American Management Association, 1601 Broadway, New York, NY 10019, www.amanet.org

Administrative Management Society, 4622 Street Road, Trevose, PA 19047

National Management Association, 2210 Arbor Boulevard, Dayton, OH 45439, www.ncssma.org

Women in Management, P.O. Box 3451, Stamford, CT 06905, www.wimonline.org

SEE ALSO *Management*

BIBLIOGRAPHY
Boone, Louis E., and Kurtz, David L. (2006). *Contemporary Business 2006*. Mason, OH: South-Western.

Certo, Samuel C., and Certo, S. Trevis (2006). *Modern Management* (10th ed.). Upper Saddle River, NJ: Pearson/Prentice Hall.

Griffin, Ricky W. (2005). *Management*. Boston: Houghton Mifflin Co.

Miller, Donald S., Catt, Steven E., and Carbon, James R. (1996). *Fundamentals of Management*. St. Paul, MN: West Publishing Company.

Mosley, Donald C., Pietri, Paul H., and Megginson, Leon C. (1996). *Management: Leadership in Action*. New York: HarperCollins.

Robbins, Steven P., and Coulter, Mary. (1999). *Management*. Upper Saddle River, NJ: Prentice-Hall.

Occupational Projections and Training Data (1996). Bulletin No. 2471. Washington, DC: U.S. Bureau of Labor Statistics Author.

Thaddeus McEwen

CAREERS IN MARKETING

Is a career in marketing for you? To be successful in a marketing career, an individual must have good communication, critical thinking, and people skills. In addition to these skills, a majority of individuals employed in marketing-related occupations possess excellent time-management skills, the ability to work with a wide variety of people, and a capacity for self-motivation. These individuals must be able to establish timelines, goals, and objectives and adhere to them.

According to the U.S. Bureau of Labor Statistics, the number of individuals who earn a living in marketing-related careers: advertising, sales, or public relations has increased rapidly. In 2005 almost one-third of all U.S. workers were employed in marketing-related positions, and marketing principles were being applied to more and

more business and nonbusiness organizations—service firms, nonprofit institutions, political candidates, and so forth. Therefore, a high demand for individuals with marketing training was emerging as a critical criterion for employment in the twenty-first century. Two major explanations have been offered for the continuously increasing demand for marketing skills: deregulation of major industries (banking, telecommunications, and transportation) and increased foreign competition.

Considering the increased role of marketing in the U.S. economy, members of the twenty-first-century workforce need to be familiar with the major marketing-related occupations. According to Philip Kotler and Gary Armstrong, in 2006, the major marketing occupations are: (1) advertising, (2) brand and product management, (3) industrial marketing, (4) international marketing, (5) marketing research, (6) new-product planning, (7) physical distribution/distribution management, (8) public relations, (9) retail marketing, and (10) sales and sales promotion marketing. A discussion of each of these major marketing occupations follows.

ADVERTISING

Advertising is a vital business activity that requires planning skills, fact-gathering ability, creativity, artistic talent, and written and oral communication skills. Individuals who are employed in advertising typically perform the following tasks:

- Search for factual information
- Read avidly
- Borrow ideas
- Talk to customers
- Develop print layouts, package designs, storyboards, corporate logotypes, trademarks, and symbols
- Specify style and size of typography
- Arrange advertisement details for reproduction

Thus, advertising involves all components of marketing—product, price, promotion, and place. Because all the above tasks require working with people who are clients or potential clients, an individual must be personable, diplomatic, and sincere. Further, to succeed in advertising, a person needs to be self-motivated and able to present information about a product to varying audiences.

BRAND AND PRODUCT MANAGEMENT

Individuals involved in brand and product management (BPM) are planners, directors, and controllers of the positioning of consumer packaged goods for sale in a dramat-

Career opportunities for which a marketing background is well suited

- Advertising Specialist
- Brand Manager
- Business to Business Sales
- Customer Service
- Distribution Specialist
- Industrial Sales
- International Sales
- Marketing Manager
- Marketing Research Analyst
- Merchandise Manager
- Product Manager
- Product Planning
- Promotion Manager
- Public Relations Manager
- Public Relations Specialist
- Purchasing Agent
- Purchasing Manager
- Receiving Specialist
- Retail Buyer
- Retail Sales
- Sales Manager
- Sales Representative
- Shipping
- Wholesale Buyer

Table 1

ically and quickly changing marketplace. BPM marketers use research as well as packaging, manufacturing, and forecasting to position products for sale to the most appropriate audience. Individuals employed in this aspect of marketing must have the leadership capability to move a product from obscurity to a national awareness in a relatively short period. Usually, the job-related responsibilities of BPM marketers increase with the growth and development of a particular product.

Thus, successful BPM marketers operate in a high-pressure, fast-paced, and constantly changing environment, since a major component of BPM marketing focuses on the financial position of the product under development. In addition, BPM marketers must be results-oriented and creative; possess strong interpersonal, communication, and analytical skills; have entrepreneurial leanings; and exhibit high levels of diplomacy, perseverance, and drive.

INDUSTRIAL MARKETING

Industrial marketing involves the planning, sale, and service of products used for commercial or business purposes. In addition to having excellent oral and written communication skills, industrial marketers must be self-reliant individuals with the ability to understand customer requirements as well as the knowledge to propose the purchase of a particular product that will satisfy customers'

needs and wants. In essence, industrial marketers are consultants who assist clients in ascertaining the appropriate product for their particular needs.

Whether employed in sales, service, product design, or marketing research positions, industrial marketers must develop and maintain ongoing business relationships with suppliers of goods and services as well as with clients. Therefore, the selling relationship is a process of maintaining and building a continuous business relationship. As in any marketing-related career, industrial marketers must have excellent people skills as well as good oral and written communication skills. In addition, a successful industrial marketer should have a broad educational background with an emphasis in technology in order to be able to link that technology to human needs and wants.

INTERNATIONAL MARKETING

With the increasing role of foreign industry in the United States, as well as increasing U.S. interests abroad, individuals with relevant foreign language skills, in addition to an understanding of selected foreign cultures, are needed to assist with the day-to-day operations of business. To be able to conduct business effectively and efficiently and to implement marketing strategies abroad, international marketers need to understand the social, economic, and political climates of foreign countries. Marketing personnel interested in this area may be required to travel and/or relocate to a foreign country to oversee company operations and to create a presence in that country's economy. In addition to the language requirement, potential international marketers need appropriate communication skills as well as diplomatic skills in order to work with foreign leaders and function in foreign economic systems.

MARKETING RESEARCH

Marketing researchers are asked to ascertain why a particular product is or is not being purchased by consumers. Based on the interpretation of data collected in marketing research, market researchers make recommendations for enhancing or eliminating existing products as well as developing new products. In addition, promotional activities are based on data collected by marketing researchers. Individuals employed in marketing research occupations must understand statistics, data/information-processing analysis, psychology, consumer behavior, and communication.

Marketing researchers interact with other marketing occupations to define problems within a particular product line as well as to identify the appropriate processes to be used to analyze and resolve those problems. A critical component of this position is the ability to present solutions to business problems in a manner that is easily understood by colleagues and constituents. Specifically, marketing researchers provide information concerning consumers, marketing environment, and competition to relevant internal and external publics. Therefore, strong analytical, methodological, and communication skills are a must for success in this arena.

NEW-PRODUCT PLANNING

New-product planning involves the creation and development of new products for an organization. Because individuals who enter this arena typically have been successful in other areas of marketing, they tend to have an excellent knowledge of and background in marketing, be familiar with the processes for conducting marketing research, be capable of generating sales forecasts, and have a background in technology. A new-product-planning marketer conceptualizes, researches, and evaluates new ideas. During the evaluation process, the new-product-planning marketer considers both the feasibility of the production of the product and the product's potential profitability. These individuals must also possess the ability to motivate, coordinate, and direct others.

New-product planning is applicable to the marketing in such areas as consumer products, consumer services, hospital and medical services, and public service programs. Because new-product development is constantly changing, a person who enters this field should have a high degree of tolerance for uncertainty and the unknown, yet nonetheless be able to develop a definite agenda and a "report card" to inform superiors about success with new products.

PHYSICAL DISTRIBUTION/DISTRIBUTION MANAGEMENT

Physical distribution is one of the largest arenas of marketing and has been defined as the analysis, planning, and control of activities concerned with the procurement and distribution of goods. Activities involved with the physical distribution process include transporting, warehousing, forecasting, processing orders, inventorying, production planning, selecting sites, and servicing customers. Individuals employed in this marketing area are concerned with the processes or methods needed to deliver the product from the manufacturer to the wholesalers to the retailers to, ultimately, the consumer.

The physical distribution process is an extensive and diverse area that involves the physical transportation of products and the various activities associated with purchasing, selling, and channel-management functions. Individuals who enter physical distribution marketing need interpersonal leadership ability in order to deal with diverse and challenging internal and external publics, as well as excellent analytical and communication skills.

PUBLIC RELATIONS

Public relations marketers either assist in the management of the images of products or individuals, or anticipate and handle public problems or complaints. Thus individuals employed in the public relations aspect of marketing create an image or message for or about an individual or organization, as well as maintaining that image with the media. This image or message needs to be communicated effectively, efficiently, and persuasively to the intended audience. To be successful in public relations, an individual needs to be people-oriented and to have excellent oral and written communication skills, as well as a background in journalism.

RETAIL MARKETING

Individuals in retail occupations deal directly with consumers or customers. Retail marketing also involves the management of sales personnel, selection and ordering of merchandise, and promotion of selected merchandise, as well as inventory control, store security, and product accounting. Typical jobs are as buyers, sales managers, department managers, and store managers. To be successful in retail marketing, individuals must be self-motivated and possess excellent people skills.

A rapidly growing component in retail marketing is direct-response marketing (DRM). DRM attempts to deliver the product from the manufacturer to the consumer by the use of direct mail, print and broadcast media, telephone marketing, catalogs, in-home presentations, door-to-door marketing, electronic ordering and funds transfer, and videotex. Attributes needed for success in the area of DRM include creativity, initiative, perseverance, and quantitative competence. In essence, retail marketers use their professional knowledge and competence to improve company profits by informing various publics of appropriate assortments of goods and service in locations that are easily accessible.

SALES AND SALES PROMOTION MARKETING

Sales and sales promotion marketers (SSPMs) need a thorough understanding of their company's products. SSPMs must not only sell a product, but also develop and maintain effective relationships with customers. The main goal of SSPMs is to inform customers about and provide them with appropriate products in an expeditious manner. Such individuals focus on providing information to potential clients/customers by interacting with them directly and personally. Beyond this, they close sales and maintain existing accounts to ensure client/customer satisfaction and loyalty.

To be successful, an individual must know the product, the customer, and the market. Further, a good understanding of people and appropriate people skills are useful in dealing with diverse and challenging internal and external publics. Because the process of selling involves persuasive two-way communication between a seller and a client, individuals in this area of marketing must be people-oriented as well as knowledgeable about the product and the manner in which the product can be used to satisfy buyers' needs and wants.

CONCLUSION

In the twenty-first century, the role of marketing in the U.S. economy will change as consumers react to ever-changing technology and as businesses respond to an ever-changing marketplace. Because of changing technology and the changing marketplace, the roles and functions of conventional marketing as it is known today will be constantly rethought and redefined. In addition, the four Ps of marketing—product, price, place, and promotion—will also be redefined and restructured. With the dynamic changes facing the marketing environment, the demand for marketing-oriented personnel will continue to increase, making marketing-related careers an exciting occupational choice for the twenty-first century.

SEE ALSO *Marketing*

BIBLIOGRAPHY

Careers in focus: Advertising and marketing. (2004). New York: Ferguson.

Kotler, Philip, and Armstrong, Gary (2006). *Principles of marketing* (11th ed.). Upper Saddle River, NJ: Pearson Prentice-Hall.

Stair, Lila B., and Stair, Leslie (2002). *Careers in marketing* (3rd ed.). Chicago: VGM Career Books.

U.S. Department of Labor. Bureau of Labor Statistics. (2005). *Occupational outlook handbook, 2004–05.* Washington, DC.

Randy L. Joyner

CELLER-KEFAUVER ANTI-MERGER ACT OF 1980

SEE *Antitrust Legislation*

CENTRALIZATION

SEE *Organizational Structure*

CERTIFICATIONS, LICENSURES, AND DESIGNATIONS

The changing global and U.S. economy, along with expectations of the workforce, has, in many instances, brought about a need for higher credentialing standards for employees in many areas of the workplace. Also, higher performance expectations have prompted some types of businesses to initiate increased standards in the area of advanced certification, licensure, and designation, so as to facilitate recognition of their work environments as professions and the employees functioning within those environments as professionals. The term *professional* denotes the individual as an expert in that field. In addition to being employed in a particular field, R. S. Poore stated that one of the factors designating a person as a professional is an earned credential. Such an earned certification, licensure, or designation places individuals at a higher knowledge and expertise level compared to their counterparts who do not possess such a credential.

The meaning of the word *profession* can examined from both sociological and philosophical perspectives. The sociological view of the definition of *profession* has its origins in the social sciences. Generally, this view is based on the perception that an occupation is a profession when a job has high social status, high income, and/or important social functions. Consequently, carpentry could not be considered a profession because the education and social status of carpenters are low. Law, however, would be considered a profession because of the perception of high income and high social status. Therefore, according to this perspective, a job is considered to be a profession when the perception by the public is that it is not a menial, repetitive task.

The philosophical view attempts to define profession in two ways—the Cartesian and the Socratic. The Cartesian view is developed by asking oneself the question of what it means in certain terms, testing the definition by the use of counterexamples, revising the belief based on the counterexamples, and continuing the process until one has one's own belief in good order. Thus, the Cartesian "approach attempts to define professions by making sense of a person's mind." Furthermore, electricians could consider their occupation a profession because individuals practice their own beliefs of professional conduct and workmanship. Conversely, the Socratic approach views a profession as a group undertaking; thus, a profession cannot consist of only one individual. Additionally, this view attempts to find a common ground between the practitioner and the philosopher whereby the process of revising the definition of the specific profession continues until everyone within the organization believes that it is the appropriate definition. Hence, individuals within the group must share a common job or occupation, such as physicians, lawyers, and dentists.

Regardless of the acceptance of the sociological view or the philosophical view, the common theme appears to be the existence of standards for individuals who are working toward a common moral endeavor. Thus, for an occupation to be considered a profession, many people are needed who earn a living performing tasks closely aligned with beliefs that enhance the completion of those tasks. Furthermore, a code of guiding ethical principles may also be used to assist with completing job-related tasks, thereby allowing individuals employed in this area to be perceived as professionals. In turn, the area can then be considered a profession.

Professions and organizations continue to seek avenues to increase the level of competence of their workforce and enhance their profession. Therefore, in order to accomplish this objective many professions have procedures in place—or are in the process of implementing such procedures—for individuals to obtain a higher credentialing certification, licensure, and designation. The certification, licensure, or designation may denote to the public more competent employees with a higher level of skills to accomplish more effectively the tasks that they are employed to perform.

Candidates seeking certification, licensure, or designation in a particular field must complete a prescribed course of study at an accredited college or university, as well as a successful score on an appropriate licensing examination. This certification, licensure, or designation ensures that individuals practicing in a particular profession have met the appropriate educational training and that they abide by the expected standards of professional conduct. Thus, many professions issue certifications, licensures, and designations based upon the successful completion of a degree from an accredited college or university and a minimum score on a national exam. Furthermore, additional certifications, licensures, and designations may be added after supplementary training.

The increased demand for excellence and recognition throughout organizations, nationally and internationally, has prompted a wave of instituting processes that require employees to become more highly skilled and more knowledgeable in their field of endeavor. B. L. Hawkins implied that one could earn a certificate, licensure, or designation from some organizations by attending a specific number of courses, where a degree is not earned. Yet, certification, licensure, or designation programs ending with degree completion have required evaluation through standardized examinations. The Chauncey Group International noted that certification

is based on the voluntary action on the part of an occupational or professional group to institute a system by which it can grant recognition to those practitioners who have met some stated level of training and experience. Such individuals are granted a certificate or diploma attesting to the fact that they have met the standards of the credentialing organization and are entitled to make the public aware of their credentialed status (Schoon and Smith, 2000, p. 146).

Thus, the impact of higher certification standards may be to increase the quality of services provided and to continue to ensure the vitality of the world's economy. A sampling of certifications, designations, and licensures available to business and finance professionals appear in Table 1.

BIBLIOGRAPHY

Davis, Michael (2003, April 25). *What can we learn by looking for the first code of professional ethics?* retrieved from http://www.iit.edu/˜schmaus/colloquium/davis.html

Hawkins, B. L. (2000). Credentials pay off. *Facilities Design and Management, 19*(6), 48–51.

Kleiner, Morris M. (2005). *Licensing occupations: ensuring quality or restricting competition?* Kalamazoo, MI: W.E. Upjohn Institute for Employment Research.

Poore, R. S. (1997). Professional certification. *Information Systems Security, 6*(1), 29–30.

Rouse, W. A., Jr. (2004). *Student achievement in a North Carolina local education agency: National board certified teachers vs. non-national board certified teachers.* Unpublished doctoral dissertation, East Carolina University, Greenville, North Carolina.

Schoon, Craig G., and Smith, I. Leon (2000). *The licensure and certification mission: Legal, social, and political foundations.* New York: Forbes Custom.

Randy L. Joyner

CERTIFIED INTERNAL AUDITOR

A certified internal auditor (CIA) is an individual who has met the requirements for certification as established by the Institute of Internal Auditors (IIA). Requirements relate to education, experience, and successful completion of an examination. Achieving the credential as a certified internal auditor is tangible evidence of meeting professional qualifications established by the IIA.

The IIA, established in 1941 at a meeting in New York City, now has a worldwide membership of more than 70,000 in more than one hundred counties. The CIA examination was first administered in 1974.

THE EXAMINATION

The CIA examination is offered twice a year, once in May and once in November. The exam has four parts:

Part I: Internal audit process

   Auditing

   Professionalism

   Fraud

Part II: Internal audit skills

   Problem solving and evaluating audit evidence

   Data gathering, documentation, and reporting

   Sampling and mathematics

Part III: Management control and technology

   Management control

   Operations management

   Information technology

Part IV: Audit environment

   Financial accounting

   Finance

   Managerial accounting

   Regulatory environment

Each part of the exam consists of eighty multiple-choice questions. To complete the examination successfully, a candidate must be familiar with the Institute of Internal Auditors' *Standards for the Professional Practice of Internal Auditing* and the institute's *Code of Ethics*. It is not necessary to be a member of the IIA in order to take the examination. However, a one-year free membership is offered to any nonmember who passes the CIA examination.

The Board of Regents, which administers the CIA exam, recognizes the accomplishments of other professional certifications. Therefore, individuals who already have a certification are eligible to receive credit for part of the exam. Part IV of the exam was designed to offer a Professional Recognition Credit. Candidates who wish to apply for the Professional Recognition Credit need to submit a registration form with a copy of the certificate or letter from the sponsoring organization noting that the person has completed the exam requirements. The sponsoring organization may be contacted to verify the information supplied by the candidate.

For example, in the United States an individual who is a certified public accountant, certified management accountant, certified information systems auditor, or certified bank auditor is eligible to receive Professional Recognition Credit for Part IV of the CIA examination. In Australia, Canada, and the United Kingdom, the char-

tered accountant designation would receive Professional Recognition Credit by the Board of Regents.

The exam is nondisclosed. Individuals taking the exam sign a statement indicating that they will not disclose questions and answers subsequent to taking the exam. The IIA considers disclosure of the exam questions by a person who took the examination to be a violation of the code of ethics.

The passing score for the exam is 75 percent. In 1996 there were 4,646 candidates. The average pass rate by exam part is 45 percent. (*Gaylord and Reid,* 1997).

EXPERIENCE REQUIREMENT

In order to become a CIA, there is an experience requirement of twenty-four months of internal auditing or its equivalent. Representative equivalent experience can include quality assurance, internal control assessment, or external auditing. A master's degree can be substituted for one year of experience. The Board of Regents determines the acceptability of equivalent work experience.

More information is available from the Institute of Internal Auditors at 247 Maitland Ave., Altamonte Springs, Florida 32701-4201, (407)937-1100, or http://www.theiia.org.

SEE ALSO *Auditing*

BIBLIOGRAPHY

Gaylord, Gloria L., and Ried, Glenda E. (2006). *Careers in Accounting* (4th ed.). New York: McGraw Hill.

Pickett, K.H. Spencer (2004). *The Internal Auditor at Work: a Practical Guide to Everyday Challenges.* Hoboken, N.J.: John Wiley & Sons.

Charles H. Calhoun

CERTIFIED MANAGEMENT ACCOUNTANT (CMA)/CERTIFIED IN FINANCIAL MANAGEMENT (CFM)

The certified management accountant (CMA) and the certified in financial management (CFM) programs are designed to recognize the unique qualifications and expertise of those professionals engaged in management accounting and financial management. These certifications provide distinction in today's economic climate and afford the opportunity to certify expertise in the business areas that are critical to the decision-making process. The CMA and CFM certifications, introduced by the Institute of Management Accountants (IMA) in 1972 and 1996, respectively, have global recognition and have received the endorsement of approximately 200 corporate and academic organizations.

The CMA and CFM Programs have four objectives:

- To establish management accounting and financial management as recognized professions by identifying the role of the professional, the underlying body of knowledge, and a course of study by which such knowledge is acquired

- To encourage higher educational standards in the management accounting and financial management fields

- To establish an objective measure of an individual's knowledge and competence in the fields of management accounting and financial management

- To encourage continued professional development

The content of the certification examinations represents the knowledge, skills, and abilities required by business professionals in the fields of management accounting and financial management. The content is validated periodically by a practice analysis conducted by the IMA. The content, covered in four examination parts for each program, encompasses:

- Economics, finance, and management

- Financial accounting and reporting (CMA) or corporate financial management (CFM)

- Management reporting, analysis, and behavioral issues

- Decision analysis and information systems

The Financial Accounting and Reporting Exam is waived, upon request, for individuals who have passed the U.S. CPA Exam; this is not the case, however, for the Corporate Financial Management Exam.

Candidates for certification must meet the following criteria to become a CMA or CFM:

- Education: Candidates must hold a baccalaureate degree, in any area, from an accredited college or university. Students attending accredited U.S. universities may take the examinations but must satisfy the education requirement prior to certification. Degrees from institutions outside the United States must be evaluated by an independent agency. The education requirement may also be satisfied by holding a CPA license to practice or other comparable professional qualification.

- Employment: Candidates must complete two continuous years of professional experience in management accounting and/or financial management. Qualifying experience consists of positions requiring judgments regularly made employing the principles of management accounting and financial management. This experience may be completed prior to or within seven years of passing the examination.

- Character references: The names of two character references must be submitted at the time of application.

- Ethics: Candidates for certification must agree to comply with the Standards of Ethical Conduct for Practitioners of Management Accounting and Financial Management.

- Membership: Candidates for certification must be a member of the IMA because the certification programs are a privilege of membership.

The CMA and CFM programs have been designed to meet the evolving needs of business and are focused on the dynamic roles that management accountants and financial managers play in business, public, and government accounting. Certified professionals are more frequently identified for promotion and have greater earning potential than those professionals who are not certified. To gather more information or to join the CMA/CFM programs, visit the IMA Web site at www.imanet.org or call (800)638-4427 for a certification information booklet.

Priscilla Payne

CERTIFIED PUBLIC ACCOUNTANT

SEE *Uniform Certified Public Accountant Examination*

CHAIN OF COMMAND

SEE *Organizational Structure*

CHANGE PROCESS

Companies that are able to compete successfully in today's rapidly changing business environment, which is characterized by globalization of the economy, exploding information technology, downsizing, restructuring, and new employer-employee relationships, must be ready to make significant changes in the way they operate. Changes can be realized in a number of areas. They can, for example, be observed in attitude or behavior. Many major organizational changes, however, are technological ones. Sometimes these changes are not intended to change behavior, but they almost always do in some respect. Another type of change is replacement of personnel; when top management is impatient with the pace of productivity, they often replace key individuals. Changes also occur in organizational structure, formal roles and jobs, control systems, work processes, and other elements of the organization's internal environment.

The motivation for change typically stems from the fact that something is not working (e.g., continued negative feedback from customers, reduced profitability, threats of acquisition, or other market pressures). For most organizations, a crisis is the catalyst for change. While a crisis may be sufficient to initiate a change, it takes much more to successfully integrate the change into the work processes. Managers must have more than an extensive knowledge of the marketplace, how to compete in it, and what internal structures must be in place to make the company successful.

Every change effort should be accompanied by an action plan. Once a compelling reason to change has been identified, it is necessary to create a picture of what the change will require, how the organization will effect it, and what the organization will look like when the change has been implemented. Although each action plan for change will be unique, all plans should follow a basic structure: (1) identification of a course of action and allocation of resources to achieve the organization's change goals; (2) designation of the authority, responsibility, and relationships that will drive the change efforts; (3) determination of who will lead the change effort and the specific roles and responsibilities of these individuals; (4) a description of the procedures and processes that will expedite implementation of the change; (5) identification of the training that will be required to enable people to incorporate the change into their work processes; and (6) identification of the equipment, tools, or machinery that will affect the way work is accomplished.

Many organizational changes are initiated and implemented through the authority of top levels of management. The problems are defined and solutions are developed by top-level managers based on information that is gathered by others with help from a limited number of people. Once a decision is made, the changes are often communicated to people in the organization through memo, speech, policy statement, or verbal command. Since only a few people, usually at the top, are involved in making the decisions, the change is usually introduced very rapidly. However, this strategy has proved

to be largely ineffective in dealing with organizational change processes, particularly for successful integration. A common misconception about carrying out a change is that it must be directed from the top. The foundation of successful change management lies in involving the people who will be affected by the change.

Sharing responsibility for change is a process whereby those at the top and those at lower levels are jointly involved in identifying problems and/or developing solutions. Virtually continual interaction takes place between top and bottom levels. The shared responsibility or participative approach can be addressed in several ways: (1) Top management defines the problem and uses staff groups or consultants to gather information and develop solutions. These identified solutions are then communicated to lower-level groups in order to obtain reactions. The feedback from the lower levels is then used to modify the solution, and the communication process starts again. The assumption underlying this approach is that although involving others in the definition of the problem or its solution may be impractical, the solution can be improved and commitment obtained by involving lower levels. (2) Top management defines the problem but seeks involvement from lower levels by appointing task forces to develop solutions. The task forces provide recommendations to top management, where the final decision is made. These task forces are composed of people who will be affected by the change and have some level of expertise in the areas that will be affected by the proposed change. The assumption here is that those who have the expertise to solve the problems are those groups that are closer to the situation. Also, the group's commitment to the change may be made deeper by this involvement. (3) Task forces composed of people from all levels are formed to collect information about problems in the organization and to develop solutions. The underlying assumptions in this approach are that people at the top, middle, and lower levels are needed to develop quality solutions and that commitment must build at about the same rate at all levels. These approaches emphasizing shared responsibility usually take longer to implement but result in more commitment from all levels of the organization and more successful integration of the change into the work processes.

Understanding the factors that drive change and how people react to change is critical to the successful implementation of change. It is part of human nature to resist change. People prefer the security of familiar surroundings and often do not react well to changes in their work or social environment. Resistance to change often takes some typical forms. One typical reaction is denial, which individuals use to protect themselves. If the change never really occurs, it does not need to be addressed. Another common reaction is passive resistance where individuals agree on the surface with the need for change but are quietly unsupportive of it. Still others may respond with active resistance by openly disagreeing with the proposed change, lobbying against it, and encouraging others to do the same.

Many managers assume that if people think the change is a good idea, they will not resist it. Why would the work force resist changes if the changes will fix what they wanted fixed? People may want change, but not necessarily the changes that have been identified in the plan. Workers may have their own ideas about what should change, and frequently the changes they think fix the problem involve someone else changing, not them. In addition workers may think the ways to make things better is simply to adjust and manipulate their work processes, not to implement the drastic changes identified in the proposed plan. Alternatively, workers may not think that is wrong with the current way of working. Often the process of changing looks too hard, looks like it will take too much energy, and seems confusing. A strictly structured change process often ignores the ingrained human resistance to change. When that happens, people who are affected by the change end up expending most of their time and energy figuring out how to stop the change or altering the change until it looks like something they can live with. If the desired change is not very desirable to the work force, managers need to find out why. Insufficient information about the driving force behind the change and the benefits expected from it is likely to cause distress among those affected by the change. People tend to act in their own perceived self-interest. Managers often think of change initiatives in broader terms, while the work force tends to think of it differently, in more narrow terms of how the change will affect their work. Sometimes managers forget or overlook this reaction to change. Effective strategies for organizational change involve an understanding of the human beings in the work force.

Cultivating a sense of involvement and ownership in all individuals affected by the proposed change is critical. The more involved people feel in shaping their future, the less likely they are to criticize the outcome. An essential factor in managing effective change is communication—no amount is too much. Managers should identify the groups/individuals affected by the proposed change in order to determine the best communication methods to use. Newsletters, focus groups, bulletin boards, intranet pages, and lunchtime seminars are all effective ways of communicating to the work force. Managers need to be aware of how information flows through the organization and which communication methods will be most effective.

Also crucial to successful integration of change in an organization is the level of support from its leaders. Top levels of management must believe that the proposed course of action is the right one for the future of the organization. At all phases of the change process, top management representatives must strongly support the change processes and communicate that support to the work force. During the planning phase, top management representatives should explain the business reasons for the changes and the costs of not changing, tell employees what they can expect to happen and when, and enlist the support of other senior managers and stakeholders in the process. During the design phase, upper level management representatives should listen and respond to feedback from the organization and provide updates on the progress of the change. During the implementation phase, top management representatives should continue to listen to resistance and respond to feedback, stay involved in the process, ensure that adequate resources and training are available, measure performance toward expected results, and reward role models.

Effective and efficient methods of communication, education/training, and rewards/reinforcements should be built into the implementation plan. Appropriate training should be incorporated into the change plan to ensure that the work force can be productive with the new work processes and systems. However, communication and training may not be the only required elements to help ensure effective change implementation. As the work force envisions the change, managers may need to ensure that rewards are in place for changing—in other words, identification of "what's in it for me?" Recognition is needed to reinforce changes in an organization. Tangible and intangible rewards for changed behavior, new attitudes, and enhanced skills can be effective both in building support and advancing the changes.

Companies and people have no choice: they must change to survive. They do have a choice, however, in how they change. Understanding the forces that effect change, the process for change, and how to manage that process is critical to an organization's survival in today's turbulent world.

SEE ALSO *Management*

BIBLIOGRAPHY

BPR OnLine Learning Center (2005). Retrieved September 29, 2005, from http://www.prosci.com.

Brill, Peter L., and Worth, Richard (1997). *The Four Levers of Corporate Change.* New York: AMACOM.

Harvard Business Review on Change (1998). Boston: Harvard Business School Press.

Hesselbein, Frances, Goldsmith, Marshall, and Beckhard, Richard, eds. (1997). *The Organization of the Future.* San Francisco: Jossey-Bass Publishers.

Johnson, Spencer (1998). *Who Moved My Cheese? An A-mazing way to deal with change in your work and in your life.* New York: G.P. Putnam's Sons.

Nixon, Bruce (1998). *Making a Difference: Strategies and Tools for Transforming Your Organization.* New York: AMACOM.

Cheryl L. Noll

CHANNELS OF DISTRIBUTION

The word *channel* might bring to mind a waterway such as the English Channel, where ships move people and cargo. Or it might bring to mind a passageway such as the Chunnel, the railroad and car tunnel under the English Channel. Either image implies the presence of paths or tracks through which goods, services, or ideas flow. This imagery offers a good starting point for understanding channels of distribution.

The term *marketing channel* was first used to describe trade channels that connected producers of goods with users of goods. Any movement of products or services requires an exchange. Whenever something tangible (such as a computer) or intangible (such as data) is transferred between individuals or organizations, an exchange has occurred. Marketing channels, therefore, make exchanges possible. How do they facilitate exchanges? Perhaps the key part of any distribution channel is the intermediary. Channel intermediaries are individuals or organizations who create value or utility in exchange relationships. Intermediaries generate form, place, time, and/or ownership values between producers and users of goods or services.

Marketing channels were traditionally viewed as a bridge between producers and users. This traditional view, however, fails to fully explain the intricate network of relationships that underlie marketing flows in the exchanges of goods, services, and information. To illustrate, consider a prescription drug purchase. To get authorization to purchase the drug, one must visit a physician to obtain a prescription. Then, one might acquire the drug from one of several retail sources, including grocery store chains (such as Kroger), mass discounters (such as Wal-Mart), neighborhood pharmacies, and even virtual pharmacies (such as Drugstore.com). Each of these prescription drug outlets is a marketing channel. Pharmaceutical manufacturers, distributors, and their suppliers are all equally important links in these channels of distribution for pharmaceuticals. Sophisticated computer systems track each pill, cap-

sule, and tablet from its point of production at a pharmaceutical manufacturer all the way to its point of sale in retail outlets worldwide.

To appreciate the complexity of marketing channels, exchange should be recognized as a dynamic process. Exchange relationships themselves continually evolve as new markets and technologies redefine the global marketplace. Consider, for example, that the World Wide Web's arrival created a new distribution channel now accounting for trillions in electronic exchanges. It may come as a surprise that the fastest-growing segment of electronic commerce involves not business-to-consumer, (called B2C in today's Web language) but business-to-business (B2B) channels.

Whether these exchange processes occur between manufacturers and their suppliers, retailers and consumers, or in some other buyer-seller relationship, marketing channels offer an important way to build competitive advantages in today's global marketplace. This is so for two major reasons:

- *Distribution strategy lies at the core of all successful market entry and expansion strategies.* The globalization of manufacturing and marketing requires the development of exchange relationships to govern the movement of goods and services. As one sips one's preferred coffee blend at the neighborhood Starbucks, consider that consumers in China, Lebanon, and Singapore may be sipping that same blend. Then consider how the finest coffee beans from Costa Rica or Colombia get to thousands of neighborhood coffee shops, airports, and grocery stores around the world.

- *New technologies are creating real-time (parallel) information exchange and reducing cycle times and inventories.* Take as an example Dell Computer, which produces on-command, customized computers to satisfy individual customer preferences. At the same time, Dell is able to align its need for material inputs (such as chips) with customer demand for its computers. Dell uses just-in-time production capabilities. Internet-based organizations compete vigorously with traditional suppliers, manufacturers, wholesalers, and retailers. Bricks-and-mortars (organizations having only a physical location) and clicks-and-orders (organizations having only a virtual presence) are in a virtual face-off.

DEFINING MARKETING CHANNELS

The Greek philosopher Heraclitus wrote, "Nothing endures but change." Marketing channels are enduring but flexible systems. They have been compared to ecological systems. Thinking about distribution channels in this manner points out the unique, ecological-like connections that exist among the participants within any marketing channel. All marketing channels are connected systems of individuals and organizations that are sufficiently agile to adapt to changing marketplaces.

This concept of a connected system suggests that channel exchange relationships are developed to build lasting bridges between buyers and sellers. Each party then can create value for itself through the exchange process it shares with its fellow channel member. So, a channel of distribution involves an arrangement of exchange relationships that create value for buyers and sellers through the acquisition (procurement), consumption (usage), or elimination (disposal) of goods and services.

EVOLUTION OF CHANNELS

Marketing channels always emerge from the demands of a marketplace. Nevertheless, markets and their needs are always changing. It is true, then, that marketing channels operate in a state of continuous evolution and transformation. Channels of distribution must constantly adapt in response to changes in the global marketplace. Remember: Nothing endures but change.

At the beginning of the nineteenth century, most goods were still produced on farms. The point of production had to be close to the point of consumption. But soon afterward, the Industrial Revolution prompted a major shift in the American populace from rural communities to emerging cities. These urban centers produced markets that needed larger and more diverse bundles of goods and services. At the same time, burgeoning industrialization required a larger assortment of production resources, ranging from raw materials to machinery parts. The transportation, assembly, and reshipment of these goods emerged as a critical part of production.

During the 1940s, the U.S. gross national product grew at an extraordinary rate. After World War II (1939–1945) ended, inventories of goods began to stockpile as market demand leveled off. The costs of dormant inventories—goods not immediately convertible into cash—rose exponentially. Advancements in production and distribution methods came to focus on cost-containment, inventory control and asset management. Marketers soon shifted from a production to a sales orientation. Such attitudes as "a good product will sell itself" or "we can sell whatever we make" receded. Marketers confronted the need to expand sales and advertising expenditures to persuade individual customers to buy their specific brands. The classic four Ps classification of marketing mix variables (product, price, promotion, and place) emerged as a marketing principle. Distribution issues were relegated to the place domain.

This innovative selling orientation inspired the development of new intermediaries as manufacturers sought fresh ways to expand market coverage to an increasingly mobile population. The selling orientation required that more intimate access be established to a now more diversified marketplace. In response, wholesale and retail intermediaries evolved to reach consumers living in rural areas, newly emerging suburbs, and densely populated urban centers.

Pioneering retailers such as John Wanamaker (1838–1922) in Philadelphia and Marshall Field (1834–1906) in Chicago quickly sprouted as Goliaths in this brave new retail world. Small retailers came of age, as well, offering specialized operations tailored to meet the needs of a changing marketplace. Retailers and their channels evolved in lockstep with the movements and needs of the consumer marketplace. As always, marketing channels were evolving in response to changing marketplace needs.

The impact of two remarkable innovations taken for granted today—the car and the interstate highway system—cannot be ignored. These transforming innovations simultaneously stimulated and satisfied Americans' desire for mobility. Manufacturers suddenly began selling their wares in previously inaccessible locations. Millions of Americans fled from the cities to the suburbs in the 1950s and 1960s. Retailers quickly followed. Yet another channel phenomenon emerged, this one involving groups of stores situated together at one site. The suburban shopping center was born. Its child, the mall, soon followed.

In 1951 the earth moved. That was the year marketers first embraced the marketing concept. The marketing concept decrees that customers should be the focal point of all decisions about marketing mix variables. It was accepted that organizations should make only what they could market instead of trying to market whatever they could make. This new perspective had a phenomenal impact on channels of distribution. Suppliers, manufacturers, wholesalers, and retailers were all forced to adopt a business orientation initiated by the needs and expectations of each channel member's customer.

The marketing concept quickly reinforced the importance of obtaining and then applying customer information when planning production, distribution, and selling strategies. A sensitivity to customer needs became firmly embedded as a guiding principle by which emerging market requirements would be satisfied. The marketing concept remained the cornerstone of marketing channel strategy for some thirty years. It even engendered the popular 1990s business philosophy known as total quality management. Small wonder, then, that in Japan the English word *customer* has become synonymous with the Japanese phrase for "honored guest."

The customer focus espoused within the marketing concept has a broad, intuitive appeal. Yet the marketing concept implicitly suggests that information should flow unidirectionally from customers to intermediaries and from intermediaries to manufacturers. This unnecessarily restrictive and reactive approach to satisfying customers' needs has been supplanted by the relationship marketing concept. As modern communication and information management technologies emerged, channel members found they could now establish and maintain interactive dialogues with customers. Ideas and information began to be exchanged—bidirectionally—in real time between buyers and sellers. Channel members learned that success comes from anticipating the needs of one's customers before they do. The earth had moved, again, as the relationship marketing philosophy was widely adopted.

How important is a customer dialogue? Sophisticated database and interactive technologies enable channel members to quickly identify changes in customers' preferences. This, in turn, allows manufacturers to modify product designs nimbly. Relationship marketing allows manufacturers to mass-customize offerings and to reduce fixed costs associated with production and distribution. Retailers and wholesalers make better-informed merchandising decisions. This is yet another lesson in the costs of carrying unwanted products. Relationship marketing yields greater customer satisfaction with the products and services they acquire and consume. And why not? The customer's voice was heard when the offering was being produced and distributed.

Relationship marketing is driven by two principles having particular relevance to marketing channel strategy:

- Long-term, ongoing relationships between channel members are cost-effective. (Attracting new customers costs over ten times more than retaining existing customers.)

- The interactive dialogue between providers and users of goods and services is based on mutual trust. (The absence of trust imperils all relationships. Its presence preserves them.)

THE ROLE OF INTERMEDIARIES

This progression from a production to a relationship orientation allowed many new channel intermediaries to emerge because they created new customer values. Intermediaries provide many utilities to customers. The provision of contractual efficiency, routinization, assortment, or customer confidence all create value in channels of distribution.

One of the most basic values provided by intermediaries is the optimization of the number of exchange relationships needed to complete transactions. Contractual

efficiency describes an aspiration shared among channel members to move toward the point where the quantity and quality of exchange relationships is optimized. Without channel intermediaries, each buyer would have to interact directly with each seller. This interaction would be extremely inefficient. Imagine its impact on the total costs of each exchange.

When only two parties participate in an exchange, the relationship is a simple dyad. Exchange processes become far more complicated as the number of channel members increases. The number of exchange relationships that can potentially develop within any channel equals:

$$\frac{3^n - 2^{n+1} + 1}{2}$$

where n is the number of organizations in a channel. When n is 2, only one relationship is possible. When n doubles to 4, up to 25 relationships can unfold. Increase n to 6, and the number of potential relationships leaps to 301. The number of relationships unfolding within a channel quickly becomes too large to efficiently manage when each channel member deals with all other members. Channel intermediaries are thus necessary to facilitate contractual efficiency. But as the number of intermediaries approaches the number of organizations in the channel, the law of diminishing returns kicks in. At that point, additional intermediaries add little new value within the channel.

McKesson Drug Company, the nation's largest drug wholesaler, acts as an intermediary between drug manufacturers and retail pharmacies. About 600 million transactions would be necessary to satisfy the needs of the nation's 50,000 pharmacies if these pharmacies had to order on a monthly basis from each of the 1,000 U.S. pharmaceutical drug manufacturers. When this example is extended to the unreasonable possibility of daily orders from these pharmacies, the number of transactions required rises to more than 13 billion. The number of transactions is nearly impossible to consummate. Nevertheless, introducing 250 wholesale distributors into the pharmaceutical channel reduces the number of annual transactions to about 26 million. This reduction in transactions is contractual efficiency.

The costs associated with generating purchase orders, handling invoices, and maintaining inventory are considerable. Imagine the amount of order processing that would be necessary to complete millions upon millions of pharmaceutical transactions. McKesson offers a computer-networked ordering system for pharmacies that provides fast, reliable, and cost-effective order processing. The system processes each order within one hour and routes the order to the closest distribution system. Retailers are relieved of many of the administrative costs associated with routine orders. Not coincidentally, the system makes it more likely that McKesson will get their business as a result of the savings.

Routinization refers to the means by which transaction processes are standardized to improve the flow of goods and services through marketing channels. Routinization has several advantages for all channel participants. To begin with, as transaction processes become routine, the expectations of exchange partners become institutionalized. The need to negotiate on a transaction-by-transaction basis disappears. Routinization permits channel partners to concentrate more attention on their own core businesses. Routinization clearly allows channel participants to strengthen their relationships.

Organizations strive to ensure that all market offerings they produce are eventually converted into goods and services consumed by members of their target market. The process by which this market conversion occurs is called sorting. In marketing channels, assortment is often described as the smoothing function. The smoothing function relates to how raw materials are converted to increasingly more refined forms until the goods are acceptable for use by final consumers. The next time you purchase a soda, consider the role intermediaries played in converting the original syrup to a conveniently consumed form. Coca-Cola ships syrup and other materials to bottlers throughout the world. Independent bottlers carbonate and add purified water to the syrup. The product is then packaged and distributed to retailers, and consumers buy it. That is assortment. That is what channels of distribution do. Two principal tasks are associated with the sorting function:

1. *Categorizing.* At some point in every channel, large amounts of heterogeneous supplies have to be converted into smaller homogeneous categories. Returning to pharmaceutical channels, the number of drugs available through retail outlets is huge. More than 10,000 legal drugs exist. In performing the categorization task, intermediaries first arrange this vast product portfolio into manageable therapeutic categories. The items within these categories are then categorized further to satisfy the specific needs of individual consumers.

2. *Breaking bulk.* Producers want to produce in bulk quantities. Thus, it is necessary for intermediaries to break homogeneous lots into smaller units. Over 60 percent of the typical retail pharmacy's capital is tied to the purchase and resale of inventory. The opportunity to acquire smaller lots means smaller capital outflows are necessary at a single time. Consequently,

pharmaceutical distributors continuously break bulk to satisfy retailers' lot-size requirements.

The role intermediaries play in building customer confidence is their most overlooked function. Several types of risks are associated with exchanges in channels of distribution, including need uncertainty, market uncertainty, and transaction uncertainty. Intermediaries create value by reducing these risks.

Need Uncertainty. The term *need uncertainty* refers to the doubts that sellers have regarding whether they actually understand their customers' needs. Usually neither sellers nor buyers understand exactly what is required to reach optimal levels of productivity. Since intermediaries act like bridges linking sellers to buyers, they are much closer to both producers and users than producers and users are to each other. Since they understand buyers' and sellers' needs, intermediaries are well positioned to reduce the uncertainty of each. They do this by adjusting what is available with what is needed.

Few organizations within any channel of distribution are able to accurately state and rank their needs. Instead, most channel members have needs they perceive only dimly, while still other firms and persons have needs of which they are not yet aware. In channels where there is a lot of need uncertainty, intermediaries generally evolve into specialists. The number of intermediaries then increases, while the roles they play become more complex and focused. The number of intermediaries declines as need uncertainty decreases.

Market Uncertainty. Market uncertainty depends on the number of sources available for a product or service. Market uncertainty is difficult to manage because it often results from uncontrollable environment factors. One means by which organizations can reduce their market uncertainty is by broadening their view of what marketing channels can and perhaps should do for them. Channels must be part of the strategic decision framework.

Transaction Uncertainty. Transaction uncertainty relates to imperfect channel flows between buyers and sellers. When considering product flows, one typically thinks of the delivery or distribution function. Intermediaries play a key role in ensuring that goods flow smoothly through the channel. The delivery of materials must frequently be timed to coincide precisely with the use of those goods in the production processes of other products or services. Problems arising at any point during these channel flows can lead to higher transaction uncertainty. Such difficulties could arise from legal, cultural, or technological sources. When transaction uncertainty is high, buyers attempt to secure multiple suppliers, although this option is not always available.

Uncertainty within marketing channels can often be minimized only through careful actions taken over a prolonged period of exchange. The frequency, timing, and quantities of deliveries typify the processes involved in matching channel functions to the need for efficient resource management within marketing channels. Channel members are often unaware of their precise delivery and handling requirement needs. By minimizing transaction uncertainty, channel intermediaries help clarify these processes. Naturally, as exchange processes become standardized, need, market, and transaction uncertainty is lessened. As exchange relationships develop, uncertainty decreases because exchange partners know one another better.

WHERE MISSIONS MEET THE MARKET

The functions performed by marketing intermediaries concurrently satisfy the needs of all channel members in several ways. The most basic way that market needs can be assessed and then satisfied centers on the role channel intermediaries can perform in helping channel members reach the goals mapped out in their strategic plans. Because they link manufacturers to their final customers, channel intermediaries are instrumental in aligning all organizations' missions with the market(s) they serve. Channel intermediaries foster relationship-building activities and are indispensable proponents of the relationship marketing concept in the marketing channel.

Channels of distribution are not all there is to marketing, but without them all the behaviors and activities known as marketing become impossible. Channels of distribution represent the final frontier within which most sustainable strategic marketing advantages can be achieved. Channels of distribution are the instruments through which organizational missions meet—come face to face with—the marketplace. Strategic success or failure will take place there.

SEE ALSO *Marketing; Retailers; Wholesalers*

BIBLIOGRAPHY

Boone, Louis E., and Kurtz, David L. (2006). *Contemporary business*. Mason, OH: Thomson/South-Western.

Boone, Louis E., and Kurtz, David L. (2006). *Contemporary marketing* (12th ed.). Eagan, MN: Thomson South-Western.

Churchill, Gilbert A., Jr., and Peter, J. Paul (1998). *Marketing: Creating value for customers* (2nd ed.). New York: Irwin McGraw-Hill.

Dickson, Peter R. (1997). *Marketing management* (2nd ed.). Fort Worth, TX: Dryden.

Hoffman, K. Douglass (2006). *Marketing principles and best practices* (3rd ed.). Mason, OH: Thomson South-Western.

Kotler, Philip, and Armstrong, Gary (2006). *Principles of marketing* (11th ed.). Upper Saddle River, NJ: Pearson Prentice Hall.

Pelton, Lou E., Strutton, David, and Lumpkin, James R. (2002). *Marketing channels: A relationship management approach* (2nd ed.). Boston: McGraw-Hill/Irwin.

Rosenbloom, Bert (2004). *Marketing channels: A management view* (7th ed.). Mason, OH: Thomson South-Western.

Allen D. Truell
Lou E. Pelton
David Strutton

CHECKING ACCOUNTS
SEE *Financial Institutions*

CHIEF FINANCIAL OFFICERS ACT OF 1990 AND FEDERAL FINANCIAL MANAGEMENT ACT OF 1994

The Chief Financial Officer Act of 1990 (CFO Act) provided tight financial control over agency operations and the central coordination of financial management functions to support an efficient administration of the executive branch. It centralized organization of federal financial management, required long-term strategic planning to sustain modernization, and began the development of projects to produce audited financial statements for the federal government. As Title IV of the Government Management Reform Act of 1994, the Federal Financial Management Act of 1994 extended the scope of the CFO Act by requiring agency-wide financial statements and a consolidated government-wide financial statement.

RATIONALE FOR CFO ACT

By the late 1980s, it was apparent that the financial systems of the federal government were in a deplorable state. The savings and loan crisis had developed undetected, financial scandals had occurred in the Department of Housing and Urban Development, numerous high-risk programs had been identified, and seriously deficient systems of internal control were common.

Financial management systems were obsolete and inefficient. Management, program funding, and revenue-generating activities were impaired. Hundreds of separate accounting systems made monitoring, comparison, and auditing difficult. Enormous investments to upgrade financial systems were failing to achieve the benefits of integration because planning and coordination were lacking.

No one federal official or agency had statutory responsibility for coordination of federal financial management practices. Congress was concerned that management functions and innovations were being neglected as a result of the preoccupation of the Office of Management and Budget (OMB) with the budget.

In 1990 the CFO Act was adopted to improve the general and financial management practices of the federal government by establishing a structure for the central coordination of financial management. The act provided for the implementation of accounting systems and internal controls to produce reliable financial information and to deter waste, fraud, and abuse. Additionally, the act required extensive changes in reporting to improve the information available to administrators and to the Congress.

REQUIREMENTS OF THE CFO ACT
AND ITS 1994 EXPANSION

The CFO Act changed federal financial management in three ways: It created a new organizational structure for financial management, it encouraged the development of new and compatible accounting systems, and it required new forms of reporting.

Three basic changes to organizational structure were introduced in the CFO Act to provide for central coordination of financial management. In addition, a coordinating council was created. First, to heighten management priorities and centralize primary accountability, the act provided for the statutory appointment by the president of a deputy director for management to report directly to the director of OMB. This individual, one of two deputy directors at OMB, is the chief financial officer of the United States with responsibility for general management and financial management policies. His or her responsibilities include guiding improvements in government-wide financial systems, monitoring the quality of financial management personnel, and working to ensure that the executive branch has a financial structure capable of producing quality financial information.

The second component of organizational reform was the creation within OMB of the Office of Federal Financial Management under the control of the deputy director for management. A controller, who functions primarily in the area of financial management, heads this office and serves as principal adviser to the deputy director for management.

The final component of organizational reform was the designation of CFOs and deputy CFOs for fourteen cabinet departments and eight major agencies of the executive branch. Accounting, budgeting, and financial activities were consolidated under agency CFOs who report directly to agency heads. These positions were created to foster organizational uniformity in management operations and to facilitate coordination of federal financial management. Additionally, the chief financial officers council was created to coordinate improvements in federal financial management among agencies.

Under the CFO Act, the deputy director of management has overall responsibility for the development of management systems, including systems to measure performance. Each agency CFO has specific responsibility to develop and maintain integrated financial management systems. These responsibilities include directing the design of agency financial management systems and enhancement projects as well as overseeing assets management systems that encompass cash management, debt collection, and inventory management and control.

In creating new financial management systems, the primary objective was to develop comprehensive financial management systems that would integrate agency accounting, financial information, and financial management systems. Priorities include the elimination of duplicate systems and establishment of strong internal controls. With respect to accounting systems, conformity with applicable accounting principles and standards were required. Integrated systems were needed to support the production of financial statements and to generate quality financial information for a variety of decision-making purposes.

To encourage the availability of sufficient resources to adequately support financial systems, the deputy director of management was required to review and monitor agency budgets for financial systems and to assess the adequacy of agency personnel. The Office of Federal Financial Management was funded under a separate and distinct line item, and agency CFOs were empowered with budget responsibility for financial management functions.

The Federal Financial Management Act provided specific improvements in financial management. To reduce the cost of disbursements, it required the use of electronic transfers in making wage, salary, and retirement payments. To encourage debt collections, it provided that agencies could retain a percentage of delinquent debts collected. To promote internal markets and competition, it established four franchise funds on a pilot basis. To reduce duplication, it empowered the OMB director to consolidate and streamline management reporting processes.

The CFO Act altered reporting by instituting five-year strategic planning reports, the production of financial statements, and issuance of annual management reports. The director of OMB was required to develop and annually to revise government-wide plans with a five-year horizon for improving the government's financial management systems. The director's report is supported by agency reports that identify changes needed to achieve modern, integrated financial systems. Deliberate long-range planning is intended to curb the proliferation of unique systems and to provide for the common elements necessary for central reporting. The five-year plans to improve financial management include details about the type and form of information that is to be produced, including kinds of projects proposed to integrate systems, equipment, and personnel needs, and the costs of implementation.

Under the CFO Act, all covered departments and agencies are required to prepare annual financial statements for trust funds, revolving funds, and commercial activities. A pilot project provided for the preparation of agency-wide statements in six agencies. A gradual pilot approach was adopted with respect to the production of agency-wide financial statements because federal accounting standards were inadequate. The Federal Accounting Standards Advisory Board (FASAB) was established one month before the CFO Act was passed.

The production of agency-wide financial statements and a consolidated government-wide financial statement for the executive branch was intended to strengthen accountability and to provide the information needed for effective management, including performance evaluation. For example, financial statements include information about the ways budgeted funds were spent, the proportion of taxes and other receivables collected, the condition of physical assets, and the extent of financial obligations associated with various commitments.

Under the CFO Act, the director of the OMB is required to submit an annual financial management report to Congress. This report analyzes the status of financial management in the executive branch; summarizes agency financial statements, audits, and audits reports; and reviews reports on internal accounting and administrative controls. Also, government corporations are required to file an annual management report in addition to financial statements, which have to include a statement about internal accounting and administrative controls. Management reports must include plans for correcting internal control weaknesses.

RESPONSIBILITIES OF AUDITORS

The Federal Financial Management Act required the production and audit of agency-wide financial statements covering all accounts and activities of the twenty-three CFO-covered agencies and a consolidated government-wide financial statement for the executive branch as a whole. Additionally, the Act provided that the director of OMB may require audited financial statements of components of agencies such as the Departments of the Army, Air Force, and Navy. All financial statements produced under the CFO and Federal Financial Management Acts must be audited in accordance with generally accepted government auditing standards.

The inspector general of an agency determines who performs the audit. In the absence of an inspector general, the agency head makes this determination. The inspector general, certified public accountant (CPA) firms, or other qualified parties may perform audits. Additionally, the comptroller general may conduct the audit at his or her discretion or at the request of Congress. The Federal Financial Management Act specifies that the comptroller general has responsibility for auditing the consolidated government-wide financial statements of the executive branch.

Special provisions apply to the auditing of government corporations. The CFO Act replaced a requirement that these corporations be audited at least once every three years by the comptroller general with a requirement of annual audits. The corporation was assigned responsibility for arranging the audit, and the comptroller general retained authority to review financial statement audits performed by others.

SEE ALSO *Government Accounting*

BIBLIOGRAPHY

Chief Financial Officers Act of 1990 (1990). *U.S. Congressional and Administrative News*, 101st Congress 2nd Session, Vol. 3, Laws (Public Law 101-576). St. Paul, MN: West.

Chief Financial Officers Act of 1990 (1990). *U.S. Congressional and Administrative News*, 101st Congress 2nd Session, Vol. 6, Legislative History (Public Law 101-576). St. Paul, MN: West.

Ewer, Sid R. (1997). "Federal Government Accountability." *CPA Journal*, 67(3): 22-27.

Government Management Reform Act of 1994 (1994). *U.S. Congressional and Administrative News*, 103rd Congress 2nd Session, Vol. 3, Laws (Public Law 103-356). St. Paul, MN: West.

Government Management Reform Act of 1994 (1994). *U.S. Congressional and Administrative News*, 103rd Congress 2nd Session, Vol. 3, Legislative History (Public Law 103-356). St. Paul, MN: West.

Hodsoll, Frank (1992). "Facing the Facts of the CFO Act." *Public Budgeting & Finance*, 12(4): 72-74.

Jones, L. R. (1993). "Counterpoint Essay: Nine Reasons Why the CFO Act May Not Achieve Its Objective." *Public Budgeting & Finance*, 13(1):,87-94.

Jones, L. R., and McCaffery, Jerry L. (1997). "Implementing the Chief Financial Officers Act and the Government Performance and Results Act in the Federal Government." *Public Budgeting & Finance*, 17(1): 35-55.

Jones, L. R., and McCaffery, Jerry L. (1992). "Federal Financial Management Reform and the Chief Financial Officers Act." *Public Budgeting & Finance*, 12(4): 75-86.

Jones, L. R., and McCaffery, Jerry L. (1993). "Implementation of the Federal Chief Financial Officers Act." *Public Budgeting & Finance*, 13(1): 68-76.

Steinberg, Harold I., and Von Brachel, John (1996). "The CFO Act: A Look at Federal Accountability." *Journal of Accountancy*, 181(3): 55-57.

Jean E. Harris

CIRCULAR FLOW

Circular flow describes how a market economy works. A market economy is one in which individuals influence directly what is produced, marketed, and consumed. Individuals do this by spending money on what they want. This then directs producers to produce goods and services that individuals will consume. The amount of goods and services that are made available is related to the laws of supply and demand.

A model that best depicts how goods and services flow in exchange for money is called the circular flow model, shown in Figure 1.

PARTICIPATION

The primary participants in the circular flow of goods and services are businesses and households. Households are made up of individuals who both spend money and are the recipients of money. Businesses do the same—they spend money and also receive money from households. It is important to note that the flow of goods and services is in one direction in Figure 1, while the flow of money expenditures is in the opposite direction. Both flows make a complete circle—hence, it is called the circular flow of goods and service.

MARKETS

There are two types of markets in the circular flow of goods and services. The resource market is where businesses purchase what they use to produce goods and services. Resources are in the form of labor, natural resources, capital, and entrepreneurship, all of which are supplied by households.

If, for example, a business wants to build a small plant to produce electronic equipment, it must have land on which to build the plant. In the process of building the plant, it uses human laborers who in turn use natural resources to construct the building. Capital to complete the building comes ultimately from households, usually by means of some type of financial institution that lends money to the entrepreneurs (who also come from households) to construct the electronics plant.

Product markets are where goods and services are sold. In the case of the plant that produces electronic equipment, the outlets for its products might be retail stores. Members of households purchase the equipment for their own use in the household. Pieces of electronic equipment are purchased by the households that also provided the resources that made it possible to build the product. The outside circle of the process shown in Figure 1 has been completed.

In the reverse direction is the flow of spending. Beginning with households, the individuals therein spend money for the purchase of goods and services that are provided by businesses. In our example, the purchase is of a finished piece of electronic equipment. The money that is spent on the equipment flows from households to the business, making it possible for the business to sustain operations.

To sustain operations, the business must pay workers and purchase resources. Money continues to flow through the business into the resource markets. Bear in mind that one of the vital resources for the operation of a business is human resources, which are supplied by households. Some of the money that passes through the business goes back into the households as pay for the use of the human resources. Once again, the circular flow is complete: money that came from households through the purchase of electronic equipment passes back to households in the form of wages.

The money flow is more extensive than just wages, as shown in Figure 1. Households do not spend all their wages on goods and services. Some of the money goes into banks, financial investments, real estate, and numerous other places. From those resources, households expect to receive interest or rent as the resource is used. Banks and other financial institutions do not simply hold the money that is deposited by the households—instead, they use it to provide capital for building electronic plants and for numerous other reasons. The money flows back and forth through the circle.

The two flows of income and expenditures are equal. Expenditures on products are ultimately someone's household income. Income that flows into households is expended in some way, either for goods and services or to

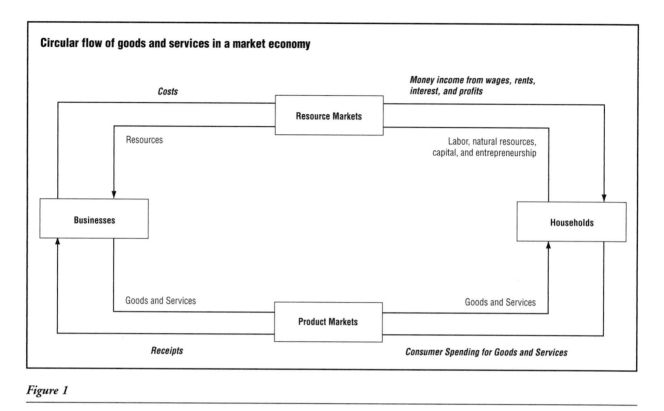

Circular flow of goods and services in a market economy

Costs

Resource Markets

Money income from wages, rents, interest, and profits

Resources

Labor, natural resources, capital, and entrepreneurship

Businesses

Households

Goods and Services

Goods and Services

Product Markets

Receipts

Consumer Spending for Goods and Services

Figure 1

purchase stock in companies, CDs, land, or another type of investment.

LIMITATIONS

The circular flow model is an accepted way to show the flow of goods and services in a market economy. In a mixed economy, the government plays an important role as well, but this is not shown in the circular flow model. Local, state, and federal governments also produce, or cause the production of, goods and services. Schools, highways, water-treatment plants, parks, and other facilities are examples of government spending. Governments take part of household incomes in the form of taxes, but they also inject money back into households in the form of wages. Some of that money goes back to the government in the form of taxes and still more goes into other places.

The government has considerable control over the economy, which in turn affects production, employment, and economic growth. If interest rates go up, households will purchase fewer goods and services. If interest rates go down, households will spend more. This spending adds to or takes away from businesses' operations and the amount of goods and services being produced.

Governments can influence the mix of goods and services offered to households. Good examples, although they might seem rather extreme, are when the government ordered the breakup of the Bell Telephone System and later of Microsoft Corporation because it was determined that they violated antitrust legislation and had become monopolies. This kind of breakup affects business operations and households.

The model that is shown in Figure 1 could also be influenced by pricing factors—that is, the laws of supply and demand. The model does not take into consideration changes in prices or how prices are determined, nor does it take into consideration how businesses choose the products or services they produce and market.

Another limitation of this model is that not all the products and services offered by businesses go to the households that provide the resources. For example, some of the electronic equipment produced in the plant described earlier might be exported to another country. In that case, the goods and services leave the circular flow and the resources to pay for the goods and services come from outside the circle. It might be easier to simplify the explanation and include all households and all businesses in the world, but most economists would not agree with that simplification.

While readers should be aware of the influence that government, exporting and importing, and pricing and production has on businesses and households, it is not necessary to alter the circular flow model. It remains a viable illustration of what happens in a macroeconomic sense without microeconomic influences.

It is also considered by some to be a limitation when money leaves the circular flow to be invested in savings, stocks, bonds, and other financial investments. However, the discussion here assumes that the money that is invested does not really leave the circle, but rather is passed on as a resource to others. It is true that some money does leave the circle because banks and other financial institutions are required by law to maintain a certain amount of money on deposit. And because some individuals in households do not trust banks or other financial institutions, they use the coffee can approach to saving their money—they simply keep their savings at home.

SUMMARY

The circular flow of goods and services is a simplified illustration of basically two flows: the flow of incomes to households from businesses and the flow of resources to businesses from households. This model excludes the more complex influences of microeconomic factors. In the macroeconomic perspective, resources flow from households to businesses, which change the resources into goods and services for consumption in the product markets. Households are rewarded for the resources they provide in the form of money. It is a circular process that flows in both directions.

SEE ALSO *Economics; Macroeconomics/Microeconomics*

BIBLIOGRAPHY

Amacher, Ryan C., and Ulbrich, Holley, H. (1995). *Principles of Economics* (6th ed.). Cincinnati, OH: South-Western Publishing.

Gitman, Lawrence J., and McDaniel, Carl (2005). *The Future of Business* (5th ed.). Mason, OH: South-Western College Publishing.

McConnell, Campbell R., and Brue, Stanley L. (2005). *Economics: Principles, Problems, and Policies* (16th ed.). Boston: McGraw-Hill/Irwin.

Roger L. Luft

CIVIL RIGHTS ACT OF 1964

The assassination of President John F. Kennedy left the United States of America in a period of turmoil and uncertainty, personified in the new and unknown President Lyndon Johnson. President Johnson was left with an

U.S. President Lyndon Baines Johnson shakes hands with civil rights leader Martin Luther King, Jr., and hands him a pen to sign the Civil Right Act, July 2, 1964. © **BETTMANN/CORBIS**

unpopular war in Vietnam, an unknown but potentially cataclysmic relationship with the Union of Soviet Socialist Republics, and the domestic time bomb of civil rights in the United States.

The era of 1954 to 1970 is known for the struggle of African Americans to gain equality de facto and under the law. The spark of the civil rights movement was the 1954 U.S. Supreme Court decision *Brown v. Board of Education of Topeka, Kansas,* when the Court decided that separate is inherently unequal. This was a reversal of an earlier decision. By making this decision the Supreme Court required that all schools desegregate with all due speed. This was the first step toward integration for the general African American population of the United States, but in many areas, especially the southern states, there was opposition to the idea of integration. Public accommodations often had separate facilities for Caucasians and African Americans.

In order to address these issues, Kennedy had called for new civil rights legislation to guarantee equal access to all public accommodations and available goods and services. Upon his death, however, there was much concern that the new civil rights law would never see the light of day. Johnson used the situation to validate Kennedy's legacy and pass the Civil Rights Act of 1964.

The Civil Rights Act of 1964 ended discrimination in all public forums based on race, color, religion, and national origin. Public accommodations included housing, entertainment, hotels, eating establishments, and businesses. The Civil Rights Act of 1964 is considered a major accomplishment for Johnson. Nevertheless, if it had not been for the death of Kennedy, many wonder if the legislation would have been passed at all.

SEE ALSO *Equal Employment Opportunity Act of 1972; Equal Pay Act of 1963; Ethics in Law for Business*

BIBLIOGRAPHY

Basic readings in U.S. democracy. Backgrounder on the Civil Rights Act. (n.d.). Retrieved November 15, 2005, from http://usinfo.state.gov/usa/infousa/facts/democrac/39.htm

Lawrence F. Peters, Jr.

CLASSIC BRANDS

Classic brands are a part of modern society that have become so deeply ingrained into our everyday experiences that they have become unobtrusive. A classic brand can be defined as one that, through careful and thorough advertising, marketing, and product positioning, has become synonymous with the product category of which it is a part. Additionally, a classic brand may also be one for which there is no other recognizable competition within its product class. In this sense, a classic brand is one that has been raised above the commodity level, creating its own product classification in the consumer's mind. This is not to say that it is the only item of its type, but rather that the other competing products hold such a small market share that they are considered obscure, making the classic brand a category killer within its market segment.

EXAMPLES OF CLASSIC BRANDS

Based on the aforementioned definition of what constitutes a classic brand, there are many products and services that may be considered classic. Coca-Cola, (or Coke, as it is commonly known) is the undisputed leader in the soft-drink industry, so much so that a consumer in a restaurant who wants a cola drink is programmed to ask for a Coke, whether the establishment serves Coke, Pepsi, or any other brand. In the same sense, an adhesive bandage is better known as a Band-Aid, facial tissue is referred to as Kleenex, and Xerox has become a verb for the act of photocopying, as well as a noun used for what the photocopy machine produces.

Household products such as Arm & Hammer Baking Soda, Clorox Bleach, and Barbie dolls provide strong examples of classic brands that have no major market competition. Of course there are other baking sodas, bleaches, and dolls on the market, but even a savvy consumer would be hard-pressed to name them. This is true not only of tangible products but of services as well. Service providers such as H&R Block and AAA (The Amer-

ican Automobile Association) are classic brands whose names are synonymous with the markets that they represent.

VISUAL IMPACT OF CLASSIC BRANDS

Much of the initial recognition of a classic brand stems not from its performance but from its visual impact on the consumer's memory. Granted, the product must perform superbly to maintain its status; however, the initial impression is often the result of a memorable logo. Classic brands generally have logos or brandmarks that have changed little since the inception of their product. The Coke bottle shape, the Golden Arches of McDonald's, and the yellow and red Arm and Hammer box are all brand identifiers that need no written words to explain what they represent. Consumers instantly recognize these symbols and associate them with the brands that they depict. In the twenty-first century, with Internet advertising becoming more and more prevalent, such simple images as these are a low-cost means of further perpetuating the brands' success.

HISTORY OF A CLASSIC BRAND

Taking a brand from common to classic is no small task and does not happen overnight. It involves strong commitment from many levels of the organization, along with a well-executed plan for remaining the leading player. A fine example of a classic brand through history is Coca-Cola, probably one of the best-known classics in the world.

Coca-Cola was created by Dr. John Smyth Pemberton, an Atlanta pharmacist, in 1886 as a beverage served at his soda fountain. He described it to his patrons as "delicious and refreshing," a line still used in Coke's advertising in the twenty-first century. In 1892, Dr. Pemberton joined forces with Asa G. Candler, an Atlanta businessman who understood the power of advertising, and registered the Coca-Cola trademark one year later. In order to create brand recognition, Candler created a wide range of promotional memorabilia for soda fountains—clocks, fans, and other novelties, all depicting the Coca-Cola trademark.

In 1915, Candler introduced the contour bottle, which itself was granted trademark protection in 1977—something not usually done for product packaging. The emergence of the contour bottle, along with bottling plants, allowed consumers to enjoy Coca-Cola in their own homes. World War II had a major impact in the building of the brand, since sixty-four of these bottling plants supplied the armed forces with more than five million bottles of Coke. It was also at this time that Coke became associated with the American spirit of a can-do attitude and became a global depiction of camaraderie and refreshment.

After the war, Coca-Cola capitalized on the technology of radio and television to continue to spread its brand imagery. Its longstanding slogans and ad campaigns, such as "It's the Real Thing," have permeated American life to the point that they are no longer just advertising; rather, they have become cultural icons. Coca-Cola's commitment to quality advertising continues in the twenty-first century through its use of not one but five well-known creative agencies whose primary focus is to maintain Coke's classic status.

This rich history, however, is not perfect. In the early 1980s, Coca-Cola tampered with perfection and launched New Coke, a reformulated version of its product with a new taste and new packaging design. Within weeks, consumers were dissatisfied with the change, and Coke moved swiftly to repair the damage that had been done. It quickly produced Classic Coke, which was the original formula that consumers had come to know and love. This proved very costly to Coke not only from the production and bottling side but also from the marketing side, where a corrective marketing plan had to be rapidly implemented. Of course, Coca-Cola rebounded with a resounding success, and it continues to be the market leader.

FORCES BEHIND CLASSIC BRANDS

The success stories of the countless other classic brands read much the same as Coca-Cola's. These classic brands all have one common thread throughout their history—successful utilization of the four Ps of marketing, which are product, placement, pricing, and promotion. It is the balance of these four significant factors that takes a brand from a name to a classic.

First and foremost is product. Brands must outperform their competition in order to become a classic. The best placement, pricing, and promotion will not raise a mediocre product to classic status, regardless of how many marketing dollars are pumped into it. Before becoming a classic brand, the product must taste better, go faster, work harder, or last longer than other products it competes against.

Second, a product must be properly placed in the market in order to overshadow the competition. Its target market must be carefully decided on and, in the case of most classic brands, be rather broad. Most classic brands appeal to a wide demographic range, rather than a small slice of consumers. People from all walks of life use most of the brands that have come to be considered classics. Band-Aids, Coke, Levi's, and Timex can be found in just

Coca-Cola Trade Card, ca. 1915–1925. ©LAKE COUNTY MUSEUM/CORBIS

about any home in America, regardless of income, geographic region, education, or age.

Next, pricing must be addressed. When looking at the cost of classic brands in comparison to their competition, the classic brands generally fall in the median price range of the product category. While higher in price than the store house brands and generics, they are not usually at the costly end of the spectrum either. In part, this is because in order to be well received by the masses, the product must be neither overpriced nor undervalued. There are many quality wristwatches on the market, but Timex, one of the least expensive, has made a name for itself as a classic brand.

Last, a product must be adequately and appropriately promoted to become a classic brand. Timex, for example, has created memorable television commercials over the years by using the same premise over and over—"Timex takes a licking and keeps on ticking." The public has grown accustomed to seeing what the wristwatch can endure and remain functional. Such a promotional idea stems from a creative department committed to the success of the brand through consistent promotional processes. Promotion must also be constant. There must always be some kind of promotional vehicle in motion to keep the brand name in the forefront of the consumer's mind. Point-of-purchase displays, radio, television, print, and Internet advertising, corporate sponsorships, and contests are all used, often simultaneously, to maintain the public's awareness of the brand.

These four traditional guidelines of product marketing are crucially important for classic brands, for the competition is generally aimed directly at them. Pepsi, for example, spends millions of dollars a year targeting itself directly against Coke. Coca-Cola cannot afford to rest on its classic brand status—they must be constantly engaged in maintaining the perfect balance of product, placement, pricing, and promotion, or risk having its market share overtaken by the hungry competition.

Classic brands are not likely to change over the next several generations. They will not disappear overnight or be swept away by increasing technology. Companies fortunate enough to have classic brands in their product lineup protect their esteemed place vigilantly through careful marketing, innovative ideas, and respect for their place in history.

SEE ALSO *Marketing; Promotion*

BIBLIOGRAPHY
"From Soda Fountain to American Icon." (1999, February 1) *Playthings.*

Karen J. Puglisi

CLASSICAL MANAGEMENT
SEE *Management*

CLAYTON ANTITRUST ACT OF 1914
SEE *Antitrust Legislation; Interstate Commerce; Marketing Mix; Sherman Antitrust Act of 1890*

CLIMATE IN ORGANIZATIONS
SEE *Organizational Behavior and Development*

CLOSED MANAGEMENT SYSTEMS
SEE *Management*

COCO (CRITERIA OF CONTROL)
SEE *Internal Control Systems*

COGNITIVE DISSONANCE
SEE *Consumer Behavior*

COLLECTIVE BARGAINING

Collective bargaining is "a process of negotiation between management and union representatives for the purpose of arriving at mutually acceptable wages and working conditions for employees" (Boone and Kurtz, 2006, pp. 424-425). Various methods may be used in the bargaining process, but the desired outcome is always mutual acceptance by labor and management of a collective bargaining agreement or contract.

United Auto Workers Vice President Nate Gooden, UAW President Ron Gettelfinger, Chrysler Group President and CEO Dieter Zetsche, and Chrysler Group COO Wolfgang Bernhard shake hands as they open talks on a new labor contract, July 16, 2003 in Auburn Hills, Michigan. © REUTERS/CORBIS

THE BARGAINING PROCESS

The collective bargaining process begins when the majority of workers of an organization vote to be represented by a specific union. The National Labor Relations Board (see Labor Unions) then certifies the union. At this point, the management of the organization must recognize the union as the collective bargaining agent for all the employees of that organization. Once this part of the process is completed, collective bargaining can begin.

Bargaining always takes place between labor and management, but negotiations can include more than one group of workers and more than one employer. Single-plant, single-employer agreements are the most common. However, if an employer has more than one plant or work site, multiplant, single-employer agreements can be bargained. Several different union groups representing the workers of the same employer can use coalition bargain-

ing. Industrywide bargaining involves one national union bargaining with several employers of a specific industry.

Many different negotiation styles can be used when union and labor representatives sit down at the bargaining table. The two basic modes of bargaining are traditional bargaining and partnership bargaining, though there are many variations of each style.

The traditional style of bargaining has been used since collective bargaining began between management and the early labor unions (see Labor Unions). It is an adversarial style of negotiating, pitting one side against the other with little or no understanding of, or education about, the other on the part of either party. Each side places its demands and proposals on the table, and the other side responds to them with counterproposals. The process is negative and involves a struggle of give-and-take on most issues. Even with its negative connotations, however, the traditional style of negotiating is still used effectively in bargaining many union contracts.

The partnership style of bargaining is the more modern approach to negotiations. It strives for mutual understanding and common education on the part of both labor and management, and it focuses on goals and concerns common to both parties. Because of its emphasis on each side's being aware of the issues concerning the other side, partnership-style bargaining is also known as interest-based bargaining. In this process, labor and management each list and explain their needs, and the ensuing discussion revolves around ways to meet those needs that will be not only acceptable but also beneficial to both parties. This style of bargaining is very positive and imparts a much more congenial atmosphere to the negotiating process. Many modern union-management contracts are bargained very successfully using the partnership style.

A blending of the traditional and partnership styles is widely used in labor-management negotiations. The combination approach is used for many reasons, including the fact that many union and management leaders are more familiar with the traditional style. However, with today's more participatory relationship between labor and management in the workplace, the partnership style is becoming more accepted and is being used more frequently. The negotiating process may also include both styles of bargaining because of the variety of issues being negotiated. The partnership style may be used to negotiate certain issues, while the traditional style may be invoked when bargaining other terms.

COLLECTIVE BARGAINING ISSUES

Labor unions were formed to help workers achieve common goals in the areas of wages, hours, working conditions, and job security. These issues still are the focus of the collective bargaining process, though some new concepts have become the subjects of negotiations. Table 1 lists the issues most often negotiated in union contracts.

THE SETTLEMENT PROCESS

Union contracts are usually bargained to remain in effect for two to three years but may cover longer or shorter periods of time. The process of negotiating a union contract, however, may take an extended period of time. Once the management and union members of the negotiating team come to agreement on the terms of the contract, the union members must accept or reject the agreement by a majority vote. If the agreement is accepted, the contract is ratified and becomes a legally binding agreement remaining in effect for the specified period of time.

If the union membership rejects the terms of the agreement, the negotiating teams from labor and management return to the bargaining table and continue to negotiate. This cycle can be repeated several times. If no agreement can be reached between the two teams, negotiations are said to have broken down, and several options become available.

Mediation is usually the first alternative when negotiations are at a stalemate. The two parties agree voluntarily to have an impartial third party listen to the proposals of both sides. It is the mediator's job to get the two sides to agree to a settlement. Once the mediator understands where each side stands, he or she makes recommendations for settling their differences. The mediator merely makes suggestions, gives advice, and tries to get labor and management to compromise on a solution. Agreement is still voluntary at this point. The mediator has no power to force either of the parties to settle the contract, though often labor and management do come to agreement by using mediation.

If mediation fails to bring about a settlement, the next step can be arbitration, which can be either compulsory or voluntary. Compulsory arbitration is not often used in labor-management negotiations in the United States. Occasionally, however, the federal government requires union and management to submit to compulsory arbitration. In voluntary arbitration, both sides agree to use the arbitration process and agree that it will be bind-

Collective bargaining issues			
Wages	**Hours**	**Working Conditions**	**Job Security**
Regular Compensation	Regular Work Hours	Rest Periods	Seniority
Overtime Compensation	Overtime Work Hours	Grievance Procedures	Evaluation
Incentives	Vacations	Union Membership	Promotion
Insurance	Holidays	Dues Collection	Layoff
Pensions			Recall

Table 1

ing. As in mediation, an impartial third party serves in the arbitration process. The arbitrator acts as a judge, listening to both sides and then making a decision on the terms of the settlement, which becomes legally binding on labor and management. Ninety percent of all union contracts use arbitration if the union and management can not come to agreement (Boone and Kurtz, 2006).

SOURCES OF POWER

If the collective bargaining process is not working as a way to settle the differences between labor and management, both sides have weapons they can use to bolster their positions. One of the most effective union tactics is the strike or walkout. While on strike, employees do not report to work and, of course, are not paid. Strikes usually shut down operations, thus pressuring management to give in to the union's demands. Some employees, even though allowed to belong to unions, are not allowed to strike. Federal employees fall into this category. The law also prohibits some state and municipal employees from striking.

During a strike, workers often picket at the entrance to their place of employment. This involves marching, carrying signs, and talking to the media about their demands. The right to picket is protected by the U.S. Constitution as long as it does not involve violence or intimidation. Problems sometimes arise during strikes and picketing when management hires replacement workers, called scabs or strikebreakers, who need to cross the picket line in order to do the jobs of the striking workers.

The boycott is another union strategy to put pressure on management to give in to the union's demands. During a primary boycott, not only union members but also members of the general public are encouraged to refuse to conduct business with the firm in dispute with the union.

Though it is rarely done, management may use the lockout as a tactic to obtain its bargaining objectives. In this situation, management closes down the business, thus keeping union members from working. This puts pressure on the union to settle the contract so employees can get back to their jobs and receive their wages.

Management sometimes uses the injunction as a strategy to put pressure on the union to give in to its demands. An injunction is a court order prohibiting something from being done, such as picketing, or requiring something to be done, such as workers being ordered to return to work.

GRIEVANCE PROCEDURES

Once a collective bargaining agreement is settled and a union contract is signed, it is binding on both the union and management. However, disagreements with contract implementation can arise and violations of the contract terms can occur. In these cases, a grievance, or complaint, can be filed. The differences that must be resolved are usually handled through a step-by-step process that is outlined in the collective bargaining agreement. The grievance procedure begins with a complaint to the worker's immediate supervisor and, if unresolved at that level, moves upward, step by step, to higher levels of management. If no resolution is found at any of these levels, the two parties can agree to have the grievance submitted to an impartial outside arbitrator for a decision binding to the union and management.

Collective bargaining is a successful way for workers to reach their goals concerning acceptable wages, hours, and working conditions. It allows workers to bargain as a team to satisfy their needs. Collective bargaining also allows management to negotiate efficiently with workers by bargaining with them as a group instead of with each one individually. Though traditional bargaining can be negative and adversarial, it does produce collective bargaining agreements between labor and management. Partnership bargaining can lead to increased understanding and trust between labor and management. It is a positive, cooperative approach to collective bargaining that also culminates in contracts between labor and management.

SEE ALSO *Labor Unions; Negotiation*

BIBLIOGRAPHY

Boone, Louis E., and Kurtz, David L. (2006). *Contemporary Business 2006*. Mason, OH: Thomson/South-Western.

Davey, Harold W., Bognanno, Mario F., and Estenson, David L. (1982). *Contemporary Collective Bargaining* (4th ed.). Englewood Cliffs, NJ: Prentice-Hall.

Miernyk, William H. (1973). *The Economics of Labor and Collective Bargaining* (2nd ed.). Lexington, MA: Heath.

Voos, Paula B., ed. (1994). *Contemporary Collective Bargaining in the Private Sector*. Madison, WI: Industrial Relations Research Association.

Wray, Ralph D., Luft, Roger L., and Highland, Patrick J. (1996). *Fundamentals of Human Relations*. Cincinnati, OH: South-Western Educational Publishing.

Paula Lee Luft

COMMAND ECONOMIES

SEE *Economic Systems*

COMMON MARKET

SEE *International Trade; Trading Blocs*

COMMUNICATION CHANNELS

In the basic communication process, a sender puts a message in words and transmits it to a receiver who interprets the message. The medium the sender chooses to transmit the message is called the communication channel.

Traditionally, it was thought that the words chosen and way they were interpreted were solely responsible for a successful message. Beginning in the 1960s with Marshall McLuhan, however, many came to believe that the medium was the message. Today, with the help of media richness theory and its extensions—and variants such as channel expansion theory—most people realize that the appropriate choice of communication channel (medium) contributes significantly, along with the words, to the success of a message. Appropriate choice helps senders communicate clearly, saving them and their businesses time and money. Therefore, examining various communication channels to understand their appropriate use is important.

Media richness theory ranks communication channels along a continuum of richness, defining highly rich channels as those handling multiple inherent cues simultaneously, such as using feedback, nonverbal cues, and several senses simultaneously. A face-to-face meeting, which employs feedback as well as audio and visual senses, is considered extremely rich. A newsletter or brochure is lean, however, involving only the visual sense and slow or no feedback. Several of these channels—brochures and Web pages, letters, electronic mail (e-mail) messages, video e-mail messages, text messaging, instant messaging, telephone conversations, videoconferencing or virtual meetings, and face-to-face meetings—will be reviewed, along with some guidelines for appropriate use.

BROCHURES/WEB PAGES

Writers usually create brochures or Web pages to provide information on a product or service. While often used for persuasive purposes, they are usually presented as routine informational documents. Writers lay out the information carefully, often designing the visual layout as carefully as they compose the text of the content. These lean channels work effectively when one-way communication in a visual medium is needed. In choosing these channels, the sender is eliminating any extraneous information a richer source might include, keeping the content of the message clear and focused.

LETTERS

Letters are primarily printed, formal business documents. They are best used when one wants to convey important, nonroutine information, such as job offers or refusals, promotions, awards and honors, and other kinds of special announcements. Also, they are an appropriate channel for certain attempts at persuasion, such as soliciting contributions to a special cause, asking someone to speak to a group, or proposing the acceptance of an idea. Print letters are still used as advertising tools; the most effective ones, however, are those that are individually customized, making them a special message.

E-MAIL MESSAGES

E-mail messages are widely used in business as well as in personal life. While e-mail is a fast and efficient channel, it is considered lean because it allows no eye contact and few nonverbal cues. Because e-mail messages are not totally secure and because they are legally discoverable, these messages are used primarily in routine contexts, leaving special or nonroutine messages for other channels. The notes writers send to family and friends are usually accounts of day-to-day activities, with more important, special messages communicated through richer channels.

VIDEO E-MAIL MESSAGES

A variant of e-mail, video e-mail is much richer than text-based e-mail, but it is still a one-way communication channel. The lack of interactivity makes it appropriate for messages that need richness but not real-time feedback. Personal use of this channel might be appropriate for such situations as showing a new haircut, introducing new friends, and even showing a new baby. On the other hand, business use of video e-mail is still evolving. Obviously, when one needs to show something, say a new package design, it would be a good choice. A short sales message might be appropriate in some contexts. At this time, the best use of this channel appears to be special messages.

TEXT MESSAGING

Text messaging is predominantly for short messages sent from one cell phone to another cell phone by typing in written messages. Because it takes time to enter the text, senders often use shortcuts such as "u" for "you" or "thx" for "thanks." Some technologies, however, are making it easier to send these messages. Not only are there Web sites where users simply enter messages via a keyboard, but the predictive technology built into phones that completes words is reducing the amount of typing needed. Additionally, voice-input software that converts voice to text is an up-and-coming technology. Sending text messages allows the senders to communicate with receivers in a way that is less disruptive than a phone call and usually more immediate than an e-mail message.

INSTANT MESSAGING

Similar to text messaging, instant messaging (IM) is used to exchange short messages, usually with abbreviated text, sent over the Internet. Most senders and receivers connect and engage in highly interactive real-time communication. Its use in business is just beginning—not only because a large percentage of young people competent at using it are just entering the workplace, but also because of the recent development of enterprise IM software, which keeps records of these messages. Until this technology became available, many businesses were reluctant to allow IM, fearing such things as problems with sexual harassment, loss of intellectual capital, and other potential problems the technology might enable. Furthermore, the Sarbanes-Oxley Act of 2002 requires that written company communications be auditable, so until enterprise IM software became available, IM's use in business was not widespread.

PHONE CONVERSATIONS

A somewhat richer channel is the phone. It transmits sound rather than printed words and sound can enrich the message's words with emphasis and emotion. It also allows for immediate feedback, qualifying it as a richer channel one would use to get important, immediate responses. The choice of this channel to transmit a message is highly contextual. Some receivers view the telephone as invasive and prefer to rely on voice-mail systems to get messages. Others view the phone as an important way of doing business. Most receivers carry cell phones so they can get important messages wherever they go. Knowing the importance of one's message, as well as the receiver's preferred way of doing business, is critical when opting to use this channel.

VIDEOCONFERENCING/VIRTUAL MEETINGS

As communication channels, videoconferencing and virtual meetings are extremely rich. These technologies allow people in different locations to interact with one another using audio and video. Users choose them for their convenience as well as cost-effectiveness. They are available in most large companies as well as on the Web by subscription for use by smaller companies and individuals. For example, a company might want to have the vice president for sales in on its planning meeting for a new product launch without asking that person to travel to its site for a thirty-minute meeting. Or a company might want to screen job candidates and then bring in only the top candidates for on-site interviews. As a rule, these channels are best used when the communication needs are special, immediate, or otherwise expensive.

FACE-TO-FACE MEETINGS

Face-to-face meetings are ranked at the top of the richness scale because they allow complete use of all senses and continuous feedback. Companies find such meetings to be a good choice for nonroutine business, such as planning new products, analyzing markets and business strategy, negotiating issues, and solving or resolving problems. Additionally, the face-to-face meetings of teams often provide a synergistic effect that improves the outcome of their actions. The collaboration efforts face-to-face meetings evoke are often worth the time and expense of using this channel.

SUMMARY

While these channels are not the only ones available, they clearly show that the sender of a message has range of choices from lean to rich. To help ensure successful communication, the sender needs to select the channel appropriate for the context. Additionally, in choosing an appropriate channel, one needs to consider not only richness but also other factors such as message content, sender and receiver competency with the channel, receiver access to the channel, and the receiver's environment. For example, while an e-mail is relatively easy to send, some people may not have easy access to receiving it, while others could easily have it forwarded to a cell phone or pick it up on a wireless device.

The appropriate choice of a communication channel leads to productivity increases and positive social effects. Understanding how the appropriate choice affects the success of a message helps senders decide which communication channel to use.

SEE ALSO *Communications in Business*

BIBLIOGRAPHY

Carlson, J. R., and George, J. F. (2004). Media appropriateness in the conduct and discovery of deceptive communication: The relative influence of richness and synchronicity. *Group Decision and Negotiation, 13*(2), 191.

Carlson, J. R., and Zmud, R. W. (1999). Channel expansion theory and the experiential nature of media richness perceptions. *Academy of Management Journal, 42*(2), 153.

Donabedian, Baorji, McKinnon, Sharon M., and Burns, William J., Jr. (1998). Task characteristics, managerial socialization, and media selection. *Management Communication Quarterly 11*(3), 372–400.

Kock, N. (2005). Media richness or media naturalness? The evolution of our biological communication apparatus and its influence on our behavior toward e-communication tools. *IEEE Transactions on Professional Communication, 48*(2), 117.

Lengel, Robert H., and Daft, Richard L. (1988). The selection of communication media as an executive skill. *The Academy of Management Executives, 2*(3):236.

McLuhan, Marshall, and Fiore, Quentin (1967). *The medium is the message.* New York: Random House.

Vickery, S. K., Droge, C., Stank, T. P., Goldsby, T. J., et al. (2004). The performance implications of media richness in a business-to-business service environment: Direct versus indirect effects. *Management Science, 50*(8), 1106.

Marie E. Flatley

COMMUNICATIONS IN BUSINESS

Communication, stated simply, is the act of conveying a message, through a channel, from one person to another; that is, connecting or sharing thoughts, opinions, emotions, and intelligence. Communication is a mechanism for all types of interaction and connectivity: communication can instantaneously bring people together, link ideas and things, deliver news and facts, and impart knowledge. Because communication can be expressed as words, letters, pictures, gestures, signals, colors, and so forth, it is credited with being the single element that has brought the world closer together.

People communicate for one of four reasons: to inform, influence, persuade, or entertain. In business, effective communication will influence outcomes and it is the critical backbone of an organization's ability to operate internally and externally as well as nationally and internationally.

COMMUNICATION BASICS

Communication, in its most basic definition, involves a sender (encoder) and a receiver (decoder). The sender encodes a message, deciding what content and relationship codes to use, and sends it via a communication channel such as face to face (verbal and nonverbal) and written (frequently using electronic technology). The receiver takes the message and, in the decoding process, attempts to understand its content and relationship meaning. After decoding, the receiver then may respond, via a communication channel, to the sender with a new message based on the receiver's perception of what the message imparted in terms of information and the relationship with the sender. It is at this point that one-way communication becomes two-way communication.

To be most effective, the feedback loop (the receiver's decoded interpretation of the original message) should go forward; that is, the receiver should respond to the sender. The feedback loop provides the sender with two vital pieces of information: (1) if the original message was correctly understood as sent and (2) the new message. The feedback loop allows for early correction of incorrectly decoded messages. The decoding, encoding, and feedback loop continue as the parties communicate.

In the decoding of a message, miscommunication and/or missed communication can occur. In the feedback loop, the receiver must clarify how that message was perceived. The greater the number of people involved in the message exchange process and the greater their differences in values, beliefs, attitudes, and knowledge of the subject matter, the greater are the chances that the message will be decoded improperly and a communication breakdown will occur.

Communication is most successful when it is understood by all persons involved in the process. That is, good communication is free from social colloquialisms, cultural mores, and gender biases. Because communication may be conveyed in many forms, it is frequently described in two general categories: verbal and nonverbal. Nonverbal communication includes body language, gestures, and signals. In general, successful communication depends on how well a sender conveys a message to a receiver relying on the six senses (seeing, speaking/hearing, intuition, smelling, touching, and tasting) and feedback.

COMMUNICATION RULES

Several rules facilitate successful communication. The following checklist provides a guide to creating successful communication:

- Make messages clear, correct, comprehensive, and concise

- In messages that require a response, include an action step with a deadline

- Select correct channels of communication based on message content and relationship components

- Structure the message so as not to overload the receiver with information

- Develop sensitivity to the receiver's communication style and create the message accordingly

- Be aware of how cultural patterns affect communication style and take this into consideration when sending and receiving messages

- Be aware that people operating in a second language may still encode/decode messages based on their first culture's communication patterns

- Enhance listening skills as an aspect of effective use of the feedback loop

- Recognize that a positive attitude enhances the effectiveness of the communication process

COMMUNICATION TRANSMISSION MODES

Technology-mediated communication has become the norm in today's worldwide business environment. Messages are communicated regularly via easy access to a wide variety of sophisticated electronic technologies, including electronic mail (e-mail), fax, and phones. People still meet face to face, but they also use express mail and courier services, messaging and paging systems, caller identification and transfer/forwarding telephony systems, and many other combinations of message transfer and delivery methods. Signaling, biometrics, scanning, imagery, and holography also have a place in business communication.

Additionally, many professionals work in virtual groups using satellite uplink/downlinks, video streaming, videoconferencing, and computer groupware. In using these technologies, one should recognize the limits of the channel of communication selected. For example, e-mail is efficient but does not convey the nuances of a message that can be gained from facial expressions, gestures, or tone of voice. The use of multiple channels of communication may be critical if the content is quite complex; thus, an oral message may not be sufficient.

The importance of using the feedback loop becomes more critical as the content and/or relational aspects of the messages expand. Also, as more workgroups operate globally in a virtual medium, cultural patterns must be considered in the quest for clear and effective communication. The expansion of global business, combined with advances in technology, has created more cross-cultural opportunities. When working in a cross-cultural, multinational/multicultural environment, it is necessary to understand that culture influences people's behavior as well as their attitudes and beliefs. People encode and decode messages with perceptions learned from their cultural filters. In intercultural situations, the professional must use the feedback loop to clarify understanding of the received message. Just because a message has been received rapidly or with use of high-level technology does not mean that the receiver has decoded it properly.

TYPES OF COMMUNICATION

Written communication usually takes such forms as letters, memos, e-mails, reports, manuscripts, notes, forms, applications, résumés, and legal and medical documents. Spoken communication includes presentations, oral exchanges (e.g., one on one or to a group), and voice mes-

saging. Speaking distinctly, with appropriate speed, as well as paying attention to voice inflection, tone, resonation, pitch clarity, and volume are important to the way a spoken message is received. Frequently, the way a spoken message is delivered is as important or even more important than the content of the message (a good example is a joke that has perfect timing). More than 90 percent of what a message conveys may actually be based on nonverbal elements; communicating a positive attitude also is helpful.

Nonverbal communication includes body language (e.g., facial expression, eye contact, posture, standing or sitting position, distance between sender and receiver, and gesturing), which can send signals to the receiver that may be much stronger than the message itself. If a picture truly speaks louder than a thousand words, communication by means other than the spoken and written word—such as clothing, signals or mannerisms reflecting personality or preferences, and gesturing—can make a big difference in the message that is conveyed.

COMMUNICATION CHANNELS

Communication in a society, whether it is personal or business communication, is essential. Individuals and organizations depend on it to function. Most businesses need both internal and external communication to be productive. Internal communication is communication that is exchanged within an organization. Usually it is less formal than communication that goes to those outside the business. Informal communication may range from chats in the hallway and lunchroom, team and group meetings, casual conversations over the phone or e-mail, and memos and preliminary reports to teleconferencing, brainstorming idea sessions, department or division meetings, and drafting documents. Informal communication also includes gossip, which relies on people passing on messages to coworkers, friends, and others outside of the organizational hierarchy.

External communication usually refers to messages that extend beyond the business organization. Because it reflects the organization's image, external communication is usually more formal. External communication is an extension of the organization and can be an important channel for marketing the company's image, mission, products, and/or services.

COMMUNICATION PARAMETERS

The selection or type of business communication takes many factors into consideration, including (1) the nature of the business (e.g., government, commerce, industry, private or public organization, manufacturing or marketing firm); (2) the mission and the philosophy of the organization (open versus limited or closed communication patterns); (3) the way the business is organized (small or large company, branch offices, subsidiaries); (4) the leadership styles of the organization's managers and supervisors (democratic, authoritarian, dictatorial, pragmatic); (5) the number and types of personnel as well as the levels of employees (hierarchy or status of positions, managerial or laborers, supervisors or team leaders); (6) the proximity of work units (closeness of departments, divisions, or groups that depend on information from each other); and (7) the need for communication (who needs to know what, when, why, where, and how for informed decision making to take place.

COMMUNICATION SYSTEMS

Every group (whether it is formal or informal, and regardless of its size) has a communication system or network. Some are very effective and efficient while others are just the opposite. Even if communication appears to be (or is) dysfunctional within an organization or group, the group has a communication system. That is, poor or dysfunctional communication still conveys a message. When dysfunctional communication is taking place, there is a lack of exchange of information or messages within the group.

COMMUNICATION STYLES

Without realizing it, most people communicate with others (verbally as well as nonverbally) according to a dominant style. Essentially, people communicate in one of four basic styles: (1) directly or authoritatively (an in-charge person or one who is a driving force to get things done); (2) analytically or as a fact finder (a person who plans, researches, and analyzes the facts and weighs the alternatives carefully); (3) amiably or as a coach (a supportive team builder who gets people to work together toward a common goal); or (4) expressively or flamboyantly (a cheerleader with a positive attitude who has an abundance of ideas and motivates others toward taking action).

Communication styles are developed over time and with practice, and they can be influenced by many environmental factors. They also may reflect cultural norms. It is important to understand one's own preferred communication style as well as those of others in order to maximize one's communication interactions.

BARRIERS TO COMMUNICATION

Effective communication relies in part on eliminating as many communication barriers as possible. Some ways to avoid common barriers to communication include the following:

- Stay focused on the topic

- Adhere to the deadline, when timing is important

- Be willing to use a communication strategy appropriate to the situation; listen, negotiate, compromise, modify, and learn from feedback

- Avoid relying on the grapevine as a source of facts, even though it may have been an accurate communication channel in the past

- Be sincere, empathetic, and sensitive to others' feelings; one's voice, confidence, actions, and other nonverbal cues speak loudly

- Seek out information about unknowns, especially when cultural and gender differences are involved

- Be tactful, polite, clear, prepared, and, above all, strive to display a positive attitude with all communication

COMMUNICATION LEGISLATION

Professional communicators should review federal legislation that provides strict parameters for direct-marketing campaigns using unsolicited faxes, e-mail, and telephone calls. The Junk Fax Prevention Act, the Can Spam Act, and the Federal Trade Commission's Do Not Call Lists are all examples of such legislation. While direct marketing continues to be an effective sales tool, some consumers demand privacy protection from unwanted solicitors. Federal legislation of privacy protection also extends to employees who use company phones, computers, and Internet capabilities.

Businesses must be clear and upfront about how employees' internal and external communications are monitored. Equally, employees must realize that their e-mail correspondence, phone conversations, and other communications may be used as evidence in a court of law, pending legal action that involves their employer.

SEE ALSO *Communication Channels; Electronic Mail; Videoconferencing; Voice Messaging; Writing Skills in Business*

BIBLIOGRAPHY

Locker, Kitty O. & Kaczmarek, Stephen Kyo. (2007). *Business communication: building critical skills* (3rd ed.). Boston, MA: McGraw-Hill.

Guffey, Mary Ellen (2006). *Business communication: process & product* (5th ed.) Mason, OH: Thomson/South-Western.

Sharon Lund O'Neil
Jerry S. Evans
Heather Bigley

COMMUNISM
SEE *Economic Systems*

COMPARISON SHOPPING
SEE *Shopping*

COMPETITION

Competition is the battle between businesses to win consumer acceptance and loyalty. The free-enterprise system ensures that businesses make decisions about what to produce, how to produce it, and what price to charge for the product or service. Competition is a basic premise of the free-enterprise system because it is believed that having more than one business competing for the same consumers will cause the products and/or services to be provided at a better quality and a lower cost than if there were no competitors. In other words, competition should provide the consumers with the best value for their hard-earned dollar.

ASPECTS OF COMPETITION

To be successful in today's very competitive business world, it is important for businesses to be aware of what their competitors are doing and to find a way to compete by matching or improving on the competitors' product or service. For example, if Pepsi-Cola offers a new caffeine-free soda, Coca-Cola may offer a new caffeine-free soda with only one calorie. By offering an improvement on the competitor's product, Coca-Cola is trying to convince soft-drink consumers to buy the new Coke product because it is an improvement on Pepsi's product.

While being aware of the competition and making a countermove is important, it is also very important to pay attention to changing consumer wants, needs, and values and to make the needed changes before the competition does. Doing research and development and being the first to provide a new product or service can give a company a competitive advantage in the marketplace. Once consumers purchase a product or service and are satisfied with it, they will typically purchase the same product again. Having a competitive advantage means that a company does something better than the competition. Having a competitive advantage might mean inventing a new product; providing the best quality, the lowest prices, or the best customer service; or having cutting-edge technology.

Neighboring gas stations compete for customers in Jersey City, New Jersey, May 20, 2004. **CHRIS HONDROS/GETTY IMAFGES**

Types of competition

Characteristics	Perfect Competition	Monopolistic Competition	Oligopoly	Monopoly
Number of competitors	Many	Few to many	Very few	No direct competition
Ease of entry into or exit from industry	Easy	Somewhat difficult	Difficult	Regulated by U.S. government
Similarity of goods/services offered by competing firms	Same	Seemingly different but may be quite similar	Similar or different	No directly competing products
Individual firm's control over price	None (set by the market)	Some	Some	Considerable (in true monopoly) Little (in regulated one)
Examples	Farmer	Fast-food restaurant	Automotive manufacturer	Power company

Table 1

To determine an area where a company might have a competitive advantage, a SWOT analysis is often done to identify the company's internal *S*trengths and *W*eaknesses and the external *O*pportunities and *T*hreats. A SWOT analysis lets the company know in which area(s) it has a competitive advantage so it can concentrate on those areas in the production and marketing of its product(s) or service(s).

In addition to staying on top of changing consumer preferences, companies must constantly be looking for ways to cut costs and increase productivity. Companies must provide consumers with the best-quality product at the lowest cost while still making a profit if they are to be successful competitors in the long run. One way to remain competitive is through the use of technology. Technology can help speed up production processes through the use of robots or production lines, move information more accurately and more quickly through the use of computer systems, and assist in research and development proceedings.

Global competition has made gaining consumer acceptance an even tougher challenge for most businesses. Firms in other countries may be able to produce products and provide services at a lower cost than American businesses. In order to compete, American businesses must find other ways to win consumers. One way for businesses to accomplish this is through competitive differentiation. Competitive differentiation occurs when a firm somehow differentiates its product or service from that of competitors. Competitive differentiation may be an actual differ-

ence, such as a longer warranty or a lower price, but often the difference is only perceived. Difference in perception is usually accomplished through advertising, the purpose of which is to convince consumers that one company's product is different from another company's product. Common ways to differentiate a product or service include advertising a better-quality product, better service, better taste, or just a better image. Competitive differentiation is used extensively in the monopolistic form of competition, discussed below.

FORMS OF COMPETITION

Although each form has many aspects, not all of which can be considered here, competition can generally be classified into four main categories: perfect competition, monopolistic competition, oligopoly, and monopoly. (Table 1 summarizes the basic differences among these four types of competition.)

Perfect Competition. Perfect competition (also known as pure competition exists when a large number of sellers produce products or services that seem to be identical. These types of businesses are typically run on a small scale, and participants have no control over the selling price of their product because no one seller is large enough to dictate the price of the product. Instead, the price of the product is set by the market. There are many competitors in a perfect competition industry, and it is fairly easy to enter or leave the industry. While there are no ideal examples of perfect competition, agricultural products are considered to be the closest example in today's economy. The corn grown by one farmer is virtually identical to the corn grown by another farmer, and the current market controls the price the farmers receive for their crops. Perfect competition follows the law of supply and demand. If the price of a product is high, consumers will demand less of the product while the suppliers will want to supply more. If the price of a product is low, the consumers will demand more of the product, but the suppliers will be unwilling to sell much at such a low price. The equilibrium point is where the supply and the demand meet and determine the market price. For example, if the going market price for wheat is $5 a bushel and a farmer tries to sell wheat for $6 a bushel, no one will buy because they can get it for $5 a bushel from someone else. On the other hand, if a farmer offers to sell wheat for $4 a bushel, the crop will sell, but the farmer has lost money because the crop is worth $5 a bushel on the open market.

Monopolistic Competition. Monopolistic competition exists when a large number of sellers produce a product or service that is perceived by consumers as being different from that of a competitor but is actually quite similar. This perception of difference is the result of product differentiation, which is the key to success in a monopolistic industry. Products can be differentiated based on price, quality, image, or some other feature, depending on the product. For example, there are many different brands of bath soap on the market today. Each brand of soap is similar because it is designed to get the user clean; however, each soap product tries to differentiate itself from the competition to attract consumers. One soap might claim that it leaves you with soft skin, while another soap might claim that it has a clean, fresh scent. Each participant in this market structure has some control over pricing, which means it can alter the selling price as long as consumers are still willing to buy its product at the new price. If one product costs twice as much as similar products on the market, chances are most consumers will avoid buying the more expensive product and buy the competitors' products instead. There can be few or many competitors (typically many) in a monopolistic industry, and it is somewhat difficult to enter or leave such an industry. Monopolistic products are typically found in retailing businesses. Some examples of monopolistic products and/or services are shampoo products, extermination services, oil changes, toothpaste, and fast-food restaurants.

Oligopoly. An oligopoly exists when there are few sellers in a certain industry. This occurs because a large investment is required to enter the industry, which makes it difficult to enter or leave. The businesses involved in an oligopoly type of industry are typically very large because they have the financial ability to make the needed investment. The type of products sold in an oligopoly can be similar or different, and each seller has some control over price. Examples of oligopolies include the automobile, airplane, and steel industries.

Monopoly. A monopoly exists when a single seller controls the supply of a good or service and prevents other businesses from entering the field. Being the only provider of a certain good or service gives the seller considerable control over price. Monopolies are prohibited by law in the United States; however, government-regulated monopolies do exist in some business areas because of the huge up-front investment that must be made in order to provide some types of services. Examples of monopolies in the United States are public utility companies that provide services and/or products such as gas, water, and/or electricity.

BIBLIOGRAPHY

Boone, Louis E., and Kurtz, David L. (2006). *Contemporary Business*. Mason, OH: Thomson/South-Western.

Bounds, Gregory M., and Lamb, Charles W., Jr. (1998). *Business*. Cincinnati, OH: South-Western College Publishing.

Burnett, John, and Moriarty, Sandra E. (1998) *Introduction to Marketing Communication: An Integrated Approach*. Upper Saddle River, NJ: Prentice Hall.

Clancy, Kevin J., and Shulman, Robert S. (1994). *Marketing Myths That Are Killing Business: The Cure for Death Wish Marketing*. New York: McGraw-Hill.

French, Wendell L. (1998). *Human Resources Management* (5th ed.). Boston: Houghton Mifflin Co.

Goldzimer, Linda Silverman, and Beckmann, Gregory, L. (1989). *"I'm First": Your Customer's Message to You*. New York: Rawson Associates.

Madura, Jeff (2004). *Introduction to Business*. Belmont, CA: Thomson/South-Western.

Moore, James F. (1996). *The Death of Competition: Leadership and Strategy in the Age of Business Ecosystems*. New York: HarperBusiness.

Nickels, William G., McHugh, James M., and McHugh, Susan M. (2005). *Understanding Business* (7th ed.). Boston: McGraw-Hill/Irwin.

Pfeffer, Jeffery (1994). *Competitive Advantage Through People*. Boston, MA: Harvard Business School Press.

Pride, William M., Hughes, Robert J., and Kapoor, Jack R. (2002). *Business* (7th ed.). Boston: Houghton Mifflin.

Zikmund, William G., Middlemist, R. Dennis, and Middlemist, Melanie R. (1995). *Business: The American Challenge for Global Competitiveness*. Homewood, IL: Austen Press.

Marcy Satterwhite

COMPETITIVE PRICING
SEE *Pricing*

COMPILATION AND REVIEW SERVICES

Public accountants are qualified to provide a range of services related to financial statements. Among the services are reviews and compilations. These services are less comprehensive than audits, which are required for publicly owned companies. Statements on Standards for Accounting and Review Services are issued by the Accounting and Review Services Committee, which is the senior technical committee of the American Institute of Certified Public Accountants (AICPA) designated to issue pronouncements in connection with unaudited financial statements or other unaudited financial information of a nonpublic entity.

NATURE OF ENGAGEMENTS PROVIDED

The most common engagements that are provided by public accountants for nonpublic entities are the compilation and review. Neither of these is as extensive as an audit. An audit requires that the public accountant obtain an understanding of internal control, assess internal control, assess fraud risk, and obtain corroborating evidence to support the figures shown in the included set of financial statements. Compilations and reviews do not have such requirements. While there are specified procedures for compilations and reviews to support the nature of report provided, such procedures are less rigorous and less extensive than those required for an audit.

COMPILATIONS

Compilations is an appropriate description of what the accountant actually does when engaged to provide this type of service. The certified public accountant (CPA) prepares—compiles—financial statements based on information supplied by the company's management. CPAs are expected to be familiar with the accounting principles and practices of the industry in which the entity operates so that the financial statements are compiled in appropriate form for that industry. This standard does not prevent an accountant from accepting a compilation engagement for an entity in an industry with which the accountant has no previous experience. It does, however, impose on the accountant responsibility for obtaining the level of understanding expected for such an engagement. Such understanding is available in AICPA guides, industry

publications, financial statements of other entities in the industry, textbooks, periodicals, and relevant Web sites.

To compile financial statements, the accountant must have an understanding of the nature of the entity's business transactions, the form of its accounting records, the stated qualifications of its accounting personnel, the accounting basis on which the financial statements are to be presented, and the form and content for the financial statements. Such knowledge is obtained through experience with the entity or through inquiry of the entity's personnel. There are instances when the accountant recognizes that other accounting services are needed, such as assistance in adjusting the books of accounting or in assuring proper classification of transactions in the accounting system. Such additional services can be provided by the accountant engaged to compile the financial statements.

If any evidence or information comes to the accountant's attention regarding fraud or an illegal act that may have occurred, the accountant should request that management consider the effect of the matter on the financial statements. Additionally, the accountant should consider the effect of the matter on the accountant's compilation report. The accountant may have to resign from an engagement if there is any question about fraud or illegal acts and the client refuses to provide additional or revised information.

The report provided states that a compilation is limited to presenting in the form of financial statements information that is the representation of management (or owners). Also, stated is that the financial statements have not been audited or reviewed and that the accountant is not expressing an opinion or any other form of assurance on them. There are circumstances that permit the accountant to limit the distribution of the report. The guidance is provided in the Statements on Standards for Accounting and Review Services.

An accountant is not precluded from issuing a report for a compilation of financial statements for an entity when the accountant is not independent in respect to that entity. When the accountant is not independent, however, there must be disclosure of the lack of independence. In the last paragraph of the report in such an instance is the need to state: "I am (we are) not independent with respect to [company name] company."

An accountant may be engaged to provide compilations for financial statements for more than one year.

REVIEWS

Reviews require that the accountant possesses a level of knowledge of the accounting principles and practices of the industry in which the entity operates and an understanding of the business of the entity that is provided primarily through inquiry and analytical procedures. Additionally, the accountant must obtain written representations from management in which, among several matters, management acknowledges responsibility for the fair presentation in the financial statements of financial position and results of operation and cash flows in conformity with generally accepted accounting practices (GAAP). A review does not provide assurance that the accountant will become aware of all significant matters that would be disclosed in an audit.

Nevertheless, accountants may become aware that information coming to their attention is incorrect, incomplete, or otherwise unsatisfactory. Furthermore, evidence or information may come to the accountants' attention regarding fraud or an illegal act that may have occurred. The accountants should request that management consider the effect of such knowledge on the financial statements. Additionally accountants should consider the effect of all information acquired on their review reports. Additional procedures may be needed if the accountants believe the financial statements are materially misstated.

An accountant must be independent in respect to the client when accepting an engagement to perform a review and provide a report. The accountant's review provides only limited assurance. This assurance is stated in the accountant's report in these words: "I am (we are) not aware of any material modifications that should be made to the accompanying financial statements in order for them to be in conformity with GAAP." The report provided by the accountant states that the scope is less than that for an audit that is performed in accordance with generally accepted auditing standards. Also stated is that the accountant does not express an opinion on the financial statements.

It is possible for an accountant to provide a report even though some modification is required. Such modification is described in a separate paragraph of the report. Also, an accountant may be asked to provide a review for financial statements for more than a single year.

WHEN COMPILATIONS AND REVIEWS ARE APPROPRIATE

When does a client hire a CPA to perform a compilation or a review instead of an audit? To understand this issue, it is first necessary to understand why some companies need audits. If the company is publicly owned and must submit financial statements to the Securities and Exchange Commission (SEC), an annual financial audit is a basic requirement for the financial statements submitted. If the management of a small public company that does not report to the SEC or a nonpublic company where the owners or shareholders are separate from the

sources for funding, there is a "monitoring" problem not unlike that for the publicly owned companies. In general, the multiple owners or the bank cannot be sure the information provided by the management of the company is reliable. Reliable information, for example, that is submitted to a bank as a source of information to be reviewed for the approval of a significant loan that is supported by a report from a public accountant, has higher value than such financial information with no involvement of a public accountant. Such information, if all other factors are satisfactory, generally means that the cost of the desired capital will be lower than if no such involvement was present.

Now, consider the case of a small sole practitioner who is both the owner and manager of the company. It might be the case that the owner/manager wants financial statements prepared so that his or her performance may be assessed, but does not require the assurance regarding the reliability of the numbers because the owner/manager is the one who provided the figures to the CPA. In essence, the person providing the information is also the user of the report. In this case, the owner/manager would probably engage a public accountant to perform a compilation. A compilation would be sufficient for the owner/manager and would be less costly than a review or an audit.

Many banks want some form of assurance from small business owners (nonpublic entities) before lending them significant sums of money, but realize that an audit is not necessary. Therefore, such a bank is likely to require that there be a review performed by an independent public accountant so that there is provided limited assurance that the financial statements are presented in accordance with GAAP.

There are instances, of course, where the banker of a small business may have multiple sources of information from the interaction between the banker and the owner of the small company. In such instances a compilation provided by an independent accountant may be sufficient.

REVIEWS REQUIRED FOR PUBLICLY OWNED COMPANIES

Publicly owned companies must have quarterly reviews. Publicly owned companies are required to file quarterly financial statements and the company's external public auditor is required to perform a review at the end of the first three quarters before the company files its quarterly financial statements with the SEC. The guidance that is followed in this review is provided by the Public Company Accounting Oversight Board (PCAOB). As of December 2005, however, the guidance required by the PCAOB is that provided by the Auditing Standards Board of the AICPA. That guidance was undergoing review by the PCAOB and was subject to modification.

SEE ALSO *Auditing*

BIBLIOGRAPHY

American Institute of Certified Public Accountants. (2005). *AICPA Professional Standards* (Vols. 1–2). New York: Author.

Konrath, Larry F. (1999). *Auditing concepts and applications: A risk analysis approach* (4th ed.). Cincinnati: South-Western.

Messier, William F., Jr., Glover, Steven M., and Prawitt, Douglas F. (2006). *Auditing and assurance services: A systematic approach* (4th ed.). Boston: McGraw-Hill/Irwin.

Vicky B. Hoffman

COMPLIANCE AUDITS

SEE *Auditing*

COMPUTER GRAPHICS

Computer graphics are found in almost every industry; individuals in all demographic, geographic, racial, political, and religious groups benefit from them. When picking up a magazine or newspaper, watching television, going to the movies, or taking a drive down the street, images produced by computer graphics are seen.

Computer graphics are used because they add color, excitement, and visual stimulation to media. They are aesthetically appealing and informative. Newspapers, magazines, brochures and reports, billboards, posters, art prints, greeting cards, and postcards incorporate digital graphics. Several movies, including *Who Framed Roger Rabbit?, Toy Story,* and *Stuart Little* have received recognition for their innovative use of digital effects and/or animation. Video games use advanced digital graphics. Scientists use computer visualizations to simulate animal movements, thunderstorms, and galaxy formation. Visual simulation is also used in training programs where people learn how to drive or fly. Physicians are able to see digital graphical representations of computerized axial tomography scan data that aid in diagnosis and treatment. Architects and product designers use computer-aided design programs to draw graphical representations of their designs. Graphic designers create digital illustrations on the computer. Across the World Wide Web computer graphics are shared around the globe.

Computer graphics are visual and, therefore, one's response to them is very different from one's response to textual or auditory communication. As children, people develop visual skills before language skills, but even as adults they respond emotionally to what they see. People bring to any viewing of an image their experience, expectations, and values. Sometimes people draw from cultural, religious, or universal symbols to help them relate the image to their experience of the world. The universal becomes personal and the personal becomes universal. Visual communication is multidimensional. People have a primal or visceral response based upon deep-seated beliefs, an emotional response based upon image content and presentation, and an associative response based upon prior experience. Then a rational response is layered on top of the rest.

FILM VERSUS DIGITAL IMAGERY

Computer graphics is the art of using computer technology to create visual images from data. One way to understand this is to contrast film and digital photography. With a film camera a roll of film is loaded into the camera. To make a picture the camera exposes some halide silver crystals on one small piece of film at a time to light. When the entire roll has been used, it may be taken to a professional who processes the film with chemicals and then shines light through the film onto light-sensitive paper. An image soon appears on the paper and a print is created.

Unlike film cameras, a digital camera does not use film. It has a minicomputer inside that records light onto a two-dimensional array of points. Each of these points is then assigned a digital value. In general all digital devices work on the same principle. The source may be light from the natural world or a piece of paper, or an image created on the computer. Each digital device turns the source input into an array of digital values. To better understand this, one needs to look more closely at how computers work.

THE BINARY SYSTEM

Computers use a binary system consisting of 1s and 0s. Conceptually this works like an on/off switch. To describe an image in black and white, white can be assigned the value "0" and black the value "1." If one takes a black-and-white image and superimposes a series of rows and columns onto it, then at each intersection of a row and column one has a point. Each point can then be assigned a value of "0," white, or "1," black. Now there is an array of 0s and 1s that taken together represent an image. Every value, that is, every 0 or 1, requires a bit of storage. An image as described above is said to have a bit depth of 1, because it takes 1 bit (either a 1 or 0) to describe any point on the image.

If one wants an image to contain shades of gray between black and white, one need more bits. If one uses 2 bits, there are four possible combinations of 1 and 0

	1960s	1970s	1980s	1990s	2000s
Computer technology	• Programs are run in batch mode using punch cards. Text characters are used to create pictures. • Printers can only print whole characters not individual dots.	• Mid 1970s: First personal computers appear. Monitors display white text against a green background the result of a P1 phosphor from a cathode ray tube. Monitors are called CRTs or greenscreens. • Graphics resolution is low, around 128 x 48 dots per screen.	• 1981: IBM introduces the first color PC. The CGA monitor is capable of displaying 4 colors using a combination of red, green, and blue. • 1984: Apple Macintosh is introduced. • Color graphics are possible, but computer memory is limited. • 1987: 256 colors and a resolution of 720 dots x 400 dots are possible.	• The number of colors a PC monitor can display jumps from 256 to 16.7 million. • PCs can use 3D graphics. • 1994: the World Wide Web becomes available to the public and provides another channel for computer graphics use.	• LCD monitors become popular. • PC Graphics Processing Units (GPU) deliver 25 times the 3D graphics performance of the 1990s.
Video	Manufacturers of video games experiment with computer graphics in games such as Pong.		• Video games have advanced to virtual reality and role playing. • In business virtual reality technology is used to evaluate and modify product designs.		• Users interact with games through real-time 3D graphical representations of users.
Movies/TV		1977: *Star Wars* incorporates 3D computer graphics into the film.	• 1984: *The Last Starfighter* displays the first photorealistic computer graphic images in a feature film. • 1988: *Who Framed Roger Rabbit* combines computer animation characters with live humans.	• 1991: *Toy Story* becomes the first computer animated full-length film. • 3D computer graphics are used in cartoons on TV and in animated movies.	• High Definition digital televisions (HDTV) become popular. • *Shark Tale* uses global illumination to render realistic shadows and reflections.
Modeling			• Early 1980s: CAD systems using 2D floor planning and rudimentary modeling are available. • Late 1980s: CAD systems offer 3D rendering and walkthrough capabilities. • 1989: Simulation and visualization programs become available. • CAT scan technology which allows physicians to see graphical representations of soft tissue aid in diagnosis and treatment of abnormalities. • 3D models of the human body are used for virtual surgery and training.	• Photographs are integrated with CAD drawings. • CAD/CAM programs are used to design, assemble and test new products.	

Figure 1

(00, 10, 01, 11), therefore four shades of gray (including black and white) can be represented. Four shades of gray are not generally enough gradation to create a realistic representation. Generally, 8 bits, or 256 shades of gray, are needed to produce a high-quality image.

COLOR AND RESOLUTION

Color poses an additional complication. All colors can be created by combining the three primary colors of light: red, green, and blue. For a computer to render color effectively it then needs to separately describe each of these three primary colors. Although any color can be created with as few as 2 bits, most computers today use 24-bit or 32-bit depth to represent a full color image, producing up to 16,777,216 colors. This surpasses the capability of the human eye, which can discern about 10 million colors.

The higher the bit depth the more accurate the color is. Even with 16 million colors, however, one may have a low-quality image unless one also has high resolution. Resolution is the density of points, or pixels, on the image array—that is, the number of columns and rows per inch. The greater the number of columns and rows the higher the density. The higher the density, the greater the resolution.

The cost of high resolution and greater bit depth is space. High-quality graphics take up a large amount of disk space in a computer and require larger memory sizes to work with and edit them. One professional digital image can easily require 50 megabytes, that is, 8,192,000 bits, or more, of space.

Display devices and printers are limited by the amount of data they can represent. The optimal resolution required for a digital image varies based upon the output medium and the number of rows and columns it can display per inch. The resulting intersection points are called dots and the number per inch are called dots per inch, or dpi. Usually a fine-art print will require high resolution, while a Web-based image will not. One of the advantages of digital images is they can be stored on the computer and used repeatedly, each reproduction being exactly the same as the last.

Until recently, before viewing a digital image it had to be converted to a nondigital or analog format because most output devices were analog. Cathode-ray tubes, most televisions, and many printers are still analog, but liquid crystal display monitors and many other printers and televisions are digital. Digital images can go directly from the computer to the output device without translation.

The capabilities and robustness of computer graphics have evolved over several decades. See Table 1 for highlights of the major advancements regarding computer graphics in the fields of computer technology, video, movies and television, and modeling.

CONCLUSION

Computer graphics will continue to get more sophisticated. Their 3-D photorealistic capabilities and ability to predict changes over time have revolutionized product development and marketing, as well as scientific research and education. They are responsible for superior special effects in movies and on television. Many newspapers and magazines use only computer-generated graphics. They add an aesthetic and emotional dimension to text. Computer graphics affect everyone's life in almost every aspect every day.

SEE ALSO *Information Technology*

BIBLIOGRAPHY

Maxwell, Marty (2004). *The Role of Visual Imagery in Advocacy Journalism.* Athens: University of Georgia.

Zenz, Dave (2002, September). Advances in graphics architectures. Retrieved November 14, 2005, from http://www1.us.dell.com/content/topics/global.aspx/vectors/en/2002_graphics?c=us&l=en&s=corp

Marty Maxwell

CONFLICT MANAGEMENT

SEE *Human Relations; Management/Leadership Styles*

CONSUMER ADVOCACY AND PROTECTION

Consumer advocacy refers to actions taken by individuals or groups to promote and protect the interests of the buying public. Historically, consumer advocates have assumed a somewhat adversarial role in exposing unfair business practices or unsafe products that threaten the welfare of the general public. Consumer advocates use tactics such as publicity, boycotts, letter-writing campaigns, Internet "gripe sites," and lawsuits to raise awareness of issues affecting consumers and to counteract the financial and political power of the organizations they target. Since even large, multinational businesses can be visibly wounded when their mistreatment of consumers or other constituencies arouses the ire of consumer advocacy organizations, it should be obvious to business owners that they can ill afford to engage in business practices that could draw the attention of consumer advocates.

Periods of vocal consumer advocacy around the turn of the twentieth century and in the late 1960s have left a legacy of federal legislation and agencies intended to protect consumers in the United States. The rights of consumers have expanded to include product safety, the legitimacy of advertising claims, the satisfactory resolution of grievances, and a say in government decisions. In the early days of industry, companies could afford to ignore consumers' wishes because there was so much demand for their goods and services. As a result, they were often able to command high prices for products of poor quality. The earliest consumer advocates to point out such abuses were called muckrakers, and their revelations of underhanded business practices spurred the creation of several federal agencies and a flurry of legislation designed to curb some of the most serious abuses. At the same time, increased competition began to provide consumers with more choices among a variety of products of higher quality. Still, some notable cases of corporations neglecting the public welfare for their own gain continued, and corporate influence in American politics enabled many businesses to resist calls for reform in advertising, worker or consumer safety, and pollution control.

This situation led to the consumer movement of the 1960s. One of the country's most outspoken and controversial consumer advocates, lawyer Ralph Nader, came to the forefront during this time. Nader's effective and well-publicized denunciations of the American automobile industry included class-action lawsuits and calls for recalls of allegedly defective products, and many of his actions served as a tactical model for future advocacy organizations.

The efforts of Nader and other activists led to the formation of several federal agencies designed to protect consumer interests. The U.S. Office of Consumer Affairs, created in 1971, investigates and resolves consumer complaints, conducts consumer surveys, and disseminates product information to the public. The Consumer Product Safety Commission, formed in 1973, sets national standards for product safety and testing procedures, coordinates product recalls, and ensures that companies respond to valid consumer complaints. Other government agencies that benefit consumers include the Federal Trade Commission (FTC) and state consumer agencies.

Richard Romero, general manager of a California Toyota dealership, shows the same contract written in English, Chinese, Korean, Vietnamese, and Tagalog. The Consumer Protection for New Californians bill requires that certain businesses including car dealers, apartment owners, bankers, and legal service providers have contracts available in four major Asian languages and Spanish. **AP IMAGES**

Nongovernmental agencies that provide information for consumers include the Better Business Bureau, a private, nonprofit organization that works to resolve complaints consumers have with businesses. The Consumer Federation of America is the one of the largest consumer advocacy groups in the United States, consisting of about 300 member organizations representing 50 million people. The International Organization of Consumers Unions, based in the Netherlands, actively promotes consumer interests on a global scale. Other well-known consumer advocacy groups include: Public Citizen, founded by Ralph Nader; the Consumers Union of the United States, which publishes *Consumer Reports*; and the National Consumers League.

CONSUMER ADVOCACY IN CYBERSPACE

In the early 1990s, the widespread use of home computers advanced consumer advocacy by making it easier for citizens to gather information and make their views known. By the early twenty-first century, the Internet had become one of the primary weapons of consumer advocates, with untold thousands of "so-called global 'gripe sites' established by campaigners or disgruntled customers with the aim of harassing and haranguing large companies," according to Simon Reeve in the *European*.

Before the advent of the World Wide Web, it was difficult for individuals or small groups, which lacked the resources of major corporations, to make their voices heard over their targets' advertising messages. "But the Internet has created a level playing field for advocacy," Reeve wrote. "With little more than a personal computer and a subscription to an Internet service provider, anyone can open a site on the World Wide Web and say more or less whatever they like." Current and potential customers of major corporations typically use common Internet search engines to access the companies' carefully prepared home pages. Yet these search engines also lead the customers to sites created by protesters—sites that are filled with complaints and allegations against the companies, ranging from the use of child labor to the exploitation of resources in less-developed countries. Thus, for consumer advocates, "the Internet means a new freedom to take on the mightiest corporations, in an environment where massive advertising budgets count for little," Reeve stated.

For businesses, on the other hand, Internet gripe sites pose a difficult problem. Although the material posted on such sites might be distorted, false, or even outright libelous, it can still prove damaging to a company's image. Moreover, few legal remedies exist as the law struggles to keep up with technology. It is often difficult for companies to trace the operators of gripe sites, for example, and suing the Internet service providers that provide a forum

for protesters has not proved successful. In addition, turning to the law for help can turn into a public relations disaster for companies, making a small problem into a much bigger one. "The Internet is an uncontrollable beast," attorney Simon Halberstam told Reeve. "While legally the firm may have recourse to law, the reality is that they may just have to accept the problem and carry on with their business."

TECHNOLOGY OFFERS MIXED BAG FOR CONSUMERS

The Internet age has provided consumers with unprecedented access to information and an often-overwhelming abundance of choices, but it has also exposed them to new types of fraud. "The deregulation and technological revolution that gave us all these new responsibilities and choices were also supposed to release the genius of the free market, which would drive down prices and create innovative comparison-shopping tools," Kim Clark wrote in *U.S. News and World Report*. "But the anticipated information explosion hasn't kept up with consumers' needs."

According to the National Consumers League, consumer losses to telemarketing and Internet scams during the first six months of 2005 were more than double the average from 2004. Telemarketing fraud victims lost an average of $4,107 during the first half of 2005, compared to $1,974 in 2004. This increase came despite efforts by the FTC to reduce consumers' exposure to unwanted telemarketing calls through registry on the National Do Not Call List, which received widespread praise from consumer advocacy groups. Similarly, Internet fraud victims lost an average of $2,579 in 2005, compared to $895 in 2004. Federal efforts to reduce spam and other sources of Internet fraud have not been particularly successful.

SEE ALSO *Consumer Bill of Rights; Consumer Protest*

BIBLIOGRAPHY

Clark, Kim (2003, August 18). Customer disservice. *U.S. news and world report*, 29.

Mayer, Robert N. (1989). *The consumer movement: Guardians of the marketplace*. Boston: Twayne.

National Consumers League. (2005, June). Mid-year fraud stats reveal alarming trends in telemarketing, Internet scams. *NCL news*. Retrived August 11, 2005, from http://nclnet.org/news/2005/fraud_trends_june2005.htm

Reeve, Simon (1998, January 26). Web attack. *European*, 20.

Unsafe at any megahertz: Ralph Nader is taking on Bill Gates. Is consumerism still a force in America? (1997, October 11). *Economist*, 80.

Laurie Collier Hillstrom

CONSUMER AND BUSINESS PRODUCTS

The classification of products and services is essential to business because it provides one of the factors for determining the strategies needed to move them through the marketing system. The two major classes are consumer products and business products.

CONSUMER PRODUCTS

Consumer products are products purchased for personal, family, or household use. They are often grouped into four subcategories on the basis of consumer buying habits: convenience products, shopping products, specialty products and unsought products.

Consumer products can also be differentiated on the basis of durability. Durable products are products that have a long life, such as furniture and garden tools. Nondurable products are those that are quickly used up or worn out, or that become outdated, such as food, school supplies, and disposable cameras.

Convenience Products. Convenience products are items that buyers want to purchase with the least amount of effort, that is, as conveniently as possible. Most are nondurable products of low value that are frequently purchased in small quantities. These products can be further divided into three subcategories: staple, impulse, and emergency items.

Staple convenience products are basic items that buyers plan to buy before they enter a store, and include milk, bread, and toilet paper. Impulse items are other convenience products that are purchased without prior planning, such as candy bars, soft drinks, and tabloid newspapers. Emergency products are those that are purchased in response to an immediate, unexpected need such as ambulance service or a fuel pump for the car.

Since convenience products are not actually sought out by consumers, producers attempt to get as wide a distribution as possible through various marketing channels—which may include different types of wholesale and retail vendors. Convenience stores, vending machines, and fast food are examples of retailer focus on convenience products. Within stores, they are placed at checkout stands and other high-traffic areas.

Shopping Products. Shopping products are purchased only after the buyer compares the various products and brands available through different retailers before making a deliberate buying decision. These products are usually of higher value than convenience goods, bought less frequently, and are durable. Price, quality, style, and color are typically factors in the buying decision. Televisions, com-

puters, lawn mowers, bedding, and appliances are all examples of shopping products.

Because customers are going to shop for these products, a fundamental strategy in establishing stores that specialize in shopping products is to locate near similar stores in active shopping areas. Promotion for shopping products is often done cooperatively with the manufacturers and frequently includes the heavy use of advertising in local media, including newspapers, radio, and television.

Specialty Products. Specialty products are items that consumers seek out because of their unique characteristics or brand identification. Buyers know exactly what they want and are willing to exert considerable effort to obtain it. These products are usually, but not necessarily, of high value. This category includes both durable and nondurable products. Specialty products differ from shopping products primarily because price is not the chief consideration. Often the attributes that make them unique are brand preference (e.g., a certain make of automobile) or personal preference (e.g., a food dish prepared in a specific way). Other items that fall into this category are wedding dresses, antiques, fine jewelry, and golf clubs.

Producers and distributors of specialty products prefer to place their products only in selected retail outlets. These outlets are chosen on the basis of their willingness and ability to provide an image of status, targeted advertising, and personal selling for the product. Consistency of image between the product and the store is also important.

Unsought Products. Unsought products are those products that consumers are either unaware of or have little interest in actively pursuing. Examples are new innovations, life insurance, and preplanned funeral services. Because of the lack of awareness of these products or the need for them, heavy promotion is often required.

The distinction among convenience, shopping, specialty, and unsought products is not always clear. As noted earlier, these classifications are based on consumers' buying habits. Consequently, a given item may be a convenience good for one person, a shopping good for another, and a specialty good for a third, depending on the situation and the demographics and attitudes of the consumer.

BUSINESS PRODUCTS

Business products are products and services that companies purchase to produce their own products or to operate their business. Unlike consumer products, business products are classified on the basis of their use rather than customer buying habits. These products are divided into six subcategories: installations; accessory equipment; raw materials; component parts and processed materials; maintenance, repair, and operating supplies; and business services.

Business products also carry designations related to their durability. Durable business products that cost large sums of money are referred to as capital items. Nondurable products that are used up within a year are called expense items.

Installations. Installations are major capital items that are typically used directly in the production process of products. Some installations, such as conveyor systems, robotics equipment, and machine tools, are designed and built for specialized situations. Other installations, such as stamping machines, large commercial ovens, and computerized axial tomography scan machines, are built to a standard design but can be modified to meet individual requirements.

The purchase of installations requires extensive research and careful decision making on the part of the buyer. Manufacturers of installations can make their availability known through advertising. Actual sale of installations, however, requires the technical knowledge and assistance that can best be provided by personal selling.

Accessory Equipment. Products that fall into the subcategory of accessory equipment are less expensive and have shorter lives than installations. Examples include hand tools, computers, desk calculators, and forklifts. While some types of accessory equipment, such as hand tools, are involved directly in the production process, most are only indirectly involved.

The relatively low unit value of accessory equipment, combined with a market made up of buyers from several different types of businesses, dictates a broad marketing strategy. Sellers rely heavily on advertisements in trade publications and mailings to purchasing agents and other business buyers. When personal selling is needed, it is usually done by intermediaries, such as wholesalers.

Raw Materials. Raw materials are products that are purchased in their raw state for the purpose of processing them into consumer or business products. Examples are iron ore, crude oil, diamonds, copper, timber, wheat, and leather. Some (e.g., wheat) may be converted directly into another consumer product (cereal). Others (e.g., timber) may be converted into an intermediate product (lumber) to be resold for use in another industry (construction).

Most raw materials are graded according to quality so that there is some assurance of consistency within each grade. There is, however, little difference between offerings within a grade. Consequently, sales negotiations focus on price, delivery, and credit terms. This negotiation, and because raw materials are ordinarily sold in large quantities, makes personal selling the principal marketing approach for these goods.

Component Parts and Processed Materials. Component parts are items that are purchased to be placed in the final product without further processing. Processed materials, on the other hand, require additional processing before being placed in the end product. Many industries, including the auto industry, rely heavily on component parts. Automakers use such component parts as batteries, sunroofs, windshields, and spark plugs. They also use several processed materials, including steel and upholstery fabric.

Buyers of component parts and processed materials have well-defined specifications for their needs. They may work closely with a company in designing the components or materials they require, or they may invite bids from several companies. In either case, in order to be in a position to get the business, personal contact must be maintained with the buyers over time. Here again, personal selling is a key component in the marketing strategy.

Maintenance, Repair, and Operating Supplies. Maintenance, repair, and operating (MRO) supplies are frequently purchased expense items. They contribute indirectly to the production of the end product or to the operations of the business. MRO supplies include computer paper, light bulbs, lubrication oil, cleaning supplies, and office supplies.

Buyers of MRO supplies do not spend a great deal of time on their purchasing decisions unless they are ordering large quantities. As a result, companies marketing supplies place their emphasis on advertising, particularly in the form of catalogs, to business buyers. When large orders are at stake, sales representatives may be used.

Business Services. Business services refer to the services purchased by companies to assist in the operation of the firm. They include financial, marketing research, promotional, legal, lawn care, and janitorial services. The decision to hire an outside business to perform needed services is often predicated on how frequently the service is needed, the specialized knowledge required, and the relative costs of providing the service internally versus contracting with an outside firm.

It is not always clear whether a product is a consumer product or a business product. The key to differentiating them is to identify the use the buyer intends to make of the product. Products that are in their final form and are ready to be purchased and consumed by individuals or households for their personal satisfaction are classified as consumer products. On the other hand, if they are bought by a business for its own use, they are considered business products. Some items, such as flour and pickup trucks, can fall into either classification, depending on how they are used. Flour purchased by a supermarket for resale is classified as a consumer good, but flour purchased by a bakery to make pastries is classified as a business product. A pickup truck bought for personal use is a consumer product; if purchased to transport lawn mowers for a lawn service, it is a business product.

SEE ALSO *Business Marketing*

BIBLIOGRAPHY

Boone, Louis E., and Kurtz, David L. (2005). *Contemporary marketing 2006.* Eagan, MN: Thomson South-Western.

Hoffman, K. Douglass (2006). *Marketing principles and best practices* (3rd ed.). Mason, OH: Thomson South-Western.

Kotler, Philip, and Armstrong, Gary (2006). *Principles of marketing* (11th ed.). Upper Saddle River, NJ: Pearson Prentice-Hall.

Pride, William M., and Ferrell, O. C. (2006). *Marketing concepts and strategies.* Boston: Houghton Mifflin.

Solomon, Michael R., Marshall, Greg W., and Stuart, Elnora W. (2006). *Marketing: Real people, real choices* (4th ed.). Upper Saddle River, NJ: Pearson Prentice-Hall.

Thomas R. Baird
Earl C. Meyer
Sharon K. Slick

CONSUMER BEHAVIOR

While in medical school, Laura Trice's one major complaint about living a vegan lifestyle and following an animal-product-free diet was the lack of "great tasting sweets." Rather than sublimating her craving for junk food, she came up with a cookie recipe that she found satisfied her sweet tooth. After graduation from medical school, Trice found a business partner who had been a self-trained vegetarian chef for over twenty years and together they started Laura's Wholesome Junk Food in 2001 (http://www.LaurasWholesomeJunkFood.com). The concept was to provide snacks that tasted as great as junk food—something most people, especially the two founders, secretly loved—that also used ingredients which were more wholesome than those used in regular products.

In July 2002 Laura's Wholesome Junk Food released their first line of energy bars priced and sized to compete with the energy bars then on the market. Their first orders were from two small stores, a vending machine company and a coffee chain. To provide samples to convince consumers that something with healthful ingredients could

taste good, Laura's Wholesome Junk Foods handed out bite-sized samples packed in plastic resealable tubs, which they subsequently named and trademarked Bite-lettes. What happened next surprised both Trice and Howard Weinthal, director of product development. "Consumers loved the Bite-lettes and kept asking how they might buy them. So we stopped making bars after 4 months and shut down for 6 months to find a place that could make the Bite-lettes for us. We didn't know if it was going to work. We thought we might be out of business" (Trice, 2005).

Figuring out not only what they wanted, but who would buy it, why they would buy it, where they would buy it, and how often they would buy it, is the cornerstone of understanding consumer behavior. Consumer behavior is the study of people: how we buy, consume and dispose of products. There were approximately 295 million people in the United States alone in 2004. Each of us is a consumer of hundreds of products every day. As consumers, we can benefit from a better understanding of how we make our decisions so that we can make wiser ones. Marketers can benefit from an understanding of consumer behavior so that they can better predict what consumers want and how best to offer it to them. Trice and Weinthal listened to consumer requests, created a new portion-controlled concept, and scrapped the full-sized energy bar. In 2005 Laura's Wholesome Junk Food sold Bite-lettes to more than 180 stores nationwide.

There are two major forces that shape who we are and what we buy. Our personal motives, attitudes, and decision-making abilities guide our consumption behavior. At the same time, our families, cultural background, the ads we see on television, and the sites we visit on the Internet influence our thoughts and actions (see Figure 1).

UNDERSTANDING CONSUMERS: INTERNAL FACTORS

Our consumption behavior is a function of who we are as individuals. Our thoughts, feelings, attitudes, and patterns of behavior determine what we buy, when we buy it, and how we use it. Internal factors have a major impact on consumer behavior.

Consumer Motivation. A marketer's job is to figure out what needs and wants the consumer has, and what motivates the consumer to purchase. Motivation is the drive that initiates all our consumption behaviors, and consumers have multiple motives, or goals. Some of these are overt, such as a physiological thirst that motivates a consumer to purchase a soft drink or the need to purchase a new suit for an interview. Other motives are more obscure, such as a student's need to plug in to an iPod or wear designer clothes to gain social approval.

Model of consumer behavior

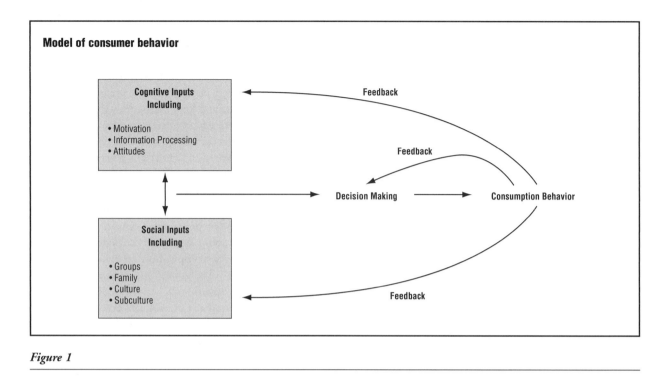

Figure 1

Most consumption activities are the result of several motives operating at the same time. Researchers specially trained in uncovering motives often use qualitative research techniques in which consumers are encouraged to reveal their thoughts (cognitions) and feelings (affect) through probing dialogue. Focus groups and in-depth interviews give consumers an opportunity to discuss products and express opinions about consumption activities. Trained moderators or interviewers are often able to tap into preconscious motives that might otherwise go undetected. Sentence completion tasks (e.g., Men who wear Old Spice are …) or variants of the thematic apperception tests, in which respondents are shown a picture and asked to tell a story surrounding it, are additional techniques that provide insight into underlying motives.

Consumer motives or goals can be represented by the values they hold. Values are people's broad life goals that symbolize a preferred mode of behaving (e.g., independent, compassionate, honest) or a preferred end-state of being (e.g., sense of accomplishment, love and affection, social recognition). Consumers buy products that will help them achieve desired values; they see product attributes as a means to an end. Understanding the means-end perspective can help marketers better position the product and create more effective advertising and promotion campaigns.

Consumer Information Processing. The consumer information-processing approach aids in understanding con-

sumptive behavior by focusing on the sequence of mental activities that people use in interpreting and integrating their environment.

The sequence begins with human perception of external stimuli. Perception is the process of sensing, selecting, and interpreting stimuli in one's environment. We begin to perceive an external stimulus as it comes into contact with one of our sensory receptors—eyes, ears, nose, mouth, or skin. Perception of external stimuli influences our behavior even without our conscious knowledge that it is doing so. Marketers and retailers understand this, and they create products and stores specifically designed to influence our behavior. Fast-food chains paint their walls in "hot" colors, such as red, to speed up customer turnover. Supermarkets steer entering customers directly into the produce section, where they can smell and touch the food, stimulating hunger. A hungry shopper spends more money.

Close your eyes and think for a moment about the hundreds of objects, noises, and smells surrounding you at this very moment. In order to function in this crowded environment, we choose to perceive certain stimuli while ignoring others. This process is called selectivity. Selectivity lets us focus our attention on the things that provide meaning for interpreting our environment or on the things that are relevant to us, while not wasting our limited information-processing resources on irrelevant items.

Did you even notice that after you decide on, say, Florida, for your vacation destination, there seems to be an abundance of ads for Florida resorts, airline promotions for Florida, and articles about Florida restaurants and attractions everywhere? Coincidence? Not really. There are just as many now as there were before, only now you are selectively attending to them, whereas you previously filtered them out. Marketers continuously struggle to break through the clutter and grab consumers' attention. Advertising and packaging is designed to grab our attention through a host of techniques, such as the use of contrast in colors and sound, repetition, and contextual placement.

Did you watch television last night? You may have paid attention to many of the ads you saw during the commercial breaks; you may even have laughed out loud at a few of them. But how many can you recall today? Consumers' ability to store, retain, and retrieve product information is critical to a brand's success. When information is processed, it is held for a very brief time (less than 1 minute) in working, or short-term, memory. If this information is rehearsed (mentally repeated), it is transferred to long-term memory; if not, the information is lost and for-

gotten. Once transferred to long-term memory, information is encoded or arranged in a way that provides meaning to the individual. Information in long-term memory is constantly reorganized, updated, and rearranged as new information comes in, or learning takes place.

Information-processing theorists represent the storage of information in long-term memory as a network consisting of nodes (word, idea, or concept) and links (relationships among them). Nodes are connected to each other depending on whether there is an association between concepts, with the length of the linkages representing the degree of the association. Figure 2 illustrates a network model of long-term memory. When Trice cofounded Laura's Wholesome Junk Food, part of her challenge was to change consumers' knowledge structures for the concept of a healthful treat, "Healthy foods and gourmet/comfort foods have often been thought of as separate entities. A person allows an occasional 'treat' of something with the assumption that the treat is a) not healthy, and b) needs to be severely limited. By opening up to the concept that being health conscious can also be

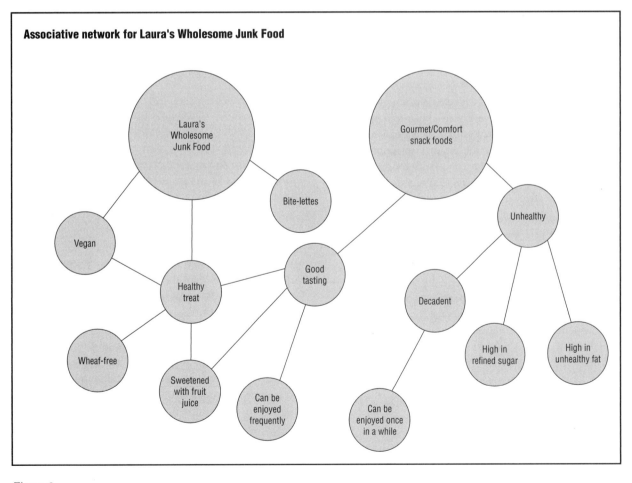

Associative network for Laura's Wholesome Junk Food

Figure 2

decadent, consumers have a new freedom to choose to incorporate treats and great tasting food for their families, their activities and for entertaining" (Trice, 2005).

The complete network brought to mind when a product is activated is called the product schema. Knowing the set of associations that consumers retrieve from long-term memory about a particular product or category is critical to a successful marketing strategy. For new products or services, marketers must first select the set of associations they want consumers to have. This is called positioning the product, or selecting the brand image. Trice's unique positioning as a "wholesome junk food" was accomplished by establishing a link between the concepts *healthful* and *decadent treat*. The brand position is then translated into clever ads, reinforced on product packaging, and integrated into all promotion and communication strategies.

Over time, a brand's image can fade or become diluted. Sometimes consumers associate concepts that are not favorable to a brand. When this occurs, marketers reposition the brand, using advertising and other marketing tools to help consumers create new links to positive association and discard links to the unfavorable ones. By rotating such catchy phrases as "Are your french fries lonely?" and "Your fish stick improvement system" on their ketchup labels, Heinz was able to reposition their ketchup as a more exciting, youth-oriented, and sparky brand.

Strategies for successful brand extensions also depend on the brand schema. Generally speaking, a brand extension is more likely to be successful if the set of associations for the extension matches the set of associations of the core product. Would Lifesavers brand toothpaste sell? Probably not, because the associations for Lifesavers (sweet, candy, sugar, fruity) are not the same as those for toothpaste (mint, clean, noncandy). On the other hand, a Lifesavers brand sugared children's cereal with colorful, fruity rings has a much better match of associations.

Attitude Formation and Change. The set of beliefs consumers have stored in long-term memory provides another critical function to marketers: It provides the basis for a consumer's attitude toward a brand or an ad. An attitude is an overall evaluation of an object, idea, or action. Attitudes can be positive or negative, and weakly or strongly held. The statement "I love Ben & Jerry's Vanilla Toffee Crunch" is a strong, positively valenced attitude toward a product. The statement "I dislike the new Toyota ad" is a weak, negatively valenced attitude toward an advertisement. Marketers work hard to continuously monitor consumer attitudes toward their products. Among other things, attitudes can indicate problems with a product or campaign, success with a product or campaign, likelihood of future sales, and overall strength of the brand or brand equity.

A popular perspective is that attitude has three components: cognitive, affective, and conative. The cognitive component reflects the knowledge and beliefs one has about the object (e.g., "Two pieces of Jolt chewing gum contains as much caffeine as one cup of coffee"), the affective component reflects feelings (e.g., "I like the energy boost I get after chewing Jolt Gum") and the conative component reflects a behavioral tendency toward the object (e.g., "I will buy Jolt Gum to take with me into my classes for exams"). Thus, attitudes are predispositions to behave in a certain way. If you have a favorable attitude toward a politician, you will likely vote for him or her in the next election. Because of this, many marketers use attitude measures for forecasting future sales.

It is important to note, however, that the link between attitudes and behavior is far from perfect. Consumers can hold positive attitudes toward multiple brands but intend to purchase only one. External economic, social, or personal factors often alter behavioral plans.

Attitudes are dynamic, which means they are constantly changing. As an individual learns new information, as fads change, as time goes on, the attitudes one once held with confidence may no longer exist. Did you ever look at old photos of yourself and wonder "What was I thinking wearing clothes like that? And look at my hairstyle!"

UNDERSTANDING CONSUMERS: EXTERNAL FACTORS

In addition to the internal factors, consumer behavior is also shaped to a large extent by social factors, such as culture, family relationships, and other aspects of the external environment. Awareness of these influences can help marketers to identify groups of consumers who tend to think, feel, or act similarly and separate them into unique market segments. Aspects of the marketing program such as product design, advertising, and pricing can then be tailored to meet the unique needs, values, and goals of these distinct groups.

Group Influences on Individual Consumer Behavior. Group influences on consumer behavior can affect motivation, values, and individual information processing; they can come from groups to which consumers already belong or from groups to which they aspire to belong. Groups can exert a variety of influences on individuals, including: (1) informational influences, where the group acts as a source for expert opinions; (2) comparative influences, such that the group provides opportunities to manage the individual's self-concept with respect to the group's identity; and (3) normative influences, whereby the group specifies guidelines and sanctions for appropriate or inappropriate individual behaviors.

The influence of groups on consumer behavior tends to vary with a variety of group- and product-related factors. For example, the more the group is perceived to be a credible, valued source of approval or disapproval to the consumer, the more likely that consumer is to conform to group values. In addition, the more frequently group members interact, and the more outwardly visible use of the product is to group and nongroup members, the greater the group's influence on individual consumption behavior.

Family Influences on Consumer Behavior. Families have a particularly significant influence on consumer behavior. For example, consumption behavior often changes substantially as family status changes over time. Thus, young unmarried adults, who are often focused on individual self-definition, tend to purchase products that enhance or define their self-concepts. In contrast, couples with children may be more interested in purchasing items or experiences that can be shared by all family members and, as a result, may spend less on individually oriented products.

Family membership also leads to a greater need for joint rather than individual decision making, further complicating consumer behavior at the household level. For example, the person who buys a product may not be the ultimate consumer of the product. Or perhaps the husband and wife have differing levels of involvement with certain product decisions, leading to different types of separate decision processes that must be integrated before a choice is ultimately made.

Understanding the dynamics involved in joint decision making and which family members influence which types of decisions has important implications for marketers interested in directing marketing efforts to the right person. Importantly, these family dynamics and lifestyle transitions are complicated by the decline in traditional households and the accompanying rise in nontraditional family structures, such as cohabiting couples or couples integrating families from previous marriages.

Cultural and Subcultural Influences on Consumer Behavior. Culture comprises the common meanings and socially constructed values accepted by the majority of members of a society or social group. It includes such things as shared values, beliefs, norms, and attitudes, as well as affective reactions, cognitive beliefs, and patterns of behavior. Typically, when we think of culture, we tend to think of differences among individuals from different countries or regions of the world. With the increasing globalization of the world economy, understanding differ-

ences and similarities in consumer behavior across cultures becomes increasingly meaningful, with important implications about the degree to which marketing strategies can be standardized across countries and cultures, or localized to reflect country- or region-specific cultural distinctions.

One important cultural difference is the degree to which the self is defined as independent from others versus interdependent with important others. Individualistic societies, such as the United States, tend to foster an independent sense of self, with the self believed to be a set of internal attributes unique to each person. Collectivist societies, however, such as China, foster an interdependent sense of self, with the self believed to be inseparable from others and the social context; person-specific attributes are less important in self-definition than are interpersonal relations. These differences in self-definition affect a variety of consumer behaviors, including emotional reactions to advertisements, the degree to which information from others is valued when making consumption decisions, and gift-giving behavior.

In addition to cultural differences that exist across countries, marketers are also increasingly recognizing the importance of subcultural differences within a society. Subcultures are distinctive groups within a society that share common meanings. Subcultures can often be identified based on demographic characteristics, such as geographic location (e.g., the southern United States), ethnicity (e.g., Hispanic Americans), or age (e.g., baby boomers). Subcultures can also be identified based on common lifestyles.

The start of the twenty-first century saw a growing emphasis on lifestyle segments based on food restrictions and food choices. For example, vegetarians, vegans, those who eat only organically grown food, and those who require gluten-free food are rapidly growing segments of the population. There are some national retailers, such as Whole Foods Market, who serve a multitude of these specialized segments.

There are also more targeted specialized products and services, such as *Gluten-Free Living,* a national magazine for people who follow a gluten-free diet (http://www.glutenfreeliving.com). Importantly, identification of lifestyle subcultures, and the corresponding development of an inventory of shared meanings, is typically more difficult than the development of such understanding of subcultures based on observable demographic characteristics.

Increasingly, Internet marketers have come to realize the value of subculture segments and have tailored product offerings and/or Web site content to appeal to particular subcultures, most often demographically based, and to foster a greater sense of community and connection among subculture members. For example, iVillage.com features content of particular interest to women and offers forums for discussion of issues relevant to its users. Similarly, Hispanic.com aims to provide services and information to Hispanic Americans as well as to provide a virtual meeting space for Hispanic Americans to meet and help one another. These represent early attempts to use the Internet to target and serve multicultural populations. Future sites are likely to target more narrowly defined subcultures (e.g., Hispanic Americans with an interest in gourmet cooking) and to focus on reaching more lifestyle-based subcultures.

THE CONSUMER DECISION-MAKING PROCESS

What consumers think and the social environment they live in determine what they buy and how that purchase decision is made. Typically, the decision process is described as a series of five stages. The first stage, need recognition, occurs when consumers perceive a difference between their ideal and actual states. Need recognition is often prompted by persuasive advertising. Consumers then begin the information search process by conducting an internal search of their own knowledge structures, followed by an external search for information from friends, family members, salespeople, and advertisements. This step can clarify the problem, providing criteria to use for assessing product alternatives and resulting in a subset, or "consideration set," of potential choices.

These options are then assessed more completely in the third stage, alternative evaluation. In this stage, products in the consideration set are compared with one another. Sometimes a simple heuristic rule of thumb, such as "I'm going to buy the cheapest product" is used. At other times a more complex strategy, such as a weighted-average model that compensates for product strengths and weaknesses, is used.

After examining each alternative, consumers are ready to purchase, the fourth step in the decision process. Finally, after buying, the consumers enter the postpurchase phase of the process, during which the performance of the chosen alternative is evaluated in light of prior expectations. Consumers will be satisfied with the product if it meets or exceeds expectations; dissatisfaction occurs if the product does not meet expectations.

This model of consumer behavior, while very useful, is highly simplified and does not always accurately reflect the decision process consumers follow. Consumers may not always proceed linearly through the five steps as described, and sometimes they may skip certain steps entirely. The model, however, is a close approximation of the process for most consumers for most purchase occasions.

We are all consumers. Understanding why we behave as we do is integral to an efficient transfer of goods and services in a market-driven economy and helps consumer needs get fulfilled. As Weinthal pointed out, "Since both founders of Laura's Wholesome Junk Food had dietary restrictions of their own and knew many individuals with limitations on what they could eat, we wanted to make the Bite-lettes accessible to as many people as possible. By making products that are all kosher, vegan, sweetened primarily with fruit, then adding a wheat-free flavor and three gluten-free ones, Laura's made something for almost every consumer" (Trice, 2005).

SEE ALSO *Marketing*

BIBLIOGRAPHY

Trice, Laura M.D. (2005). Personal correspondence.

Wilkie, William L. (1994). *Consumer Behavior* (3rd ed.). New York: Wiley.

Lauren G. Block
Patricia Williams

CONSUMER BILL OF RIGHTS

Webster's dictionary defines consumerism as "a movement for the protection of the consumer against defective products, misleading advertising, etc." Limited consumer protection was present until the 1950s and early 1960s. In the 1950s, a significant breakthrough occurred with the establishment of the product-liability concept, whereby a plaintiff did not have to prove negligence but only had to prove that a defective product caused an injury. In his 1962 speech to Congress, President John F. Kennedy outlined four basic consumer rights, which later became known as the Consumer Bill of Rights. In 1985, the United Nations endorsed Kennedy's Consumer Bill of Rights and expanded it to cover eight consumer rights. Consumer protection can only survive in highly industrialized countries because of the resources needed to finance consumer interests.

Kennedy's Consumer Bill of Rights included the right to be informed, the right to safety, the right to choose, and the right to be heard. The right to be informed involves protection against misleading information in the areas of financing, advertising, labeling, and packaging. Several laws of the 1960s and 1970s were aimed at this right. The Cigarette Labeling Act (1965), Fair Packaging and Labeling Act (1966), and the Wholesome Meat Act (1967) all addressed packaging. This legislation dealt with the accurate identification of the content of the product and any dangers associated with the product. The Truth-in-Lending Act required full disclosure of all costs and the annual percentage rate on installment loans. Prior to Truth-in-Lending, the actual cost was hidden and confusing to calculate. Another significant piece of legislation, the Magnuson-Moss Warranty Act, requires a warranty that states that a product will meet performance standards and affirms that a warranty can be stated or implied. Other regulation took place at the state level. Forty states have a cooling-off law, which allows a consumer to change his or her mind when purchasing products from direct salespeople.

The second consumer right, the right to safety, is aimed at injuries caused by using products other than automobiles. To address this problem, the government established the Consumer Product Safety Commission (CPSC) in 1972. The CPSC has jurisdiction over 13,000 diverse products. The powers of the CPSC include the right to require warning labels, to establish standards of performance, to require immediate notification of a defective product, and to mandate product testing. However, its greatest power is product recall.

The right of consumer choice means the consumer should have a range of products from various companies to choose from when making a purchasing decision. To ensure these rights, the government has taken a number of actions, such as imposing time limits on patents, looking at mergers from the standpoint of limiting consumer choice, and prohibiting unfair price cutting and other unfair business practices.

The final consumer right is the right to be heard. Presently, no government agency is responsible for handling consumer complaints. However, a number of government agencies do attempt to protect certain consumer rights. The Office of Consumer Affairs publishes a Consumer's Resource Handbook listing agencies that work in the area of consumer rights. In addition, a number of consumer groups issue complaints to the government and industry groups.

The growth of consumerism in the United States has not been without opposition. Although corporations have taken positive steps in many areas, they have also opposed advancement of some consumer rights. Because corporations can have deep pockets, they are able to appeal court cases and slow down litigation. Today, however, because of past successes, the need for consumer protection is not nearly as great as it was in previous years.

SEE ALSO *Consumer Advocacy and Protection*

BIBLIOGRAPHY

Alexander, Richard (1999). "The Development of Consumer Rights in the United States Slowed by the Power of Corporate Political Contributions and Lobbying." Retrieved September 29, 2005, from http://consumerlawpage.com/article/lobby.shtml.

"Consumer Rights." Retrieved September 29, 2005, from http://www.nolo.com.

Mary Jean Lush
Val Hinton

CONSUMER PRICE INDEX

The consumer price index (CPI) provides a method for calculating the price changes that consumers and household managers face over a stated period. Even though the CPI focuses primarily on consumer prices, its calculations are also of great direct value to governmental and business groups. Yet, at the same time, the CPI is the most commonly used price-level indicator. The CPI is a nationwide measure of a weighted measure of prices. It has the capability of consistently measuring changes in prices over periods.

The CPI serves two population groups: urban wage earners (CPI-U) and clerical workers (CPI-W). The CPI-U represents about 87 percent of the U.S. population and is based on the expenditures of all families living in urban areas. The CPI-W is a subset of the CPI and is based on the expenditures of families living in urban areas who meet additional requirements. At least one person in the family has to earn more than one-half of the family's income from clerical or hourly wage occupations. The CPI-W represents about 32 percent of the total U.S. population.

COST-OF-LIVING INDEX

Occasionally the term *cost-of-living index* is substituted for the term *CPI*. Nevertheless, to take in all the factors of paying to live would require the inclusion of calculations including every consumer's goods and services. Thousands of items are already included, and sheer volume forbids including all of them.

CONSTRUCTION OF THE CONSUMER PRICE INDEX

The basic CPI is calculated monthly by the U.S. Bureau of Labor Statistics. To construct the CPI, a theoretical market basket is filled with several thousands of carefully selected goods and services that reflect amounts and types of purchases by consumers. The purchases made will be included in the calculations on a sample basis. The sample data come from interviews with several families selected at random from the two population groups: CPI-U and CPI-W.

The goods and services are divided into more than 800 categories and then arranged into eight major groups: food and beverages, travel, apparel, transportation, medical care, recreation, education, and communication.

In an overly simplified example, the CPI would work like this:

Suppose you purchase one each of five different items and services at the prices indicated below. Since the quantity of items and service are all the same, it will not be necessary to weight the items.

Item	Cost	Quantity purchased	Cost x Quantity
A	$21.00	1	$21.00
B	$36.00	1	$36.00
C	$18.00	1	$18.00
D	$43.00	1	$43.00
E	$36.00	1	$36.00
Total	—	5	$154.00
Average cost is $30.80 (154/5 = $30.80)			

Now suppose the quantity purchased differs with the various items. It will be necessary to weight the items.

Item	Cost	Quantity purchased	Cost x Quantity
A	$21.00	1	$21.00
B	$36.00	3	$108.00
C	$18.00	1	$18.00
D	$43.00	4	$172.00
E	$36.00	10	$360.00
Total	—	19	$679.00
Average cost is $35.74 (679/5 = $35.74)			

The average cost is then compared to a base-year cost to calculate the CPI.

BASE YEAR

To calculate the CPI, a base year (usually a starting time such as a month and a year) should be selected. The base-year value is ordinarily shown as a percentage with the percentage symbol omitted, often 100.0. An example might be Base Year percentage 100.0 and Current Value 139.9. The base-year value is usually some time in the past. The point of the base year is to serve as a factor in calculating price changes.

CHALLENGES IN SECURING THE DATA

Consumers vary their retail buying decisions based on many criteria—such as convenience, color, size, and taste. Nevertheless, they do change their minds. "Change" is one of the most important factors with which the CPI must deal in its quest to ensure that the price data reported are accurate. As brand-new major items begin appearing in retail stores, the CPI may "suddenly" need to investigate nationwide for items that a short time ago were not even on store shelves. Even beyond this, the timing for the newly arrived products and/or services may not be predictable. The CPI obviously lives in a world of challenges.

INFLATION

Prices of goods and services are tracked by the CPI because significant increases in retail prices may affect the overall results and create a grand total increase in prices. This, of course, suggests inflation. Retailers take note of price increases that are affecting the products with which they deal. They may very likely consider this as justification for raising their own prices, which results in inflation. The role of the CPI has been to measure change in prices.

Before the 1970s the average consumer did not tend to devote much attention to changes in the price levels. With the advent of the CPI, however, any strong rises in inflation and reporting of such by the newspapers and other media literally made headlines. More citizens sought to increase their knowledge of inflation.

Escalation is a technique of using strategies to handle inflationary data as positively as possible. Escalation agreements may use the CPI to adjust payments planned and subject to adjustment based upon results of the periodically published the CPI reports.

EFFECT OF SEASONAL FLUCTUATION

The CPI has found it necessary to calculate seasonal fluctuation so as to distinguish bona fide changes in the value of money as contrasted to changes that make their appearances on a repetitious basis.

SAMPLING ERRORS

The CPI measures price changes based on sampling. This means that even when data are handled accurately, the "luck of the draw" may cause the sample mean to differ from the population mean. Sampling "errors" are not mistakes. They are actually "differences."

PRODUCER PRICE INDEXES

Producer price indexes are the calculated values of items that are added to manufacturing work in progress. After the items are added in, they become part of the total retail price of the goods and/or services (the CPI).

DISSEMINATION OF CPI DATA

It is quite easy to obtain information about the CPI. An annual index is published every January. Indexes are also published for geographical areas for both the CPI-U and CPI-W.

SEE ALSO *Pricing*

BIBLIOGRAPHY

Schultze, Charles L., and Mackie, Christopher (Eds.) (2002). *At what price?: Conceptualizing and measuring cost-of-living and price indexes.* Washington, DC: National Academy Press.

U.S. Department of Labor. Bureau of Labor Statistics. Consumer Price Index Home Page. http://www.bls.gov/cpi

G. W. Maxwell

CONSUMER PRODUCT SAFETY ACT OF 1972

Congress passed the Consumer Product Safety Act in 1972 to "assist consumers in evaluating the comparative safety of consumer products; to develop uniform safety standards for consumer products and to minimize conflicting state and local regulations; and to promote research and investigation into the causes and prevention of product related death, illnesses, and injuries." The act also established the Consumer Product Safety Commission (CPSC) to "protect the public against unreasonable risks associated with consumer products." The CPSC has authority to set mandatory standards, ban products, order recalls of unsafe products, and institute labeling requirements.

The CPSC is an independent regulatory agency charged with protecting consumers from unreasonable risk of injury associated with consumer products. The most serious risks include amputation, electrocution, burns, asphyxiation, and cancer. Examples of recent product liability lawsuits in which defendant companies lost include breast implants that leaked silicone gel and football helmets that did not have enough padding. The commission has jurisdiction over about 15,000 types of consumer products, such as automatic coffeemakers, toys, furniture, clothing, and lawn mowers. The CPSC works to reduce the risk of injury and death from consumer products by:

U.S. Consumer Product Safety Commission Chairman Hal Stratton warns against recalled toys and other products that pose serious safety threats to children (Bethesda, MD, November 25, 2003). AP IMAGES

- Developing voluntary standards with industry
- Issuing and enforcing mandatory standards and banning consumer products if no feasible standard would adequately protect the public
- Obtaining the recall of products or arranging for their repair
- Conducting research on potential product hazards
- Informing and educating consumers through the media, state and local governments, and private organizations, and by responding to consumer inquiries

The CPSC has three key program areas:

1. The Office of Hazard Identification and Reduction, which collects and analyzes consumer injury and death data to determine trends in consumer product hazards.

2. The Office of Compliance and Enforcement, which supervises compliance and administrative activities related to the act. This office also reviews proposed standards and rules with respect to their enforceability.

3. The Office of Information and Public Affairs, which is responsible for the development, implementation, and evaluation of a comprehensive national information and public affairs program designed to promote product safety.

In addition, the commission has also written rules to establish performance, design, composition, packaging, and construction standards for many products. Examples of products with mandatory safety standards include matchbooks, walk-behind power lawn mowers, residential garage-door openers, swimming-pool slides, chain saws, home-use pesticides, and cellulose insulation.

The CPSC has been involved in actions to protect U.S. citizens. For example, Polaris Industries was fined $950,000 for allegedly continuing to make certain engines on all-terrain vehicles after receiving injury and accident reports. Also, Hamilton Beach/Proctor-Silex agreed to pay a $1.2 million civil penalty to settle allegations that they failed to report defects in countertop toasters, juice extractors, and slow cookers.

Consumers have benefited in the areas where the CPSC has taken action. The commission is constantly challenged to keep abreast of new products and potential hazards that may be associated with them. The commission is usually able to react, however, only after a consumer has been injured or died. The CPSC has changed the way many products are designed and manufactured. Continuing education by consumer groups, the media, and the CPSC has helped increase public awareness of possible consumer safety hazards. The CPSC is an important consumer protection agency, protecting consumers by ensuring that products they use every day are safe.

SEE ALSO *Consumer Bill of Rights*

BIBLIOGRAPHY

Consumer Product and Safety Act. (1972). Section 2051.

Consumer Product Safety Commission Web site. http://www.cpsc.gov

Fise, M. E. R. (2003). Consumer product safety regulation. In K. J. Meier, E. T. Garman, and L. R. Keiser (Eds.), *Regulation and consumer protection: Politics, bureaucracy and economics* (4th ed.). Mason, OH: Thomson Custom Solutions.

Garman, E. T. (2005). *Consumer economic issues in America* (8th ed.). Mason, OH: Thomson Custom Solutions.

Hamilton Beach agrees to pay $1.2 M civil penalty. (2005, April 11). *HNF: The Weekly Newspaper for the Home Furnishing Network*, p. 123.

Polaris to pay fine for ATV failures. (2005, January 24) *Powersports business, 8*(2), 1.

Sushinsky, George (2004). Growing together. *ASTM International standardization news*. Retrieved October 24, 2005, from http://astm.org/SNEWS.

Phyllis Bunn
Laurie Barfitt

CONSUMER PROTEST

The United States was built on the philosophy of ensuring citizens' rights as set forth in the Constitution and Bill of Rights. Throughout history, American citizens and consumers have expended considerable energy toward ensuring that organizations, retailers, and governments recognize and adhere to these rights. When citizens believe one of those rights has been overlooked or denied, they join in protest to rectify the perceived injustice, as was evidenced by the pre–American Revolution Boston Tea Party.

Since the Boston Tea Party, consumers have determined to attain and maintain an undercurrent of resistance to unfair business and industry practices directly affecting consumers' health, welfare, and safety. Specifically, during certain volatile times (the 1890s Progressive era, the Great Depression in the 1930s, and the 1960s through the 1970s), consumer concerns have been more strongly emphasized. Women's magazines (e.g., *McClure's* and *Ladies' Home Journal*) awakened women to the activist movement as a way of ensuring safe products, achieving justice, and attaining a level of equality.

Upton Sinclair's 1906 graphic novel *The Jungle* exposed unsanitary food-processing and meat-packing conditions. As a result, the U.S. Congress passed the Pure Food and Drug Act of 1906, which created the U.S. Food and Drug Administration (FDA). In 1937 more than 100 people died after using a liquid sulfur drug, Elixir Sulfanilamide, which proved the inadequacy of the Pure Food and Drug Act. A new law, the federal Food, Drug, and Cosmetic Act of 1938, was enacted. Before marketing new drugs, manufacturers were required by this law to prove their safety to the FDA.

World War II (1939–1945) minimized consumer concerns until the early 1960s. President John F. Kennedy, who considered consumer protection to be an important issue, suggested improvements in existing programs and also proposed two new consumer protection programs: a special assistant for consumer affairs (which was carried out by President Lyndon B. Johnson in 1964) and a national oversight board made up of labor, cooperative,

Ralph Nader (1934–). Social activist and consumer protestor in Cambridge, Massachusetts, October 4, 2004. © **RICK FRIEDMAN/CORBIS**

and consumer groups, the Consumer Federation of America (established in 1967).

Individuals such as Ralph Nader (1934–) and his advocacy groups have crusaded to ensure consideration and enforcement of consumer rights since the mid-twentieth century. Often these activities have resulted not only in important consumer victories, but have also brought about positive changes in the political climate and in the institution of self-regulation.

AUTOMOBILE SAFETY

From the time of the appearance of the automobile on the American landscape until 1966, when a federal auto safety law was enacted, manufacturers had determined the level of safety for their automobiles. From the first death in 1899 until 1966, about 2 million automobile-related deaths and about 100 million injuries—a figure three times greater than U.S. combat losses in all military actions—occurred. Consumer advocates postulated that

many of those deaths and injuries could have been avoided had automobile producers included certain safety features as part of the standard package. Consumers began to demand automobile safety features such as air bags, seat belts, and turn signals.

The National Highway and Traffic Safety Administration (NHTSA) was established to ensure highway and automobile safety. It was responsible for setting minimal safety standards for automobiles, as well as ensuring consumer notification of automobile safety defects. NHTSA developed and issued thirty standards in 1967 aimed at reducing crash potential and resulting damage.

TAXES AND CONSUMER ISSUES

Based on the initial successes of his Public Interest Research Group, Nader formed the Public Citizen Tax Reform Research Group in 1972. The tax group's *People and Taxes* was the first publication to explain the manipulation of the tax system to subsidize big corporations, thereby burdening the average taxpayer. In 1976, after many successful tax-reform actions, Robert Brandon and his colleagues Tom Stanton and Jonathan Rowe published a succinct, understandable tax analysis, *Tax Politics: How They Make You Pay and What You Can Do about It.*

Nader and his Raiders have played major roles in addressing and resolving consumer issues on the rights of consumers, workers, and airline passengers; telecommunications; education; banking; automobile safety; environmental protection; and legal issues. Their campaigns, publications, and books have also resulted in the emergence of public opinion supporting environmental protection. Additionally, John C. Esposito's 1970 book, *The Vanishing Air,* declared that the Clean Air Act of 1967 had failed to initiate effective air pollution controls. At about the same time, the Environmental Protection Agency increased its focus on environmental issues, and the Clean Water Act (1972) was passed, both resulting from public reaction to the publication of David Zwick and Marcy Benstock's *Water Wasteland,* which critiqued the failures of pollution-control laws. Further, in response to 1970 statistical findings that worker deaths and disabilities totaled over 14,000 annually, Nader sponsored Joseph Page's report *Bitter Wages,* which helped turn the public and political tide toward enacting the Occupational Safety and Health Act (OSHA) of 1970.

While OSHA has often been perceived by consumer activists as being slow to act or react, it has established standards that ensure business compliance with workplace safety mandates. Additionally, OSHA standards aid in reducing and minimizing cancer risks resulting from the use of ordinary carcinogens, including industrial chemicals, such as benzene; pesticides, such as DBCP; ethylene oxide, a carcinogenic gas that is used for medical equipment sterilization; and formaldehyde, which is used in countless educational and industrial environments. All these standards stemmed from the work (from 1974 through 1983) of the Public Citizen Health Research Group headed by Sidney M. Wolfe.

BOYCOTTS

In 1995 Monroe Friedman (1934–) defined a consumer boycott as an action that threatens an organization's survival by depriving it of sales. Such action is "an attempt by one or more parties to achieve certain objectives by urging individual consumers to refrain from making selected purchases in the marketplace" (p. 199). Local, state, and international boycotts appear to be less common than national boycotts. The duration of boycotts varies: Short-term boycotts usually last three months or less, whereas long-term boycotts sometimes last more than a year. Friedman also noted that boycott characteristics evolve over time. From the beginning announcement that a boycott is being considered, the level of militancy builds, and many media-oriented boycotts combine the power of the media with their own actions to achieve the desired outcome.

In 1994 protesters boycotted dairy products in an effort to prevent products from cows injected with bovine growth hormone (BGH), a hormone to increase bovine milk production, from being marketed. The hormone has the potential to create other medical complications, which could result in health risks to consumers. The FDA affirmed that the concerns expressed by boycott participants might be valid. In response to the boycott, several national food distributors and grocery chains announced that they would not sell goods from BGH-treated cows. BGH, however, continues to be used by some dairy farmers.

SELF-REGULATION

As mentioned earlier, self-regulation through codes of ethical conduct and establishing, reviewing, and maintaining product standards has become essential for maintaining fruitful customer/organizational interaction. Self-regulation has engendered creation of such consumer-focused organizations as Better Business Bureaus, the International Business Ethics Institute, and the Internet Law and Policy Forum.

Since the 1990s consumers have become more confident in the power of their joint efforts to protect their collective interests. Numerous new consumer-interest groups have organized, and the Internet has been recognized as a forum for both sharing information in educating private citizens about the impact of various big-business and governmental activities on their quality of life, and as a means to register various individual complaints with companies and governmental representatives. Consumers have come to recognize the Internet as an efficient, effective, and immediate tool for sharing concerns with their state and national legislators. Some legislators have indicated that they receive thousands of e-mails daily from their constituents.

LEGISLATIVE INITIATIVES

Examples of legislative initiatives resulting from consumer-generated efforts include California Senator Dianne Feinstein's bipartisan Internet Pharmacy Consumer Protection Act (the Ryan Haight Bill), which required new Internet pharmacy disclosure standards and minimized instances where domestic Internet pharmacies can sell drugs without authentic prescriptions. The passing of the Electricity Deregulation and Blackout Prevention Act Initiative of 2004 was an effort by California citizens to restore the concept of customer service by the utility companies by eliminating deregulation legislation that had been passed in 2001. That deregulation resulted in the 2001 energy crisis and left many Californians without electric service, ultimately costing California billions of dollars. BlackBoxVoting.org, a consumer protection Web site for elections, is funded by citizen donations (http://www.blackboxvoting.org). The National Consumers League works to protect consumers from telephone and online fraud.

Public Citizen, founded by Nader, is a public-interest, watchdog organization frequently critical of corporations. The efforts of Public Citizen are largely responsible for passage of the Lobbying Disclosure Act and the Lobbying and Ethics Reform Act of 2005. Another Nader-founded nonprofit organization, Essential Information, encourages private citizens to become active and engaged in their communities. The Citizen Works Web site (http://www.citizenworks.org), founded in April 2001 by Nader—recruits and trains citizen activists and directs them to focused action campaigns.

Issues that may have been paramount in consumers' minds prior to September 11, 2001 (such as genetically modified crops, Congressional ethics and election reform, and corporate welfare), became less prominent after day. Consumers began to refocus their activities on more bread-and-butter issues and the economy, such as changes in Medicaid and Medicare, prescription drugs, health-care management organizations, identity theft, homeland security, and utility costs (particularly gasoline and heating oil prices). Media outlets of all kinds, particularly since 9/11, have articulated growing consumer concerns in these areas. Further, changes in consumer attitudes toward these issues is also reflected in not only refocused national governmental agendas but also through the directions taken in activities of state governments, which are most directly affected and contacted by concerned consumers.

SEE ALSO *Consumer Advocacy and Protection*

BIBLIOGRAPHY

Alexander, Richard (1999). The development of consumer rights in the United States slowed by the power of corporate political contributions and lobbying. Retrieved January 11, 2006, from http://consumerlawpage.com/article

Brobeck, Stephen (1990). *The modern consumer movement: References and resources.* Boston: G. K. Hall.

Cannarozzi, M. (2000). Cyber-patrols threaten Internet liberties. Retrieved January 11, 2006, from http://www.chronicleworld.org/archive/cyberpat.htm

Consumer@action. (2005). The evolution of consumer action: The history of the organization. Retrieved January 11, 2006, from http://www.consumer-action.org/English/evolutionofCA.php

Esposito, John C. (1970). *Vanishing air: The Ralph Nader study group report on air pollution.* New York: Grossman.

Friedman, Monroe (1995). On promoting a sustainable future through consumer activism. *Journal of Social Sciences, 51*(4), 197–215.

Friedman, Monroe (1999). *Consumer boycotts: Effecting change through the marketplace and the media.* New York: Routledge.

It-Pays-to-Complain.com. http://www.it-pays-to-complain.com

Nader, Ralph (1965). *Unsafe at any speed.* New York: Grossman.

Page, Joseph A., and O'Brien, Mary-Win (1973). *Bitter wages: Ralph Nader's study group report on disease and injury on the job.* New York: Grossman.

Public Citizen Congress Watch. http://www.citizen.org

U.S. Consumer Product Safety Commission. http://www.cpsc.gov

Zwick, David, and Benstock, Marcy (1971). *Water wasteland: Ralph Nader's study group report on water pollution.* New York: Grossman.

Mary Jean Lush

CONTEMPORARY MANAGEMENT THOUGHTS

SEE *Management*

CONTINGENCY MODEL

SEE *Management/Leadership Styles*

CONTINUING PROFESSIONAL EDUCATION

SEE *Professional Education*

CONTRACTS

A contract is a promise or a set of promises for the breach of which the law gives a remedy, or the performance of which the law in some way recognizes as a duty.

The freedom to contract has not existed throughout history. In medieval England, the courts did not engage in the enforcement of agreements between individuals. Rather, the feudal society that ruled personal interaction was relied upon for all forms of trade. As society evolved to emphasize individual freedoms over social caste, the ability to contract was viewed as a fundamental tenet of individual liberty. Writers and economic theorists such as Adam Smith, David Ricardo, Jeremy Bentham, and John Stuart Mill "successively insisted on freedom of bargaining as the fundamental and indispensable requisite of progress; and imposed their theories on the educated thought of their times."

Article I, Section 10 of the U.S. Constitution protects the individual right to contract by stating that, "No State shall … pass any … law impairing the obligations of Contracts." Many state constitutions contain similar provisions.

Generally, the law of contracts does not come from statutes passed by Congress or by state legislatures, but rather is a product of the common law, the continuing line of court decisions dating back to pre-colonial English courts. The common law is living and constantly evolving, as modern courts continue to analyze, revise and even disagree on its application. The American Law Institute, a collection of legal scholars and practitioners, attempted to catalogue the common law of contracts in its Restatements of the Law of Contracts in 1932. The Restatement, Second, of the Law of Contracts was published in 1979. The Restatement, although it does not have the force of law itself, is generally regarded as an excellent source. The law of contracts is also significantly influenced by the Uniform Commercial Code (UCC), which has been adopted in forty-nine states. The UCC is an attempt to standardize laws dealing with contracts and commerce. The UCC is beyond the scope of this article.

FORMATION OF A CONTRACT

A contract consists of one individual making an offer, another accepting the offer, and the existence of consideration between the contracting parties.

OFFER

An offer is the expression of a willingness to enter into a bargain. An offer must be directed to a particular offeree and be sufficiently clear so as to justify another individual in the belief that acceptance of the offer would constitute an agreement. Although an offer need not set forth all terms of the potential bargain (even the price may be left to be later determined), a valid offer must identify the fundamental elements of the proposed agreement. An offer may be revoked at any time before it is accepted or before it is reasonably relied upon by another individual.

ACCEPTANCE

Acceptance of an offer is the communication by the offeree of mutual assent, that is, the agreement to be bound by the terms of an offer. An offer may be accepted only by a person to whom the offer was directed and only before the offer terminates or is revoked. A valid acceptance must be communicated to the offeror by the same or similar means under which the offer was communicated, and must be unequivocal to make the agreement binding. At common law, it is generally held that any deviation from the terms of the offer is not an acceptance, but rather a rejection and a counteroffer. If the offer identifies a specific mode of acceptance, such as form, date, time, or place, that mode must be followed for an acceptance to be valid. Generally, an acceptance is not effective until it comes into the possession of the offeror, although some states employ the *mailbox rule*, which makes acceptance sent by U.S. mail effective upon its deposit in the mail. If an offer specifically invites acceptance by performance of a specified act, performance of that act by the offeree constitutes acceptance without notification of the offeror. Except in very limited circumstances, such as where the parties have a pattern of previous dealings or where it would be inequitable to find otherwise, silence does not constitute acceptance.

CONSIDERATION

An offer and acceptance alone do not create a valid and binding contract. A third element, consideration, must exist. Consideration is a bargained-for exchange, that is, the existence of mutuality of obligation. Both parties must derive some benefit—or, alternatively, both parties must experience some detriment or forbearance—for a contract to exist. Without consideration, an offer and acceptance represent merely a naked, unenforceable promise.

While the existence of consideration is critical to the enforceability of a contract, the quantity or quality of consideration is immaterial. Generally, courts are not concerned with the value or adequacy of consideration and will not interfere with a bargain entered into between the parties because of insufficient consideration. Certain acts or forbearance cannot constitute consideration. A preexisting duty to perform or refrain from performing may not be consideration for a contract. Therefore, fulfilling an existing contractual obligation or refraining from an unlawful act cannot constitute consideration. An exception to this rule is that the agreement to pay a preexisting debt may be consideration. A promise to make a gift is not consideration, nor is a moral obligation. A promise not to sue, so long as the right to sue actually exists, may be consideration.

DEFENSES

In its most basic form, a contract exists where there is an offer, an acceptance of the offer, and consideration to support the contract. Despite the existence of these three elements, enforcement of a contract may be denied if a sufficient defense to the formation of a contracts is present.

In order for an individual to enter into a contract, that person must have the legal capacity to do so. At common law, minors, individuals who are mentally ill, persons under the influence of alcohol or drugs, and those under a legal guardianship lack legal capacity to contract. The rule as to minors is that a contract of a minor is voidable, not void. That is, a minor has the option to make a contract valid or not. However, if a minor enjoys the benefit of a contract, the minor is obligated either to repay the other party or to fulfill the minor's obligations under the contract. In addition to capacity, an individual must have the legal competency to enter a contract. Competency is generally defined as the mental ability of a party to contract. In other words, a legally competent person is one who possesses the ability to recognize and understand the contractual obligations that will result. Courts will assume that capacity and competency exist until it is proved otherwise.

If the parties to a contract make a mutual mistake with regard to that contract, such as a mutual misunderstanding, there is no mutual assent and therefore no contract. Clerical errors, known as scrivener's errors, will generally be corrected by a court. That is, rather than finding the contract invalid, the court will merely correct the error.

A contract that is based on a fraudulent misrepresentation of a material term is unenforceable. A fraudulent misrepresentation is material if the maker intended for the misrepresentation to induce the other party to enter the contract and if the misrepresentation would likely induce a reasonable person to so enter the contract.

Duress may make a contract unenforceable. Physical duress, or forcing a person to accept an offer, invalidates the contract, while the threat of physical harm makes the contract voidable at the election of the victim. Courts are divided on whether economic duress is sufficient to deny the enforceability of a contract.

A contract that is entered into under undue influence is also voidable at the election of the victim. Undue influence exists where one improperly takes advantage of one's relationship with another to coerce the other person to enter a contract. Examples are the influence that an adult child may have over an elderly parent who is dependent on the child for care, or the reliance of an unsophisticated individual on a sophisticated adviser, where the adviser is aware of the reliance.

As a general rule, an illegal bargain is void as a matter of law and may not be enforced. Therefore, a contract to commit murder, to rob a bank, or to steal a car is void as a matter of law.

A contract may be void because enforcement of the contract would be unconscionable. It is important to understand that mere disproportionality of the benefits of a contract, no matter how great, does not make the contract void as unconscionable. Unconscionability may be found only where there is grossly disproportionate bargaining power to the extent that one of the parties had virtually no choice in accepting the terms of the contract. Contracts are rarely found to be unconscionable unless a significant public policy issue is involved.

CONTRACT INTERPRETATION

An offer, acceptance, and consideration must be present to form a contract. The defenses to contract formation, as discussed above, may be used to show that no contract exists. However, even if it is shown that a contract does exist, questions may arise as to the content and meaning of that contract.

RULES OF CONSTRUCTION

In interpreting contracts, courts generally follow certain fundamental rules of construction. Under the four corners rule, courts will restrict their analyses to the written terms of the agreement itself, wherever possible. Ambiguities will be construed against the drafter. Courts will generally seek to harmonize the terms of a contract in a manner that makes those terms consistent. Courts will generally find that specifics in a contract will control over generalities. Words and phrases used in a contract are given their plain meaning absent evidence to the contrary.

PAROL EVIDENCE RULE

The parol evidence rule provides that if the parties to a contract intended for their contract to be a complete integration, that is, if the parties intended that the written agreement be the full extent of the understanding between them, then evidence other than the contract itself may not be admitted to contradict the written terms. Therefore, in interpreting a contract, the court should generally not look beyond the contract itself for interpretation. The parol evidence rule permits evidence intended to prove or disprove the legitimacy of contract formation, such as evidence showing a party's capacity or showing fraud or mutual mistake, but prohibits evidence intended to vary, contradict, or change the terms of the written agreement. Of course, if a contract refers to another document, that other document may be admitted to explain the terms of the contract at issue.

STATUTE OF FRAUDS

A common mistake is the belief that oral contracts are not enforceable. In fact, most oral contracts, if they fulfill all of the requirements of a contract, are indeed enforceable. However, the statute of frauds requires that in certain specific circumstances, contracts must be in writing. While the requirements vary from state to state, generally the statute of frauds requires the following contracts to be in writing: contracts by executors, administrators, or other personal representatives; contracts in consideration of marriage; contracts for the sale of real estate; contracts for the sale of goods exceeding $500; and contracts that will not be performed within one year of the making of the contract. The statute of frauds generally does not require any particular written form, and generally a contract will suffice so long as it identifies the parties, describes the subject matter, states the essential and material terms, states that consideration exists, and is signed by the party against whom enforcement is sought.

REMEDIES AND DAMAGES

Throughout this article, reference has been made to the court's enforcement of a contract. This, of course, begs the question of what course of action may be taken to enforce a contract, to repay the victim of a breach of contract, or to punish those who breach.

Generally, the victim of a breached contract is entitled to be made whole, or put in the same position as that party would have been in had the contract been fulfilled. Commonly, this is done by forcing the breaching party to pay the aggrieved party compensatory damages. Compensatory damages are intended to compensate the non-breaching party for the actual damages suffered. Normally, compensatory damages are measured by the party's expectancy, or what the parties should have reasonably foreseen as flowing from the breach. Expectancy damages are often described as conferring the benefit of the bargain upon the nonbreaching party. Where expectancy damages are difficult to determine or otherwise impractical, a party may receive reliance damages, which are intended to compensate for the losses incurred in relying on the breaching party's fulfillment of the contract. A third alternative for compensation is restitution, where the breaching party must compensate the victim for the benefit conferred upon the breaching party.

Liquidated damages are a method used by contracting parties to estimate the damages that will result in the event of a breach. Liquidated damages may not serve as a penalty against the breaching party, but so long as they are a reasonable estimate of the damages that would be suffered by the nonbreaching party, they will be enforced. A clause in an apartment rental contract that requires a breaching party to pay two months rent is a common form of liquidated damages.

Punitive damages are those intended to punish the breaching party. Punitive damages are available only in very rare cases; they generally are not awarded in contract disputes.

Finally, equitable relief is available to nonbreaching parties where none of the above remedies would be sufficient. Under the concept of equity, a court may take corrective action other than by awarding money. In rare circumstances where none of the above described compensatory damages would be sufficient, a court may order specific performance. That is, the court will order the parties to fulfill their obligations under the contract. This method is not favored because of the practical difficulty of enforcement, but in some cases, such as the purchase of real estate, art, and the like, it is the only remedy that is sufficient. Also available is an injunction, which is a court order preventing a party from taking further action, such as a continued breach of a contract.

SEE ALSO *Law in Business*

Keith A. Bice

COOPERATIVE

A cooperative (also referred to as a co-op) is a form of business ownership that consists of a group of people who have joined together to perform a business function more efficiently than each individual could do alone. The purpose of a cooperative is not to make a profit for itself, but to improve each member's situation. However, members of certain types of cooperatives do make a profit by selling

IGA Cooperative in Ste Foy, Quebec, 2005. **PHOTOGRAPH BY MIRANDA H. FERRARA. THE GALE GROUP.**

their product and/or service to customers who are not co-op members.

Cooperatives can take many forms. For example, a group of single parents may decide to band together to provide a child-care facility so they will have reliable day care for their children. Each parent contributes a certain amount of money and/or time, and in exchange they all have a safe place to leave their children. A credit union is also a type of cooperative. The purpose of a credit union is not to make a profit for itself, but to help each member be more financially secure. By creating their own financial institution, members can receive a higher interest rate on the money they have placed in savings and receive a lower interest rate on loans. Retailers have also started establishing co-ops. Ace Hardware, for example, is a co-op of independent hardware store owners. By banding together, the hardware owners can share advertising costs and receive discounts for bulk ordering of materials and supplies. Sharing costs and discounts allows small hardware stores to compete with large chain hardware stores.

While cooperatives can be found in many different areas of the economy, they are most commonly found in the agricultural area. A group of farmers may band together to allow themselves to be more competitive and to achieve more economic power. Agricultural cooperatives allow members to save money on materials needed to produce and market their product, which means a larger profit margin for all members. Ocean Spray Cranberries, Inc., for example, is a cooperative of several hundred cranberry and citrus growers from all over the country. Other well known cooperatives include Blue Diamond, Sunkist,

IGA (Independent Grocers Association), and Land-O-Lakes.

BIBLIOGRAPHY

Boone, Louis E., and Kurtz, David L. (2006). *Contemporary Business*. Mason, OH: Thomson/South-Western.

Bounds, Gregory M., and Lamb, Charles W., Jr. (1998). *Business*. Cincinnati, OH: South-Western College Publishing.

Madura, Jeff (2004). *Introduction to Business*. Belmont, CA: Thomson/South-Western.

"NCBA.coop … National Cooperative Business Association." Retrieved October 15, 2005, from http://www.ncba.org/index.cfm.

Nickels, William G., McHugh, James M., and McHugh, Susan M. (2005). *Understanding Business* (7th ed.). Boston: McGraw-Hill/Irwin.

Pride, William M., Hughes, Robert J., and Kapoor, Jack R. (2002). *Business* (7th ed.). Boston: Houghton Mifflin.

Marcy Satterwhite

COOPERATIVE ADVERTISING

SEE *Advertising; Marketing Mix*

COPYRIGHTS

A copyright gives the owner the exclusive right to reproduce, distribute, perform, display, or license original material. Further, the owner also receives the exclusive right to produce or license the production of derivatives of that material. In essence, a copyright provides protection to the owner guaranteeing that material cannot be copied without the owner's permission. Under the current law, materials are covered whether or not a copyright notice is attached and whether or not the material is registered.

However, an exception exists for the fair use of the material. The fair use of copyrighted material includes such use as reproduction for purposes of criticism, comment, news reporting, teaching (including multiple copies for classroom use), scholarship, or research and is not considered an infringement of a copyright. Thus, fair use allows an individual to reproduce the material for nonprofit activities.

Originally, copyrights referred only to written materials. However, copyrights have been extended to include: (1) literary materials; (2) musical materials, including any accompanying words; (3) dramatic materials, including any accompanying music; (4) pantomimes and choreographic materials; (5) pictorial, graphic, and sculptural materials; (6) motion pictures and other audiovisual materials; (7) sound recordings; and (8) architectural materials. Thus, material must be original and published in a concrete medium of expression to be covered by a copyright. In other words, for material to be eligible for copyright protection, a tangible product must exist. Consequently, copyright protection does not extend to any original material for ideas, procedures, processes, systems, methods of operation, concepts, principles, or discovery, regardless of the form in which the material is described, explained, illustrated, or embodied.

The owner of a copyright has the right to do and authorize any of the following: (1) to reproduce the copyrighted material in copies; (2) to prepare derivative materials based on the original copyrighted material; (3) to distribute copies of the copyrighted material to the public by sale or other transfer of ownership, or by rental, lease, or lending; (4) in the case of literary, musical, dramatic, and choreographic materials, pantomimes, and motion pictures and other audiovisual materials, to perform the copyrighted material publicly; and (5) in the case of literary, musical, dramatic, and choreographic materials, pantomimes, and pictorial, graphic, or sculptural materials, including the individual images of a motion picture or other audiovisual materials, to display the copyrighted material publicly.

The Berne Convention was a convention for the protection of literacy and artistic materials and the Universal Copyright Convention is a convention to provide for the adequate and effective protection of the rights of authors and other copyright proprietors in literary, scientific, and artistic materials, which includes writings; musical, dramatic, and cinematographic materials; and paintings, engravings, and sculpture. As a result, international guidelines for identifying materials that were subject to copyright protection were established, and those guidelines included an administrative process for redress if an author believed material to be reproduced without permission. Not only were the materials subject to copyright protection expanded from written materials to audiovisual materials; pictorial, graphic, or sculptural materials; architectural materials; collective materials; and compilation materials; but reproduction of materials was refined to include performing or displaying material as well as transmitting the work without the author's permission. The United States joined the Berne Convention for the Protection of Literary and Artistic Materials in 1989.

The federal agency charged with administering the act is the Copyright Office of the Library of Congress. Materials are subject to copyright protection with or without copyright notice attached to the material. To obtain a copyright for an original work, an application for copyright registration should be filed with the Register of Copyrights in the Copyright Office of the Library of Congress. The application requests the following information: (1) the name and address of the author of the material; (2) in the case of materials other than anonymous of pseudonymous work, the name and nationality or domicile of the author or authors and, if one of more of the authors is deceased, the dates of their deaths; (3) if the work is anonymous or pseudonymous, the nationality or domicile of the author or authors; (4) in the case of material made for hire, a statement to that effect; (5) if the copyright claimant is not the author, a brief statement of how the claimant obtained ownership of the copyright; (6) the title of the work, together with any previous or alternative titles under which the material may be identified; (7) the year in which creation of the work was completed; (8) if the work has been published, the date and nation of its first publication; (9) in the case of a compilation or derivative material, an identification of any pre-existing material(s) that it is based upon, and a brief, general statement of the additional materials covered by the copyright claim being registered; and (10) in the case of published documents containing materials manufactured in the United States, the names of the individuals or organizations who performed the manufacturing process and the location where the manufacturing process was performed. Simply, an author of an original work must file the required information and form to register the copyright with the Register of Copyrights in the Copyright Office of the Library of Congress. The appropriate fee must accompany the form to register the copyright. In addition, the Copyright Office of the Library of Congress has been charged with overseeing the copyright process and reviewing any reported violations. While this office has the major responsibility for adjudicating any alleged copyright violations, the U.S. Supreme Court and the U.S. Circuit Court of Appeals have both rendered decisions affecting copyrights.

BIBLIOGRAPHY

United States Copyright Office, http://www.copyright.gov/ accessed January 31, 2006.

Randy L. Joyner

CORPORATE EDUCATION

In corporate America the acquisition and dissemination of knowledge is at the core of most business, industry, and government entities. These organizations either provide knowledge (e.g., software, information technology, biotechnology) or process knowledge (e.g., telecommunications, banking, advertising). In an era where information is critical, the emphasis is on speed, flexibility, technical expertise, and innovation. These factors drive business processes and affect the bottom line. Successful organizations continually update their knowledge base and the skills of their workforce to keep pace with the changing demands of the global marketplace and the technological advances that provide a competitive advantage.

A corporation's future is determined in part by its involvement in the development of its intellectual resources. Enterprises are expanding the education and training segments of their business activities. Chief executive officers (CEOs) realize that without this effort, they will lose their edge in the highly competitive global economy. Continuing education is vital to the future success of any organization, but it is of equal or greater importance that employees remain adaptable and agile learners, able to profit personally and professionally from opportunities generated by the global economy. Investing in the right course of study for the right people at the right time continues to be a challenge for businesses as they plan and prepare for the future.

Corporate restructuring and technological advances give employees broader responsibilities that require more skills and training for self-managed, cross-functional teams. In the past, frontline staff would communicate with middle management who made decisions and solved problems. Today, middle management is disappearing. Frontline workers are expected to process information, make decisions, and solve problems as they occur. Entry-level workers are required to be skilled, knowledgeable, and adaptable. If they do not have these skills when they are hired, the company must provide the education necessary for these employees to be successful.

TYPES OF CORPORATE EDUCATION

Typically, four types of corporate education are used to enhance employees' knowledge and skills. These include independent study, apprenticeships and on-the-job training, traditional classroom instruction, and unconventional training programs.

Independent Study. Independent study is a growing trend in corporate education. Interactive Web-based training allows participants to acquire new skills without leaving their desks. This reduces time and travel costs compared with traditional classroom training. Employees are given the flexibility to learn at their convenience, at their own pace, and from almost any location. This method is beneficial for those who lack the time to attend regularly scheduled classes or those who are uncomfortable in traditional classroom situations.

The value of an independent-study program is enhanced when used in conjunction with electronic mail, synchronous chat discussions, asynchronous discussion forums, and desktop videoconferencing. These tools allow employees to participate in electronic discussion groups that serve to reinforce learning objectives. Online learning via the "virtual classroom" relies more on students' learning from collaborative discussions and team projects than from traditional lectures. As high-speed forms of communication become more readily available, CEOs and chief learning officers or chief information officers of many large corporations are encouraging their workforce to be trained in online skills. In terms of a forward-thinking public image, these organizations project an aura of familiarity and competency with cutting-edge technology. This earns confidence from customers and associates and respect from rivals.

Apprenticeships and On-the-Job Training. Apprenticeships are a form of on-the-job training (OJT) where individuals with little or no experience are prepared for

occupations as skilled craftspeople and earn hourly wages as they learn. Experienced workers train novice employees to become, for example, accomplished electricians, machinists, operating engineers, carpenters, or tool-and-die makers. These programs usually require a prescribed number of hours of related classroom instruction. Examples of coursework include safety, mathematics, schematic reading, and technical courses to meet particular state or federal licensing or certification requirements.

Other OJT programs are customized for participants who have some job-related skills but need to become more knowledgeable and proficient in a particular trade. As with apprenticeships, employees benefit because they are paid to learn. In addition, employers benefit from hosting OJT programs because they have the full-time services of motivated individuals who are training to fulfill specific company needs. Participants also include long-time employees who need to adapt to new technologies and procedures to maintain their job security.

Traditional Classroom Instruction. Traditional classroom instruction is similar to most postsecondary learning environments in which an instructor or trainer presents mate-

On-site corporate education class. **PHOTOGRAPH BY KELLY A. QUIN. THE GALE GROUP.**

rial by lecturing, demonstrating a skill, or leading a discussion. In-class activities may encourage collaborative learning, but for the most part, traditional classroom instruction is often a passive learning experience.

Corporations with frequent employee turnover, such as the hotel and resort industry, find traditional classroom education to be inefficient and expensive. This type of industry must train its staff to properly and uniformly satisfy customer service requirements; employees, however, may be seasonal workers, making repeat training a continuous necessity. Training days require employees to miss work, which creates additional problems for hotel managers and guests. Additionally, tight budgets limit the number of corporate trainers available. Lack of proper training prevents workers from excelling at their jobs, which negatively impacts the business.

For these reasons, organizations are shifting from traditional classroom instruction to Web-based interactive training that actively involves students in the learning process. These programs are always accessible from designated locations and are easily modified to reflect cultural and language differences.

A growing trend is the corporate for-profit university offering degree programs entirely in an online setting. These educational entities allow working individuals to pursue bachelor's and master's degrees and certificate programs with less disruption in their work schedules or home life. Examples of these types of organizations include Walden University, the University of Phoenix, and Laureate Education.

Unconventional Training Programs. Unconventional methods may be used if the purpose of a training program is to modify employee attitudes or work ethics. This is done to transform the internal corporate culture into one that is compatible with the corporation's external image and direction. Among the programs that may be appropriate for this type of application are leadership development, team building, and conflict resolution.

Corporate outdoor training is less conventional than the traditional classroom approach, but it is gaining in popularity with many international businesses as an informal method of conveying corporate values across a diverse range of cultures. Moving the training experience from the classroom to the outdoors provides a unique learning environment where individual challenges encourage positive team behaviors. Outdoor activities such as outward-bound trips, ropes courses, white-water rafting, and rock climbing require individual initiative and team problem-solving skills. Communication, trust, teamwork, and camaraderie are stressed during these courses.

Another unconventional corporate education program emphasizes the usefulness of humor in the work-

place. This program encourages employees from all levels of the organization including upper management to laugh and have fun, making work more enjoyable for everyone. The motivation behind this type of training is to create an atmosphere in which employees want to work as a team, are proud of their contributions, and enjoy the company of their managers and coworkers. Participating organizations benefit from a reduction in stress-related absenteeism and an increase in workforce creativity and innovation. Many corporations have become successful because they realized in the early stages of their development that a happy team is a winning team.

ONGOING VALUE OF EDUCATING WORKERS

Corporations cannot afford to become complacent. The perception that they have an abundance of educated employees who are motivated, content, and comfortable with existing technologies is seldom correct. As demonstrated throughout the twentieth century, technological developments have altered the fortunes of once-thriving companies by outdating products and business practices that were once considered state of the art. Ongoing employee education is a critical component in determining an industry's ability to survive and prosper. Evolving information systems and peripheral equipment will improve business communications and transactions, allowing instant access to many types of data from a variety of locations. Speed and proficiency in the use of these systems, which are attained mainly through continuous workforce education, will help to determine an organization's status within the business community.

It is unlikely that this trend will reverse. Clients are accustomed to information on demand and, in the long run, technology is cost-efficient. A primary goal of most corporations is to increase profits. Without an ongoing commitment to workforce education, businesses cannot meet their full potential.

SEE ALSO *Professional Education; Training and Development*

Diane M. Clevesy
Mark J. Snyder
Lisa E. Gueldenzoph

CORPORATE RESTRUCTURING

SEE *Reengineering*

CORPORATIONS

A business corporation is a legal entity permitted by law in every state to exist for the purpose of engaging in lawful activities of a business nature. It is an artificial person created by law, with many of the same rights and responsibilities possessed by humans. Corporations are widely prevalent in the United States and virtually every large enterprise is a corporation.

RIGHTS AND PRIVILEGES OF A CORPORATION

Within legal guidelines, corporations may issue stock, declare dividends, and provide owners with limited liability.

Stocks A corporation can issue and attempt to sell stock. Every share of stock owned represents a share of the corporation's ownership.

From the standpoint of stock sale, there are two kinds of corporations: public and private. With a public corporation, anyone can buy shares of stock, which may very well be traded on a stock exchange. With a private corporation, however, sale of stock may be limited to stipulated persons, such as members of the principal stockholder's family.

A corporation can own "treasury stock"; that is, it may repurchase its own stock that it had previously issued and sold.

A corporation may even give its stock away for any reason; for example, as a donation to a charity, or as a reward to employees for industrious service.

Dividends. A corporate board of directors has the authority to declare and pay dividends in the form of cash or stock. Cash dividends are ordinarily payable from current net income, although net income "kept" from previous years may also be used. A common name for net income kept is "retained earnings." Recipients of stock dividends receive shares of stock in the corporation, thereby increasing the total number of shares they own. Stock dividends are declared from capital stock that has been authorized but not issued.

Rules exist regarding eligibility for receipt of a dividend. For example, assume that a cash dividend is declared on August 15, payable on September 15. If Stockholder A owns the stock on August 15, he or she receives the dividend on September 15. If Stockholder A sells the stock on August 27, Purchaser B buys it "ex-rights," meaning that on September 15 the dividend still goes to Stockholder A. Purchaser B would not receive a dividend until the next one is declared, perhaps on November 15.

Example of stock split			
2 for 1 stock split	Shareholder owns	Value of shareholder's shares on corporation's records	
		Per share	Total value
Before	100 shares	$80	$8,000
After	200 shares	$40	$8,000

Figure 1

Recipients of cash dividends pay income tax as of the year the dividends are received. Income tax on stock dividends, however, is postponed until the recipients sell the stock.

Occasionally, corporations split their stock. However, this does not change the value of the shareholder's shares on the corporation records or the corporation's net worth. A stock split is a good sign as it is often done to reduce the price of a stock that has risen to a point at which its marketability is impaired. (See Figure 1)

Limited Liability. If a corporation suffers large financial losses or even terminates its existence, the shareholders might lose part or all of their total investment. However, that is ordinarily the extent of their loss. Creditors cannot satisfy their claims by looking to the personal assets of corporate shareholders as they can with a sole proprietorship or an ordinary partnership.

Limited liability can be advantageous because it encourages investment in the corporation. With personal assets of $1.1 million, a potential investor might willingly invest $50,000 in a corporation knowing that no risks exist beyond the $50,000.

The limited liability advantage, however, can be lost if the owners directly engage in the company's management and play an influential role in causing corporate losses.

Additional Rights of a Corporation. Corporations have the basic right to conduct a business in which they sell products or services and to engage in either a profit-seeking or a non-profit-seeking enterprise.

Corporations have the right to own, sell, rent, or lease real or personal property.

Corporations may sue other business entities, such as another corporation, a partnership, or a sole proprietorship.

Corporations may merge with other corporations.

Corporations may make contracts with either another business or a person.

Corporations may hire or discharge employees of any rank, from entry-level employees to the chief executive officer (CEO).

Corporations may borrow money, and they often do so by issuing corporate bonds. Owning a corporate bond does not grant the bondholder any form of ownership in the company. Instead, corporate bondholders have actually loaned money to the corporation, virtually always with a stated interest rate and with terms regarding dates and methods of repayment. Bondholders may ordinarily sell their bonds to other persons, most often through stockbrokers.

In addition to issuing bonds, corporations may borrow directly from any loan source, such as banks. On occasion, corporations raise needed cash by authorizing and selling additional stock.

Corporations may make any lawful investment. They often invest in the stock and/or bonds of other corporations, personal or real property, mutual funds, money market accounts, certificates of deposit, and government securities.

REQUIREMENTS OR LIMITATIONS OF A CORPORATION

Corporations are subject to risk, to suits, and to income tax liabilities.

Risk. By engaging in business activities, corporations are at risk, great or small. Profit-seeking corporations may very well find the large profits they seek. But they risk huge economic losses and even bankruptcy.

Suits. Corporations may be sued by any business, including other corporations. They may also be sued by individuals or groups of persons.

Income Tax. Corporations must pay federal and state income taxes on the net profit they make during a calendar or fiscal year. People who receive cash dividends must also pay income tax for the year they are received. Thus it is often said that corporation profits are subject to double taxation. Corporations receive no deduction for any cash dividends that they pay. Recipients of stock dividends, however, postpone payment of income tax on stock dividends until they sell the stock.

REGULATION OF CORPORATIONS

Corporations are subject to two kinds of regulation: regulation by the state in which they are incorporated and reg-

ulation by the individual corporation's articles of incorporation and bylaws.

State Regulation. Corporations are regulated by business corporation laws that exist in all fifty states. Although the statutes prescribe what corporations may and may not do, they are written in broad and general language. In essence, then, the states permit articles of incorporation to be written in a manner that permits corporations to engage in business for almost any legal purpose.

Articles of Incorporation. The Articles are filed publicly and are available to the public. They are subject to amendment. Bylaws are not filed publicly. Consequently, they tend be more detailed than articles of incorporation.

Board of Directors. Members of the board of directors make the major decisions of the corporation. When corporations are formed, they draw up the Articles of Incorporation, usually for approval by shareholders. The board of directors also draws up the initial and ensuing bylaws.

Board members are most often shareholders and officers of the corporation. They are elected by the shareholders. They may be "internal" directors or, for reasons of good public relations or of obtaining of expertise, may work on the "outside" and be selected on the basis of their prominent role in the community.

Policies made by the board of directors are carried out by the corporation's executives, who direct the work of employees under their jurisdiction.

CLASSES OF STOCK

Corporations ordinarily have two classes of stock: common and preferred. The two classes differ in many respects but both also share a number of common characteristics. There is no limit to how many classes of stock a corporation may have.

Common Stock. Common stockholders participate more in the governance of a corporation than do preferred stockholders. This is accomplished by giving common stockholders the right to vote for members of the board of directors as well as on major decisions (e.g., a merger with another corporation). Common stock, however, can be issued without voting rights.

Cumulative voting, which permits shareholders to cast one vote for each share of common stock owned in any combination, is prevalent. In an election for members of the board of directors, for example, a shareholder owning 2000 shares of common stock could cast all 2000 votes for one candidate or divide them in any way among candidates (e.g., 400 votes for each of five candidates).

Cumulative voting offers some protection for smaller stockholders.

The market value of common stock tends to fluctuate more than that of preferred stock.

Preferred Stock. Preferred stockholders are not ordinarily granted the voting rights given to common stockholders. They cannot participate in elections for members of the board of directors or in major decisions of the corporation.

However, preferred stockholders are almost always given prior rights over common stockholders in the matter of dividends.

Dividends for preferred stockholders are often stated in advance and do not tend to fluctuate as much as those for common stock. Preferred dividends may be stated as a percentage of par value or as a dollar amount per share.

However, preferred dividends are not guaranteed in the same sense as is bond interest. Neither preferred nor common stock dividends can be paid without approval of the board of directors. Boards may "skip" declaring dividends if the directors feel the financial situation so warrants.

Preferred stock is often "cumulative." With this provision, a preferred stock dividend that is not declared or paid is considered to be "owed." As long as the preferred dividend is "owed," no common stock dividend may ordinarily be declared or paid. But even if the preferred stock is not cumulative, a frequently applied policy is that common stock dividends cannot be declared as long as the preferred dividends are "in arrears."

Sometimes preferred stock is "convertible." Shareholders who own convertible preferred stock may, at a price announced when the stock is purchased, turn in their preferred stock and receive common stock in its place. Assume, for example, that an investor purchases preferred stock at $36.50 per share. The stock is convertible four years from its issuance at a ratio of 3:1; that is, three shares of preferred stock can be traded at the shareholder's option for one share of common stock. At the 3:1 ratio, after discounting any related transfer costs, the preferred stockholder would find it profitable to convert if the common stock value rises above $109.50 per share ($36.50 × 3).

Preferred stock may be "callable." At the option of the corporation, callable preferred stock may be surrendered to the corporation, usually at a price a little above par value (or a stated value). If the stated value is $50, the callable price on or after a specified date might be $51.25. If the stock's market value rises to, say, $55, it might be profitable for the corporation to call for its surrender.

Occasionally preferred stock is given the right to "participate" with common stock in being granted dividends above a stated value. For example, assume the board of directors declares a regular preferred stock dividend at $3 per share and a common stock dividend at $13 per share. With participating rights, it would have been stipulated that preferred stockholders would receive $1 per share more for every additional $5 given to common stockholders.

If a corporation closes down its operation, preferred stockholders have prior claim over common stockholders upon dissolution of the assets. A sufficient amount of the corporation's assets would need to be turned over to the preferred stockholders before common stockholders could claim any part of the assets. In practice, however, assets of a closed-down corporation are rarely sufficient to pay off the preferred shareholders in full.

RELATED FORMS OF BUSINESS OWNERSHIP

Five types of business entities have regulations similar to those of corporations.

Professional Corporations. Professional corporations, organized under corporation laws of their respective states, involve incorporation by persons engaged in professional practice, such as medical doctors, lawyers, and architects. They are granted limited liability against claims from their clients, except for malpractice.

Not-for-Profit Corporations. Not-for-profit corporations, formed under the nonprofit laws of their respective states, have members instead of stockholders. Any income made cannot be distributed to the members.

Some apply to the Internal Revenue Service for tax-exempt status, becoming 501(c)(3) organizations, which permits donor gifts to be declared tax-deductible.

Closed Corporations. Closed corporations, not permitted by statute in all states, limit shareholders to fifty. They permit the firm to operate informally either by eliminating the board of directors or curtailing its authority. Closed corporations also restrict transferability of the owners' shares of stock.

Limited-Liability Companies. Limited-liability companies enjoy the benefits of limited liability while being taxed like a general partnership. Owners' net income is taxed at an individual personal rate rather than at the rate of a corporation (taxation of both corporate net income and dividends).

Not all states permit formation of limited-liability companies. They are neither a partnership nor a corporation. They generally have a limited life span. Management must be by a small group. States do not restrict the number or the type of members. Unlimited transferability of ownership is not permitted.

S Corporations. S corporations' major benefit is that they are taxed like partnerships. The owners' income tax is based on their share of the firm's total net income, whether or not it is distributed to them. The second huge benefit is limited liability.

However, an S corporation is limited to thirty-five shareholders, none of whom can be nonresident aliens. Only one class of stock may be issued or outstanding. The S corporation may own only 80 percent of a subsidiary business firm.

BIBLIOGRAPHY

Dicks, J. W. (1995). "Corporation." In J. W. Dicks, *The Small Business Legal Kit and Disk.* Holbrook, MA: Adams Medica Corporation.

Sniffen, Carl R. J. (2001). *The Essential Corporation Handbook* (3rd ed.). Central Point, OR: Oasis Press/PSI Research.

Spadaccini, Michael (2005). *The Essential Corporation Handbook* (4th ed.). Irvine, CA: Entrepreneur Media.

G. W. Maxwell

COST ACCOUNTING

SEE *Accounting*

COST ALLOCATION

A cost is generally understood to be that sacrifice incurred in an economic activity to achieve a specific objective, such as to consume, exchange, or produce. All types of organizations—businesses, not-for-profits, governmental—incur costs. To achieve missions and objectives, an organization acquires resources, transforms them in some manner, and delivers units of product or service to its customers or clients. Costs are incurred to perform these activities. For planning and control, decisions are made about areas such as pricing, program evaluation, product costing, outsourcing, and investment. Different costs are needed for different purposes. In each instance, costs are determined to help management make better decisions.

When incurred, costs are initially reviewed and accumulated by some classification system. Costs with one or more characteristics in common may be accumulated into cost pools. Costs are then reassigned, differently for specified purposes, from these cost pools to one or more cost objects. A cost object is an activity, a unit of product or service, a customer, another cost pool, or a segment of an organization for which management needs a separate measurement and accumulation of costs. Costs assigned to a cost object are either direct or indirect. A direct cost can be traced and assigned to the cost object in an unbiased, cost-effective manner. The incurrence of an indirect cost cannot be so easily traced. Without such a direct relationship to the cost object, an indirect cost requires an in-between activity to help establish a formula relationship. When the indirect cost is assigned through the use of this formula, the cost is considered allocated. The activity used to establish the in-between linkage is called the basis of allocation.

TYPES OF ALLOCATIONS

Cost allocations can be made both within and across time periods. If two or more cost objects share a common facility or program, the cost pool of the shared unit is a common cost to the users and must be divided or allocated to them. Bases of allocation typically are based on one of the following criteria: cause-and-effect, benefits derived, fairness, or ability to bear. The selection of a criterion can affect the selection of a basis. For example, the allocation of the costs of a common service activity across product lines or programs based on relative amounts of revenue is an ability to bear basis, whereas the same allocation based on the relative number of service units consumed by each product line or program would reflect either the benefits derived or the cause-and-effect criteria. Cost allocation then is the assignment of an indirect cost to one or more cost objects according to some formula. Because this process is not a direct assignment and results in different amounts allocated depending on either the basis of allocation or the method (formula) selected, some consider cost allocation to be of an arbitrary nature, to some extent.

Costs of long-lived assets are allocated and reclassified as an expense across two or more time periods. For anything other than land, which is not allocated, the reclassification of tangible assets is called depreciation (for anything other than natural resources) or depletion (for natural resources) expense. The bases for these allocations are normally either time or volume of activity. Different methods of depreciation and depletion are available. The costs of long-lived intangible assets, such as patents, are allocated across time periods and reclassified as amortization expense. The basis for these allocations is normally time.

Cost allocations within a time period are typically across either organizational segments known as responsibility centers or across units of product or service or programs for which a full cost is needed. Allocations may differ depending on whether a product or program is being costed for financial reporting, government contract reimbursement, reporting to governmental agencies, target pricing or costing, or life-cycle profitability analysis. Allocations to responsibility centers are made to motivate the centers' managers to be more goal-congruent in their decisions and to assign to each center an amount of cost reflective of all the sacrifices made by the overall organization on behalf of the center. These allocations can be part of a price or transfers of cost pools from one department to another.

ETHICAL CONSIDERATIONS

Allocations can involve ethical issues. Often the federal government issues contracts to the private sector on a cost-plus basis; that is, all the actual costs incurred to complete a contract plus a percentage of profit is reimbursed to the contractor performing the contract. A contractor completing both governmental and private-sector contracts may select a formula that tends to allocate more indirect costs to governmental contracts than to nongovernmental ones. A contractor may also try to include in reimbursement requests costs that are not allowable by the governmental agency. A contractor may even try to double-count a cost item by including it as a direct cost of the contract and as a part of an indirect cost pool allocated to the contract. Lastly, a contractor may attempt to have a reimbursement cover some of the costs of unused capacity. Audits are made of costs of government contracts to identify inappropriate costs.

SERVICE FIRMS, NOT-FOR-PROFIT ORGANIZATIONS, AND MERCHANDISERS

Service and not-for-profit organizations also allocate costs. The cost object can be a unit of service, an individual client, or a cluster (category) of clients. The costs of a service firm are typically professional labor and indirect costs in support of the labor. The basis for allocating these indirect costs is often professional labor hours (either billable or total) or the cost of such, reflective of either cause-and-effect or benefits-received criteria. For not-for-profit organizations, the proportions to be allocated are best figured in terms of units of the resource on hand, such as the number of full-time equivalents, amount of square footage, or number of telephone lines. An important point to remember is that the principles of allocation are the same for for-profit and not-for-profit organizations. The only difference is that the cost objects will be dissimilar.

Merchandisers, unlike most service and not-for-profit organizations, have inventory that must be costed for external and internal reporting purposes. In these cases, the cost object is a unit of inventory. Incidental costs associated with the acquisition and carrying of the inventory are mostly direct costs easily traceable clearly assignable to the entire inventory, if not to individual units.

MANUFACTURERS

Manufacturers need to cost the resources required to complete their products. In costing a unit of product for inventory valuation, costs of production are assigned. With the unit of product as the cost object, production costs are either direct costs (traceable usage of materials and labor) or indirect costs (all of the other production costs, referred to as overhead). The indirect production costs are allocated. Traditionally, manufacturers using labor-intensive technologies used a single basis of allocation based on labor, either in hours or in cost, associated with a single indirect cost pool. A manufacturer using a more capital intensive technology might use a nonlabor basis such as machine hours. Today many firms produce a varied set of products, using varied technologies with many levels of complexity. Such firms need a more refined cost assignment system that uses multiple bases of allocation with multiple indirect cost pools, such as activity based costing.

While a unit of output remains the final cost object for product costing, the technology a producer uses can require a cost assignment to an intermediate cost pool (object) prior to an assignment to a unit of output. For instance, a batch technology has a cost assignment first to an individual job order (batch), and the total cost assigned to the job order is then unitized over the units in the batch to determine cost of one unit of output. Alternatively, for a given period in a process technology, costs are accumulated by (assigned to) each production process; the total cost assigned is then unitized across the total number of (equivalent) units produced by that process to cost-out a unit of output.

Manufacturers also incur service department costs (such as computer center costs) in support of production departments. These service department costs are indirect to a unit of production and for full costing must be allocated, first to respective production areas and then to the units of output. Such allocations are called service department allocations, and the basis of allocation is normally an activity reflective of the nature of demands made on the service department by other departments, both service and production.

JOINT PRODUCTION ALLOCATIONS

Allocations are also required in a joint production process. When two or more separately identifiable final products initially share a common joint production process, the products are called joint products. The point at which they become separately identifiable is referred to as the split-off point. Manufacturing costs incurred prior to this split-off point are referred to as joint costs and need to be allocated across the different joint products for product costing purposes. The bases for allocating the joint costs typically include (1) relative sales value at split-off, (2) net realizable value at split-off (as an approximation of the sales value at split-off), (3) final sales value at the completion of the production process, and (4) the number of physical units of the joint products at split-off.

Many would consider this list of bases to be in an order of descending preference of use. Normally there are additional production costs beyond the split-off point. These additional costs are incurred in order to complete each joint product. For a given joint product, the net realizable value at split-off is calculated by subtracting the additional costs to complete from the final sales value of the finished joint product.

SERVICE DEPARTMENT (RE)ALLOCATIONS

There are three basic methods to allocate service department costs to production departments or programs in a not-for-profit: (1) the direct method; (2) the step method; and (3) the reciprocal method. The basis for allocation of service area costs should ideally be causally related to the demands made on that area by other areas. Both cause-and-effect and benefits-received criteria are taken into account. If the service areas provide service to each other (referred to as reciprocal services), the reciprocal method is the most accurate, the step method next, and the direct method the least accurate. With different service and production departments as cost objects, costs are initially accumulated on a department-by-department basis. Departments working directly on programs or units of product or service are production departments. The other departments are service departments. The allocation problem then is to reassign service department costs to production departments or programs for both performance evaluation and product or program costing. Within a production department, these allocated service costs are then reallocated to units of service or product according to the bases of allocation that each respective production department uses for its indirect costs.

The direct method ignores reciprocal services. A service department's costs are allocated to the production departments according to the extent to which each pro-

duction department uses (or, for budgeting purposes, intends to use) the services of the service department. This extent is determined on a percentage basis by either the amount of services actually provided by the service department to all the production departments or by the amount of services the service department is capable of providing at normal or full capacity. Variable and fixed costs may be allocated separately, resulting in a dual allocation process (for example, variable costs based on actual usage and fixed costs based on budgeted usage).

The step method partially takes reciprocal services into account by allocating service department costs to production departments on a sequential basis. The service department that provides the greatest amount of service to the other service departments is allocated first; the one providing the second greatest amount of service to the other service departments is allocated second; and so forth. The absolute dollar amounts of costs incurred within service departments can be used to break a tie in usage, the larger amount allocated first. Once a service department has been allocated, it is ignored for all subsequent allocations.

The reciprocal method takes into account all the reciprocal services by setting up a set of simultaneous equations, one equation per service department. For any given service department, its equation is: Total allocable cost = direct costs of the service department + costs allocated from each of the other service departments based on this department's use of the other service departments. Once these equations are solved, the resultant allocable cost (sometimes referred to as the reciprocal or artificial cost) is reallocated across all the other departments, service and production, according to the original percentage usages.

Two additional issues, fairness and acquiring the service from the inside or from the outside, concern the allocation of a common cost. The amount of common service cost allocated to a using department may be greater that what it would cost that department to obtain the same service from the outside. A variation of the reciprocal method provides an analysis to help the manager of a using department decide whether to obtain the service from another department within the organization or to contract outside for the service from another organization. The amount of a particular service department's cost allocated to a using department may be dependent on the extent to which other departments also use this service department.

SEE ALSO *Costs*

BIBLIOGRAPHY

Blocher, Edward J., Chen, Kung H., and Lin, Thomas W. (2005). *Cost Management: A Strategic Emphasis.*Boston: McGraw-Hill/ Irwin.

Horngren, Charles T., Foster, George, and Datar, Srikant M. (2005). *Cost Accounting: A Managerial Emphasis* (12th ed.). Upper Saddle River, NJ: PrenticeHall.

Ijiri, Yuji (1975). *Theory of Accounting Measurement*. Sarasota, FL: American Accounting Association.

Kaplan, Robert S., and Atkinson, Anthony A. (1998). *Advanced Management Accounting* (3rd ed.). Upper Saddle River, NJ: PrenticeHall.

Willson, James D., Colford, James P., Roehl-Anderson, Janice M., and Bragg, Steven M. (1999). *Controllership: The Work of the Managerial Accountant*. New York: J. Wiley.

Lawrence A. Klein
Clifford Brown

COST-BENEFIT ANALYSIS

Cost-benefit analysis is used for determining which alternative is likely to provide the greatest return for a proposed investment. Sometimes referred to as cost-effectiveness analysis, it is relevant to businesses as well as to not-for-profit entities and governmental units.

A business might find it helpful to use cost-benefit analysis to determine if additional funds should be invested in a facility in the home country or in another country. A community not-for-profit organization that provides a variety of programs for children might use cost-benefit analysis to assist management in determining which activities will provide the most services for the costs specified. A federal governmental agency might use cost-benefit analysis to determine which of several projects planned for the national parks is likely to be most used by interested citizens, given the costs.

Because resources such as money and time are limited, an organization usually cannot undertake every project proposed. To decide whether to undertake a project, decision makers weigh the benefits from the project against the cost of the resources it requires, normally approving a project when its benefits exceed its costs. Cost-benefit analysis provides the structure and support for making such decisions.

Benefits increase the welfare of the organization. Some benefits are monetary benefits, such as the dollar amount of cash inflows from additional sales of a product or the saving in cash outflows that a project enables. Other benefits are important but harder to quantify. For example, a project may increase customer satisfaction; increased customer satisfaction may increase future sales, but the exact relationship between sales and satisfaction is often hard to specify.

Costs are the outlays or expenditures made in order to obtain a benefit. Many costs are measured monetarily, such as the cost of buying a new machine or of hiring an additional employee.

COST-BENEFIT ANALYSIS IN BUSINESS

A cost-benefit analysis is straightforward when all costs and benefits are measurable in monetary terms. Assume that Company A must decide whether to rent an ice cream machine for the summer for $900. The ice cream machine will produce additional cash inflows of $1,000 during the summer. The benefit of additional cash inflows ($1,000) exceeds the additional cost ($900), so the project should be undertaken. Not all cost-benefit analyses are this simple, however. If the benefits and costs occur in different time periods, it may be necessary to discount the future cash flows to their current equivalent worth.

In another example, cost savings is a benefit. Assume that Company B makes about 100,000 photocopies a year. Company B does not have its own copy machine and currently pays 4 cents per copy, or $4,000 a year, to Copycat Copiers. Company B can lease a copy machine for $2,500 a year. It must also pay 2 cents per page for paper for the leased machine, or $2,000. In this example, the cost of leasing the machine and buying paper ($2,500+$2,000=$4,500) exceeds the benefit of saving the $4,000 normally paid to Copycat Copiers. Company B should continue to use Copycat Copiers for its photocopies. However, Company B must have a pretty good estimate of the number of copies it needs to be comfortable with its decision. If Company B needs 150,000 copies this year instead of 100,000, the cost of the leasing the machine and buying paper ($2,500+$3,000=$5,500) is cheaper than the $6,000 (150,000×$0.04) savings in fees to Copycat Copiers.

A third example involves a project with benefits that are difficult to quantify. Assume that Company C is deciding whether to give a picnic costing $50,000 for its employees. Company C would receive the benefit of increased employee morale from the picnic. Better employee morale might cause employees to work harder, increasing profits. However, the link between increased morale and increased monetary profits is tenuous. The decision maker must use his or her judgment to compare the nonmonetary benefit to the monetary cost, possibly deciding that increased employee morale is worth the $50,000 cost but would not be worth a $100,000 cost.

In the preceding examples, cost-benefit analysis provided a framework for decision making. The range of objectivity related to measurement of the factors is typical. Techniques used in business as a basis for determining costs and benefits, such as return on investment, are generally quantifiable and thus appear to be objective. However, it is not uncommon for qualitative factors to enter into the decision-making process. For example, providing a product that individuals with limited incomes will be able to purchase may not provide the highest monetary return on investment in the short run, but might prove to be a successful long-term investment. Careful decision makers attempt to deal with a difficult-to-quantify factor in as objective a manner as possible. However, cost-benefit analysis in most situations continues to introduce measurement problems.

COST-BENEFIT ANALYSIS IN NONBUSINESS ENTITIES

Cost-benefit analyses are also common in nonbusiness entities. Boards of not-for-profit organizations establish priorities for their programs, and such priorities often specify desired program outputs. For example, assume a not-for-profit organization is interested in reducing the level of illiteracy among the citizens of a rural community in a state that has one of the lowest per-capita incomes in the United States. As alternative programs for those who need to learn to read are considered, there will be cost-benefit analyses that focus on a number of factors, including the extent to which a particular program can attract those who are illiterate. A program in the downtown area of a small town might be considered because a facility is available there at low cost, and that low cost is appealing. Focus on cost is not sufficient, however. When benefits are considered, it might become clear that those who are eager for such a program do not have cars and that there is no public transportation from where they reside to the center of the small town. Further consideration of relevant factors and of alternatives, undertaken in good faith, should result in cost-benefit analyses that provide valuable information as the agency makes decisions.

At all levels of government in the United States, cost-benefit analyses are used as a basis for allocating resources for the public good to those programs, projects, and services that will meet the expectations of citizens. For example, decision makers at the federal level who have policy responsibility for environmental standards, air-quality rules, or services to the elderly often find information from cost-benefit analyses to be critical to the decision-making task.

CONTINUING EFFORTS TO QUANTIFY COST-BENEFIT FACTORS

As possibilities for the use of funds increase, there is motivation for better measurement of both costs and benefits as well as for speedier ways of accomplishing analyses for

alternatives that are appealing. All types of entities, including businesses, not-for-profit organizations, and governmental units, strive to improve the measurements used in cost-benefit analyses. The capabilities of electronic equipment provide promising assistance in accumulating data relevant for analyses. Wise use of resources is an important goal in every organization; cost-benefit analyses make a key contribution to this goal. Therefore, attention is given to improving both the effectiveness and efficiency of such analyses.

BIBLIOGRAPHY

Boardman, Anthony, E. (2006). *Cost-Benefit Analysis: Concepts and Practice.* Upper Saddle River, NJ: Pearson/Prentice-Hall.

Nas, Tevik F. (1996). *Cost-Benefit Analysis: Theory and Application.* Thousand Oaks, CA: Sage Publications.

Mary Michel
Mary Ellen Oliverio

COST OF LIVING INDEX

SEE *Consumer Price Index*

COST-VOLUME-PROFIT ANALYSIS

Cost-volume-profit analysis (CVP), or break-even analysis, is used to compute the volume level at which total revenues are equal to total costs. When total costs and total revenues are equal, the business organization is said to be breaking even. The analysis is based on a set of linear equations for a straight line and the separation of variable and fixed costs.

Total variable costs are considered to be those costs that vary as the production volume changes. In a factory, production volume is considered to be the number of units produced, but in a governmental organization with no assembly process, the units produced might refer, for example, to the number of welfare cases processed. There are a number of costs that vary or change, but if the variation is not due to volume changes, it is not considered to be a variable cost. Examples of variable costs are direct materials and direct labor. Total fixed costs do not vary as volume levels change within the relevant range. Examples of fixed costs are straight-line depreciation and annual insurance charges. Total variable costs can be viewed as a 45° line and total fixed costs as a straight line. In the break-even chart shown in Figure 1, the upward slope of line DFC represents the change in variable costs. Variable costs sit on top of fixed costs, line DE. Point F represents the breakeven point. This is where the total cost (costs below the line DFC) crosses and is equal to total revenues (line AFB).

All the lines in the chart are straight lines: linearity is an underlying assumption of CVP analysis. Although no one can be certain that costs are linear over the entire range of output or production, this is an assumption of CVP. To help alleviate the limitations of this assumption, it is also assumed that the linear relationships hold only within the relevant range of production. The relevant range is represented by the high and low output points that have been previously reached with past production. CVP analysis is best viewed within the relevant range, that is, within our previous actual experience. Outside of that range, costs may vary in a nonlinear manner. The straight-line equation for total cost is:

Total cost = total fixed cost + total variable cost

Total variable cost is calculated by multiplying the cost of a unit, which remains constant on a per-unit basis, by the number of units produced. Therefore the total cost equation could be expanded as:

Total cost = total fixed cost + (variable cost per unit × number of units)

Total fixed costs do not change.

A final version of the equation is:

$$Y = a + bx$$

In this equation, a is the fixed cost, b is the variable cost per unit, x is the level of activity, and Y is the total cost. Assume that the fixed costs are $5,000, the volume of units produced is 1,000, and the per-unit variable cost is $2. In that case the total cost would be computed as follows:

$$Y = \$5,000 + (\$2 \times 1,000) \ Y = \$7,000$$

It can be seen that it is important to separate variable and fixed costs. Another reason it is important to separate these costs is because variable costs are used to determine the contribution margin, and the contribution margin is used to determine the break-even point. The contribution margin is the difference between the per-unit variable cost and the selling price per unit. For example, if the per-unit variable cost is $15 and selling price per unit is $20, then the contribution margin is equal to $5. The contribution margin may provide a $5 contribution toward the reduction of fixed costs or a $5 contribution to profits. If the business is operating at a volume above the break-even point volume (above point F), then the $5 is a contribution (on a per-unit basis) to additional profits. If the business is operating at a volume below the break-even point

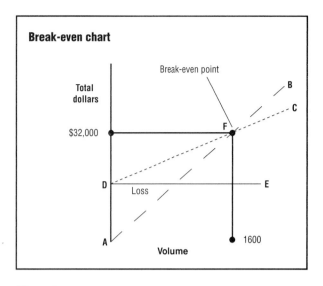

Figure 1

(below point F), then the $5 provides for a reduction in fixed costs and continues to do so until the break-even point is passed.

Once the contribution margin is determined, it can be used to calculate the break-even point in volume of units or in total sales dollars. When a per-unit contribution margin occurs below a firm's break-even point, it is a contribution to the reduction of fixed costs. Therefore, it is logical to divide fixed costs by the contribution margin to determine how many units must be produced to reach the break-even point:

$$\text{Break-even in units} = \frac{\text{total fixed costs}}{\text{contribution margin per unit}}$$

Assume that the contribution margin is the same as in the previous example, $5. In this example, assume that the total fixed costs are increased to $8,000. Using the equation, we determine that the break-even point in units:

$$\text{Break-even point in units} = \frac{\$8000}{\$5}$$
$$= 1600 \text{ units}$$

In Figure 1, the break-even point is shown as a vertical line from the x-axis to point F. Now, if we want to determine the break-even point in total sales dollars (total revenue), we could multiply 1600 units by the assumed selling price of $20 and arrive at $32,000. Or we could use another equation to compute the break-even point in total sales directly. In that case, we would first have to compute the contribution margin ratio. This ratio is determined by dividing the contribution margin by selling price. Referring to our example, the calculation of the ratio involves two steps:

$20 (selling price)
-15 (variable cost)
$ 5 (contribution margin)

$$\text{Contribution margin ratio} = \frac{\text{contribution margin}}{\text{selling price}}$$

$$= \frac{5}{20}$$

$$= 25\%$$

Going back to the break-even equation and replacing the per-unit contribution margin with the contribution margin ratio results in the following formula and calculation:

$$\text{Break-even in total sales} = \frac{\text{total fixed costs}}{\text{contribution margin ratio}}$$

$$= \frac{\$8000}{.25}$$

$$= \$32,000$$

Figure 1 shows this break-even point, at $32,000 in sales, as a horizontal line from point F to the y-axis. Total sales at the break-even point are illustrated on the y-axis and total units on the x-axis. Also notice that the losses are represented by the DFA triangle and profits in the FBC triangle.

The financial information required for CVP analysis is for internal use and is usually available only to managers inside the firm; information about variable and fixed costs is not available to the general public. CVP analysis is good as a general guide for one product within the relevant range. If the company has more than one product, then the contribution margins from all products must be averaged together. But, any cost-averaging process reduces the level of accuracy as compared to working with cost data from a single product. Furthermore, some organizations, such as nonprofit organizations, do not incur a significant level of variable costs. In these cases, standard CVP assumptions can lead to misleading results and decisions.

SEE ALSO *Costs*

G. Stevenson Smith

COSTS

The word "cost" appears in many accounting, economics, and business terms with subtle distinctions in meaning. The word by itself rarely has a clear meaning. (Likewise the word "value" has no clear meaning. Avoid using "value" without a modifying adjective, such as "market," "present," or "book.") The word cost, without modifying adjectives, typically means the sacrifice, measured by the price paid or required to be paid, to acquire goods or services. Hence, the word often carries the meaning more precisely represented by the following:

- *Acquisition cost; historical cost.* Net price plus all expenditures to ready an item for its intended use at the time the firm acquired the item. The other expenditures might include legal fees, transportation charges, and installation costs.

Accountants can easily measure acquisition cost, but economists and managers often find it less useful in making decisions. Economists and managers more often care about some measure of current costs, which accountants find harder to measure.

- *Current cost.* Replacement cost or net realizable value.

- *Replacement cost.* Acquisition cost at the date of measurement, typically the present, in contrast to the earlier date of acquisition.

- *Net realizable value.* The amount a firm can collect in cash by selling an item, less the costs (such as commissions and delivery costs) of disposition.

Accountants most often refer to current costs as fair value.

- *Fair value.* Price negotiated at arm's length between willing buyers and willing sellers, each acting rationally in their own self-interest. Sometimes measured as the present value of expected cash flows.

Accountants often contrast (actual) historical cost with standard cost.

- *Standard cost.* An estimate of how much cost a firm should incur to produce a good or service. This measurement plays a role in cost accounting, in situations where management needs an estimate of costs incurred before sufficient time has elapsed for computation of actual costs incurred.

The following terms desegregate historical cost into components.

- *Variable cost.* Costs that change as activity levels change. (The term "cost driver" refers to the activity that causes cost to change.) Strictly speaking, variable costs are zero when the activity level is zero. Careful writers use the term "semivariable costs" to mean costs that increase strictly linearly with activity but have a positive value at zero activity level. Royalty fees of 2 percent of sales are variable; royalty fees of $1,000 per year plus 2 percent of sales are semivariable.

- *Fixed cost.* A cost that does not change as activity levels change, at least for some time period. In the long run, all costs can vary.

In accounting for the costs of product or services or segments of a business, accountants sometimes desegregate total costs into those that benefit a specific product and those that benefit all products jointly produced.

- *Traceable cost; direct cost.* A cost the firm can identify with a specific product, such as the cost of a computer chip installed in a given personal computer, or with some activity.

- *Common cost; joint cost; indirect cost.* A cost incurred to benefit more than one product or activity, such as the cost of rent of a factory building in which the firm makes several different kinds of personal computers or the cost of a steer from which the firm manufactures leather and hamburger. Some restrict the term common cost to situations such as the first, where the firm chooses to produce products together, while restricting "joint costs" to situations, such as the second, where the firm must incur the cost simultaneously. The major problem in cost accounting is allocation of common and joint costs to individual products. Managers and regulators (e.g., the Securities and Exchange Commission and the IRS) often insist on such allocations, while economists and some accountants recognize that such allocations do not aid decision making.

Virtually all costs recorded by accountants require a cash outlay at some time. Analysts sometimes need to distinguish between costs associated with current or future cash expenditures and those where the expenditure already occurred.

- *Out-of-pocket cost; outlay cost; cash cost.* An item requiring a current or future cash expenditure.

- *Book cost; sunk cost.* A cost incurrence where the cash expenditure has already occurred, such as the cost of depreciation for a machine purchased several years ago. (In accounting, depreciation is an allocation of a previous expenditure, while in economics depreciation represents a decline in current value.)

In decision making, the cost concepts above often get further refined, as follows.

- *Incremental cost; marginal cost; differential cost; avoidable cost.* The firm will incur (save) incremental costs if it carries out (or stops) a project. These four terms tend to have the same meaning, except that the economist restricts the term "marginal cost" to the cost of producing one more unit. Thus the next unit has a marginal cost; the next week's output has an incremental cost. If a firm produces and sells a new product, the related new costs would properly be called "incremental," not marginal. If a factory is closed, the costs saved are incremental, not marginal.

- *Unavoidable cost; inescapable cost; sunk cost.* Unavoidable costs will occur whether the decision is made to go ahead or not, because the firm has already spent, or committed to spend, the cash. Not all unavoidable costs are book costs; consider a salary promised, but not yet earned, that the firm will pay if it makes a no-go decision. Sunk costs are past costs that current and future decisions cannot affect and, hence, are irrelevant for decision making (aside from income tax effects). For example, the acquisition cost of machinery is irrelevant to a decision of whether to scrap the machinery. In making such a decision, one should consider only the sacrifice of continuing to own it and the cost of, say, the electricity to run the machine, both incremental costs. Sunk costs become relevant for decision making when the analysis requires taking income taxes (gain or loss on disposal of asset) into account, since the cash payment for income taxes depends on the tax basis of the asset. Avoid using the ambiguous term "sunk costs." Consider, for example, a machine costing $100,000 with current salvage value of $20,000. Some would say that $100,000 is sunk; others would say that only $80,000 is sunk. Those who say $100,000 have in mind a gross cost, while those who say $80,000 have in mind a net cost—original amount reduced by current opportunity cost.

In deciding which employees to reward, management often cares about desegregating actual costs into those that are controllable and those not controllable by a given employee or division. All costs can be affected by someone in the firm; those who design incentive schemes attempt to hold a person responsible for a cost only if that person can influence the amount of the cost.

A firm incurs costs because it perceives that it will realize benefits. Careful usage of cost terms distinguishes between incurrences where the firm will enjoy the benefits in the future from those where the firm has already enjoyed the benefits. Accounting distinguishes costs that have future benefits by calling them *assets* and contrasting them with costs whose benefits the firm has already consumed, by calling them *expenses*. Other pairs of terms involving this distinction are *unexpired cost* versus *expired cost* and *product cost* versus *period cost*.

Economists, managers, and regulators make further distinctions between cost concepts, as follows.

- *Fully absorbed cost* versus *variable cost*. Fully absorbed costs refer to costs where the firm has allocated fixed manufacturing costs to products produced or divisions within the firm as required by generally accepted accounting principles. Variable costs, in contrast, may be more relevant for making decisions, such as in setting prices or deciding whether a firm has priced below cost for antitrust purposes.

- *Fully absorbed cost* versus *full cost*. In full costing, the analysis allocates all costs, manufacturing costs as well as central corporate expenses (including financing expenses), to products or to divisions. In full absorption costing, the firm allocates only manufacturing costs to product. Only in full costing will revenues, expenses, and income summed over all products or divisions equal corporate revenues, expenses, and income.

- *Opportunity cost* versus *outlay cost*. Opportunity cost refers to the economic benefit forgone by using a resource for one purpose rather than another. If the firm can sell a machine for $200,000, then the opportunity cost of using that machine in operations is $200,000 independent of its outlay cost or its book cost or its historical cost.

- *Future cost* versus *past cost*. Effective decision making analyzes only present and future outlay costs, or out-of-pocket costs. Optimal decisions result from using future costs, whereas financial reporting uses past costs.

- *Short-run cost* versus *long-run cost*. For a given configuration of plant and equipment, short-run costs vary as output varies. The firm can incur long-run costs to change that configuration. This pair of terms is the economist's analogy of the accounting pair, above, variable and fixed costs. The analogy is inexact because some short-run costs are fixed, such as property taxes on the factory.

- *Imputed cost* versus *book cost*. Imputed costs do not appear in the historical cost accounting records for financial reporting. The actual cost incurred is recorder and is called a *book cost*. Some regulators

calculate the cost of owners' equity capital, for various purposes; these are imputed costs. Opportunity costs are imputed costs and are relevant for decision making.

- *Average cost* versus *marginal cost*. This is the economic distinction equivalent to fully absorbed cost of product and variable cost of product. Average cost is total cost divided by number of units. Marginal cost is the cost to produce the next unit (or the last unit).

- *Differential cost* versus *variable cost*. Whether a cost changes or remains fixed depends on the activity basis being considered. Typically, but not invariably, analysts term costs as *variable*, or *fixed*, with respect to an activity basis such as changes in production levels. Typically, but not invariably, analysts term costs as *incremental*, or not, with respect to an activity basis, such as the undertaking of some new venture. Consider the decision to undertake the production of food processors, rather than food blenders, which the manufacturer has been making. To produce processors requires the acquisition of a new machine tool. The cost of the new machine tool is incremental with respect to a decision to produce food processors instead of food blenders, but, once acquired, becomes a fixed cost of producing food processors. Consider a firm that will incur costs of direct labor for the production of food processors or food blenders, whichever the firm produces. Assume the firm cannot produce both. Such labor is variable with respect to production measured in units, but not incremental with respect to the decision to produce processors rather than blenders. This distinction often blurs in practice, so a careful understanding of the activity basis being considered is necessary for understanding of the concepts being used in a particular application.

Analysis of operating and manufacturing activities uses the following subdivisions of fixed (historical) costs. Fixed costs have the following components:

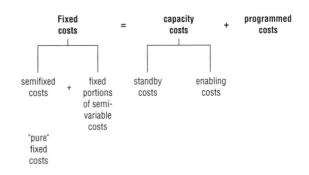

Capacity costs (committed costs) give a firm the capability to produce or to sell, while *programmed costs (managed costs, discretionary costs)*, such as for advertising or research, may be nonessential, but once the firm has decided to incur them, they become fixed costs. The firm will incur *standby costs* even if it does not use existing capacity; examples include property taxes and depreciation on a building. The firm can avoid *enabling costs*, such as for a security force, if it does not use capacity. A cost fixed over a wide range but that can change is a *semifixed cost* or "step cost." An example is the cost of rail lines from the factory to the main rail line, where fixed cost depends on whether there are one or two parallel lines but are independent of the number of trains run per day. *Semivariable costs* combine a strictly fixed component cost plus a variable component. Telephone charges usually have a fixed monthly component plus a charge related to usage.

SEE ALSO *Cost Allocation; Cost-Benefit Analysis; Cost-Volume-Profit Analysis*

BIBLIOGRAPHY

Buchanan, James M., and Thirlby, G. F. (1973). *L.S.E. Essays on Cost*. London: Weidenfeld and Nicholson.

Horngren, Charles T., Foster, George, and Datar, Srikant M. (2005). *Cost Accounting: A Managerial Emphasi* (12th ed.). Upper Saddle River, NJ: Prentice-Hall.

Maher, Michael W., Stickney, Clyde P., and Weil, Roman L. (2006). *Managerial Accounting: An Introduction to Concepts, Methods, and Uses* (9th ed.). Mason, OH: Thomson/South-Western.

Stickney, Clyde P., and Weil, Roman L. (2006). *Financial Accounting: An Introduction to Concepts, Methods and Uses* (11th ed.). Mason, OH: Thomson/South-Western.

Roman L. Weil

COTTAGE INDUSTRIES

Cottage industries is a term that was prevalent during the eighteenth and nineteenth centuries to describe the home-based system of manufacturing. This term is also used today to refer to goods or services that are produced at home. Sewing, craft production, sales and marketing, typing, bookkeeping, and auto repair are just a few examples of home-based employment.

HISTORY

Rural families were some of the first to become involved in the cottage industry. They added to their agricultural income by making products at home. Merchants provided the raw materials to the families, collected and marketed the finished product, and then paid the family a percentage of the price charged to the end consumer. Some of the items made by these at-home workers were cloth and clothing, shoes, cigars, and hand-decorated items.

Cottage industries developed in cities around 1870, resulting in the harsh tenement housing system. Immigrant families lived and worked in these crowded, unsafe apartment buildings. They worked for extremely low wages, usually making garments. This system lasted until around 1920, when better management of factories made home-produced goods less competitive.

Hand-decorating of items, sewing, and other highly specialized activities still operate as cottage industries today. Economists point to the rise of a new type of cottage industry whereby people can stay at home to perform work on their computers that formerly had to be done at the office. Telecommuters is another term used more frequently today to refer to home-based employment. Many jobs that used to require workers' physical presence in the office can now be performed from home. Running a business from home today requires only a couple of phone lines with call forwarding and call waiting, a computer with e-mail and a modem, a fax machine, a copier, and office supplies. For executives on the go, a cell phone and laptop computer can keep them up and running from just about any location.

HOME EMPLOYMENT BENEFITS

There are many reasons that people choose to work from their homes. They can be experienced or inexperienced, young or elderly, healthy or physically challenged, single or married, with or without children.

Many mothers and/or fathers of young children find it more productive, more cost-effective, and safer to keep their children with them while they work at home. They can have the flexibility of arranging their job around their family's needs. Many parents enjoy being able to spend time with their children during the day. Parents maintain responsibility for the safety of their own children and can keep abreast of how much they are learning, know who they are playing with, and save money on day-care expenses at the same time.

Another reason people choose to work from home is that they do not have to commute to and from their workplace. By not commuting to work, they can save on wear and tear of their vehicle, get lower insurance rates, and spend less money on gas.

Working from home also saves money that would normally be spent on a workplace wardrobe. Much more informal clothing can be worn when working at home. Not spending money on uniforms, suits, and/or dresses provides more money for other expenses.

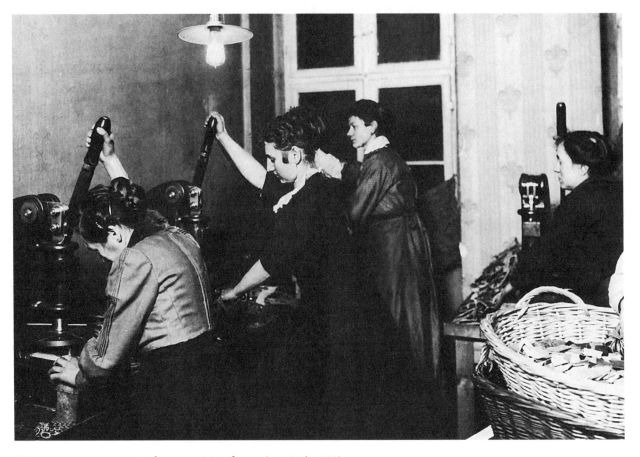

Women operating a cottage industry munitions factory (ca. 1914–1918). © CORBIS

Home employment gives control of one's life to oneself. There is freedom and flexibility in setting work schedules. Parents can be home for their children, there are no commuting hassles, and no one looks over shoulders or determines break time. The individual, not the employer, determines the work schedule. A parent has the flexibility of scheduling work flow around school activities such as field trips and sports activities.

DECISIONS TO MAKE

Despite all of the benefits, home employment is not for everyone. For example, those who start their own business must be able to generate work. There are advertising costs involved in getting the company name out to the general public. Careful consideration should be given to the possible advertising avenues to use. Advertising can be very expensive and may not generate enough business if it does not reach potential customers. People who do good work but cannot get others to recognize this or cannot do well in promoting themselves may be spending more than they are earning.

Detailed record keeping is a must for the self-employed as well as the work-at-home person. Some deductions are available only if the business is making a profit, while others are used yearly to determine expenses. Depending on the type of business a person wishes to become involved in, start-up costs need to be considered and information gathered on the best equipment/tools necessary. Some businesses may require a starting inventory, while others do not. When considering start-up costs, one should shop wisely and consider purchasing used equipment and supplies. This will save money for other expenses, and the depreciation on these items will be more reasonable. Advertising, mileage expenses, cost of supplies, phone, electricity, and entertainment are just some of the expenses for which records must be maintained. Tax laws can and do change frequently. The person who is unsure about what records need to be kept should contact a tax adviser for detailed and up-to-date information.

Another factor to consider before deciding to work from home is motivation. One must be able to set one's own schedule and follow through on it. If a person is used to working for someone else and having supervision and direction provided, it can be very easy to let work slide. Setting goals and following through on them is a necessity when working for oneself.

Finally, one should check local authorities before starting a home-based business as towns vary greatly in their local ordinances. They will explain any rules the town has established regarding home-based businesses and give guidance in the necessary paperwork or approval process.

HOME EMPLOYMENT RESOURCES

For those people who wish to become self-employed and work out of their home, there are several organizations available to help get started.

One major resource for the self-employed is an association called SCORE (Service Corps of Retired Executives). SCORE is a nonprofit group sponsored by the U.S. Small Business Administration that has provided successful, free business counseling since 1964. SCORE matches volunteer counselors with clients needing their expert advice. It also maintains a national skills roster to help identify the best counselor for a particular client. SCORE is made up of more than 13,000 retired or active executives and has more than 400 chapters nationwide. These executives volunteer their time, skills, and experience to help the self-employed get started in their own business or help those who are already in business when they have problems or need advice. SCORE also offers many seminars and workshops and posts this information at its local chapters. Since its inception, SCORE has advised, counseled, and mentored more than 300,000 small businesses, helping nearly 4 million Americans with face-to-face counseling, e-mail counseling, and training. For more information on SCORE, contact a local chapter personally or visit its Web site at http://www.score.org/.

Home Employment Resource is an organization dedicated to helping people who want to work at home. It provides information on companies nationwide that hire people to work from home. A partial listing of jobs that have been available to the home-employed include typists, graphic artists, auto appraisers, editors, reporters, financial analysts, cartoonists, claims processors, photographers, proofreaders, recruiters, and writers. There are many jobs available for home-based workers if one knows where to look. This organization assists in contacting the companies that hire work-at-home people. The Web site for Home Employment Resource is http://www.home-employment.com/.

The Independent Homeworkers Alliance (IHA) is an organization dedicated to helping people who want to work from home. The IHA offers its members valuable benefits that are designed specifically for the work-at-home person. Included in its database are more than 43,000 job listings. Membership and maintenance fees that are charged to members are applied directly to the organization itself to improve, enhance, and add to the existing services provided to its members, who number more than 27,000. More information about Independent Homeworkers Alliance is available through their Web site at http://www.homeworkers.org/.

There are also home study schools that offer training in fields such as medical billing and claims processing, medical transcription, bookkeeping, and paralegal work. For more information on home-study schooling, contact At-Home Profession ... America's First Home Study School for Work-at-Home Careers, 2001 Lowe Street, Fort Collins, CO 80525.

BIBLIOGRAPHY

"Home Employment Resource". Retrieved October 15, 2005, from http://www.home-employment.com/.

"IHA". Independent Homeworkers Alliance. Retrieved October 15, 2005, from http://www.homeworkers.org/.

"SCORE 'Counselors to America's Small Business" Retrieved October 15, 2005, from www.score.org.

The World Book Encyclopedia (2005). Chicago: World Book, Inc.

Julie A. Watkins

COUPONS
SEE *E-Marketing; Marketing Mix; Pricing; Promotion*

CPI
SEE *Consumer Price Index*

CREDIT/DEBIT/TRAVEL CARDS

Until the 1920s, consumer purchases in the United States were made primarily in one of two ways: cash or personal check. However, in that decade, a new means of payment was introduced—the credit account. While credit transactions had been common for a long time in business to business dealings, they were new to the consumer market. The credit account allowed a consumer to defer payment on a purchase made today to some time in the future: thus, the expression "buy now, pay later" was born. Evidence of the credit account typically took the form of a card—the credit card.

Since the 1920s, different types of credit cards have emerged. In addition, related types of cards have also appeared on the consumer scene: the debit card, as well as the ATM card and the smart card, and the travel card and charge card.

CREDIT CARDS

A credit card is a pocket size, plastic card that allows the holder to make a purchase on a credit account that will be repaid at some time in the future. Repayment may be in a single amount or in a series of amounts. At a minimum, the credit card will include identification of the user by name, account number, and signature.

The earliest issuance of credit cards in the United States was by gasoline companies and retail stores. Thus, it was quite common in the first half of the twentieth century to carry a credit card from Esso, Sears, and/or a local department store. These early cards were issued by the private company itself based on the credit policy of that company. Many of the accounts were expected to be paid in the month following purchase. Others were revolving charge accounts in which partial payment was expected every month, with a charge for interest on amounts not paid promptly.

If the balances of the credit accounts were not paid, the issuing firm took the loss. Thus, deciding to issue a credit card was a thoughtful process on the part of the firm. Often, the three Cs of credit were applied to a credit applicant: character, capacity, and capital. Character referred to the record of the applicant in paying previous accounts— his or her credit history. Capacity meant the earnings potential (salary) of the applicant. Capital referred to the net assets (assets minus liabilities) of the person. Obtaining a credit card was far from an automatic process.

Major changes in the nature and types of credit cards occurred in the 1950s. Two types of credit cards emerged in that decade: the charge card and the bank credit card.

The bank credit card expanded the idea of a credit card company to a much broader usage—virtually every merchant and service provider worldwide. The 1959 BankAmericard from the Bank of America in California became the VISA card. The 1970s saw the birth of Master Charge, which became MasterCard. These cards are issued by banks, so one applies to a bank for the credit card. A preset credit limit is assigned to the card user. After an item is charged at a firm, the firm receives payment from the bank. The bank charges a fee to the firm, pays the firm the net amount, and then collects from the consumer. The consumer usually pays an annual fee to the bank and is charged interest on the unpaid balance at the

end of each month. Credit cards may also be used to make a cash advance from the bank. However, it should be remembered that interest rates on cash advances using a credit card can be much higher than the rates for credit card purchases. Thus, the cash advance feature should be used wisely.

While at one time it was difficult to earn credit, the process is far easier at the present time. Banks compete for customers for their credit cards and often solicit college students with limited capital and offer them credit cards. Telemarketing of credit cards is frequent. Low credit limits are relatively easy to obtain. Demonstrating a solid payment record and growth in earnings then leads to higher limits.

Managing one's credit is important to the consumer. It is critical never to get into a position in which one has so many credit cards and so many high balances that the credit bills never get paid off. For example, if you have a bank credit card with a balance of $1,000 and an interest rate of 18 percent a year or 0.083 percent a month (18 percent divided by twelve months), the interest for the current month will be $15 ($1,000 × .015). If the payment made on the account this month is only $25, then the first $15 is for interest; the remaining $10 ($25–$15) reduces the principal of $1,000 to $990 for the next month. In other words, more has been paid for interest than for what was purchased; the situation in the following month will change very little. At this rate of payment, it could be several years before the balance is reduced to zero. In the meantime, if the card has been used for more purchases, the cycle of remaining in debt continues. Credit card management is critical to a consumer. In fact, one who has difficulty in dealing with credit cards might be better off with debit cards.

DEBIT CARDS

A debit card is also issued by a bank and looks like a credit card, but it works very differently. When one uses a debit card, the amount spent is deducted immediately from the user's bank account. It is as if one is paying by check without having to write a check. There will be no unpaid future bills, for the payment is made at the time of the expenditure. For example, many people today purchase groceries with the debit card by running it through the card reader at the grocery store check out counter. In addition, people often get extra cash while paying for the groceries with that debit card.

It is helpful to know how a bank account works from the bank's point of view to fully understand the debit card. When an amount is added to a bank account, such as by a deposit, the individual's account is credited; when an amount is subtracted from that bank account, such as by writing a check, the account is debited. Thus, the term

Credit Cards. © ALAN SCHEIN PHOTOGRAPHY/CORBIS

debit card states what happens to the bank account when the card is used—an immediate subtraction.

A common function of the debit card is as an ATM card. ATM stands for the Automated Teller Machine that so many use today. ATMs allow for 24-hour banking. The card holder is able to make deposits, find out bank balances, transfer money from account to account, and make a loan payment. The ATM/debit card can also be used to obtain cash; the amount withdrawn is subtracted immediately from the bank account and thus is another use of a debit card.

The user of the debit card must take particular care in keeping records of expenditures with the debit card. Unlike the check that usually is recorded at the time of payment, the debit card expense has its record in the form of a sales slip, a register receipt, or a record of an ATM withdrawal or deposit. Debit card expenditures must be deducted from the bank account balance by the user in a regular accurate manner to avoid losing track of the account balance.

A variation on the debit card is the smart card. While the debit card uses a magnetic strip, the smart card typically uses an embedded semiconductor to store and main-

tain information. Smart cards have many uses, but in general are used for prepayment of an expense, such as when a phone card is purchased. The phone card has so many dollars in it that have been paid for in advance of use. As the card is used, money value is deducted. Other applications of the smart card are for the payment of tolls and for the purchase of gasoline. In both cases, the card can be waved at a reader that will record the toll or the purchase of gasoline. Food plans at colleges and transit cards on subway systems are other uses of the smart card. Using a smart card saves that sudden search for change to pay a toll or to make a phone call.

TRAVEL CARDS

Travel cards, also called travel and entertainment cards, fall into two categories. The first is the charge card mentioned earlier. A charge card is issued by a firm whose main product is credit granting in order to purchase a service. The first two companies in this field were Diners' Club, Inc., and American Express Company. In both cases, one is issued a card based on a credit check and then uses the card at designated establishments and with designated types of firms to pay for services or products. Payment is made not to a store nor to a bank, but rather to Diners' Club or to American Express. Diners' Club cards are used primarily at eating establishments. American Express cards are used for airlines, hotels, and other travel-related activities. No credit limits are established for charge cards, but payment is expected in full within the next billing period to maintain one's credit record. However, a current change in the approach to the charge card has been made by American Express to allow monthly payments, just as if it were a bank credit card account.

A second type of travel card is issued by airlines or hotel chains. This card does not have direct money use, but serves instead as an upgraded service provider. Thus, included in this category are such cards as frequent flyer cards, with which airline mileage is accumulated, to be later used for upgraded or free flights. In addition, services are provided to the cardholder such as early boarding of flights and/or other amenities. Also included in this category are hotel chain cards that accumulate services at hotels in that chain. Room upgrades, speedy check in and check out, and help with reservations are among the benefits of this type of card. Furthermore, many hotels are partners with airlines, so money spent at a hotel can result in additional miles on the airline mileage account.

A growing trend among the airlines is the issuance of airline MasterCards or VISA cards. The airlines work with a bank to issue standard bank credit cards with one modification: every dollar spent using that credit card is turned into airline mileage that can be turned in for airline tickets and/or upgrades in travel classification. Thus, the benefit of the bank credit card is joined with the value of the airline travel card.

SUMMARY

From a time when what was bought was paid for on the spot, "plastic" has changed the way that consumers do business and handle personal financial functions. Credit cards allow a purchase now with payment in the future. Debit cards result in an immediate deduction from a bank account without writing a check. Smart cards allow for prepayment of expenses to aid in convenience when the expense needs to be paid. Travel cards permit charging of travel related expenses and the accumulation of travel services and benefits. All of these items are part of a paperless financial society accessed by cards of various types. In fact, it is possible that the day of cards will at some point end and another means will be found to connect payments for purchases. Until then, given the many ways to purchase, wise consumerism is needed for the correct choice of cards for an individual.

Burton S. Kaliski

CREDIT UNIONS
SEE *Financial Institutions*

CRIME AND FRAUD

Both individuals and businesses commit many criminal activities that cost businesses, consumers, government agencies, and stockholders considerable sums of money each year. Business crime is not new; in fact, fraudulent activities have been a common part of business operations for thousands of years. For instance, in 360 B.C.E. in Syracuse, Sicily (then a Greek colony), Xenothemis and a ship owner, Hegestratos, persuaded a customer to advance cash by claiming that a vessel was fully laden with corn. Maritime trade was at that time very risky, and many vessels were subsequently lost at sea. Hegestratos intended to exploit this risk of loss at sea three days after the ship sailed from port by sinking it. When the other passengers discovered Hegestratos's plot, he panicked, jumped overboard, and drowned. This early example illustrates that criminal, and especially fraudulent, activities have existed within the world of business for some time and, unfortunately, will probably continue to do so.

Under modern law, for a crime to have occurred, an illegal act must have been committed and intent to commit the act must be shown. A crime is a violation of local, state, federal, or international law and is punishable by the appropriate government authority. Criminal activities are usually defined as applying to a specific type of behavior or action. Criminal activities can be committed by individuals against a business as well as by businesses through the actions of their employees against consumers, the general public, and/or stockholders. Statistics regarding a variety of crimes committed in the United States can be found on the Federal Bureau of Investigation's Web site (http://www.fbi.gov).

CRIMES COMMITTED BY INDIVIDUALS AGAINST BUSINESSES

Business-related individual criminal activities are normally broken down into two categories: internal and external.

Internal Crimes. Internal crime occurs when an employee steals from or commits some other offense against the business. For example, depending on their jobs, employees may have access to business files, records, or sensitive financial information. The dishonest employee could then use this information to commit a crime against the business. Generally, the higher in the business the employee, the greater the potential for serious criminal activities against the firm.

A number of internal crimes are frequently committed against a business. Among the most common are abuse of power, embezzlement, misuse of business time, computer and electronic information manipulation, intellectual property theft, supply and equipment pilferage, travel expense abuse, and vandalism and sabotage.

Abuse of power. Making inappropriate financial decisions on behalf of the business that are really intended to benefit the employee is one form of employee criminal activity. An example of this may be seen when an employee is empowered to sign purchase contracts on behalf of the employer with the objective of getting the lowest price available from outside vendors. Instead of doing this, an employee could sign contracts with more expensive outside vendors and receive a kickback in return. Acceptance of kickbacks is an abuse of power and, depending on the size of the contracts, may cost a business a considerable amount of money.

Embezzlement. One of the most common internal criminal activities is the manipulating of accounting records to steal business funds. Employees who are well trained in accounting techniques may be able to devise sophisticated schemes to cover their connection to the stolen business funds. Such criminal accounting violations can go on for years and end up costing a business many thousands of dollars. These criminal accounting practices can be detected through a variety of methods, such as changes in accounting procedures, coworker concerns, and regular internal and/or external audits. Examples of embezzlement warning signs may be viewed on the Find-Law for Small Business Web site (http://smallbusiness.findlaw.com/business-operations/accounting/accounting-embezzlement-signs.html).

Accounting crimes are very serious matters that have adverse consequences for a business. The stealing of funds hurts the business's profit margin and, in turn, stockholders. Stock value is harmed because of the reduced profits showing on the books, which, in turn, can cost a business the lost value of its securities. Such internal accounting crimes must be reported to the appropriate law enforcement agencies, making the embezzlement part of the business's public record. Thus the business faces the embarrassment associated with having been a victim of accounting crimes, possibly weakening its image and public confidence in it. An employee who gets caught committing such crimes faces severe penalties if convicted. Depending on the amount of funds stolen, an employee could be charged with and convicted of a felony and face a long prison sentence. In addition, once convicted of such a crime, it will be next to impossible for a person to get another job in the business world.

Misuse of business time. Employees who perform non-work-related functions while at work are involved in fraudulent activities because they are getting paid to do work for the business but in reality are not performing those functions. An example of this practice is an employee who surfs the Internet for several hours a day for personal reasons, depriving the business of employee production during that time. A few hours of lost time here and there may not seem like much to an employee, but the aggregate loss of work time in the business as a whole can add up to a sizable loss. The misuse of business time by employees surfing the Internet is has become known as cyberslacking. For more information about cyberslacking and its potential impact on business, see the bCentral Web site (http://www.bcentral.co.uk/newsletters/bulletins/cyberslacking.mspx).

Computer and electronic information manipulation. The advent of modern technology has provided more opportunities for employees to commit computer or electronic fraud. One of the most common forms of embezzlement involves the electronic manipulation of business funds so as to deposit them into personal or other third-party accounts. Once the rerouted business funds are deposited into such an account, the employee may withdraw them and spend them at will. Initially, such electronic fraud might seem easy to carry out, but computers leave behind clues that will lead auditors to the final destination of the funds and to the dishonest employee. For more information regarding the use of computers in criminal activity, see an article available on the Web site of the company Natural Security Institute (http://nsi.org/Library/Compsec/crimecom.html).

Intellectual property theft. One of the fastest-growing areas of business-related criminal activity is the theft of cutting-edge technology by workers from their employers. Typically, dishonest employees will sell the stolen technological knowledge to a competing firm. Criminal activity in this area can be extremely damaging to any business. One reason is that most businesses invest considerable sums of money in research and development to improve or create new technology. The theft and resale of this information to competitors could easily cost a business many thousands of dollars in lost profits. Another is that the business's competitors can stay competitive for only a fraction of the price and thus reap even larger profits. In response to this serious issue, businesses have tightened security and have asked law enforcement to vigorously prosecute anyone involved with this type of criminal behavior. Statistics regarding intellectual property theft can be found at the U.S. Department of Justice's Office of Justice Programs Web site (http://www.ojp.usdoj.gov/bjs/abstract/ipt02.htm).

Supply and equipment pilferage. Another example of internal employee criminal activity is the theft of business supplies and office equipment. Businesses are concerned with employees who steal supplies and office equipment, such as laptop computers, paper, paper clips, pens, printers, and so forth. The theft of such business property reduces business profits and, if its stock is publicly traded, earnings for its stockholders. The consequences for dishonest employees who are caught engaging in these activities include job termination and criminal prosecution. For more information about preventing employee pilferage, see the National Federation of Independent Business Web site (http://www.nfib.com/object/3289337.html).

Travel expense abuse. Employees who travel for a business as part of their jobs may commit fraud by putting personal items on the firm's expense account. For example, employees may include higher amounts on their expense voucher than were actually paid. This practice is common when reporting the amount paid in the form of a tip, as usually no receipt is involved. Individually, the funds embezzled by one employee in this way might not add up to much, but collectively this type of crime could cost a business many thousands of dollars each year.

Vandalism and sabotage. Another type of internal crime is an employee's intentional destruction of business property or equipment. The employee does not receive any monetary benefit from destroying business property; rather, it is done to get back at a business or a supervisor for a myriad of reasons, such as being passed over for promotion, a pending layoff, or a poor performance evaluation. Traditional employee vandalism involves destruction of physical property, including computer equipment, office furniture, business vehicles, or other business property. Physical destruction of business property can be deterred by the use of surveillance equipment and the visible presence of adequate security staff. For more information on preventing vandalism see the Boulder, Colorado, Police Department Web site (http://www.ci.boulder.co.us/police).

A real threat to modern businesses is efforts to sabotage computer systems. An employee with extensive knowledge of a business's computer system could create a computer virus or some other highly technical method to incapacitate some or all of the business's computer system. The destruction or failure of a business's computer system would cause enormous trouble for the business. In addition, if business files were to be damaged or erased, it could cost the business a considerable amount of time and resources to fix them, not to mention the lost sales or poor customer service that might occur as a result. Since the computer security issue is so important, businesses normally discontinue computer access for employees who are going to be separated from the firm. In addition, business security typically monitors employees who have exhibited strong negative feelings toward the business or a supervisor.

External Crimes. Among the more common external crimes committed against a business are burglary, robbery, shoplifting, and walk-in office/factory thefts.

Burglary. Burglary is usually thought of as breaking into a building with the intent of committing a felony, or, in particular, stealing something. Although any business may be burglarized, individuals who commit burglary tend to target those firms where they are likely to receive a high monetary return for their efforts. Financial institutions, such as banks, are often targeted because they normally have large amounts of cash or valuable securities on hand. Almost every major financial business uses a variety of elaborate antiburglary devices to deter potential burglaries. Financial institutions also use extensive networks of electronic equipment to notify law enforcement when burglaries do occur. Most major businesses now employ a wide variety of antiburglary strategies in order to provide maximum security to their offices and employees. For further information on burglary prevention strategies, see the Los Angeles, California, Police Department Web site (http://www.lapdonline.org).

Robbery. Robbery is committed when a criminal uses force or the threat of force—usually with a weapon, such as a gun or knife—to steal from a business during its normal operating hours. Robberies are very serious because of their potential for bodily injury of employees and/or customers who are on the premises at the time the robbery is committed. Moreover, any property or money that is stolen also hurts the business from a profit-and-loss point of view. For further information on robbery prevention strategies, see the Colorado Association of Robbery Investigators Web site (http://www.co-asn-rob.org/Default.htm).

Shoplifting. One of the most prominent threats to any retail business is shoplifting, which costs businesses millions of dollars in lost sales and stolen merchandise each year. Unfortunately, the cost associated with this type of criminal activity is passed on to honest consumers in the form of higher prices. Because of the high costs associated with shoplifting, many retail businesses use sophisticated electronic surveillance systems in order to deter shoplifting and to catch those who commit the crime. Most retailers have adopted a zero-tolerance policy relative to shoplifting and will prosecute anyone caught stealing regardless of the amount. The combination of strong antitheft measures and vigorous prosecution of those caught has resulted in fewer numbers of shoplifting cases. For further information on shoplifting prevention, see the Web sites for the National Association for Shoplifting Prevention (http://www.shopliftingprevention.org/main.asp)

and the Seattle, Washington, Police Department (http://www.ci.seattle.wa.us/police/default.htm).

Walk-in office/factory thefts. Some individuals commit thefts simply by walking into an office and stealing something of value. The criminal then walks out of the office or factory with the item and tries to resell the product. Individuals who commit such crimes often try to look as if they belong there (such as a delivery person) in order to get past business security and to not look suspicious to the employees.

CRIMES COMMITTED BY BUSINESSES

Occasionally, businesses are sources of crime against consumers, the general public, government, and/or stockholders. Examples of crimes committed by businesses include fraudulent reporting, price fixing, and product misrepresentation.

Fraudulent Reporting. A business might partake in fraudulent activities by manipulating or misrepresenting business accounting records, profit information, sales data, or other pertinent financial information. This type of behavior is usually an attempt to hide serious financial problems in order to prevent the general public, regulatory agencies, or stockholders from getting poor status reports. Unfavorable financial information can be devastating to a business's stock value, which, in turn, will likely cause the business to lose a considerable amount of money in business equity. For example, business X might intentionally misreport higher profits than were actually accrued to maintain the stock price and value of the business. If the actual lower profits had been reported, then the stock would almost surely go down, causing a decrease in the value of the business.

Another reason a business might report inaccurate financial data is because most corporate officers have some form of stock options, and a serious drop in the stock price might be very costly on a personal basis. This type of fraud is usually carried out at the top levels of the business. When this type of crime is committed by a business through its officers, serious consequences accrue to both. Once the crime is uncovered, regulatory and law enforcement agencies at both the federal and state levels may begin an investigation of the alleged fraudulent activities. If the criminal activities are substantiated and convictions occur, the business, at a minimum, faces large fines, while the officers face long prison terms. In addition, the business faces a humiliating defeat in the arena of public opinion that will, in turn, hurt future sales.

Price Fixing. Businesses may engage in another type of crime known as "price fixing," or conspiring with competitors to charge a minimum price for their products. This practice forces consumers to pay more for a particular product than would be charged in a "nonprice-fixing" competitive environment. Businesses are rewarded with higher profit margins because this practice does not force them to conform to market forces. Price fixing is a violation of the Sherman Antitrust Act of 1890, which was passed to ensure that a competitive free market exists, allowing for competitive pricing. The Federal Trade Commission and the U.S. Department of Justice have primary jurisdiction over businesses that engage in violations of the Sherman Antitrust Act. When a business and its officers are prosecuted for price fixing, the business often faces large fines while individual officers usually go to prison.

Product Misrepresentation. When a business knowingly produces a defective or substandard product and sells it to the public anyway, the firm has committed product fraud. Product fraud is extremely serious because consumers depend on safe products in every aspect of daily life. Defective or unsafe products can cause serious harm to both the individual consumer and the general public. An example of product fraud would be when an automobile manufacturer produces and markets a vehicle that has shown, in presale trials, to be unsafe. For instance, a vehicle may be unsafe when hit from behind or from the side, causing the gas tank to explode because of design flaws. The obvious results of such flaws in vehicle design are the severe injury and/or death of people. Naturally, responses to product fraud include numerous lawsuits and lack of public trust in businesses that knowingly release defective or poorly designed products.

SUMMARY

Business-related criminal activity is not new. Crimes in business, such as fraud, can be traced back thousands of years. Crimes can be committed both by and against a business. Common crimes that influence the health of businesses and their customers include burglary, embezzlement, fraud, robbery, and shoplifting. Since crimes, both by and against businesses, are so costly, elaborate measures have been put in place to decrease the likelihood of their occurrence.

SEE ALSO *Cyber Crime; Fraudulent Financial Reporting; Identity Theft; Privacy and Security*

BIBLIOGRAPHY
Bologna, G. Jack, and Shaw, Paul (2000). *Avoiding cyber fraud in small businesses: What auditors and owners need to know.* New York: Wiley.

Boni, William C., and Kovacich, Gerald L. (1999). *I-way robbery: Crime on the Internet*. Boston: Butterworth/Heinemann.

Boni, William C., and Kovacich, Gerald L. (1999). *Netspionage: The global threat to information*. Boston: Butterworth/Heinemann.

Callahan, D. (2004). *The cheating culture: Why more Americans are going wrong to get ahead*. New York: Harcourt.

Coleman, J. W. (2002). *The criminal elite: Understanding white-collar crime* (6th ed.). New York: Worth.

Comer, M. J. (1998). *Corporate fraud* (3rd ed.). Brookfield, VT: Gower.

Hunter, R. (2002). *World without secrets: Business, crime, and privacy in the age of ubiquitous computing*. New York: Wiley.

Loewy, A. H. (2004). *Criminal law in a nutshell* (4th ed.). St. Paul, MN: Thomson/West.

Mann, R. A., and Roberts, B. S. (2005). *Essentials of business law and the regulation of business* (8th ed.). Mason, OH: Thomson/South-Western/West.

Rezaee, Zabihollah (2002). *Financial statement fraud: Prevention and detection*. New York: Wiley.

Silverstone, Howard, and Sheetz, Michael (2004). *Forensic accounting and fraud investigation for non-experts*. Hoboken, NJ: Wiley.

Twomey, David P., Jennings, Marianne Moody, and Fox, Ivan (2002). *Anderson's business law and the legal environment* (18th ed.). Mason, OH: West/Thomson Learning.

Allen D. Truell
Michael Milbier

CRITERIA OF CONTROL (COCO)

SEE *Internal Control Systems*

CURRENCY EXCHANGE

Money is any medium that is universally accepted in an economy by sellers of goods and services as payment and by creditors as payment for debts. Money serves as a medium of exchange; indeed, without money, we would have to resort to barter in doing business. Barter is simply a direct exchange of goods and services for other goods and services. For instance, a wheat farmer who wants a pair of eyeglasses must find an optician who, at exactly the same time, wants a dozen bushels of wheat; that is, there must be a double coincidence of wants, and the elements of the desired trade must be of equal value. If there is not a double coincidence of wants, the wheat farmer must go through several trades in order to obtain the desired eyeglasses; for example, this might involve trading wheat for a computer, then the computer for several lamps, then the lamps for the desired eyeglasses.

The existence of money means that individuals do not need to hold a diverse collection of goods as an exchange inventory. Money allows them to specialize in any area in which they have a comparative advantage and to receive money payments for their labor. Money can then be exchanged for the fruits of other people's labor. The use of money as a medium of exchange permits individuals to specialize and promotes the economic efficiencies that result from specialization.

In the same way that money facilitates exchange in a single economy, exchange of currencies facilitates the exchange of goods and services across the boundaries of countries. For instance, when you buy a foreign product, such as a Japanese car, you have dollars with which to pay the Japanese carmaker. The Japanese carmaker, however, cannot pay workers in dollars. The workers are Japanese, they live in Japan, and they need Japanese yen to buy goods and services in that country. There must be some way of exchanging dollars for the yen that the carmaker will accept in order to facilitate trade. That exchange occurs in a foreign-exchange market, which in this case specializes in exchanging yen for dollars.

The particular exchange rate between yen and dollars that would prevail depends on the current demand for and supply of yen and dollars (see Figure 1). If one cent per yen is the equilibrium price of yen, then that is the foreign-exchange rate determined by the current demand for and supply of yen in the foreign-exchange market. A person going to the foreign-exchange market would need one hundred yen (1/.01) to buy one dollar or one dollar to buy one hundred yen.

SUPPLY AND DEMAND FOR FOREIGN CURRENCY

Suppose you want to buy a Japanese car. To do so, you must have Japanese yen. You go to the foreign-exchange market or your American bank. Your desire to purchase the Japanese car causes you to offer supply dollars to the foreign-exchange market. Your demand for Japanese yen is equivalent to your supply of U.S. dollars to the foreign-exchange market. Indeed, every U.S. import leads to a supply of dollars and a demand for some foreign currency. Likewise, every U.S. export leads to a demand for dollars and a supply of some foreign currency by the purchaser.

For the moment assume that only two goods are being traded—Japanese cars and U.S. steel. Thus, the U.S. demand for Japanese cars creates a supply of dollars and a demand for Japanese yen in the foreign-exchange market. Similarly, the Japanese demand for U.S. steel cre-

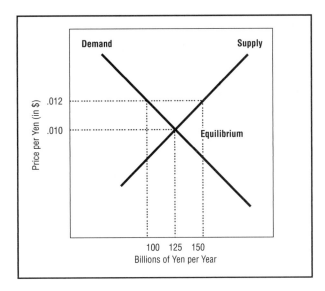

Figure 1

DETERMINANTS OF THE VALUE OF FOREIGN EXCHANGE

Supply and demand in the foreign-exchange market are determined by changes in many market variables, including relative price levels, real interest rates, productivity, product preferences, and perceptions of economic stability.

Different countries have different rates of inflation, which are an important factor in determining exchange rates. Purchasing power parity (PPP) is one widely used theory of the determination of exchange rates. PPP exists between any two currencies whenever changes in the exchange rate exactly reflect relative changes in price levels in two countries. In the long run, the average value of exchange rates depends on their purchasing power parity because in that way the relative prices in the two countries will stay the same (when measured in a common currency). That is, changes in the relative values of the two currencies compensate exactly for differences in national exchange rates. The PPP theory seems to work well in the long run when the differences in inflation rates between two countries are relatively large. When differences in inflation rates are relatively small, other market-oriented forces may dominate and often distort the picture.

A factor that may affect equilibrium currency prices is the interest rate of a country. If the U.S. interest rate, corrected for people's expectations of inflation, abruptly increased relative to interest rates in the rest of the world, international investors elsewhere would increase their demand for dollar-denominated assets, thereby increasing the demand for dollars in foreign-exchange markets. An increased demand in foreign-exchange markets, other things held constant, would cause the dollar to appreciate and other currencies to depreciate.

Another factor affecting equilibrium is a change in relative productivity. If one country's productivity increased relative to another's, the former country would become more competitive in world markets. The demand for its exports would increase, and so would the demand for its currency.

Changes in consumers' tastes also affect the equilibrium prices of currencies. If Japan's citizens suddenly developed a taste for a U.S. product, such as video games, this would increase the demand for U.S. dollars in foreign-exchange markets.

Finally, economic and political stability affect the supply of and demand for a currency, and therefore the equilibrium price of that currency. If the United States looked economically and politically more stable than other countries, more foreigners would want to put their savings into U.S. assets than in assets of another country. This would increase the demand for dollars.

ates a supply of yen and a demand for dollars in the foreign-exchange market. The equilibrium exchange rate will tell us how many yen a dollar can be exchanged for (the dollar price of yen) or how many dollars a yen can be exchanged for (the yen price of dollars).

The demand for and supply of foreign-exchange determine the equilibrium foreign exchange rate. For the moment, ignore any speculative aspects of foreign exchange; that is, assume that there are no individuals who wish to buy yen simply because they think that the price of yen will go up in the future.

The idea of an exchange rate is similar to the idea of paying a market-determined price for something you want to buy. If you like soda, you know you have to pay about fifty cents a can. If the price went up to one dollar, you would probably buy fewer sodas. If the price went down to twenty-five cents, you might buy more. In other words, the demand curve for soda, expressed in terms of dollars, slopes downward, following the law of demand.

The demand curve for Japanese yen also slopes downward. Suppose it costs you one cent to buy one yen—this would be the exchange rate between dollars and yen. If tomorrow you had to pay two cents for a yen, then the exchange rate would have changed. Looking at such an increase with respect to the yen, we would say that there has been an appreciation in the value of the yen in the foreign-exchange market. But this increase in the value of the yen means that there has been a depreciation in the value of the dollar in the foreign-exchange market. When one currency appreciates, the other currency depreciates.

Money traders in Tokyo AP IMAGES

FIXED- VERSUS FLEXIBLE-EXCHANGE-RATE SYSTEMS

Under the flexible-exchange-rate system, the equilibrium exchange rate reflects the supply and demand for the currency. Under a fixed-exchange-rate system, a country's central bank intervenes by buying or selling its currency to keep its foreign-exchange rates from changing. As with most systems in which the price of a good or service is fixed, the only way that it can remain so is for the government to intervene. Consider the two-country example above. Suppose that there were an increase in the prices of all goods and services made in the United States, including steel. The Japanese yen would now buy less steel than before. The Japanese would supply fewer yen to the foreign-exchange market and demand fewer dollars at the fixed exchange rate. However, suppose Americans continued to demand Japanese cars. In fact, they would demand more Japanese cars because, at the fixed exchange rate, the relative price of Japanese cars would fall. Americans would now supply more dollars to the foreign-exchange market

and demand more yen. In the absence of intervention by a central bank, the exchange rate would change. In order to maintain the foreign-exchange price of the yen, the Japanese central bank would buy (demand) dollars and sell (supply) yen.

If the central bank did not act to support the stated foreign-exchange rate, then too much or too little of one currency would be supplied or demanded. This lack of balance (i.e., disequilibrium) in the foreign-exchange market would impede trade between the two countries and could potentially result in a black market (i.e., underground market or illegal trade) in the two currencies.

CURRENCY CRISES

The only way for the United States to support the price of the dollar is to buy up excess dollars with foreign reserves—in our case, with Japanese yen. But the United States might eventually run out of Japanese yen. If this happened, it would no longer be able to stabilize the price of the dollar, and a currency crisis would result. A currency crisis occurs when a country can no longer support the price of its currency in foreign-exchange markets under a fixed-exchange-rate system. Many such crises have occurred in the past several decades when countries have attempted to maintain a fixed exchange rate that was in disequilibrium.

One alternative to a currency crisis or to continuing to try to support a fixed exchange rate is to devalue unilaterally. Currency devaluation is equivalent to currency depreciation, except that it occurs under a fixed-exchange-rate regime. The country officially lowers the price of its currency in foreign-exchange markets; this is a deliberate public action by a government following a fixed-exchange-rate policy. Revaluation is the opposite of devaluation. This occurs when, under a fixed-exchange-rate regime, there is pressure on a country's currency to rise in value in foreign-exchange markets. Unilaterally, that country can declare that the value of its currency in foreign-exchange markets is higher than it has been in the past. Currency revaluation is the equivalent of currency appreciation, except that it occurs under a fixed exchange rate regime and is mandated by the government. Managed exchange rates, sometimes referred to as dirty float, occur when a central bank or several central banks intervene in a system of flexible exchange to keep the exchange rate from undergoing extreme changes.

SUMMARY

A well-functioning foreign-exchange market is vital for worldwide trade. In a flexible-exchange-rate system, supply of and demand for a currency determine the exchange rate. In a fixed-exchange rate system, a government imposes the exchange rate, and given the mandated exchange rate, consumers determine how much of the currency they wish to supply or demand. In a managed-exchange-rate system, the exchange rate is determined through the markets, but the central bank will intervene by buying and selling the currency in order to influence the price.

SEE ALSO *International Trade*

Denise Woodbury

CUSTOMER SERVICE

In the very competitive world of marketing a product or service, what consumers will buy and when, where, and how they will purchase it is often determined by the type, level, and quality of customer service provided by competing marketers. This purchase determination has become even more of a strategic issue with the advent of new mar-

keting channels such as the Internet and television-shopping networks. A growing number of organizations are giving increased attention to customer service. Financial institutions, hospitals, public utilities, airlines, retail stores, restaurants, manufacturers, and wholesalers are just a few of the businesses that face the problem of attracting new customers and retaining the patronage of existing customers.

Building long-term relationships with customers has been given a high priority by the majority of America's most successful enterprises. These companies realize that customer satisfaction is an important key to success. Customer service can be defined as those activities that enhance or facilitate the purchase and use of the product or service. Today's emphasis on customer satisfaction can be traced to a managerial philosophy that has been described as the marketing concept.

THE MARKETING CONCEPT AND CUSTOMER SERVICE

The significant increase in the desire to provide effective consumer service is a direct result of a shift to the marketing concept in the early 1950s. The marketing concept has three major components: (1) identifying what the consumer needs and wants, (2) developing products/services to meet those needs/wants, and (3) designing marketing plans to effectively and efficiently deliver the products/services in a manner that will satisfy the customer and the long-term objectives of the organization. The foundation for the success of the marketing concept is a business philosophy that leaves no doubt in the mind of every employee that customer satisfaction is of primary importance. All energies are directed toward satisfying the consumer. The degree to which customer satisfaction is dependent on the quality of service varies greatly with different products/services. The service continuum (see Figure 1) shows the significant difference between a necktie (tangible product with little service involved) and a lawn mowing service (no tangible product).

SERVICE QUALITY

Whether consumers patronize an organization on a continuing basis is often strongly influenced by the level and quality of service they receive from that firm. Since this service experience is an important determinate of future purchase behavior, then it becomes important to examine how consumers evaluate the service provided and how a business might assess how well they deliver quality service.

Research has found that consumers often evaluate the quality of the service they receive based on five criteria. Businesses and organizations should consider these crite-

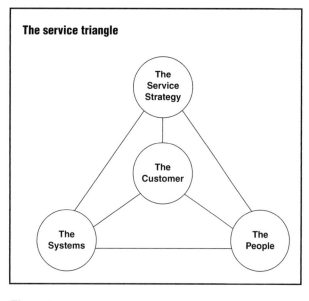

The service triangle

The
Service
Strategy

The
Customer

The
Systems

The
People

Figure 1

ria when they examine how well they are satisfying their customer's needs:

- *Tangibles*—Physical facilities, equipment, employees' appearance, etc.

- *Reliability*—Dependable and accurate service

- *Responsiveness*—Prompt customer assistance

- *Empathy*—Firm/employees show concern about the individual needs of the customer

- *Assurance* —Employees instilling trust and confidence in the service provider through their knowledge, courtesy, and helpfulness

Gap Theory. One method of examining the degree to which a firm is meeting the service expectations of the consumer on these five dimensions is called the gap theory. The gap theory first determines the difference between the customer's service expectations and the customer's perception of the service actually received. This gap is referred to as the service gap and is considered the most important because it determines the level of satisfaction/dissatisfaction with the service and, ultimately, the organization.

If a service gap exists, management should examine four other gaps that most likely are the reason for the service gap. These four gaps are:

1. *Knowledge gap*—The difference between the consumer's service expectations and management's perception of consumer's expectations

2. *Standards gap*—The difference between the management's perception of consumer's expectation and the standards established by the organization for service delivery

3. *Delivery gap*—The difference between the established standards and the actual quality of service delivered by employees

4. *Communications gap*—The difference between the actual quality of service provided and the quality of service communicated to consumers through promotional material and activities

If any of these gaps exist, a service gap will follow—with the probability of customer dissatisfaction.

THE NEW CUSTOMER

Customers, and the type and quality of service they demand, are constantly changing. This requires businesses to stay alert for changes and adjust to meet new service challenges. In an article by Ron Zemke (2002), the consumer of the twenty-first century was briefly characterized by customer service professionals. Zemke described new consumers as more knowledgeable about the products they purchase, possessing more sophistication, being a little more impulsive and less patient, wanting to be treated as individuals rather than numbers, and desiring to be treated fairly and like everyone else or knowing a clear reason why not.

At the end of the article Zemke presented a laundry list of fourteen customer needs identified by Chip Bell, a Dallas-based consultant and author of *Customer Love: Attracting and Keeping Customers for Life.*

1. Make me smarter.

2. Help me do it myself.

3. Make the response fast … but don't sacrifice quality—quick and rushed aren't the same.

4. Help me customize the experience like I want it.

5. Anchor your offering to a cause I like and believe in. Good works sell.

6. Entertain me. Make the experience bright, shiny, and memorable.

7. Don't invade my privacy; never let me worry about whether you know too much about me.

8. Respect my time by making your offer super easy to deal with.

9. Anticipate my needs.

10. Treat me with respect when things go wrong … not some cheap, generic atonement that is unmatched to the incident.

11. Never take me for granted. I will drop you in a heartbeat.

12. My time is as important as my funds … maybe more.

13. Help me integrate … link stuff together to increase the efficiency of my life.

14. Life is complex: Make service simple. Life is harried: Make service calm. Life can be shallow: Make service have resonance and depth. Life can be painful: Make service joyful. Life is too fast: Help me keep up. Life can be lonely: Make service a value connection. (quoted in Zemke, 2002, p. 49)

SEE ALSO *Marketing*

BIBLIOGRAPHY

Albrecht, Karl, and Zemke, Ron (2002). *Service America in the new economy* (rev. ed.). New York: McGraw-Hill.

Bell, Chip R. (2000). *Customer love: Attracting and keeping customers for life.* Provo, UT: Executive Excellence.

Hoffman, K. Douglass (2006). *Marketing principles and best practices* (3rd ed.). Mason, OH: Thomson South-Western.

Lascu, Dana-Nicoleta, and Clow, Kenneth E. (2004). *Marketing frontiers: Concepts and tools.* Cincinnati: Atomic Dog.

Lovelock, Christopher, and Wirtz, Jochen (2004). *Services marketing: People, technology, strategy* (5th ed.). Upper Saddle River, NJ: Pearson Prentice Hall.

Manning, Gerald L., and Reece, Barry L. (2004). *Selling today: Creating customer value* (9th ed.). Upper Saddle River, NJ: Pearson Prentice Hall.

Pride, William M., and Ferrell, O. C. (2006). *Marketing concepts and strategies.* Boston: Houghton Mifflin.

Reece, Barry L., and Brandt, Rhonda (2005). *Effective human relations: Personal and organizational applications* (9th ed.). Boston: Houghton Mifflin.

Sewell, Carl, and Brown, Paul B. (2002). *Customers for life: How to turn that one-time buyer into a lifetime customer* (rev. ed.). New York: Doubleday.

Solomon, Michael R., Marshall, Greg W., and Stuart, Elnora W. (2006). *Marketing: Real people, real choices* (4th ed.). Upper Saddle River, NJ: Pearson Prentice Hall.

Zemke, Ron (2002). The customer service revolution. *Training, 39*(7), 44–49.

Thomas Baird
Barry L. Reece

CYBER CRIME

Cyber crime refers to criminal conduct occurring in cyberspace—computerized, networked environments such as those in an office or on the Internet and the World Wide Web. According to U.S. law, cyber crimes have been committed if someone intentionally accesses a network facility without authorization or intentionally exceeds his or her given level of authorization to access that facility. If the crime is committed for commercial advantage, malicious destruction, private commercial gain, or in furtherance of any criminal act, the punishment is a fine and/or imprisonment for up to five years for a first offense. For any subsequent offense, the punishment is a fine and/or imprisonment for up to ten years.

TYPES OF CYBER CRIMES

Cyber crimes fall into three categories: (1) when computers or computer systems are the targets of crimes, such as hacking, denial of service, and viruses and Trojan horses; (2) when computers are the medium by which criminal activity is committed, such as phishing, sniffing, spamming, and spoofing; and (3) when computers are abused by rogue employees to illegally access organizational networks and steal valuable information. The following is a discussion of these cyber crimes.

Crimes against Computers and Computer Systems.

- *Hacking:* Breaking into a computer network or Web site such as a bank's intranet by using a software program that can generate multiple login usernames and passwords until a valid combination is found and access is granted. Once in the system, the hacker is able to steal, alter, or delete any files within the system.

- *Denial of service:* By using a computer to flood a given Web site with so much useless traffic (e-mail, interactions, etc.) the site becomes frozen and stops the regular service thus losing business for a period.

- *Viruses, worms, and Trojan horses:* Small, malicious software programs that are sent as attachments to e-mails with the intent of paralyzing the receiving computer(s). Once an e-mail recipient opens such an attachment, the virus, worm, or Trojan horse is released, disabling computers and replicating itself by contaminating the whole e-mail system.

Crimes Using Computers to Deceive Users.

- *Phishing:* Cyber criminals send legitimate looking e-mails to customers of banks and credit card companies asking them to update their account information by clicking on a Web link that sends the customer to an official-looking but actually fake site. By doing so, the criminals can steal customers' account information and thus masquerade as that customer.

- *Sniffing:* Criminals use their software to monitor the traffic on a Web site and steal valuable information traveling through it.

- *Spamming:* The unethical sending of millions of e-mail promotions to recipients who have never asked for the information. Spamming becomes illegal when a person sends numerous unsolicited e-mails containing illegal or objectionable messages such as pornography, threats, or harassments.

- *Spoofing:* The practice of deceiving online shoppers with a fake site of a legitimate company in order to get their identities and credit card numbers.

Crimes by Employees. Organizations need to be increasingly aware of employees who exceed authorization to access their company network and steal information for criminal use.

COUNTERMEASURES

Users need to use caution before handing over personal information and should think twice before "updating" information when they have not initiated the transaction. To protect individual computers, corporate networks, and Web sites, the following measures should be adopted: (1) users (both institutions and individuals) should install antivirus software and firewalls on their computers; (2) users should not use their birthday, social security number, or phone number as passwords to their accounts; (3) users should use different passwords for different accounts and change them periodically; (4) users should not open e-mail attachments or click on links from unknown sources; (5) to prevent phishing and spoofing, consumers should check Web sites' legitimacy and security before giving personal information and credit card numbers; (6) users should monitor their credit card usage and immediately report any unfamiliar transactions; (7) organizations should have clearly defined employee Internet policies; and (8) users should immediately report to the police when they experience a cyber crime.

SEE ALSO *Identity Theft*

BIBLIOGRAPHY

Awad, Elias M. (2004). *Electronic commerce: From vision to fulfillment* (2nd ed.). Boston: Pearson/Prentice Hall.

McNurlin, Barbara C., and Sprague, Ralph H., Jr. (2004). *Information systems management in practice* (6th ed.). Upper Saddle River, NJ: Prentice Hall.

U.S. Department of Justice (2005). *United States code annotated: Title 18. Crimes and criminal procedure.* Retrieved December 1, 2005, from http://www.usdoj.gov/criminal/cybercrime

Jensen J. Zhao

D

DATABASES

Databases are designed to manipulate large amounts of information by inputting, storing, retrieving, and managing that information. Databases use a table format, with Microsoft Access being one of the most widely used.

Databases consist of rows and columns. Each piece of information is entered into a row, which creates a "record." Databases are commonly used when saving addresses or other types of long lists of information. Once the records are created in the database, they can be sorted and manipulated in a variety of ways that are limited primarily by the software being used.

The word *data* is normally defined as facts from which information can be derived. For example, "Fred Crouse lives at 2209 Maple Avenue" is a fact. A database may contain millions of such facts. From these facts the database management system (DBMS) can derive information in the form of answers to questions such as "How many people live on Maple Avenue?" The popularity of databases in business is a direct result of the power of DBMSs in deriving valuable business information from large collections of data.

Databases are somewhat similar to spreadsheets, but databases are more powerful than spreadsheets because of their ability to manipulate the data. It is possible to do a number of functions with a database that would be more difficult to do with a spreadsheet. Consider these actions that are possible to do with a database:

- Perform a variety of cross-referencing activities
- Complete complicated calculations
- Bring current records up to date
- Retrieve large amounts of information that match certain criteria

RELATIONAL DATABASES

Most modern databases are relational, meaning that data are stored in tables, consisting of rows and columns, and that data in different tables are related by the meanings of certain common columns. (The tables in a database are sometimes called files, the rows are called records, and the columns are called fields. Nevertheless, this is an older terminology, left over from the early days of business computer systems.) The following is an example of a simple relational database consisting of three tables: one for customers, one for products, and one for sales:

Customers			
customer_no	name	address	phone
1001	Jones	320 Main	555-8811
1002	Smith	401 Oak	555-8822
1003	Brown	211 Elm	555-8833
1004	Green	899 Maple	555-8844

Products		
product_no	description	price
25	Ring	3.25
33	Gasket	1.23
45	Shaft	4.55

Sales			
sale_no	date	customer_no	product_no
841	3/11	1002	45
842	3/12	1001	25
843	3/12	1002	45
844	3/13	1004	33
845	3/14	1003	25
846	3/15	1002	33

Suppose one wants to know the customer's name for sale number 845. Looking in the customer number column of the Sales table, one will see that it was customer 1003. Next, one refers to the Customers table and finds customer 1003. Here one see the customer's name is Brown. So, Brown was the customer for sale number 845.

STRUCTURED QUERY LANGUAGE

The foregoing is a simple example of a database query. In a modern database, queries are expressed in a query language, which requires a particular format that can be recognized and interpreted by the DBMS. The standard query language for relational databases, as adopted by the American National Standards Institute (ANSI), is SQL, which is generally understood to be an abbreviation for "structured query language." Here are a few examples of queries expressed in SQL:

Query: Which products have a price over $2?

SQL solution: Select product_no, description
From Products
Where price > 2.00

Result:
product_no	description
25	Ring
45	Shaft

This query's SQL solution illustrates the SQL format. In general, SQL "statements" have a Select "clause," a From "clause," and a Where "clause." The Select clause lists the columns that are to be shown in the result, the From clause lists the database tables from which data are to be taken, and the Where clause gives the condition to

be applied to each row in the table. If a row satisfies the condition, then it is selected, and the values in that row for the columns listed in the Select clause are included in the result.

Query: When have we sold product number 45 to customer 1002?

SQL solution: Select date
From Sales
Where product_no = 45 and customer_no = 1002

Result:
date
3/11
3/12

In this example one can see that the condition in the Where clause includes the connector "and," which indicates that both conditions (product_no = 45 and customer_no = 1002) must be fulfilled. In the sample database there are two rows that satisfy this condition, and the query's result yields the dates from those two rows.

The next query gives the SQL solution to the original query discussed above.

Query: What is the customer's name for sale number 845?

SQL solution: Select name
From Customers, Sales
Where sale_no = 845 and Sales.customer_no = Customers.customer_no

Result: Brown

This query illustrates how one can query more than one table at once in SQL. First, one lists all tables needed to answer the query. In this case then, one lists the Customers and the Sales tables. Then in the Where clause, one states two conditions:

sale_no = 845 and
Sales.customer_no = Customers.customer_no

The first condition indicates that the sale_no column must have a value of 845. Because there is only one row in the Sales table having that value, one has limited one's query to that single row. The second condition indicates that one wants only that row in the Customers table which has the same value for its customer_no column as the Sales row has for its customer_no column. This condition then limits one's result to the joining together of one row from the Sales table and one row from the Customers table. Finally, the Select clause,

Select name

tells one that one should give the value from the name column as one's result. As shown before, the resulting customer name is "Brown."

Queries can also be used to perform calculations:

Query: What is the average price of our products?

SQL solution: Select Avg (price)
From Products
Result: 3.01

SQL also provides statements that can be used to make changes to data in the database. For example, suppose one wanted to increase the price of one's products by 3 percent. Then the following statement can be used:

Update Products
Set price = 1.03 * price

This statement will cause the price of every product in the Products table to be increased by 3 percent. Note that it does not matter whether one has 3 products, as shown in the sample database, or 300,000 products. A single statement will update the prices of all products. Of course, if one wants to change only the prices of selected products, one can do that, too:

Update Products
Set price = 1.03 * price
Where product_no = 33

This statement will change only the price of product number 33. SQL also provides statements to Insert new rows into tables and to Delete rows from tables.

These queries show only a very small number of the capabilities of SQL. The Where clause can be used to select rows based on where names are in the alphabet, whether dates are before or after certain other dates, based on averages, and based on many other conditions.

SMALL AND LARGE DATABASES

Databases can be single-user or multiuser. A single-user database exists on a single computer and is accessible only from that computer. Many single-user databases exist, and there are a number of commercial database manufacturers that address this market. A multiuser database may exist on a single machine, such as a mainframe or other powerful computer, or it may be distributed and exist on multiple computers. Multiuser databases are accessible from multiple computers simultaneously.

With the rise of the Internet, many databases are publicly accessible. For example, the holdings of university libraries are maintained on databases that can be browsed from remote locations. A person interested in locating a book in a library can enter the book's title, author, or subject, and a database query will be automatically performed. Information on the desired book or list of books will be returned to the person's computer.

SELECTING A DATABASE SYSTEM

A person or business seeking to purchase a DBMS for use in managing a database should consider the following factors:

Relational: Virtually all major commercial DBMSs are relational, because the desirability of relational databases is well-accepted in the database community.

SQL: In addition, because the ANSI has adopted SQL as it standard for relational databases, the desired DBMS should support SQL.

Capacity: As noted above, DBMSs are designed for a variety of environments. Some are designed to be single-user systems, while others are designed for medium-sized businesses, while still others are designed for large businesses. The system selected should naturally be one that has been shown to be successful in and appropriate for the environment for which it is chosen.

Disaster recovery capability: More sophisticated systems are more capable of recovering from power outages, computer hardware failure, and the like than are the single-user systems. They use sophisticated logging and database locking facilities that make such recovery possible. Often, these facilities are unnecessary for single-user systems.

SUMMARY

Databases and DBMSs are central to modern business information systems. Relational databases using SQL provide substantial logical power to help businesses make informed decisions based on their own data. Database systems can be small and handled by a single user, or they can be large and available to multiple users. They are even publicly available through the Internet. DBMSs can be sophisticated and expensive, and consequently their purchase requires careful, informed consideration.

SEE ALSO *Information Technology; Software*

BIBLIOGRAPHY

About Databases Guide Site. http://databases.about.com

Dunham, Jeff (1998). *Database performance tuning handbook.* New York: McGraw-Hill.

Groff, James R., and Weinberg, Paul N. (2002). *SQL: The complete reference* (2nd ed.). Berkeley, CA: Osborne/McGraw-Hill.

Hansen, Gary W., and Hansen, James V. (1996). *Database management and design* (2nd ed.). Upper Saddle River, NJ: Prentice Hall.

Kroenke, David M. (2006). *Database processing: Fundamentals, design, and implementation* (10th ed.). Upper Saddle River, NJ: Pearson Prentice Hall.

Post, Gerald V. (2005). *Database management systems: Designing and building business applications* (3rd ed.). Boston: McGraw-Hill/Irwin.

Rob, Peter, and Semaan, Elie (2004). *Databases: Design, development and deployment* (2nd ed.). Boston: McGraw-Hill.

Dorothy Maxwell
Gary Hansen

DEBIT CARD
SEE *Credit/Debit/Travel Cards*

DECA

DECA, Inc. is a national student organization for individuals preparing for marketing, management, and entrepreneurship careers. With over 185,000 members in 2006, DECA serves as the companion to marketing education programs within secondary and postsecondary schools across all fifty states of the United States, its territories, two provinces of Canada, and Germany. As a cocurricular organization, DECA is an integral part of classroom instruction—a vehicle through which students learn marketing and management and are motivated to succeed.

In partnership with businesses throughout the country, DECA offers learning experiences that contribute to the integration of academic and career-focused instruction, resulting in heightened student achievement and student recognition. For example, each year thousands of student members participate in a competitive events program, culminating in state and national secondary and postsecondary international career development conferences that allow members to demonstrate academic and marketing excellence. Also, a host of leadership development programs are offered.

Organized in 1946, DECA meets the needs of marketing (at the time called distributive) education students seeking professional and personal growth. The association is governed by a board of directors. Until 1991, DECA was referred to as the Distributive Education

Clubs of America. Although that continues to be the legal name, the organization uses the commonly recognized acronym DECA, along with the tag line, "An Association of Marketing Students." DECA is advised by a national advisory board, consisting of business representatives, and a congressional advisory board, comprised of federal legislators.

The official publications of DECA are the *DECA Advisor, Dimensions, Chi Connection,* and the *DECA Guide.* Such scholarships as the Harry Applegate, Hilton, Marriott International, Otis Spunkmeyer, Safeway, and Sears Scholarships are available to support the academic endeavors of members. More information is available from DECA at 1908 Association Drive, Reston, VA 20191; 703-860-5000 (phone); 703-869-4013 (fax); or, http://www.deca.org.

SEE ALSO *Business Professionals of America; Future Business Leaders of America; SkillsUSA*

BIBLIOGRAPHY
Berns, Robert G. (1996). *DECA: A continuing tradition of excellence.* Reston, VA: DECA.

Robert G. Berns
Jewel E. Hairston

DECENTRALIZATION
SEE *Organizational Structure*

DECISION MAKING

Decision making, also referred to as problem solving, is the process of recognizing a problem or opportunity and finding a solution to it. Decisions are made by everyone involved in the business world, but managers typically face the most decisions on a daily basis. Many of these decisions are relatively simple and routine, such as ordering production supplies, choosing the discount rate for an order, or deciding the annual raise of an employee. These routine types of decisions are known as programmed decisions, because the decision maker already knows what the solution and outcome will be. However, managers are also faced with decisions that can drastically affect the future outcomes of the business. These types of decisions are known as nonprogrammed decisions, because neither the appropriate solution nor the potential outcome is known. Examples of nonprogrammed decisions include merging with another company, creating a new product, or expanding production facilities.

Decision making typically follows a six-step process:

1. Identify the problem or opportunity
2. Gather relevant information
3. Develop as many alternatives as possible
4. Evaluate alternatives to decide which is best
5. Decide on and implement the best alternative
6. Follow-up on the decision

In *step 1*, the decision maker must be sure he or she has an accurate grasp of the situation. The need to make a decision has occurred because there is a difference between the desired outcome and what is actually occurring. Before proceeding to step 2, it is important to pinpoint the actual cause of the situation, which may not always be obviously apparent.

In *step 2*, the decision maker gathers as much information as possible because having all the facts gives the decision maker a much better chance of making the appropriate decision. When an uninformed decision is made, the outcome is usually not very positive, so it is important to have all the facts before proceeding.

In *step 3*, the decision maker attempts to come up with as many alternatives as possible. A technique known as "brainstorming," whereby group members offer any and all ideas even if they sound totally ridiculous, is often used in this step.

In *step 4*, the alternatives are evaluated and the best one is selected. The process of evaluating the alternatives usually starts by narrowing the choices down to two or three and then choosing the best one. This step is usually the most difficult, because there are often many variables to consider. The decision maker must attempt to select the alternative that will be the most effective given the available amount of information, the legal obstacles, the public relations issues, the financial implications, and the time constraints on making the decision. Often the decision maker is faced with a problem for which there is no apparent good solution at the moment. When this happens, the decision maker must make the best choice available at the time but continue to look for a better option in the future.

Once the decision has been made, *step 5* is performed. Implementation often requires some additional planning time as well as the understanding and cooperation of the people involved. Communication is very important in the implementation step, because most people are resistant to change simply because they do not understand why it is necessary. In order to ensure smooth implementation of the decision, the decision maker should communicate the reasons behind the decision to the people involved.

In *step 6*, after the decision has been implemented, the decision maker must follow-up on the decision to see if it is working successfully. If the decision that was implemented has corrected the difference between the actual and desired outcome, the decision is considered successful. However, if the implemented decision has not produced the desired result, once again a decision must be made. The decision maker can decide to give the decision more time to work, choose another of the generated alternatives, or start the whole process over from the beginning.

STRATEGIC, TACTICAL, AND OPERATIONAL DECISIONS

People at different levels in a company have different types of decision-making responsibilities. Strategic decisions, which affect the long-term direction of the entire company, are typically made by top managers. Examples of strategic decisions might be to focus efforts on a new product or to increase production output. These types of decisions are often complex and the outcomes uncertain, because available information is often limited. Managers at this level must often depend on past experiences and their instincts when making strategic decisions.

Tactical decisions, which focus on more intermediate-term issues, are typically made by middle managers. The purpose of decisions made at this level is to help move the company closer to reaching the strategic goal. Examples of tactical decisions might be to pick an advertising agency to promote a new product or to provide an incentive plan to employees to encourage increased production.

Operational decisions focus on day-to-day activities within the company and are typically made by lower-level managers. Decisions made at this level help to ensure that daily activities proceed smoothly and therefore help to move the company toward reaching the strategic goal. Examples of operational decisions include scheduling employees, handling employee conflicts, and purchasing raw materials needed for production.

It should be noted that in many "flatter" organizations, where the middle management level has been eliminated, both tactical and operational decisions are made by lower-level management and/or teams of employees.

GROUP DECISIONS

Group decision making has many benefits as well as some disadvantages. The obvious benefit is that there is more input and therefore more possible solutions to the situation can be generated. Another advantage is that there is shared responsibility for the decision and its outcome, so one person does not have total responsibility for making a decision.

The disadvantages are that it often takes a long time to reach a group consensus and that group members may have to compromise in order to reach a consensus. Many businesses have created problem-solving teams whose purpose is to find ways to improve specific work activities.

SEE ALSO *Management*

BIBLIOGRAPHY

Boone, Louis E., and Kurtz, David L. (2005). *Contemporary Business* (11th ed.). Mason, OH: Thomson/South-Western.

Bounds, Gregory M., and Lamb, Charles W., Jr. (1998). *Business*. Cincinnati, OH: South-Western College Publishing.

Clancy, Kevin J., and Shulman, Robert S. (1994). *Marketing Myths That are Killing Business: The Cure for Death Wish Marketing*. New York: McGraw-Hill.

French, Wendell L. (2003). *Human Resources Management* (5th ed.). Boston: Houghton Mifflin Co.

Madura, Jeff (1998). *Introduction to Business* (3rd ed.). Belmont, CA: Thomson/South-Western.

Nickels, William G., McHugh, James M., and McHugh, Susan M. (2004). *Understanding Business* (7th ed.). Boston: McGraw-Hill.

Pride, William M., Hughes, Robert J., and Kapoor, Jack R. (1999). *Business* (6th ed.). New York: Houghton Mifflin.

Marcy Satterwhite

DEFLATION
SEE *Business Cycle*

DELEGATION
SEE *Mangement: Authority and Responsibility*

DEMAND
SEE *Supply and Demand*

DEMOGRAPHICS
SEE *Market Segmentation*

DEPARTMENTALIZATION
SEE *Organizational Structure*

DEPRESSION
SEE *Business Cycle*

DEREGULATION

Most societies rely on competitive markets to handle the allocation of scarce resources to their highest and best uses. Yet markets are not without their shortcomings. For this reason, governments sometime institute regulatory control. In 1887, the first regulatory agency, the Interstate Commerce Commission, was created to regulate monopolistic pricing policies of railroads.

When private firms gain monopoly power, usually because of economies of scale, they are in a position to restrict production and raise price with little worry of competition; these are known as natural monopolies. The government may permit a single producer (e.g., of natural gas or electricity) to exist in order to gain lower production costs but simultaneously empower a regulatory agency to set the firm's prices.

A second reason for regulation stems from the fact that society declares certain activities illegal. Prostitution, gambling, and certain drugs are either not permitted or allowed only under certain conditions. Through a licensing system, government agencies control who enters such industries, their prices, and their methods of operation.

Another reason for government regulation arises because society establishes standards for particular professions, such as medicine, law, accounting, and real estate. The government guarantees compliance with these standards by imposing tests and other requirements. Those failing to meet these standards are not permitted to engage in that business. Hundreds of agencies administer tests and police the professions, all done ostensibly in the interest of protecting the consumer. Interestingly, license holders often push for even higher licensing requirements, often grandfathering in all current license holders, because higher salaries are possible when the number of competitors is restricted.

Many government regulations are designed to protect people from the negative consequences (i.e., externalities) of buyers and sellers who have little incentive to look out for the welfare of third parties. For example, slaughterhouses may have the freedom to kill animals for sale to their customers in grocery stores without taking into account obnoxious odors or sounds emanating from the slaughterhouse. Neighborhood residents, however, incur externality costs. Through agencies such as the Environmental Protection Agency (EPA), the government controls what slaughterhouses can and cannot do in order to lessen the negative effects on the population.

Although government regulation is pervasive, it is apparent that regulation may not achieve the lofty goals set out in the initial effort to regulate. Governments can also fail, and government failure often aggravates the problems it sets out to solve. Public choice economists have identified several specific causes of government failure. Voters are often rationally ignorant about many things, and they vote for political candidates who are uninformed or misinformed. Also, politicians are often indebted to their financial supporters, some of whom are regulated industries, and will often enact laws favorable to their supporters regardless of the negative impact on the public. Politicians may even be willing to sacrifice the future for the sake of short-term benefits for their financial supporters. Recognition of such limitations to government regulation has caused Congress to rethink regulation, especially as it relates to certain industries.

Beginning in the mid-1970s, increased dissatisfaction with the burdens of regulation, especially the costs imposed on consumers, led to the deregulation of a number of industries, including the airlines (Airline Deregulation Act of 1978), natural gas (Natural Gas Policy Act of 1978), trucking (Motor Carrier Act of 1980), and banking (Depository Institutions Deregulation and Monetary Control Act of 1980).

In 1997 some states began deregulating the production and sale of electricity. Technologies permit small companies to produce electricity at reduced costs. Under the new system (much like the system in the telephone industry), local utilities must permit competitors to use their electric lines for a fee.

Benefits from deregulation include reduced prices and increased choices for consumers. Competition among long-distance telephone suppliers is keen, no longer requiring government regulation, and is demonstrated by the fact that from 1985 to 1998 prices declined 72 percent. Expanded service and reduced prices have occurred in both airlines and trucking. Eleven thousand new trucking lines started up within three years of deregulation, and savings may be as high as $50 billion per year.

Some concerns have arisen about deregulation, however. The airline industry has become more concentrated since deregulation. In 1978 eleven carriers handled 87 percent of the traffic, while in 1995 seven carriers handled 93 percent of the traffic. Although some feared reduced safety, that has not materialized. Some of the bank failures in the 1980s were attributed to deregulation, yet depositors receive higher interest. On balance, deregulation effects have been positive.

A significant change in direction has also taken place with regard to government regulation of industries producing externalities. Many externalities arise because of the lack of property rights; consequently there is greater emphasis on establishing clearly defined property rights, which allows the market to automatically internalize the cost to buyers and sellers, making government regulation costly and unnecessary. The EPA depends less heavily on its command-and-control approach and more heavily on tradable permits, reducing the overall level of pollution and allowing firms to avoid pollution in a more cost-effective way.

Although Congress has deregulated specific industries, social regulation designed to protect consumers has expanded. Through such agencies as the Occupational Safety and Health Administration, the Consumer Product Safety Commission, the Food and Drug Administration, the Equal Employment Opportunity Commission, and the EPA, the government is attempting to provide safer products, better health care, fairer employment practices, and a cleaner environment. Government at federal, state, and local levels has also continued to increase license requirements for numerous occupations and professions.

Many economists wonder if the benefits are high enough to warrant the cost of regulation. In addition to regulatory-imposed limits on consumer freedom, product prices rise, administrative costs are high, and some firms are driven out of business, thereby reducing competition. To further complicate things, many special-interest groups use such laws to increase their wealth at the expense of others. It has been estimated that federal regulation costs each household $6000 per year. Clearly the issues surrounding regulation/deregulation will continue to be discussed into the twenty-first century.

BIBLIOGRAPHY

Kahn, Alfred E. (1988). *The Economics of Regulation: Principles and Institutions.* Cambridge, MA: MIT Press.

Kahn, Alfred E. (2004). *Lessons from Deregulation: Telecommunications and Airlines After the Crunch.* Washington, DC: Brookings Institution Press.

Teske, P., Best, S., and Mintrom, M. (1995). *Deregulating Freight Transportation.* Washington, DC: AEI Press.

Winston, C. (1993, September). "Economic Deregulation" *Journal of Economic Literature*, 1263-1289.

James R. Rinehart
Jeffrey J. Pompe

DERIVATIVES

Derivative instruments are used as financial management tools to enhance investment returns and to manage such risks relative to interest rates, exchange rates, and financial instrument and commodity prices. Several local and international banks, businesses, municipalities, and others have experienced significant losses with the use of derivatives. However, their use has increased as efforts to control risk in complex situations are perceived to be wise strategic decisions.

SFAS 133'S DEFINITION OF A DERIVATIVE INSTRUMENT

In 1998, the Financial Accounting Standards Board (FASB) issued Statement on Financial Accounting Standards No. 133 (SFAS 133), *Accounting for Derivative Instruments and Hedging Activities,* which is effective for companies with fiscal years beginning after June 15, 2000. SFAS 133 establishes new accounting and reporting rules for derivative instruments, including derivatives embedded in other contracts, and for hedging activities. Derivatives must now be reported at their fair values in financial statements. Gains and losses from derivative transactions must be reported currently in income, except from those transactions that qualify as effective hedges.

According to Statement on Financial Accounting Standards (SFAS) 133, a derivative instrument is defined as a financial instrument or other contract that represents rights or obligations of assets or liabilities with all three of the following characteristics:

- It has (1) one or more underlyings and (2) one or more notional amounts or payment provisions or both. Those terms determine the settlement amount of the derivative. An underlying is a variable (i.e., stock price) or index (i.e., bond index) whose market movements cause the fair value market or cash flows of a derivative to change. The notional amount is the fixed amount or quantity that determines the size of the change caused by the change in the underlying; possibly a number of currency units, shares, bushels, pounds, or other units specified in the contract. A payment provision specifies a fixed or determinable settlement to be made if the underlying behaves in a specified manner.

- It requires no initial net investment or an initial net investment that is smaller than would be required for other types of similar instruments.

- Its terms require or permit net settlement (SFAS 133, paragraph 6).

USERS OF DERIVATIVES

The derivatives market serves the needs of several groups of users, including those parties who wish to hedge, those who wish to speculate, and arbitrageurs.

- A hedger enters the market to reduce risk. Hedging usually involves taking a position in a derivative financial instrument, which has opposite return characteristics of the item being hedged, to offset losses or gains.

- A speculator enters the derivatives market in search of profits, and is willing to accept risk. A speculator takes an open position in a derivative product (i.e., there is no offsetting cash flow exposure to offset losses on the position taken in the derivative product).

- An arbitrageur is a speculator who attempts to lock in near riskless profit from price differences by simultaneously entering into the purchase and sale of substantially identical financial instruments.

Other participants include clearinghouses or clearing corporations, brokers, commodity futures trading commission, commodity pool operators, commodity trading advisors, financial institutions and banks, futures exchange, and futures commission merchants.

TYPES OF DERIVATIVE INSTRUMENTS

Derivative instruments are classified as:

- Forward Contracts
- Futures Contracts
- Options
- Swaps

Derivatives can also be classified as either forward-based (e.g., futures, forward contracts, and swap contracts), option-based (e.g., call or put option), or combinations of the two. A forward-based contract obligates one party to buy and a counterparty to sell an underlying asset, such as foreign currency or a commodity, with equal risk at a future date at an agreed-on price. Option-based contracts (e.g., call options, put options, caps and floors) provide the holder with a right, but not an obligation to buy or sell an underlying financial instrument, foreign currency, or commodity at an agreed-on price during a specified time period or at a specified date.

Forward Contracts. Forward contracts are negotiated between two parties, with no formal regulation or exchange, to purchase (long position) and sell (short position) a specific quantity of a specific quantity of a commodity (i.e., corn and gold), foreign currency, or financial instrument (i.e., bonds and stock) at a specified price (delivery price), with delivery or settlement at a specified future date (maturity date). The price of the underlying asset for immediate delivery is known as the spot price.

Forward contracts may be entered into through an agreement without a cash payment, provided the forward rate is equal to the current market rate. Forward contracts are often used to hedge the entire price changed of a commodity, a foreign currency, or a financial instrument. irrespective of a price increase or decrease.

Futures Contracts. Futures are standardized contracts traded on a regulated exchange to make or take delivery of a specified quantity of a commodity, a foreign currency, or a financial instrument at a specified price, with delivery or settlement at a specified future date. Futures contracts involve U.S. Treasury bonds, agricultural commodities, stock indices, interest-earning assets, and foreign currency.

A futures contract is entered into through an organized exchange, using banks and brokers. These organized exchanges have clearinghouses, which may be financial institutions or part of the futures exchange. They interpose themselves between the buyer and the seller, guarantee obligations, and make futures liquid with low credit risk. Although no payment is made upon entering into a futures contract, since the underlying (i.e. interest rate, share price, or commodity price) is at-the-market, subsequent value changes require daily mark-to-marking by cash settlement (i.e. disbursed gains and daily collected losses). Similarly, margin requirements involve deposits from both parties to ensure any financial liabilities.

Futures contracts are used to hedge the entire price change of a commodity, a foreign currency, or a financial instrument since the contract value and underlying price change symmetrically.

Options. Options are rights to buy or sell. For example, the purchaser of an option has the right, but not the obligation, to buy or sell a specified quantity of a particular commodity, a foreign currency, or a financial instrument, at a specified price, during a specified period of time (American option) or on a specified date (European option). An option may be settled by taking delivery of the underlying or by cash settlement, with risk limited to the premium.

The two main types of option contracts are call options and put options, while some others include stock (or equity) options, foreign currency options, options on futures, caps, floors, collars, and swaptions.

- American call options provide the holder with the right to acquire an underlying product (e.g., stock) at an exercise or strike price, throughout the option term. The holder pays a premium for the right to benefit from the appreciation in the underlying.

- American put options provide the holder with the right to sell the underlying product (e.g., stock) at a certain exercise or strike price, throughout the option term. The holder gains as the market price of the underlying (stock price) falls below the exercise price.

- An interest rate cap is an option that allows a cap purchaser to limit exposure to increasing interest rates on its variable-rate debt instruments.

- An interest rate floor is an option that allows a floor purchaser to limit exposure to decreasing interest rates on its variable-rate investments.

Generally, option contracts are used to hedge a one-directional movement in the underlying commodity, foreign currency, or financial instrument.

Swaps. A swap is a flexible, private, forward-based contract or agreement, generally between two counterparties to exchange streams of cash flows based on an agreed-on (or notional) principal amount over a specified period of time in the future.

Swaps are usually entered into at-the-money (i.e., with minimal initial cash payments because fair value is zero), through brokers or dealers who take an up-front cash payment or who adjust the rate to bear default risk. The two most prevalent swaps are interest rate swaps and foreign currency swaps, while others include equity swaps, commodity swaps, and swaptions.

Swaptions are options on swaps that provide the holder with the right to enter into a swap at a specified future date at specified terms (stand-alone option in a swap) or to extend or terminate the life of an existing swap (embedded option on a swap).

Swap contracts are used to hedge entire price changes (symmetrically) related to an identified hedged risk, such as interest rate or foreign currency risk, since both counterparties gain or lose equally.

RISK CHARACTERISTICS OF DERIVATIVES

The main types of risk characteristics associated with derivatives are:

- Basis Risk. This is the spot (cash) price of the underlying asset being hedged, less the price of the derivative contract used to hedge the asset.

- Credit Risk. Credit risk or default risk evolves from the possibility that one of the parties to a derivative contract will not satisfy its financial obligations under the derivative contract.

- Market Risk. This is the potential financial loss due to adverse changes in the fair value of a derivative.

Market risk encompasses legal risk, control risk, and accounting risk.

SEE ALSO *Investments*

BIBLIOGRAPHY

Hull, John (1998). *Introduction to Futures and Options Markets* (3rd ed.). Upper Saddle River, NJ: Prentice Hall.

Kolb, Robert (2003). *Futures, Options and Swaps* (4th ed.). Malden, MA: Blackwell.

Statement of Financial Accounting Standards (SFAS) No. 133, Accounting for Derivatives Instruments and Hedging Activities. (1998). Norwalk, CT: Financial Accounting Standards Board (FASB).

Patrick Casabona

DESKTOP PUBLISHING

Before 1985 the process of creating and publishing a professional-looking document was quite different from what it has evolved into since that time. Before the invention of the laser printer and then in 1985 desktop-publishing software, the publishing process involved numerous professionals performing various tasks—typically in a variety of locations. Writers and editors created the text for a project; designers and artists created the layout and necessary photographs and other artwork; typesetters created galleys of finished type that then had to be cut and pasted into place on an art board; camera operators, "strippers," and other printing professionals produced negatives, flats, and printing plates; press operators printed the finished project.

All that changed significantly with the advent of laser printing and desktop-publishing software. Aldus Corporation founder Paul Brainerd coined the phrase *desktop publishing* to refer to a new publishing process—a combination of technology that now allowed the functions of writing, editing, designing, typesetting, illustrating, formatting, and printing a document to be accomplished by one person (if desired) working at one location—his or her own desktop!

The process of desktop publishing can be accomplished with word-processing software or with sophisticated desktop-publishing software. Desktop publishing includes projects printed on desktop printing equipment (black-and-white laser printers, ink-jet printers, and color laser printers) as well as those prepared in electronic form for final printing on high-end commercial printing presses. The use of personal computers (PCs) has become so widespread that the traditional publishing process described earlier is obsolete—and rarely seen. Essentially, all professional printing projects are created on PCs with word-processing or desktop-publishing software (or both).

As a result, *desktop publishing* is taking on a new meaning. Rather than referring to the process that was such a revolution in 1985 or even to the type of software used to produce a project, the term is now generally used to refer to the type of document produced. Generally speaking, desktop publishing refers to a "designed" document that effectively integrates type and visual elements for printing either on desktop-printing equipment or on traditional or digital professional-printing equipment. Thus, desktop publishing could be summarized simply as the combination of design principles, type, and visual elements into a professional-looking document. By contrast, *word processing* refers to such basic text-intensive documents as business letters, memos, and reports created with word-processing software that facilitates efficient entry, editing, and layout of the text.

The term *desktop-publishing software* refers to PC programs designed to facilitate professional document design and creation. Also referred to as page-layout programs, Adobe InDesign, Adobe FrameMaker, QuarkXPress, and Corel Ventura were the leading professional-level desktop-publishing programs in the early twenty-first century. In addition, Adobe PageMaker—producing basic documents such as brochures and newsletters—was targeted to business, education, and small- and home-office users.

Desktop-publishing software targeted to small- and home-office users included such programs as Microsoft Office Publisher and Serif PagePlus. Another category of desktop-publishing software is home-publishing and specialty programs—programs not considered to be serious desktop-publishing programs—designed for home users to create such projects as calendars, greeting cards, business cards, and fliers. Such programs included Print Shop, PrintMaster, Calendar Creator, and Greeting Card Factory.

HOW WORD-PROCESSING AND DESKTOP-PUBLISHING PROGRAMS DIFFER

Understanding the essential differences between the functionality of word-processing software and that of desktop-publishing software can help an organization or individual make a good choice between the two types of software for use in creating desktop-publishing projects.

Both word-processing and desktop-publishing programs include basic word-processing capabilities such as these:

- Copy, cut, move, and paste functions
- Spell-checking

Desktop publisher at work. © MARTHA TABOR/WORKING IMAGES PHOTOGRAPHS

- Find-and-replace functionality
- Automatic generation of tables of contents and indexes
- Styles for formatting characters and paragraphs
- Tables and columns

Despite the inclusion of such features in desktop-publishing software, word-processing software is nearly always a much better choice for basic word processing, as it allows the user to focus more on editing and developing content efficiently than on creating the document layout and implementing design elements.

Where word-processing and desktop-publishing programs begin to differ most noticeably is in the way the programs handle the integration of graphical elements and text elements. In word-processing software, all the text of a document is treated as one long "string" of words running through the entire document. If a new paragraph is inserted on the first page of the document, all the text in the document (and often the graphical elements as well) typically moves down by the length of that inserted paragraph, and the text on the last page of the document may even move to the top of a new page that is automatically added to the document. Even if the document contains sections, chapters, or other "unmovable" breaks, the insertion of the paragraph on the first page can significantly alter the layout of the entire document.

In most word-processing applications (basic documents such as letters and memos), this string of text running through the document works just fine, because the document is not layout- or format-intensive. Likewise, designed documents that do not include extensive graphical elements and that are not adversely affected by the flow-through-text effect of word-processing software can often be created more easily in word-processing software than in desktop-publishing software.

On the other hand, when documents are carefully designed and formatted to integrate text and graphics in specific ways on each page, the string effect of word processing can be frustrating and inefficient. That is where desktop-publishing software is much more effective.

Desktop-publishing software is designed as a page-layout tool, meaning that its emphasis is not on processing words but on laying out and integrating textual and graphical elements in a document. Text is generally placed in a desktop-publishing document in text boxes or "frames" that can be positioned in exact locations on specific pages. A "story" or unit of text (such as an individual article in a newsletter) may be broken into several frames in a document, and the text will "flow" like a string through these frames—but the frames retain their original sizes, shapes, and positions, and graphical elements are not moved or otherwise affected.

If the addition of a paragraph to a story pushes text through the associated frames and causes the text to exceed the capacity of those frames, the user is warned that some text is not "placed" and must be positioned or placed by the user. But the overall document layout is not affected by the new text as it can be in word-processing software. In short, the desktop-publishing-software user has greater control over the layout of document elements than does the word-processing-software user.

TYPICAL DESKTOP-PUBLISHING-SOFTWARE FUNCTIONALITY

Functions and features that are typically present only in desktop-publishing software and that therefore set desktop-publishing software apart from word-processing software include the following:

Grids and guidelines: Document layout is facilitated by nonprinting guidelines and underlying document grids. Graphical and textual elements placed in the document may "snap" to these guidelines and grids to ensure alignment with other document elements, creating a more-professional, consistent look in the document.

Printing-industry measurements: Although type size is measured in points in both word-processing and desktop-publishing software, word-processing software typically uses inches for all other measurements. In desktop-publishing software, units of measure more common to the traditional printing industry are used for greater ease and accuracy. For example, indentations and margins may be set using picas and points rather than inches. (One pica is 12 points, and 6 picas is an inch. Thus, an inch is 72 points.) A margin of three-quarters of an inch would be designated as 54 points or, more typically, 9p0 (9 picas and 0 points). A line height of just over one-sixth of an

inch could be designated either as 14 points or as 1p2 (1 pica and 2 points).

Sophisticated typographic control: Desktop-publishing programs often have very sophisticated typographic control that results in the most professional typesetting possible. For example, individual character widths and heights can be expanded or condensed as needed, and line spacing and word spacing can be set to custom specifications. The appearance of fully justified text (text lines that are either "stretched out" or "compressed" to make them all exactly the same length) is enhanced by multiline "composition" rather than single-line composition typical of word processing. That is, the desktop-publishing software evaluates multiple lines of type at a time to determine the optimal places to break each line for the most-pleasing overall look of a paragraph.

Other advanced features: Desktop-publishing software may include such other advanced features as book and chapter management, built-in manipulation of graphical elements (such as the addition of key-line borders, drop shadows, rounded or beveled corners, and feathered edges), text set on a curved line, and easy overlapping or "wraparound" of graphical and textual elements for the desired effect.

USING DESKTOP-PUBLISHING SOFTWARE EFFECTIVELY

An experienced word-processing operator can probably learn to be proficient in using desktop-publishing software fairly quickly with the right training. Most people find that the learning curve for desktop-publishing software is much steeper than it is for word-processing software because of the advanced features of desktop-publishing software.

One of the most-useful practices for effective use of desktop-publishing software is that of using both word-processing and desktop-publishing software in the overall process of creating a desktop-publishing project. Since word-processing software is especially suited to entering, editing, and collaborating with others on the basic copy or text of a project, it should generally be used to complete those copy-intensive tasks. Then, when the copy is completely edited and ready for layout and formatting, it can be imported into desktop-publishing software, where it can be laid out on the page along with graphical elements much more efficiently because of the advanced page-layout functionality of desktop-publishing software.

SEE ALSO *Information Technology; Software*

BIBLIOGRAPHY

Conover, Charles (2003). *Designing for print: An in-depth guide to planning, creating, and producing successful design projects.* Hoboken, NJ: Wiley.

Hinderliter, Hal (2003). *Desktop publishing primer.* Sewickley, PA: GATFPress.

Lake, Susan E. L. (2006). *Desktop publishing* (2nd ed.). Mason, OH: Thomson South-Western.

Ray L. Young

DIGITAL DIVIDE

The digital divide is a term that describes access, or lack thereof, to technology for completing a task. Having the proper equipment and knowing how to use the accompanying technology efficiently has become increasingly important. As more of the world goes online, individuals and businesses that are digitally literate and able to access technology effectively are reaping great rewards both personally and professionally, leaving behind those who are not digitally literate.

Among the major concerns in bridging the digital divide is the need for becoming information literate in terms of reading, writing, and applying skills when using computers. This is especially true in lower socioeconomic areas of the United States and in third world countries.

Moving the term *digital divide* to another level recognizes that aging computers often cause a significant slowdown in Internet access, thus creating considerable problems in communication online.

WHY SHOULD THE DIGITAL DIVIDE BE CLOSED?

Increasing knowledge and efficient access to the Internet are two related forces that need to be addressed to close the digital divide. The need for developing realistic and meaningful digital skills and knowledge is extremely important for all people, regardless of their age. More and more business and communication are being conducted via the Internet. Information that relates to daily life and involves personal development and safety are often available on the Internet as opposed to being sent through the postal system or even phoned to new or regular customers.

Learning to access information online provides an opportunity for business growth and development. Online education is becoming an increasingly common offering of a college's curriculum in an attempt to better serve potential and current students. Because more people are working at home, there is a pressing need to bridge the digital divide in providing this population with all the essential tools in order to complete their work.

Having greater access to read and research information online provides the opportunity to become an informed citizen at local, state, and national levels. Even beyond that is the opportunity to think globally in studying topics that apply to the entire world.

THE FUTURE OF THE DIGITAL DIVIDE

The digital divide is beginning to be decreased by providing greater access to technology and the Internet. Cyber-cafes are available in most large cities. Most libraries in the United States provide Internet access. Wireless capabilities and laptop computers along with phenomenal cell phone interface capabilities make access to communication easier than it has ever been historically. While public areas seem to provide better grounds for equalizing the digital divide, many homes because of a lack of connectivity and affordability do not have the technology, which can instantly create a digital divide.

BIBLIOGRAPHY

Cooper, Joel, and Weaver, Kimberlee D. (2003). *Gender and computers: Understanding the digital divide.* Mahwah, NJ: Lawrence Erlbaum Associates.

Definition of *digital divide.* http://www.reed.edu

Digital divide. http://www.answers.com

Kuttan, Appu, and Peters, Laurence (2003). *From digital divide to digital opportunity.* Lanham, MD: Scarecrow.

Smith, Craig Warren (2002). *Digital corporate citizenship: The business response to the digital divide.* Indianapolis: Center on Philanthropy at Indiana University.

Warschauer, Mark (2003). *Technology and social inclusion: Rethinking the digital divide.* Cambridge, MA: MIT Press.

Webopedia. Digital divide. http://www.webopedia.com

Dorothy A. Maxwell

DIRECT MAIL ADVERTISING

SEE *Advertising*

DISCOUNT STORES

Discount stores are often defined as retail outlets that sell brand-name and private-brand merchandise at prices significantly lower than prices at conventional retailers. To offset the lower prices, a number of different strategies and tactics are used, depending on the type of discount retailer. Some of these strategies and tactics include: maintaining a high sales volume; keeping expenses down; negotiating lower wholesale prices; and cutting profit margins. Other tactics are: using inexpensive fixtures, decorations, and displays; minimizing free customer services and maximizing the use of self-service; carrying overstocks and discontinued products from other retailers and producers; and stocking off-season merchandise.

In addition, improvement of operational efficiency is continually sought to control costs. Modern discount stores may range from specialty shops (such as discount bookstores) to major discount chains that typically sell a wide variety of products including hard goods (e.g., major electronics, automobile supplies, toys, and small appliances), soft goods (e.g., apparel, bedding, and bath products), groceries, and other general merchandise.

HISTORY OF DISCOUNT STORES

Discount stores evolved from a series of retailing changes that began in the United States in the late nineteenth century. Following the Civil War (1861–1865), the development of mass-production processes and a mass-distribution system, along with population increases, paved the way for a new approach to retailing—mass merchandising. The first type of mass-merchandising operation was the department store. The second was the chain store, which included variety stores and "junior department stores." The third was the mail-order house. These patterns for mass merchandising remained relatively constant through the 1920s. The genesis of discount retailers, known as "undersellers," also occurred in the early 1900s. S. Kline (1912), J. W. May (1924), and Alexander's (1928) were the early undersellers of soft goods (e.g., apparel).

The Great Depression of the 1930s and the accompanying economic hardships set the stage for another retailing change and the further emergences of discount operations. Grocery supermarkets, the fourth type of mass-merchandising operation, appeared in 1930s. Early supermarkets, pioneered by Fred Meyer (1922) and Hendrik Meijer (1934), were comprehensive grocery stores that were designed for self-service and consumer accessibility. Size and low-cost facilities enabled these supermarkets to operate on low margins and sell below the competition. The inventories of supermarkets expanded to include nonprescription drugs during this time. The starting point for the fifth type of mass merchandising, discount stores, is often traced to the opening of a radio and appliance store by the Masters brothers in Manhattan in 1937.

The development of supermarkets, chain stores, and the predecessors of the discount stores that caused greater price competition in the 1930s, and concern, in the midst of the Depression, for maintaining employment brought about legislative constraints in several states to protect small retailers. These resale-price-maintenance, or "fair-trade," laws provided that manufacturers could establish retail prices for products that carried their brand name, thus legally fixing prices. In 1937 these laws were strengthened by federal legislation, the Miller-Tydings Resale Price Maintenance Act. Even though the laws were difficult to enforce, they would present a major challenge to discount merchandisers over the years to come.

After World War II (1939–1945), discount merchandising grew rapidly. This explosion in growth was fueled by consumer bargain hunting in the face of rising prices, the pent-up demand for goods created by wartime shortages, and the establishment of homes and families by returning GIs. Many consider E. J. Korvette, opened in 1948 by Eugene Ferkauf, as the first discount store. Soon regional discount stores, such as Zayres, Arlans, Gibson's and Two Guys, sprang up across the country to satisfy the demand for consumer goods, including television sets and other new products. Many of these new discounters sold their merchandise out of other existing businesses or set up in low-cost facilities such as abandoned factories and lofts. Despite these often makeshift origins, the modern discount industry was beginning to take shape.

Sparked by increased consumer confidence in discount stores and increased availability of goods from manufacturers, discounting continued to grow rapidly during the 1950s and became an important part of the retail landscape. New chains were drawn to the field, and established chains opened new outlets. Variety stores, specialty retailers, traditional department stores, and supermarkets were looking into discounting and, in some cases, launching ventures.

Mid-Twentieth Century. The look of discount stores also began to change in the 1950s as leading discounters (e.g., Masters, Two Guys, Korvette) took on a department-store-like appearance by adding household goods, apparel, and other soft goods. "Mill store" discount operations further contributed to this change as they began to surface with their base of soft goods.

In addition to the national and regional chains that entered the industry in the 1950s, several others opened their doors in the early 1960s. Many of the new additions were inexperienced and underfinanced, but among the new entries were four that would become the giants of the industry: Kmart, Woolco, Target, and Wal-Mart. All four began their operations in 1962.

Kmart was formed by Kresge, one of the nation's leading chain stores, in response to competition from drugstores, supermarkets, and the new discount stores. Kresge's new venture was unique in two respects. First, the marketing plan was based on the idea of offering quality merchandise—predominantly national brands—at discounted prices. Second, the location strategy was to "surround" cities with their stores.

Woolco was organized by Woolworth, another long-time leader among variety stores. Faced with the same problem as Kresge, they also responded by shifting their efforts to discounting. Their strategy was built around carrying department store merchandise, auto parts and accessories, and soft goods, all at discount prices.

Target was a spin-off of the Dayton Corporation, a Minneapolis-based regional department-store chain. It was conceived as a chain of regional upscale discount stores designed to attract affluent suburbanites. The product lines were higher quality and higher priced, with an emphasis on furniture and household appliances.

Wal-Mart was started from scratch by Sam Walton, the owner of a group of Ben Franklin variety stores in the south-central states. Walton's strategy was to establish stores only in small- and medium-size towns so that he could capture a substantial part of the total local market. His key policy was to sell at "everyday low prices," rather than hold periodic sales.

In addition to their marketing innovations, these four industry leaders played a major role in setting the pattern for other aspects of the industry. In particular, they established large facilities with standardized layouts in or near shopping centers. Their merchandise lines included both hard and soft goods and once they were established, they reduced the number of leased departments to a minimum.

Many discount businesses failed in the early 1960s because of the fierce competition brought on by the proliferation of new discounters and the experimentation of other retailers in discounting. In spite of the failures, the industry continued to expand in the mid-1960s, both in terms of number of stores and amount of sales.

The 1970s were a decade of expansion for the successful chains. Woolco and Kmart focused on national expansion and by 1974 Kmart had become the first truly national chain, with stores in each of the forty-eight contiguous states. Wal-Mart expanded into the Southeast and Midwest and Target established a strong presence in the Midwest. Some chains were forced into bankruptcy by the recessions of the 1970s, but their stores were bought up by the major chains and others. The decade also witnessed the end of federal fair-trade laws.

Late Twentieth and Early Twenty-first Centuries. Two distinct trends were underway as the discount industry entered the 1990s. One was the bankruptcy of several remaining discounters. The other was the spectacular growth of the (now) three major players: Target, Kmart, and Wal-Mart. Target sales more than doubled between 1987 and 1993. Kmart sales grew by more than $8.3 billion during the period 1988–1993. Meanwhile, in 1991 Wal-Mart passed Sears to become the nation's largest retailer. Their combined sales had increased by more than $46.7 billion during the period 1988–1993. As a result of these trends, the industry fragmented into four segments: the three major chains and a group of regional operators.

The beginning of the twenty-first century finds continued growth and consolidation as well as new applications in the discount retail business. Electronic commerce discount retailing has grown significantly, rapidly changing the shape of discounting and affecting the current industry members. Along with the departure of a number of discounters and the acquisition of others by stronger chains, new kinds of discounters have emerged.

TYPES OF DISCOUNT STORES

Although the full-line department-discount retailers such as Wal-Mart and Target are what first come to mind when discussing discount stores, there are as number of other types of discount stores. The following are the common types of discount retailers.

Food-Oriented. *Box (limited line) stores:* Limited number of product lines; very limited assortment of brands and sizes; few national brands; few perishables; products displayed in boxes with sides and tops cut off; very low prices; little atmosphere and few services; very little promotion (e.g., Aldi and Save-a-Lot).

Warehouse stores: Moderate number of product lines but a low depth of assortments; carry manufacturer's brands bought discount wholesale at very low prices; limited atmosphere; few services; minimal promotion (e.g., Cub Foods).

General Merchandise. *Full-line discount stores:* Extensive width and depth of assortments; average-to-good-quality products, often less fashionable; very competitive prices; average atmosphere and minimal services; significant advertising (e.g., Wal-Mart, Target, and Kmart).

Off-price chains: Moderate width and very low depth of assortments; average to good quality; lower continuity; low prices; little atmosphere and few services; some limited promotion (e.g., T.J. Maxx and Burlington Coat Factory).

Selected discount stores listed in the Top 100 Retailers with their rank

Rank	Retailer	2004 Revenues (000's)
Discount department store		
1	Wal-Mart	$288,189,000
5	Target	$46,839,000
14	Kmart	$19,701,000
28	Meijer	$11,500,000
72	Mervyn's	$3,200,000
Wholesale clubs		
4	Costco	$47,145,712
38	BJ's Wholesale Club	$7,375,301
Internet discount sites		
40	Amazon.com	$6,921,124
Off-Price		
21	TJX	$14,913,483
Discount variety store		
36	Dollar General	$7,660,927
47	Family Dollar	$5,281,888
75	Dollar Tree Stores	$3,126,009
Closeout merchandise		
54	Big Lots	$4,375,072

SOURCE: Triversity Top 100 Retailers. (2005) *Stores*. Retrieved October 24, 2005 from http://www.stores.org

Figure 1

Factory outlets: Owned and operated by the manufacturer; often located in outlet malls; moderate width but poor depth of assortment; some irregular merchandise; lower continuity; very low prices; some atmosphere and service; some promotion (e.g., Bass, Levi's, and Totes).

Membership clubs: Often referred to as wholesale clubs; charge a modest membership fee; broad assortment of food and nonfood items; lower continuity; low to very low prices; some atmosphere and service; some promotion (e.g., Costco, Sam's, and BJ's Wholesale).

Closeout retailers: Broad, but inconsistent, assortment of general merchandise and apparel; low prices; little atmosphere and service; some limited promotion (e.g., Big Lots and Tuesday Morning).

Discount variety store: Sometimes referred to as value retailers; limited assortment of foods and general merchandise; caters to the lower-income market; low prices; little atmosphere and few services; minimal promotion (e.g., Dollar Tree, Family Dollar Store, and Dollar General).

Internet discount sites: Electronic discount retailing, also called e-tailing; sells at discount prices over the Internet; large assortment of merchandise; good service; generally delivered by mail or parcel service (e.g., Amazon.com).

Figure 1 shows the gross revenues of selected major discount retailers in each of the different types. The ranking is the rank of the retailer in the Top 100 Retailers listed in *Stores* in July 2005.

SEE ALSO *Market Segmentation; Retailers*

BIBLIOGRAPHY

Berman, Barry, and Evans, Joel R. (2004). *Retail management: A strategic approach* (9th ed.). Upper Saddle River, NJ: Prentice Hall.

Boone, Louis E., and Kurtz, David L. (2004). *Contemporary marketing* (11th ed.). Mason, OH: Thomson South-Western.

Discounting: Chronicles of its evolution (30 years of discounting). (1992, September). *Discount Store News*, pp. 49–50.

Discount Stores Information at Business.com. http://www.business.com/directory/retail_and_consumer_services/conglomerates/discount_stores

Hoffman, K. Douglass (2006). *Marketing principles and best practices* (3rd ed.). Mason, OH: Thomson South-Western.

Kotler, Philip, and Armstrong, Gary (2006). *Principles of marketing* (11th ed.). Upper Saddle River, NJ: Pearson Prentice Hall.

Levy, Michael, and Weitz, Barton A. (2004). *Retailing management* (5th ed.). New York: McGraw-Hill/Irwin.

Ogden, James R., and Ogden, Denise T. (2005). *Retailing: Integrated retail management.* Boston: Houghton Mifflin.

Pride, William M., and Ferrell, O. C. (2006). *Marketing concepts and strategies.* Boston: Houghton Mifflin.

Solomon, Michael R., Marshall, Greg W., and Stuart, Elnora W. (2006). *Marketing: Real people, real choices* (4th ed.). Upper Saddle River, NJ: Pearson Prentice Hall.

Stone, Kenneth E. (1995). *Competing with the retail giants: How to survive in the new retail landscape.* New York: Wiley.

Triversity. (2005, July). Top 100 retailers. *Stores*. Retrieved March 1, 2006 from http://www.stores.org

Vance, Sandra S., and Scott, Roy V. (1994). *Wal-Mart: A history of Sam Walton's retail phenomenon.* New York: Twayne.

Thomas Baird
Earl C. Meyer
Winifred L. Green

DISPLAYS

SEE *Advertising; Promotion*

DISPOSABLE INCOME

SEE *Income*

DISTRIBUTION

SEE *Channels of Distribution; Transportation*

DIVERSITY IN THE WORKPLACE

Diversity means having distinct or unlike elements. In a workplace, diversity means employing people who may be different from each other and who do not all come from the same background. The differences may be those of national origin, physical appearance, religion, education, age, gender, or sexual orientation.

Corporate culture previously focused on a very narrow range of differences, but the range has become broader. Diversity in the workplace has now become a reality for all employers. Managing that diversity is an idea whose time has come. Employers of all kinds are awakening to the fact that a diverse workforce is not a burden, but a potential strength.

THE CHANGING FACE OF AMERICA

Changing demographics is an urgent reason for the increased interest in managing diversity in the workplace. When the 2000 census results were reported, business received a jolt: Hispanics had become nearly 13 percent of the U.S. population and had surpassed African Americans as the largest minority group. With more diversity come varied expectations of service as well as language barriers. Customer service training consultants are adding diversity to their curriculum because customers have varied backgrounds and expect customized service. Employers realize they must attract, retain, and promote a full spectrum of people to be successful. So great is their need that advice on management of diversity is a growth industry.

Progressive employers have developed specialized programs to deal with the workforce diversity. Some of these programs, known as "valuing differences programs," are geared to the individual and interpersonal level. Their objective is to enhance interpersonal relationships among employees and to minimize blatant expressions of prejudice. Often these programs focus on the ways that men and women or people of different races or cultures have unique values, attitudes, behavior styles, and ways of thinking. These educational sessions can vary in length from one day to several days or they can occur on an ongoing basis. They usually concentrate on one or several of the following general objectives:

- Fostering awareness and acceptance of human differences

A diverse workplace leads to a stronger company. © BILL VARIE/CORBIS

- Fostering a greater understanding of the nature and dynamics of individual differences

- Helping participants understand their own feelings and attitudes about people who are different from themselves

- Exploring how differences might be tapped as assets in the workplace

HARASSMENT

The Equal Employment Opportunity Commission (EEOC) is the federal agency responsible for enforcing antidiscrimination efforts. The EEOC has identified what constitutes unlawful harassment: It is verbal or physical conduct that denigrates or shows hostility or aversion toward an individual because of his or her race, color, religion, gender, national origin, age, or disability or that of his or her friends, relatives, or associates. It must also create a hostile work environment, interfere with work performance, and affect one's employment opportunities. Many states, cities, and employers have also included sexual orientation in their antidiscrimination policies.

Examples of harassment include epithets, slurs, negative stereotyping, or threatening acts toward an identified person or group. Other examples include written or graphic material placed on walls, bulletin boards, or elsewhere on the employer's premises that denigrates or shows hostility or aversion toward an individual or group. Included in this definition are acts that purport to be pranks but in reality are hostile or demeaning.

To be illegal, harassment must be sufficiently severe or pervasive to alter the conditions of employment and create an intimidating or abusive work environment. Although courts do not usually hold employers liable for violations based on isolated derogatory remarks in the workplace, many recognize that in the right context one slur can effectively destroy a working relationship and can create a hostile environment, particularly if the comment is made by a supervisor.

At the organizational level, employers must be sensitive to local, state, and federal regulations that address all types of discrimination in employment. With today's diverse workplace, the goal is to increase the chances of equal opportunity for all workers and mutual respect in the workplace.

EMPLOYER RESPONSIBILITIES

Providing a workplace free from harassment is one of the basic responsibilities of an employer. Although sexual harassment has received most of the public attention, harassment can take many forms. As employers add staff from a variety of ethnic, religious, age, and cultural groups, maintaining a harmonious workplace is critical. Given our increasing litigious society, it is inevitable that court decisions related to other forms of harassment will increase.

A major challenge for all employers is to assimilate a variety of employees into the mainstream of corporate life. Women and minorities are sometimes excluded from social activities or left out of informal communications networks. The result appears to be a sense of isolation, lower organizational commitment, and ultimately a decision to seek employment in a more welcoming environment. For example, a woman feeling left out may think that too much emphasis is placed on getting along with others in senior management: "As a woman, I do not fit into the group of males who go to lunch together and play golf together. These are the guys who get the promotions."

As workforce diversity increases, exclusion and isolation may disappear. In the meantime, a few organizations are encouraging women's support groups, black caucuses, and other ways to help subgroups tie into social and communications networks. More importantly, organizations are becoming more sensitive to sponsoring social activities that will allow full participation by all employees.

DISCRIMINATION

Making prejudgments is part of human nature because a person cannot anticipate every event freshly in its own right. Although prejudgments help give order to daily living, a person's mind has a habit of assimilating as much as it can into categories, which may result in irrational judgments. A person acts with prejudice because of his or her personality, which has been formed by family, school, the media and community environments.

Prejudice has been defined as an attitude based partly on observation and partly on ignorance, fear, and cultural patterns, none of which has a rational basis. A prejudiced person tends to think of all members of a group as being the same, giving little consideration to individual differences. This kind of thinking gives rise to stereotypes.

Stereotypes, like prejudices, are based partly on observation and partly on ignorance and tradition. For example, a person who assumes that all women are overly emotional is subscribing to a widely held but false stereotype.

Stereotypes are difficult to overcome because they usually develop over a long time. Some stereotypes are shared by many people, giving them an illusion of rationality. Many people, however, are trying to rid themselves of stereotyped thinking about others. This effort reflects a growing consciousness that people are individuals and can and should be treated as such.

The basis of prejudice toward a subgroup of society is often found in economic or psychological factors. Most free-market countries have a diversity of social groups. The social mobility concept postulates that as one subgroup moves up in economic terms, it is replaced by a less fortunate subgroup that is seeking a better way of life.

Since the mid-1800s, various ethnic groups have immigrated to the United States in waves. Tension between subgroups is often a result of economic competition for jobs, shelter, and social status. When physical differences, religious beliefs, ethical values, and traditions differ, subgroups can feel threatened and can sometimes take inappropriate actions.

Sometimes, there is a short-term macroeconomic gain for employers in aiding and abetting discrimination in the workplace. Competition for jobs among workers can help employers to lower wages and neglect working conditions. Employers often threaten striking workers with the prospect of being replaced, since there are usually members of minority groups who are willing to take jobs that pay lower wages.

As the United States becomes more involved in international markets, business managers are becoming aware that discrimination can make a disastrous impression on potential buyers and sellers. When one promotes democracy but practices discrimination, one's credibility is lost. Establishing oil trade with African countries, for example, becomes more complex when Africans see the U.S. establishment discriminating against African Americans.

RACIAL PREJUDICE

The United States has a history of divisiveness. White settlers drove out Native Americans and, in the South, set up a system of labor based on slavery. Some racism toward blacks and Native Americans still exists in the United States.

Minority groups come from subcultures that often have their own norms and values, which are not always understood by the majority group. For example, African Americans' social relations are sometimes characterized by an outlook they describe as ecosystem distrust. Ecosystem distrust subsumes such phenomena as lower interpersonal trust and suspicion of authority figures. When this type of outlook is brought into a traditional white, middle-class work environment, there can be misunderstandings and mistrust. Lack of awareness of these phenomena can easily lead to false assumptions by management about the worker. Because of cultural differences, many employers are conducting cross-cultural training for employees from both majority and minority groups.

GENDER ISSUES

Many women have felt discriminated against in the workplace. Advancement into management positions for women has been difficult. Since the 1990s, more and more women have not only entered the workforce but also have been promoted into management positions. Some would argue that men and women influence the workplace differently. Women are perceived as exercising leadership through strong interpersonal skills. Male leadership can be perceived as more direct, impersonal, and focused on results. A diverse team incorporating different styles of leadership will do more to help employers succeed in today's marketplace.

Traditionally, women have been discriminated against in terms of pay. The wage gap continues to narrow slowly. For various reasons, women's pay is gaining parity with men's. For example, many high-paying manufacturing jobs have disappeared, forcing many men into jobs in lower-paying service industries.

Americans continue to mature; an increasing number of minority youths are becoming part of the workforce; gay men and lesbians are becoming an important part of the workforce and marketplace; people with disabilities are also increasingly entering the labor force; and business is becoming more global. Organizations that continue to exclude some segments of the population from their workforce risk sending the less-than-subtle message that some employees and perhaps some customers are less valued, less important, and less welcome. This will have a negative effect on the bottom line.

SEE ALSO *Americans with Disabilities Act of 1990; Organizational Behavior and Development*

BIBLIOGRAPHY

Equal Employment Opportunity Commission. http://www.eeoc.gov

Hymowitz, Carol (2005, October 24). "Too many women fall for stereotypes of selves, study says." *The Wall Street Journal,* p. B1.

Katz, Judith H., Miller, Frederick A., and Seashore, Edith W. (1994). *The promise of diversity: Over 40 voices discuss strategies for eliminating discriminatin in organizations.* Burr Ridge, IL: Irwin.

Rout, Lawrence (Ed.). (2005, November 14). Leadership [Special section]. *The Wall Street Journal,* section R.

Tatum, Beverly Daniel (2003). *"Why are all the black kids sitting together in the cafeteria?": And other conversations about race.* New York: Basic.

U.S. Census Bureau. http://www.census.gov

Patrick J. Highland

DIVISION OF LABOR

In the early 1900s, Max Weber (1864–1920), one of the pioneers of modern sociology, designed a perfectly rational organizational form, called a bureaucracy. Among the characteristics of this ideal organization were specialization, division of labor, and a hierarchical organizational design.

Division of labor is a form of specialization in which the production of a product or service is divided into several separate tasks, each performed by one person. According to Weber's design, inherent within the specialization and division of labor is knowledge of the precise limit of each worker's "sphere of competence," and the authority to perform individual tasks without overlapping the tasks of others.

Adam Smith (1723–1790), an early economist, suggested that productivity would rise significantly when the division of labor principle was used. Output per worker would be raised while costs per unit produced would be reduced. Division of labor was applied, for example, in manufacturing plants that incorporated mass production techniques. In organizations that used mass production, each worker specialized in completing one specialized task, and the combined work of several specialized workers produced the final product. For example, in manufacturing an automobile, one worker would assemble the dashboard, another would assemble the wheels, and yet another would paint the exterior.

Since the time of Adam Smith, division of labor has been perceived as a central feature of economic progress. Two aspects of labor exist. First is the division of labor within firms, which concerns the range of tasks performed

Max Weber (1864–1920). *German sociologist Max Weber defined the beaucratic model in the early 1900s.*

by workers within a particular firm. Second is the division of labor between firms, which concerns the range of products or services the firm produces.

CURRENT APPLICATION OF DIVISION OF LABOR

Fred Luthans (2005) describes the bureaucratic model proposed by Max Weber as an "historical starting point" for organizational analysis. Citing "complex, highly conflicting relationships, advanced information technology, and empowered employees," Luthans (p. 519) discusses the functional and dysfunctional consequences of specialization uncovered in several research studies. For example, although specialization has enhanced productivity and efficiency, it has also led to conflict between specialized units, hindering achievement of the overall goals of the organization. Further, specialization can impede communication among units, as highly specialized units tend to "withdraw into themselves and not fully communicate with other units above, below, or horizontal to it" (p. 519). In addition, highly specialized jobs can lead to employee boredom and burnout.

Given these concerns, a significant change is under way in management of work in organizations. According to Richard Walton (1991), the work force can be managed in two ways, one based on control and the other based on commitment. Key factors that differ between the control and commitment approaches are job design principles, performance expectations, management organization (structure, systems, and style), compensation policies, employment assurances, employee input in policies, and labor-management relations (Walton, 1995).

The control-oriented approach is based on the classic bureaucratic principles of specialization and division of labor. In the control-oriented environment, worker commitment does not flourish. Division of labor can ultimately reduce productivity and increase costs to produce units. Several reasons are identified as causes for reduction in productivity. For example, productivity can suffer when workers become bored with the monstrous repetition of a task. Additionally, productivity can be affected when workers lose pride in their work because they are not producing an entire product they can identify as their own work. A breakdown in the mass production line can bring an entire production line to a standstill. Also, with highly specialized jobs, worker training can be so narrowly focused that workers cannot move among alternate jobs easily. Consequently, productivity can suffer when one key worker is absent. Finally, discontent with control is increasing in today's work force, further hindering the long-term success of the classic bureaucratic application of specialization and division of labor.

In contrast to the control-oriented approach, the commitment-oriented approach proposes that employee commitment will lead to enhanced performance. Jobs are more broadly designed and job operations are upgraded to include more responsibility. Control and coordination depend on shared goals and expertise rather than on formal position. The control and commitment-oriented approaches are only one way to view the concepts of division of labor and specialization. These concepts influenced organizations in the late 1990s by a complex array of organizational dynamics.

In response to such complex organizational dynamics as intense competitive pressures, organizations were being restructured. Hierarchies were becoming flatter, meaning that fewer levels of management existed between the lowest level of worker and top management. In some organizations, web-like and network organizational structures were replacing traditional hierarchical organizations (Kerka, 1994). In these redesigned organizations, the shift was away from departments that focused on traditional organizational functions such as production, administration, finance, design, and marketing (Lindbeck and Snower, 1997).

In the restructured organizations, highly-specialized jobs disappeared in favor of workers performing a multitude of tasks within relatively small autonomous customer-oriented teams. In these working groups, workers were given a broad task specification by management and within those loose constraints, the teams were allowed to organize, to allocate roles, to schedule tasks, and so forth (Bessant, 1991). With this design, traditional occupational barriers and clear-cut specialized job descriptions began evaporating as workers were empowered to define their own job tasks. This movement resulted in a decrease of the division of labor and specialization within firms.

As a consequence of these changes, during the 1990s increased division of labor between firms was often accompanied by a reduction in the division of labor within firms. In other words, while firms were becoming more specialized in the products and services they offered, individual workers within firms were handling an increasing range and depth of job responsibilities. As mentioned earlier, this work was often completed in autonomous teams.

EFFECTS OF SIZE, COST, AND PERFORMANCE ON DIVISION OF LABOR

In some organizations, division of labor and the degree of specialization are being reduced, while in other organizations, division of labor and specialization are increasing. A number of factors can influence this discrepancy among organizations.

For example, the degree of specialization and division of labor can be related to the size of the organization; typically, small and mid-sized employers are not able to cost justify specialized division of labor. Lindbeck and Snower (1997) report that, as the costs of communication among workers declines, the degree of specialization, and consequently, division of labor within organizations, may rise. Some literature reports that, as the size of the market increases, it supports more division of labor. The degree of division of labor within firms can also depend on the degree to which performance on particular tasks is measurable, and the degree to which wages affect task performance. Implementation of technology can also have a profound influence on the division of labor in organizations.

EFFECTS OF TECHNOLOGY ON DIVISION OF LABOR

Computerization has enabled organizations to increase the variety of tasks performed by workers, consequently reducing specialization and division of labor. For example, information technology—flexible machine tools and programmable multipurpose equipment—can reduce the division of labor within firms as workers transfer their knowledge from task to task more easily. Information and manufacturing technology can also enable individual workers or work teams to combine different tasks more readily to meet a customer's needs while enhancing productivity. For example, customer information gained from production activities can be used to improve financial accounting practices, and employee information gained from training activities can be used to improve work practices.

Eric Alsene (1994) reported that increased integration of computer databases has the potential to profoundly alter task and functional assignments in organizations, consequently affecting division of labor and specialization. Originally, the purpose of integrating computers into organizations was to merge the various functions of labor. Computer integration was designed to restructure businesses around their core business processes, outsourcing some activities to specialized external organizations and strengthening partnerships with suppliers and subcontractors. In the new culture shaped by computer integration, every worker was to have a broader view of the organization. Workers were expected to work in teams with enhanced communication, participation, teamwork, and an enhanced sense of belonging and continuous learning. In this new organizational model enabled by technology, the classic bureaucratic mass production model in which workers performed functions separately and sequentially was eliminated.

The computer integration model was designed to ultimately lead to the dismantling of vertical and horizontal barriers while supervisory control concentrated increasingly on work methods rather than on final products (Child, 1987). In other words, the new design enabled organizations to focus on how products and services were delivered rather than on what products or services were delivered. This design facilitated continuous improvement in the organization. The new technologies assisted in blurring the boundaries among departments while information flowed freely throughout the organization, thereby disregarding the traditional bureaucratic hierarchy. As work groups and task forces were formed, units no longer worked in isolation.

The new model enabled by technology calls into question the traditional division of labor in organizations. For example, flexible manufacturing systems eliminate the barrier between maintenance and production. This increased automation supports the movement described earlier of work becoming more diversified, independent, intellectual, and collective.

SUMMARY

The classic principles of division of labor and specialization still exist. However, their application produces both functional and dysfunctional consequences in the increasingly complex organizations of the twenty-first century. A number of factors affect the modern application of division of labor. Along with other complex organizational and market dynamics, these factors include information technology, worker empowerment, human factors, communication systems, organizational size, competitive pressures, and organization structure.

SEE ALSO *Management: Historical Perspectives*

BIBLIOGRAPHY

Alsene, Eric (1994). "Computerization Integration and Organization of Work in Enterprises." *International Labor Review.* 133(5/6): 657-676.

Bessant, J.R. (1991). *Managing Advanced Manufacturing Technology: The Challenge of the Fifth Wave.* Manchester, UK: NCC Blackwell.

Child, J. (1987). "Organizational Design for Advanced Manufacturing Technology," in Wall, T.D., Clegg, C.W. and Kemp, N.J., eds. *The Human Side of Advanced Manufacturing Technology.* Chichester: Wiley.

Kerka, Sandra (1994). "New Technologies and Emerging Careers. Trends and Issues Alerts." Columbus, OH: ERIC Clearinghouse on Adult, Career, and Vocational Education.

Lindbeck, Assar, and Snower, Dennis J. (1997). "The Division of Labor Within Firms." Stockholm, Sweden: Institute for International Economic Studies, University of Stockholm.

Luthans, Fred (2005). *Organizational Behavior* (10th ed.). Boston, MA: McGraw-Hill.

Walton, Richard E. (1985). *From Control to Commitment in the Workplace: In Factory After Factory, There Is a Revolution Under Management of Work.* Boston: Harvard Business Review.

Donna L. McAlister-Kizzier

DOCUMENT PROCESSING

A document is any written, printed, or electronically prepared business communication that conveys information. In the information age, documents are essential products that are becoming larger and more complex. Document processing involves the equipment, software, and procedures for creating, formatting, editing, researching, retrieving, storing, and mailing documents.

HISTORY OF DOCUMENT PREPARATION

The advent of a writing system coincided with the transition from a hunter-gatherer society to agrarian encampments where it became necessary to count one's property—whether it was parcels of land, animals, or measures of grain—or to transfer that property to another individual or another settlement. Letters were being handwritten as early as 2686 B.C.E. Prior to the inventions of the typewriter and the computer, all documents were handwritten, whether they were letters, bills of lading, property deeds, or reports.

The invention of the typewriter changed the way people communicated—moving from handwritten documents to typed ones. The typewriter was invented in 1714 by Henry Mill. Christopher Latham Sholes, a Milwaukee inventor, is the person most often associated with the invention of the typewriter in the United States. In 1868 Sholes produced the first practical typewriter to be patented.

At that time, however, correspondence was deeply rooted in etiquette and penmanship. Individuals were of the mindset that letter writing was the most private, complete, and encompassing form of communication between people. Individuals who dared to type letters risked rejection. Typewritten letters were viewed as insulting, implying that the recipient could not read. Even as late as 1922, the etiquette authority Emily Post was still describing letter writing as an art—even as she saw that art shrinking until "the letter threatens to become a telegram, a telephone message, a post-card" (Post).

Nonetheless, sales of the typewriter became lucrative, and with its acceptance, individuals found the process of preparing documents a far simpler one. The typewriter gave operators a faster means of writing than a person could do by hand.

In 1961 IBM introduced the first electric typewriter, the Selectric. Instead of the standard movable carriage and individual type strikers, this typewriter had a revolving type ball. The use of the revolving type ball allowed the Selectric to print faster than traditional typewriters. Following on the heels of the electric typewriter, IBM introduced the Magnetic Tape Selectric Typewriter (MT/ST) in 1964. The MT/ST was one of the earliest attempts to convert the regular Selectric typewriter into a word processor.

TYPES OF DOCUMENT PROCESSING

Different definitions have been ascribed to document processing. Several business education courses with document processing in their titles describe courses as being designed to teach students how to create a variety of computer-based documents—anything from business, technical, medical, and/or legal documents, tables, forms, reports, presentations documents, to documents for electronic publishing.

Nonetheless, computer science or library and information science show marked differences in their definition of document processing. In these areas, document processing might "explore the issues involved in building natural-language-processing applications that operate on large bodies of real text such as the ones found in the World Wide Web" (Dras and Cassidy, 2005, para. 2). Others find document processing to relate to electronic publishing—and to include such topics as typography, computer languages, file formats, specifications for document style and semantics, and electronic document standards.

Document processing has also been described as processing text documents, including methods of indexing for retrieving text based on content. Thus, document processing appears akin to nonverbal language in that it is learned terminology, one not easily or readily defined—one whose meaning varies with the culture of the organization and/or individual.

While an administrative assistant considers document processing as using a computer to keyboard a letter, memo, electronic mail (e-mail), or report, other individuals see document processing as a means of coordinating and conducting business transactions. An order submitted to purchase a certain product, for example, becomes a document for processing.

From the word-processing perspective, in its simplest form the term *document processing* means the production of paperwork. Originally the term encompassed all business equipment concerned with the handling of text. The term *word processor* came to represent stand-alone units. In 1981, with the advent of the IBM personal computer (PC), the playing field for word processors changed. Software-based word processors gradually replaced dedicated word processors. In this fashion, the term went from representing hardware to referring to software.

THE FUTURE OF DOCUMENT PROCESSING

In 1980 R. I. Anderson reported that "an even broader concept of word processing is emerging which ties automatic typing equipment into a communications network for input and output" (p. 55). At this time, optical character recognition, output to phototypesetting equipment, output onto microfilm, or output routed to automatic filing systems were separate units that were being tied together into a total information system of which word processing was a part.

Advances in technology have made it easier for individuals to create and manage documents. Tablet PCs, scanners, voice-recognition software, and the Internet are all changing the face of document processing.

Doctors' offices use wireless tablet PCs for inputting patient data during examinations. Prior to this technological development, patient reports would have been dictated by the physician and transcribed by an assistant. The hard-copy form of the patient's report would have then been stored in the patient's file. The use of the tablet PC also eliminates the need for storage space for hard-copy records and makes retrieval of materials faster and simpler. Also archiving stored records from a computer is a simpler process because older files may be stored on compact disks, jump drives, or external hard drives so that the data is available if needed but is not consuming space on an active hard drive.

Prior to the advent of scanners, documents were stored in file folders, file cabinets, file centers, and departments. Hard copies of documents can now be scanned and stored in an electronic file. This technological advance decreases the space formerly needed for document storage. Also, when a customer or other individual needs a document, a copy can be sent immediately by scanning the requested document and attaching it to an e-mail message.

Voice-recognition software is an important development, particularly to physically challenged individuals. Through the use of a microphone, individuals can dictate letters, memos, e-mail, and reports and have those documents convert to type on the computer screen. The use of voice-recognition software in industry reduces the number of repetitive stress injuries (such as carpal tunnel syndrome) and decreases the amount of time required to input data.

Companies are using e-mail as their official communication channel, thereby eliminating the need for hard copies of interoffice memorandums. In addition to being a faster means of communication, e-mail messages provide a hard-copy record, when needed, by simply printing the message. E-mail messages may also be stored electronically, reducing the required storage space for hard-copy documents.

SEE ALSO *Word Processing; Writing Skills in Business*

BIBLIOGRAPHY
Anderson, R. I. (1980). *Word processing: The changing office environment* (Margaret H. Johnson, Ed.). Reston, VA: National Business Education Association.

Dras, M., and Cassidy, S. (2005). *Document processing and the semantic Web.* Retrieved October 13, 2005, from Macquarie University, Department of Computing Web site: http://www.comp.mq.edu.au/units/comp348

Ober, Scot, Johnson, Jack E., and Zimmerly, Arlene (2006). *Gregg college keyboarding and document processing* (10th ed.). New York: McGraw-Hill Irwin.

Post, Emily (1922). *Etiquette in society, in business, in politics, and at home.* New York: Funk & Wagnalls.

Shelly, Gary B., Cashman, Thomas J., and Vermaat, Misty E. (2003). *Discovering computers 2004: A gateway to information.* Boston: Course Technology.

Szul, L. F., and Bouder, M. (2003, February). Speech recognition: Its place in business education. *Business Education Forum,* pp. 54–56.

K. Virginia Hemby-Grubb

DOUBLE-ENTRY ACCOUNTING
SEE *Accounting*

DOW JONES INDUSTRIAL AVERAGE
SEE *Stock Indexes*

DURABLE GOODS
SEE *Goods and Services; Marketing Mix*

E

E-MAIL

SEE *Electromic Mail*

EARNINGS MANAGEMENT

Earnings management is the practice of inappropriately managing the earnings number reported in the company's income statement, and is quite different from the process of managing the company's underlying business. The Panel on Audit Effectiveness, established by the Public Oversight Board in response to a concern expressed by the Securities and Exchange Commission (SEC), found no single definition of the term, but cited several examples, including this from attorney Michael R. Young:

> There are two types of managed earnings. One type is simply conducting the business of the enterprise in order to attain controlled, disciplined growth. The other type involves deliberate manipulation of the accounting in order to create the *appearance* of controlled, disciplined growth when, in fact, all that is happening is that accounting entries are being manipulated [italics in original]. (Panel on Audit Effectiveness, 2000)

In an interesting overview article, Patricia Dechow and Douglas Skinner suggested that there is a fine distinction between fraudulent accounting and earnings management: Both involve the intent, by reporting management, to distort their company's earnings picture, but fraudulent accounting does so by violating generally accepted accounting standards (GAAP) while earnings management does so within GAAP. (Technically, fraud requires scienter—proof of an intent to injure. It is a legal determination, and would be subject to an analysis of all surrounding circumstances.)

INTENSIFIED PRESSURES FOR EARNINGS MANAGEMENT

In a landmark 1998 speech, the then chairman of the SEC, Arthur Levitt, Jr., said:

> While the problem of earnings management is not new, it has swelled in a market that is unforgiving of companies that miss their [earnings] estimates. I recently read of one major U. S. company that failed to meet its so-called "numbers" by one penny and lost more than six percent of its stock value in one day.... the different pressures and expectations placed by, and on, various participants in the financial community appear to be almost self-perpetuating.

Also in that speech, the chairman suggested this slippery slope:

- Analysts ask managements of the companies they follow for guidance, as they project future earnings for the company and projections are influential in analysts' recommendations.

- Investors use those research reports in their decisions.

- The management people running those companies try to meet the analysts' earnings projections to (i)

213

maintain their credibility with the analyst community, and (ii) maintain the relative price of the company's stock.

- Where the normal operations of the business do not produce earnings equal to the investment community's expectations, managements are pressured to find ways to manage the reported earnings.

- Auditors, who want to retain their clients, bend under their own set of pressures to let this process continue.

APPROACHES TO MANAGING EARNINGS

Many strategies are used by companies to manage earnings in ways that are inappropriate. These are strategies that have as their outcome the achievement of predetermined earnings figures. Only a few of the most popular will be discussed here.

Decisions Solely to Meet Earnings Goal. Perhaps the simplest way to manage earnings is to control the expense spigot. Even the most lean company can find discretionary expenses that can be trimmed to help meet the earnings target for a period. Advertising, research, staff training, or maintenance programs can be deferred, at least in the short run. There is a great temptation to cut these programs "in the short run" on the assumption that business will pick up in subsequent periods and the deferred programs can then be resumed.

In well-run companies, managements are focused on the long-run success of the entity, and they avoid temptations to enhance, artificially, the results for any single quarter or year.

Making Necessary Judgments to Meet Earnings Goal. Opportunities for earnings management are inherent in accrual accounting. Under the accrual method, management is asked to look beyond the simple cash inflows and outflows the company experienced during a period and give a more nuanced picture of the company's operations. But the application of accrual accounting requires some difficult judgments. For example:

- Revenues are recorded when the sale transaction is complete, not when the customer makes payment, but management must then estimate what proportion of those credit sales will not be collected in the future.

- When the company pays cash for a fixed asset, that cash outflow is allocated as an expense over future years; but management must then estimate how many years will be benefited from the acquisition.

- If the company is sued, management must estimate the likelihood that the suit will result in an assessment against the company, and how much that assessment is likely to be.

The financial community has agreed that an accrual-based measure of earnings, subject to these judgments, is a much better measure of business success than a simple measure of cash results. The increase in information in an accrual-based income statement is largely the result of the exercise of managements' judgments.

In well-run companies, managements exercise those judgments, issue by issue, without regard to the effect those judgments have on the entity's reported earnings. To make sure that those judgments are free from bias, well-run companies outline—in formal policies and written accounting manuals—the processes to be followed in developing accrual judgments. Earnings management occurs when the decision makers skew issue-by-issue judgments, perhaps skirting their own policies, with an objective of forcing the earnings to a predetermined number.

Changing Accounting Principles to Meet Earnings Goal. The opportunity to manage earnings is also inherent in U.S. accounting standards. For many reasons, the financial community has agreed that it was better if the standards to be followed in preparing financial statements—and measuring earnings—were set by community consensus, rather than by government fiat. That notion of an underlying consensus is embedded in the name given to that body of standards—GAAP.

Understandably (and perhaps unfortunately), that consensus approach has allowed different accounting rules to be available for similar transactions. There are, for example, at least three different generally accepted ways to account for the cost of inventory items; there are also at least three different generally accepted ways to allocate the cost of a fixed asset over its useful life.

In well-run companies, management selects among the alternative accounting standards the one that most closely reflects the underlying relevant economic factors. Earnings management occurs when those making decisions select among the allowable alternatives of a particular generally accepted accounting standard the one that will result in earnings that meet the predetermined number.

FULL DISCLOSURE IS A KEY DEFENSE

Most financial and accounting personnel accept at least the semistrong version of the efficient market hypothesis—that is, an understanding that the financial marketplace will incorporate all available information in the prices it sets for stocks, it will do so promptly, and without regard to the source of that information.

Even if the final net income number on a company's income statement has been enhanced by earnings management, the efficient market hypothesis holds that analysts and other readers of the financial statements will correct for that overstatement, preparing an adjusted or pro forma income statement backing out the items that artificially benefited the reported results. That will be true only so long as information about the artificial enhancements is fully disclosed. Information about earnings management can be disclosed to the readers of the income statement in several ways:

- The impact of material, unusual events or transactions should be highlighted as separate line items in the income statement (Accounting Principles Board Opinion 30)

- The footnotes to the financial statements should describe the earnings impact of any changes in accounting policy, or changes in estimates (Financial Accounting Standards Board Statement No. 154)

- The management's discussion and analysis (MD&A) segment of SEC filings should "Describe any unusual or infrequent events or transactions or any significant economic changes that materially affected the amount of reported income" and "The discussion and analysis shall focus specifically on material events ... that would cause reported financial information not to be necessarily indicative of future operating results" (U.S. SEC Regulation S-K)

A company's management might argue that they had good reasons for changing the process they had followed in establishing reserves, or even for offering sales incentives at the end of a period. Such moves cannot be—and should not be—constrained under the flexibility that is inherent in accrual accounting systems. The market should not be deceived so long as the effect of those adjustments is fully detailed in the notes or the MD&A. But without full disclosure, the enhanced income statement may well present a misleading picture of the company's operations. An income statement, enhanced by earnings management without adequate disclosure, may well be a fraudulent income statement.

A HIGH-INTEGRITY FINANCIAL ORGANIZATION IS THE BEST DEFENSE

As Levitt said, the pressure to practice earnings management is not new—what is new is the intensity of that pressure. With the passage of the Sarbanes-Oxley Act of 2002, the community has established some contrapressures:

strengthening the hand of the board of directors and the audit committee; enhancing the professionalism of outside auditors; and requiring fairness sign-offs by the chief executive officer (CEO) and the chief accounting officer. Those regulations may help keep the pressures in balance, and reduce the incidence of earnings management.

But in the end, fair financial reporting depends on the integrity of the company's financial team. Every CEO needs a well-respected accountant at his or her side, to help temper the temptation within the company to manage earnings. Every company needs a high-integrity chief accounting officer who is prepared to say, "No, we shouldn't give in to the pressure—I can't let our company go down that path."

BIBLIOGRAPHY

American Institute of Certified Public Accountants. (1973). Reporting results of operations. *Accounting Principles Board Opinion No. 30.* New York: Author.

Dechow, Patricia M., and Skinner, Douglas J. (2000). Earnings management: Reconciling the views of accounting academics, practitioners and regulators. *Accounting Horizons, 14*(2), 235–250.

Financial Accounting Standards Board. (1978, November). *Statement of financial accounting concepts no. 1.* Norwalk, CT: Author.

Financial Accounting Standards Board. (2005, May). *FASB statement 154: Accounting changes and error corrections—A replacement of Accounting Principles Board (APB) opinion no. 20 and FASB statement no. 3.* Norwalk, CT: Author.

Levitt, Arthur, Jr. (1998, September 28). *The "Numbers game."* Speech given at New York University Center for Law and Business. Also, reprinted in *The CPA Journal,* December 1998.

McKee, Thomas E. (2005). *Earnings management: An executive perspective.* Mason, OH: Thomson.

Panel on Audit Effectiveness. (2000). Earnings management and fraud. In *Report and Recommendations.* Stamford, CT: Author.

U.S. Securities and Exchange Commission. (2004). Regulation S-K, Section 229.0 Retrieved February 15, 2006, from http://www.sec.gov/divisions/corpfin/forms/regsk.htm

Robert J. Sack

ECONOMIC ANALYSIS

Economic forces affect decisions made in personal business activities, as well as within business organizations, government entities, and nonprofit organizations. Changes in economic conditions affect and are affected by supply and demand, strength of buying power and the willingness to spend, and the intensity of competitive efforts. These changes propel fluctuations in the overall state of the economy and influence courses of action and the timeliness of actions. Nonprofit organizations, for example, may find that fund-raising efforts fueled by personal contributions are more successful during periods of economic prosperity. A first-time home buyer may be more inclined to purchase a house when interest rates are low and prices are likely to increase in future months. Since decision makers cannot control economic forces, a concerted effort should be made to monitor such forces. All business executives know that it is important to gain some idea of what general business conditions will be in the months or years ahead. Fortunately, certain economic indicators or indices enable decision makers to forecast oncoming changes in economic forces. Since both individuals and organizations operate in a dynamic economic environment, losing sight of what is going on can be disastrous for either.

THE BUSINESS CYCLE

Fluctuations in the economy tend to follow a general pattern that is commonly referred to as the business cycle. The business cycle, in the traditional view, consists of four stages—each of which may vary in terms of duration and intensity. The four stages are prosperity, recession, depression, and recovery.

Up-to-date charts, tabulations, and measures of relevant economic indicators are published by the Bureau of the Census in the monthly report, *Business Cycle Developments*. Economic indicators are predictors or gauges that signal cyclical movement of the economy within each stage of the business cycle or from one stage to another. A few examples of economic indicators include average workweek in manufacturing, new building permits for private housing, new orders for durable goods, and changes in consumer installment debt. While various government agencies collect and report monthly, quarterly, semi-annual, and annual measures of numerous economic indicators, economists representing various industries and other decision makers analyze and interpret the data.

Timing is everything when it comes to making good business cycle-sensitive decisions. Just as a truck driver starts braking before reaching an intersection with a flashing red light, decision makers need to make appropriate plans before the business cycle passes from one stage to the next. Prosperity, a period characterized by low unemployment and relatively high incomes, is followed by recession, a period during which unemployment rises and total buying power declines, leading to decreased spending by business firms and consumers. A production manager should make appropriate cutbacks prior to the onset of a recession. Failure to do so, in the face of decreasing sales, leads to bloated inventories and idle productive resources. On the other hand, when a period of recession (during which unemployment is extremely high and wages are very low), gives way to a period of recovery (characterized by increases in employment and income), a production manager should begin to plan for increased outputs. Just as the truck driver saw the red light and recognized it as a signal to start braking, decision makers must see changing economic conditions and make appropriate responses.

THE PROCESS OF CONDUCTING AN ECONOMIC ANALYSIS

Conducting an economic analysis requires the application of scientific methods to break down economic events into separate components that are easier to analyze. The remainder of this article discusses the steps included in this process.

Step 1—Identify Appropriate Economic Indicators. The first step in the process of conducting an economic analysis is to identify appropriate economic indicators for specific economic forecasts or trends. While various indicators may be selected, they are usually classified as indicators that lead, lag, and/or are coincident with economic conditions. Measures of data derived from economic indicators yield valuable information for the identification of economic trends and the preparation of specific economic forecasts.

Step 2—Collect Economic Data. Once the identification of indicators has been completed, the second step, which is the collection of economic data yielded by the indicators, can begin. Data collection is accomplished through observation and/or by reviewing measures of economic performance, such as unemployment rates, personal income and expenditures, interest rates, business inventories, gross product by industry, and numerous other economic indicators or indices. Such measures of economic performance may be found in secondary sources such as business, trade, government, and general-interest publications. The Bureau of Economic Analysis (BEA), contained in the U.S. Department of Commerce, provides economic information via news releases, publications, diskettes, CD-ROMs, and the Internet. The information may be accessed through the Bureau's Web site (http://www.bea.doc.gov), on recorded telephone messages, and in printed *Bureau of Economic Analysis Reports*. Such economic data are also available online through STAT-USA's Economic Bulletin Board.

Step 3—Prepare or Select an Economic Forecast. Of course, simply gathering information about economic indicators is not enough. Decision makers must use the data to identify trends and project forecasts. Decision makers know that it is important to gain some idea of what economic conditions will be in months or years ahead. As a result, they either use the collected data to prepare their own forecasts or they use economic forecasts that have been prepared by experts who monitor economic activity. Regardless of its origin, the forecast itself is essential if the decision maker is to recognize opportunities and threats posed by the economic environment. Thus, using economic data to predict the future is the third step in the process.

Economic forecasting can be and often is a complicated process. While accurate, relevant data are the basis for predictions, forecasters must be careful not to gather so much data that sheer volume makes analyzing impossible. Forecasts may be classified as short term (with spans or distances to the target period of up to one or two years), intermediate (two to five years), and long term (relating to more persistent developments and distant occurrences). Because of the possibility of unforeseen events occurring over a long interval, short-term forecasts are usually more accurate than long-range ones. There are four principal techniques used to forecast:

- Judgmental forecasting is the oldest and still the most important method of forecasting the future. Judgmental forecasters often blend several forecasters' judgments together to produce a forecast. This may be a complicated process, since various "Delphic" methodologies are used to integrate inputs from people experienced in forecasting.

- Indicator forecasts are nearly as old as judgmental forecasts. This technique requires that economic indicators be used to estimate the behavior of related variables. The index of leading indicators published by the Commerce Department is the best-known overall measure, but decision makers can use many other indicators for their own purposes.

- Time-series techniques use trend projections of past economic activity to extend into the future. Projecting is done by plotting data for the past years on a chart and, from the latest data, extending a line into future time periods that follows the pattern of prior years.

- Structural models of the economy try to capture the interrelationships among many variables, using statistical analysis to estimate the historic patterns. Large models of the U.S. economy, used by major forecasting firms and the government, may have up to a thousand interlinked equations. Simple models used by individual organizations, however, can have as few as one equation.

These four methods are not mutually exclusive. Combinations of methodologies are perhaps more commonly used in formulating forecasts today.

Step 4—Interpret the Economic Data. The fourth step requires decision makers to examine, assess, and interpret the economic data collected and the subsequent forecast generated from the economic data. Decision makers evaluate the data and forecast for accuracy, try to resolve inconsistencies in the information, and—if it is warranted—assign significance to the findings. By analyzing economic data and forecasts, decision makers should be able to recognize and identify potential opportunities and threats linked to economic changes and developments. As a result, they are better able to understand the influence that the economy is exerting and better prepared to make decisions and plan strategy. The process, however, should not be viewed in an oversimplified manner. Today's global economic links make economic forecasting and analysis especially complex.

Step 5—Monitor Intervening Forces. Then, too, intervening forces can and do influence economic activity. Such forces can shift or alter economic performance and trends and must be anticipated by decision makers. Thus, anticipating and monitoring the government's manipulation of two powerful sets of economic instruments, fiscal policy and monetary policy, becomes the fifth step in the process. Fiscal policy is the government's combined spending and taxation program, while monetary policy represents actions by the Federal Reserve System that affect the supply and availability of money and credit. The two arms of policy can work to supplement each other when powerful stimulus or restraint is sought. Or they can work in beneficial or damaging opposition, when one or the other is driven off-course into excessive stimulation or excessive restraint. Observers can often anticipate the government's implementation of fiscal and/or monetary policies based on prevailing economic conditions. The outcomes of such implementations must be considered by analysts.

Step 6—Use the Economic Analysis for Decision Making. Finally, decision makers use the results of an economic analysis for decision making. Astute decision makers recognize that economic forces are uncontrollable and that current strategies may need to be adjusted to cope with or overcome obstructing economic changes. They approach with caution opportunities and threats discovered as a result of economic scanning and analysis. They pursue a proactive approach, however, knowing that an economic analysis enables them to choose from alternative approaches how to employ scarce or uncommon resources and achieve objectives in the most efficient and cost effective manner.

SEE ALSO *Economics*

BIBLIOGRAPHY

Cross, Wilbur (1999). *Dictionary of Business Terms.* Englewood Cliffs, NJ: Prentice Hall.

"Economic Statistics Briefing Room." Retrieved October 18, 2005, from http://www.whitehouse.gov/fsbr/esbr.html.

"FEDSTATS." Retrieved October 18, 2005, from http://www.fedstats.gov.

Geahigan, Priscilla Cheng, ed. (1994). *American Business Climate and Economic Profiles.* Detroit, MI: Gale Research.

Maddison, Angus (1995). *Explaining the Economic Performance of Nations: Essays in Time and Space.* Brookfield, VT: Edward Elgar Publishing.

"Office of Economic Analysis". Retrieved October 18, 2005, from http://www.sec.gov/about/economic.shtml.

Schumpeter, Joseph A. (1994). *History of Economic Analysis.* New York: Oxford University Press.

STAT-USA/Internet. Retrieved October 18, 2005, from http://www.stat-usa.gov.

Trueman, Richard E. (1981). *Quantitative Methods for Decision Making in Business.* Chicago: Dryden Press.

Tummola, V.M. Rao (1973). *Decision Analysis with Business Applications.* New York: Intext Educational Publishers.

Ralph D. Wray

ECONOMIC CYCLE

SEE *Business Cycle*

ECONOMIC DEVELOPMENT

Economic development, generally speaking, is a process of change that is focused on the betterment of the community, state, and/or nation. Defining economic development can be difficult. The first term in this phrase—economic—refers to an accepted paradigm for organizing the business and financial and even to some extent the governmental sectors of a nation. Economics is viewed as the foundation for building a prosperous society. However, it is the second term—development—over which there is considerable debate. People's perceptions of development vary. For some, development has the appearance of successful commercial enterprise; for others, the face of development is one of economic equality. Nevertheless, the concept of economic development has the attention of government, the business sector, and the citizenry. Economic development is pursued as one of the goals of a successful country, state, or city. It captures the attention of the news media and impacts, as well as is impacted by, political objectives.

MEASUREMENT OF ECONOMIC DEVELOPMENT

Economic development in a community can take many forms. However, before discussing the process of economic development, we must first understand how economic development has been measured, particularly at the national level. It is within this framework that communities have pursued their goal of improving the local economic environment. In fact, standardized measures of economic development are being used throughout the world, not just in the United States.

Standardized measures of economic development are used to identify the status of one's country, state, or local community. We use these measures for a number of different purposes, including identifying trends and understanding patterns of economic development in communities that face different resource opportunities and constraints.

One of the most common methods of measuring economic growth is by calculating the gross national product of a country. Gross national product (GNP) is the value of goods and services produced *by* an economy's factors in a given period of time (e.g., the value of all goods and services produced by U.S. operations throughout the world in a given year). Gross domestic product (GDP), on the other hand, is the value of goods and services produced *in* an economy in a given period of time (e.g., the value of goods and services produced in the United States in a given year). When these measures are adjusted for inflation, we correct for any changes in the GNP or GDP that are due simply to increases in the price level in the economy. Real GDP, for example, is the value of goods and services produced in an economy adjusted for changes in the price level. This is particularly important when comparing across different economies because changes in price levels will not necessarily be uniform from one country to the next.

The general purpose of using measures such as real GNP or real GDP is to collect and analyze information related to a country's economic transactions. Real GNP or real GDP provides analysts with an indication of how quickly the business sector of the economy is growing in a country. It also serves as a guidepost for local communities as they address economic development issues at a local level.

Trends in national economic development reflect changes occurring at the state and local levels and can

Economic Development in Seattle, Washington. © JOEL W.
ROGERS/CORBIS

impact local economic development planning. For instance, if the real GDP of a country has increased, then we conclude that the country has experienced economic growth and the economy has improved. This information sends a signal to local economies suggesting that the national economy is in the growth phase of the business cycle. Communities can use this information to identify their position relative to the current trend and to plan future economic development. If, however, real GNP has declined, then the economy is thought to have experienced an economic downturn and a community can use this information to anticipate the impact of future economic downturns.

TRENDS IN ECONOMIC DEVELOPMENT IN THE UNITED STATES

Positive trends in growth at the national level do not guarantee that individual communities are or will be successful in developing their local economies. The needs of local communities have changed as the patterns of growth at

the local level have changed. Thus the rules of local economic development as they relate to attracting new business in order to promote economic growth also have changed. As communities compete with each other to attract new businesses and hence jobs to the local environment, they are discovering that the traditional methods of tax abatement and low-interest loans, coupled with job training, are not sufficient to guarantee a level of development that improves the economic base of the community. In fact, communities are looking for ways to ensure that they will get more from the investment than it will cost them in terms of tax abatements and infrastructure costs.

As firms increasingly engage in multilocation operations, communities are finding that, in addition to attracting new businesses, encouraging local firms to develop is a valuable economic development tool. The community's view of its resources has expanded beyond providing the traditional tax incentives to expand a community's economic resources to include factors such as a well-educated work force and adequate public services. Communities are more likely to target the type of firm that is right for the community. The emphasis on locating manufacturing enterprises has diminished as communities look to healthy businesses that fit the changing needs of the work force and infrastructure. Explicit consideration of the impact of the new business on economic equity in the community is also becoming more important, and growth and equity are increasingly recognized as complementary rather than opposing goals.

Many of these changes can be summarized in the phrase "sustainable development." The case of sustainable development is appearing more and more frequently in discussions of community economic development. Sustainable development is a process of development that "ensures the needs of the present are met, without compromising the ability of future generations to meet their own needs" (World Commission on Environment and Development, 1987, p. 9). The vision of sustainable development is one of developing within the capacity of our resources an ability to replenish themselves; by analogy to the financial sector, it means living off of the interest as opposed to the capital of our investment.

In the context of sustainable development, economic development is managed and controlled in a way that recognizes the dynamic nature of social, political, technological, and economic factors in a local community. Ultimately, the process of economic development is changed from one of identifying incentives for business growth to one of comprehensive planning to address social, economic, and environmental concerns. The themes of economic development also change. Traditional local economic development policies pursue increases in economic activity and thus in the income levels of local residents. A larger tax base and lower levels of unemployment are equated with business expansion. Sustainable development means that growth occurs alongside community goals of increased self-sufficiency and improved environmental quality. In fact, different forms of growth are encouraged. The sustainable development initiative is not opposed to growth but rather focuses its efforts on answering the question, "*How* do we grow?"

Successful economic development has been achieved in many communities pursing a sustainable development approach. Among the success stories is Kansas City, Missouri, which faced one of the most urgent economic development problems of urban areas—urban sprawl. From 1960 to 1990, the population in the metropolitan area grew by less than one-third while the land area developed more than doubled. The city's population was moving to the suburbs while the inner city was slowly being abandoned. As a result, the jobs moved with the population, and the communities in the outer ring of the city used traditional economic development tools, such as tax incentives, to attract new business. The central city attempted to compete by providing additional incentives. The burden, however, was clearly felt by taxpayers, as this increased over this period.

A Metropolitan Development Forum was formed to address the community development issues associated with urban sprawl. The forum has been successful in many areas: they have identified regional transportation needs, achieved agreement on the role of tax incentives in the region as a whole, created a metropolitan greenway, and created local initiatives for economic development planning.

One community that has achieved long-term success is Portland, Oregon. Portland has channeled the economic growth in the city such that employment in the formerly dying downtown area grew from 50,000 jobs in 1975 to 105,000 jobs in 1998. This strategy has been successful because they focused the development of business in areas that are close to developed transit systems, limited commuter parking, and controlled the expansion of growth into the rural areas.

Kansas City and Portland are only two of many examples of successful sustainable development initiatives across the country. As a community's needs change and as development is more broadly defined to include social as well as economic indicators of progress, sustainable development and planned growth initiatives will continue to take hold. There are many opportunities ahead for local economies to grow and prosper in ways that recognize the importance of improving the quality of life as well as the economy's overall productivity and income levels.

SEE ALSO *Economics*

BIBLIOGRAPHY

Parkin, Michael (2005). *Macroeconomics* (7th ed.). Boston: Addison-Wesley.

Shaffer, Ron (1998). "Playing by New Rules in Local Economic Development." *Community Economics Newsletter*, No. 263. Center for Community Economic Development, University of Wisconsin-Madison.

Shaffer, Ron (1995). "Sustainable Community Economic Development." *Community Economics Newsletter*, No. 224. Center for Community Economic Development, University of Wisconsin-Madison.

Thomas, Margaret G. (1999). "Strategies for Sustainable Economic Development." *Community Economics Newsletter*, No. 267. Center for Community Economic Development, University of Wisconsin-Madison.

World Commission on Environment and Development (1987). *Our Common Future.* Oxford: Oxford University Press.

Ellen Jean Szarleta

ECONOMIC SYSTEMS

The fundamental economic problem in any society is to provide a set of rules for allocating resources and/or consumption among individuals who cannot satisfy their wants, given limited resources. The rules that each economic system provides function within a framework of formal institutions (e.g., laws) and informal institutions (e.g., customs).

In every nation, no matter what the form of government, what the type of economic system, who controls the government, or how rich or poor the country is, three basic economic questions must be answered. They are:

- *What and how much will be produced?* Literally, billions of different outputs could be produced with society's scarce resources. Some mechanism must exist that differentiates between products to be produced and others that remain as either unexploited inventions or as individuals' unfulfilled desires.

- *How will it be produced?* There are many ways to produce a desired item. It may be possible to use more labor and less capital, or vice versa. It may be possible to use more unskilled labor to substitute for fewer units of skilled labor. Choices must be made about the particular input mix, the way the inputs should be organized, how they are brought together, and where the production is to take place.

- *For whom will it be produced?* Once a commodity is produced, some mechanism must exist that distributes finished products to the ultimate consumers of the product. The mechanism of distribution for these commodities differs by economic system.

MARKET VS. COMMAND SYSTEMS

One way to define economic systems is to classify them according to whether they are market systems or command systems. In a market system, individuals own the factors of production and individually decide how to use them. The cumulative decisions of these individuals are reflected in constantly changing prices, which result from the supply and demand for different commodities and, in turn, impact that supply and demand. The prices of those commodities are signals to everyone within the system indicating relative scarcity and abundance. Indeed, it is the signaling aspect of the price system that provides the information to buyers and sellers about what should be bought and what should be produced.

In a market system the interaction of supply and demand for each good determines what and how much to produce. For example, if the highest price that consumers are willing to pay is less than the lowest cost at which a good can be produced, output will be zero. That does not mean that the market system has failed. It merely implies that the demand is not high enough in relation to supply to create a market; however, it might be someday.

In a market economy the efficient use of scarce inputs determines how output will be produced. Specifically, in a market system, the least-cost production method will have to be used. If any other method were used, firms would be sacrificing potential profit. Any firm that fails to employ the least-cost technique will find that other firms can undercut its price. That is, other firms can choose the least-cost or any lower-cost production method and be able to offer the product at a lower price, while still making a profit. This lower price will induce consumers to shift purchases from the higher-priced firm to the lower-priced firm, and inefficient firms will be forced out of business.

In a market system, individuals make the choice about what is purchased; however, ability to pay, as well as the consumer's willingness to purchase the good or service, determine that choice. Who gets what is determined by the distribution of money income. In a market system, a consumer's ability to pay for consumer products is based on the consumer's money income. Money income in turn depends on the quantities, qualities, and types of the various human and non-human resources that the individual owns and supplies to the marketplace. It also depends on the prices, or payments, for those resources. When you are selling your human resources as labor services, your money income is based on the wages you can earn in the labor market. If you own non-human resources—capital and land, for example—the level of interest and rents that you are paid for your resources will influence the size of your money income, and thus your ability to buy consumer products.

Critics commonly argue that in a market system the rich, who begin with a disproportionately large share of resources, tend to become richer while the poor, who begin with a disproportionately small share of resources, tend to become poorer. They further argue that a government, which is designed to protect private-property rights, will tend to be exploited by those in power, which tends to be the economically wealthy. These critics argue that a market economy leads to selfish behavior rather than socially desirable outcomes.

In contrast, a command system is one in which decision making is centralized. In a command system, the government controls the factors of production and makes all decisions about their use and about the consumption of output. The central planning unit takes the inputs of the economy and directs them into outputs in a socially desirable manner. This requires a careful balancing between output goals and available resources.

In a command system the central planners determine what and how much will be produced by first forecasting an optimal level of consumption for a future period and then specifically allocating resources projected to be sufficient to support that level of production. The optimal level of production in a command economy is determined by the central planners and is consistent with government objectives rather than being a function of consumer desires.

As a part of the resource allocation process, the central planners also determine how production will take place. This process could focus on low-cost production or high quality production or full-employment of relatively inefficient resources or any number of other governmental objectives.

Finally, the command system will determine for whom the product is produced. Again, the focus is on socially desirable objectives. The product can be allocated based on class, on a queuing process, on a reward system for outstanding or loyal performance, or on any other socially-desirable basis for the economy.

Critics commonly argue that because planned economies cannot effectively process as much relevant information as a market does, command economic systems cannot coordinate economic activity or satisfy consumer demand as well as market forces do. For example, consider an economic planning board of twenty people that must decide how many coats, apartment buildings, cars, trains, museums, jets, grocery stores, and so forth should be built in the next five years. Where should these planners begin? How would they forecast the future need for each of these? Critics argue that, at best, planners would make a guess about what goods and services would be needed. If they guess wrong, resources would be misallocated and too much or too little production would take place. These critics argue that private individuals, guided by rising and falling prices and by the desire to earn profits, are better at satisfying consumer demand.

CAPITALISM

Under a capitalist economic system, individuals own all resources, both human and non-human. Governments intervene only minimally in the operation of markets, primarily to protect the private-property rights of individuals. Free markets in which suppliers and demanders can enter and exit the market at their own discretion are fundamental to the capitalist economic system. The concept of laissez-faire, that is, leaving the coordination of individuals' wants to be controlled by the market, is also a tenet of capitalism.

What and how much will be produced? How will it be produced? For whom will it be produced? In a capitalist system, individuals own resources, either through inheritance or through industry. The individual receives compensation for the use of resources by others. This, combined with inherited wealth of the person, determines an individual's spending power. The accumulated spending power and the willingness of individuals to allocate resources to consumption determine demand. The availability and costs of resources, together with the potential for profits of firms, determine supply. In a market system the demand of consumers combined with the supply of producers determine what and how much will be produced.

Because of the economic competitiveness of the market system, the lowest-cost production method will be used. If anything other than the lowest-cost production method was being used, a competing firm would have an incentive to enter production to earn a greater profit and could afford to sell at a lower price, thus driving the original firm out of production. Consumers could then purchase more of the product at a lower price, allowing their limited resources to purchase more.

Production will be allocated to those with available resources and a willingness to purchase the output of production. These purchases then become information for suppliers in determining what and how much to produce in the future.

Thus, pure capitalism is an economic system based upon private property and the market in which, in principle, individuals decide how, what, and for whom to produce. Under capitalism, individuals are encouraged to follow their own self-interests, while the market forces of supply and demand are relied upon to coordinate economic activity. Distribution to each individual is according to his or her ability, effort, and inherited property.

Typically the economies of Canada, the United States, and Western Europe are considered to be capitalist.

SOCIALISM

Under a socialist economic system, individuals own their own human capital and the government owns most other, non-human resources—that is, most of the major factors of production are owned by the state. Land, factories, and major machinery are publicly owned.

What and how much will be produced? How will it be produced? For whom will it be produced? A socialist system is a form of command economy in which prices and production are set by the state. Movement of resources, including the movement of labor, is strictly controlled. Resources can only move at the direction of the centralized planning authority. Economic decisions about what and how much, how, and for whom are all made by the state through its central planning agencies.

In theory, socialism is an economic system based upon the individual's good will toward others, rather than a function of his or her own self-interest. Socialism attempts to influence individuals to take other people's needs into account and to adjust their own needs in accordance with what is available. In socialist economies, individuals are urged to consider the well-being of others. If individuals do not behave in a socially desirable manner, the government will intervene. In practice, socialism has become an economic system based on government ownership of the means of production, with economic activity governed by central planning. The economies of Sweden and France are examples of a socialist economic system.

COMMUNISM

Under a communist economic system, all resources, both human and non-human, are owned by the state. The government takes on a central planning role directing both production and consumption in a socially desirable manner.

What and how much will be produced? How will it be produced? For whom will it be produced? Central planners forecast a socially beneficial future and determine the production needed to obtain that outcome. The central planners make all decisions, guided by what they believe to be good for the country. The central planners also allocate the production to consumers based on their assessment of the individual's need. Basic human needs and wants would be met according to the Marxist principle, "From each according to his ability to produce, to each according to his need."

The economies of China, the former Soviet Union, and the former East Germany are examples of communist economies.

MIXED ECONOMIC SYSTEMS

In practice, most economies blend some elements of both market and command economies in answering the three fundamental economic questions:

- What and how much will be produced?
- How will it be produced?
- For whom will it be produced?

Furthermore, within any economy, the degree of the mix will vary.

The economy of the United States is generally considered to be a free market or capitalist economic system. However, even in the United States the government has determined a minimum wage, has set rules and regulations for environmental protection, has provided price supports for agricultural products, restricts the imports of items that might compete with local production, restricts the exports of sensitive output, provides for public goods such as a park system, and provides health and retirement services through Medicaid and Medicare. All of these detract from the essential nature of a capitalist economy. However, most decisions continue to be left to free markets, leaving the United States as a mixed economy that leans heavily toward the capitalist economic system.

In contrast, the economy of the former Soviet Union is generally considered to be communist. However, the strict controls of the central planning unit of the country tended to be more intensely focused on heavy industry, including the defense and aerospace industries, than on agricultural industries. Farmers often had significant freedom to produce and sell (or barter) what they wished.

SUMMARY

Countries have scarce resources. The economic systems of countries are designed to allocate those resources, through a production system, to provide output for their citizens. The fundamental questions that these systems answer are:

- What and how much will be produced?
- How will it be produced?
- For whom will it be produced?

Market economies leave the answers to these questions to the determination of the forces of supply and demand while command economies use a central planning agency to direct the activities of the economy. Pure capitalist economies are market economies in which the role of government is to ensure that the ownership of the resources used in production are privately held. Socialist economies are primarily command economies where most non-human resources are owned by the state but human capital is owned by the individual. Communist economies are also command economies but all resources, both human and non-human, are owned by the state.

In practice, all economies are actually mixed economies, incorporating some facets of both market and command economies. The relative importance of the particular economic system in the country is the determinant of the type of economic system that it is generally considered to be.

SEE ALSO *Economics*

Denise Woodbury

ECONOMICS

Economics is often described as a body of knowledge or study that discusses how a society tries to solve the human problems of unlimited wants and scarce resources. Because economics is associated with human behavior, the study of economics is classified as a social science. Because economics deals with human problems, it cannot be an exact science and one can easily find differing views and descriptions of economics. In this discussion, the focus is an overview of the elements that constitute the study of economics, that is, wants, needs, scarcity, resources, goods and services, economic choice, and the laws of supply and demand.

Every person is involved with making economic decisions every day of his or her life. This occurs when one decides whether to cook a meal at home or go to a restaurant to eat, or when one decides between purchasing a new luxury car or a low-priced pickup truck. People make economic decisions when they decide whether to rent or purchase housing or where they should attend college.

WANTS, NEEDS, AND SCARCITY

As a society, and in economic terms, people have unlimited wants; however, resources are scarce. Do not confuse wants and needs. Individuals often want what they do not need. In the automobile example used above, someone might want to drive a large luxury car, but a small pickup truck may be more suited to the purchaser's needs if he or she must have a vehicle for hauling furniture. Economic decisions must be made.

A resource is scarce when there is not enough of it to satisfy human wants. And human wants are endless.

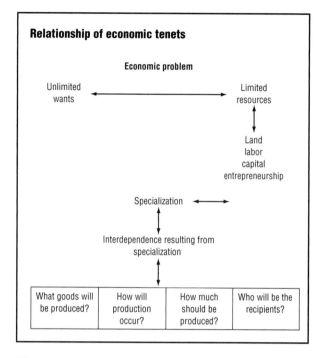

Relationship of economic tenets

Economic problem

Unlimited wants ↔ Limited resources

Land labor capital entrepreneurship

Specialization ↔

Interdependence resulting from specialization

What goods will be produced?	How will production occur?	How much should be produced?	Who will be the recipients?

Figure 1

Because of unlimited wants and limited resources to satisfy those wants, economic decisions must be made. This problem of scarcity (limited resources) must be addressed, which leads to economics and economic problems.

Figure 1 illustrates the relationships that exist relative to wants and scarcity. Many elements influence economic decisions. To better understand economics, it is critical to understand what is shown in Figure 1.

RESOURCES

Economic resources, often called factors of production, are divided into four general categories. They are land, labor (sometimes referred to as human resources), capital, and entrepreneurship.

Land. Land describes the ground that might be used to build a structure such as a factory, school, home, or church, but it means much more than that. Land is also the term used for the resources that come from the land. Trees are produced by the land and are used for lumber, firewood, paper, and numerous other products, so they are referred to as land. Minerals that come from the ground, such as oil that is used to make gasoline or to lubricate automobile engines, or gold that is used to make jewelry, or wheat that is grown on the land and is used in the production of bread and other products, or sheep that are raised for the wool they produce that is used to make sweaters are all described as land.

Labor (Human Resources). Labor is the general category of the human effort that is used for the production of goods and services. This includes physical labor, such as harvesting trees for lumber, drilling for oil or mining for gold, growing wheat for bread, or raising the sheep that produce wool for a sweater. In addition to physical labor, there is mental labor, which is necessary for such activities as planning the best ways to harvest trees and making decisions about which trees to harvest. Labor is also involved when a doctor or surgeon analyzes and diagnoses (mental labor) before performing a medical procedure, then performs the procedure (physical labor).

Capital. Capital is input that is often viewed in two ways, much as is labor. Capital might be viewed as human capital—the knowledge, skills, and attitudes that humans possess that allow them to produce. The other type of capital is physical capital, which includes buildings, machinery, tools, and other items that are used to produce goods and service. Traditionally, physical capital has been a prerequisite for human capital; however, because of rapid changes in technology, today human capital is less dependent on physical capital.

Entrepreneurship. One special form of human capital that is important in an economic setting is entrepreneurship (often thought of as the fourth factor of production). Entrepreneurial abilities are needed to improve what we have and to create new goods and services. An entrepreneur is one who brings together all the resources of land, labor, and capital that are needed to produce a better product or service. In the process of doing this, the entrepreneur is willing to assume the risk of success and failure.

Many people associate entrepreneurship with creating or owning a new business. That is one definition of entrepreneurship but not the only one. An entrepreneur might create a new market for something that already exists or push the use of a natural resource to new limits in order to maximize efficiency and minimize consumption.

GOODS AND SERVICES

It takes land, labor, and capital that are used by an entrepreneur to produce goods and services that will ultimately be used to satisfy our wants. Goods are tangible, meaning they are something that can be seen or touched. The production of goods requires using limited resources to produce in order to satisfy wants. An example might be a farmer who grows grain. The farmer uses farm equipment manufactured from resources; ground is a natural resource that is used to grow the grain; and because the growth of grain depletes the nutrients in the soil, the farmer must use fertilizers to restore the nutrients. Limited resources are used to produce natural or chemical fertilizers, but they are necessary for crop production. Water might be used to irrigate the crop and enhance production. When the crop is ready for harvest, the farmer uses additional resources to complete the process—equipment, gasoline, labor, and so on—which results in a good that can be used or sold for use by others.

Services are provided in numerous ways and are an intangible activity. There is no doubt that one can often see someone providing a service, but the service is not something that someone can pick up and take home to use. An example of a service is a ride in a taxi through a crowded city. It takes resources for the owner or driver to provide the service, and a passenger is consciously aware of riding in a taxi. When the ride is completed and the provider has been paid, the passenger does not have anything tangible to hold except the receipt. However, resources have been used to provide the service. The automobile used as the cab, the fuel used to operate the cab, and the labor of the driver are all examples of resources being used to provide a service that will satisfy a want.

It is important to understand that because goods and services utilize resources that are limited, goods and services are also scarce. Scarcity results when the demand for a good or service is greater than its supply. Remember that society has unlimited wants but scarce resources. It is scarcity, then, that causes consumers to have to make choices. If individuals cannot have everything they want, they must decide which of the goods and services are most important and which they can do without.

ECONOMIC CHOICE

Opportunity Cost. When one makes economic decisions, it is because of limited resources. Alternatives must be considered. People make such decisions based on expecting greater benefits from one alternative than another. There is an opportunity cost involved in the choice. Opportunity cost is the benefit forgone from the best alternative that is *not* selected: individuals give up an opportunity to use or enjoy something in order to select something else.

Opportunity costs cannot always be measured, because it might be satisfaction that is lost. At other times, however, opportunity cost can be measured. Here are examples of each. Perhaps a student is studying hard for a final examination in a difficult course because a good exam score is critical to achieve the desired grade. Friends call to invite the student out for the evening. The alternatives are to study or to have fun. Being wise, the student selects studying instead of going out. It is difficult to measure the opportunity cost of having fun with friends. In the second example, the same studying student is asked to help someone clean a garage. If the person offers to pay the student $50 to clean the garage and the student chooses to study, the opportunity cost is easily measured at $50. In both these examples, opportunity cost is directly related to what was given up, not any other benefits that might result from the decision.

Circumstances also play a role in opportunity cost. Sometimes people are forced into a decision because of circumstances and the results may not always be optimal. For example, if someone is planning to relocate to a new city to start a new job and wants to sell a house before the move in order to be able to purchase a new house in the new location, the person may sell the house for less than the market price in order to complete the process. The opportunity cost is the value of what was given up in order to be able to purchase a new home. Every time a choice is made, opportunity costs are assumed.

Production. Another economic choice that must be made is related to production. This is illustrated in Figure 1. All four of the decisions must be made: What goods will be produced? How will production occur? How much should be produced? Who will be the recipients? All are decisions that influence production efficiency.

Efficiency is the primary element in deciding what to produce and how to go about the production process. Efficiency is producing with the least amount of expense, effort, and waste, but not without cost. If you take something away from a person to satisfy another person, one will be less happy and the other will be more happy. If a way can be found to make one person more happy without making the other person less happy, this would be efficient.

An example of economic efficiency might be the following. Assume someone owns a car and a friend does not own a car but does drive. The friend needs transportation regularly for a week. It happens to be a time when the car owner will be away on a business trip and therefore will not be using the car. It makes no sense for the friend to buy a car to use for such a short period of time, so the owner loans the friend the car for that week. The car owner is no worse off and the friend is better off. Economic efficiency has occurred in this situation. If the car owner had not loaned the car to the friend, there would have been waste because the friend would have had to buy or rent a car. It is wasteful to fail to take advantage of opportunities in which there is no loss of satisfaction to either party.

Production efficiency is a situation in which it is not possible to produce any more units of a good without giving up the opportunity to produce another good unless a change occurs in available productive resources. If a farmer is growing wheat to be sold for the production of bread, there is a point at which adding additional fertilizer to the soil would do no good. If the fertilizer were used on an oat crop in a different field, production could be increased for that crop. The way to increase the wheat production is to find different resources to make the crop better, such as irrigating the land to provide more moisture.

In the above example, it was suggested that different or additional resources might be used to increase production. This is necessary only after efficiency has been achieved. Additional resources would have to come from land, labor, capital, or entrepreneurship. It is most common that capital will be used most often to increase production. Capital is productive input that is increased by people. This is known as investment. Investment involves giving up what might presently be consumed in favor of producing something to consume in the future. If the farmer wants to increase wheat production in the future, something will have to be given up now in order to increase the resources available for future production.

Increasing human capital is critical to increasing production. This does not mean that more people must be produced, but rather that the knowledge and skills of humans must be increased. This can happen because of improvements in technology and new ways of satisfying wants. This involves the entrepreneurial factor that was described previously—the human element that figures out ways to improve and expand the resources that already exist.

Product Distribution. Getting goods into the hands of those who want them involves many choices. The economic system must decide how to divide the products that are produced among the potential recipients. Sometimes products can be divided equally among recipients, but normally this is not the situation. It must then be determined how the division will take place. In a capitalistic economic system, distribution is often determined by wealth. If two people have the same wants, the person who can most afford something will be able to acquire it.

THE LAW OF SUPPLY AND DEMAND

Production decisions are made based on demand for goods and services. Supply of goods and services is dependent upon demand for the same. Why do movies that are much more popular stay at theaters longer than those that are not as popular? Demand for the movie causes the theater operators to supply the showings that the consumer wants. Why does the room rate in a convention hotel go down on weekends? There is less demand on weekends because most convention-goers leave on Friday or Saturday and others do not arrive until Monday, so the supply of available rooms goes up. Hotel operators try to

create more demand for their vacant weekend rooms by lowering prices and offering attractive amenities.

The law of demand states that during a specific time period the quantity of a product that is demanded is inversely related to its price, as long as other things remain constant. The higher the price, the lower the demand; the lower the price, the higher the demand. Do not confuse demand with wants. Consumers have unlimited wants, as was established at the beginning of this discussion. Nor are demands and wants the same as needs. A consumer may need to have a crown put on a tooth but may not want to have it done because of the high cost. At some point, the suffering patient may demand the services be provided regardless of the price.

Often when prices are too high and demand for a product or service lessens, it is because consumers have found a suitable substitute. Substitution happens all the time as a result of economic decisions that are made by consumers. For example, if someone needs a winter coat and likes one with a designer name and a price that reflects that name, the purchase may not be made. Instead, the person finds a similar coat that does not have a designer label and purchases it instead at a much lower cost.

Demand for goods or services determines the amount that will be supplied. The law of supply states that the greater the demand, the more that will be supplied; the lower the demand, the less that will be supplied. The amount that will be supplied by a producer of the good or service is based on capacity and willingness to supply the product at a specific price. A producer will not supply goods and services just because there is demand for them—price for the good or service is an important consideration.

If consumers are willing to pay more for a good or service, the producer will likely be willing to shift more resources in order to increase the supply of the demanded product. If a rancher is raising prime beef cattle and there is high demand for this good and consumers are willing to pay more for high-quality beef, then the rancher might be willing to supply more even if it is necessary to shift resources or acquire additional resources to be able to do so.

Demands change, supplies change, and prices change. So how does a producer know how much is enough and what price to charge for the goods and services? Very simply, the demand for and supply of goods and services can be plotted on graphs using different prices. The supply and demand for a good or service intersect on the graph at what is called the equilibrium price, or the price where all of what is supplied will be demanded. If the price is below equilibrium, there will be a shortage of the good or service, and if the price is above equilibrium, there will be a surplus of the good or service. For a more detailed explanation on this aspect of economics, see the discussion of supply and demand.

SUMMARY

Economics is a complex topic that is studied constantly and thoroughly. This article has given an overview of some of the main tenets of economics; however, there is much that was not even introduced. There are other topics throughout this encyclopedia, such as macroeconomics and microeconomics, that will further define and expand the topic of economics.

SEE ALSO *Business Cycle; Careers in Economics; Economics: Historical Perspectives; Ethics in Economics; Macroeconomics/Microeconomics*

BIBLIOGRAPHY

Dolan, Edwin G., and Lindsey, David E. (1994). *Economics* (7th ed.). Fort Worth: Dryden Press.

Heilbroner, Robert L., and Thurow, Lester C. (1998). *Economics Explained*. New York: Simon & Schuster.

Lipsey, Richard G., Steiner, Peter O., Purvis, Douglas D., and Courant, Paul N. (1993). *Economics*. New York: Harper-Collins College Publishers.

McEachern, William A. (2006). *Economics: A Contemporary Introduction*. Mason, OH: Thomson/South-Western.

Roger L. Luft

ECONOMICS: HISTORICAL PERSPECTIVES

Economics has been around since the beginning of time, but the study of economics dates back only a few hundred years. Since the beginning of human history, people have had to confront the problem of scarce resources and unlimited wants. The study of economics will continue until the end of time because each day uncovers new evidence that supports or revolutionizes economic theory.

THE DEVELOPMENT OF ECONOMIC SYSTEMS

The United States has a capitalistic economic system. Sometimes this system is called the free-enterprise system because that term is more acceptable to certain individuals. A capitalistic system includes a market society, or market system—a system of mercantilism in which participants react freely to the opportunities and challenges of the marketplace. This is in contrast to systems in which participants follow tradition or the commands of others. In a market system, anyone can buy land or sell it of his or her own free will or produce products and/or services that are sold at a market price. In earlier societies, participants responded not to the demands of the marketplace but to the demands of tradition or law as well as the threat and fear of punishment.

The factors of production, key to a capitalistic system, are the result of historical changes that made labor a key to creating wealth, made real estate out of land that had been in families for generations, and made capital out of possessions. Capitalism, a free-market system, was the cause of much unrest and insecurity, but it also gave birth to progress and, ultimately, fulfillment. There have been several key individuals whose work and economic writing help to clarify current thought about economic systems. The ideas of four are presented here.

ADAM SMITH (1723–1790)

Perhaps the best known and one of the most revered economists, Adam Smith wrote *The Wealth of Nations* in 1776, the same year the Declaration of Independence was signed. In this famous work, Smith explained how an independent society works. He answered several questions that people had at the time regarding the concepts of a free-market system.

Of primary concern was the question of how those consumed with greed might be controlled so they would not take over society. Smith introduced the concept of competition. Anyone bent on bettering only him- or herself with no regard for others will be confronted by others with the same goals. In this new system, those who are buying or selling are forced to meet the prices offered by competitors.

Smith also illustrated that a market system also has another important function. That function is to produce goods and services that society wants, and in quantities that society wants. A good example of this is when products such as Hula Hoops, Cabbage Patch dolls, or Beanie Babies became the rage, there were not enough being produced to satisfy all the potential buyers. As a result, the manufacturers had to increase production and were also able to increase prices because the demand for the products was so great and buyers were willing to pay higher prices. In fact, many buyers bought quantities they did not need precisely so they could, in turn, sell the high-demand products to others who were willing to pay the higher price. That is the capitalistic market system.

Smith was extremely visionary and foresaw that if a free market is to grow and prosper, there must be little government intervention. He saw that a free market must be self-regulating in order to become wealthy and robust. He made it clear that it was truly individuals' greed and

Karl Marx (1818–1883). *German social, political and economic theorist Marx stressed the instability of capitalism.*
© GETTY IMAGES

desire for profits that would create a working free-enterprise system that is self-regulating.

KARL MARX (1818–1883)

The mere mention of Karl Marx might be disturbing to some. However, his thoughts and writings on economics have stirred many to more intense economic analysis. His role in economic history is quite different from that of Adam Smith. Smith was the visionary regarding the orderly processes and growth of capitalism while Marx diagnosed its disorderliness and eventual demise. Marx believed that growth is fraught with crises and pitfalls.

Marx was the first economic theorist to stress the instability of capitalism, maintaining that economic growth is wavering and uncertain. He pointed out that even though accumulation of wealth is primary in a free-market system, it may not always be possible. Marx believed that increasing instability would occur until the system collapsed.

Marx discussed how the size of businesses would continue to grow because of the inherent instability and

demise of smaller, noncompetitive businesses. Failing businesses would be bought by successful ones; hence, the growth cycle would continue. He realized that a trend toward larger businesses is typical in a capitalistic system.

Marx also speculated that there would be a class struggle in a capitalistic society. He thought that as small businesses were forced out of the marketplace and acquired by larger businesses, the social structure would also evolve into two classes. He predicted that there would be one class of wealthy property owners and another class of propertyless workers. There are arguments for and against Marx's economic beliefs, but he has more critics than supporters in capitalistic countries.

JOHN MAYNARD KEYNES (1883–1946)

John Maynard Keynes was the father of a "mixed economy" in which the government plays a crucial role. Many believe that government should not have a role in a capitalistic system, viewing such a role with considerable distrust and suspicion. As a result, many find Keynes's theories to be as offensive as those of Marx.

One of the main tenets of Keynes's theory—in conflict with both Smith and Marx—is that economic problems in a capitalistic society are not self-correcting and that economies cannot keep growing indefinitely. He believed that if there is nothing to support capital growth, a depressed economy requires outside intervention or a substitute for business capital spending. Keynes believed that only government intervention could get a country out of a depression and the economy back on track.

ALFRED MARSHALL (1842–1924)

Alfred Marshall was a mathematician who applied his mathematical training to his explanation of economics. Marshall's economic theories, although very elaborate, have been viewed as eclectic and lacking in internal consistency. He was noted for taking a series of formal economic thoughts and analyses and linking them. He thought that his writings would present a detailed picture of economic reality.

His complex thoughts are extremely detailed, and he developed theories of value and distribution that combine marginal utility with real cost. The forces behind both supply and demand determine value. Behind demand is marginal utility, which is reflected in the prices at which given quantities will be demanded by buyers. Marshall stated that behind supply is marginal effort and sacrifice, reflected in the prices at which given quantities will be produced.

John Maynard Keynes (1883–1946). *Keynes defined the theory of a "mixed economy," in 1941.* © **BETTMANN/CORBIS**

SUMMARY

There are, of course, many other noted economists who have influenced the study of economics. Many contemporary economic theorists have used the writings of the early economists to further develop economic thought. Economics is a continually evolving study, and its history will be constantly changing.

SEE ALSO *Economics*

BIBLIOGRAPHY

Blaug, Mark, ed. (1990). *The History of Economic Thought.* Brookfield, VT: E. Elgar Publishing.

Deane, Phyllis (1978). *The Evolution of Economic Ideas.* New York: Cambridge University Press.

Galbraith, John Kenneth (1987). *Economics in Perspective: A Critical History.* Boston: Houghton Mifflin.

Heilbroner, Robert L., and Thurow, Lester C. (1998). *Economics Explained.* New York: Simon and Schuster.

Heimann, Eduard (1964). *History of Economic Doctrines: An Introduction to Economic Theory.* New York: Oxford University Press.

Rostow, W.W. (1990). *Theorists of Economic Growth from David Hume to the Present With a Perspective on the Next Century.* New York: Oxford University Press.

Roger L. Luft

EDUCATION

SEE *Corporate Education; Online Education; Professional Education; School to Career Movement; Training and Development*

ELECTRONIC COMMERCE

Electronic commerce, e-commerce or ecommerce consists primarily of the distributing, buying, selling, marketing, and servicing of products or services over electronic systems such as the Internet and other computer networks. The information technology industry might see it as an electronic business application aimed at commercial transactions. It can involve electronic funds transfer, supply chain management, e-marketing, online marketing, online transaction processing, electronic data interchange, automated inventory management systems, and automated data–collection systems. It typically uses electronic communications technology such as the Internet, extranets, e-mail, Ebooks, databases, and mobile phones. (Electronic commerce, n.d.)

It is fitting that this entry begins with the definition of e-commerce from a free encyclopedia, self-described as "the largest encyclopedia in history, in terms of both breadth and depth," entirely created by the voluntary contributions of the Internet community—for that is a very good indication of the revolutionary basis upon which e-commerce has thrived. The entry on e-commerce in the previous edition of this work also began with a quote, but one in which it was seen more as a promise than a reality: "No single force embodies our electronic transformation more than the evolving medium known as the Internet. Internet technology is having a profound effect on the global trade in services" ("The U.S. Government's Framework," 1997). At that time Forrester Research, a market research company, estimated that e-commerce would increase to $1,444 trillion by 2003. In reality, e-commerce in the United States totaled $1,679 trillion in 2003, having met that earlier forecast several years ahead of schedule (see Figure 1).

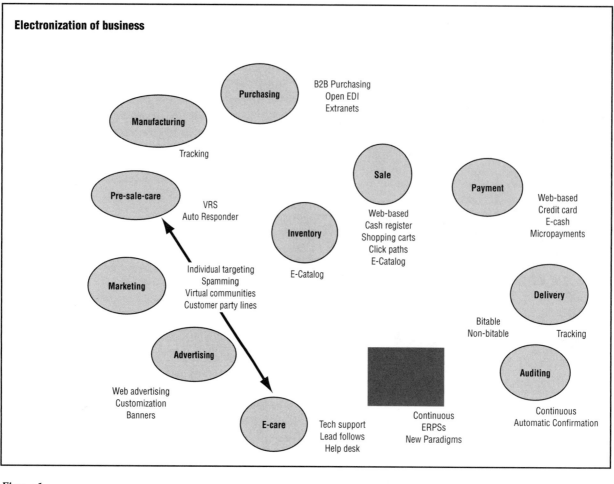

Electronization of business

Manufacturing
Tracking

Purchasing
B2B Purchasing
Open EDI
Extranets

Pre-sale-care
VRS
Auto Responder

Sale
Web-based
Cash register
Shopping carts
Click paths
E-Catalog

Payment
Web-based
Credit card
E-cash
Micropayments

Inventory
E-Catalog

Individual targeting
Spamming
Virtual communities
Customer party lines

Marketing

Delivery
Bitable
Non-bitable
Tracking

Advertising
Web advertising
Customization
Banners

E-care
Tech support
Lead follows
Help desk

Continuous
ERPSs
New Paradigms

Auditing
Continuous
Automatic Confirmation

Figure 1

And e-commerce, which encompasses both business to business (B2B) and business to consumer (B2C), is no longer a purely U.S. phenomenon. For example, Internet sales in the United Kingdom in 2004 totaled £71.1 billion in 2004, an increase of 81 percent from 2003, while purchases by consumers totaled £18.1 billion in 2004, a tripling in three years. On the other hand, the European Union had notably less e-commerce activity, when one excludes the United Kingdom. Thus contrast the thriving business to consumer growth in the United Kingdom and the United States with the astonishingly low numbers in the first quarter of 2003—in France of just 75 million euros and in Spain of a mere 40 million euros. Obviously the story of e-commerce is one of mixed success, which indicates that the barriers to its growth are no longer technological, but the economic, legal, social, and perhaps even cultural infrastructure needed to support it.

As this illustrates, the basis of e-commerce is the extraordinary power of the Internet as a transformative force not just on business and the economy, but of the human imagination itself. It serves not just as a medium for the communication of information, but for bringing together like-minded people with a degree of transparency and economy never contemplated before. The above works on the assumption that many heads are better than one: that information that is aggregated through evolution is more than the sum of its parts. The same is true of e-commerce. At its most basic, e-commerce is simply an "electronic storefront" that replicates the printed catalog of the pre–Internet age. At its most innovative, though, e-commerce makes full use of the power of the Internet to create a unique type of commerce that has never existed before.

The quintessential example of the latter is eBay (http://www.ebay.com), which began, as its name suggests, as an online extension of the familiar American tradition of the garage sale. But it rapidly grew to become an institution because of the realization that this was a mechanism for people with even the most esoteric tastes to meet and exchange with each other for profit in a way that was not feasible, let alone economic, before. Today it is the site of choice for anyone looking for the most unlikely of items that previously could be found only by searching through obscure shops. But eBay is far more than a boon for collectors, as it exploits a key driver of e-commerce: the economic externality of the network effect.

NETWORK EFFECT

When a good or service possesses a network effect, then its value to a consumer depends on the number of other consumers who also purchase that item. Indeed, Metcalfe's law states that the total value of a good or service that possesses a network effect is roughly proportional to the square of the number of customers already owning that good or using that service. When eBay brings together potential consumers for one product, then they also serve as a potential market for other products. One consequence of this effect is that there is a tendency for a natural monopoly to be created, with anyone wishing to auction a product having little to gain and a lot to lose from going to an auction site other than the one with the most customers. EBay is now widely used by large businesses for B2B, as well as by auction houses for rare art and such high-value items as automobiles, boats, and even real estate, a far cry from its garage-sale origins.

Many dot-coms during the Internet boom of the 1990s claimed to be exploiting network effects, even to the extent of sacrificing current profits in order to buy the "eyeballs" needed to reach a critical mass of users. While much of that turned out to be illusory, there is little doubt that network effects are a fundamental driver of e-commerce, taking advantage of the Internet's abolition of time and distance to bring together large numbers of customers in one place. Sites such as Amazon.com take that effect into account when they use buyer recommendations as the selling point for their products. Allowing for the inclusion of such comments creates an online community in which potential buyers and owners can compare experiences. Similar practices are used to police buyers and sellers on eBay, or to rank the integrity of sites and products on epinions.com, illustrating again the tremendous variety of the Internet when driving commerce.

A MAINSTAY OF THE ECONOMY

As e-commerce has matured and become ubiquitous, it has attracted attention as a mainstay of the economy rather than as a novelty. Thus e-commerce sales are watched as closely as in-store sales for the health of the retail economy, with the traditional "black Friday" (the day after Thanksgiving) sales being followed by the "black Monday" the following week when workers allegedly use their office Internet connections to do their holiday shop-

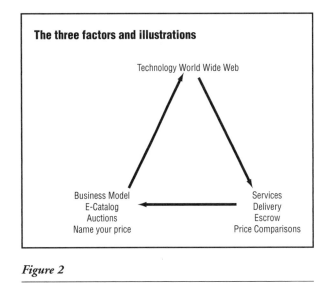

The three factors and illustrations

Technology World Wide Web

Business Model
E-Catalog
Auctions
Name your price

Services
Delivery
Escrow
Price Comparisons

Figure 2

ping online. Moreover, e-commerce is now the subject of extensive academic research, which is archival rather than speculative as it was in the late 1990s.

One of the most interesting findings of this research is that relating to why consumers buy books from Amazon. Professor Erik Brynjolfsson of the Massachusetts Institute of Technology has shown that the reason is not predominantly lower prices. Rather it is the variety of books that Amazon sells, especially of hard-to-find titles that dwarf on all dimensions what can be found at even the largest brick-and-mortar bookstore. "[Consumers] got about 10 times as much value from the selection as they got from the lower prices and competition.... more value was created from the increased choice and selection," said Professor Brynjolfsson (quoted in Postel, 2004, p. C11).

In other words, value comes not just from the lower prices that more transparent competition allows on the Internet, but from the combination of greater choice and easy searching. These effects, Internet-based versions of economies of scale and scope, undoubtedly exist for many other e-commerce applications, from business-to-business marketplaces to online recruiting, music downloads, and even Internet dating. Evidently the dot-com collapse in 2000 has fulfilled its Darwinian purpose in winnowing out from e-commerce those firms that had no coherent business plan for the Internet, leaving behind firms that have a compelling logic in being online.

B2B E-COMMERCE

Although this discussion has focused thus far on examples from B2C, businesses are some of the most highly valued users of eBay and even Amazon. It needs to be kept in mind that B2B is really where all the action is, even if it does not receive the publicity of B2C. In 2003, 94.3 percent of all e-commerce activity in the United States was B2B, with a figure of 75 percent for the United Kingdom in 2004.

Businesses have found the Internet the ideal platform for conducting supply-chain management, fostering competition in suppliers, and reaching their sophisticated business buyers. This is especially the case since in today's economy what firms are mainly selling to each other is information, not just in the case of services such as banking and digital applications, but even when the product concerned is a physical product; the real value added comes from optimizing price and specification, as opposed to the physical transfer of the product. That is the role of the huge B2B marketplaces created by large companies, or even entire industries, which can be roughly described as eBay's for businesses (indeed, many firms have simply outsourced to eBay itself).

SEE ALSO *E-Marketing*

BIBLIOGRAPHY

Electronic commerce. (n.d.). Retrieved February 17, 2006, from Wikipedia Web site: http://en.wikipedia.org/wiki/Electronic_commerce

Metcalfe's useful equation. (n.d.) Retrieved November 11, 2005, from Killer-apps Web site: http://www.killer-apps.com/contents/booktour/metcalfes_useful_equation.htm

Postel, V. (2004, April 22). Selection in ranks above price among the benefits of shopping online. *The New York Times,* p. C11.

U.K. National Statistics. (2006, February 9). Information and communication technology activity of UK businesses, 2004. Retrieved February 17, 2006, from http://www.statistics.gov.uk/downloads/theme_economy/ecommerce_report_2004.pdf

U.S. Department of Commerce. (2005, May 11). E-stats. Retrieved February 17, 2006, from http://www.census.gov/eos/www/papers/2003/2003finaltext.pdf

The U.S. government's framework for electronic commerce. (1997). Retrieved March 1, 2006, from http://www.technology.gov/digeconomy/framewrk.htm

VisaEurope. (2003, May 20). Online spending in Europe doubles [Press release]. Retrieved February 17, 2006, from http://www.visaeurope.com/pressandmedia/press154_pressreleases.html

Miklos A. Vasarhelyi
Michael Alles

ELECTRONIC MAIL

Electronic mail (e-mail) is mail that is sent electronically from one electronic mailbox to another. E-mail differs from postal mail in the areas of speed of delivery, privacy, security, and access. Other issues relating to e-mail include organization, etiquette, junk mail and fraud attempts, legal matters, and trends.

SPEED OF DELIVERY

One of the biggest attractions of e-mail is the speed with which a message may be sent. When a message is sent from a computer in Houston, Texas, it arrives instantly in London and New Zealand. E-mail has been a true factor in making the global business environment a smaller place. A virtual team can communicate across the globe. Sending an e-mail message across the ocean before leaving work one day can result in a response from another time zone before one's next workday begins.

Postal mail requires several days for a message to arrive and additional time for a response. The speed of delivery of e-mail has had negative effects as well as positive ones. For example, those sending the message expect a very fast response. Frequently if the response is not fast enough, a second message is sent asking why there has been no response. So, patience in communication has become an issue. Because a fast response is demanded, sometimes the response is rushed, incomplete, and less tactful and or politically polished than it should be. Advantages of e-mail are the elimination of telephone tag plus the convenience of reading and responding to e-mail at the recipient's convenience.

As the popularity and expectations for e-mail have increased, so have the daily demands to read and respond to e-mail. Many employees find that they spend hours each day responding to their e-mail.

Instant Messaging. Instant messaging (IM) is frequently viewed as the upstart, even speedier cousin of e-mail. Those who use IM often employ abbreviations and codes to quickly get their messages across. The advantage of IM is the interactive nature of the messages, which work much like a written telephone call. While early IM systems were not always linked to the corporate communication paths, IM was considered the same as a conversation. Employees were not necessarily careful with what they said or how they said it. Now, however, companies have the ability to capture IM if they wish, so it is no longer a quick, safe way to complain about the boss or colleagues.

PRIVACY

Mail from the U.S. Postal Service comes with a guarantee of privacy. If a third party opens mail intended for someone else without the addressee's permission, that person has committed a crime punishable by law. No such privacy exists in e-mail. Courts have held that employees sending e-mail on company computers, with company accounts and software, and using company time have no expectations of privacy. Companies feel free to examine an employee's e-mail. In addition, e-mail has been summoned on court cases to prove work environment status.

Employees should never write anything in an e-mail that they would not say face-to-face to the concerned parties. E-mail is not like private letters that are received in the mail, torn up, and thrown away. E-mail is backed up, placed on other servers, and will be retrievable for a long time. Also, the person to whom e-mail is sent may decide to forward it to others without the sender's permission.

SECURITY

E-mail is now available in many venues. Checking e-mail on office or home computers is no longer the only option. E-mail can be transmitted to personal digital assistants, pagers, and cell phones. These media frequently use wireless networks. Wireless signals have more security issues than wired systems. Just as a cell phone call can be intercepted and heard by others, so can the related e-mail be compromised. When dealing with issues that should be secure, how the e-mail will be received should be considered. Most companies would not want third parties to be able to easily glance at a cell phone display and see proprietary company information.

ACCESS

E-mail is of value only if it is sent to a valid e-mail address where it will be reviewed by the person one is attempting to contact. Addresses may be changed and if an address is not current, the e-mail will not be delivered, resulting in a communication delay. One cannot communicate effectively if one is missing e-mail addresses or has bad addresses, the other parties do not use e-mail, or the other parties are not checking their e-mail.

ORGANIZATION

In order to keep up with a barrage of e-mail arriving daily, it is a good idea to organize one's e-mail. E-mail is received in chronological order, but most e-mail software will let users sort the chronological list by name of sender or subject. This way users can find that message they remember getting but cannot see in their mailbox at first glance. Another option is to move messages one is finished with to specific folders. Users can even designate that certain incoming messages be sent directly to a folder or mailbox rather than their inbox. Users do have to remember to check their e-mail in that special folder or mailbox, though.

Handling e-mail in a prompt and effective manner is increasingly important as the volume of e-mail continues to build. Accuracy in responses, as well as attention to important message details such as grammar and spelling, will indicate professionalism in corporate communication.

ETIQUETTE

When communicating with e-mail, etiquette is an important convention that should not be overlooked. E-mail lends itself naturally to brief messages. A message can be so brief, however, that it is terse and may seem both rude and abrupt to the receiver. Tone, therefore, is an important issue of etiquette. This is especially true in communicating with international audiences who may expect a more extensive exchange of courtesies in the e-mail message.

Correct use of e-mail etiquette includes such courtesies as asking a message sender for permission before forwarding the sender's message to others, using an appropriate and clearly understood subject line, and sending messages only to people who have an interest in receiving them.

Some message senders use emoticons or symbols to indicate nonverbal communication cues, for instance, :-) (which indicates happiness). Reviews are mixed on whether emoticons are acceptable in the business use of e-mail.

JUNK MAIL AND FRAUD ATTEMPTS

Along with receiving a large volume of e-mail is the issue of junk mail including spam, viruses, and phishing. Spam is unsolicited e-mail that is delivered usually in mass mailings to the electronic mailbox. The sheer volume of spam can cause systems to crash. In 2003 the CAN-SPAM Act was passed in an attempt to better regulate spam. Spam filters have been taking a bite out of spam by excluding suspicious e-mail messages and sending them to a quarantine area. The e-mail reader should go to the quarantine area periodically to see if important messages have been sent there by accident. Because the spam filter looks for a wide variety of subject lines, care must be taken to include an explicit and appropriate subject line. Using something such as "hi" or "it's me" might send messages straight to the receiver's quarantine box.

Viruses can be attached to e-mail messages, usually through attachments. A good plan is to scan attachments with a current virus scanner before opening any that might be suspicious. As more computer users use strong antivirus programs, this issue may become less important in the future.

Phishing occurs when a message is received that purports to be from an entity e-mail readers would know, such as their banks, popular shopping sites, or auction services. If the message is not examined closely, the screen image and presentation may seem authentic. The message is phishing for information by trying to get users to reveal valuable personal information such as account numbers and passwords that the phisher can use for schemes involving fraud and identity theft.

LEGAL ISSUES

Increasingly, e-mail is becoming involved when legal issues arise. When a company is the subject of a lawsuit, a subpoena for e-mail and IM is often served. Having a responsible program to track and save e-mail and IM is critical to a company's success. Some companies have even made the decision to outsource the management of electronic resources including e-mail and IM to ensure that an acceptable program exists in case of legal issues. Companies should have policies concerning electronic communication so that employees will know what kind of messages are acceptable and what are not. Regular training for employees will result in increasing quality of messages.

TRENDS

Trends in e-mail include better filters and restrictions on spam in the workplace, control and accountability for both e-mail and newer technology such as IM, an escalation in the demand to supply e-mail records when legal issues arise, and more ways to use e-mail in the future. The ability to manage e-mail effectively will be increasingly important as a workplace skill.

SEE ALSO *Communication Channels; Ethics in Information Processing; Writing Skills in Business*

BIBLIOGRAPHY

Brandt, A. (2005). Phishing anxiety may make you miss messages. *PC World, 23*(10), 34.

Dvorak, J. C. (2005). Truth, magic, and the Internet. *PC Magazine, 24*(15), 77.

FTC: Subject-line labeling ineffective against spam. (2005, September/October). *The Information Management Journal, 39*(5), 11.

Gonsalves, Antone (2005, June 3). High-tech industry is unresponsive to online customers. *InternetWeek.*

Greenemeier, Larry (2005, July 27). E-mail analysis is key to catching terrorists and corporate crooks. *Information Week.*

Greer, D. (2005). Locking down IM. *Computerworld, 39*(35), 31–32.

How outsourcing e-mail management helps financial services companies. (2005, June 1). *Business Credit, 107*(6), 42–43.

Pomeroy, Ann (2004, November). Business "fast and loose" with e-mail, IMs-study. *HR Magazine, 49*(11), 32–34.

Vijayan, J. (2005). Training needed to halt "spear-phishing" attacks. *Computerworld, 39*(34), 6.

Winning the war on spam. (2005). *Economist, 376*(8440), 50–51.

Marsha L. Bayless

E-MARKETING

E-marketing is a process of planning and executing the conception, distribution, promotion, and pricing of products and services in a computerized, networked environment, such as the Internet and the World Wide Web, to facilitate exchanges and satisfy customer demands. It has two distinct advantages over traditional marketing. E-marketing provides customers with more convenience and more competitive prices, and it enables businesses to reduce operational costs.

As businesses offer e-marketing and online shopping, customers can get market information from their computers or cell phones and buy goods or find services without leaving home twenty-four hours a day and seven days a week (24/7). They can read ads on the Web or from e-mail, get e-coupons, view pictures of goods, compare prices, and make purchases with a few clicks of their mouse, saving the time and money it would take to shop in person at a brick-and-mortar store. At the same time, e-businesses can reduce costs in distribution channels and physical store space and thus pass the savings on to customers.

To make e-marketing effective and efficient, managers of e-businesses need to know online customer behavior, e-marketing techniques, costs and benefits of e-marketing over traditional marketing, and pitfalls and legal issues of e-marketing. A discussion of each of these aspects follows.

ONLINE CUSTOMER BEHAVIOR

In the late 1990s online shoppers were mainly well-educated, high-earning, twenty- to forty-year-olds. By 2003 online shoppers represented a broader demographic, with an average age of forty-four years and an average annual household income of $65,000. Of these shoppers, 50 percent were female and 50 percent were college graduates. According to a 2004 report from the U.S. Department of Commerce, in 2003 searching for product/service information was the second most popular online activity after e-mailing or instant messaging and 77 percent of U.S. Internet users age fifteen and older shopped online. E-customers researched products and services that they were considering for purchase online. Their final purchases, however, may not have been made online.

Several reasons are behind the reluctance to purchase online. Studies published in 2003 and 2004 reported that 25 percent of e-commerce sites do not display a phone number clearly on the customer service page; 49 percent of online shoppers could not readily find the answers to a question; and 88 percent of shoppers abandoned their online shopping carts before reaching the checkout. The Yankee Group, a Boston-based research firm, indicated that up to the first quarter of 2003, the average conversion rate from shopping in brick-and-mortar stores to buying on e-commerce sites was just 10 percent.

E-customers' most serious concern is security and privacy, followed by price, delivery cost, return policy, customer service, site design, navigation, one-click shopping, and personalization. E-marketers must assure customers that their sites use cybercrime-proof systems to protect e-customer information and clearly display the security/privacy statement on their sites. Competitive prices, discounts, e-coupons, free delivery, and standard return policies motivate initial online purchases and repeat purchases. Nevertheless, requiring too many mouse clicks for navigating on a site, a lack of easily accessible help, technical difficulties, and requesting too much customer information for purchasing goods often causes shoppers to abandon their online shopping carts before reaching the checkout.

E-MARKETING TECHNIQUES

E-marketing techniques can be broken down to pull and push marketing. Pull marketing is a passive technique by which online shoppers take the initiative requesting specific information on the Web. Search engines, product/service advertising, e-coupons, and e-samples are part of pull marketing. For example, e-marketers can register their e-commerce sites, products, and services with search engines such as Google and or Yahoo, thereby enabling online shoppers to search for product/service information using Google or Yahoo and link to their sites. Similarly, e-marketers can also register their e-coupons and e-samples with e-coupon sites such as ecoupons.com and e-sample sites such as yes-its-free.com.

Push marketing is a proactive technique that enables e-marketers to "push" their product/service information to Web visitors or shoppers without their requesting it. Banner advertising, pop-up advertising, e-mail promotion, and spamming belong to push marketing. For instance, e-marketers can rent designated space from Internet service providers such as America Online or MSN for their banner or pop-up ads. Using animated graphics, appealing messages, and links, e-marketers try to lure visitors to their sites to buy their products or services. Many Internet users, however, find such ads annoying and employ software that blocks pop-ups and banner ads.

E-mail promotion is widely used by e-marketers to send new product/service information to their registered customers. For example, airline companies periodically e-mail their registered customers about their e-fares and promotional vacation packages. Spamming refers to sending millions of e-mail promotions to recipients who have never asked for the information. These recipients' e-mail addresses are often purchased or swapped with other businesses. Spamming is at best unethical and at worst illegal.

COSTS AND BENEFITS OF E-MARKETING

E-marketing can offer more competitive prices than traditional marketing because e-marketing reduces costs by not having to maintain physical store space and by strategically placing distribution centers throughout the country. Second, because the Internet is available 24/7, e-marketing enables shoppers to search for product/service information and buy goods at their convenience, not just when the store is open. Third, research indicates that the cost of Internet-based promotion is one-fourth of traditional promotion, because it does not incur the costs of paper, printing, handling, and mailing. Fourth, e-marketing enables buyers to custom-build products such as shoes, clothes, computers, and automobiles on the Web, options often not available in stores.

PITFALLS AND LEGAL ISSUES

Failures and successes in e-marketing have shown that when marketing goods online results in distribution, storing, or shipping and handling costs higher than the value of the goods, an exclusively online enterprise may be headed for a short life. In addition, e-marketers need to be aware of cultural pitfalls when designing e-commerce sites for foreign markets.

E-marketers must operate their businesses in compliance with numerous laws. For example, e-marketers are responsible for protecting customers' privacy; without customers' permission, they are not legally allowed to share or sell customers' information to a third party. Copying other businesses' Web information for commercial use is also in violation of copyright law.

SEE ALSO *Cyber Crime; Electronic Commerce*

BIBLIOGRAPHY

Awad, Elias M. (2004). *Electronic commerce: From vision to fulfillment* (2nd ed.). Boston: Pearson/Prentice Hall.

Strauss, Judy, El-Ansary, Adel, and Frost, Raymond (2005). *E-marketing*. Upper Saddle River, NJ: Pearson/Prentice Hall.

Zhao, Jensen J. (2003). *Web design and development for e-business*. Upper Saddle River, NJ: Prentice Hall.

Zhao, Jensen J., Whitesel, Joel A., Alexander, Melody W., et al. (2004). The quality of *Fortune 500* B2C e-commerce Web sites: An experiential assessment by online shoppers. *Issues in information systems, 5*(1), 359–365.

Jensen J. Zhao

EMPLOYEE ASSISTANCE PROGRAMS

The term employee assistance program (EAP) refers to a program that provides business and industry with the means of identifying employees whose job performance is negatively affected by personal or job-related problems. The EAP arranges for structured assistance to solve those problems, with the goal of reestablishing the employee's effective job performance. The services of an EAP may be contracted, or the program may be an employer's own creation, designed to fit the unique needs of a company. EAPs typically provide professional, confidential, no- or low-cost assistance for employees with personal problems.

EAPs help employers by identifying troubled workers, by either supervisory referrals or self-referrals. Each referred employee is assessed, and a plan of action is designed to suit his or her needs. The ability to uncover the employee's primary problem is required. The goal is to enable the employees to work again at peak levels. An effective EAP requires a knowledge of resources available in the community.

HISTORY

No one knows when the first employer offered counseling and social work services to its employees. But in 1917 Macy's, the New York City department store, opened an office specifically devoted to helping employees deal with personal problems. Metropolitan Life Insurance Company and Western Electric were also pioneers in the field, but it was not until the years immediately following World War II that a limited form of EAP became relatively common.

In those days, Alcoholics Anonymous was a new organization gaining widespread attention. For the first time, alcohol abuse was perceived by business to be a workplace problem, and many companies started alcoholism programs for their workers. These programs were usually staffed by recovering alcoholics who trained supervisors to spot alcoholics by looking for such symptoms as shaking hands, bloodshot eyes, and alcohol on the breath. These early programs produced gratifying results, but they were severely limited because they identified only late-stage problems. Alcoholics in the early stage whose hands

AT&T employee assistance center counselor provides advice to an 18-year employee who has been laid off. **ROB NELSON//TIME LIFE PICTURES/GETTY IMAGES**

did not shake and who did not drink on the job did not receive help.

Today, most EAPs pay close attention to the specific needs of clients. For example, until recently few EAPs dealt with gambling-related issues; but now counselors are being trained to deal with gambling addiction and related problems. A number of companies also have EAPs that offer financial and legal referrals to employees with consumer credit or bankruptcy problems and legal concerns. These services are in addition to assistance offered for emotional, family, work, and substance-abuse problems.

Another area that EAPs frequently deal with is critical incident intervention—helping workers handle deaths, suicides, hostage situations, major accidents, and natural disasters, including fires, earthquakes, mudslides, floods, and hurricanes. Employees often need assistance in dealing with the emotional and physical trauma of these natural disasters.

MODERN PROGRAMS

Organizational development, managed care, workers' compensation, child care, and catastrophic disasters are just a few of the issues that are expanding the scope of today's EAPs. The changes going on in corporate America are tremendous. As a result, the role and scope of the company's employee assistance program has evolved with the times. Some EAPs offer workers professional organizational counseling. This service runs the gamut from counseling work-group members who are having problems getting along with one another to counseling survivors of downsizing on how to handle stress.

Managers may have to terminate good employees as well as difficult ones. Besides the emotional effects, there is also a practical side to letting workers go: There is documentation and a procedure to follow. Human resources staff members are stretched to the limit in some cases.

Many EAPs provide disability management services. Companies today want to complement the traditional disability arrangement with a whole-person approach. In many cases workers' self-esteem is tied to their jobs. As workers sit at home recuperating from injuries or disabilities, they may become bored and depressed. In some cases their disabilities may put financial strains on their families. Therefore, there is a need to supplement the medical care a person is receiving with counseling on issues he or she is facing. The goal is to keep the worker connected to the workplace.

Today's EAPs have grown in size and sophistication. In some businesses EAPs are operated through employee associations. Sometimes professional groups or similar businesses and small industries unite to form a consortium. Although all EAPs aim to help both management

and employees, there are differences in how they do it. Boiled down to the essentials, these differences come under two headings: who is helped and how that help is provided.

SINGLE-ISSUE PROGRAMS

Single-issue programs aim to help only employees impaired by a specific problem. Their focus is clear, and they are generally small enough to cost the employer relatively little. A disadvantage of single-issue programs is that they may become stigmatized because of the negative connotations of terms such as addiction and alcoholism. Some people may be afraid to use the program for fear of being labeled drunks or addicts. Since the per-person cost of an EAP decreases with the number of people who use it, this stigmatization is an important issue to consider. Furthermore, supervisors tend to look only for symptoms of abuse instead of concentrating on declining job performance.

The greatest weakness of single-issue programs is their lack of preventative power. Late-stage alcoholics and addicts have the highest relapse rate and the least chance for permanent recovery. Single-issue programs tend to find these late-stagers, but recognizing those in the early stages for whom help can be most effective is much more difficult.

BROAD-BRUSH EAPS

Broad-brush EAPs offer help to employees suffering from all kinds of problems, including chemical dependency. For example, a broad-brush program may provide crisis-management services for those whose problems can be dealt with over the short term. Sometimes all that is needed is a chance to talk a problem over with a sympathetic listener. The great advantage of broad-brush programs is their ability to uncover drug and alcohol problems in their early stages. Often early-stagers come to their EAP presenting problems that make no mention of alcohol or drugs. At first clients complain about financial trouble, a stressful marriage, or abuse of problem children. It is only after working with a skilled counselor that the truth is revealed: cocaine bankrupting an executive; a marriage in trouble because the wife drinks and the husband enables her; children acting out because they cannot get the nurturing they need from addicted parents.

One disadvantage of broad-brush programs is that they are usually more expensive than single-issue programs. There are, however, ways to minimize costs by designing a program customized to specialized businesses. Costs can be reduced when multiple businesses form an EAP alliance. In the long run, EAPs can save businesses money by making them more efficient and productive, by reducing accidents, by reducing employee absenteeism/turnover, by raising employee morale and decreasing grievances, and by cutting back on the number of unnecessary insurance claims.

MODES OF SERVICE

Today's EAPs differ from their predecessors in the mode of service they deliver. It would be impossible to describe all variations that exist, but a short description of several of the most common varieties will provide some insight.

Some EAPs are just a hotline. Employees are encouraged to call a particular number and ask for help. The EAP provides the names and numbers of local public service agencies that may be able to address employees' personal problems. Alone, this just barely qualifies as employee assistance. However, a hotline in conjunction with other services may prove helpful in attracting fearful employees for whom anonymity is essential. And hotlines can be extremely beneficial when depression is a serious problem.

Other EAPs amount to no more than a single individual in the personnel department or the medical office who can direct an employee off-site on the basis of his or her problem. This is not much better than the hotline, and employees may not go near the office for fear of being labeled. Employees required to report to this office because of poor performance evaluations and fear of losing their livelihoods may complain about the lack of confidentiality.

A few very large companies have elaborate on-site EAP divisions with full staffs, including doctors and nurses. Or several geographically close companies with similar concerns or products may join together to form an EAP consortium that contracts with a consulting EAP organization to provide services to employees from each site.

Most EAP providers emphasize the confidential nature of their services and will give the employer numerical information only, without divulging names of EAP-assisted employees. Otherwise, many employees would be hesitant, if not totally unwilling, to admit a personal problem for fear that it would jeopardize their job status or chances for promotions.

However, there may be situations in which an employer may need to know certain types of information. For example, when an employee is engaged in dangerous duties, supervisory personnel may need to know general information about the employee's condition for safety reasons. Therefore, the employer's promise of confidentiality and privacy to employees is extremely important. Whatever level of confidentiality the employer establishes must be maintained; notice must be given to employees and consent obtained for variances. Also, it is important that an employer give employees clear warnings that such disclosures are permitted. Specific state privacy laws may affect the availability of such information.

Some EAP programs provide services to groups of employees during a crisis. For example, a team of counselors from an EAP may work with an entire department affected by a violent workplace incident.

EAPS CAN DETER VIOLENCE

Stress at home or on the job, burnout, or relationships that have soured can result in violent acts at work. Experts estimate that more than 100,000 incidents of workplace violence occur annually in the United States. The typical workplace killer is a middle-aged man, most likely a loner frustrated by problems on the job with few personal contacts outside the workplace. One study showed men were responsible for 98 percent of all violence committed at work. The average age was 36, and firearms were used 81 percent of the time. Following workplace homicides, one-fourth of the murderers killed themselves.

Workplace violence, whether it involves harassment, threats, or physical attack, is a serious and growing problem for employers. Lack of attention to the issue can mean lost lives, discontent, and fear among employees, as well as tremendous cost to companies.

Corporations without preventive measures are particularly subject to lawsuits and higher costs. The best way to prevent workplace violence is to have an effective employee assistance program. Other precautions companies can take to prevent violence are establishing clear guidelines on appropriate behavior, screening applicants carefully, training employees to identify warning signs, and setting up procedures for managers to respond to cries for help. Companies also should look closely at the procedures they use when they terminate employees. Perhaps most important is maintaining a healthy work environment. It really boils down to one person's relationship with another and whether or not the environment fosters mutual respect.

EXTERNAL PROVIDERS

A unique feature of employee assistance programs is the dual responsibility that its professionals have toward both the companies they work for and the individual workers in those organizations who require assistance. The special responsibilities toward the organization go beyond those that social workers have toward their agencies because the occupational setting also is a client to which they have service obligations. At times this dual responsibility creates ethical dilemmas for practitioners. The very existence of a well-functioning EAP is a major source of assistance to the organization as a whole, not just the individual clients who receive direct services.

Both managers and employee clients expect staff members of in-house EAPs to be especially adept in matching an employee's needs with resources that provide prompt and effective intervention. The depth and thoroughness of the assessment is a means of increasing the probability that key problems will be identified and prioritized accurately. Failure to meet these expectations can adversely affect the credibility of the EAP. As a result, most EAPs devote a significant part of program resources to locating, evaluating, and updating their network of providers. The referral function is distinct from the procedures governing the internal services. Referring is the process of locating one or more providers external to the employer to supply ongoing services to deal with employee concerns. These external resources may assume responsibility for all of a client's needs or they may be ancillary to the work being done in-house by an EAP counselor.

Most employees are not well informed about treatment programs, community agencies, or even self-help groups. EAPs must educate them about available services, their relative benefits, and how these resources are viewed in the community. In addition, clients often need to be encouraged to assume a consumer orientation regarding referral sources. Having to apply for any kind of help is intimidating, and it is difficult for the uninitiated to recognize appropriate or inappropriate requirements. Clients should be told that if they decide a resource is not acceptable they may return to the EAP for other options.

PERSONAL PROBLEMS

People thrive on things they do well. Often it is their work. A happy, healthy worker is likely to be a productive one. Conversely, personal problems can hamper an employee's performance. Sometimes problems can be alleviated quickly, but often the problems extend over long periods of time. The impact on the employee will vary, but there will usually be noticeable change in behavior and attitude. Personal problems are significant hurdles that every person living in today's complex society will confront in one fashion or another.

Employees' personal problems can have many sources. Most can be categorized into one of the following categories: substance abuse, health related, family related, and financial. Almost every adult will deal with one or more of these problems. It is how individuals deal with these problems, and the level of support they receive in addressing the issue, that will determine the intensity of the problem's impact.

SEE ALSO *Employee Benefits*

BIBLIOGRAPHY
Browning, Darrell (1994). "Stamping Out Violence." *Human Resources Executive*, 22-25.

Patrick J. Highland

EMPLOYEE BENEFITS

Employee benefits are compensations given to employees in addition to regular salaries or wages. These compensations are given at the entire or partial expense of the employer. Benefit packages usually make up between 30 and 40 percent of an employee's total compensation for employment, which makes them an important aspect of the terms of employment. While some employee benefits are required by law, many employers offer additional benefits in order to attract and retain quality workers and maintain morale. Some types of benefits are also used as incentives to encourage increased worker productivity.

LEGALLY REQUIRED BENEFITS

While some benefits are offered as incentives to attract workers, some are legally required. For example, employers must provide workers' compensation insurance, which pays the medical bills for job-related injuries and provides an income for employees who become disabled because of a job-related injury. Social Security must be paid by the employer (in addition to the amounts deducted from employees' pay) to help meet employees' retirement needs, and employers must pay for unemployment insurance to compensate workers in the event that their job is eliminated. The Family and Medical Leave Act, passed by Congress in 1993, requires large employers to provide workers with unpaid leave for family or medical emergencies (up to twelve weeks of unpaid, job-protected leave per year). Under this law, employees are guaranteed that they can return to the same or a comparable position and that their health care coverage will be continued during the leave.

TRADITIONAL TYPES OF EMPLOYEE BENEFITS

Because of continually rising health care costs, one of the most desirable types of benefits for employees to have is a health insurance plan. These plans can be set up to cover the individual worker and, in many cases, the worker's family as well; they may or may not include such options as dental, eye, chiropractic, hospital, and other types of health care. Health insurance plans may be provided at no cost to employees, or they may be made available at a more desirable rate than employees could get on their own. The health insurance aspect of a benefit package is often the major deciding factor in whether a person accepts a position with a company. The degree of health insurance is often more important to a potential employee than the salary level, especially when children are involved.

Most benefit plans also include a certain number of paid sick days, personal days, and/or vacation days. Many companies are finding ways of increasing the flexibility of employee benefits. One way to increase flexibility is to group vacation, personal, and sick days into a certain amount of paid time off (PTO). PTO allows employees to take days off—for example, to care for a sick child, observe a religious holiday, or go on vacation—without explanation. The PTO benefit helps employees because their time is more flexible, and it helps employers by maintaining morale and reducing unanticipated absenteeism.

Life insurance and retirement options are another type of benefit many companies offer their employees. These types of benefits often encourage employees to remain with the same company because they do not want to cash in their life insurance or retirement plans. This tends to make employees more loyal to the company because their future is invested with the company. It also gives the employee a feeling of power by having some control over planning for retirement.

EXPANDED TYPES OF EMPLOYEE BENEFITS

While health care, paid time off, and retirement plans are the most common types of benefits employees receive, some companies offer even more types of benefits to help attract and retain employees as well as increase employee morale and improve job performance. One example of this type of benefit is tuition reimbursement, which allows employees to further their education while working. Motivating employees to better themselves at the employer's expense, helps the company keep knowledgeable employees.

With the growing number of single parents and dual-career couples in the work force, many companies have opened day-care facilities in the workplace where employees can feel safe about leaving their children. On-site child care is obviously a very desirable benefit for parents because it allows them to check up on the children, cut down on travel time, and be available in case of an emergency. However, some childless workers feel that this benefit discriminates against them because they get no use out

Retailers like Target offer discounts on merchandise to their employees. **PHOTOGRAPH BY KELLY A. QUIN. THE GALE GROUP.**

of the day-care facility. One way many companies are handling this type of concern is through a cafeteria plan. While there are several different ways to set up a cafeteria plan, such as setting aside pre-tax dollars for medical expenses, one of the most useful ways is to give employees many different benefit options to choose from. Each employee is given a set allowance that can be used toward any benefit the employee chooses, allowing the employees to pick the options that will most benefit them. The cafeteria plan is one fair way to handle benefits for everyone concerned.

Another characteristic of the work force is its increasingly older age. As a result, there are an increasing number of workers with aging parents who need care. Many companies recognize the need for elder care and are providing benefits to help, such as referral services for quality nursing homes and flexible work hours and/or days off so employees can care for aging parents.

Other benefits provided by some employers include credit unions to help employees with financial needs, gym facilities to allow employees to fit exercise into their busy schedules, cafeterias that sell reduced price meals to working employees, and on-site laundry services where employees can have laundry done while they are at work. Making the work environment seem more like a family helps boost employee morale and improve working relationships. Many companies provide uniforms for their employees, so that workers do not have to worry about ruining their own clothing. The uniforms also help with the feeling of unity because everyone in the company is dressed similarly. Because transportation can often be a problem for employees, some companies are even providing transportation options as a benefit to employees. Disney World, in Orlando, Florida, has a shuttle that picks employees up from their living quarters and takes them to work. Corn detasslers meet in a central location and a bus takes them to the site. Sales people are often provided with a company car.

While these types of benefits are meant to attract and retain employees as well as create a positive work environment, some types of employee benefits are used to encourage increased performance. The following are the four main types of benefits used as incentives to encourage employees to exhibit superior performance:

1. *Profit sharing* gives the employee a portion of the company profits. Profit sharing is often done through making shares of company stock part of the employee benefit package. Employees receive a certain number of shares of stock each year, which provides employees an incentive to help the company succeed. This might also be accomplished through a yearly profit-sharing bonus.

2. *Gain sharing* rewards employees for exceeding a predetermined goal by sharing the extra profits. If profits exceed the goal, employees share in the extra profits.

3. *Lump-sum bonuses* are a one-time cash payment based on performance. Lump-sum bonuses may be an annual reward, such as a Christmas bonus, where the purpose is to share profits with the employees, and thus motivate them.

4. *Pay for knowledge* rewards employees for continuing their education and/or learning new job tasks. The more education or experience an employee has, the higher he/she moves up on the pay-for-knowledge pay scale. Pay for knowledge is an incentive for employees to continue their education because it results in immediate rewards on the job.

PERKS

In addition to what are typically considered employee benefits, many employers also offer perks to their employees. Typically limited to employees in management positions, these perks include such benefits as country club or health club memberships, a company car, special parking privileges at work, tickets for sporting events, first-class travel accommodations, and generous expense accounts. However, certain types of perks are also being extended to employees in many different types of positions. One type of perk that is common in many retail stores is an employee discount on merchandise bought from the place of employment. For example, Dayton Hudson's Target stores offer a 10 percent discount to employees and their immediate families when purchasing merchandise from any Target store. Employees of local movie theaters often receive free movie tickets as a perk, while many restaurant employees receive free or reduced-price meals. By offering employees such perks, the company is providing a strong incentive for employees to continue working there.

FLEXIBLE WORK PLANS

A flexible work plan is another type of employee benefit that has been proven to have a positive influence on employee productivity, attendance, and morale. A flexible work plan allows employees to adjust their working conditions within constraints set by the company and may include such options as flex-time, a compressed workweek, job sharing, and home-based work. Flex-time involves adjusting an employee's daily time schedule; it can be as simple as allowing a worker to come into work an hour earlier and leave an hour earlier than the normal 8-to-5 workday. Usually there are some time constraints set up by the company, but employees who work within those constraints can basically set their own schedules. A compressed workweek involves working longer hours each day for fewer days than the normal Monday-through-Friday workweek. For example, at many businesses employees work ten-hour days, four days a week.

Job sharing allows two or more people to divide the tasks of one job. It allows the same consistency as a full-time person, because the work is simply divided among the people who share the job responsibility. Job sharing is popular among people who only want to work part time but want a job with full-time responsibilities. These types of people include older workers, retirees, students, and working parents. Home-based work programs allow employees to perform their jobs at home instead of in an office setting. These people are often known as telecommuters, because they commute to work through electronic mail, faxes, and other types of telecommunications. Home-based work is popular with disabled workers, elderly workers, parents with small children, and workers who have had to relocate far away from the workplace because of a spouse's job change. Through home-based work, all of these types of employees are able to take care of personal and family responsibilities while maintaining and enjoying their job and/or career.

CONCLUSION

It should be noted that the various types of benefits offered to employees can depend greatly on the size and type of the business as well as its geographic location. For example, a small business might be unable to afford to provide complete health care coverage for employees because there are not enough employees to divide the risk. This would cause the cost of the insurance to be high. On the other hand, a large company may not want to give all 1,000 employees a turkey for Thanksgiving because of the enormity of the undertaking. A video store would be more likely to give employees free movie rentals, while a restaurant would offer employees free or reduced-price meals. Employee benefits may be the major deciding factor for many people when choosing a company for employment. In order to attract and retain the best-quality employees, companies must be willing to offer flexible and extensive types of benefits to meet various employee needs.

SEE ALSO *Employee Compensation*

BIBLIOGRAPHY

Boone, Louis E., and Kurtz, David L. (2006). *Contemporary Business*. Mason, OH: Thomson/South-Western.

Bounds, Gregory M., and Lamb, Charles W., Jr. (1998). *Business*. Cincinnati, OH: South-Western College Publishing.

French, Wendell L. (2003). *Human Resources Management*. Boston: Houghton Mifflin.

Jenks, James M., and Zevnik, Brian (1993). *Employee Benefits Plain and Simple*. New York: Collier.

Madura, Jeff (2004). *Introduction to Business*. Belmont, CA: Thomson/South-Western.

Nickels, William G., McHugh, James M., and McHugh, Susan M. (2005). *Understanding Business* (7th ed.). Boston, MA: McGraw-Hill/Irwin.

Pfeffer, Jeffery (1994). *Competitive Advantage Through People*. Boston, MA: Harvard Business School Press.

Pride, William M., Hughes, Robert J., and Kapoor, Jack R. (2002). *Business* (7th ed.). Boston: Houghton Mifflin.

Marcy Satterwhite

EMPLOYEE COMPENSATION

In exchange for job performance and commitment, an employer offers rewards to employees. Adequate rewards and compensations potentially attract a quality work force, maintain the satisfaction of existing employees, keep quality employees from leaving, and motivate them in the workplace. A proper design of reward and compensation systems requires careful review of the labor market, thorough analysis of jobs, and a systematic study of pay structures.

There are a number of ways of classifying rewards. A commonly discussed dichotomy is intrinsic versus extrinsic rewards. Intrinsic rewards are satisfactions one gets from the job itself, such as a feeling of achievement, responsibility, or autonomy. Extrinsic rewards include monetary compensation, promotion, and tangible benefits.

Compensation frequently refers to extrinsic, monetary rewards that employees receive in exchange for their work. Usually, compensation is composed of the base wage or salary, any incentives or bonuses, and other benefits. Base wage or salary is the hourly, weekly, or monthly pay that employees receive. Incentives or bonuses are rewards offered in addition to the base wage when employees achieve a high level of performance. Benefits are rewards offered for being a member of the company and can include paid vacation, health and life insurance, and retirement pension.

A company's compensation system must include policies, procedures, and rules that provide clear and unambiguous determination and administration of employee compensation. Otherwise, there can be confusion, diminished employee satisfaction, and potentially costly litigation.

DETERMINANTS OF COMPENSATION

Fair and adequate compensation is critical to motivating employees attracting high-potential employees, and retaining competent employees. Compensation has to be fair and equitable among all workers in the same company (internal equity). Internal equity can be achieved when pay is proportionate to the individual employee's qualifications and contributions to a company. On the other hand, compensation also has to be fair and equitable in comparison to the external market (external equity). If a company pays its employees below the market rate, it may lose competent employees. In determining adequate pay for employees, a manager must consider the three major factors: the labor market, the nature and scope of the job, and characteristics of the individual employee.

Potential employees are recruited from a certain geographic area—the labor market. The actual boundary of a labor market varies depending on the type of job, company, and industry. For example, an opening for a systems analyst at IBM may attract candidates from across the country, whereas a secretarial position at an elementary school may attract candidates only from the immediate local area of the school.

Pay for a job even within the same labor market may vary widely because of many factors, such as the industry, type of job, cost of living, and location of the job. Compensation managers must be aware of these differences. To help compensation managers understand the market rate of labor, a compensation survey is conducted. A compensation survey obtains data regarding what other firms pay for specific jobs or job classes in a given geographic market. Large companies periodically conduct compensation surveys and review their compensation system to assure external equity. There are professional organizations that conduct compensation surveys and provide their analysis to smaller companies for a fee.

Several factors are generally considered in evaluating the market rate of a job. They include the cost of living of the area, union contracts, and broader economic conditions. Urban or metropolitan areas generally have a higher cost of living than rural areas. Usually, in calculating the real pay, a cost-of-living allowance (COLA) is added to the base wage or salary. Cost-of-living indexes are published periodically in major business journals. During an economically depressed period, the labor supply usually exceeds the demand in the labor market, resulting in lower labor rates.

The characteristics of an individual employee are also important in determining compensation. An individual's job qualifications, abilities and skills, prior experiences, and even willingness to work in hardship conditions are determining factors. Within the reasonable range of a market rate, companies offer additional compensation to attract and retain competent employees.

In principle, compensation must be designed around the job, not the person. Person-based pay frequently

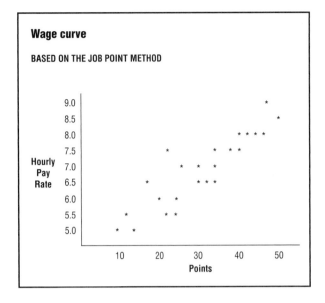

Figure 1

results in discriminatory practices, which violates Title VII of the Civil Rights Act, and job-based compensation is the employer's most powerful defense in court. For job-based compensation, management must conduct a systematic job analysis, identifying and describing what is happening on the job. Each job must be carefully examined to list the necessary tasks and actions, identify skills and abilities required, and establish desirable behaviors for successful completion of the job.

With complete and comprehensive data about all the jobs, job analysts must conduct systematic comparisons of them and determine their relative worth. Numerous techniques have been developed for the analysis of relative worth, including the simple point method, job classification method, job ranking method, and the factor comparison method.

Information resulting from the comprehensive job analysis will be used for establishing pay or wage grades. Assume that twenty-five jobs range from 10 to 50 points in their job scores based on the job point method. All twenty-five of these jobs are reviewed carefully for their relative worth and plotted on Figure 1. The x-axis represents job points and the ordinate (y-axis) represents relative worth or wage rates. Once a manager can identify fair and realistic wages of two or more jobs, desirably top and bottom ones, then all the rest can be prorated along the wage curve in the diagram.

In order to simplify the administration of a wage structure, similar jobs in the approximate cluster are grouped together into a class or grade for pay purpose. Figure 2 shows how twenty-five jobs are grouped into five pay grades. Employees move up in their pay within each grade, typically by seniority. Once a person hits the top pay in the grade, he or she can only increase the pay by moving to a higher grade. Under certain unusual circumstances, it is possible for an outstanding performer in a lower grade to be paid more than a person at the bottom of the next-highest level.

INNOVATIONS IN COMPENSATION SYSTEMS

As the market becomes more dynamic and competitive, companies are trying harder to improve performance. Since companies cannot afford to continually increase wages by a certain percentage, they are introducing many innovative compensation plans tied to performance. Several of these plans are discussed in this section.

Incentive Compensation Plan. Incentive compensation pays proportionately to employee performance. Incentives are typically given in addition to the base wage; they can be paid on the basis of individual, group, or plant-wide performance. While individual incentive plans encourage competition among employees, group or plant-wide incentive plans encourage cooperation and direct the efforts of all employees toward achieving overall company performance.

Skill-Based or Knowledge-Based Compensation. Skill-based pay is a system that pays employees based on the skills they possess or master, not for the job they hold. Some managers believe that mastery of certain sets of skills leads to higher productivity and therefore want their employees to master a series of skill sets. As employees gain one skill and then another, their wage rate goes up until they have mastered all the skills. Similar to skill-based pay is knowledge-based pay. While skill-based pay evolved in the manufacturing sector, pay-for-knowledge developed in the service sector (Henderson, 1997). For example, public school teachers with a bachelor's degree receive the lowest rate of pay, those with a master's degree receive a higher rate, and those with a doctorate receive the highest.

Team-Based Compensation. As many companies introduce team-based management practices such as self-managed work teams, they begin to offer team-based pay. Recognizing the importance of close cooperation and mutual development in a work group, companies want to encourage employees to work as a team by offering pay based on the overall effectiveness of the team.

Performance-Based Compensation. In the traditional sense, pay is considered entitlement that employees

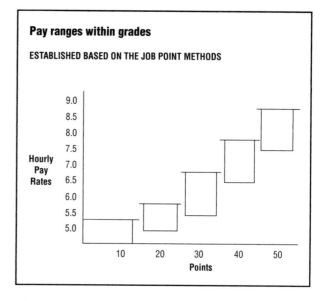

Figure 2

deserve in exchange for showing up at work and doing well enough to avoid being fired. While base pay is given to employees regardless of performance, incentives and bonuses are extra rewards given in appreciation of their extra efforts. Pay-for-performance is a new movement away from this entitlement concept (Milkovich and Newman, 2005). A pay-for-performance plan increases even the base pay—so-called merit increases—to reflect how highly employees are rated on a performance evaluation. Other incentives and bonuses are calculated based on this new merit pay, resulting in substantially more total dollars for highly ranked employee performance. Frequently, employees also receive an end-of-year lump sum bonus that does not build into base pay.

EXECUTIVE COMPENSATION

Recently, people have been concerned with the excessively high level of executive compensation. According to *Business Week*'s annual executive pay survey, in 1997 Sanford Weill, CEO of Travelers Group, collected $7.5 million in salary and bonuses plus $223.2 million for long-term compensation, totaling $230.7 million. In the same year, Roberto Goizueta, CEO of Coca-Cola, earned a total of $111.8 million, including annual salary, bonuses, and long-term compensation. Compensation for the twenty highest-paid executives ranged from $28.4 million to $230 million.

Frequently, executive compensation becomes controversial. Are these compensations excessive? What justifies such a large compensation for executives? Justification of such a large sum of compensation is linked to the company's performance. In fact, a significant portion of executive compensation results from exercising stock options, which were quite valuable in the recent bull market. Yet ordinary working-class Americans are outraged by the shocking contrast in pay raises: annual executive pay at large companies rose 54 percent in 1996, whereas the pay raises of most working-class people were in the 3 percent to 5 percent range during the same period.

An executive compensation package is typically composed of (1) base salary, (2) annual incentives or bonuses, (3) long-term incentives (e.g., stock options), (4) executive benefits (e.g., health insurance, life insurance, and pension plans), and (5) executive perquisites. Considering the high turnover rate of competent executives, offering a competitive salary is crucial in attracting the top candidates.

Frequently, annual bonuses play a more important role than base salary in executive compensations. They are primarily designed to motivate better performance. In order to underscore the importance of financial performance, usually measured by the company's stock price, top executives are offered stock options. Sometimes, exercising stock options yields more cash benefits to executives than do annual salaries.

In addition to monetary compensation, executives enjoy many different types of perquisites, commonly called perks. Such executive perks include the luxurious office with lush carpets, the executive dining room, special parking, use of a company airplane, company-paid membership in high-class country clubs and associations, and executive travel arrangements. Many companies even offer executives tax-free personal perks, including such things as free access to company property, free legal counseling, free home repairs and improvements, and expenses for vacation homes or boats.

Another perk that became popular recently is the so-called golden parachute—a protection plan for executives in the event that they are forced out of the organization. Such severance frequently results from a merger or hostile takeover of the company. The golden parachute provides either a significant one-time sum to the departing executive or a guaranteed executive position in the newly merged company.

SEE ALSO *Employee Benefits*

BIBLIOGRAPHY

Henderson, Richard I. (2006). *Compensation Management in a Knowledge-Based World* (7th ed.). Upper Saddle River, NJ: Pearson/Prentice Hall.

Henderson, Richard I. (1994). *Compensation Management: Rewarding Performance* (6th ed.). Englewood Cliffs, NJ: Prentice Hall.

Klein, Andrew L. (1996). "Validity and Reliability for Competency-Based Systems: Reducing Litigation Risks." *Compensation and Benefits Review*, 28(4): 31-37.

Milkovich, George T., Newman, Jerry M., and Milkovich, Carolyn (1996). *Compensation* (8th ed.). New York: McGraw-Hill/Irwin.

Pauline, George B. (1997, March/April). "Executive Compensation and Changes in Control: A Search for Fairness." *Compensation and Benefits Review* 29: 30-40.

Reingold, Jennifer, and Borrus, Amy. (1997, May 12). "Even Executives Are Wincing at Executive Pay." *Business Week*, 40-41.

Reingold, Jennifer, and Melcher, Richard A. (1998, April 21). "Executive Pay." *Business Week*, 58-66.

Lee Wonsick Lee

EMPLOYEE DISCIPLINE

Discipline refers to the actions imposed by an organization on its employees for failure to follow the organization's rules, standards, or policies. Traditional approaches to discipline, based on punishment, are known to promote adversarial relationships between leaders and followers. A more effective approach now being used by many companies recognizes good performance and encourages employee commitment to the organization and its goals. Once employees see the discrepancy between actual and expected performance, the burden is on the employee to change. Even with more positive approaches to discipline, organizations still need to have some form of disciplinary procedure, whether formal or informal, that carries successively stiffer penalties for repeated or more serious offenses.

ESTABLISHING AND COMMUNICATING WORK RULES

A first step in the disciplinary procedure is to establish work rules that are in line with the organization's goals or objectives. These work rules become the basis for disciplinary actions when the rules are broken. They are generally established jointly by management, the organization's human resources unit, and employees, who should have an opportunity for input to ensure that rules are fair and can reasonably be followed. Work rules are directly related to work behavior and productivity. Employees who continually violate the rules are candidates for a disciplinary procedure.

Employees must know the rules that have been established. Even though employees might have had input in the development of the rules, it is the employer who creates the final version. The organization's work rules should be presented in a printed format, and each employee should be given a copy. This is usually accomplished in the form of an employee handbook. The handbook may have other information, but the work rules are a critical part of it.

In some organizations, these work rules are discussed at meetings, seminars, or training sessions. Employees with long tenure in the organization typically review the rules periodically. Work rules should be reviewed from time to time and, if necessary, revised. If an organization makes major changes in the way it operates because of new equipment, expansion or contraction, or new ownership, it will need to revise its work rules accordingly. Small companies with only a few employees also need to have written work rules. Such companies may not have an employee handbook, but it is still wise for the rules to be written and presented to each employee. Additionally, these rules may be posted in a spot where all employees can read them easily.

EVALUATING EMPLOYEES

In the employee evaluation process, either formal or informal, behaviors requiring disciplinary actions are often revealed. Informal evaluation might occur at all times as supervisors monitor employees. Formal evaluations of each employee should be completed regularly so that deficiencies can be discovered and discussed with the employee. When employees violate work rules, a change of behavior is sought. Although small companies with only a few employees may not use a formal written evaluation, it is still important that employees be evaluated regularly. Small companies may find it easier to take corrective actions than large companies because of the closeness of the supervisor to each of the work situations. In contrast, a supervisor in a large organization might be responsible for from fifty to one hundred or more workers.

When employees break the rules of the organization, they often need assistance to change their behavior so as to operate within the established parameters. Counseling and coaching could be a part of this process, but they usually take place prior to disciplinary actions. If employees change their behavior as a result of disciplinary actions and conform to the established work rules, there is no need for further discipline. If a change in behavior does not occur, then a harsher disciplinary procedure will need to be implemented.

The need to resort to disciplinary procedures may be lessened by (1) smart hiring, using background checks and extensive interviews; (2) performance evaluations with clear goals and objectives; (3) training and development to improve skills and increase performance; and (4) rewarding performance and goal achievement.

USING THE DISCIPLINARY PROCEDURE

Although most employees do follow the organization's rules and regulations, there are times when the employer must use the discipline procedure. Frequent reasons for using the procedure include the following:

Absence from work

Absenteeism

Abusing customers

Abusive language toward supervisor

Assault and fighting among employees

Causing unsafe working conditions

Damage to or loss of machinery or materials

Dishonesty

Disloyalty to employer (includes competing with employer, conflict of interest)

Falsifying company records (including time records, production records)

Falsifying employment application

Gambling

Horseplay

Incompetence (including low productivity)

Insubordination

Leaving place of work (including quitting early)

Loafing

Misconduct during a strike

Negligence

Obscene or immoral conduct

Participation in a prohibited strike

Possession or use of drugs or intoxicants

Profane or abusive language (not toward supervisor)

Refusal to accept a job assignment

Refusal to work overtime

Sleeping on the job

Slowdown

Tardiness

Theft

Threat to or assault of management representative

A formal disciplinary procedure usually begins with an oral warning and progresses through a written warning, suspension, and, ultimately, discharge. Formal disciplinary procedures also outline the penalty for each successive offense and define time limits for maintaining records of each offense and penalty. For instance, tardiness records might be maintained for only a six-month period. Tardiness prior to the six months preceding the offense would not be considered in the disciplinary action. Less formal procedures generally specify the reasons for disciplinary action as being for just or proper cause.

Preventing the disciplinary procedure from progressing beyond the oral warning stage is obviously advantageous to both the employee and management. Discipline should be aimed at correction rather than punishment. If the behavior can be corrected by a friendly talk between the supervisor and the employee, there is less chance that the problem will become a source of bitterness. Formal oral or written warnings are less likely to cause animosity than would a suspension. Of course, the most costly and least acceptable form of discipline is discharge. Disciplinary procedures should be viewed as a means of encouraging employees to abide willingly by the rules and standards of the organization.

The importance of having a procedurally correct performance evaluation system receives constant emphasis. There is a need to adopt procedural due process for performance evaluation systems in order to rate employee job performance accurately because those ratings might be challenged. Legal problems regarding employee disciplinary measures can be prevented by making sure that these measures follow prescribed guidelines, such as:

- Employees are given advance notice of disciplinary action.
- Disciplinary rules are reasonable.
- Offenses are properly investigated.
- Investigations are conducted objectively.
- Rules are enforced equally.
- Penalties are related to the severity of offenses.

LABOR UNION INVOLVEMENT

Numerous employees in the United States are represented by labor unions. In a unionized organization, the supervisor is the primary link between the organization and union members. The supervisor's first responsibility is to uphold the interests of management. At the same time, the supervisor must fulfill the contractual obligations of management and see that the union fulfills its obligations. Collective bargaining between management and the union determines terms of worker contracts, legal documents that cover a specified period of time. Union contracts include provisions for a worker grievance and disciplinary procedures. For example, the union contract may stipulate that an employee can be disciplined for just cause. To fulfill this provision, management must develop a system of discipline that supervisors must follow.

FEATURE OF AN EFFECTIVE DISCIPLINARY PROCESS

A disciplinary procedure is directed against the worker's behavior rather than the person. Key features of an effective process include the following principles of disciplining workers.

1. The length of time between the misconduct and the discipline should be short. For discipline to be most effective, it must be administered as soon as possible, but without making an emotional, irrational decision.

2. Disciplinary action should be preceded by advance warning. Noting rule infractions in an employee's record is not sufficient to support disciplinary action. An employee who is not advised of an infraction is not considered to have been given a warning. Noting that the employee was advised of the infraction and having the employee sign a discipline form are both valid employment practices. Failure to warn an employee of the consequences of repeated violations of a rule is a frequently cited reason for overturning a disciplinary action.

3. Consistency in the discipline procedure is key. Inconsistency lowers morale, diminishes respect for the supervisor, and leads to grievances. Consistency does not mean that an absence of past infractions, long length of service, a good work record, and other mitigating factors should not be considered when applying discipline. However, an employee should feel that under essentially the same circumstances any other employee would have received the same punishment/penalty.

4. Supervisors should take steps to ensure impartiality when applying discipline. The employee should feel that the disciplinary action is a consequence of behavior, not of personality or relationship to the supervisor. The supervisor should avoid arguing with the employee and should administer discipline in a straightforward, calm manner. Administering discipline without anger or apology and then resuming a pleasant relationship aid in reducing the negative effects of discipline.

5. Ordinarily, the supervisor should administer discipline in private. Only in the case of gross insubordination or flagrant and serious rule violations is a public reprimand desirable. Then a public reprimand helps the supervisor regain control of a situation. Even in such situations, however, the supervisor's objective should be to regain control, not to embarrass the employee.

6. The supervisor should warn the employee of the result of repeated violations. Sometimes suggestions to the employee on ways to correct behavior are beneficial. Supervisors should be very reluctant to impose disciplinary suspensions and to discharge workers. Usually, discipline of this degree is reserved for higher levels of management. However, even though supervisors usually lack the power to administer disciplinary suspensions or to discharge workers, they are nearly always the ones who must recommend such action to higher management.

7. Finally, it is necessary to document the action taken and inform others in the organization. Any time an organization takes disciplinary action, it must consider the possibility of an Equal Employment Opportunity complaint. The documentation should be sufficiently detailed that another manager at a similar level in the organization would come to the same conclusions or least see clearly why the decision was made. Sufficient documentation does not mean that every detail of an individual's work needs to be recorded. Rather, the manager should keep accurate records of those elements that significantly contribute to or hamper the work effort. In addition, this information, both positive and negative, should be communicated to the employee either orally or in writing.

SUMMARY

If a company is to have a successful employee disciplinary procedure, both the organization and the manager have important roles to play. In practice, companies assume the responsibility of establishing rules, communicating them to employees, and developing a penalty system for enforcing them. The manager's role in the disciplinary procedure is distinct from that of the organization, yet the two overlap and support each other. Managers are responsible for implementing the organization's discipline procedure. This requires them to do several things: They must compare their organization's rules with employee behavior to determine whether a rule has been broken; they must determine whether they have sufficient proof that the employee did indeed break the rule; they must decide what corrective action should be taken and then take it; and they must document whatever action is taken. To the extent that all managers perform these steps effectively, the disciplinary procedure will be effective and there is a very good chance that employee behavior on the job can be significantly improved.

SEE ALSO *Motivation*

BIBLIOGRAPHY

Benton, Douglas A. (1998). *Applied Human Relations* (6th ed). Upper Saddle River, NJ: Prentice-Hall.

Champagne, Paul J., and McAfee, R. Bruce (1989). *Motivating Strategies for Performance and Productivity*. New York: Quorum Books.

Greenberg, Jerald (1999). *Managing Behavior in Organizations: Science in Service to Practice*. Upper Saddle River, NJ: Prentice-Hall.

Hersey, Paul, Blanchard, Kenneth H., and Johnson, Dewey E. (2001). *Management of Organizational Behavior*. Upper Saddle River, NJ: Prentice Hall.

Rue, Leslie W., and Byars, Lloyd L. (2004). *Supervision: Key Link to Productivity*. Boston: McGraw-Hill.

Whetten, David A., and Cameron, Kim S. (2005). *Developing Management Skills*. Upper Saddle River, NJ: Pearson/Prentice Hall.

Wray, Ralph D., Luft, Roger L., and Highland, Patrick J. (1996). *Fundamentals of Human Relations*. Cincinnati, OH: South-Western Educational Publishing.

Yukl, Gary (2005). *Leadership in Organizations*. Upper Saddle River, NJ: Pearson/Prentice-Hall.

Marcia Anderson

EMPLOYEE MOTIVATION

SEE *Motivation*

ENTREPRENEURSHIP

A subject taught in many high schools and colleges, entrepreneurship is actually defined as "the state of being an entrepreneur." An entrepreneur is an individual who owns, organizes, and manages a business and, in so doing, assumes the risk of either making a profit or losing the investment. According to the Small Business Administration (1999), the total number of businesses in the United States in 1995 was somewhere between 16 million and 24 million, of which approximately 15,000 were large. In 1997, there were an estimated 8.5 million businesses owned by women.

For any business to be successful, an adequate level of funding must be furnished. The amount needed varies according to the scope and nature of the business. Another key factor in the success of an entrepreneurial organization is planning, including planning for the marketing, management, and financial aspects of the business.

From a personal perspective, becoming an entrepreneur is not a simple task. It certainly has its drawbacks. However, it can also be quite rewarding.

BENEFITS AND DRAWBACKS OF ENTREPRENEURSHIP

Choosing to create a new business, or even to purchase an existing one, is a decision that has a far-reaching impact. Long hours, poor pay, and an unclear future are only three of the challenges a budding entrepreneur must face. And, of course, losing everything one invests in a business is a very real risk. In fact, while 885,416 new employer firms were created in 1997, as reported by the U.S. Department of Labor, 857,073 businesses were terminated during the same year, with 53,826 of these being bankruptcies and 83,384 being failures. Failures and bankruptcies are business closures that occur while the business owes debts.

However, the potential rewards are unlimited. Business owners can profit greatly. Many of the wealthiest people on earth are entrepreneurs, including William Henry Gates III (1955–), the world's richest person and cofounder, chairman, and CEO of Microsoft Corporation. Another reward entrepreneurs tend to appreciate is independence. However, entrepreneurs' time is not necessarily their own. The work of the business must be completed, and often the entrepreneur is the one who must perform the most complex tasks of the business. Although others may work for the owner and manager of the business, it is ultimately the responsibility of the entrepreneur to make sure that the work gets done. Other rewards cited by entrepreneurs include personal satisfaction gained while performing the duties of the business and the resulting prestige.

BUSINESS PLAN

Planning is a key ingredient in the success of an entrepreneur. A business plan helps to guide the decision making needed to operate a business. The first decision is to choose what sort of business to own. The business may be:

- A retail business that markets a tangible product (such as clothing, houses, food)
- A wholesale business that acquires goods from a producer and distributes requested quantities to retailers
- A service business that offers an intangible product (such as insurance, haircuts, consultant services, construction, financial services)
- A manufacturing business that produces a product

Of course, a business may perform more than one of these functions. The scope of the business will also be

William Henry Gates, III (1955–). *Entrepreneur Bill Gates speaks in Dearborn, Michigan, April 29, 2005.* © **REBECCA COOK/REUTERS/CORBIS**

dependent on the breadth and depth of the products or services offered as well as the geographic region served.

One option available to someone interested in purchasing a business is a franchise. A franchise is a license to organize a business that markets products manufactured or owned by a parent company, such as a Kwik Copy, Sleep Inn, McDonald's, Play It Again Sports, or other businesses.

Another early decision involves choosing the legal form of ownership. Three options are sole proprietorship, partnership, and corporation. In a sole proprietorship, a single person owns and operates the business. The owner assumes all risks and responsibilities for the business, including debts. Two or more individuals may form a partnership and serve as co-owners of the business. If the partnership is a general partnership, all partners assume unlimited liability. However, if the partnership is a limited partnership, one or more of the partners assumes unlimited liability while the remaining partner(s) do(es) not. Instead, they may lose up to the amount of their investment, while having limited involvement in the business.

The third form of ownership is the corporation. A corporation is a group of individuals who obtain a charter giving the organization formed by the group legal rights and privileges. This organization can perform such functions as buying and selling, as well as owning property, as if the group were an individual person. The corporation is actually owned by individuals who purchase stock. A major advantage of this form of ownership is that the stockholders themselves have limited liability, thus minimizing financial risks.

The Small Business Administration (1999) reports that in 1996, according to the Internal Revenue Service, 16,471,000 sole proprietorships, 1,679,000 partnerships, and 5,005,000 corporations filed nonfarm business tax returns.

A business plan often contains three major sections: the marketing plan, the management plan, and the financial plan.

Marketing Plan. Marketing is a process in which the decisions of the business are based upon the goals of the organization. One of these goals is usually that of satisfying the needs and wants of potential customers or a target market. Potential customers can be divided into specific market segments that represent groups based on specified characteristics. For example, a business may strive to serve those in their late teens and early twenties who live primarily in large cities. Narrowing the segment even further, the business may offer goods or services for those interested specifically in sports—both as active players and as spectators or fans. Thus the business may sell athletic shoes and clothing, sports equipment, and how-to books. The owner(s) would locate this business in an area with a large number of people in that age group. Other factors to consider when defining a target market include such demographic factors as income level, sex, marital status, and ethnic group, and such geographic factors as climate and region of the country.

Part of the marketing plan is the marketing mix. A marketing mix has four basic components: product, place, price, and promotion.

Product: The product is the goods and/or services offered by the business. A travel agent may offer the service of arranging any type of trip to anywhere in the world or may specialize specifically in cruises. Choosing products is dependent on the market segment the business intends to serve. Other considerations include the amount of physical space available for storing the product, the amount of funds needed to purchase the product from the wholesaler or manufacturer, and the profitability potential of offering the product. Another important consideration is the product's life cycle. A life cycle has four sections: introduction, growth, maturity, and decline. When a new product is introduced to the market, it is in the introduction phase. Over time, it may grow in popularity and sales, reaching a point of maturity. Maturity is then followed by decline. An entrepreneur must be careful to avoid offering products or services that are in decline. That is one of the reasons for continually monitoring the sales of products and adjusting the product mix to reflect such changes in the product life cycle.

Place: Another factor in the marketing mix is place. Marketers often say that the success of a business is dependent upon "location … location … location." Choosing the location of the business is an important decision that must take into consideration such factors as the chosen target market, traffic patterns, parking availability, population trends, competitive businesses, rental costs, and other expenses. The place function also includes business activities that involve physical distribution, such as transporting goods, handling the goods, storing the goods, and keeping track of the goods (inventory).

An increasing number of businesses are locating on the Internet. Entrepreneurs create World Wide Web pages on which they promote their offerings. Consumers may either telephone the business to order the product or service or use a credit card to purchase the item over the Internet. The actual location of the business is less important since the Web is available throughout the country and, indeed, the world. However, the location still must be considered relative to business expenses (e.g., rent, utility prices) and transportation prices (e.g., cost of transporting products purchased on the Internet from the business to the customer).

Businesses can also be located in the home. In fact, home-based businesses represent a large portion of businesses in the United States. Many entrepreneurs begin their businesses in the home and eventually outgrow the space available there, at which point the owner usually seeks an outside facility.

Price: Price is the third component of the marketing mix. A pricing structure must be developed that includes specific goals and reflects policies of the business. A goal may reflect an intended image of the business or a particular profit margin that is sought. Factors to consider when identifying goals and policies related to price are: the amount of sales that are sought, pricing policies of competitors, profits that are projected, supply of the product that is available and projected demand for that product, the location of the business, and the expenses of the business.

Promotion: The fourth component of the marketing mix is promotion—the activities of the business that are intended to inform potential customers about the product or service and persuade them to purchase it. Methods include personal selling, advertising, visual merchandising (the coordination of all physical elements in a business such as displays, counters, offices, windows, signs, fixtures, lighting, and such), and publicity. The effectiveness of promotional strategies must be monitored so that promotional dollars are spent on strategies that are contributing to the achievement of business goals.

Management Plan. Another major section of a business plan is the management plan. The four basic functions of management are planning, organizing, directing, and controlling.

Planning involves the determination of goals and objectives for the business, including the actual results sought by the firm. A set of policies and procedures are determined that guide the identification of specific activities that will lead to these goals. Planning does not end with the creation of a business plan, however, as it continues throughout the life of the business.

To implement the plan, the entrepreneur organizes the personnel and other resources of the business. An organizational chart is created that shows the hierarchy of the people working in the business. After the number of employees and their qualifications are determined, applicants are recruited and, once hired, are trained. Other types of resources that are organized by management are facilities, equipment, materials, and supplies.

The third management function is directing. Managers direct the work of the business by applying leadership and management skills. They model desired behavior while supervising, motivating, and evaluating their employees. Finally, comparing the plan with the actual results is called controlling. By observing and studying financial statements, managers can understand the status of the business and adjust activities where necessary to contribute toward the achievement of the business goals. The controlling function also includes evaluation of employees.

Financial Plan. The financial aspects of the business must also be planned. The financial plan includes several financial statements. One of these statements is the statement of financial requirements, which identifies the projected expenses and the assets they will create for a specified time period. Among the expenses listed are those for rent, insurance, telephone, and inventory. The entrepreneur also needs money to meet personal expenses as the business grows. These expenses are also included in this statement. The expenses are used to create assets. Assets are items of value that are owned by the business. For example, if a business purchases land upon which to place a facility for the business, the money needed for the purchase is an expense that then creates the asset of land.

The financial plan also includes the source(s) of the funds needed to meet the financial requirements. Sometimes an entrepreneur will already have all the funds needed, but more often these must be acquired from family members, private lending agencies, and/or governmental loan programs.

Another statement included in the financial plan is the income statement, which may be referred to as a profit-and-loss statement or operating statement. This statement is a projection of the sales expected in a given period of time, the cost of the merchandise that will be sold, and the operating expenses of the business. From this information, projected profits or losses are determined.

A financial plan also includes a beginning balance sheet. This form provides a list of the assets, liabilities, and net worth of a business on a given day. Assets are tangible items that are owned by the business, liabilities are the debts of a business, and net worth is the amount of investment that the owner(s) has in the business.

The financial plan also includes a cash-flow analysis and a break-even analysis. The cash-flow analysis identifies the cash generated after expenses and loan principal payments are deducted. This projection is calculated for several years into the future. The break-even analysis identifies the break-even point, which is the level of sales and expenses, including loan principal payments, at which a business has no profit and no loss.

RESOURCES

Information that can help the budding entrepreneur is available from people, printed material, and the Internet. All entrepreneurs need people they can go to for advice. Accountants and attorneys are especially important. An accountant not only provides the financial data and statements for the business but also interprets the information for the entrepreneur. This is important because business decisions must be based on a variety of considerations, including financial ones. Attorneys provide legal advice throughout the process of purchasing or creating a business and owning and managing it.

Other sources of information include financial institutions, the Chamber of Commerce, educational institutions, insurance agents, and suppliers of products used in the business. Publications provide up-to-date information: books from major publishers, magazines such as *Entrepreneur* and *Inc.*, and newsletters and journals offered by associations are available. Many types of businesses are served by trade associations such as the American Hotel and Motel Association, which is comprised of owners and operators of lodging businesses throughout the country. Along with providing publications, these organizations hold conferences and workshops and provide networking opportunities. Various government agencies are also available for advice, such as the Small Business Administration and the Internal Revenue Service.

The Internet provides information from a variety of people and organizations. Although the Internet is a valuable resource, the information available on it is not screened for accuracy. Relevant Web sites can be located by use of search engines that pinpoint specification on categories and topics.

Although it is important that the entrepreneur seeks advice throughout the planning and operation of a business, the ultimate decision maker on matters related to the business is the entrepreneur.

SUCCESSFUL ENTREPRENEURS

Successful entrepreneurs can be found in just about every community in the country. From small businesses employing only a few persons to megabusinesses employing thousands, successful entrepreneurs abound. The following successful entrepreneurs represent a few of those at the high end of success as measured by wealth:

William (Bill) H. Gates is the co-founder, chairman, and CEO of Microsoft Corporation, the world's leading provider of software for personal computers. Gates was a student at Harvard when he developed BASIC, a programming language for the first microcomputer. He founded Microsoft in 1975 with a childhood friend, Paul Allen (1953–). According to Microsoft Corporation, Gates's determination to develop Microsoft stemmed from his belief that the personal computer would be a valuable tool for every home and office; thus he began developing software for personal computers.

Mary Kay Ash (1918–2001) launched Mary Kay Cosmetics on September 13, 1963. Mary Kay, Inc. reports that, with a life savings of $5,000, Ash launched what is now the largest direct seller of skin care products and the best-selling brand of skin-care and color cosmetics in the United States. Mary Kay Cosmetics originated from an idea of writing a book to help women survive in the male-dominated business world. From there, Ash inadvertently created the marketing plan for Mary Kay Cosmetics.

Gozi Samuel Oburota (1957–) founded the Gozi Samuel Oburota Certified Public Accountancy Corporation (GSO) in 1994. According to the GSO Corporation, before founding the company, Oburota had served as a senior accountant at IBM, trusted with worldwide accounting responsibility for the DASD 3390 mainframe computer project from product development through manufacturing and general availability. GSO is a full service certified public accounting firm with offices in San Jose, Los Angeles, and Washington, D.C. By 1999, GSO was one of the fastest-growing professional firms headquartered in Silicon Valley. GSO is 100 percent minority owned.

SEE ALSO *Factors of Production; Sole Proprietorship*

BIBLIOGRAPHY

Ely, Vivien K., Berns, Robert G., Lynch, Richard L., and Popo, Debbi (1993). *Entrepreneurship.* New York: Glencoe/McGraw-Hill.

Entrepreneur Magazine, Entrepreneur Media, Inc., 2445 McCabe Way, Ste. 400, Irvine, CA 92614.

Kent, Calvin A., ed. (1990). *Entrepreneurship Education Current Developments, Future Directions.* New York: Quorum Books.

Inc. 375 Lexington Ave., New York, NY 10017.

Longenecker, Justin G., Moore, Carlos W., and Petty, J. William (2003). *Small Business Management: An Entrepreneurial Emphasis.* Mason, OH: Thomson/South-Western.

Mary Kay, Inc. (2005). Retrieved October 18, 2005, from http://www.marykay.com/home.aspx.

Meyer, Earl C., and Allen, Kathleen R. (1994). *Entrepreneurship and Small Business Management.* Mission Hills, CA: Glencoe.

Microsoft Corporation (2005). Retrieved October 18, 2005, from http://www.microsoft.com. 1999.

Moorman, Jerry W., and Halloran, James W. (1995). *Contemporary Entrepreneurship.* Cincinnati, OH: South-Western Educational Publishing.

United States Small Business Administration (2005). Retrieved October 18, 2005, from http://www.sba.gov.

Robert G. Berns
Jewel E. Hairston

ENVIRONMENTAL MARKETING
SEE *Green Marketing*

ENVIRONMENTAL PROTECTION AGENCY

In December 1970, the U.S. Environmental Protection Agency (EPA) was established as an independent agency. Reorganization Plan #3 of 1970 consolidated fifteen components from five agencies for the purpose of grouping all environmental regulatory activities under a single agency. Most of these functions were housed in the Department of the Interior, Department of Agriculture, and the Department of Health, Education and Welfare.

The purpose of the EPA is to ensure that all Americans and the environment in which they live are safe from health hazards. The EPA has a number of goals: clean air, clean and safe water, safe food, preventing and reducing pollution, water management and restoration of waste sites, redirection of international pollution, and credible deterrents to pollution. Also, the EPA engages in education about pollution and its environmental risks.

The first four goals deal with the immediate environment of people: clean air; clean and safe water; safe food; and preventing pollution and reducing risks in our environment. The remaining goals deal with education, the clean-up of existing pollution, and efforts in the global arena. They involve better water management, the reduction of cross-border environmental risks, the expansion of Americans' right to know about their environment, sound service, improved understanding of environmental risks, credible deterrents to pollution, and greater compliance with the law and effective management.

In addition to these goals, the EPA has adopted a number of principles to guide management in establishing priorities. These guidelines are to reduce environmental risks, to prevent pollution, to focus on children's health, to establish partners with local governments, to maximize public participation, to emphasize community-based solutions, to work with Indian tribes, and to choose cost-effective solutions. The EPA also is engaged in ongoing educational programs, which emphasize the community's right to know about its environmental risks.

The EPA has to enforce fifteen or more statutes or laws, including the Clean Air Act; the Clean Water Act; the Federal Food, Drug, and Cosmetic Act; the Endangered Species Act; the Pollution Prevention Act; and the Federal Insecticide, Fungicide, and Rodenticides Act. The EPA also enforces other laws dealing with pollution and toxic substances.

The EPA has had some major successes since its inception. In the area of air quality: (1) More than half of the large cities now meet air-quality standards; (2) emissions of common air pollutants have dropped by an average of 24 percent; and (3) blood lead levels in children have declined by 75 percent. In the area of water quality: (1) 60 percent of the nation's waterways are safe for fishing and swimming; (2) ocean dumping has been banned; and (3) standards for wastewater have been established for fifty industries. In the area of toxic and pesticide management: (1) DDT has been banned; (2) safer pesticides have been introduced; and (3) toxic emissions have been reduced by 39 percent. Finally, the EPA has been able to

American Electric Power's Muskingum River Plant, Beverly, Ohio, was named in an Environmental Protection Agency lawsuit in 1989. **AP IMAGES**

set many standards covering a wide range of pollutants. More information is available from the EPA at Araiel Rios Building, 1200 Pennsylvania Avenue, NW, Washington, D.C. 20460, (202)260-2090, or http://www.epa.gov.

SEE ALSO *Green Marketing*

BIBLIOGRAPHY

Environmental Protection Agency (EPA) (2005). "EPA's Mission." Retrieved October 18, 2005, from http://www.epa.gov/epahome.

EPA. "Frequently Asked Questions" (2005). Retrieved October 18, 2005, from http://www.epa.gov/history. 1999.

EPA. "Research Programs." (2005) Retrieved October 18, 2005, from http://www.epa.gov/epahome/program2.htm.

"About EPA" (2005) Retrieved October 18, 2005, from http://www.epa.gov/epahome/aboutepa.htm.

Val Hinton
Mary Jean Lush

EQUAL EMPLOYMENT OPPORTUNITY ACT OF 1972

The Equal Employment Opportunity Act (Public Law 92-261) of 1972 was designed to prohibit job discrimination for reasons of race, religion, color, national origin, and sex. The term *equal*, however, must be interpreted correctly as it applies to this legislation. It does not mean that every applicant or employee must be considered equal in ability or competency. Rather, it means that the law looks at all applicants or employees as equals, who deserve fair treatment.

Specifically, it requires that no applicant or employee may be rejected from employment or treated unfairly solely because of race, religion, color, national origin, or sex. The law requires that the most competent applicants be hired and the most competent employees be promoted.

Donald Dickman, president of Black Males for Justice, leads a news conference outside the Equal Employment Opportunity Commission in Washington, D.C., April 19, 1999. AP IMAGES

The law does not promise a job or a promotion. It is meant to level the playing field and make the rules the same for all applicants and employees. Equal employment opportunity programs include affirmative action for employment, as well as means for handling discrimination complaints. The law applies to everyone who is in a position to hire individuals.

Laws relating to equal employment opportunity date back to the Civil Rights Act of 1883, which prohibited favoritism in federal employment. In 1940 Executive Order 0948 prohibited discrimination in federal agencies based on race, creed, or color. In 1961 Executive Order 10925 required that positive steps be taken to eliminate workplace discrimination in federal agencies. The next landmark act influencing equal employment opportunity was the Equal Pay Act of 1963, which prohibited the payment of different wages to workers for substantially similar work on the basis of sex. Title VII of the Civil Rights Act of 1964—which prohibited discrimination based on race, color, sex, religion, or national origin and established the Equal Employment Opportunity Commission—was a very important piece of legislation for the movement.

The Equal Employment Opportunity Act of 1995 prohibits discrimination based on the following items: impairment, marital status, political belief or activity, race, religion, sex, social status as a person, age, role in business dealings, lawful sexual activity, physical features, pregnancy, position or past employment position, and association with a person who is identified by reference to any of the foregoing thirteen grounds. Also prohibited is sexual harassment, which applies to both employers and employees.

SEE ALSO *Diversity in the Workplace; Sexual Harassment*

BIBLIOGRAPHY
U.S. Equal Employment Opportunity Commission. http://www.eeoc.gov/ retrieved February 3, 2006.

Lawrence F. Peters, Jr.

EQUAL PAY ACT OF 1963

The Equal Pay Act of 1963, a federal U.S. law, was introduced and passed to ensure that women and men involved in the same job, with the same job description, got paid equally. The act was meant to address the wage gap between men and women. As the gap increased it became obvious that many women were excluded from certain jobs in order to maintain the status quo of men, and those women who did break into the business world were getting paid less than men doing the same job.

During World War II (1939–1945), many women answered the call of the U.S. government and went to work in droves to produce needed supplies for the war effort. Prior to World War II, many women were expected to stay home to tend to their households; after the war, however, women found that they enjoyed working outside their home, they needed the income, or they chose to work to supplement the family income for some of the extras that disposable income could provide. The U.S. Congress determined that different pay based on sex tended to cause many economic and social problems. Allowing wage differences based on sex kept the living standards low, prevented the workforce from reaching its full potential, and tended to cause labor disputes based on the inequity of pay. By requiring equal pay, families were able to buy more goods, thus boosting the economy.

During the 1970s two court cases further defined the Equal Pay Act of 1963. *Schultz v. Wheaton Glass Company* was heard by the Third Circuit of the U.S. Court of Appeals, and *Corning Glass Works v. Brennan* was heard by the U.S. Supreme Court. In *Schultz v. Wheaton,* the Third Circuit Court of Appeals determined that jobs do not need to be identical but rather "substantially equal" in order to be protected under the Equal Pay Act.

Furthermore, in 1974 the Supreme Court determined in *Corning Glass Works v. Brennan* that women could not be paid less simply because they would work at a lower pay rate than men. At the same time the Supreme Court confirmed the constitutionality of the Equal Pay Act.

Even with the Equal Pay Act and the subsequent rulings by the Supreme Court and other lower courts, equity has not been reached between men and women. According to the U.S. Census Bureau, women earned approximately 77¢ for every $1.00 their male counterpart earned in 2004.

SEE ALSO *Diversity in the Workplace; Sexual Harassment*

BIBLIOGRAPHY
Butts, Cassandra Q. (2004, May 7). Marching on for equal pay. Retrieved February 17, 2006, from Center for American Progress Web site: http://www.americanprogress.org/site/pp.asp?c=biJRJ8OVF&b=68060
U.S. Census Bureau. (2005, August 30). Income Stable, Poverty Rate Increases, Percentage of Americans Without Health Insurance Unchanged. (News Release). Retrieved March 1,

Iowa Senator Tom Harkin speaks at a press conference addressing the Equal Pay Act, June 12, 2001 in Washington, D.C. **ALEX WONG/GETTY IMAGES**

2006, from http://www.census.gov/Press-Release/www/releases/archives/income_wealth/005647.html

U.S. Equal Employment Opportunity Commission. (1997). The Equal Pay Act of 1963. Retrieved February 17, 2006, from http://www.eeoc.gov/policy/epa.html

Lawrence F. Peters, Jr.

EQUILIBRIUM

SEE *Supply and Demand*

EQUITY THEORY

SEE *Motivation*

ERGONOMICS

Ergonomics is the science of fitting the job to the worker and adapting the work environment to the needs of humans. An overall goal of ergonomics is to promote health and safety and to optimize productivity.

The term ergonomics comes from the Greek words *ergon*, meaning work, and *nomos*, meaning laws—thus, laws of work. The study of ergonomics as a way to reduce human error began in the military during the Korean War. In planes used for pilot training, the eject button was poorly placed and pilots sometimes accidentally ejected themselves—often at too low an altitude for their parachutes to open. The button's location was changed and fewer lives were lost.

Principles of ergonomics are applied to the design of many elements of everyday life, from car seats to garden tools. Many different occupations are involved in implementing these human factor principles in the workplace, such as human factors/ergonomics specialists; safety engineers; industrial hygienists, engineers, designers; human resource managers; occupational medicine physicians and therapists; and chiropractors. Research in ergonomics is ongoing.

Knowledge of basic ergonomics principles is important for both workers and employers because both share responsibility for a safe work environment. One can easily imagine the potential hazards in manufacturing settings where equipment is operated and heavy materials are handled, but hazards exist in other environments, too. And technology (especially computer use) has brought about widespread changes in how work is accomplished.

Attention to ergonomics principles helps to reduce workplace injuries and illnesses that result in workers' compensation costs, medical claims, and lost work time. Many disorders and injuries are preventable when work conditions are designed for human safety and comfort. People need training in how to recognize hazards and safety problems as well as how to control their own behaviors for maximum comfort and health.

One of the key considerations in ergonomics is adjustability of physical elements. People come in all shapes and sizes, and the average workstation configuration will not fit everyone. Making changes during a workday in the physical setup of equipment, such as adjusting chair height, can alleviate discomfort and fatigue. Work surfaces should be at comfortable heights in relationship to a chair or to a standing position. Equipment and related items should be arranged conveniently.

Whenever a mismatch occurs between the physical requirements of a job and the physical capacity of a worker, musculoskeletal disorders can result. People working with intense concentration or at high speeds often work with poor posture. Cumulative trauma disorders (also called repetitive strain injuries) are caused by repeating the same motion in awkward positions or with noticeable force, such as in lifting heavy objects. Carpal-tunnel syndrome, a disorder affecting nerves in the wrist that has the potential to permanently disable, is a condition affecting people in a variety of occupations from meatpackers to musicians. Wrist pain can be severe, with treatment involving wrist splints, anti-inflammatory drugs, or even surgery. And people who use a computer extensively are especially prone to developing carpal-tunnel syndrome. Computer use often contributes to vision problems, too.

Ergonomic computer keyboards help ease the strain on hands and wrists. **PHOTOGRAPH BY KELLY A. QUIN. THE GALE GROUP.**

Posture in standing and in seated positions is important to avoid musculoskeletal disorders. The natural curve of the spine should be maintained, with the head balanced over the spine. When a person is seated:

- Feet should rest on the floor, with legs and body forming 90° to 110° angles

- The body should be straight, with the neck upright and supporting the head balanced on the spine (not forward or twisted to the sides)

- Upper arms should be perpendicular to the floor; forearms should parallel the floor

Symptoms of musculoskeletal disorders can begin as numbness or stiffness in joints or tingling, aching sensations in muscles. Pain or burning sensations may be evident, too. Often symptoms progress gradually, becoming more severe with prolonged exposure to the condition causing them. Damage to nerves, tendons, joints, or soft tissue can result.

With computer use so prevalent, poor work habits will contribute to musculoskeletal disorders for many people who spend long hours seated at a computer. These include the following:

- Wrists misaligned or excessive force used with a keyboard

- Poor posture used with an incorrect seating height

- A monitor incorrectly positioned, resulting in eye strain and vision problems

- Inappropriate lighting, causing glare on monitors and other work surfaces

- High concentration, causing infrequent breaks

Guidelines for working conditions when using a computer include:

Chair: A well-designed chair with easy-to-implement adjustability is essential. A user can vary angles of back support and the seat pan to control the degree of pressure on the thighs and back. Weight should be evenly distributed, with no extreme pressure points. An upright posture is a little easier to achieve if the seat pan is tilted slightly forward of horizontal. When a person is seated, feet should rest on the floor and the chair seat pan should be even with the back of the knee, ranging from 13 to 19 inches above the floor depending on an individual's height. A foot rest may be used to relieve pressure on the thighs. Both lumbar and mid-level back support are needed. Arm rests, adjustable for height, are helpful to many people. The chair should have a five-point base for stability and casters for easy movement.

Keyboard: The keyboard provides the primary means of interacting with a computer. The keyboard should be in a comfortable position, and wrists should float over the keyboard when keying with a light touch so wrists and forearms remain straight. Although wrist pads are helpful for resting when not keying, they can actually create problems when a user keeps wrists on them when keying because the wrists can bend down. Different opinions exist on the appropriate angle of the keyboard; some people prefer a flat position while others find a reverse incline more comfortable. Split and curved keyboards are available, too. However, the most important part of keyboard use is keeping the wrists straight in line with the forearm and not bent to the side. When voice-recognition technology becomes commonly used, dependency on the keyboard will be reduced.

Mouse: A mouse should be positioned next to the keyboard, reachable without extending the arm in an awkward position. Again, a light touch is needed and users should avoid gripping or squeezing the mouse. A wrist support or adjustable mouse platform may be helpful if a user begins to develop wrist problems. A variety of shapes are available for these pointing devices, and a trackball can be used for the same purpose.

Monitor: A monitor should be directly in front of the user, with the top of the screen at or below the line of sight, 18 to 30 inches away from the eyes, and tiltable to avoid glare from overhead lighting and windows. If necessary, antiglare filters can be added. Screen size should be large enough for easy reading of screen character sizes with a screen refresh rate fast enough to avoid a visible flicker. An individual can experience blurred vision or fatigue from a poor monitor viewing angle, reflected glare, or a low-quality monitor. Because glands in the eyelids produce tears that cleanse eyes as the eyelids blink and the eyes move, irritated eyes can develop because one's blink rate tends to decrease when one is concentrating.

To avoid neck and eyestrain, an individual should:

- Use a copyholder positioned near the monitor to support material used with computer work.

- Use lower levels of lighting to reduce glare on monitors. Many older offices have high illumination levels that are necessary for paper-intensive tasks—but are too highly lighted for computer work. Softer overall, or ambient, lighting should be used, with task lighting added to surfaces as needed for more illumination.

- Relax eye muscles by shifting focus from the computer screen to distant objects for a few seconds every 5 to 10 minutes.

- Take microbreaks to stretch the neck, shoulders, hands, wrists, back, and legs as well as to rest the eyes. Stretching exercises can be simple neck rotations, shoulder shrugs, fists clenched and then released, or arms hanging down naturally for a few moments. Get up and move around about every 30 minutes. Take a brisk walk if possible. Exercises with hand weights will help with stretching and will give the body isometric exercise.

While it may be ideal to have individually adjustable temperature controls, this is not feasible in many work situations. For business offices, most people are comfortable with temperature levels at 68° to 72° in the winter and 72° to 76° in the summer. Humidity levels should be maintained between 40 to 60 percent not only for comfort but also for proper functioning of office equipment. Indoor air quality involves more than heating and cooling—air should be cleansed of pollutants (bacteria, dust, fumes, etc.), with fresh air added before circulation. Many factors affect the efficiency of HVAC (heating, ventilation, and air conditioning) systems. These systems must be designed for the number of people and the equipment to be used in each area because computers and other devices can produce almost as much heat as a human body produces.

Another important concept is adjustability of work pace. Jobs may require redesign to allow workers to accomplish tasks at varying speeds or to enable workers to rotate to different tasks or to use a variety of work methods that permit different movements. Rest breaks are important, too, and microbreaks can be taken to interrupt intense situations, to rest arms and wrists, or to rest eyes.

Much ergonomics information is available in print and on the Internet, published by organizations such as the Occupational Safety and Health Administration (OSHA), the National Institute of Occupational Safety and Health (NIOSH), the National Safety Council, the Human Factors and Ergonomic Society, and others. OSHA is developing ergonomics program standards that were to be published in 2000 (OSHA 1999). Consultants can provide technical expertise to help with all phases of ergonomics assessment and the implementation of corrective measures and/or training programs.

SEE ALSO *Office Layout*

BIBLIOGRAPHY
"Occupational Safety and Health Administration." Retrieved October 18, 2005, from http://www.osha.gov/SLTC/ergonomics/index.html. 1999.

Patricia R. Graves

ETHICS: AN OVERVIEW

Ethics is the study of questions of morality, the search to understand what is right, wrong, good, and bad. It is the branch of philosophy that systematically studies moral ideals and goals, motives of choice, and patterns of good and bad conduct. The word ethics is derived from the Greek *ethikos*, meaning "character." Issues of personal character, and the search for the best patterns for living, were at the core of Greek ethical philosophy. In contrast, the word moral is from the Latin *more* (MOR-ay). The Romans used this term to describe the customary ways that people tended to act. Thus, though the two terms are often used interchangeably today, morality has evolved to mean the social norms that people are taught and conditioned to follow, while ethics has come to refer to the rational investigating and questioning of these norms. This view of ethics is said to be normative, since it assumes the existence of at least some universal moral principles and standards.

Ethics tends to be a cross-disciplinary field of study. Theologians study ethics and morality in light of religious teachings and divine commands. Psychologists seek to understand how people's values influence their thinking, behavioral motivations, and personal development. Sociologists attempt to identify and explain varying cultural norms and practices. Business educators try to help companies, employees, and professionals avoid expensive and counterproductive ethical misdeeds. However, the study of normative ethics has historically been dominated by philosophers, who have applied rules of reason and logic to find answers to humanity's perplexing moral questions.

One apparent obstacle to this process is that logical reasoning, at least at first glance, does not seem to lead different people to the same ethical conclusions and answers. If people, ideally, used reason correctly, what would it tell us about ethics? This search for the best, most logical principles to follow is the realm of general ethics. The end results of this search are ethical systems or theories—groups of systematically related ethical principles that attempt to describe and prescribe human morality. Scholars in applied ethics then take these ethical systems and principles and apply them to contemporary moral questions, dilemmas, and life-situations. Examples of specific studies in applied ethics include business, government, and professional ethics (medical, legal, etc.).

RELIGIOUS AND PHILOSOPHICAL ETHICS

Perhaps the greatest continual struggle related to ethics throughout history has been between followers of religious ethics and proponents of philosophical ethics. Religious ethics gives preeminence to divine authority. Actions that conform to the will or teachings of this authority are considered good or right; actions that do not conform are seen as bad, wrong, or evil. It is believed that people can find or discover this divine will through sacred scriptures, the teachings of religious leaders, prayer, and personal revelation. On the other hand, philosophical ethics places its primary emphasis on rational thought and the rules of logic. This view assumes that individuals can use reason to find answers to moral questions, making religious authority unnecessary.

This conflict can reach critical proportions. Many philosophers who have challenged the religious authorities of their times have been branded as dangerous heretics. Foreshadowing the pattern that would repeat itself for centuries, the central charge leading to the conviction and eventual execution of Socrates was that he questioned the gods of Athens and taught others to do the same. However, it is also worth noting that some of history's most influential ethical thinkers have argued that the perceived conflict between reason and faith may only be illusionary and that faith and reason need not be adversaries, but can support and even validate each other.

ETHICAL SYSTEMS

There have been about as many different philosophical viewpoints on ethics as there have been people thinking about them. However, these can be roughly grouped into three main families of ethical systems. The first are virtue-

Socrates (c. 470–399 B.C.E.). Along with Greek philosophers Plato and Aristotle, Socrates was a poineer in virtue-ethical thinking. © GIANNI DAGLI ORTI/CORBIS

ethics theories, founded on the teachings of the three great lights of ancient Greek philosophy—Socrates (c. 469–399 B.C.E.), Plato (427?–347? B.C.E.), and Aristotle (384–322 B.C.E.). Most attempts to chronicle Western ethical thinking begin with these three men because of their emphasis on reason and logic as essential tools for finding answers to ethical questions. This assumption has been the cornerstone of philosophical thinking ever since. The central focus in virtue-ethics is personal character. The ancient Greeks believed it was a mandate from nature itself that the purpose of life for humans was to achieve happiness and fulfillment. The goal of ancient Greek ethics, then, was the search for "the good life," the pattern of specific character traits (virtues) that people should integrate into their lives to make happiness and fulfillment most likely. Plato and Aristotle wrote that the virtues of wisdom, courage, temperance, and justice were the most logical choices to help people achieve this goal.

One evidence of the profound influence of these Greek thinkers is that so many other philosophers have adopted and adapted their approach. Cicero (106–43 B.C.E.), the most well known of the Roman intellectuals, leaned heavily on Aristotle's principles and concepts. The Catholic theologian Thomas Aquinas (1225?–1274) took

Aristotle's writings about the essential roles of reason and nature in ethics and integrated them with medieval Roman Catholic dogma. In doing so, he helped to usher in the Enlightenment, revolutionizing Catholic thinking and doctrine in ways still evident today. Aquinas's ethical system (natural law) remained the most influential view throughout much of the Middle Ages, supported in no small part by the power of the Church. This domination continued until the seventeenth and eighteenth centuries, when philosophers began attempting to restore the pre-eminence of reason over religious authority, perhaps the most significant event in the development of ethical thinking since the time of Plato.

One early leader was the British philosopher John Locke (1632–1704). Locke stretched natural law's tenets to include the assumption that all humans are endowed by nature (or God) with certain basic human rights. This fact gives people a clear moral duty to respect the rights of others. Thus, violating the rights of others becomes the only real moral wrong, and all actions that do not violate the rights of other persons must be ethically permissible. Among the most ardent supporters of Locke's natural rights system were the founders of the United States, who viewed his principles and assumptions as the moral bedrock of their new republic. These principles, evident throughout the Declaration of Independence and Constitution, remain at the heart of the American legal system.

The second family of ethical systems is made up of deontology theories. These approaches share the view that ethics should be based primarily on moral duty. This approach is probably best exemplified by the writings of the great German philosopher and writer Immanuel Kant (1724–1804). Kant maintained that at the heart of ethics lies the moral duty to obey the dictates of reason. People can know what reason commands through intuition and moral reason. Kant's central ethical principle is the categorical imperative, which says that the only moral actions are those consistent with the moral standards that we would want everyone else to follow. For example, Kant argued that lying is always wrong, since no rational person would want lying to become the moral standard for everyone. (Kant recognized no exceptions, arguing that even lying to save a life was immoral.) A corollary to this principle is Kant's respect for persons, the maxim that it is always wrong to exploit others. People, he argued, must be treated as ends (goals) in themselves, not merely as means to our own ends.

The third major family of ethical systems comprises the utilitarian theories. This approach sees the proper goal of ethics as producing good, pleasure, or happiness. Early proponents of utilitarianism were the British philosophers Jeremy Bentham (1748–1832) and John Stuart Mill (1806–1873). According to utilitarian reasoning, the morally right (or best) action is the one that produces the greatest possible happiness for the greatest possible number. Thus, behaviors are not always moral or always immoral. Instead morality is based on specific variables unique to each situation. In some situations, lying might produce more overall good than telling the truth (e.g., deceiving a kidnapper to save a child). In other situations, truth would clearly produce more good.

BUSINESS AND PROFESSIONAL CODES OF ETHICS

These classical ethical systems are expressed and affirmed in contemporary society in many ways. Codes of ethics are practical examples. A code of ethics is a written document intended to serve as a guideline to those who would follow it. Most larger businesses and corporations have codes of ethics for their employees, as do most professions for their members. Professional codes are usually written by members of the profession through a central national organization. For example, it is generally understood that American doctors are subject to the American Medical Association code of ethics, and American lawyers follow their bar association codes. But many other professions have codes of ethics as well, including such diverse fields as journalism, pharmacy, business management, education, accounting, engineering, nursing, law enforcement, and psychology. Even the best codes of ethics cannot guarantee ethical behavior. Indeed, many codes do not even contain methods of enforcement, but merely express the ideals and values of their respective corporations and professions. The decision to act ethically or unethically is, as it has been through the ages, up to the individual.

BIBLIOGRAPHY

DeGeorge, Richard T. (1999). *Business Ethics* (5th ed.). Upper Saddle River, NJ: Prentice Hall.

Frost, S. E. (1962). *Basic Teachings of the Great Philosophers*. New York: Anchor.

Goree, Keith (1995). *Ethics in American Life*. Mason, OH: South-Western.

Gorlin, Rena A. (1994). *Codes of Professional Responsibility* (3rd ed.). Washington, DC: Bureau of National Affairs.

Holmes, Robert L. (2003). *Basic Moral Philosophy*. Belmont, CA: Thomson/Wadsworth.

Denise, T.C., Peterfreund, Sheldon P., and White, Nicolas P., eds. (1999). *Great Traditions in Ethics* (7th ed.) Belmont, CA: Wadsworth.

DeVries, Paul, Veatch, Robert M., Newton, Lisa H., Baker, Emily V., and Richardson, Michael (2000). *Ethics Applied* (ed. 3.0.). Boston: Pearson.

Ruggiero, Vincent R. (2004). *Thinking Critically About Ethical Issues* (6th ed.). Boston: McGraw Hill Higher Education.

Shaw, William H. (2005). *Business Ethics*. Belmont, CA: Thomson/Wadsworth.

Wagner, Michael E., ed. (1991). *An Historical Introduction to Moral Philosophy*. Englewood Cliffs, NJ: Prentice Hall.

Keith Goree

ETHICS IN ACCOUNTING

At least as far back as ancient Greece, when the Hippocratic oath was instituted for medical practitioners, a hallmark of a profession has been its claim to integrity. When the public thinks of the accounting profession, they usually think of certified public accountants (CPAs) who work in big national or regional firms that audit the financial statements of publicly listed companies. But many CPAs work in smaller partnerships, auditing or organizing the books and records of private companies and not-for-profit and governmental organizations. CPAs may also perform other services, most notably tax services. Some work as financial officers and management accountants in corporations, large and small, as well as governmental and not-for-profit institutions. In addition, many accountants who do not have a CPA designation perform services similar to some of the services—but not audits—performed by CPAs.

ROLE OF ETHICS IN THE WORK OF PUBLIC ACCOUNTANTS

As noted, only CPAs can audit the financial statements of publicly owned companies that have to report to the federal government's Securities and Exchange Commission (SEC). CPAs who audit the financial statements of an organization have a clear ethical responsibility to all those who use audited financial statements. But public accountants are in a peculiarly difficult position compared with those in the legal and medical professions, because the parties that rely on their work extend beyond the client (often a corporation) who pays them, to the business and financial community, including stockholders, investors, creditors, suppliers, customers, employees, and government regulators. These parties rely on the objectivity and integrity of CPAs to make sure that the financial statements fairly present in accordance with generally accepted accounting principles.

In the early days of the public accounting profession in the United States, many accountants came to the United States to audit new and growing enterprises on behalf of British investors. These auditors clearly knew to whom they owed their loyalties. They also brought with them strict principles that, when many of these auditors founded U.S.-based audit firms, influenced the formation of the accounting profession in the United States. Almost from the beginning, however, professional ethical standards were not left to the individual CPAs to determine.

To protect the public, states instituted educational standards and examinations, as well as admission standards for CPAs and the rescindment of professional licenses for breaches of professional standards. The American Association of Public Accountants formed an ethics committee in 1906 to develop ethics standards for its members. Its modern successor body, the American Institute of Certified Public Accountants (AICPA), is an organization of all state societies of CPAs. Its Professional Ethics Executive Committee (established in 1971) promulgates a code of professional conduct and investigates, threatens, and punishes AICPA members for infringements of the code.

Consequently, for much of the twentieth century the accounting and auditing profession was largely self-regulating, with a professional code of conduct and a mechanism for investigating and punishing those whose conduct fell below professional standards. A separate investigation might also be conducted by the state licensing organization (e.g., the Department of Education in New York State).

The federal legislation that ensued after the 1929 stock market crash (the Securities Act of 1933 and the Securities Exchange Act of 1934) set up a federal agency, the SEC, with broad powers of regulating public securities markets. All public companies are required by these acts to register with the SEC and to file annual audited financial statements. The SEC largely delegated accounting standard setting to the private sector but retained enforcement action. It may regulate the most powerful members of the profession who audit the financial statements filed with the SEC directly, by enforcement actions including bans on auditing or working for public companies; it can also ban trading in the securities of public companies. For the most part though, throughout the twentieth century, the audit profession continued to be self-regulating at the federal level, by agreement and cooperation between the SEC and the AICPA.

ETHICAL CONCERNS BEGINNING IN THE 1990S

During the 1990s the growth of management consulting by audit firms caused many observers to question whether those firms were sufficiently independent to conduct their audits of public companies in the interest of the investing public. Anecdotal evidence of an increasing willingness by auditors to agree with corporate management's dubious accounting treatments, strained the relationship between the profession and the SEC. Its chairman, Arthur Levitt, was so concerned about the growing threat to the integrity of financial reporting and hence to the operation of capital markets that he instituted a new regulatory body in 1997, the Independence Standards Board (ISB). The ISB attempted to shore up audit firms' independence from corporate management by instituting stricter regulation of professional conduct. Unfortunately, the board received little more than lip service from leading CPA firms and was abolished in 2001.

The corporate scandals of 2001–2002 resulted in major federal legislation and regulation not seen since the 1933 and 1934 securities acts, principally the Sarbanes-Oxley Act (SOX) of 2002. SOX transferred the regulation of accountants auditing the financial statements of public corporations from the AICPA to the Public Companies Accounting Oversight Board (PCAOB), a new private sector, not-for-profit body. The PCAOB is funded from fees paid by registrants. SOX requires accounting firms, including international firms and foreign firms that play a substantial role in the preparation of audit reports of U.S. public companies, to register with the PCAOB. As of November 2005 more than 1,500 firms were registered.

Section 103 of SOX directed the PCAOB to establish auditing and related attestation, quality control, ethics, and independence standards and rules for registered public accounting firms. To meet this requirement for ethical standards under rule 3500T, the board adopted the AICPA's Code of Professional Conduct Rule 102, and passed interpretations and rulings (as Section 191) as of April 16, 2003, as interim ethics standards, unless superseded or amended by the board. The board also adopted (under rule 3600T) the AICPA code of Professional Conduct Rule 101 as its interim Independence Standard, along with Standards 1, 2, and 3 and their interpretations issued by the ISB. It is the responsibility of users to determine if a particular rule has been amended or superseded.

AICPA CODE OF ETHICS

The AICPA Code of Ethics covers general principles as well as more explicit rules of conduct. It is based on six principles, which are translated into a set of specific rules that AICPA members must observe. The code is supported by interpretations and rulings that apply in specific circumstances. The overriding objective of the six principles is to commit members to honorable behavior, even at the sacrifice of personal advantage. The preamble states that by accepting membership in the institute "a CPA assumes an obligation of self-discipline above and beyond the requirements of laws and regulations."

The six principles to which the CPA must adhere are:

1. *Commitment*—to the public interest and honoring public trust

2. *Integrity*—sensitivity to professional and moral judgments

3. *Objectivity*—requires the CPA to be unbiased and impartial in assessing facts, making estimates and arriving at judgments

4. *Independence*—unbiased, impartial, and free of conflicts of interest (independence in fact and appearance) when providing auditing or other attestation serves. CPAs may not audit a company if they (or spouse or dependents) own stock in that company and/or have financial or employment relationships with the client (apart from financial interest in timely receipt of audit fees).

5. *Confidentiality*—information known to accounting professionals may not be disclosed to outsiders except when professional work papers are subpoenaed by a court. (Accountants do not have attorney-client privilege.)

6. *Professional competence*—exercising due care, including observing professional technical and ethical standards. Accounting professionals should undertake only tasks that they can complete with professional competence, and they must carry out their responsibilities with sufficient care and diligence, usually referred to as due care.

As the AICPA Code of Ethics has been adopted as the interim standard by the PCAOB, it governs behavior of all AICPA members, in all types of practice—auditing public companies, private companies, not-for-profit and governmental institutions, as well as attestation and tax practices. Accountants who are not members of the AICPA but who belong to other professional bodies are governed by similar codes of ethics. Those who are not members of any professional body are still subject to professional codes promulgated by state governments, for example, the New York State code.

In so far as the PCAOB amends their rules of ethics, however, there may be an increasing gulf between the demands made on registered firms by that board, and the requirements of the AICPA for CPA firms not involved in audit of public companies. For example, on November 23, 2005, the board proposed a change in rule 3502 from "Responsibility not to Cause Violations" (of tax shelter laws) to "Responsibility not to Knowingly or Recklessly Contribute to Violations." Unless the AICPA adopts the same higher standard, CPAs auditing public firms will in the future have to conform to higher ethical standards than those who do not.

ETHICS ENFORCEMENT

Enforcement varies with the type of accountant (CPA or non-CPA) and the type of practice (audit of publicly listed companies or not). For non-CPAs, state governments and professional societies may be responsible for ethics enforcement, but the penalty imposed by professional societies is limited to expulsion. CPAs face higher penalties.

Section 105 of SOX makes the PCAOB responsible for the enforcement of the professional standards for accountants auditing the financial statements of corporations issuing securities in public markets. The PCAOB adopted rules, approved by the SEC in May 2004, that allow it to investigate:

> any acts or practices, or omissions to act, by registered public accounting firms and persons associated with such firms, or both, that may violate any provision of the Act, the rules of the Board, the provisions of the securities laws relating to the preparation and issuance of audit reports and the obligations and liabilities of accountants with respect thereto, including the rules of the Commission issued under the Act, or *professional standards* [italics added]

Registered firms must cooperate with PCAOB investigations, the results of which are private and not released to the public. If a potential breach of professional standards is found, though, the PCAOB may hold public hearings and may impose sanctions—including revoking a firm's registration, barring a person from participating in audits of public companies, and invoking fines and imposition of remedial measures, such as training, quality-control procedures, and appointment of independent monitors.

Following SOX the AICPA membership voted to permit the AICPA to sanction members without investigation, if the SEC, Internal Revenue Service, PCAOB, or a state board sanctioned the member. In addition, the institute will allow more public disclosure and transparency on disciplinary matters.

CPAs who do not audit the financial statements of publicly listed companies do not fall under the jurisdiction of the SEC and the PCAOB. Ethical standards for these CPAs are enforced by the state societies of CPAs (if they are members) and by individual state enforcement mechanisms of codes of ethics. For example, in New York State, the Office of the Professions of the Department of State Education investigates and prosecutes professional misconduct. Penalties include censure, reprimand, fines of up to $10,000 for each violation, suspension of license and, in severe cases, revocation of license. The state board deals with about thirty cases of all types of professional misconduct by CPAs per year, about nine of which involve breaches of professional duties. State societies of CPAs also have enforcement mechanisms for their codes of ethics, and violations can lead to public expulsion.

ETHICS FOR ACCOUNTANTS NOT IN PUBLIC PRACTICE

Not all accountants work as public auditors. Those who work for corporations as financial managers, management accountants, and internal auditors may be CPAs, but a significant number are not. Over time, these accountants and internal auditors have founded their own professional societies without state or federal legislation. These societies also promulgate professional standards ensuring all members are appropriately qualified to do the work required of them and that all members adhere to a code of conduct or ethics somewhat similar to those of the AICPA. Examples include the Institute of Management Accountants' Standards of Ethical Conduct, which apply to practitioners of management accounting and financial management in corporations and not-for-profit institutions, and the Institute of Internal Auditors' (IIA) Code of Ethics, which applies to all IIA members and to certified internal auditors.

SEE ALSO *Accounting*

BIBLIOGRAPHY

American Institute of Certified Public Accountants. (2006, January). *AICPA code of professional conduct.* Retrieved February 20, 2006, from http://www.aicpa.org/about/code/index.html

Institute of Internal Auditors. (n.d.) *Code of ethics.* Retrieved February 20, 2006, from http://www.theiia.org/index.cfm?doc_id=604

Institute of Management Accountants. (n.d.). *IMA's statement of ethical professional practice.* Retrieved February 20, 2006, from http://www.imanet.org/ima/sec.asp?TRACKID=&CID=191&DID=323

New York State Education Department, Office of the Professions. (n.d.). *Professional misconduct and discipline.* Retrieved February 20, 2006, from http://www.op.nysed.gov/opd.htm

Public Company Accounting Oversight Board. (2005, February 15). *Bylaws and rules of the Public Company Accounting Oversight Board.* Retrieved February 20, 2006, from http://www.pcaobus.org/Rules/Rules_of_the_Board/Bylaws.pdf

Jan Sweeney

ETHICS IN ECONOMICS

As might be suspected, early writings on ethics were centered not on economics or business, but personal beliefs and actions. It becomes readily apparent from early discussions of ethics that philosophers and writers viewed ethics as a matter of choice. Individuals must make choices in their lives. This is important to note—businesses do not make choices. Choices are made and/or implemented by individuals within the economic enterprise. People in government make choices, people in educational institutions make choices, people in businesses make choices, people with churches make choices; everyone is forced to make choices, and even the choice not to choose is a decision.

ETHICS IN ORGANIZATION

Velasquez (2002) illustrated some important points regarding organizations and their acts relative to individuals in the organization. He stated:

I. A corporate organization exists only if (1) there exist certain human individuals placed in certain circumstances and (2) our linguistic rules lay down that when those kinds of individuals exist in those kinds of circumstances, they shall count as a corporate organization.

II. A corporate organization acts only if (1) certain human individuals in the organization performed certain actions in certain circumstances and (2) our linguistic rules lay down that when those kinds of individuals perform those kinds of actions in those kinds of circumstances, this shall count as an act of their corporate organization. (p. 16)

Linguistic rules are the rules of either written or spoken language. In the above quote, it is pointed out that individuals make up the corporation or business and that the corporation acts when these individuals carry out their assigned duties within the scope of the corporate authority. However, since it is human individuals on whom the corporation depends, it is these individuals who are seen to be responsible for moral duties and issues.

Businesses are the most significant institution in the economic structure. As such, businesses are expected to produce goods and services that are demanded by members of society, and once produced, these goods and services must be distributed to the numerous societal groups. Decisions are made within the business structure about who will produce, how much will be produced, how production will be implemented, how the work will be organized, and how the finished good or service will be made available to the consuming members of society. All these decisions are necessary in the day-to-day operation of an economic institution, and all these choices are made by people. It could be argued that computer models are used to make decisions, but it can be further counter-argued that computer models are developed by people and people are the ones who implement recommendations made by computer modeling.

In order for people in all institutions to make choices, there must be some guidelines or principles upon which the choices are based. These guidelines are often referred to as values. Everyone develops a set of values, or preferences, beginning in early childhood—or perhaps even immediately from birth. These values stem from how people are raised, where they live, their ancestry, and all the other factors that influence everyone's lives. If everyone has a value system, everyone must have an ethical system upon which to base judgments and choices. Stemming from this personal set of values will come policies and procedures that will guide all organizations within the economic structure.

Boulding (1968) argued that individuals have a real personal ethic, which can be deduced from a person's actual behavior, and a verbal ethic, which can be deduced from a person's statements. Boulding found that it is basically a universal phenomenon that a person will talk about one set of ethical principles but act according to another. The old statement "Do as I say, not as I do" seems to reflect an accurate perception of reality.

Ethics, from an economist's perspective, is a matter of choice. Economics is a matter of choice. There are several alternatives from which a choice must be made. A business owner or manager might have to decide between producing weapons for military use or firearms for use by private individuals who pursue the sport of wild game hunting. These decisions are not always easy, especially when guided by the need for the organization to make a profit. The choice that is ultimately made is based on a value system that influences policies and procedures in the organization. In an economic environment, the decision is often made based on values that have been determined to be most important or that are ranked on a scale of best to worst.

A dilemma that faces all decision makers, especially when group decision making is used, is the different value systems that are held by individuals. While organizations have policies and procedures, not every option from which to choose is necessarily easily defined or clearly understood. Many organizations have mechanisms through which those affected by the decision can appeal it for further consideration. In the case of a university student who receives a failing grade but thinks the grade was undeserved because of a conflict with the professor, an appeal by the student might be heard and a decision could be made to overturn the professor's decision. Or the decision might be made in favor of the professor and the student's appeal denied. Such a decision is based on value systems that guide ethical behaviors.

Decisions made by economic institutions do not always match what the general populace thinks is correct. When this happens, the result can be new laws or rules that are passed to try to contain those who are perceived as violating the public trust. For example, many laws have been passed to curb problems with pollution. Antipollution laws are designed to reduce the harmful effects of pollution; when a business does not follow the laws, it can be severely penalized. In some cases, the new laws force the closure of business enterprises because conformity to the laws is cost-prohibitive. This was the case when laws went into effect requiring underground gasoline tanks at service stations to meet Environmental Protection Agency requirements. Many businesses could not meet the requirements because of the expenses involved and they closed their doors.

At other times, businesses choose to violate the laws in order to save money. In the long run, this can cost more than the business would have had to pay had the changes been made to comply with the laws. This occurred when a chemical manufacturing company was caught dumping hazardous waste into an Illinois River. The company was told to stop the dumping and was fined a large sum of money. However, during the time the environmental inspectors were on the premises, the company chose to dump more waste into the river, saying that if they had not done it, there could have been a fatal accident in the plant. They were fined an additional sum. These examples illustrate choices that must be made—not by businesses in economic systems, but by individuals in the businesses.

Whereas businesses are the most significant institution within the economic structure, it should also be noted that businesses are not the only institutions within an economic structure. There are many other important groups, such as the family, government, churches, and schools. All these institutions play an important role in developing value systems and the moral influences on individuals in businesses.

Because many other institutions influence the thinking of individuals in organizations, different value systems are developed. Some value systems are inconsistent with what is necessary for successful business operations and become a threat to a business and economic system. An example of that is honesty. An individual whose value system does not include complete honesty becomes a threat to successful business operations. Because of threats like these to economic entities, rules are established to deal with those who have different value systems. The rules are called laws, and the government is the largest enforcer of laws.

Governments are important to successful business and economic operations. Governments help to assure fair trade and commerce within a country and internationally.

A good example of this is when the U.S. government ordered the breakup of the Bell Telephone System several years ago. It was felt that the system had grown too large and that fair competition was not possible. When companies become monopolies, they can set prices and control supplies of goods and services in ways that might not be fair to consumers. A government can intervene to assure fair trade practices. Many laws have been written to influence fair economic trade.

SETTING BUSINESS ETHICAL STANDARDS

Businesses make decisions that influence consumers, employees, and society in general. It is people who make up the businesses, and it is people who must set the standards for ethical conduct. The process for setting standards needs to be a top-down approach—management must develop and support an ethical code. Employees must understand what is expected of them in order to follow the codes. Managers and employees must be trained to interpret and consider alternatives relative to established ethical codes. In larger businesses, compliance offices are often established to assure that ethical codes are followed.

People outside the business must also know what ethical standards are being followed, and they must know that individuals within the company who do not follow the prescribed ethical codes will be dealt with in a manner appropriate to the violation. This illustrates the need to enforce the ethical codes. If a business establishes an ethical code but does not enforce it, the code will not be followed.

SOCIAL RESPONSIBILITY

Closely related to ethical codes are responsibilities that economic enterprises have to society. This is known as social responsibility. This is a difficult element of business operations because it normally means additional costs to the business. Social responsibility could mean making contributions to charitable organizations. An example might be a corporation donating land it is not using to a conservation group for the development of a nature preserve.

Social responsibility also includes internal considerations, such as hiring minorities, establishing on-site child-care facilities, controlling pollution, ensuring safe working conditions, providing substance-abuse programs for employees, and manufacturing safe products. These are all economic decisions that have social effects both within and outside the business.

Businesses that are concerned about social responsibility will conduct social audits. This is a systematic evaluation of the organization's progress toward implementing socially responsible programs. This is not a precise science and depends on interpretations of what is socially responsive behavior. Again, these decisions must be made by individuals within the business. Social audits do illustrate that a business is at least concerned about the social impact it has.

SUMMARY

Ethics is not easy for any business, and there will always be individuals and/or groups who question the behaviors of institutions in our economic system. Our discussion has focused on businesses in the economic system, but other systems such as churches, schools, and governmental agencies are also subjected to critical ethical scrutiny. Ethics and social responsibility are the concern of everyone, and it is up to individuals to establish ethical codes and to follow them.

SEE ALSO *Economics*

BIBLIOGRAPHY

Baylis, Charles A. (1958). *Ethics: The Principles of Wise Choice.* New York: Holt.

Boulding, Kenneth E. (1968). *Beyond Economics: Essays on Society, Religion, and Ethics.* Ann Arbor: University of Michigan Press.

Bowne, Borden P. (1979). *The Principles of Ethics.* New York: AMS Press.

Brandt, Richard B. (1998). *A Theory of the Good and the Right.* Amherst, NY: Prometheus Books.

Facione, Peter A., Scherer, Donald, and Attig, Thomas. (1991). *Ethics and Society.* Englewood Cliffs, NJ: Prentice Hall.

Velasquez, Manuel G. (2002). *Business Ethics: Concepts and Cases.* Upper Saddle River, NJ: Prentice Hall.

Roger L. Luft

ETHICS IN FINANCE

Ethics in general is concerned with human behavior that is acceptable or "right" and that is not acceptable or "wrong" based on conventional morality. General ethical norms encompass truthfulness, honesty, integrity, respect for others, fairness, and justice. They relate to all aspects of life, including business and finance. Financial ethics is, therefore, a subset of general ethics.

Ethical norms are essential for maintaining stability and harmony in social life, where people interact with one another. Recognition of others' needs and aspirations, fairness, and cooperative efforts to deal with common issues are, for example, aspects of social behavior that contribute to social stability. In the process of social evolution, we have developed not only an instinct to care for ourselves but also a conscience to care for others. There may arise situations in which the need to care for ourselves runs into conflict with the need to care for others. In such situations, ethical norms are needed to guide our behavior. As Demsey (1999) puts it: "Ethics represents the attempt to resolve the conflict between selfishness and selflessness; between our material needs and our conscience."

Ethical dilemmas and ethical violations in finance can be attributed to an inconsistency in the conceptual framework of modern financial-economic theory and the widespread use of a principal-agent model of relationship in financial transactions. The financial-economic theory that underlies the modern capitalist system is based on the rational-maximizer paradigm, which holds that individuals are self-seeking (egoistic) and that they behave rationally when they seek to maximize their own interests. The principal-agent model of relationships refers to an arrangement whereby one party, acting as an agent for another, carries out certain functions on behalf of that other. Such arrangements are an integral part of the modern economic and financial system, and it is difficult to imagine it functioning without them.

The behavioral assumption of the modern financial-economic theory runs counter to the ideas of trustworthiness, loyalty, fidelity, stewardship, and concern for others that underlie the traditional principal-agent relationship. The traditional concept of agency is based on moral values. However, if human beings are rational maximizers, then agency on behalf of others in the traditional sense is impossible. As Duska (1992) explains it: "To do something for another in a system geared to maximize self-interest is foolish. Such an answer, though, points out an inconsistency at the heart of the system, for a system that has rules requiring agents to look out for others while encouraging individuals to look out only for themselves, destroys the practice of looking out for others" (p. 61).

The ethical dilemma presented by the problem of conflicting interests has been addressed in some areas of finance, such as corporate governance, by converting the agency relationship into a purely contractual relationship that uses a carrot-and-stick approach to ensure ethical behavior by agents. In corporate governance, the problem of conflict between management (agent) and stockholders (principal) is described as an agency problem. Economists have developed an agency theory to deal with this problem. The agency theory assumes that both the agent and the principal are self-interested and aim to maximize their gain in their relationship. A simple example would be the case of a store manager acting as an agent for the owner of the store. The store manager wants as much pay as possi-

ble for as little work as possible, and the store owner wants as much work from the manager for as little pay as possible. This theory is value-free because it does not pass judgment on whether the maximization behavior is good or bad and is not concerned with what a just pay for the manager might be. It drops the ideas of honesty and loyalty from the agency relationship because of their incompatibility with the fundamental assumption of rational maximization. "The job of agency theory is to help devise techniques for describing the conflict inherent in the principal-agent relationship and controlling the situations so that the agent, acting from self-interest, does as little harm as possible to the principal's interest" (DeGeorge, 1992). The agency theory turns the traditional concept of agency relationship into a structured (contractual) relationship in which the principal can influence the actions of agents through incentives, motivations, and punishment schemes. The principal essentially uses monetary rewards, punishments, and the agency laws to command loyalty from the agent.

Most of our needs for financial services—management of retirement savings, stock and bond investing, and protection against unforeseen events, to name a few—are such that they are better entrusted to others because we have neither the ability nor the time to carry them out effectively. The corporate device of contractualization of the agency relationship is, however, too difficult to apply to the multitude of financial dealings between individuals and institutions that take place in the financial market every day. Individuals are not as well organized as stockholders, and they are often unaware of the agency problem. Lack of information also limits their ability to monitor an agent's behavior. Therefore, what we have in our complex modern economic system is a paradoxical situation: the ever-increasing need for getting things done by others on the one hand, and the description of human nature that emphasizes selfish behavior on the other. This paradoxical situation, or the inconsistency in the foundation of the modern capitalist system, can explain most of the ethical problems and declining morality in the modern business and finance arena.

ETHICAL VIOLATIONS

The most frequently occurring ethical violations in finance relate to insider trading, stakeholder interest versus stockholder interest, investment management, and campaign financing. Businesses in general and financial markets in particular are replete with examples of violations of trust and loyalty in both public and private dealings. Fraudulent financial dealings, influence peddling and corruption in governments, brokers not maintaining proper records of customer trading, cheating customers of their trading profits, unauthorized transactions, insider trading, misuse of customer funds for personal gain, mispricing customer trades, and corruption and larceny in banking have become common occurrences.

Insider trading is perhaps one of the most publicized unethical behaviors by traders. Insider trading refers to trading in the securities of a company to take advantage of material "inside" information about the company that is not available to the public. Such a trade is motivated by the possibility of generating extraordinary gain with the help of nonpublic information (information not yet made public). It gives the trader an unfair advantage over other traders in the same security. Insider trading was legal in some European countries until recently. In the United States, the 1984 Trading Sanctions Act made it illegal to trade in a security while in the possession of material nonpublic information. The law applies to both the insiders, who have access to nonpublic information, and the people with whom they share such information.

Campaign financing in the United States has been a major source of concern to the public because it raises the issue of conflict of interest for elected officials in relation to the people or lobbying groups that have financed their campaigns. The United States has a long history of campaign finance reform. The Federal Election Commission (FEC) administers and enforces the federal campaign finance statutes enacted by the Congress from time to time. Many states have also passed lobbying and campaign finance laws and established ethics commissions to enforce these statutes.

ETHICAL CODES

Approaches to dealing with ethical problems in finance range from establishing ethical codes for financial professionals to efforts to replace the rational-maximizer (egoistic) paradigm that underlies the modern capitalist system by one in which individuals are assumed to be altruistic, honest, and basically virtuous.

It is not uncommon to find established ethical codes and ethical offices in American corporations and in financial markets. Ethical codes for financial markets are established by the official regulatory agencies and self-regulating organizations to ensure ethically responsible behavior on the part of the operatives in the financial markets.

One of the most important and powerful official regulatory agencies for the securities industry in the United States is the Securities and Exchange Commission (SEC). It is in charge of implementing federal securities laws, and, as such, it sets up rules and regulations for the proper conduct of professionals operating within its regulatory jurisdiction. Many professionals play a role within the securities industry, among the most important of which are accountants, broker-dealers, investment advisers, and investment companies. Any improper or unethical conduct on the part of these professionals is of great concern to the SEC, whose primary responsibility is to protect investor interests and maintain the integrity of the securities market. The SEC can censure, suspend, or bar professionals who practice within its regulatory domain for lack of requisite qualifications or unethical and improper conduct. The SEC also oversees self-regulatory organizations (SROs), which include stock exchanges, the National Association of Security Dealers (NASD), the Municipal Securities Rulemaking Board (MSRB), clearing agencies, transfer agents, and securities information processors. An SRO is a membership organization that makes and enforces rules for its members based on the federal securities laws. The SEC has the responsibility of reviewing and approving the rules made by SROs.

Other rule-making agencies include the Federal Reserve System, the Federal Deposit Insurance Corporation (FDIC), and state finance authorities. Congress has entrusted to the Federal Reserve Board the responsibility of implementing laws pertaining to a wide range of banking and financial activities, a task that it carries out through its regulations. One such regulation has to do with unfair or deceptive acts or practices. The FDIC has its own rules and regulations for the banking industry, and it also draws its power to regulate from various banking laws passed by Congress.

In addition to federal and state regulatory agencies, various professional associations set their own rules of good conduct for their members. The American Institute of Certified Public Accountants (AICPA), the American Institute of Certified Planners (AICP), the Investment Company Institute (ICI), the American Society of Chartered Life Underwriters (ASCLU), the Institute of Chartered Financial Analysts (ICFA), the National Association of Bank Loan and Credit Officers (also known as Robert Morris Associates), and the Association for Investment Management and Research (AIMR) are some of the professional associations that have well-publicized codes of ethics.

TOWARD A PARADIGM SHIFT

There has been an effort to address the ethical problems in business and finance by reexamining the conceptual foundation of the modern capitalist system and changing it to one that is consistent with the traditional model of agency relationship. The proponents of a paradigm shift question the rational-maximizer assumption that underlies the modern financial-economic theory and reject the idea that all human actions are motivated by self-interest. They embrace an alternative assumption that human beings are to some degree ethical and altruistic and emphasize the role of the traditional principal-agent relationship based on honesty, loyalty, and trust. Duska (1992) argues: "Clearly, there is an extent to which [Adam] Smith and the economists are right. Human beings are self-interested and will not always look out for the interest of others. But there are times they will set aside their interests to act on behalf of others. Agency situations were presumably set up to guarantee those times."

The idea that human beings can be honest and altruistic is an empirically valid assumption; it is not hard to find examples of honesty and altruism in both private and public dealings. There is no reason this idea should not be embraced and nurtured. As Bowie (1991) points out: "Looking out for oneself is a natural, powerful motive that needs little, if any, social reinforcement … Altruistic motives, even if they too are natural, are not as powerful: they need to be socially reinforced and nurtured" (p. 19). If the financial-economic theory accepts the fact that behavioral motivations other than that of wealth maximization are both realistic and desirable, then the agency problem that economists try to deal with will be a nonproblem. For Dobson (1993), the true role of ethics in finance is to be found in the acceptance of "internal good" ("good" in the sense of "right" rather than in the sense of "physical product"), which, he adds, is what classical philosophers describe as "virtue"—that is, the internal good toward which all human endeavor should strive. He contends: "If the attainment of internal goods were to become generally accepted as the ultimate objective of all human endeavor, both personal and professional, then financial markets would become truly ethical" (p. 60).

SEE ALSO *Finance*

BIBLIOGRAPHY

Bowie, Norman E. (1991). "Challenging the Egoistic Paradigm." *Business Ethics Quarterly*. 1:1, 1-21.

Bowie, Norman E., and Freeman, Edward R., eds. (1992). *Ethics and Agency Theory: An Introduction*. New York: Oxford University Press.

DeGeorge, Richard T. (1992). "Agency Theory and the Ethics of Agency." In *Ethics and Agency Theory: An Introduction*, Norman E. Bowie and Edward R. Freeman, eds. New York: Oxford University Press.

Dobson, John (1993). "The Role of Ethics in Finance." *Financial Analysis Journal*. 49:6, 57-61.

Duska, Ronald R. (1992). "Why Be a Loyal Agent? A Systematic Ethical Analysis." In *Ethics and Agency Theory: An Introduction*. Norman E. Bowie and Edward R. Freeman, eds., New York: Oxford University Press.

Frowen, S.F., and McHugh, F.P., eds. (1995). *Financial Decision-Making and Moral Responsibility*. New York: St. Martin's Press.

Goodpaster, Kenneth E. (1991). "Business Ethics and Stakeholder Analysis." *Business Ethics Quarterly*. 1:1, 52-71.

Anand G. Shetty

ETHICS IN INFORMATION PROCESSING

New technologies in information processing often raise ethical concerns, resulting from their creating new possibilities for human action. Computer ethics can be defined as moral philosophy concerning the ethical dilemmas involved in areas of information processing, including theories, approaches in decision-making situations, and methods of increasing awareness of ethics. These ethical and moral issues are among the most socially important aspects of information processing. There are two major problems in the area: (1) unethical behavior leading to immoral acts such as virus creation and software piracy and (2) lack of awareness about information technology security and information technology-related crimes.

Ethics in information processing is considered so important that the Computer Ethics Institute developed the following Ten Commandments of Computer Ethics.

> Thou shalt not use a computer to harm other people.
>
> Thou shalt not interfere with other people's computer work.
>
> Thou shalt not snoop around in other people's computer files.
>
> Thou shalt not use a computer to steal.
>
> Thou shalt not use a computer to bear false witness.
>
> Thou shalt not copy or use proprietary software for which you have not paid.
>
> Thou shalt not use other people's computer resources without authorization or proper compensation.
>
> Thou shalt not appropriate other people's intellectual output.
>
> Thou shalt think about the social consequences of the program you are writing or the system you are designing.
>
> Thou shalt always use a computer in ways that ensure consideration and respect for your fellow humans.

Use of information

		% Ethical		% Would You Do It?	
		High School Yes	Univ Yes	High School Yes	Univ Yes
1.	You are the payroll clerk and know what everyone's salary is. A raise will be given next month. You feel that it would be OK to tell a few of your closest friends what they will be getting.	0.36	0.27	0.54	0.29
2.	Your job is in jeopardy because you have displayed very little initiative. You need this job because you have a family to support. You use a colleague's computer and see a proposal for a new product. You write it up as your own.	0.15	0.12	0.25	0.15
3.	Today is the third day you have had trouble getting to work on time. You can punch in by computer from your home. You do it "just for today" so that you do not lose your job.	0.15	0.10	0.48	0.35
4.	You work for the phone company and have access to private/unlisted numbers. A friend calls you saying he must make an emergency call and he needs to know a number that is unlisted. You give your friend the number.	0.17	0.17	0.39	0.42
5.	A really nice word processing program is on the computer in your office. You would like to have it on your home computer, so you copy it.	0.33	0.33	0.59	0.56
6.	You work in a bank and have access to all bank account records. Out of curiosity, you check to see what your friends' bank balances are.	0.10	0.13	0.23	0.21

Table 1

INFORMATION-PROCESSING ETHICS AND BUSINESS

Ethical issues raised by information processing in business include confidentiality of data, software piracy, hacking, and stealing the property of others. In order to determine the ethical knowledge and behavior of young people, a survey of 780 high school and university business students was conducted (Vincent and Meche, 2003). The ethical knowledge survey was made up of nineteen questions, six of which were the information-processing questions shown in Table 1.

All of the actions in Table 1 are unethical. The responses shown in the table demonstrate that ethical problems exist among young people. As can be seen, some do not recognize ethical dilemmas, and many would participate in unethical behavior regardless. For instance, revealing confidential information, stealing the ideas of others, copying software, and punching the time clock from home are unethical behaviors. Unauthorized copying of software—software piracy—is stealing. Besides being strictly illegal in many countries, it is morally wrong, because it violates the right of the owners of the software to receive payment for the use of their invention. The presence of illegal software used is highest in some Asian countries, followed by Eastern Europe, and the United States. Additionally, according to a *Computerworld* survey of 255 information systems professionals in

corporate America, 53 percent have made unauthorized copies of commercial software ("Results of a Survey," 1995). The typical reason given was to try it out before buying it.

Hacking and virus creations are serious crimes that must be treated just like other criminal offenses. Generally speaking, hacking is breaking into other people's property; it is an immoral action that cannot be justified under any circumstances. One of the most popular hackers' arguments is that "electrons are free—they do not belong to anybody." This premise is invalid; there is no reason why electrically committed crimes should be treated differently from physical crimes.

Information on the Internet, including thousands of databases and more than four hundred magazines, is extremely hard to control. Search engines or robots have been designed to search for specific information in this immense collection of data. When a search engine filters or controls all the information that a person accesses, there is the danger that the person's view of the topic will become narrowed. This offers the designers of search engines an opportunity to manipulate people's minds by controlling the information they receive. Additionally, online shopping creates the possibility of disclosure of financial information, such as credit card information, to unauthorized parties.

Questions have arisen concerning computer graphics. For example, should graphical re-creations of incidents such as automobile accidents be allowed to be used in courtrooms? Is it right for an individual to electronically reproduce and then alter an artistic image originally created by someone else. It is apparent that there should be clear rules and regulations concerning cyberspace (Johnson, 2001).

INFORMATION-PROCESSING ETHICS AND ETIQUETTE

Courtesy in information processing is often referred to as Netiquette—or etiquette on the Internet. E-mail and chat room etiquette is central to courtesy in cyberspace. In both situations people should follow the Golden Rule: "Do unto others as you would have them do unto you."

Regarding e-mail, one should respond promptly to e-mail messages; think twice before sending personal information and private letters on business systems; not send flame mail (mail written in anger); not send duplicate copies of private e-mail without letting the recipient know who else is getting it; and not send unsolicited mail, such as pyramid schemes, chain letters, and junk mail.

Schools and employers should establish e-mail policies, present them in writing, and have training sessions for all involved. Lack of an e-mail policy creates legal risks. Often, the company is responsible for the e-mail of its employees. Additionally, e-mail is not a secure medium. Many company policy statements say that e-mail is owned or co-owned by the company and that the company has a right to inspect it. The federal Electronic Communication Privacy Act of 1986 prohibits the interception of any wire, oral, or electronic communication, but there is a business exception to the law that allows employers to intercept such communications that are deemed work-related.

Chat room etiquette involves communicating with others over the Internet. The same etiquette used in personal conversation should be observed here. Anonymity does not excuse bad behavior.

INFORMATION-PROCESSING ETHICS AND PORNOGRAPHY

Computer pornography means depiction of actual sexual contact (hard-core) and depiction of nudity or lewd exhibition (soft-core). The courts and numerous U.S. statutes concur with the distinction between hard-core and soft-core pornography. Not all pornography meets the legal test for obscenity, however, nor are all depictions of sexual activity deemed pornographic (Albee, 1999). Pornography and obscenity certainly raise a few moral questions: Are pornographic materials morally objectionable or not? Is it right for the state to regulate access to pornographic

material by consenting adults? In all the confusion one point should be made: Pornography degrades human beings.

Feminists consider pornography to be demeaning to women, contributing to their being seen as objects of desire and control for men. Some religious leaders maintain that pornography ought to be banned because it is morally wrong. Meanwhile pornography continues to be a huge force in the social and personal context (Albee, 1999).

CODES OF ETHICS IN INFORMATION PROCESSING

The following guidelines should be considered when developing codes of ethics for schools and businesses:

1. Identify prevailing social values before addressing current issues in the school or workplace. Examples of ethical values important to society might include trustworthiness, responsibility, respect, empathy, fairness, and citizenship.

2. In composing the code of ethics, give examples of behaviors that reflect each value.

3. Have key members of the organization review the code and provide input.

4. Review any rules or values incorporated into the code to assure that they adhere to relevant laws and regulations; this ensures that the school or organization is not breaking any of them.

5. Indicate that all employees are expected to conform to the values stated in the code of ethics.

6. Announce and distribute the new code of ethics to all involved.

7. Update the code at least once a year.

Examples of topics typically addressed in codes of ethics include: dressing appropriately; avoiding illegal drugs; following the instructions of superiors; being reliable and prompt; maintaining confidentiality; not accepting personal gifts from stakeholders; avoiding discrimination based on race, gender, age or sexual orientation; avoiding conflicts of interest; complying with laws and regulations; not using the organization's property for personal use; and reporting illegal or questionable activity (McNamara, 1998).

TEACHING INFORMATION PROCESSING ETHICS

In direct and indirect ways people begin to learn ethical values from birth. While the family and religious institutions are assigned the primary responsibility for ethical education, schools have traditionally been charged with teaching and reinforcing moral values, especially those directly related to school behaviors. Since many of the ethical issues that surround technology deal with school behaviors, they are an appropriate and necessary part of the school curriculum. Schools must create technology environments that help students avoid temptations. Computer screens that are easily monitored, use of passwords, and logging in and out of secure network systems, along with videotaping of lab areas, all help remove the opportunities for technology misuse in the media center or classroom.

Teachers and leaders of student groups who want to promote good ethical behavior can use methods such as creating codes of ethics, using stories of good or bad ethical behavior as examples in discussions, inviting speakers, and using case studies, role playing, games, simulations, and mock trials. Of primary importance is the teacher's or student leader's own behavior, which should be exemplary. Technology privileges should not be given to students until they have demonstrated that they know and can apply ethical standards and school policies.

Finally, measures should be taken to improve the solutions to the ethical dilemmas that arise in information processing. There is a need for more specific professional guidelines and codes of ethics; research on ethical problems; education and training; and cooperation among all who are involved with information-processing ethics, including, but not limited to, theologians, philosophers, computer scientists, educators, business people, and attorneys.

SEE ALSO *Information Processing*

BIBLIOGRAPHY

Albee, Reid D. (1999). "Ethical Dimensions: Ethical Considerations of Pornography." Retrieved October 18, 2005, from http://www.umm.maine.edu/resources/beharchive/bexstudents/ReidAlbee/ra360.html.

Johnson, Deborah G. (2001). *Computer Ethics* (3rd ed.). Upper Saddle River, NJ: Prentice Hall.

McNamara, Carter (1998). "Complete Guide to Ethics Management: An Ethics Toolkit for Managers." Retrieved October 18, 2005, from http://www.mapnp.org/library/ethics/ethxgde.htm#anchor41892.

Vincent, Annette, and Meche, Melanie (2003). "Knowledge of Ethics Among Teens and Young Adults." *Ethics and Critical Thinking*, 2003(4) 1-11.

Annette Vincent
Melanie A. Meche

ETHICS IN LAW FOR BUSINESS

This article deals with ethical problems in law in the context of business operations. A lawyer is professionally qualified to give businesspersons advice on what the law is; judges are authorized to decide what the law is; and legislatures, within the limits of the Constitution, may make the law. Religious organizations and other organizations make many statements about what is ethical, but unless the ethical norms are written into law, they are not enforceable and, to some extent, remain a matter of personal opinion.

This article is intended to raise issues of ethics in law for business that may be discussed and debated. It also provides a framework from Aristotle (384–322 B.C.E.) to aid in the discussion of determining the most ethical course. In each case questions may be asked as follows:

1. What are the ethical choices in making this decision?

2. Does the law require the businessperson to make ethical choices?

3. Should the law require the businessperson to make ethical choices?

WHAT IS LAW?

Law for business consists of a set of required norms of behavior. The essence of law is that it commands behavior under threat of punishment or sanction. Tax law requires the payment of money to the government; there is no choice. Contracts are entered into voluntarily, but once entered into they may be enforced through the courts. Many laws have no particular ethical content. Many laws require ethical behavior, and, in rare cases, some laws may require unethical behavior. Frequently the law allows the businessperson the choice to be either ethical or unethical. In those cases the question arises: Should the law require ethical behavior?

WHAT IS ETHICS?

The Greek word *ethos* means habit. The Greek philosopher Aristotle taught that the ethical person is one who has virtuous habits. Among the virtues are courage, temperance, honor, good temper, truthfulness and justice. Virtues can be learned through education and practice. Aristotle believed virtue and consequent ethical behavior can be learned. He went on to say that we all seek "the good life," which comes when we live in a society of ethical persons—that is, those who behave virtuously. This philosophy can serve as a model for our discussion. We must decide what the elements of "the good life" are (wealth, security, freedom, opportunity). Next, what in a given business situation would be ethical (virtuous behavior), and does the law require or should the law require ethical behavior? In the following paragraphs areas of business law that have ethical issues are considered. The reader is invited to examine the issues in light of the above ethical model.

CONTRACTS AND ETHICS

Business is about making and selling products and exchanging goods and services. When a contractor orders a load of bricks to build a house and then in turn sells the house or hires a worker, it is a constant process of making and fulfilling contracts. A contract is a promise to do something. It may be to deliver goods, to perform a service (say, to paint a house), or possibly to employ or be employed by another. The very process of business is making and fulfilling contracts. Without contracts, no business would be possible. There are many ethical issues involved in making contracts.

For most legal purposes, a person becomes an adult at age eighteen. Before that, a minor may disaffirm an otherwise legal agreement, a provision that exists to protect minors from abuse by overreaching adults. What should the rights and responsibilities of minors be? What about adults who are mentally incompetent or insane?

What about adults of normal intelligence and capacity? Suppose a loan is made on the following terms: "Here is a loan of $20. You will give me $21 back in a week." This is an interest rate of 5 percent a week, which is 5 percent × 52, or 260 percent a year. This contract is illegal in most states. Suppose a fast-talking but honest salesperson sells goods on credit in the buyer's home. Buyers must be told in writing that they have three days to change their minds. Is this ethical?

Under the law of contract, when a transaction is completed, it is final. Suppose a person buys a set of green towels and then decides a couple of days later that red towels would look better. The store could legally say, "you bought them, there is nothing wrong with them; they are yours." If a sign in the store said, "All returns must be made within 30 days," that sign becomes part of the contract. Frequently signs warn, "No returns on prom and party dresses." This reinforces the contract. A good return policy is simply good business, but the law leaves the ethics of returns up to the store. What return policy is the most ethical for business?

WARRANTIES

A warranty is part of a business contract. It is essentially a binding promise that the product is fit for its intended purposes, is free of defects, and works. Most products of any complexity come with a "limited warranty," which most commonly warrants parts and labor for one year. Also common these days are the sales of extended warranties that extend the one-year warranty up to three or even five years. This allows manufacturers and sellers to write warranties in almost any fashion. The ethical questions are: To what extent should a company stand behind its products? At what point is it ethically correct for the customer to accept the risk of a defective product?

The way warranties are written can raise ethical problems. In an automobile, tires and batteries wear out and are subject to very limited warranties; however, a modern automobile consists of thousands of parts—any one of which may give out or be defective. Warranty descriptions, even when plainly written, can be confusing as to what is included and what is excluded. What, then, is an ethical automobile warranty?

ADVERTISING

Everyone is aware that there is much criticism of the ethics of advertising. False advertising is against the law, and all would agree it is unethical. Famous cases involve a product that was beneficial in many ways but was falsely claimed to prevent colds. In another case, an aspirin company claimed its aspirin was more effective than others.

If a store advertises "apples—5 pounds for $2.50," it must have a reasonable quantity on hand; it is considered good business practice to give rain checks, but doing so is not legally required. It is also against the law to advertise a product at a very low price with the intention of trying to talk customers into higher-priced products. This is known as bait and switch.

The law allows what is known as sales puffery. This is an emphasis on subjective qualities, such as that a car is beautiful and will make you feel good, or that a high-fat food tastes good without mentioning the health risks of excess fat. It is easy to look at advertisements and identify sales puffery and half-truths. What is the ethical line?

It is against the law to advertise illegal products, such as controlled substances, but what about legal products that are harmful? Cigarettes may not now be advertised on television or on billboards. Should the ban be extended to advertising in magazines?

Truthful advertising is part of freedom of speech. What other restrictions, if any, should be part of law? What about advertisements for alcohol?

EMPLOYMENT LAW

Few areas of law mix law and ethics as much as employment law. Surely employment is critical to our welfare and thus is of keen interest and subject to much emotional debate.

Employment-at-Will. While government employees and unionized workers enjoy more job protection, most employees in the United States are employed at will. The law allows them to be fired for cause or for no cause. A boss, under the law, may fire even a long-term employee simply because the boss does not like the person. In most other industrialized countries employees, after a probationary period, can be fired only for cause (e.g. they are incompetent or steal company property). U.S. law seems to be less ethical. What arguments can be made for U.S. law?

Employment Discrimination Law. The United States made a major commitment to putting ethics into law through the Civil Rights Act of 1964, which forbids employment discrimination based on race, religion, creed, national origin, or sex. Other categories, including age and disability status, have been added since then. Most people agree that the United States had great problems of employment discrimination and that today, despite substantial progress, many problems remain. There are many ethical questions. Virtually everyone would agree that it is unethical to discriminate both because it is wrong and because it violates the law. Should the law compel businesses to be ethical and not discriminate?

Jobs Overseas. Since almost everyone agrees the U.S. civil rights laws serve an ethical purpose, should American business voluntarily implement these laws as policy in their operations in foreign countries that do not have similar laws?

Wages are substantially lower in many countries, such as Mexico, than in the United States. Many companies have moved all or part of their operations to Mexico. The law allows this. What ethical obligation does a company have to U.S. workers who in many cases will not find comparable employment? What do managers ethically owe to workers and what to the shareholders or owners? What, then, are the ethical obligations to potential Mexican workers who may be eager to take the jobs even though the pay, benefits, and protection are well below U.S. standards? This, in fact, is a whole area of ethical discussion. What standards of employment (pay, benefits, job protection) should U.S. companies and consumers demand when we make or buy goods produced in a foreign country?

ENVIRONMENT

Along with civil rights, the environmental movement has been another great crusade. The purpose of environmentalism is to protect the planet not only for ourselves but also for those who come after us. Compliance with environmental law would seem a basic ethical norm. How far should environmental law go? Chemical companies that make products we all use everyday, by the nature of their business, pollute the environment. What is the ethical position of a chemical company in spending money lobbying the public and Congress on new laws and enforcement of existing ones? Automobiles still pollute the atmosphere, although much less than in the past. Gasohol is a motor fuel made in part from ethanol, which is made from corn, but it is more expensive than gasoline. What are the ethical issues surrounding ethanol?

Global warming is an important environmental issue. According to some, our planet is gradually growing warmer due to pollutants. This could end or radically change life on earth. Others say that the earth naturally warms and cools and that there is no evidence to suggest that there has been any significant change because of pollution. What should be the ethical position of citizens, especially companies that stand to either lose or gain by governmental measures taken?

As with civil rights law, many countries have less stringent laws than the United States regarding environmental issues. U.S. companies with operations in these countries can pollute much more than in the United States. It is also an important point that pollution does not respect national borders. What are the ethical norms that a company should consider in making its policy?

CONCLUSIONS

Aristotle said that deciding what is the best ethical course is not easy. Reasonable people will disagree on what is right. This article is intended to raise questions, not to provide answers. Many more issues of ethics in law for business could be considered. The ultimate, overreaching questions are: What is an ethical company and to what extent should law require ethics?

SEE ALSO *Law in Business*

BIBLIOGRAPHY

Bagley, Constance E., and Savage, Diane W. (2006). *Managers and the Legal Environment: Strategies for the 21st Century* (5th ed.). Mason, OH: Thomson/West.

Corley, Robert N. (1999). *The Legal and Regulatory Environment of Business* (11th ed.). New York: Irwin/McGraw-Hill.

Cheeseman, Henry R. (2000). *Contemporary Business Law* (3rd ed.). Upper Saddle River, NJ: Prentice-Hall.

Mann, Richard A., Roberts, Barry S., and Smith, Len Y. (2000). *Smith and Roberson's Business Law* (11th ed.). Australia; Cincinnati, OH: West Legal Studies in Business.

McGuire, Charles. (1998). *The Legal Environment of Business* (3rd ed.). Dubuque, IA: Kendall/Hunt Publishing Company.

Carson Varner

ETHICS IN MANAGEMENT

Managers in today's business world increasingly need to be concerned with two separate but interrelated concerns—business ethics and social responsibility.

BUSINESS ETHICS

Perhaps the most practical approach to view ethics is as a catalyst that causes managers to take socially responsible actions. The movement toward including ethics as a critical part of management education began in the 1970s, grew significantly in the 1980s, and is expected to continue growing. Hence, business ethics is a critical component of business leadership. Ethics can be defined as our concern for good behavior. We feel an obligation to consider not only our own personal well-being but also that of other human beings. This is similar to the precept of the Golden Rule: Do unto others as you would have them do unto you. In business, ethics can be defined as the ability and willingness to reflect on values in the course of the organization's decision-making process, to determine how values and decisions affect the various stakeholder groups, and to establish how managers can use these precepts in day-to-day company operations. Ethical business leaders strive for fairness and justice within the confines of sound management practices.

Many people ask why ethics is such a vital component of management practice. It has been said that it makes good business sense for managers to be ethical. Without being ethical, companies cannot be competitive at either the national or international level. While ethical management practices may not necessarily be linked to specific indicators of financial profitability, there is no inevitable conflict between ethical practices and a firm's emphasis on making a profit. Our system of competition presumes underlying values of truthfulness and fair dealing.

The employment of ethical business practices can enhance overall corporate health in three important areas. The first area is productivity. The employees of a corporation are stakeholders who are affected by management practices. When management considers ethics in its actions toward stakeholders, employees can be positively affected. For example, a corporation may decide that busi-

Former Tyco CEO L. Dennis Kozlowski leaves court in New York, June 17, 2005, after being convicted of looting the industrial products and services company of more than $600 million in corporate bonuses and loans. **AP IMAGES**

ness ethics requires a special effort to ensure the health and welfare of employees. Many corporations have established employee advisory programs (EAPs) to help employees with family, work, financial, or legal problems, or with mental illness or chemical dependency. These programs can be a source of enhanced productivity for a corporation.

A second area in which ethical management practices can enhance corporate health is by positively affecting outside stakeholders, such as suppliers and customers. A positive public image can attract customers. For example, a manufacturer of baby products carefully guards its public image as a company that puts customer health and well-being ahead of corporate profits, as exemplified in its code of ethics.

The third area in which ethical management practices can enhance corporate health is in minimizing regulation from government agencies. Where companies are believed to be acting unethically, the public is more likely to put pressure on legislators and other government officials to regulate those businesses or to enforce existing regulations. For example, in 1990 hearings were held on the rise in gasoline and home heating oil prices following Iraq's invasion of Kuwait, in part due to the public perception that oil companies were not behaving ethically.

A CODE OF ETHICS

A code of ethics is a formal statement that acts as a guide for how people within a particular organization should act and make decisions in an ethical fashion. Ninety percent of the *Fortune* 500 firms, and almost 50 percent of all other firms, have ethical codes. Codes of ethics commonly address such issues as conflict of interest, behavior toward competitors, privacy of information, gift giving, and making political contributions. According to a recent survey, the development and distribution of a code of ethics within an organization is perceived as an effective and efficient means of encouraging ethical practices within organizations (Ross, 1988).

Business leaders cannot assume, however, that merely because they have developed and distributed a code of ethics an organization's members have all the guidelines needed to determine what is ethical and will act accordingly. There is no way that all situations that involve ethical decision making an organization can be addressed in a code. Codes of ethics must be monitored continually to determine whether they are comprehensive and usable guidelines for making ethical business decisions. Managers should view codes of ethics as tools that must be evaluated and refined in order to more effectively encourage ethical practices.

CREATING AN ETHICAL WORKPLACE

Business managers in most organizations commonly strive to encourage ethical practices not only to ensure moral conduct but also to gain whatever business advantage there may be in having potential consumers and employees regard the company as ethical. Creating, distributing, and continually improving a company's code of ethics is one usual step managers can take to establish an ethical workplace.

Another step managers can take is to create a special office or department with the responsibility of ensuring ethical practices within the organization. For example, management at a major supplier of missile systems and aircraft components has established a corporate ethics office. This ethics office is a tangible sign to all employees that management is serious about encouraging ethical practices within the company.

Another way to promote ethics in the workplace is to provide the work force with appropriate training. Several companies conduct training programs aimed at encouraging ethical practices within their organizations. Such programs do not attempt to teach what is moral or ethical but, rather, to give business managers criteria they can use to help determine how ethical a certain action might be. Managers then can feel confident that a potential action will be considered ethical by the general public if it is consistent with one or more of the following standards:

1. *The Golden Rule*: Act in a way you would want others to act toward you.

2. *The utilitarian principle*: Act in a way that results in the greatest good for the greatest number.

3. *Kant's categorical imperative*: Act in such a way that the action taken under the circumstances could be a universal law, or rule, of behavior.

4. *The professional ethic*: Take actions that would be viewed as proper by a disinterested panel of professional peers.

5. *The TV test*: Always ask, "Would I feel comfortable explaining to a national TV audience why I took this action?"

6. *The legal test*: Ask whether the proposed action or decision is legal. Established laws are generally considered minimum standards for ethics.

7. *The four-way test*: Ask whether you can answer "yes" to the following questions as they relate to the decision: Is the decision truthful? Is it fair to all concerned? Will it build goodwill and better friendships? Will it be beneficial to all concerned?

Finally, managers can take responsibility for creating and sustaining conditions in which people are likely to behave ethically and for minimizing conditions in which people might be tempted to behave unethically. Two practices that commonly inspire unethical behavior in organizations are giving unusually high rewards for good performance and unusually severe punishments for poor performance. By eliminating such factors, managers can reduce much of the pressure that people feel to perform unethically. They can also promote the social responsibility of the organization.

SOCIAL RESPONSIBILITY

The term social responsibility means different things to different people. Generally, corporate social responsibility is the obligation to take action that protects and improves the welfare of society as a whole as well as organizational interests. According to the concept of corporate social responsibility, a manager must strive to achieve both organizational and societal goals. Current perspectives regarding the fundamentals of social responsibility of businesses are listed and discussed through (1) the Davis model of corporate social responsibility, (2) areas of corporate social responsibility, and (3) varying opinions on social responsibility.

A model of corporate social responsibility developed by Keith Davis (1975) provides five propositions that describe why and how businesses should adhere to the obligation to take action that protects and improves the welfare of society and the organization:

Proposition 1: Social responsibility arises from social power.

Proposition 2: Business shall operate as an open system, with open receipt of inputs from society and open disclosure of its operation to the public.

Proposition 3: The social costs and benefits of an activity, product, or service shall be thoroughly calculated and considered in deciding whether to proceed with it.

Proposition 4: Social costs related to each activity, product, or service shall be passed on to the consumer.

Proposition 5: Business institutions, as citizens, have the responsibility to become involved in certain social problems that are outside their normal areas of operation (pp. 20-23).

The areas in which business can become involved to protect and improve the welfare of society are numerous and diverse. Some of the most publicized of these areas are urban affairs, consumer affairs, environmental affairs, and employment practices. Although numerous businesses are involved in socially responsible activities, much controversy persists about whether such involvement is necessary or appropriate. There are several arguments for and against businesses performing socially responsible activities.

The best known argument supporting such activities is that because business is a subset of and exerts a significant impact on society, it has the responsibility to help improve society. Since society asks no more and no less of any of its members, why should business be exempt from such responsibility? Additionally, profitability and growth go hand in hand with responsible treatment of employees, customers, and the community. However, studies have not indicated any clear relationship between corporate social responsibility and profitability (Aupperle, Caroll, and Hatfield, 1985; McGuire, Sundgren, and Schneeweis, 1988).

One of the better known arguments against such activities is advanced by the distinguished economist Milton Friedman. Friedman (1989) argues that making business managers simultaneously responsible to business owners for reaching profit objectives and to society for enhancing societal welfare represents a conflict of interest that has the potential to cause the demise of business. According to Friedman, this demise almost certainly will occur if business continually is forced to perform socially responsible behavior that is in direct conflict with private organizational objectives. He also argues that to require business managers to pursue socially responsible objectives may be unethical, since it requires managers to spend money that really belongs to other individuals.

Regardless of which argument or combination of arguments particular managers might support, they generally should make a concerted effort to perform all legally required socially responsible activities, consider voluntarily performing socially responsible activities beyond those legally required, and inform all relevant individuals of the extent to which their organization will become involved in performing socially responsible activities.

Federal law requires that businesses perform certain socially responsible activities. In fact, several government agencies have been established to develop such business-related legislation and to make sure the laws are followed. The Environmental Protection Agency has the authority to require businesses to adhere to certain socially responsible environmental standards. Adherence to legislated social responsibilities represents the minimum standard of socially responsible performance that business leaders must achieve. Managers must ask themselves, however, how far beyond the minimum they should attempt to go—a difficult and complicated question that entails assessing the positive and negative outcomes of performing socially responsible activities. Only those activities that contribute to the business's success while contributing to the welfare of society should be undertaken.

Social Responsiveness. Social responsiveness is the degree of effectiveness and efficiency an organization displays in pursuing its social responsibilities. The greater the degree of effectiveness and efficiency, the more socially responsive the organization is said to be. The socially responsive organization that is both effective and efficient meets its social responsibilities without wasting organizational resources in the process. Determining exactly which social responsibilities an organization should pursue and then deciding how to pursue them are perhaps the two most critical decision-making aspects of maintaining a high level of social responsiveness within an organization. That is, managers must decide whether their organization should undertake the activities on its own or acquire the help of outsiders with more expertise in the area.

In addition to decision making, various approaches to meeting social obligations are another determinant of an organization's level of social responsiveness. A desirable and socially responsive approach to meeting social obligations involves the following:

- Incorporating social goals into the annual planning process

- Seeking comparative industry norms for social programs

- Presenting reports to organization members, the board of directors, and stockholders on progress in social responsibility

- Experimenting with different approaches for measuring social performance

- Attempting to measure the cost of social programs as well as the return on social program investments

S. Prakash Sethi (1975) presents three management approaches to meeting social obligations: (1) the social obligation approach, (2) the social responsibility approach, and (3) the social responsiveness approach. Each of Sethi's three approaches contains behavior that reflects a somewhat different attitude with regard to businesses performing social responsible activities. The social obligation approach, for example, considers business as having primarily economic purposes and confines socially responsible activity mainly to conformance to existing laws The social responsibility approach sees business as having both economic and societal goals. The social responsiveness approach considers business as having both societal and economic goals as well as the obligation to anticipate upcoming social problems and to work actively to prevent their appearance.

Organizations characterized by attitudes and behaviors consistent with the social responsiveness approach generally are more socially responsive than organizations characterized by attitudes and behaviors consistent with either the social responsibility approach or the social obligation approach. Also, organizations characterized by the social responsibility approach generally achieve higher levels of social responsiveness than organizations characterized by the social obligation approach. As one moves from the social obligation approach to the social responsiveness approach, management becomes more proactive. Proactive managers will do what is prudent from a business viewpoint to reduce liabilities whether an action is required by law or not.

Areas of Measurement. To be consistent, measurements to gauge organizational progress in reaching socially responsible objectives can be performed. The specific areas in which individual companies actually take such measurements vary, of course, depending on the specific objectives of the companies. All companies, however, probably should take such measurements in at least the following four major areas:

1. *Economic function*: This measurement gives some indication of the economic contribution the organization is making to society.

2. *Quality of life*: The measurement of quality of life should focus on whether the organization is improving or degrading the general quality of life in society.

3. *Social investment*: The measurement of social investment deals with the degree to which the organization is investing both money and human resources to solve community social problems.

4. *Problem solving*: The measurement of problem solving should focus on the degree to which the organization deals with social problems.

The Social Audit: A Progress Report. A social audit is the process of taking measurements of social responsibility to assess organizational performance in this area. The basic steps in conducting a social audit are monitoring, measuring, and appraising all aspects of an organization's socially responsible performance. Probably no two organizations conduct and present the results of a social audit in exactly the same way. The social audit is the process of measuring the socially responsible activities of an organization. It monitors, measures, and appraises socially responsible performance.

SEE ALSO *Management*

BIBLIOGRAPHY

Aupperle, K. E., Caroll, A. B., and Hatfield, J. D. (1985). "An Empirical Examination of the Relationship Between Corporate Responsibility and Profitability." *Academy of Management Journal* 28(2): 446-463.

Davis, K., and Blomstrom, R.L. (1975, June). "Five Propositions for Social Responsibility." *Business Horizons*, 19-24.

Friedman, M. (1989). "Freedom and Philanthropy: An Interview with Milton Friedman." *Business and Society Review* 71: 11-18.

McGuire, J. B., Sundgren, A., and Schneeweis, T. (1988). "Corporate Social Responsibility and Firm Financial Performance." *Academy of Management Journal* 31: 854-872.

Sethi, S. P. (1975). "Dimensions of Corporate Social Performance: An Analytical Framework." *California Management Review*, 17(3): 58-64.

Thomas Haynes

ETHICS IN MARKETING

Ethics are a collection of principles of right conduct that shape the decisions people or organizations make. Practicing ethics in marketing means deliberately applying standards of fairness, or moral rights and wrongs, to marketing decision making, behavior, and practice in the organization.

In a market economy, a business may be expected to act in what it believes to be its own best interest. The purpose of marketing is to create a competitive advantage. An organization achieves an advantage when it does a better job than its competitors at satisfying the product and service requirements of its target markets. Those organizations that develop a competitive advantage are able to satisfy the needs of both customers and the organization.

As our economic system has become more successful at providing for needs and wants, there has been greater focus on organizations' adhering to ethical values rather than simply providing products. This focus has come about for two reasons. First, when an organization behaves ethically, customers develop more positive attitudes about the firm, its products, and its services. When marketing practices depart from standards that society considers acceptable, the market process becomes less efficient—sometimes it is even interrupted. Not employing ethical marketing practices may lead to dissatisfied customers, bad publicity, a lack of trust, lost business, or, sometimes, legal action. Thus, most organizations are very sensitive to the needs and opinions of their customers and look for ways to protect their long-term interests.

Second, ethical abuses frequently lead to pressure (social or government) for institutions to assume greater responsibility for their actions. Since abuses do occur, some people believe that questionable business practices abound. As a result, consumer interest groups, professional associations, and self-regulatory groups exert considerable influence on marketing. Calls for social responsibility have also subjected marketing practices to a wide range of federal and state regulations designed to either protect consumer rights or to stimulate trade.

The Federal Trade Commission (FTC) and other federal and state government agencies are charged both with enforcing the laws and creating policies to limit unfair marketing practices. Because regulation cannot be developed to cover every possible abuse, organizations and industry groups often develop codes of ethical conduct or rules for behavior to serve as a guide in decision making. The American Marketing Association, for example, has developed a code of ethics (which can be viewed on its Web site at www.ama.org). Self-regulation not only helps a firm avoid extensive government intervention; it also permits it to better respond to changes in market conditions. An organization's long-term success and profitability depends on this ability to respond.

UNFAIR OR DECEPTIVE MARKETING PRACTICES

Marketing practices are deceptive if customers believe they will get more value from a product or service than they actually receive. Deception, which can take the form of a misrepresentation, omission, or misleading practice, can occur when working with any element of the marketing mix. Because consumers are exposed to great quantities of information about products and firms, they often become skeptical of marketing claims and selling messages and act to protect themselves from being deceived. Thus, when a product or service does not provide expected value, customers will often seek a different source.

Deceptive pricing practices cause customers to believe that the price they pay for some unit of value in a product or service is lower than it really is. The deception might take the form of making false price comparisons, providing misleading suggested selling prices, omitting important conditions of the sale, or making very low price offers available only when other items are purchased as well. Promotion practices are deceptive when the seller intentionally misstates how a product is constructed or performs, fails to disclose information regarding pyramid sales (a sales technique in which a person is recruited into a plan and then expects to make money by recruiting other people), or employs bait-and-switch selling techniques (a technique in which a business offers to sell a product or service, often at a lower price, in order to attract customers who are

Marketing of tobacco products, as seen on this billboard along Chicago's Dan Ryan Expressway, has been the target of government regulation. **AP IMAGES**

then encouraged to purchase a more expensive item). False or greatly exaggerated product or service claims are also deceptive. When packages are intentionally mislabeled as to contents, size, weight, or use information, that constitutes deceptive packaging. Selling hazardous or defective products without disclosing the dangers, failing to perform promised services, and not honoring warranty obligations are also considered deception.

OFFENSIVE MATERIALS AND OBJECTIONABLE MARKETING PRACTICES

Marketers control what they say to customers as well as and how and where they say it. When events, television or radio programming, or publications sponsored by a marketer, in addition to products or promotional materials, are perceived as offensive, they often create strong negative reactions. For example, some people find advertising for all products promoting sexual potency to be offensive. Others may be offended when a promotion employs stereotypical images or uses sex as an appeal. This is particularly true when a product is being marketed in other countries, where words and images may carry different meanings than they do in the host country.

When people feel that products or appeals are offensive, they may pressure vendors to stop carrying the product. Thus, all promotional messages must be carefully screened and tested, and communication media, programming, and editorial content selected to match the tastes and interests of targeted customers. Beyond the target audience, however, marketers should understand that there are others who are not customers who might receive their appeals and see their images and be offended.

Direct marketing is also undergoing closer examination. Objectionable practices range from minor irritants, such as the timing and frequency of sales letters or commercials, to those that are offensive or even illegal. Among examples of practices that may raise ethical questions are persistent and high-pressure selling, annoying telemarketing calls, and television commercials that are too long or run too frequently. Marketing appeals created to take advantage of young or inexperienced consumers or senior citizens—including advertisements, sales appeals disguised as contests, junk mail (including electronic mail), and the use and exchange of mailing lists—may also pose ethical questions. In addition to being subject to consumer-protection laws and regulations, the Direct Marketing Association provides a list of voluntary ethical guidelines for companies engaged in direct marketing (available at their Web site at www.the-dma.org).

ETHICAL PRODUCT AND DISTRIBUTION PRACTICES

Several product-related issues raise questions about ethics in marketing, most often concerning the quality of products and services provided. Among the most frequently voiced complaints are ones about products that are unsafe, that are of poor quality in construction or content, that do not contain what is promoted, or that go out of style or become obsolete before they actually need replacing. An organization that markets poor-quality or unsafe products is taking the chance that it will develop a reputation for poor products or service. In addition, it may be putting itself in jeopardy for product claims or legal action. Sometimes, however, frequent changes in product features or performance, such as those that often occur in the computer industry, make previous models of products obsolete. Such changes can be misinterpreted as planned obsolescence.

Ethical questions may also arise in the distribution process. Because sales performance is the most common way in which marketing representatives and sales personnel are evaluated, performance pressures exist that may lead to ethical dilemmas. For example, pressuring vendors to buy more than they need and pushing items that will result in higher commissions are temptations. Exerting influence to cause vendors to reduce display space for competitors' products, promising shipment when knowing delivery is not possible by the promised date, or paying vendors to carry a firm's product rather than one of its competitors are also unethical.

Research is another area in which ethical issues may arise. Information gathered from research can be important to the successful marketing of products or services. Consumers, however, may view organizations' efforts to gather data from them as invading their privacy. They are resistant to give out personal information that might cause them to become a marketing target or to receive product or sales information. When data about products or consumers are exaggerated to make a selling point, or research questions are written to obtain a specific result, consumers are misled. Without self-imposed ethical standards in the research process, management will likely make decisions based on inaccurate information.

DOES MARKETING OVERFOCUS ON MATERIALISM?

Consumers develop an identity in the marketplace that is shaped both by who they are and by what they see themselves as becoming. There is evidence that the way consumers view themselves influences their purchasing behavior. This identity is often reflected in the brands or products they consume or the way in which they lead their lives.

The proliferation of information about products and services complicates decision making. Sometimes consumer desires to achieve or maintain a certain lifestyle or image results in their purchasing more than they need or can afford. Does marketing create these wants? Clearly, appeals exist that are designed to cause people to purchase more than they need or can afford. Unsolicited offers of credit cards with high limits or high interest rates, advertising appeals touting the psychological benefits of conspicuous consumption, and promotions that seek to stimulate unrecognized needs are often cited as examples of these excesses.

SPECIAL ETHICAL ISSUES IN MARKETING TO CHILDREN

Children are an important marketing target for certain products. Because their knowledge about products, the media, and selling strategies is usually not as well developed as that of adults, children are likely to be more vulnerable to psychological appeals and strong images. Thus, ethical questions sometimes arise when they are exposed to questionable marketing tactics and messages. For example, studies linking relationships between tobacco and alcohol marketing with youth consumption resulted in increased public pressure directly leading to the regulation of marketing for those products.

The proliferation of direct marketing and use of the Internet to market to children also raises ethical issues. Sometimes a few unscrupulous marketers design sites so that children are able to bypass adult supervision or control, or sometimes they present objectionable materials to underage consumers or pressure them to buy items or provide credit card numbers. When this happens, it is likely that social pressure and subsequent regulation will result. Likewise, programming for children and youth in the mass media has been under scrutiny recently.

In the United States, marketing to children is closely controlled. Federal regulations place limits on the types of marketing that can be directed to children, and marketing activities are monitored by the Better Business Bureau, the Federal Trade Commission, consumer and parental groups, and the broadcast networks. These guidelines provide clear direction to marketers.

ETHICAL ISSUES IN MARKETING TO MINORITIES

The United States is a society of ever-increasing diversity. Markets are broken into segments in which people share some similar characteristics. Ethical issues arise when marketing tactics are designed specifically to exploit or manipulate a minority market segment. Offensive practices may take the form of negative or stereotypical representations of minorities, associating the consumption of harmful or questionable products with a particular minority segment, and demeaning portrayals of a race or group. Ethical questions may also arise when high-pressure selling is directed at a group, when higher prices are charged for products sold to minorities, or even when stores provide poorer service in neighborhoods with a high population of minority customers. Such practices will likely result in a bad public image and lost sales for the marketer.

Unlike the legal protections in place to protect children from harmful practices, there have been few efforts to protect minority customers. When targeting minorities, firms must evaluate whether the targeted population is susceptible to appeals because of their minority status. The firm must assess marketing efforts to determine whether ethical behavior would cause them to change their marketing practices.

ETHICAL ISSUES SURROUNDING THE PORTRAYAL OF WOMEN IN MARKETING EFFORTS

As society changes, so do the images of and roles assumed by people, regardless of race, sex, or occupation. Women have been portrayed in a variety of ways over the years. When marketers present those images as overly conventional, formulaic, or oversimplified, people may view them as stereotypical and offensive.

Examples of demeaning stereotypes include those in which women are presented as less intelligent, submissive to or obsessed with men, unable to assume leadership roles or make decisions, or skimpily dressed in order to appeal to the sexual interests of males. Harmful stereotypes include those portraying women as obsessed with their appearance or conforming to some ideal of size, weight, or beauty. When images are considered demeaning or harmful, they will work to the detriment of the organization. Advertisements, in particular, should be evaluated to be sure that the images projected are not offensive.

CONCLUSION

Because marketing decisions often require specialized knowledge, ethical issues are often more complicated than those faced in personal life—and effective decision making requires consistency. Because each business situation is different, and not all decisions are simple, many organizations have embraced ethical codes of conduct and rules of professional ethics to guide managers and employees. However, sometimes self-regulation proves insufficient to protect the interest of customers, organizations, or society. At that point, pressures for regulation and enactment of

legislation to protect the interests of all parties in the exchange process will likely occur.

SEE ALSO *Marketing*

BIBLIOGRAPHY

American Marketing Association Code of Ethics (2005). New York: American Marketing Association.

Barnett, Tim, Bass, Ken, and Brown, Frederick (1998, May 1). "Ethical Ideology and the Ethical Judgments of Marketing Professionals." *Journal of Business Ethics*, 715-723.

Berman, Barry, and Evans, Joel R. (2004). *Retail Management: A Strategic Approach.* Upper Saddle River, NJ: Prentice Hall.

Bone, Paula F., and Corey, Robert J. (1998). "Moral Reflections in Marketing." *Journal of Macromarketing*, 25(1), 104-114.

Ferrell, O. C., Hartline, Michael D., and McDaniel, Stephen W. (1998). "Codes of Ethics Among Corporate Research Departments, Marketing Research Firms, and Data Subcontractors: An Examination of a Three-Communities Metaphor." *Journal of Business Ethics*, 17(5), 503-516.

"FTC Guides Against Deceptive Pricing." (1998). Retrieved October 18, 2005, from http://www.ftc.gov/bcp/guides/decptprc.htm.

Gustafson, Robert, Popovich, Mark, and Thomsen, Steven (1999, March 15). "The 'Thin' Ideal Study." *Marketing News*, 22.

Jones, Thomas M., and Ryan, Lori V. (1998). "The Effect of Organizational Forces on Individual Morality: Judgment, Moral Approbation, and Behavior." *Business Ethics Quarterly* 8(3), 431-445.

Koehn, Daryl (1999, January 11). "Business Ethics Is Not a Contradiction." *San Antonio Business Journal*, 38.

Kotler, Philip, and Armstrong, Gary (2005). *Principles of Marketing* (11th ed.). Upper Saddle River, NJ: Pearson Prentice Hall.

Mahoney, Ann I. (1999, March). "Talking About Ethics." *Association Management*, 45.

Murphy, Patrick E. (1998). "Ethics in Advertising: Review, Analysis, and Suggestions." *Journal of Public Policy and Marketing*, 17(2), 316-319.

Murphy, Patrick E. (1999). "Character and Virtue Ethics in International Marketing: An Agenda for Managers, Researchers, and Educators." *Journal of Business Ethics* 18(1), 107-124.

Rieck, Dean (1998, October 1). "Balancing Ethics and Profitability." *Direct Marketing*, 53-56.

Rose, Gregory M., Bush, Victoria D., and Kahle, Lynn (1998). "The Influence of Family Communication Patterns on Parental Reactions Toward Advertising: A Cross-National Examination." *Journal of Advertising* 27(4), 71-85.

Russell, J. Thomas, King, Karen W., and Lane, W. Ronald (2004). *Kleppner's Advertising Procedure* (16th ed.). Upper Saddle River, NJ: Prentice Hall.

Self-Regulatory Guidelines for Children's Advertising. (2003). New York: Children's Advertising Review Unit of the Council of Better Business Bureaus.

Sirgy, M. Joseph, Lee, Dong-Jin, Kosenko, Rustan, and Lee, H. (1998, Spring). "Does Television Viewership Play a Role in the Perception of Quality of Life?" *Journal of Advertising*, 125-142.

United States Code, Title 15, Section 45. Retrieved October 18, 2005, from
http://www4.law.cornell.edu/uscode/15/45.text.html.

John A. Swope

EUROPEAN UNION

The European Union is a rapidly changing economic and political union of mostly western European nations that arose out of the European Community in 1993. This international organization is not meant to replace the sovereignty of the individual countries but rather to unify them under a common currency and economic structure, as well as under some shared principles of law and human rights. One of the cornerstones of the European Union has been the new currency, known as the euro, and the creation of a new European Central Bank. This new group of nations is to rival the United States and to increase trade among its member nations. This is no easy feat because of the strong national identities of these nations, including language barriers and long-standing cultural disputes.

HISTORY

The beginnings of the European Union were cultivated soon after the end of World War II (1939–1945), when it appeared that Europe would once again be a battleground between the United States and the Union of Soviet Socialist Republics. On May 9, 1950, the French foreign minister, Robert Schuman, proposed the first agreement to pool coal and steel resources. In 1952 the European Coal and Steel Community was established, and it included Belgium, France, Italy, Luxembourg, the Netherlands, and West Germany. It was hoped that this new spirit of cooperation would not only prevent war from breaking out between member nations but also present a strong economic face to the United States.

With this newfound success, the European Coal and Steel Community evolved in 1958 to become the European Economic Community. This was an attempt to integrate further other parts of these varied economies in order to remove other trade barriers. The Treaty of Maastricht in 1992 continued the evolution by introducing new areas of cooperation including defense, justice, and home affairs. These combined areas created the "community" relationship that exists today. Also in 1992, twelve of the fifteen nations agreed to a single European currency,

called the euro, which was to have been managed by the new European Central Bank.

In 2005 the members of the European Union included: Austria, Belgium, Cyprus, the Czech Republic, Denmark, Estonia, Finland, France, Germany, Greece, Hungary, Ireland, Italy, Latvia, Lithuania, Luxembourg, Malta, the Netherlands, Poland, Portugal, Slovakia, Slovenia, Spain, Sweden, and the United Kingdom. The candidate countries were Bulgaria, Croatia, Romania, and Turkey. Macedonia, formerly a part of Yugoslavia, had a pending application. A new constitution was being proposed for 2006, but by 2005 France and Belgium had turned it down. The United Kingdom delayed the vote in that country pending a hearing to determine what the possible ramifications of the failure could be.

GOVERNMENT MAKEUP

Three main institutions make up this union of nations. The first one is the Council of the European Union. This body represents the individual member states. The second body is the European Parliament meant to represent the citizens of the European Union. The third body is the European Commission, which is to represent the common interests of the continent of Europe. These three parts are to represent all parts of the constituency of Europe.

The Council of the European Union is the main decision-making body in which the control of the body rotates every six months to another member nation. Depending on what the agenda is for particular meetings determines which minister from each nation attends. For instance, if there is a meeting on agriculture, the agriculture ministers from each nation would attend. There are nine different policy areas that the council considers. The General Secretariat is the administrative part of the council, and it is based in Brussels. The ambassadors of the member nations determine the agenda for the council.

The council and the European Parliament share legislative authority and responsibility for the budget. On important events such as amending treaties, a unanimous decision must be met; on other votes, however, only a qualified majority of 232 votes is required. Voting rights are based on the size of the population of the member state.

The European Parliament is the representative arm of the European Union. Every five years the people of Europe elect the membership in a direct election. In 2005 the European Parliament had 732 members, which was expected to be increased to 786 in 2007. The European Parliament is also the body responsible for open debate. It has become the area where the people's opinion meets the democratic process, creating some of the most innovative

The European Parliament in Brussels during British Prime Minister Tony Blair's address, June 23, 2005. © **YVES HERMAN/REUTERS/CORBIS**

policies. Because of its representative nature, the Parliament most accurately reflects the ideals and opinions of its people.

The European Commission is an independent political body meant to act upon the interests of the European Union as a whole. The commission is made up of one person from each nation. It is also the executive arm of the European Union and follows through with the decisions made by the council. In the event of censure by the Parliament, the entire body must resign. Censure requires a two-thirds vote by the Parliament in order to be passed and is an effective check on the balance of power within the European Union.

The judicial branch is known as the Court of Justice of the European Union. It meets in Luxembourg and is made up of one judge from each country serving an initial term of six years with additional terms of three years. The role of the Court of Justice is not only to make sure the laws created are fair and just, but also to guarantee that member nations fulfill their European Union obligations.

MONETARY POLICY

The primary strength of the European Union lies within its strong currency known as the euro. It has become the second most important currency along with the U.S. dollar. While the U.S. dollar has become less important because of world events such as stock market scandals and terrorist attacks, the euro has become more widely sought after. The euro began circulation in January 2002, replacing the individual currencies being used at the time in twelve nations. What is remarkable about the new currency is that it not only replaced the currencies of these nations, but also replaced icons of national and cultural symbols. This contributed to the new "European identity." One of the other benefits was the ability to travel within member nations without having to exchange currencies.

The process of bringing member nations on board with the single currency was not easy or painless. The new currency requires economic discipline by reducing budget deficits, curbing inflation, curbing interest rates, and reducing public borrowing to below 60 percent of gross domestic product to ensure the stability of the new currency. In order to make this happen, the European Central Bank was created in 1999. The bank set was ordered to set and maintain the value of the euro interest rates, and develop sound fiscal policy. One of the tenets of the fiscal policy is to maintain budget discipline in order to remain vigilant over the budget deficits of other member nations. A second tenet of the European Central Bank is that employment be a priority of the bank. Not all nations agreed to take on the euro as its national currency. Some nations such as the United Kingdom, Denmark, and Sweden did not accept the currency until they gave it much thought and discussion.

AREAS OF DISAGREEMENT

The goals of the European Union include banishing trade barriers detrimental to free trade among member nations while at the same time supporting the people of these individual countries in their everyday lives. Difficulties arise when differing cultures must cooperate and make joint decisions. The areas of agriculture and immigration are of particular concern. Some nations have long histories of protectionist philosophies for their food as well as with the issue of illegal immigrants.

In agriculture there have been other questions concerning issues that have to do with monetary policy, language barriers, and long-standing feuds. Of particular importance are the addition of the former Eastern European nations into the European Central Bank and the management of the euro in the global economy. Significant concerns include whether these nations can appropriately manage their economies to qualify for inclusion into the European Central bank and if they can, whether they will be able to maintain economic discipline. If they cannot, the concern is that their collective economies could sabotage what the European Union has worked so hard to establish since the mid-twentieth century.

Other concerns are how the roles of terrorism, the rising demand for oil, and the rise of other large economies such as China may affect the stability of the currency and the world economy in general. These challenges are indeed unique and will present a future of cooperative communication.

SEE ALSO *Trading Blocs*

BIBLIOGRAPHY

Fontaine, Pascal (2003, October). Europe in 12 lessons. *Europa.* Retrieved November 2, 2005, from http://europa.eu.int/abc/12lessons/index2_en.htm

European Union. http://www.answers.com/topic/european%20union

Kagan, R. (2003). *Of paradise and Power: America and Europe in the new world order.* NewYork: Knopf.

Smith, N. (ed) (2005). *The European Union.* Bronx, NY.

Lawrence F. Peters, Jr.

EXECUTIVE COMPENSATION

SEE *Employee Compensation*

EXPECTANCY THEORY

SEE *Motivation*

EXPORTS

SEE *Global Economy; International Investment; International Trade; Trading Blocs*

F

FACSIMILE REPRODUCTION

Facsimile reproduction means making an exact copy of anything imprinted on paper (words, pictures, graphics, maps, charts, or other types of pictorial media) using electronic devices such as copiers, facsimile (fax) machines, printers, scanners, digital cameras, and any other similar reprographic equipment. Whether reproducing information either electronically or on paper, producing quality copies that are acceptable to the task being performed is of the utmost importance.

HISTORICAL FACTS OF FACSIMILE REPRODUCTION

- One of the earliest methods used to make a printed copy was the invention of carbon paper by a Briton named J. W. Swan around 1862; it was not used in offices, however, until sometime later. This type of carbon paper provided a somewhat less than perfect copy of typed material and provided a choice between very messy carbon paper that made several copies or single-use carbon paper that was much easier to use.

- A duplicating machine called the mimeograph began to be used in the late 1890s. Copies were produced by typing on a lightly oiled surface called a master. This process involved retyping an original document, a very time-consuming process. As time passed, the mimeograph machine was improved enough to permit masters to be reused if stored properly.

- In 1906 the Haloid Company (which later became the Xerox Corporation) was founded to sell photographic paper for its early version of today's copier. It was expensive, impractical, and difficult to use.

- In 1913 Edouard Belin invented the Belinograph, a portable facsimile machine capable of using ordinary phone lines.

- In the 1920s, a copying machine called a duplicating machine, considered one of the first modern examples of efficient industrial design was introduced by the Gestetner Company.

- The death knell for carbon paper was sounded in 1937 when American law student Chester Carlson invented the electrostatic dry-copying process of duplication that became known as xerography. This process used the effect of light on photoconductivity and led to the phenomenal success of the Xerox Corporation's commercial copy machine introduced in 1959. The major problem with this copier was that it was heat-sensitive and resulted in paper scorching.

- After World War II (1939–1945), 3M and Eastman Kodak introduced the Thermo-Fax and Verifax copiers. While the machines were relatively inexpensive and easy to use, they required special paper that was extremely expensive, and the copies were of poor quality.

- Dot-matrix printers were introduced in 1971, providing a reasonably efficient way to reproduce computer-generated information on paper.

- In 1974 the first international fax standard was set by the United Nations allowing for fax messages to be transmitted at a rate of one page every six minutes. Special paper that was light sensitive was required for these early fax machines.

- The first laser printer was introduced by IBM in 1975. This process of copying used light lasers and improved both the process and the product.

Reprographic technology of the early twenty-first century involves using fax machines, copiers, printers, scanners, digital cameras, and other digital-related equipment in conjunction with phones and computers to reproduce pictures, sounds, and other images electronically and on paper. As a specific reprographic method is refined, its quality improves and propels the reprographic process forward to a higher level and a future with endless boundaries supported by ongoing research.

FAX MACHINES

Fax machines have emerged as an essential piece of communication equipment to be used both personally and professionally because of their convenience and efficiency in transmitting specific types of information. Fax machines are unique in that they can make or transmit exact copies of words, pictures, graphics, or other types of pictorial media electronically via phone lines. Most fax machines can produce plain paper copies, but it is not advisable to consider using a fax machine as a replacement for a regular copier machine because of cost.

COPIERS

User-friendly copiers are standard pieces of equipment for reproduction and provide a wide array of capabilities. Copiers are sold by a wide variety of vendors who offer an array of products and services to meet individual needs. When selecting a copier for possible lease or purchase, individual features and individual needs should be major considerations. The cost of a copier is determined by the model selected and the options desired. Prices range from a few hundred dollars to more than $100,000.

The number of copies that can be produced in a minute is an important feature. Ease of use in loading paper is also important. Paper is usually loaded in the front of the machine using one or more paper tray configurations. Most copiers are capable of producing two-sided copies as well as copying books or bound documents without distortion of the copy. Most copiers also provide an option that allows copied material to be enlarged or reduced in scale within certain percent increments.

All copiers have a push-button digital control panel that provides the user with the opportunity to select the

Combination copier, fax, scanner by Xerox®. *Machines like this one have multiple document reproduction capabilities.*
PHOTOGRAPH BY KELLY A. QUIN. THE GALE GROUP.

functions desired in an easy and efficient manner, and offer service information as well. Copiers use toner cartridges that need to be replaced when the toner powder is used up.

PRINTERS

A printer is an essential piece of reproduction equipment to accommodate information printed via a computer. Printers vary in price depending on the features desired. The three most commonly used types of printers are ink-jet printers, bubble-jet printers, and laser printers.

Ink-Jet Printers. Ink-jet printers are among the most popular types of printers used because of their affordability and performance. Ink-jet printers operate by spraying small amounts of ink on paper to create images. Ink-jet printers use small replaceable cartridges that come in both color and black and white.

Bubble-Jet Printers. Bubble-jet printers are somewhat similar to ink-jet printers in that with a bubble-jet printer, heat that is created with tiny resistors vaporizes the ink into a bubble. The formed bubble then ejects from the print head onto the paper.

Laser Printers. Laser printers operate using the concept of static electricity, which allows electricity to stick to a device inside the printer called the drum, which in turn creates electrostatic images. As paper moves through the printer, the electrostatic images are coated with a black powder called toner, similar to that of a copier which produces an image. Toner comes in cartridges and is available in both color and black and white.

SCANNERS

Scanners are electronic devices that can automatically read but not distinguish in any way material being scanned. This process is known as optical character recognition. From there a scanner uses software to convert the image and/or words into a pattern of dots known as a bitmap. The quality of the scanned material depends on the number of dots per inch and the depth of each dot (known as a pixel). Scanners come in several sizes depending on the amount of material to be scanned. One of the most common is the flatbed scanner.

Scanners have a wide variety of applications including copying photographs and medical records. The files can then be edited and formatted and then sent electronically. Major considerations when selecting a scanner should include ease of use as well as image and quality resolution.

DIGITAL CAMERAS

Of all the reprographic devices invented in the late twentieth century, the digital camera, because of its construction, has become one of the fastest-growing methods of reproducing images and data. Among the digital camera's many advantages is the capability of seeing instantly what the picture looks like, thus allowing the user to delete or keep the picture for printing. It is also possible to print one picture or several pictures, depending on preference. Because there is no film, digital cameras can be reused easily. With proper computer equipment, digital camera chips can be inserted into the computer and pictures can be printed immediately.

Digital cameras operate with specific types of rechargeable batteries. Keeping the batteries charged is important to remember when using a digital camera. Digital cameras have no film but operate using a sensor chip and flash memory. Chip size affects the resolution of the picture and the hues and intensities of colors. Digital cameras come in a wide variety of configurations and prices. When shopping for a digital camera, consumers should carefully consider both the resolution quality, which is very important in guaranteeing a high-quality picture, and the amount of memory.

SUMMARY

The history of facsimile reproduction is rich with research that intertwines with the many diversified methods of reproduction today. While electronics are used in new and creative ways daily in reproducing material, the need for high-quality production of the printed word continues to be of the utmost importance.

SEE ALSO *Office Technology*

BIBLIOGRAPHY

Brain, Marshall (n.d.). How fax machines work. Retrieved November 3, 2005, from Howstuffworks Web site: http://electronics.howstuffworks.com/fax-machine.htm

Digital camera. (n.d.) Retrieved November 3, 2005, from Answers.com Web site: http://www.answers.com/Digital Camera

Harris, Tom (n.d.). How laser printers work. Retrieved November 3, 2005, from Howstuffworks Web site: http://computer.howstuffworks.com/laser-printer.htm

How does a bubble jet printer work? (n.d.). Retrieved November 3, 2005, from Howstuffworks Web site: http://electronics.howstuffworks.com/question163.htm

Meeker-O'Connell, Ann (n.d.). How photocopiers work. Retrieved November 3, 2005, from Howstuffworks Web site: http://electronics.howstuffworks.com/photocopier.htm

Tyson, Jeff (n.d.). How inkjet printers work. Retrieved November 3, 2005, from Howstuffworks Web site: http://computer.howstuffworks.com/inkjet-printer.htm

Tyson, Jeff (n.d.). How scanners work. Retrieved November 3, 2005, from Howstuffworks Web site: http://computer.howstuffworks.com/scanner.htm

Wilson, Tracy V., Nice, K., and Gurevich, G. (n.d.) How digital cameras work. Retrieved November 3, 2005, from Howstuffworks Web site: http://electronics.howstuffworks.com/digital-camera.htm

Dorothy A. Maxwell

FACTORS OF PRODUCTION

Land, labor, capital, and entrepreneurship: These are four generally recognized factors of production. Of course, in a literal sense anything contributing to the productive process is a factor of production. However, economists seek to classify all inputs into a few broad categories, so standard usage refers to the categories themselves as factors. Before the twentieth century, only three factors making up the classical triad were recognized: land, labor, and capital. Entrepreneurship is a fairly recent addition.

The factor concept is used to construct models illustrating general features of the economic process without getting caught up in inessential details. These include models purporting to explain growth, value, choice of production method, income distribution, and social classes. A major conceptual application is in the theory of production functions. One intuitive basis for the classification of the factors of production is the manner of payment for their services: rent for land, wages for labor, interest for capital, and profit for entrepreneurship.

LAND

This category sometimes extends over all natural resources. It is intended to represent the contribution to production of nonhuman resources as found in their original, unimproved form.

For the French physiocrats led by Francois Quesnay in the 1750s and 1760s, land was the only factor yielding a reliable gain to its owner. In their view, laborers and artisans were powerless and in excess supply, and hence they earned on average only a subsistence-level income. In the same way, what they produced outside of agriculture fetched enough to cover only their wages and input costs with no margin for profit. Only in agriculture, due to soil fertility and other gifts of nature, could a laborer palpably produce more than required to cover subsistence and other costs, so only in agriculture could proprietors collect surplus. Thus the physiocrats explained land rent as coming from surplus produced by the land. They recommended taxes on land as the only sound way to raise revenue and land-grabbing as the best means to increase the government's revenue base.

In 1821 David Ricardo, in *The Principles of Political Economy and Taxation*, stated what came to be known as the classical view: that rent reflects scarcity of good land. The value of a crop depends on the labor required to produce it on the worst land under cultivation. This worst land yields no rent—as long as some of it remains unused—and rent collected on better land is simply its yield in excess of that on the worst land. Ricardo saw rent as coming from differences in land quality (including accessibility) and scarcity. The classical economists assumed only land—understood as natural resources—could be scarce in the long term.

Marginalism, as expounded in 1899 by John Bates Clark in *The Distribution of Wealth*, takes a different approach. It declares that rent reflects the marginal productivity of land—not, as with Ricardo, the productivity of good versus marginal land. Marginal productivity is the extra output obtained by extending a constant amount of labor and capital over an additional unit of land of uniform quality. Marginalists held that any factor of production could be scarce. Their theory is based on the possibility of substituting among factors to design alternative production methods, whereby the optimal production method allocates all the factors to equalize their marginal productivity with their marginal costs.

Long thought of as a self-sustaining input, land might depreciate just like produced assets do. In 1989 Herman Daly and Jonathan Cobb, in *For the Common Good*, distinguished between nonrenewable resources that are consumed or depreciate irretrievably, and renewable resources where the rate of natural renewal is important. One consequence of this work in environmental econom-

ics is that natural resource accounting increasingly resembles capital accounting.

LABOR

The classical "labor theory of value" was an innovative theory in response to the physiocratic doctrine that only land could yield surplus. In 1776 Adam Smith, in *The Wealth of Nations*, observed that with expansion of production and trade, enterprises were making profits over long periods of time, although they either had nothing to do with agriculture or else as agricultural enterprises. Classical economists tried to answer the question: Where does profit come from? Their answer was that it came from labor. At prevailing prices, labor can yield a surplus over subsistence costs in many industries.

The question arises of why proprietors, but not laborers, earn profit. Ricardo arrived at one answer: technical innovation increases labor productivity. Owners of innovative equipment, until its general adoption, get the premium from reduced costs. In 1867 Karl Marx in *Capital*, added that wages reflect the cost of subsistence, not what laborers can produce, and that profit is the difference between the two. Even without innovation proprietors would reap surpluses, Marx held, since laborers lack market power and cannot afford their own equipment.

Why do wages differ for different types of labor? Marx's answer was that higher wages cover costs, beyond personal subsistence, of training and cultivation of skills, acknowledging that one kind of equipment, known as human capital, was available at least to some laborers.

Marginalist economists noticed the advance of technology, which according to classical and Marxist views made labor ever more productive, continually throws laborers out of work. This led them to attribute productivity to equipment rather than only to labor. Referring to equipment as capital, they developed production functions featuring labor and capital as substitutes for each other. Choice among production techniques involving different combinations of labor and capital became a major theme in marginalist growth theory.

CAPITAL

This most controversial of factors is variously defined as produced equipment; as finance used to acquire produced equipment; as all finance used to begin and carry on production, including the wage fund; and as the assessed value of the whole productive enterprise, including intangibles such as goodwill. In 1960 Piero Sraffa, in *Production of Commodities by Means of Commodities*, showed that capital in the sense of produced equipment can fail to behave as expected in marginalist production functions when an entire economy is modeled. Specifically, equip-

Joseph Alois Schumpeter (1883–1950). Schumpeter's 1912 *work contrasted the entrepreneur with the capitalist.* © BETTMANN/CORBIS

ment adopted to replace labor after wages rise from a low level, relative to interest on capital, may be abandoned again in favor of labor as wages rise still higher. This counterintuitive reswitching can happen because the equipment used is itself a product of labor and equipment, and because the ratio of labor to equipment varies for different products.

Frequently capital is treated as finance, associated with the payment of interest. Yet the connection with equipment, in spite of Sraffa's demonstration, has never been severed entirely. One still studies capital depreciation, distinguishing wear-and-tear from obsolescence, and from the present value of investments in capital. Increasingly, theory has come to treat any investment as a capital investment. Furthermore, acquired skills (as opposed to know-how, an attribute of society rather than individuals) have come to be viewed as analogous to physical equipment, capable of yielding their owners a return. This analogy suggests their current designation as human capital. Thus capital is a concept still mired in confusion, and care must be taken in its use to be sure what it means.

ENTREPRENEURSHIP

Until the twentieth century, this function was assigned to the capitalist and frequently conflated with capital. In the classical view, profit rather than interest was attributed to ownership of capital. In the marginalist view, capital earned interest, and profit was a mere residual after all the factors of production were compensated. In his *Principles of Economics*, first published in 1890, Alfred Marshall made extensive references to "organization" and "management," referring to the coordination function of entrepreneurship but to neither risk-assuming nor innovation. However, in 1912 Joseph Schumpeter, in *The Theory of Economic Development*, featured the revolutionary role of organizer and innovator and contrasted it with that of the conservative financier, thus vividly distinguishing the entrepreneur from the capitalist. The entrepreneur's role in this view is not merely that of manager and risk-taker, but also of visionary—someone who seeks as much to destroy the old order as to create something new. Since innovation usually requires destroying old ways of doing things, Schumpeter gave it the name creative destruction. Profit is now assigned to entrepreneurship, to innovation. With the rise of venture capitalists and other financiers willing to take on more risk and do more for innovation in the hope for supernormal returns, the distinction between capitalist and entrepreneur has again become fuzzier. Now there are entrepreneurial financiers as well as entrepreneurial producers and distributors.

Although in business usage stock dividends are distributed profits, in economic analysis they figure as returns to capital, a kind of interest payment, since they are a return to finance rather than to entrepreneurship. The fact that stocks are legally equity rather than debt shares is thereby ignored. Similarly, salaries of corporate executive officers are treated as profit, a return to entrepreneurship, rather than as wages for labor services.

SEE ALSO *Entrepreneurship*

BIBLIOGRAPHY
Clark, John Bates (1965). *The Distribution of Wealth* (3rd ed.). New York: A.M. Kelley.
Daly, Herman E., and Cobb, John B., Jr. (1994). *For the Common Good: Redirecting the Economy Toward Community, the Environment, and a Sustainable Future.* Boston: Beacon Press.
Marshall, Alfred (1997). *Principles of Economics* (8th ed.). Amherst, NY: Prometheus Books.
Marx, Karl (1977). *Capital.* New York: Vintage Books.
Ricardo, David (2004). *The Principles of Political Economy and Taxation.* Mineola, NY: Dover Publication.
Schumpeter, Joseph (1934/1912). *The Theory of Economic Development.* Cambridge, MA: Harvard University Press.
Schumpeter, Joseph (1994). *History of Economic Analysis.* New York: Oxford University Press.

Smith, Adam (2003). *An Inquiry into the Nature and Causes of the Wealth of Nations.* New York: Bantam Classic.

Sraffa, Piero (1960). *Production of Commodities by Means of Commodities.* London: Cambridge University Press.

Michael Brun

FADS

The Hula Hoop, Pet Rock, and Cabbage Patch Kids were all crazes known as fads. These products, like most fads, entered the market quickly, created a consumer obsession, sold millions of units in a short amount of time, and declined just as rapidly. Their special product life cycle of quick, dramatic sales and a sharp, drastic decline differs from the five stage product life cycle concept of product development, introduction, growth, maturity, and decline. Fads have a limited following and tend to die quickly because they do not satisfy a strong consumer need.

THE PRODUCT LIFE CYCLE

The course that a product's sales and profits take over its lifetime is the product life cycle (PLC). Marketers know that all products will have some type of life cycle, but the shape and length is not known in advance. In the first stage of the cycle, product development, an idea for a product is formulated and development of the product begins. During this stage sales are zero, consumer research begins, and promotion consists of public relations.

The next stage, introduction, is characterized by a period of slow sales growth, but no profits are made because of the high initial investment and promotional costs. The company begins to inform consumers about the product through advertising, and distribution of the product is selective.

The third stage of the PLC, growth, is a time of rapid market acceptance and increasing profits. Product distribution becomes more widespread, and advertising shifts from being informative to being persuasive. Realizing the opportunity for profit, competitors will enter the market, creating market expansion. Promotional spending remains the same or increases slightly. Prices

Called the "greatest fad of them all" the Hula Hoop was developed in 1957.

ENCYCLOPEDIA OF BUSINESS AND FINANCE, SECOND EDITION

may be lowered during the growth stage to attract new customers.

The fourth stage of the PLC, maturity, is a period of slow sales growth and leveling-off or declining profits. Most potential buyers have been reached, so no new customers are buying the product. This stage presents the greatest challenges to marketers. To prevent entering the decline stage, research and development departments may make product modifications to meet the changing needs of consumers, distribution becomes selective again, and advertising becomes competitive because of the number of competitors who have entered the market.

Sales slow and profits drop in the decline stage, usually because of advances in technology, a shift in consumer taste, or increased competition. Distribution becomes exclusive, and sales promotions are developed. Products in the decline stage should have their sales, market share, costs, and profit trends regularly reviewed so that managers can decide whether to maintain the product, harvest the product (reduce various costs associated with the product), or drop the product from the product line.

THE PRODUCT LIFE CYCLE OF FADS

The Hula Hoop has been called the "greatest fad of them all." Developed in 1957 by Wham-O creators Richard Knerr and Arthur "Spud" Melin, it was modeled after an Australian toy. A prototype was developed and tested on U.S. playgrounds and was found to have the longest play value. After only four months on the market, 25 million Hula Hoops had been sold. In less than a year, sales had almost completely stopped and competition was increasing, so Wham-O entered foreign markets and its success continued. Collectively, toy manufacturers made $45 million off the Hula Hoop.

The life cycle of the Hula Hoop was not typical of most products. A prototype was developed and tested during the product development stage, but the Hula Hoop bypassed the introduction stage and, with rapid sales, the toy quickly entered the growth stage. Again, the Hula Hoop skipped the maturity stage and went directly into the decline stage, with sales coming to an almost immediate halt. Other fads' life cycles have followed this model.

Gary Dahl created the Pet Rock in the 1970s, complaining that dogs, cats, and other pets were too messy, misbehaved, and expensive. Instead, Dahl had a pet rock that was easy to care for and cheap; it also had a great personality. Dahl wrote the *Pet Rock Training Manual* and created the Pet Rock out of a Rosarita Beach Stone that cost him a penny. In October 1975, Dahl packaged the Pet Rock in a gift box shaped like a pet carrying case, included the training manual, and sold it for $3.95.

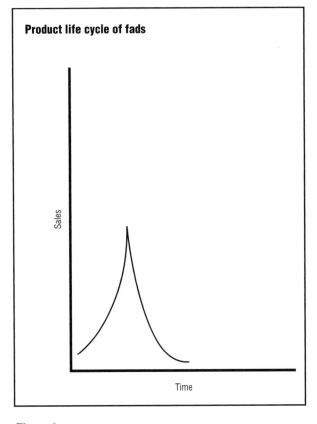

Product life cycle of fads

Sales

Time

Figure 1

Within a few months, Dahl had sold a million rocks and became an instant millionaire. By the next February, sales had stopped.

Unlike the Hula Hoop, the Pet Rock was not tested during the product development stage. Dahl had the idea for the product and quickly produced it with no market testing. Similar to the Hula Hoop, the Pet Rock caught on quickly with consumers, reached its life-cycle peak at the growth stage, and dipped down into the decline stage in a very short period of time.

Artist Xavier Roberts created Cabbage Patch Kids, originally called "Little People," in 1977. The cloth doll was "delivered" at BabyLand General Hospital, a former medical clinic in Cleveland, Georgia, where Roberts had his employees dress in white nurses' and doctors' uniforms. Sales of the dolls were termed adoptions, and each doll came with a birth certificate and adoption papers. Roberts sold 250,000 dolls at prices ranging from $125 to $1,000. National Cabbage Patch mania struck when Roberts signed a contract with Coleco in 1982, and $25 models started selling all over the United States. Approximately 2.5 million Cabbage Patch Kids were sold in the first year on the market, but, like the fads before it, Cabbage Patch Kids had lost a dominating position in the market by 1985.

The Cabbage Patch Kids had a standard product development stage, but its introduction stage was short. Shortly after hitting the toy store shelves, sales skyrocketed and the product entered the growth stage with full force. It entered the maturity stage when sales starting leveling off and the supply was greater than the demand. In an effort to prevent the product from entering the decline stage, marketers at Coleco experimented with product extensions—but to no avail. Eventually, profits began to drop and the Cabbage Patch Kids fell into the decline stage. Figure 1 shows the product life cycle of fads.

Fads are generally mysterious both to their creators and to the public. Although their products were unique, Wham-O, Dahl, and Roberts had no idea they would experience such rapid success. Past fads have included the Rubik's Cube, Beanie Babies, and Furbee. Most fads never really completely die, but they never regain their initial popularity. To understand consumer obsessions with fads, marketers must understand consumer buying behavior.

CONSUMER BUYING BEHAVIOR

There are four types of buying behavior: complex buying behavior, dissonance-reducing buying behavior, habitual buying behavior, and variety-seeking buying behavior. Complex buying behavior occurs when the consumer is purchasing something expensive or risky, such as a personal computer. The consumer must learn about the product line, is highly involved in the buying process, and perceives significant differences among brands. Marketers must differentiate their products' features from other brands. Dissonance-reducing buying behavior occurs when an expensive or risky purchase is being made, but the consumer perceives no difference in brands. They may purchase the brand that offers the best price or that is the most convenient to buy. Habitual buying behavior involves low consumer involvement and little concern for brand differences. Variety-seeking buying behavior is characterized by low consumer involvement but significant differences in brands. Consumers displaying this type of buying behavior often switch brands to experience variety rather than because of dissatisfaction.

Fad purchasers display variety-seeking buying behavior. Buyers of Beanie Babies are loyal to the Ty brand; they will not buy competing brands. Many consumers who buy Beanie Babies switch to the next craze when it hits the shelves. PokeMon became the latest fad in 2000, and the variety seekers shifted again to this latest trend. Until consumer demands and obsessions cease to exist, fads are here to stay.

SEE ALSO *Marketing; Promotion*

BIBLIOGRAPHY

Kotler, Philip, and Armstrong, Gary (2005). *Principles of Marketing* (11th ed.). Upper Saddle River, NJ: Prentice Hall.

Friedrich, Otto (1983, December 12). "The Strange Cabbage Patch Craze". *Time*, 122.

Jennifer L. Scheffer

FAIR PACKAGING AND LABELING ACT OF 1966

Many consumer problems have been, and in some instances still are, caused by incorrect and even fraudulent information disclosure on products and through advertising. The Fair Packaging and Labeling Act of 1966 was passed during the Johnson administration to ensure that consumers have the information they need to choose wisely among competing products. The act directs businesses to disclose necessary information truthfully. Product labels must include such basic information as ingredients and contents, quantity, and maker of the product. Therefore, any business engaged in producing and distributing consumer products must comply with the Fair Packaging and Labeling Act of 1966. This act comes under the consumer-protection charge of the Federal Trade Commission, which bears the primary responsibility for making sure that labeling is not false and misleading. Textiles and food products are two examples of products regulated under this act, which not only prevents consumer deception but also provides consumers with the opportunity to compare value.

Amendments to the Fair Packaging and Labeling Act of 1966, passed in 1992 and enforced beginning in 1994, require labels to include conversion of quantities into a metric measurement in addition to the customary U.S. system of weights and measures. There was a great deal of opposition to this act from both private and public-sector manufacturers that sold their products only in the United States. For example, some paint manufacturers said that labeling contents in pints and gallons should be sufficient since their paint was sold only in the United States. The minimum federal penalty for not including metric measurements was established at $10,000. State regulators have the authority to remove products from store shelves if they were not compliant with the established guidelines.

Under the George H.W. Bush administration, the Nutrition Labeling and Education Act of 1990 was passed, which requires detailed information on labels and standardized descriptive phrases such as "low fat" and "light." Manufacturers had to comply with this act by 1994. Since the passage of the Nutrition Labeling and

Education Act, people are better satisfied with the information printed on food and drug labels (Kristal, Levy, Patterson, Li, & White, 1998). While manufacturers were initially opposed to the new nutrition labeling, mainly because of cost, it was predicted that consumer health benefits would exceed the cost.

In 1993 the Food and Drug Administration issued additional regulations to the Nutrition Labeling and Education Act, stating that restaurant menus must comply with regulations for nutrient and health claims that appear on signs, placecards, and menus. The rule was finalized in 1996, establishing criteria under which restaurants must provide nutrition information for menu items. Thus, healthier or low-fat menu choices must be highlighted with claims such as no more than 5 grams of fat per serving. Restaurants are getting excellent customer response, better than expected, to providing healthy food choices. Consumers today are demanding higher quality. Fair labeling and packaging help assure consumers that they are getting the high quality they are demanding.

SEE ALSO *Packaging*

BIBLIOGRAPHY
Baker, H. (2001). "Worth the weight." *Global Cosmetic Industry,* 163(3), 18-19.
Federal Trade Commission. "The Fair Packaging and Labeling Act, 15 U.S.C.§§1451-1461." Retrieved from www.ftc.gov/os/statutes/fplajump.html.
Kristal, A. R., Levy, L., Patterson, R. E., Li, S. S., & White, E. (1998). "Trends in food use associated with new labeling regulations." *American Journal of Public Health,* 88(8), 1212-1216.
Kurtzweil, P. (1997). "Today's special nutrition information." *FDA Consumer,* 31(4), 21-26.
U.S. Food and Drug Administration (FDA). "Guide to nutrition labeling and education act." Retrieved from www.fda.gov/ora/inspect_ref/igs/nleatxt.html.

Phyllis Bunn
Laurie Barfitt

FASB

SEE *Financial Accounting Standards Board*

FEDERAL RESERVE SYSTEM

To promote the development of a sound economy and a reliable banking system, Congress passed, and President Woodrow Wilson signed, the Federal Reserve Act on December 23, 1913. The act was a response to the recurring bank failures and financial panics that had plagued the nation.

After much disagreement and eventual compromise, all parties to the discussions—the government, banks, other financial institutions, and a few business and labor leaders—agreed that a central U.S. bank was essential for the economic health of the country. Starting with the goal of stabilizing the nation's monetary and financial system, the Federal Reserve System (commonly called the Fed) has undertaken a number of responsibilities.

STRUCTURE OF THE SYSTEM

Designed by Congress and subject to congressional authority, the Fed is a politically independent and financially self-sufficient federal agency. It consists of the following components:

1. A central bank, sometimes called the government's bank, located in Washington, D.C.

2. Twelve regional Reserve Banks, located in Atlanta, Boston, Chicago, Cleveland, Dallas, Kansas City, Minneapolis, New York, Philadelphia, Richmond, San Francisco, and St. Louis. Each Reserve Bank relies on advisory groups for information and suggestions. Some of the more important ones concern operations, small business and agriculture, and thrift institutions (savings banks, savings and loan associations, and credit unions). Reserve Bank officials also meet periodically to discuss mutual problems. These groups include the Conference of Presidents, the Conference of First Vice Presidents, the Conference of Chairmen, and the Financial Services Policy Committee.

3. Twenty-five branch banks, located within defined areas of the Reserve Banks. For example, branch banks within the San Francisco Reserve Bank area are located in Los Angeles, Portland (Oregon), Salt Lake City, and Seattle.

4. Member banks, located throughout the country. Some are national banks (all of which are commercial banks) chartered by the federal government and, by law, are members of the Fed. Others are state commercial banks that have chosen to be members. Of the more than 9,000 commercial banks in the country, more than 3,700 are members of the Fed. Other depository institutions, including nonmember commercial banks and thrift institutions, are subject to many of the Fed's rules and regulations. A member bank is required to purchase stock from its Reserve Bank in an amount equal to 3 percent of its combined capital and surplus. However, this investment does not represent control of or a financial

The Federal Reserve Building in Washington, D.C. © LEE SNIDER/PHOTO IMAGES/CORBIS

interest in the Reserve Bank. In return for its investment, however, a member bank receives a 6 percent annual dividend and the right to vote in elections of directors of its Reserve Bank.

GOVERNANCE OF THE SYSTEM

These are three basic components in the governance structure of the Fed:

1. The Fed's primary policy-making group is the seven-member Board of Governors. Appointed by the president and confirmed by the Senate, members serve for one fourteen-year term only. A member who is appointed to fill an unexpired term may be appointed for an additional full term. From among the seven members, the Board's chairman and vice chairman are also appointed and confirmed by the president and the Senate for four-year terms.

2. There are three advisory groups that aid the Board of Governors:

    a. Federal Advisory Council, consisting of one member from each Reserve Bank. Its major concerns involve banking and economic issues.

    b. Consumer Advisory Council, consisting of thirty specialists in consumer and financial matters.

    c. Thrift Institutions Advisory Council, consisting of people representing thrift institutions. This Council is concerned with issues affecting those institutions.

3. The Federal Open Market Committee (FOMC) consists of the seven-member Board of Governors, the New York Federal Reserve Bank president, and an additional four Reserve Bank presidents who serve on a one-year rotating basis. By tradition, the Committee elects the Board of Governors chairperson as its chairperson and the New York Reserve Bank president as its vice chairperson. Although all twelve Reserve Bank presidents attend the FOMC's eight-times-a-year formal meetings, only the Board, the New York Reserve Bank president, and the four rotating presidents are voting members.

ACTIVITIES AND RESPONSIBILITIES OF THE FEDERAL RESERVE SYSTEM

In conjunction with the FOMC and the twelve Reserve Banks, the Board of Governors' main concern is the development of monetary policy, which it carries out through three means:

1. The establishment of reserve-level rates (amounts that member banks must set aside to be reserved against deposits). These amounts depend on the nation's economic activity status, with emphasis placed on price levels and the volume of business and consumer expenditures. By the lowering of the required reserve-level rate, banks can increase the proportion of funds they are able to lend to customers. By raising the required reserve-level rate, the opposite effect takes place. Thus, the Fed can influence such factors as economic activities, the money supply, interest rates, credit availability, and prices. However, a change in a reserve-level rate usually causes banks to change their strategic plans. In addition, a reserve-level rate increase is costly to banks. Consequently, changes in reserve-level rates are uncommon.

2. The approval of discount rates (interest rates at which member banks may borrow short-term funds from their Reserve Bank). When inflation threatens, a discount-rate increase tends to dampen economic activity because then banks charge higher interest rates to borrowers. On the other hand, a discount-rate decrease is designed to stimulate business activity. The term discount window is often used when describing a Reserve Bank facility that extends credit to a member bank.

3. Another rate, the federal funds rate, is an important factor affecting day-to-day bank operations. This is the rate charged by one depository institution to another for the overnight loan of funds. This happens when one bank is short of funds while another has a surplus. The rate is not fixed; it may change from day to day and from bank to bank.

4. Open-market operations (the purchase and sale of U.S. government securities in the open market). These activities are conducted by the FOMC, of which the Board of Governors comprises the majority. The Fed buys and sells U.S. government securities such as Treasury bills from banks and others several times a week. As a result, the amounts banks have available to lend to borrowers are affected. For example, when the Fed buys securities, banks have more funds, so interest rates tend to drop. The opposite occurs when the Fed sells its securities. By

Ben S. Bernanke (1955–). *Chairman of the Federal Reserve Board 2006–.* AP IMAGES

and large, open-market operations comprise the most powerful tool the Fed has to influence monetary policy.

Other activities and responsibilities of the Federal Reserve System include the following:

1. Supervision of the twelve Reserve Banks and their branches. With regard to the latter, the Board of Governors, through the Reserve Banks, uses both on- and off-site examinations to maintain awareness of each member bank's activities. These activities include the quality of loans, capital levels, and the availability of cash.

2. Cooperative efforts of the U.S. Treasury and the Fed. For example, the Fed acts as the Treasury's fiscal agent by putting paper money and coins into circulation, handling Treasury securities, and maintaining a checking account for the Treasury's receipts and payments.

3. Oversight of banking organizations, such as bank holding companies (companies that own or control one or more banks).

4. Provision of an efficient payments system such as check collections and electronic transactions. With billions of checks in circulation each year, the Fed plays a major role in assuring their efficient processing. By arrangements among the Reserve Banks, member banks and nonmember banks, checks are credited or debited (added to or subtracted from) to depositors' accounts speedily and accurately. Electronic methods are being used increasingly to transfer funds (and securities, too). One such method, involving very large sums, is called Fedwire. Another is the Automated Clearinghouse (ACH), which is used by the government, businesses, and individuals for the receipt or payment of recurring items, such as Social Security.

5. Enforcement of consumer credit protection laws. These laws include the Community Reinvestment Act, which promotes community credit needs; the Equal Credit Opportunity Act, which prohibits discrimination in credit transactions on the basis of marital status, race, sex, and so forth; the Fair Credit Reporting Act, which allows consumers access to their credit records for the purpose of correcting errors; and the Truth in Lending Act, which enables consumers to determine the true amount they are paying for credit.

6. Establishment of banking rules and regulations.

7. Determination of margin requirements (the amount of credit granted investors for the purchase of securities, such as shares of stock). The borrowed funds are usually secured from a bank or a brokerage firm (a company that sells stocks and/or bonds). Margin requirements that are too liberal can damage the stock market and the economy.

8. Approval or disapproval of applications for bank mergers (two or more banks joining together to form one new bank). The Fed also acts if the new bank is to become a state member bank of the Federal Reserve System.

9. Approval and supervision of the Edge Act (named for Senator Walter Edge of New Jersey) and agreement corporations. Both cases involve corporations that are chartered to engage in international banking. Edge Act corporations are chartered by the Fed, while agreement corporations secure their charters from the states. The latter are so named because they must agree to conform to activities permitted to Edge Act corporations. The Fed is also responsible for approving and regulating foreign branches of member banks and for developing policies regarding foreign lending by member banks.

10. Issuance and redemption of U.S. savings bonds. Regardless of how the bonds are purchased—for example, through an employer savings plan or a bank—it is the Fed that processes the applications and sends the bonds.

SUMMARY

Since it holds substantial U.S. government securities, the Federal Reserve System earns sufficient interest to operate without government appropriations. Consequently, it is both a financially self-sufficient and politically independent agency that exerts great influence on the nation's economy. It bolsters domestic consumer confidence and is a major player in global economic activities.

SEE ALSO *Financial Institutions*

BIBLIOGRAPHY

Board of Governors of the Federal Reserve System. (2002) *The Federal Reserve System: Purposes and Functions.* Washington, DC: Books for Business.

Federal Reserve System (2003). "The Structure of the Federal Reserve System". Retrieved October 18, 2005, from http://www.federalreserve.gov.

Feinman, Joshua N. (1993, June). "Reserve Requirements: History, Current Practice, and Potential Reform." *Federal Reserve Bulletin*, 569-589.

Melvin Morgenstein

FEDERAL TRADE COMMISSION ACT OF 1914

The Federal Trade Commission Act of 1914 prohibits unfair methods, acts, and practices of competition in interstate commerce. It also created the Federal Trade Commission, a bipartisan commission of five presidential appointees, confirmed by the Senate, to police violations of the act. The Federal Trade Commission's (FTC) function is to counter deceptive acts and practices and anticompetitive behavior by businesses. The FTC enforces the Clayton and Federal Trade Commission Acts as well as a number of other antitrust and consumer-protection laws. The FTC's rulemaking authority enables it to issue rules interpreting the antitrust laws that govern either all members of industry or apply to specific business practices. When a rule is violated, the FTC can initiate civil proceedings in a federal district court to obtain injunctive relief and civil damages.

The Federal Trade Commission Act of 1914 (and the provisions of the antitrust acts that preceded it) promotes free and fair trade competition by investigating and preventing violations of the law. Key areas covered by the act, as well as other antitrust laws, include:

Price fixing: There are two types of price fixing: vertical and horizontal. Vertical price fixing occurs when manufacturers make express or implied agreements with their customers obligating them to resell at a price dictated by the manufacturer. Manufacturers can suggest retail prices but not fix them by agreement. Few sellers are caught vertically fixing prices; instead, they intimidate retailers by cutting off sales (Garman, 2005). Horizontal price fixing occurs when competitors make direct agreements about the quantity of goods that will be produced, offered for sale, or bought. According to Garman (2005), in one case, an agreement by major oil refiners to purchase and store the excess production of small independent refiners was found to be illegal because the purpose of the agreement was to affect the market price for gasoline by artificially limiting the availability of supply. The government can take action, civil and/or criminal, in cases of price fixing.

Unfair competition: The FTC and antitrust policies that preceded it are in agreement on concepts of unfair competition. Examples of unfair competition are larger businesses using their size or market power to gain lower prices from suppliers or a manufacturer granting discounts for the same products sold to larger firms without granting similar discounts to smaller businesses when selling costs do not vary.

Merger prohibition: A merger is the acquisition of one company by another. The FTC established guidelines and criteria that challenge mergers that lessen competition. The judgment of the courts is that a restraint of trade occurring through a merger must be undue and unreasonable before it is held illegal.

Deceptive practices: False advertising is one example of deceptive practice. The FTC considers an advertisement deceptive if it contains misrepresentation or omission that is likely to mislead consumers acting reasonably under the circumstances to their detriment.

Even though there are differences of opinion as to the effectiveness of antitrust policy, everyone (consumers, competitors, and prospective business owners) benefits from a more competitive economy. Thus, antitrust policy is an important element in public policy regarding business. Unfortunately, there are limits to what is accomplished mainly because the amount of funds provided by Congress for antitrust issues has a significant impact on enforcement.

SEE ALSO *Antitrust Legislation*

BIBLIOGRAPHY

Garman E. T. (2005). *Consumer Economics Issues in America* (8th ed.). Mason OH: Thomson Custom Solutions.

Meier, K. J., Garman, E. T., and Keiser, L. R. (2003). *Regulation and Consumer Protection: Politics, Bureaucracy and Economics* (4th ed.). Mason, OH: Thomson Custom Solutions.

Phyllis Bunn
Laurie Barfitt

FEEDBACK

SEE *Communications in Business; Job Enrichment; Operations Management; Performance Appraisal; Standard-Based Work Performance*

FINANCE

Corporate or Business Finance is basically the methodology of allocating financial resources, with a financial value, in an optimal manner to maximize the wealth of a business enterprise. There are three major decisions to be made in this allocation process: capital budgeting, financing, and dividend policy. Capital budgeting is the decision regarding the choice of which investments are to be made with the resources that have been brought into the business or earned and retained by the business. The choice depends on the returns to be made from the investment exceeding the cost of capital. The method used to do this is the discounted time-value of money of the cash flow from the investment. This value is the internal rate of return (IRR), a measure of return on investment. When the IRR exceeds the required return, which is equal to the cost of the funds invested (see weighted average cost of capital, below) then the investment should be made. If such a required return is used as the discount rate, then that is the same as saying the investment will yield a positive net present value (NPV). If there are two or more investments that can be made, but they are mutually exclusive, then they must be ranked, and the one with the highest NPV should be chosen. If there is a limited amount of funds to be invested, then some bankers or advisers who obtain additional funds for a business may require that the business choose among the investments so as not to exceed the limited level of funds available. This selection process, which is called capital rationing, should be done in a similar manner to rank the projects by selecting the combination of investments that do not exceed the total funds available and that yield the maximum total net present value.

Financing is the decision of which resources or funds are to be brought into the business from external investors and creditors in order to be invested in profitable projects. The first external source of finance is debt, which includes loans from banks and bonds purchased by bondholders. The debt creditors take less risk of nonrepayment because the business must repay them if there are funds available to do so when the debt becomes due. The second external source of finance is equity, which includes common stock and preferred stock. The equity investors in the business take more business risk and may not receive payment until the creditors are repaid and the management of the business decides to distribute funds back to the investors. The goal of the financing decision is to obtain all the resources necessary, to make all the investments that yield a return in excess of the cost of the funds invested or the required rate of return, and to obtain these funds at the lowest average cost, so as to reduce the required rate of return and increase the net present value of the projects selected.

Dividend policy is the decision regarding funds to be distributed or returned to the equity investors. This can be done with common stock dividends, preferred stock dividends, or stock repurchase by the business of its own stock. The aim of this decision is to retain the resources in the business that are required to run the business or make additional investments in the business, as long as the returns earned exceed the required return. In theory, management should return or distribute all resources that cannot be invested in the business at levels in excess of the required return. In practice, however, dividends are often maintained at or changed to certain levels in order to convey the proper signals to the investors and the financial markets. For example, dividends can be maintained at moderate levels to demonstrate stability, maintained at or reduced to low levels to demonstrate the growth opportunities for the business, or increased to higher levels to demonstrate the restoration of a strong financial (capital) structure (debt and equity capital) for the business.

Capital is the total of financial resources invested in the business. In terms of the sources, there are two types of capital: interest-bearing debt funds, such as loans, bonds, short-term notes, and interest-bearing payables to trade suppliers; and equity, such as common and preferred stock and the earnings retained in the business that add to stockholders' share of the entities. In terms of uses, there are also two types of capital: net working capital, such as operating cash, inventory, and receivables, less interest-free payables to trade suppliers; and fixed capital, such as property, plant, and equipment. Capital is managed to

maximize wealth by maximizing the rates of return on investments of capital and thus maximizing the total net present value of the business. This can be done by minimizing the amount of capital used for given business investments with given business returns.

Weighted average cost of capital is the weighted average of the returns on investment or future dividends for the stockholders and interest rates on debt for the creditors. This average return should be used as the required return for investments, as mentioned earlier, because it represents the weighted average of the required returns of all the different debt creditors and equity investors. It also represents the weighted average of the costs that can be saved by the business if the resources or financial funds are returned to the creditors and investors instead of being used for investments within the business.

Capital structure is represented by the types of sources of capital funds invested in the business. A common measure of sources is the percentage of debt relative to equity that appears on a company's balance sheet. Usually, the cost or required returns for the debt is much less than the equity, especially on an after-tax basis. Thus, the total cost of capital declines when some debt funds from creditors are substituted for equity funds from investors. Yet as more debt is added, the business becomes riskier because of the higher amount of fixed payments that must be made to creditors, whether or not the business is generating adequate funds from earnings; and then the costs of both the debt and equity funds are increased to the point where the weighted-average cost increases.

Acquisitions, which are purchases of other businesses, are merely another type of capital budgeting investment for a business. Such purchases should be evaluated in the same manner as any other capital investment, as outlined earlier, to obtain the maximum positive net present value, though the issues and data are often more complex to analyze.

Price/earnings ratio is often used in making acquisitions as an abbreviated measure of valuation. This ratio is of the value or price of a business or its stock to its earnings. Yet the actual decision to make an acquisition is a capital budgeting decision; the resultant determination of price or net present value can then be described in relative terms to the earnings in the price/earnings ratio.

Returns for any business or particular debt or investment made in the business are merely the cash flows that will ultimately be earned by the business or particular creditors and stockholders. These can be expressed in dollar terms or as percentages, with the latter being the average annual percentage of the cash flows relative to the overall investment in the business or the particular amounts of debt or stock involved. For debt instruments, these percentage rates are called interest rates. For specific investment decisions, the returns used should be those that are incremental of the specific investment.

Return/interest rates are based on three components: pure return for the investor or creditor providing funds; coverage of inflation rates, so that the purchasing power of the proceeds is maintained apart from the true return; and additional return for additional risk, such as an equity investment in a risky business as opposed to a bond from the U.S. government. These components are then compounded with each other, rather than merely added together, to obtain the overall interest rate or required return on equity investment. When calculating return or interest rates, any additional up-front money, such as closing costs, must also be added to the investment; this amount increases or reduces the return, depending on who pays for it.

Residual values are a portion of the returns to be earned in an investment that is returned to the business when the investment is sold or the project is terminated. This can be most important in the liquidation of inventory and receivables when operations of a portion of a business are terminated or when real estate ceases to be required and thus can be sold, for example, when a factory is closed or when a lease term is complete.

Maturities of debt instruments, such as bonds, loans, or notes payable, are the amounts of time outstanding before the debt becomes due. The financial management rule with respect to maturities is to match the duration of the funds being borrowed by the debtor, or invested by the creditor, with the timing of his or her own business needs for funds in the future. Thus, the financing of a new business—with the likely future expansions of property, plant, equipment, inventory, and receivables—can be done with longer-term debt funds. Yet the financing of a specific shorter-term need, such as the outlays on a construction project before completion payments are made, should be comparably shorter in maturity. Similarly, the investment of temporary excess cash should be in shorter-term instruments, such as short-term CDs or Treasury bills. If maturities are not matched, then the additional time before the debt becomes due from or to the investor becomes a period of speculation on the rise or fall of future interest rates.

International finance is concerned with the same methodology of allocating financial resources, but with modifications or areas of emphasis required by the restrictions of currency and capital movements among countries and the differences in the currencies used in different countries. The following paragraphs represent some of the major changes to the basic financial decisions:

1. Foreign capital budgeting requires the use of foreign cash flows and local tax rates, but U.S. inflation rates and U.S. dollars at the current exchange rates can be used. The required return or cost of capital then need only be adjusted, as with any investment, for the greater or lesser risk of the project in which the investment is made, which includes the greater or lesser risk of the country in which the investment is being made.

2. Foreign capital markets are a source for both debt and equity funds, for both foreign subsidiary operations and the general needs of the overall business. Foreign subsidiary capital structures often utilize more local debt when legally and practically available in order to reduce the risk of blockages of earned funds from repatriation to the parent company in another country. In addition, local-currency debt reduces the risk for the parent company if the exchange rates for the local currency change adversely.

3. Foreign-exchange rates can change dramatically and therefore pose a significant risk for the value of assets held in or future payments from foreign countries. These exposures may be in dealings with third parties or within a company's own foreign subsidiaries. Forward currency contracts or currency options, instruments used to purchase one currency for another currency in the future at guaranteed exchange rates, can be used to protect against such risk. While these contracts are often also used to make profits by managers who believe the exchange rates will change in a manner different from the expectations implicit in the overall currency market, such use should be viewed as risky speculation.

4. Personal finance is concerned with the same methodology of allocating resources, but with a greater emphasis on allocating some of them to obtain the maximum consumption satisfaction at the lowest cost, as opposed to earning income and cash flow returns on the investments.

5. Budgeting and financial planning are the processes used by financial managers to forecast future financial results for a business, a person, or a particular investment. Usually, the major components of earnings, cash flow, and capital are projected in the form of forecasted income statements, cash-flow statements, and balance sheets. The latter show where the capital funds are invested in the components of fixed and working capital, as well as the sources of these capital funds in terms of the debt, stock, and retained earnings.

ISSUES IN APPLIED CORPORATE FINANCE AND VALUATION

Estimation of the Cost of Capital. In recent decades, theoretical breakthroughs in such areas as portfolio diversification, market efficiency, and asset pricing have converged into compelling recommendations about the cost of capital to a corporation. The cost of capital is central to modern finance, touching on investment and divestment decisions, measure of economic profit, performance appraisal, and incentive systems. Each year in the United States, corporations undertake more than $500 billion in expenditures, so how firms estimate the cost is not a trivial matter. A key insight from finance theory is that any use of capital imposes an opportunity cost on investors; namely, funds are diverted from earning a return on the next-best equal risk investment. Since investors have access to a host of financial market opportunities, corporate use of capital must be benchmarked against these capital market alternatives. The cost of capital provides this benchmark. Unless a firm can earn in excess of its cost of capital, it will not create economic profit or value for investors. A recent survey of leading practitioners reported the following best practices:

- Discounted cash flow (DCF) is the dominant investment-evaluation technique

- Weighted average cost of capital (WACC) is the dominant discount rate used in DCF analyses

- Weights are based on market, not book, value mixes of debt and equity

- The after-tax cost of debt is predominantly based on marginal pretax costs, as well as marginal or statutory tax rates

- The capital asset pricing model (CAPM) is the dominant model for estimating the cost of equity

Discounted Cash Flow Valuation Models. The parameters that make up the DCF model are related to risk (the required rate of return) and the return itself. These models use three alternative cash-flow measures: dividends, accounting earnings, and free cash flows. Just as DCF and asset-based valuation models are equivalent under the assumption of perfect markets, dividends, earnings, and free cash-flow measures can be shown to yield equivalent results. Their implementation, however, is not straightforward. First, there is inherent difficulty in defining the cash flows used in these models. Which cash flows and to whom do they flow? Conceptually, cash flows are defined differently depending on whether the valuation objective is the firm's equity or the value of the firm's debt plus equity. Assuming that one can define cash flows, one is left with another issue. The models need future cash flows as inputs. How is the cash-flow stream estimated from present data? More important, are current and past dividends, earnings, or cash flows the best indicators of that stream? These pragmatic issues determine which model should be used. Although the dividend model is easy to use, it presents a conceptual dilemma. Finance theory says that dividend policy is irrelevant. The model, however, requires forecasting dividends to infinity or making terminal value assumptions. Firms that currently do not pay dividends are a case in point. Such firms are not valueless. In fact, high-growth firms often pay no dividends, because they reinvest all funds available to them. When firm value is estimated using a dividend discount model, it depends on the dividend level of the firm after its growth stabilizes. Future dividends depend on the earnings stream the firm will be able to generate. Thus, the firm's expected future earnings are fundamental to such a valuation. Similarly, for a firm paying dividends, the level of dividends may be a discretionary choice of management that is restricted by available earnings. When dividends are not paid out, value accumulates within the firm in the form of reinvested earnings. Alternatively, firms sometimes pay dividends right up to bankruptcy. Thus, dividends may say more about the allocation of earnings to different claimants than valuation. All three DCF approaches rely on a measure of cash flows to the suppliers of capital (debt and equity) to the firm. They differ only in the choice of measurement, with the dividend approach measuring the cash flows directly and the others arriving at them in an indirect manner. The free cash-flow approach arrives at the cash-flow measure (if the firm is all-equity) by subtracting investment from operating cash flows, whereas the earnings approach expresses dividends indirectly as a fraction of earnings.

The Capital Asset Pricing Model. This is a set of predictions concerning equilibrium expected returns on risky assets. Harry Markowitz established the foundation of modern portfolio theory in 1952. The CAPM was developed twelve years later in articles by William Sharpe, John Lintner, and Jan Mossin. Almost always referred to as CAPM, it is a centerpiece of modern financial economics. The model provides a precise prediction of the relationship that we should observe between the risk of an asset and its expected return. This relationship serves two vital functions. First, it provides a benchmark rate of return for evaluating possible investments. For example, if one is analyzing securities, one might be interested in whether the expected return we forecast for a stock is more or less than its "fair" return given its risk. Second, the model helps one to make an educated guess as to the expected return on assets that have not yet been traded in the marketplace. For example, how does one price an initial public offering of stock? How will a new investment project affect the return investors require on a company's stock? Although the CAPM does not fully withstand empirical tests, it is widely used because of the insight it offers and because its accuracy suffices for many important applications. Although the CAPM is a quite complex model, it can be reduced to five simple ideas:

- Investors can eliminate some risk (unsystematic risk) by diversifying across many regions and sectors

- Some risk (systematic risk), such as that of global recession, cannot be eliminated through diversification. So even a basket with all of the stocks in the stock market will still be risky

- People must be rewarded for investing in such a risky basket by earning returns above those that they can get on safer assets

- The rewards on a specific investment depend only on the extent to which it affects the market basket's risk

- Conveniently, that contribution to the market basket's risk can be captured by a single measure—beta—that expresses the relationship between the investment's risk and the market's risk

Finance theory is evolving in response to innovative products and strategies devised in the financial marketplace and in academic research centers.

SEE ALSO *Careers in Finance; Ethics in Finance; Finance: Historical Perspectives*

BIBLIOGRAPHY
Bodie, Zvi, Kane, Alex, and Marcus, Alan J. (1999). *Investments* (6th ed.). Boston: McGraw-Hill/Irwin.

Bruner, Robert F. (2003). *Case Studies in Finance: Managing for Corporate Value Creation* (4th ed.). Boston: McGraw-Hill/Irwin.

Bruner, Robert F., Eades, Kenneth M., Harris, Robert S., and Higgins, Robert C. (1998). " 'Best Practices' in Estimating the Cost of Capital: Survey and Synthesis." *Journal of Financial Practice and Education* 8:1, 13-28.

Kaushik, Surendra K., and Krackov, Lawrence M. (1989). *Multinational Financial Management*. New York: New York Institute of Finance.

Stein, Jeremy (1996). "Rational Capital Budgeting in an Irrational World." *The Journal of Business* 69:4, 429-55.

White, Gerald I., Sondhi, Ashwinpaul C., and Fried, Dov (2003). *The Analysis and Use of Financial Statements* (3rd ed.). Hoboken, NJ: Wiley.

Surendra K. Kaushik
Lawrence M. Krackov
Massimo Santicchia

FINANCE: HISTORICAL PERSPECTIVES

Finance is a field of specialization that studies all aspects of obtaining money and making decisions about the allocation of that money. There are many segments of this field by type—corporate finance, federal government finance, municipal finance, not-for-profit finance, and personal finance. This brief discussion will be an overview of corporate finance in the economy in the United States.

In the United States, major corporations and the financial institutions with which they associate are regulated by the U.S. Treasury, which implements fiscal and monetary policies; and the U.S. Congress, which enacts laws and regulations, intersect in their interests. A driver of finance in the United States is the goal to maintain full employment and to achieve a specified level of economic growth. Corporate finance is critical to such a goal.

The history of corporate finance in the United States began with rudimentary, unregulated means of securing funds in the early years of the newly established nation. By the end of the twentieth century, a level of progress that made the United States a financial leader in the global community was reached. The success of the finance function in corporate America is the result of a combination of business innovation in the design and strategies of securing funds and the governmental regulations that ensure integrity in financial markets. Yet, problems persist in what has become since the twentieth century a complex, fast-changing field of specialization.

EARLY AMERICAN FINANCE

In colonial United States, businesses were, for the most part, small and self-financed. The first settlers, however, who had been British subjects, were well acquainted with the corporate form of organization. As Joseph Davis noted, "before the end of the colonial period a considerable number of truly private corporations had been established for ecclesiastical, education, charitable, and even business purposes" (1917, p. 4).

Many of these early efforts were unsuccessful, and individuals who invested in them often lost their total contributions. The nature of financing problems in these early efforts is illustrated by the story of an organization called the Society for Establishing Useful Manufacturers. In November 1791, the legislature of New Jersey passed an act incorporating this enterprise, which likely manufactured such products as paper, textiles, pottery, and wire. Davis identified this company as "one of the pioneer industrial corporations of the United States and the largest and most pretentious of these" (p. 349). Plans for the new corporation were publicly announced, including the much-criticized strategy of raising capital by issuing public stocks. The emphasis on developing domestic industry and reducing dependence on imports was appealing to potential investors, and private citizens were getting encouragement from the newly formed federal government to undertake business activity on a broader scale than had been common at the time.

At the time the prospectus for this new enterprise was being circulated, Alexander Hamilton, the secretary of the Treasury, presented his *Report on Manufacturers,* which was prepared in response to President George Washington's direction "to prepare and report to the House, a proper plan for the encouragement and promotion of such manufactories as will tend to render the United States independent of other nations" (quoted in Davis, p. 362).

The requisite capital was indeed raised, with most of the subscriptions secured in New York. Shortly thereafter, panic ensued because the new enterprise was not progressing as intended. Leading officers and directors were involved in the speculative boom and had not given attention to the actual business of the new enterprise. Thereafter, the leaders, who were in possession of most of the paid-in funds, went bankrupt. This story reveals the lure of becoming wealthy quickly and of general incompetence among leadership. There were virtually no rules to restrain the behavior of the leaders; they readily, therefore, appropriated the funds for their own personal use.

The society was saved by a loan of $10,000 from the Bank of New York, and there is evidence that the secretary of Treasury was responsible in securing this financing. Nevertheless, there continued to be serious financial problems, throughout the period when facilities for the envisioned textile mills were being constructed. The newly appointed treasurer was supposed to be bonded, but he refused. He continued in the position nonetheless. When he retired in 1796, the treasurer's books and the funds were supposed to be left with the deputy-governor. The books, though, were never recovered. It is not clear whether all the funds were recovered. The operations were unprofitable and were discontinued in the same year.

R. E. Wright (2002) presents an interesting analysis of colonial business behavior using the framework of the theory of asymmetry in the principal/agent relationship. Wright concluded "that colonists did little to reduce moral hazard in colonial financial markets. Borrowers often acted in ways that were not in the best interests of lenders" (p. 27). It is Wright's position, however, that most colonial banks in the early national period learned to limit moral hazard by monitoring depositors' accounts and noting the use of funds that had been provided through loans.

FINANCE IN THE 1800S

On the brink of the nineteenth century the United States had a dismal record of successful corporations, as illustrated by the effort in New Jersey discussed above. The country was a world of small mercantile businesses. As of 1790, for example, there were only three banks, three bridge companies, a few insurance associations, and a dozen canal companies. Some businesspeople, however, began to see the value of the corporation: The risks of manufacturing made the limited liability of the corporation appealing.

Several states enacted useful laws. In 1811 New York passed a law that allowed for the incorporation of certain kinds of manufacturing concerns with less than $100,000 of capital. Connecticut, in 1817, and Massachusetts, in 1830, granted limited liability, which was the first step in movement for general incorporation acts. The intent of such acts was to encourage the financing of entities through the corporate structure and to protect the public that might be inclined to invest in these new enterprises. In the same period, the government was significantly involved in the financing of businesses. As Thomas C. Cochran noted:

> The capital needs of banking and transportation brought state participation in business organization. Few such pioneer enterprises seemed possible without substantial state, county, or municipal purchases of stocks and bonds. The credit of the state was generally substituted in part for that of the private company by issuance of state bonds and use of the proceeds to buy the company's securities. (1966, p. 219)

At the same time, Cochran noted some of the serious drawbacks of the new ownership:

> Free and secret transferability of corporate ownership encouraged grave abuses on the part of unscrupulous financiers. It was possible for managing groups to profit personally by ruining great companies and then selling out before the situation became known. (p. 219)

Nevertheless, there were conscientious men who were interested in productive efficiency as well as the quest for wealth. Among the individuals Cochran identified was Nathan Appleton:

> Nathan Appleton ... turning from mercantile pursuits in 1813, joined with some of the Lowells and Jacksons, put his capital into large-scale textile manufacture.... Appleton came to be looked upon as the business leader of Massachusetts.... By 1840 he and his Boston associates had created in eastern Massachusetts a miniature of the corporate industrial society of the twentieth century.

They controlled banking, railroad, insurance, and power companies as well as great textile mills scattered all over the state. It was the large "modern" corporation controllable by strategically organized blocs of shares, and virtually self-perpetuating boards of directors that made this concentration of power possible, but it must be remembered that it was also this device for gathering together the savings of thousands of small investors that had produced the great development. (p. 220)

There were remarkable developments throughout the 1800s. Jonathon Baskin and Paul Miranti, for example, pointed out that the "last quarter of the eighteenth century saw the start of a great economic expansion that changed corporate finance in fundamental ways" (1997, p. 127). It was during this period that there was extensive development of railroads, which independently became strong bastions of finance capitalism. During this period, preferred stock and debt became popular means of financing corporations. During the final decades of the 1800s, relatively widely distributed financial journals and newspapers began to appear. Such publications provided information for prospective investors.

U.S. FINANCE IN THE 1900S

The economic success of the United States at the turn of the twentieth century was reflected in the optimism evident in the U.S. secretary of the Treasury Lyman Judson Gage's comment in the *Annual Financial Review,* a supplement to the *New York Times* (January 1, 1900). His observation was that "the year we have just passed through has been one of great prosperity, the future has no cloud."

Much credit in providing resources was given to banks. Joseph Schumpeter, in his theory of economic development, highlighted the role of bankers as the source of funds for entrepreneurs, who themselves often lack financial resources. Schumpeter noted: "In an economy without development there would be no such money market.... The kernel of the matter lies in the credit requirements of new enterprises.... Thus, the main function of the money or capital market is trading in credit for the purpose of financing development" (1934, pp. 122–127).

Schumpeter undoubtedly was fully aware of the U.S. experience and the influence of American bankers in the impressive growth of the American economy from the mid-1800s through the early decades of the twentieth century. Of the leaders in finance, some of the most impressive of the bankers were the Morgans. As Ron Chernow, in his history of the Morgans, concluded: "The old pre-1935 House of Morgan was probably the most formidable financial combine in history. It financed many industrial giants, including U.S. Steel, General Electric,

General Motors, Du Pont, and American Telephone and Telegraph" (1990, p. xi).

A VIEW FROM ENGLAND

An English journalist, William Lawson, wrote an interesting account of finance in the United States in 1906. He declared in his introduction that he had studied American finance for twenty-five years, traveled throughout the United States, and seen most of its financial institutions from the inside. He developed a highly favorable opinion of the astuteness of the leadership in finance. Among his comments was:

> It is only a few years ago that New York was a financial satellite of London. How long will it be before London becomes a financial satellite of New York?... Till lately the idea prevailed that it was to grow in the ordinary grooves, and was to be like other countries, only much bigger. But that is not to be its prosaic destiny. It is to be a country of its own—a nation by itself.... Gradually, it is breaking loose from all European models and precedents.... [T]he U.S ... probably always will be, a country by itself is particularly true of its finance. (p. 7)

DISCONTENT EXPRESSED

The success of the American economy at the brink of the twentieth century also introduced alarm because of the growth of monopolies and the abuses of business as revealed by muckrakers, for example. Reporters, such as Ida Tarbell (the story of Standard Oil) and Lincoln Steffens (an account of civic corruption in Minneapolis) when published in *McClure* in 1903 captured the attention of the public. The reform efforts of President Theodore Roosevelt in first decade were appealing to many citizens.

At the same time, investors became increasingly interested in corporate common stocks, as reported by Baskin and Miranti. As these historians noted, "New York Stock Exchange statistics: total annual share turnover rose from 159 million in 1900 to 1.1 billion at the height of the 1929 boom" (1997, p. 167). The role of finance continued to be impressive.

IMPETUS FOR REGULATION OF SECURITIES IN THE UNITED STATES

Prior to 1929 there was little support for federal regulation of securities markets in the United States. As noted on the Securities and Exchange Commission (SEC) Web site, "During the 1920s, approximately 20 million large and small shareholders took advantage of post-war prosperity and set out to make their fortunes in the stock market. It is estimated that of the $50 billion in new securities offering during this period, half became worthless" (SEC).

Public confidence shifted dramatically with the stock market crash of 1929. For the economy to recover, the public's faith in the capital markets needed to be restored. The outcome was the passage of two acts by Congress, the Securities Act of 1933 and the Securities Exchange Act of 1934. These laws were established to provide structure in the functioning of financial markets and to provide government oversight.

CHANGES IN FINANCIAL STRUCTURE

The role of banks changed during the twentieth century as businesses became larger and the types of financial institutions increased. Raymond Goldsmith's 1969 study provided a comparison of the main types of U.S. financial institutions in 1900 and 1963. Goldsmith's analysis revealed that in 1900, 62.9 percent of total assets of all the financial institutions were held by commercial banks; by 1963 that percentage was 32.2. Thrift institutions, including mutual savings banks, savings and loan associations, credit unions, finance companies, insurance organizations, and investment companies were active participants in financial services.

Shares of assets held by banks and thrift institutions continued to decline. While the two types of financial institutions held 55 percent of total assets in 1963, the two types held only 22.7 percent by the end of 1999, as reported by the Federal Reserve Board. The Federal Reserve Bank has been a critical participant in all aspects of finance in the United States through its monetary and credit policies.

THE ROLE OF THE SEC

The Securities Exchange Act of 1934 included the establishment of the SEC, which was charged with enforcing the newly passed securities laws, promoting stability in the markets, and protecting investors. The SEC operates on the premise that all investors should have access to certain basic facts about investments prior to purchase. The key means of achieving this is through requiring that all publicly owned companies disclose relevant financial and other information to all citizens.

The SEC oversees key participants in the financial world, including stock exchanges, broker-dealers, and investment advisers. Through its enforcement authority, the SEC brings civil enforcement actions against individuals and companies that violate securities laws. Typical infractions relate to insider trading, accounting fraud, and providing false or misleading information about securities and the companies that issue them.

THE ROLE OF STOCK EXCHANGES

Stock exchanges have played a significant role in the financing of U.S. business enterprises through providing a means of buying and selling securities. The first stock exchange in the United States was established in 1790 in Philadelphia. Two years later, the New York Stock Exchange (NYSE) was formed when twenty-four stockbrokers signed an agreement to trade with one another beneath a buttonwood tree outside what is now 68 Wall Street. The NYSE is the largest stock exchange in the world.

The NYSE's first client, in 1792, was the Bank of New York, and its first office, set up in 1817, was a rented room at 40 Wall Street. It achieved its first million-share day on December 15, 1886, and its first billion-share day on October 28, 1997.

A study of all securities markets by the SEC in 1961 revealed that the over-the-counter securities market was fragmented and obscure, leading the SEC to propose to the National Association of Securities Dealers that it develop an automated over-the-counter securities system. Such a system was completed and began operations in February 1971; it is known as the National Association of Securities Dealers Automated Quotations (NASDAQ) system. The world's first electronic stock market, by the end of 1999 it ranked second, below the NYSE, among the world's securities markets in terms of dollar volume. Technological advances have introduced online buying and selling of securities.

THE BEGINNING OF THE TWENTY-FIRST CENTURY

The new century began with stunning disclosures of corporate scandals. Such disclosures vividly revealed the inadequacy of the rules and regulations of corporation reporting. No objective, thorough investigation of the alleged fraud in financial reporting existed.

Congress, however, passed the Sarbanes-Oxley Act of 2002, which changed markedly the regulatory environment in which publicly owned corporations function in the United States. The act established a new governing board, the Public Company Accounting Oversight Board. That board assumed all professional responsibilities, including those earlier delegated to the public accounting profession. The board has responsibility for auditing rule making and for monitoring of all publicly owned corporations reporting to the SEC.

The opinions of the success of the new regulations are mixed. As of the end of 2005, there continued to be shocking disclosures of misrepresentation of financial information, insider trading, appropriation of company funds for personal use by top executives—including chief executive officers—and other violations of corporate governance in the United States.

THE PLACE OF THE FINANCE INDUSTRY

The finance industry continues to be of central importance in the United States. The Bureau of Economic Analysis, part of the U.S. Department of Commerce, reanalyzed gross domestic product (GDP) by industry data based on the North American Industry Classification System, which was introduced in the 1990s. The analysis for the period from 1987 to 2000 showed that the industry category, "Finance, insurance, real estate, rental, and leasing (FIRE)," was the number-one contributor to "value added by industry group in current dollars as percentage of Gross Domestic Product for selected years."

These are the figures for the finance category:

	1987	1997	2000
Gross domestic product	100.0	100.0	100.0
Finance, insurance, real estate, rental and leasing	17.7	19.2	19.7

The advance-industry estimates for 2004 noted that FIRE comprised a larger share of current-dollar GDP (20.7 percent) than goods-producing industries (19.6 percent) in 2004.

THE GLOBALIZATION OF FINANCE

The transformation of capital markets from the national level to the global level increased considerably during the final decade of the twentieth century. Leadership is provided through the International Organization of Securities Commissions (IOSCO), which was organized in the early 1970s. More than 90 percent of the world's financial activity was represented among the more than 181 national security regulators who were members of IOSCO in 2005. One of the key goals for 2005 was to strengthen capital markets against financial fraud.

SEE ALSO *Finance*

BIBLIOGRAPHY

Baskin, Jonathon Barron, and Miranti, Paul J., Jr. (1997). *A history of corporate finance.* New York: Cambridge University Press.

Chernow, Ron (1990). *The house of Morgan: An American banking dynasty and the rise of modern finance.* New York: Atlantic Monthly Press.

Cochran, Thomas C. (1966). Business organization and the development of an industrial discipline. In Thomas C. Cochran and Thomas B. Brewer (Eds.), *Views of American economic growth: The agricultural era.* New York: McGraw-Hill.

Davis, Joseph Stancliffe (1917). *Essays in the earlier history of American corporations* (Vol. 1). Cambridge, MA: Harvard University Press.

Gage, Lyman Judson (1900, January 1). Secretary Gage reviews the nation's finances. *The New York Times Supplement: Annual Financial Review.*

Goldsmith, Raymond (1969). *Financial structure and development.* New Haven, CT: Yale University Press.

International Organization of Securities Commissions. http://www.iosco.org

Lawson, William Ramage (1906). *American finance: Part first.— domestic.* Edinburgh and London: Blackwood.

National Association of Securities Dealers Automated Quotations. http://www.nasdaq.com

New York Stock Exchange. http://www.nyse.org

Schumpeter, Joseph A. (1934). *The theory of economic development: An inquiry into profits, capital, credit, interest, and the business cycle.* Cambridge, MA: Harvard University Press.

Securities and Exchange Commission. (n.d.). The investor's advocate: How the SEC protects investors and maintains market integrity. Retrieved November 14, 2005, from http://www.sec.gov/about/whatwedo.shtml

U.S. Department of Commerce. Bureau of Economic Analysis. http://www.bea.gov

Williamson, Harold F. (1951). *Growth of the American economy* (2nd ed.). Englewood Cliffs, NJ: Prentice-Hall.

Wright, R. E. (2002) *The wealth of nations rediscovered: integration and expansion in american financial markets 1780-1850.* New York: Cambridge University Press.

Mary Ellen Oliverio

FINANCIAL ACCOUNTING STANDARDS BOARD

The United States has a longstanding tradition of accounting standards being set by the private sector as opposed to the government. Although the federal government's Securities and Exchange Commission (SEC) has the legal authority to establish accounting standards for public companies, the SEC has historically looked to the private sector to set accounting standards.

The first two standard-setting organizations in the United States were the Committee on Accounting Procedure (CAP), which was established in 1938, and the Accounting Principles Board (APB), which replaced the CAP in 1959. Both organizations were committees of the

American Institute of Certified Public Accountants (AICPA) and included approximately twenty representatives of the accounting profession who served on a part-time basis. Pronouncements issued by those two bodies are considered to be generally accepted accounting principles (GAAP) unless they have been specifically amended or replaced by a subsequent pronouncement.

Largely as a result of criticisms concerning the perceived lack of independence of the APB and the part-time involvement of its members, a major reconsideration of the standard-setting structure in the United States occurred in the early 1970s. This led to the creation in 1973 of a new standard-setting body designed to be independent of all other business and professional organizations. That new group was the Financial Accounting Standards Board (FASB).

The FASB is funded by revenues from the sales of its publications and by voluntary contributions, primarily from public accounting firms and corporations. The board consists of seven full-time members. The usual composition of the board is three members with extensive public accounting experience, two from a corporate background, one academic, and one financial analyst.

The three pillars on which the FASB was built are independence, openness (or sunshine), and neutrality. Although independence can never be totally assured, the FASB charter did attempt to protect the board from as much external pressure as possible. The charter gives the FASB exclusive authority to set its own agenda and establish accounting standards. Board members are insulated from external pressures by fixed five-year terms with a two-term maximum, by the requirements to end all past employment relationships, and by disclosure of and certain limitations on investments and outside activities that might create a conflict of interest.

Sunshine characterizes the open process that the board follows. It means that all its technical business is conducted in meetings that are announced in advance and are open to the public. Because the board's Rules of Procedure require a supermajority of five votes to approve the issuance of any new standard, no more than four board members can meet privately to discuss technical issues.

Neutrality means that accounting standards should be designed to provide the best possible information for economic decision making without regard to how that information may affect economic, political, or social behavior. Put another way, accounting standards should not be intentionally biased for the purpose of promoting either private special interests or government policy goals. Neutrality has been reinforced by adoption and adherence to a broad set of principles called the conceptual framework. That framework was designed to produce standards that result in neutral information that is useful in decision making.

An independent group, the Financial Accounting Foundation, oversees the activities of the FASB. It is responsible for selecting members of the FASB, raising money to fund the FASB's operations, and providing general oversight of the FASB to assure that it is performing its mission. The foundation is composed of a sixteen-member board of trustees that represent the majority of the groups interested in, or affected by, the accounting standard-setting process.

The FASB has the authority to establish GAAPs but has no authority to enforce its standards. The SEC and the AICPA are the organizations that provide the enforcement mechanism. The SEC requires compliance with FASB standards by all public companies, that is, those whose securities are traded in public markets, either on stock exchanges or over-the-counter. The AICPA requires public accounting firms that audit either public or private companies to express an opinion as to whether those companies' financial statements conform with GAAPs.

STANDARD-SETTING PROCESS

Within this overall structure, the FASB has developed an extensive structure of due process to conduct its standard-setting activities. The process usually starts by determining what financial reporting issues are sufficiently pervasive and important that they warrant consideration by the board.

The FASB has a professional staff of approximately forty-five persons; once a project is added to the agenda, staff members are assigned to begin research on the topic. On most larger projects, a task force of outside advisers is appointed; they assist in the staff's research and the board's deliberations by providing expertise, a diversity of viewpoints, and a mechanism for communication with those who may be affected by the proposed standard.

The FASB sometimes asks for written comments from constituents during the research phase through the issuance of a Discussion Memorandum. Such a document analyzes the problem in depth, delineates the issues, identifies alternative solutions, and discusses the merits of those solutions in an objective way. Alternatively, the board may issue what is known as a Preliminary Views document, which includes tentative decisions on a few basic issues and again seeks input from constituents.

After completion of initial research by the staff and consideration of comments on a Discussion Memorandum or Preliminary Views, if one of those documents is issued, the board members begin deliberating the issues in earnest. This process can take anywhere from a few months to several years, depending on the number and complexity of the issues involved as well as the strength of the convictions of individual board members. Once at least five board members agree on an overall answer, the board issues an Exposure Draft (ED) of a proposed standard for public comment. The comment period is at least ninety days.

While the ED is out for public comment, the FASB will often conduct a field test, which is designed to test the application of the proposed standard using actual financial information provided by volunteering companies.

The number of comment letters received on an ED can range from a few dozen to more than a thousand, depending on how pervasive and how controversial the proposal is. Comment letters are received primarily from corporations, large public accounting firms, government regulators, academics, and financial analysts, although any interested party is free to express his or her views. After reading the letters, the board redeliberates all the issues in the ED and any additional issues that may have arisen in the comment and field-test processes. At the end of those deliberations, the board again votes; if there is sufficient support among the board members, it issues a final Statement of Financial Accounting Standards.

The steps described above are just an overall outline of the process. Throughout a project's life, discussions are held with the FASB's advisory council, the project task force, and various other interested parties. In addition, the process does not end with the issuance of a Statement. The FASB monitors the application of a Statement to ensure that it is working as planned. Should the standard not work in practice, then the board may consider amending it to provide clarification, issuing additional interpretive guidance, or taking some other action to address problems that arise.

Most FASB projects are controversial. For example, pronouncements on topics such as accounting for employee stock options, postretirement health care benefits, and derivative financial instruments were strongly opposed by many corporations and other affected parties. The board does its best to consider the reasonable arguments expressed by all parties. But in the final analysis, the FASB endeavors to act in the public interest by issuing accounting standards that will result in the most informative and unbiased financial statements possible. Thus investors, creditors, and all others who use financial statements in making economic decisions can take comfort in the fact that the FASB puts the general public interest above any concerns of individual corporations or other self-interested parties.

Despite disagreement over some specific pronouncements, the board's various constituents remain generally supportive. They know that their views are carefully weighed during the FASB's deliberations, but they also recognize that the ultimate determinant of a new standard must be the board's judgment. As the FASB's mission statement states, "The FASB is committed to following an open orderly process for standard setting that precludes placing any particular interest above the interests of the many who rely on financial information."

COMMUNICATING WITH THE FASB

In addition to the Statements, EDs, Discussion Memoranda, and Preliminary Views documents referred to above, the FASB publishes a variety of other documents that provide guidance on financial accounting and reporting. For example, its Emerging Issues Task Force (EITF) develops consensus positions on accounting matters that demand prompt solutions. EITF materials and other FASB publications can be ordered by individual item or through a variety of subscription programs that the organization offers. Special discounts on publications are available to parties who make voluntary contributions to support the overall work of the FASB.

More information on publications or any other related matters is available from the FASB at 401 Merritt 7, P.O. Box 5116, Norwalk, CT 06856-5116, (203)847-0700, or at http://www.fasb.org.

SEE ALSO *Accounting*

BIBLIOGRAPHY

Miller, Paul B. W., Redding, Rodney J., and Bahnson, Paul R. (1998). *The FASB: The People, the Process, and the Politics* (4th ed.). Boston: Irwin/McGraw-Hill.

Van Riper, Robert (1994). *Setting Standards for Financial Reporting: FASB and the Struggle for Control of a Critical Process.* Westport, CT: Quorum Books.

Dennis R. Beresford

FINANCIAL FORECASTS AND PROJECTIONS

Business entities need to plan for the future, must consider alternative management strategies and prepare capital and operating budgets, and must also consider alternative funding and cash budget possibilities. An important part of the planning process is the preparation of prospective financial statements that attempt to predict the outcome of the business entity's activities in future periods.

Financial forecasts and financial projections are prospective financial statements that present an entity's expected financial position, results of operations, and cash flows in future periods under two different conditions. Financial forecasts assume that the entity will continue to function in the manner in which it is currently functioning. For example, if the entity is a retail store chain, then it will continue to do business in the manner in which it is currently engaged. The financial forecast presents the predicted results for the next year. Financial projections, on the other hand, make one or more hypothetical assumptions about an entity's future course of action. For example, if the retail store chain were considering a Web site at which it would also sell merchandise in addition to the merchandise sold in the stores, a financial projection would provide expected results. Financial forecasts and projections should be distinguished from *pro forma* financial statements, which show the effect of a hypothetical future event on the historical financial statements results.

PREPARATION OF PROSPECTIVE FINANCIAL STATEMENTS

The preparation of prospective financial statements requires considerable knowledge of the entity's business and the factors that are likely to determine its future results. The following key factors related to future results must be considered in the preparation of such statements:

- Factors related to the specific entity
- Factors related to the industry
- Factors related to the market
- Factors related to the economy

Factors Related to the Specific Entity. The principal cost elements of the entity's doing business must be considered. Depending on the entity, these elements may include such costs as payroll and benefits, needed employees, raw materials, products the entity sells, freight or shipping, and advertising.

Another consideration is the availability of resources. For example, are the expert, specialized, or skilled workers available to meet the needs of the entity under the plan as initially proposed? Are the raw materials and/or products for resale available? Can the delivery system be organized to accomplish the task? Are the company's physical facilities sufficient for the uses and for the capacities contemplated?

Factors Related to the Industry. Factors related to the industry in which the entity is operating must be considered. Is the industry one in which companies are very competitive? Are competitive industries emerging? Is obsolescence emerging within the industry? Are there regulatory considerations and requirements? Is new technol-

ogy being introduced into the industry? What are the economic conditions within the industry?

Factors Related to the Market. Market factors must be considered. What are the trends in business or consumer demand related to the services or goods being sold by the entity? Are competitive companies emerging, perhaps with new or different products? Is unique marketing required? Are there pricing developments to be factored into the forecast?

Factors Related to the Economy. Numerous factors related to the economy must be considered. What are the economic conditions in the country? What are critical economic trends? Is the economy inflationary, deflationary, or stable? What is the trend with regard to labor availability? What are the financing considerations in relation to the economy? What are interest rates? Are there significant factors related to long-term versus short-term financing? Is a public stock offering a possible financing option?

ATTESTATION SERVICES PROVIDED FOR FINANCIAL FORECASTS AND FINANCIAL PROJECTIONS

Forecasts and projections are important in an organization. They are also of great interest to financial analysts and others in the business environment who make decisions about future business behavior. Because of outsider interest, public accountants are engaged to provide professional services. There are three types of engagements that a certified public accountant may undertake in relation to financial forecasts and projections:

1. Examination: An accountant evaluates the preparation, underlying support, and presentation of the financial statements, and expresses an opinion on them

2. Applying agreed-upon procedures: Users establish the nature and scope of the engagement, and only the results of the procedures performed are provided

3. Compilation: An accountant prepares the prospective statements from information and assumptions provided, and no assurance is given

Examination. The American Institute of Certified Public Accountants (AICPA) has prepared guidelines for prospective financial statements engagements. The person or persons who prepare the financial statements, called the responsible party, are usually the management of the company but may be outsiders, such as the management of an entity considering acquiring the company. The accountants who examine such statements must consider whether the sources of information used by the client are sufficient to support the assumptions reflected in the prospective statements. For example, external sources that should be considered include industry and government publications; reports on new information; digital, electronic, and mechanical technology; reports on new scientific developments; micro and macroeconomic forecasts; and reports on present and proposed legislation. Examples of internal sources that accountants consider include strategic plans, budgets, contractual agreements, purchase and sale agreements and commitments, intellectual property rights such as copyrights and patents, royalty and commission agreements, employee contracts and labor agreements, and financing and debt agreements.

When the examination is of a financial projection, the accountants must determine whether the hypothetical condition or course of action (which will not necessarily occur) is consistent with the purpose of the projection. The accountants must evaluate the support underlying assumptions in the same manner as is done for a forecast.

Upon completion of a financial forecast examination, assuming the accountants have collected sufficient evidence to provide a reasonable basis for the standard report to be issued, that report will state in part:

> In our opinion, the accompanying forecast is presented in conformity with guidelines for presentation of a forecast established by the American Institute of Certified Public Accountants, and the underlying assumptions provide a reasonable basis for management's forecast.

Upon completion of a financial projection examination, the standard report would include a description of the hypothetical assumption and the opinion would state that the underlying assumptions provide a reasonable basis for management's forecast assuming the occurrence of the hypothetical assumption. The report will state in part:

> In our opinion, the accompanying projection is presented in conformity with guidelines for presentation of a projection established by the American Institute of Certified Public Accountants, and the underlying assumptions provide a reasonable basis for management's projection [then the hypothetical assumption would be described and assumed to have occurred, for example, "assuming the establishment of a Web site which will … "]

Financial forecasts are considered general-purpose financial statements that may be distributed to any interested party, whereas financial projections are considered limited-purpose financial statements only to be used by the responsible party who prepared the statements or by

knowledgeable third parties. In both forecasts and prospective financial statement opinions, a warning must be included in the opinion that the prospective results may not be achieved.

If, in the accountants' opinion, the prospective financial statements depart from AICPA guidelines, or one of the significant assumptions does not provide a reasonable basis for the prospective statements, or the accountants could not apply some procedures that were considered necessary, the report would have to be modified.

Applying Agreed-Upon Procedures. Another type of engagement that certified public accountants may undertake is to apply only some procedures, which have been specified by the users, to the financial forecast or projection. An example of such an engagement might be to review the forecast in regard to sales, or payroll costs, or both. Limiting the procedures to only one item, or some of the items, on the prospective financial statements does not enable the accountants to provide an overall opinion. Because of the limitation in regard to the procedures performed, the report is restricted to the users who specified the procedures to be applied.

The standard applying agreed-upon procedures report will state in part:

> At your request, we have performed certain agreed-upon procedures, as enumerated below, … we make no representation regarding the sufficiency of the procedures described … [a list of the procedures performed and related findings would be stated] … we do not express an opinion on whether the prospective financial statements … provide a reasonable basis for the presentation.

Compilation. A compilation of prospective financial statements by certified public accountants involves only the service of preparing the statements in whole or part from information and significant assumptions provided by the responsible party, usually a member of management. Because such an activity does not envision an examination or even applying agreed-upon procedures, no assurance is provided.

The standard compilation report on a forecast would state in part:

> We have not examined the forecast and, accordingly, do not express an opinion or any other form of assurance on the accompanying statements or assumptions.

IMPORTANCE OF FORECASTS AND PROJECTIONS

Forecasts and projections have assumed extraordinary significance in U.S. business. The release of corporate managers' earnings forecasts has become common. Management forecasts have become an important source of information for financial analysts and investors. Stock prices show significant movements after the release of information that shows earnings will be higher or lower than current expectations.

However, some skepticism in regard to these forecasts exists on the part of financial analysts and governmental agencies, such as the Securities and Exchange Commission, because of the fear that forecasts may be biased at times in order to influence capital markets or may simply be inaccurate. In addition, prospective financial information is considered vital in relation to mergers and acquisitions as well as to such business entity management activities as budgeting. In these circumstances, it would appear advisable to obtain certified public accountant examinations and reports before the public release of prospective financial information.

SEE ALSO *Budgets and Budgeting; Finance; Forecasing in Business*

BIBLIOGRAPHY

Coller, Maribeth, and Yohn, Teri Lombardi (1998). "Management Forecasts: What Do We Know?" *Financial Analysts Journal* (January/February): 58-62.

Guide for Prospective Financial Information (2002). New York: American Institute of Certified Public Accountants.

Hirst, D. Eric, Koonce, Lisa L., and Miller, Jeffrey S. (1998). "The Joint Effect of Management's Prior Forecast Accuracy and the Form of Its Financial Forecasts on Investor Judgment." *Journal of Accounting Research* 37 (Supplement): 101-124.

Bernard H. Newman

FINANCIAL INSTITUTIONS

A financial institution is one that facilitates allocation of financial resources from its source to potential users. A large number of different types of financial institutions in the United States create a rich mosaic in the financial system. Some institutions acquire funds and make them available to users. Others act as middlemen between deficit and surplus units. Still others invest (manage) funds as agents for their clients. The key categories of financial institutions are: deposit taking; finance and insurance; and investment, pension, and risk management. There are also government and government-sponsored institutions that carry out regulatory, supervisory, and financing functions. Historically, each type has performed a specialized function in the financing and investment management needs of different industries and economic activities, as well as development of regional areas of the country.

DEPOSIT TAKING

Deposit-taking institutions take the form of commercial banks, which accept deposits and make commercial, real estate, and other loans; savings and loan associations and mutual savings banks, which accept deposits and make mortgage and other types of loans; and credit unions, which are cooperative organizations that issue share certificates and make member (consumer) and other loans. Altogether, there were more than 9,000 deposit-taking institutions with more than 92,000 branches spread across the U.S. economy in 2005.

The U.S. commercial banking system practiced competition through a large number of firms in the industry from 1776 to 1976. It was designed to be a unit-banking system in which state charters of banks allowed only one-office banking. The system also encouraged thrift and use of local savings for investment in the local economy. The unit-banking system not only forced competition among existing and new banks in a given banking market, it deliberately avoided the emergence of monopolies in the industry. The founding fathers in the original thirteen states understood the harm monopolies could inflict on the economic and financial systems. In due course the U.S. Congress passed the Sherman Antitrust Act of 1890—and subsequent laws and regulations—making monopoly and monopolistic practices unacceptable and therefore illegal.

The commercial banking industry dominated the U.S. financial industry from the beginning to the 1970s when financial product innovation and the resulting business and consumer financial choices exploded to create competition across financial services industries. The commercial banking industry and its limited product offerings on both sides of the balance sheet were the only choices available to the general public until the late 1960s. This is because the commercial banks specialized in taking checking account deposits on the liability side and making commercial loans on the asset side. For the safety of their operations, they relied on maturity-based hedging of mostly short-term liabilities with short-term self-liquidating commercial loans as assets. This also meant that households, farmers, students, and other groups did not have access to financial capital as commercial banks were not equipped to manage risks inherent in such loans.

Savings and loan associations, mutual savings banks and credit unions, and money market mutual funds are other deposit-taking institutions. Savings and loan associations take savings deposits and primarily make mortgage loans throughout the country. They have provided funds to create millions of housing units in the country. Their key function is maturity intermediation when they accept short-term deposits and make long-term mortgage loans. Mutual savings banks exist mainly in the eastern part of the United States. Like savings and loan associations, they, too, accept short-maturity deposits and make long-term mortgage loans. They also issue consumer and other loans, making them somewhat more diversified, and therefore their loan portfolio is less risky in terms of loan defaults. Credit unions specialize in member savings and loans, although they also make mortgage-type loans and other investments similar to other deposit-taking institutions.

FINANCE AND INSURANCE INSTITUTIONS

Finance (credit) companies are different from deposit-taking banking institutions in that their sources of funds are not deposits. They acquire funds in the market by issuing their own obligations, such as notes and bonds. They make loans, however, on the other side of the balance sheet in full competition with deposit-taking and other types of financial institutions, such as insurance companies. Finance companies specialize in business inventory financing, although they also make consumer loans, mostly indirectly through manufacturers and distributors of goods and services. Some of the finance companies are huge and operate in domestic as well as foreign markets. Several are bigger than most of the commercial banks in the United States.

Insurance companies provide the dual services of insurance protection and investment. There are two types of insurance companies: life insurance companies and casualty and property insurance companies. Insurance companies' sources of funds are primarily policy premiums. Their uses of funds range from loans (thus competing with finance companies, commercial banks, and savings and loan associations) to creation of investment products (thus competing with investment companies). Life insurance companies match their certain mortality-based needs for cash outflows with longer-term riskier investments such as stocks and bonds. Casualty and property insurance companies have more uncertainty of cash outflows and their timing. Therefore they have more conservative investment policies in terms of maturity and credit risk of their investments in a diversified portfolio of assets.

INVESTMENT, PENSION, AND RISK MANAGEMENT

Investment companies pool together funds and invest in the market to achieve goals set for various types of investments, matching liquidity, maturity, return, risk, tax, and other preferences of investors on the one hand and users of funds on the other. Investment companies are organized as open-end or closed-end mutual funds. Open-end funds accept new investments and redeem old ones, while closed-end funds accept funds at one time and then do not take in new funds. Investment companies have become very popular with investors, and thus they have mobilized trillions of dollars.

Another type of company is investment banks, which provide investment and fund-raising advice to potential users of funds, such as commercial, industrial, and financial companies. They also create venture capital funds or companies. Some of them also have brokerage and dealerships in securities. Many of them underwrite securities and then place them in the market or sell them to investors.

Pension funds in the private and the government sectors collect pension contributions and invest them according to goals of the employees for their funds. Increasingly, employees are able to indicate their personal preferences for risk and reward targets with respect to their own and sometimes their employers' contributions.

Other institutions that are significant participants in the U.S. financial system are the stock, bond, commodity, currency, futures, and options exchanges. The various types of exchanges make possible not only creation and ownership of financial claims but also management of liquidity and risk of price changes and other risks in underlying commodities in the market. They greatly expand investment opportunities for savers and access to funds by small, medium, and large business enterprises. They have deepened and broadened markets in financial products and services, helped manage price risk, and improved allocation efficiency in financial markets where every attribute desired in a financial product has a counterparty with which to trade. The banking and investment intermediaries have extended their services to the global saver-investor with the cross-border flow of funds and trading of financial products facilitated by cross-border investing, listing, and trading of securities in home and foreign markets in home and foreign currencies.

HISTORICAL DEVELOPMENT OF THE U.S. FINANCIAL SYSTEM

Specialization and division of labor, identified as sources of creativity and efficiency by Adam Smith, led to the creation of other specialized deposit-taking and investment-type financial institutions that began to meet the demand not fulfilled by the commercial banking industry. Similar institutions were created to finance agriculture and housing in rural areas, public works, and education. Laws and regulations recognized and strengthened the separation, and thus specialization, of the financial function different intermediaries performed in the financial system.

The system was further strengthened by establishing government and semigovernment intermediaries to increase liquidity in the market, manage maturity risk, and broaden the sharing of the market (price) risk through secondary markets for mortgages, agency (government and sponsored) securities, and other asset-based securities. Examples of these institutions are: Commodity Credit Corporation, Farm Credit Banks, Farm Credit Financing Assistance Corporation, Farmers Home Administration, Federal Home Loan Mortgage Corporation, Federal Financing Corporation, Federal National Mortgage Association, Federal Housing Administration, Federal Home Loan Banks, Government National Mortgage Association, Resolution Funding Corporation, Small Business Administration, and Student Loan Marketing Association.

THE MONETARY SYSTEM

The U.S. monetary system is based on credit. The U.S. currency is issued by its central bank, the Federal Reserve System, as a liability on itself. The value of the currency is based on its purchasing power in the economy and around the world and has not been linked to or defined in terms of any particular commodity or an index since 1968. The issuance of currency was tied to the U.S. gold holdings prior to 1968. The U.S. money supply consists of currency and coins and checkable public deposits in the banking system.

The Federal Reserve System, created in 1913, was established to furnish elastic currency to the economy and to supervise the banking system. Prior to 1913 there had been financial crises that were due to absence of a systematic way to provide money and credit in the economy. Large bank failures—due to fraud and mismanagement, as well as economic fluctuations and boom and bust in commodity prices—had also occurred.

The Federal Reserve System consists of the Board of Governors of the Federal Reserve and the twelve regional or district Federal Reserve banks. The Board of Governors in Washington, D.C., is the central decision-making organization. The board has seven members who are nominated by the president of the United States and confirmed by the Senate. Each board member is appointed for fourteen years, so as to ensure that the board remain immune from political influence of any administration in office. The board is set up as an independent agency; it does not report to the president, but it does report to

Congress. Nevertheless, it actively coordinates its research and analysis with the White House and the secretary of the U.S. Department of Treasury in formulating policy. The regional Federal Reserve banks' Board of Directors is also structured to represent banking, industry and commerce, and the general public. There is a formal statutory requirement to have three directors from the three groups in the district area on the board.

The monetary policy-making body within the Federal Reserve is the Federal Open Market Committee (FOMC), which meets regularly (generally eight times per year). Its voting members are the seven governors of the board of governors and five presidents of the regional banks. The president of the Federal Reserve Bank of New York is a permanent member of FOMC, and the other four presidents serve on annual rotation from among four groups formed from the remaining eleven regional banks.

The regional banks are located in Boston, New York, Philadelphia, Richmond, Atlanta, Cleveland, Chicago, Dallas, St. Louis, Kansas City, Minneapolis, and San Francisco. These cities were chosen as representatives of the regional economies of the United States in 1913. It was thought at the time that the regional economies had different characteristics in terms of the type and level of economic activity, so they needed different accommodation with respect to supply of money and finance, rediscounting mechanisms, and interest rates. In other words, it was thought that there were twelve different money markets in the U.S. economy, so each one needed special attention for its needs.

This structure of the Federal Reserve System continues to this day, even though the money market has become one market because of institutional and technological advancements. Now there are truly national financial institutions, not just in terms of their national charter, with interstate deposit taking and lending of commercial and numerous other types of loans to businesses and households.

The Federal Reserve policy serves the needs of the entire economy and all its parts by taking into account economic and financial information concerning all economic segments and activities in the U.S. economy. There are many advisory committees, such as the Federal Advisory Committee representing the interests of the banking industry, the Consumer Advisory Committee representing consumer interests, and similar other committees representing interests of other segments to the Federal Reserve System. Legislative, regulatory, monetary policy, and day-to-day operations of the central bank consider relevant details in their deliberations and policy decisions, including research from a wide variety of sources—private and public—about the economy.

LEGAL AND REGULATORY STRUCTURE

The key laws governing the U.S. financial institutions are: National Bank Act of 1863; Federal Reserve Act of 1913; McFadden Act of 1927; Banking Act (Glass-Steagall) of 1933 and 1935; Securities Act of 1933; Securities Exchange Act of 1934; Federal Credit Union Act of 1934; Investment Advisers Act of 1940; Investment Company Act of 1940; Bank Holding Company Act of 1956 and Douglas Amendment of 1970; Bank Merger Act of 1966; Employment Retirement Income Security Act of 1974; Depository Institutions Deregulation and Monetary Control Act of 1980; Depository Institutions (Garn–St. Germain) Act of 1982; Competitive Equality in Banking Act of 1987; Financial Institutions Reform, Recovery, and Enforcement Act of 1989; Federal Deposit Insurance Corporation Improvement Act of 1991; Interstate Banking and Branching Efficiency Act of 1994; and Financial Services Modernization Act of 1999.

The federal agencies that regulate depository institutions are: Office of the Comptroller of the Currency, Federal Reserve System, Federal Deposit Insurance System, National Credit Union Administration, and Office of Thrift Supervision. The Securities and Exchange Commission, the Commodity Futures Trading Commission, and the U.S. Department of Justice monitor and enforce relevant laws and regulations concerning securities and futures markets. State authorities regulate, monitor, and enforce laws concerning depository, insurance, finance companies, and other financial institutions. The laws and regulations on financial institutions in the United States have made them competitive, efficient, fair, safe and sound, and transparent with the use of both carrots and sticks.

FINANCIAL SERVICES MODERNIZATION ACT OF 1999

The U.S. financial system in the twenty-first century has evolved into the largest, most developed, most efficient, and most sophisticated financial system in the world. The financial system has grown enormously since the founding of the first insurance company by Benjamin Franklin, as Philadelphia Contributionship, in 1752. The first banks in the United States were the Bank of New York, founded by Alexander Hamilton in 1784; the Bank of Boston, also founded in 1784; and the First Bank of the United States, chartered in 1791.

The economic structures and forces that have made this success possible are the concepts (or the foundation stones) of competition, specialization, thrift, entrepreneurial culture, and innovation. These concepts were just as well understood and vigorously practiced in the American colonies as they were expounded on by Adam Smith in Scotland in 1776 in *An Inquiry into the Nature and Causes of the Wealth of Nations,* his synthesis of a competitive market system. The United States has structured its economic and financial systems on Smith's economic model since its founding in 1776.

The Financial Services Modernization Act, signed into law by President Bill Clinton in late 1999, removed many of the restrictions on the banking and securities institutions imposed in the 1920s and 1930s. For example, financial conglomerates were again be able to organize commercial banking, insurance business, investment banking, securities underwriting, and other financial services under the umbrella of a holding/parent company. The McFadden Act and the Glass-Steagall Act are now in the history books. Financial innovation made possible by computer and communications technologies and spawned by competition and deregulation has brought U.S. financial institutions and the entire financial system to the exciting financial structure of the twenty-first century.

SEE ALSO *Federal Reserve System*

BIBLIOGRAPHY

Federal Deposit Insurance Corporation, Division of Research and Statistics. (2005). *Statistics on banking: A statistical profile of the United States banking industry.* Washington, DC: Author.

Federal Reserve System. (1994). *Purposes and functions* (8th ed.). Washington, DC: Board of Governors of the Federal Reserve System.

Kidwell, David S., Blackwell, D. W., Whidbee, D. A., and Peterson, D. W. (2006). *Financial institutions, markets, and money* (9th ed.). Hoboken, NJ: Wiley.

Kohn, Meir G. (2004). *Financial institutions and markets* (2nd ed.). New York: Oxford University Press.

Madura, Jeff (2006). *Financial markets and institutions* (7th ed.). Mason, OH: Thomson South-Western.

Mayo, Herbert B. (2004). *Financial institutions, investments, and management: An introduction* (8th ed.). Mason, OH: Thomson South-Western.

Mishkin, Frederic S. (2004). *The economics of money, banking, and financial markets* (7th ed.). Boston: Pearson.

Rose, Peter S., and Marquis, Milton H. (2006). *Money and capital markets* (9th ed.). Boston: McGraw-Hill/Irwin.

Surendra Kaushik

FINANCIAL LITERACY

Financial literacy encompasses the knowledge and skills for personal financial planning, the selection of financial services, budgeting and investing, developing an insurance program, credit management, consumer purchases, consumer rights and responsibilities, and decision-making skills for all aspects of life as consumers, workers, and citizens. Financial literacy affects all aspects of an individual's planning and spending: income, money management, the use of credit, saving and investing, and decision making for the wise use of resources. A lifelong process, financial literacy is a critical area of knowledge and skills for all consumers who must make choices about their financial resources. From a child's earliest spending to a senior citizen's retirement decisions, individuals apply their knowledge and skills to financial choices. Managing finances has become increasingly complex.

ORGANIZATIONS PROMOTING FINANCIAL LITERACY

A number of organizations are active supporters of financial literacy, and many focus on financial education for young people. The Jump$tart Coalition for Personal Financial Literacy was convened in 1995 to promote personal financial literacy, particularly among young adults, and is a major source of financial literacy information. Membership in the coalition includes more than 160 organizations committed to improving young people's knowledge and skills. A few of the member organizations are: American Institute of Certified Public Accountants, American Council on Consumer Interest, Federal Deposit Insurance Corporation, Girl Scouts of the USA, NAACP, Social Security Administration, and the Foundation for Financial Literacy.

RESOURCES FOR FINANCIAL LITERACY

A function of Jump$tart is to serve as a clearinghouse for educational tools and resources, prekindergarten through adult, for all types of educational programs. These tools and resources, available from members of the coalition, include audiotapes, books, textbooks, booklets/pamphlets, periodicals, posters, simulations/games, software/compact disks, student workbooks, lesson plans, teaching guides, videos, and Web site links. Jump$tart maintains an online database of national training programs available to consumers and educators. The materials available from the Jump$tart clearinghouse help educators and students with financial literacy programs. The materials can also assist adults to develop financial literacy—an important point, since financial matters change throughout one's life. Materials are organized by topic: income, money management, saving and investing, and the use of credit.

INCOME

What income is to be managed? This question is a first step in wise management of financial resources. All con-

sumers must manage their finances, but incomes vary. "Stretching" income to meet needs and wants is a part of financial management; knowing how to develop goals for spending, based on a realistic understanding of income, is a basic part of financial literacy.

MONEY MANAGEMENT

Money management is the process of planning how to get the most from money—how to use money to meet needs and wants. Budgeting, either by a formal or informal plan, is a first step in deciding what needs and wants must be met and what resources are available. Money management includes plans for saving and investing, not just spending. Too often consumers spend all of their income, which means no money is left for saving.

SAVING AND INVESTING

Consumers must set goals for saving and investing, because their choices of vehicles for saving and investing depend on those goals. Saving, contrasted to investing, may be thought of as safeguarding money for future use. Saving may not provide a return on money. Investing, however, may be defined as putting money to use in order to earn a return. Providing for the future can mean short-term savings and long-term investments. If a goal is to provide retirement income, a consumer should consider long-term investment. Buying a new small appliance, on the other hand, may require only short-term saving.

Income, money management, saving and investing, and the use of credit require consumer planning and decision-making skills. Underlying all aspects of financial literacy is the knowledge and skills for wise use of all financial resources a consumer may accumulate over a lifetime.

USE OF CREDIT

Knowledge about credit is a major part of financial literacy. Consumers use credit to buy durable and nondurable goods, large and small. Credit provides a convenient way to "buy now, pay later." Buying on credit enables a consumer to build a credit rating, a necessity for mortgages and loans. All consumers should be aware of the ways in which they can use credit as a convenient way to purchase goods and services, but they should also know the costs of credit and how to avoid the pitfalls of unwise use of credit.

SOME CONSEQUENCES OF FINANCIAL LITERACY

In 2003 and in 2004, Bankrate conducted financial literacy surveys of 1,000 Americans about what they know about and how they act upon twelve concepts basic to financial well-being. The 2004 survey showed that Americans were getting better at knowing what they need to do to achieve financial well-being, but they did not always act on their knowledge.

Bankruptcy is one of the severe consequences of a lack of financial literacy. In reaction to the number of bankruptcies declared after the Bankruptcy Reform Act of 1978, in 2005 the U.S. government tightened bankruptcy laws.

Financial literacy is a long-term solution to consumer problems with finances. In the Bankrate survey, individuals who were "financially literate" earned more, paid less for loans, used credit cards more wisely, had savings for emergencies, had prepared a will, lived by a monthly budget, and were more constant and careful shoppers for financial services. "Financially literate consumers" accepted the key concepts that:

- Money management is a long-term responsibility

- Consumers should be savers instead of spenders and must live within a budget

- Comparison shopping pays off

- Smart consumers pay bills on time, read their bank statements regularly, and shop for the best rates on credit

- Buying on a whim and snap decisions about buying must be avoided

- Individuals must regularly save and invest for retirement

These concepts are part of the foundation for financial literacy.

BIBLIOGRAPHY

Bankrate.com. (2004, April 6). Bankrate survey: Americans nearly flunk financial literacy. Retrieved December 1, 2005, from http://www.bankrate.com/brm/news/financial-literacy2004/grade-home.asp

Jump$tart Coalition for Personal Financial Literacy. http://www.jumpstart.org

Mandell, Lewis (2005). *Financial literacy—Does it matter?* Washington, DC: Jump$tart Coalition for Personal Financial Literacy.

National Endowment for Financial Education. (2005). Education programs. Retrieved December 1, 2005, from http://www.nefe.org/pages/educationalprograms.html

U.S. Courts. (2005). Bankruptcy statistics. Retrieved December 1, 2005, from http://www.uscourts.gov/bnkrpctystats/bankruptcystats.htm

Betty J. Brown

FINANCIAL MARKETS

SEE *Capital Markets*

FINANCIAL STATEMENT ANALYSIS

Financial statement analysis is the process of examining relationships among financial statement elements and making comparisons with relevant information. It is a valuable tool used by investors and creditors, financial analysts, and others in their decision-making processes related to stocks, bonds, and other financial instruments. The goal in analyzing financial statements is to assess past performance and current financial position and to make predictions about the future performance of a company. Investors who buy stock are primarily interested in a company's profitability and their prospects for earning a return on their investment by receiving dividends and/or increasing the market value of their stock holdings. Creditors and investors who buy debt securities, such as bonds, are more interested in liquidity and solvency: the company's short- and long-run ability to pay its debts. Financial analysts, who frequently specialize in following certain industries, routinely assess the profitability, liquidity, and solvency of companies in order to make recommendations about the purchase or sale of securities, such as stocks and bonds.

Analysts can obtain useful information by comparing a company's most recent financial statements with its results in previous years and with the results of other companies in the same industry. Three primary types of financial statement analysis are commonly known as horizontal analysis, vertical analysis, and ratio analysis.

HORIZONTAL ANALYSIS

When an analyst compares financial information for two or more years for a single company, the process is referred to as horizontal analysis, since the analyst is reading across the page to compare any single line item, such as sales revenues. In addition to comparing dollar amounts, the analyst computes percentage changes from year to year for all financial statement balances, such as cash and inventory. Alternatively, in comparing financial statements for a number of years, the analyst may prefer to use a variation of horizontal analysis called trend analysis. Trend analysis involves calculating each year's financial statement balances as percentages of the first year, also known as the base year. When expressed as percentages, the base year figures are always 100 percent, and percentage changes from the base year can be determined.

VERTICAL ANALYSIS

When using vertical analysis, the analyst calculates each item on a single financial statement as a percentage of a total. The term vertical analysis applies because each year's figures are listed vertically on a financial statement. The total used by the analyst on the income statement is net sales revenue, while on the balance sheet it is total assets. This approach to financial statement analysis, also known as component percentages, produces common-size financial statements. Common-size balance sheets and income statements can be more easily compared, whether across the years for a single company or across different companies.

RATIO ANALYSIS

Ratio analysis enables the analyst to compare items on a single financial statement or to examine the relationships between items on two financial statements. After calculating ratios for each year's financial data, the analyst can then examine trends for the company across years. Since ratios adjust for size, using this analytical tool facilitates intercompany as well as intracompany comparisons. Ratios are often classified using the following terms: profitability ratios (also known as operating ratios), liquidity ratios, and solvency ratios. Profitability ratios are gauges of the company's operating success for a given period of time. Liquidity ratios are measures of the short-term ability of the company to pay its debts when they come due and to meet unexpected needs for cash. Solvency ratios indicate the ability of the company to meet its long-term obligations on a continuing basis and thus to survive over a long period of time. In judging how well on a company is doing, analysts typically compare a company's ratios to industry statistics as well as to its own past performance.

CAVEATS

Financial statement analysis, when used carefully, can produce meaningful insights about a company's financial information and its prospects for the future. However, the analyst must be aware of certain important considerations about financial statements and the use of these analytical tools. For example, the dollar amounts for many types of assets and other financial statement items are usually based on historical costs and thus do not reflect replacement costs or inflationary adjustments. Furthermore, financial statements contain estimates of numerous items, such as warranty expenses and uncollectible customer balances. The meaningfulness of ratios and percentages depends on how well the financial statement amounts depict the company's situation. Comparisons to industry statistics or competitors' results can be complicated because companies may select different, although equally acceptable, methods of accounting for inventories and other items. Making meaningful comparisons is also hampered when a company or its competitors have widely diversified operations.

The tools of financial statement analysis, ratio and percentage calculations, are relatively easy to apply. Understanding the content of the financial statements, on the other hand, is not a simple task. Evaluating a company's financial status, performance, and prospects using analytical tools requires skillful application of the analyst's judgment.

SEE ALSO *Accounting; Analytical Procedures; Financial Statements*

Mary Brady Greenawalt

FINANCIAL STATEMENTS

Financial statements provide information of value to company officials as well as to various outsiders, such as investors and lenders of funds. Publicly owned companies are required to periodically publish general purpose financial statements that include a balance sheet, an income statement, and a statement of cash flow. Some companies also issue a statement of stockholders' equity and a statement of comprehensive income, which provide additional details on changes in the equity section of the balance sheet. Financial statements issued for external distribution are prepared according to generally accepted accounting principles (GAAP), which are the guidelines for the content and format of the statements. In the United States, the Securities and Exchange Commission (SEC) has the legal responsibility for establishing the content of financial statements, but it generally defers to an independent body, the Financial Accounting Standards Board (FASB), to determine and promote accepted principles.

The balance sheet, also known as the statement of financial position or condition, presents the assets, liabilities, and owners' equity of the company at a specific point in time. The assets are the firm's resources, financial or nonfinancial, such as cash, receivables, inventories, properties, and equipment. The total assets (balance) equal the sources of funding for those resources: liabilities (external borrowings) and equity (owners' contributions and earnings from firm operations). The balance sheet is used by investors, creditors, and other decision makers to assess the overall composition of resources, the constriction of external obligations, and the firm's flexibility and ability to change to meet new requirements.

Firms frequently issue a separate statement of stockholders' equity to present certain changes in equity rather than showing them on the face of the balance sheet. The statement of stockholders' equity itemizes the changes in equity over the period covered, including investments by owners and other capital contributions, earnings for the period, and distributions to owners of earnings (dividends) or other capital. Sometimes companies present a statement of changes in retained earnings rather than a statement of stockholders' equity. The statement of changes in retained earnings, also known as the statement of earned surplus, details only the changes in earned capital: the net income and the dividends for the period. Then the changes in contributed capital (stock issued, stock options, etc.) must be detailed on the balance sheet or in the notes to the financial statements.

The income statement, also known as the statement of profit and loss, the earnings statement, or the operations statement, presents the details of the earnings achieved for the period. The income statement separately itemizes revenues and expenses, which result from the company's ongoing major or central operations, and the gains and losses arising from incidental or peripheral transactions. Certain irregular items, such as discontinued operations, extraordinary items, and effects of accounting changes, are presented separately, net of tax effect, at the end of the statement. When revenues and gains exceed expenses and losses, net income is realized. Net income for the period increases equity. The results of the firm's operating activities for the period as presented in the income statement provide information that can be used to predict the amount, timing, and uncertainty of future cash flows. This statement is useful to investors, creditors, and other users in determining the profitability of operations. The income statement must also show earnings per share (EPS), where the net income is divided by the weighted average number of shares of common stock outstanding. Since EPS scales income by the magnitude of the investment, it allows investors to compare diverse companies of different sizes; hence, investors commonly use it as a summary measurement of firm performance.

In 1998, the FASB required that companies present a separate statement that classifies all items of other comprehensive income by their nature. Other comprehensive income includes all equity changes not recorded in the income statement or in the statement of changes in retained earnings and that do not result from contributions by owners. In addition to providing a separate statement, companies must display the total of other comprehensive income separately from retained earnings and additional paid-in capital in the equity section of the balance sheet.

The statement of cash flows replaced the statement of changes in financial position in 1987 as a required financial statement for all business enterprises. The statement of cash flows presents cash receipts and payments classified by whether they stem from operating, investing, or financing activities and provides definitions of each category. Information about key investing and financing activities not resulting in cash receipts or payments in the period must be provided separately. The cash from operating activities reported on the statement of cash flows must be reconciled to net income for the period. Because GAAP requires accrual accounting methods in preparing financial statements, there may be a significant difference between net income and cash generated by operations. The cash-flow statement is used by creditors and investors to determine whether cash will be available to meet debt and dividend payments.

Financial statements include notes, which are considered an integral part of the statements. The notes contain required disclosures of additional data, assumptions and methodologies employed, and other information deemed useful to users.

The financial statements of publicly owned companies also include an auditor's report, indicating that the statements have been audited by independent auditors. The auditor's opinion is related to fair presentation in conformity with GAAP.

The external financial statements required for not-for-profit organizations are similar to those for business enterprises, except that there is no ownership component (equity) and no income. Not-for-profit organizations present a statement of financial position, a statement of activities, and a statement of cash flows. The financial statements must classify the organization's net assets and its revenues, expenses, gains, and losses based on the existence or absence of donor-imposed restrictions. Each of three classes of net assets—permanently restricted, temporarily restricted, and unrestricted—must be displayed in the statement of financial position, and the amounts of change in each of those classes of net assets must be displayed in the statement of activities. Governmental bodies, which are guided by the Governmental Accounting Standards Board (GASB), present general-purpose external financial statements that are similar to those of other not-for-profit organizations, but they classify their financial statements according to fund entities.

SEE ALSO *Accounting; Financial Statement Analysis*

BIBLIOGRAPHY

Engstrom, J., and Copley, Paul A. (2004). *Essentials of Accounting for Governmental and Not-for-Profit Organizations* (7th ed.). Boston: McGraw-Hill/Irwin.

Financial Accounting Standards Board (1987). *Statement of Financial Accounting Standards No. 95: Statement of Cash Flows.* Norwalk, CT: Financial Accounting Foundation.

Financial Accounting Standards Board (1993). *Statement of Financial Accounting Standards No. 117: Financial Statements of Not-for-Profit Organizations.* Norwalk, CT: Financial Accounting Foundation.

Financial Accounting Standards Board. (1997). *Statement of Financial Accounting Standards No. 130: Reporting Comprehensive Income.* Norwalk, CT: Financial Accounting Foundation.

Gross, M., McCarthy, John H., and Shelmon, Nancy E. (2005). *Financial and Accounting Guide for Not-for-Profit Organizations.* Hoboken, NJ: Wiley.

Revsine, L., Collins, D.W., and Johnson, W.B. (2005). *Financial Reporting and Analysis.* Upper Saddle River, NJ: Pearson/Prentice-Hall.

Victoria Shoaf

FISCAL POLICY

Fiscal policy is a term that denotes the approach that government takes to managing the income it collects—usually termed *taxes*—and the expenditures of those taxes. It refers ordinarily to any level of government, including federal, state, municipality, and occasionally private organizations such as Girl Scouts and Boy Scouts, private and public organizations, and many other thousands of similar organizations.

The term *fiscal* refers to timing. It is an invention designed to maximize the convenience of establishing various beginning and ending times. An example would be a fiscal year that begins on October 1 and ends on September 30. Fiscal policy is manifested in a government's policies on taxation and expenditures. To obtain funds for their operation, government units generally collect some form of taxes.

Particularly in the case of the federal government, the expenditure of these funds not only provides goods and services for constituents, but, additionally, has a direct impact on the economy. For example, the expenditures of the tax dollars may exceed the amount of the funds received by the government. (The government spends more than it receives.) The resulting deficit tends to stimulate the economy. As goods and services are produced for government purchase, it puts extra money into the economy and into the hands of the producers of those goods and services.

But what if the expenditures of the government are fewer than the tax dollars received? (The government spends less than it receives.) The resulting governmental surplus curtails the economy because now the government does not buy as much, and fewer dollars get into the economy.

THE FEDERAL BUDGET

In the United States, the fiscal process of the federal government begins each February with the president sending to Congress a proposed federal budget for the coming fiscal year, which begins in October. Congress then develops a budget resolution, which is to be completed by April. The budget resolution contains overall revenue and spending budgets as well as the budget amount of discretionary and mandatory spending for each functional area, such as discretionary and mandatory spending.

BILLS THAT PROVIDE BUDGET AUTHORITY

Bills that provide budget authority for annual discretionary spending must be completed by June each year. Legislative changes can also be made for mandatory spending or tax provisions at this time. Any legislation that would cut taxes or increase mandatory spending, however, must be accompanied by legislation that would raise revenue or cut spending in other areas to pay for these changes. Consequently, any new legislation in this area must be "budget neutral" (income and spending must be equal).

According to the Financial Management Office, in fiscal year 2004, receipts for the U.S. budget totaled $1,879,799 billion. Outlays totaled $2,292,352 billion. The deficit was $412,553 billion. (Differences between any two figures may not be equal because of rounding differences. Sources of the above data are the Financial Management Service, U.S. Department of the Treasury; and the Congressional Budget Office.)

FEDERAL GOVERNMENT REVENUE

Individual income taxes have been the federal government's largest source of funds for many years. Individual income taxes for the years 1999–2004 are as follows:

1999 $879,480 billion

2000 $1,004,461 billion

2001 $994,339 billion

2002 $858,545 billion

2003 $793,699 billion

2004 $808,958 million

The enormous impact of the Social Security system on the federal government's budget is without question as it is the largest outlay of the federal government every year. In 2004 total Department of Health and Human Services outlay was $543,215 billion. In 1998 the same outlay was $359,700 billion.

Defense spending was the largest item of discretionary spending in the federal budget. In 2004 the amount was $437,111 billion.

INTEREST ON THE FEDERAL GOVERNMENT'S DEBT

In 2004 the public debt of the United States was $739.1 billion. This amounted to $25,182 per capita for the United States. In contrast, the debt per capita in 1990 was $13,000. The interest paid in 2004 was $321.6 billion.

Though fiscal policy could be an automatic stabilizer for the economy because it automatically responds to changes in economic activity, government spending on such items as unemployment benefits generally increases during a recession, moderating the extremes of the business cycle, whereas government receipts such as income taxes will fall during a recession, also moderating the extremes of the business cycle. Consequently, fiscal policy, along with monetary policy—which is dictated by the Federal Reserve—has an important influence on the health of the economy in the United States.

SEE ALSO *Government Role in Business*

BIBLIOGRAPHY

Bruce, Neil (2001). *Public finance and the American economy* (2nd ed.). Reading, MA: Addison-Wesley.

Citizen's guide to the federal budget: Budget of the United States government (1996—). Retrieved March 5, 2006, from http://www.gpoaccess.gov/usbudget/citizensguide.html

G. W. Maxwell

FOOD AND DRUG ADMINISTRATION

The Food and Drug Act of 1906, which prohibited the interstate trade of misbranded or tainted food, drinks, and drugs, was passed by Congress on the same day as the Meat Inspection Act. At this time there was no Federal Drug Administration, but there was a Bureau of Chemistry. In 1927 a separate enforcement agency known as the Food, Drug and Insecticide Administration was create and in 1930 it was renamed the Food and Drug Administration (FDA). In 1938 after five years of battle with

Congress, the Federal Food, Drug, and Cosmetic Act was passed. According to the FDA's Web site, it contained the following new provisions:

- Extending control to cosmetics and therapeutic devices

- Requiring new drugs to be shown safe before marketing—starting a new system of drug regulation

- Eliminating the Sherley Amendment requirement to prove intent to defraud in drug misbranding cases

- Providing that safe tolerance is set for unavoidable poisonous substances

- Authorizing standards of identity, quality, and fill-of-container for foods

- Authorizing factory inspections

- Adding the court injunctions to the previous penalties of seizures and prosecutions

Later the FDA's jurisdiction was expanded to include microwaves and any radiation-emitting consumer products, as well as veterinary drugs and pet food. The agency monitors the manufacture, transportation, and sale of food and drugs. To ensure its efficiency, the FDA operates in 157 cities and employs approximately 9000 people. Among its employees are chemists, microbiologists, and investigators who visit 15,000 locations each year.

FDA inspectors visit businesses that are regulated by the FDA. If a problem exists, the FDA allows the company to voluntarily correct the problem or recall the faulty product. If the company refuses to cooperate, the FDA can go to court to force cooperation. Court action can include criminal prosecution if necessary.

In the area of drug control, the FDA does not conduct its own experiments but closely examines the results of the company's research. FDA inspectors conduct three types of inspections: study oriented, investigation oriented, and bioequivalence inspections. Study-oriented inspections are needed in case of new drug or new-product applications for approval. An investigator-oriented inspection may be ordered if other investigators looking at the same study think the findings are inconsistent. If one study is the sole basis for a marketer request, a bioequivalence study is conducted.

Once a drug or device is approved, the agency's responsibility does not end. The FDA monitors any complaints and looks for any adverse reactions associated with the product. As a result, approximately 3,000 products are recalled each year.

In addition to ensuring the quality of the product itself, the FDA has had a major influence on businesses

"*Nutrition Facts*" *label from a package of pasta.* PHOTOGRAPH BY KELLY A. QUIN. THE GALE GROUP.

and the way goods are packaged. For example, medicines and products dangerous to children are now packaged in childproof bottles, and labels on containers of food products must list the nutritional contents and their amounts.

Any company that produces a product that is under the jurisdiction of the FDA has felt the pressure of its regulations, and complaints have been made about the slowness of the FDA's procedures. However, no country's citizens enjoy more protection regarding the products they use than U.S. citizens.

More information is available from the Food and Drug Administration, 5600 Fishers Lane, Rockville, MD 20857, or http://www.fda.gov.

SEE ALSO *Consumer Advocacy and Protection*

BIBLIOGRAPHY

Food and Drug Administration. *Frequently Asked Questions.* Retrieved October 18, 2005, from http://www.fda.gov/opacom/faqs/faqs.html.

Food and Drug Administration. *Information Sheets,* "Guidance for Institutional Review Boards and Clinical Investigators". Retrieved October 18, 2005, from http://www.fda.gov /oc/oha/IRB/toc.html.

Food and Drug Administration. *Milestones in United States Food and Drug Law History.* Retrieved October 18, 2005, from www.fda.gov/opacom/backgrounders/miles.html.

Food and Drug Administration. *Small Business Guide to FDA.* Retrieved October 18, 2005, from http://www.fda.gov /ora/fed_state/Small_Business/sb_guide/default.htm.

Food and Drug Administration. *Warning Letters.* Retrieved October 18, 2005, from http://www.fda.gov/foi/warning.htm.

Val Hinton
Mary Jean Lush

FOOD, DRUG, AND COSMETIC ACT OF 1938

The Food, Drug, and Cosmetic Act of 1938 is the most important of the pure food and drug acts passed and administered by the U.S. Food and Drug Administration (FDA) of the U.S. Department of Health and Human Services. Food and drug laws were enacted to ensure the safety, proper labeling, and purity of foods, drugs, vaccines, devices, and cosmetics. The 1938 act is a revision of the first food and drug law, passed in 1906, which brought attention to many abuses in the form of poor health practices and excessive pricing. The revised law of 1938 and subsequent amendments give consumers greater protection from dangerous and impure foods and drugs; these laws require labeling that discloses the nature of the contents of the package, informing the buyer as to the product's composition and giving the buyer some insight as to the value of the product. These laws also provide safeguards against the introduction of untested new drugs.

The Food, Drug, and Cosmetic Act of 1938 addressed the wholesomeness of the food supply by giving the FDA powers to engage in economic regulation, set legally enforceable food standards, and establish affirmative labeling requirements. Consequently, the FDA examines food products' adulteration from the perspectives of both wholesomeness and safety. For example, the FDA has investigated several cases involving the alteration of fruit juices by dilution with sugar water or less expensive juices that represent both reductions in wholesomeness and economic fraud.

Another condition of economic fraud covered by the Food, Drug, and Cosmetic Act is misbranding of food by manufacturers: The food is not adulterated, but the consumer is deceived. In 1993 the FDA seized 2,400 cases of Procter & Gamble's Citrus Hill orange juice because the label used the word *fresh* when the product was produced from concentrate.

Since the passing of the first food and drug law, food laws and regulations have evolved from:

1. concern about food fraud, to

2. concerns about food safety, to

3. protection of the nutritional integrity of food, to

4. truth in labeling, to, most recently,

5. concern about the relationship between health and food.

Many amendments to the Food, Drug, and Cosmetic Act of 1938 and other food-related laws and acts have been passed by Congress and will continue to be enacted in response to future technological changes and developments. Manufacturers of food, drugs, cosmetics, and their related products must comply with the law. Penalties for violations include seizure of illegal goods, injunctions, restraint of shipments that violate the law, and criminal prosecution of those responsible for the violation.

SEE ALSO *Consumer Advocacy and Protection*

BIBLIOGRAPHY
Food, Drug and Cosmetic Act of 1938. Essential Documents in American History; Essential Documents, 1492–Present. 1–24. EBSCO Publishing.

Meier, Kenneth J., Garman, E. Thomas, and Keiser, Lael R. (2003). *Regulation and consumer protection: Politics, bureaucracy and economics* (4th ed.). Mason, OH: Custom Thomson.

U.S. Food and Drug Administration. (n.d.). *The 1938 Food, Drug, and Cosmetic Act.* Retrieved February 20, 2006, from http://www.fda.gov/oc/history/historyoffda/section2.html

Phyllis Bunn
Laurie Barfitt

FORECASTING IN BUSINESS

Business leaders and economists are continually involved in the process of trying to forecast, or predict, the future of business in the economy. Business leaders engage in this process because much of what happens in businesses today depends on what is going to happen in the future. For example, if a business is trying to make a decision about developing a revolutionary new automobile, it would be nice to know whether the economy is going to be in a recession or whether it will be booming when the automobile is released to the general public. If there is a recession, consumers will not buy the automobile unless it can save them money, and the manufacturer will have

spent millions or billions of dollars on the development of a product that might not sell.

The process of attempting to forecast the future is not new. Most ancient civilizations used some method for predicting the future. In the twenty-first century, computers with elaborate programs are often used to develop models to forecast future economic and business activity. Contemporary models of economic and business forecasting have been developed in the last century. Forecasting models are considerably more statistical than they were hundreds of years ago when the stars and mystical methods were used to predict the future. Almost every large business or government agency performs some type of formalized forecasting.

Forecasting in business is closely related to understanding the business cycle. The foundations of modern forecasting were laid in 1865 by William Stanley Jevons, who argued that manufacturing had replaced agriculture as the dominant sector in English society. He studied the effects of economic fluctuations of the limiting factors of coal production on economic development.

Forecasting has become big business around the world. Forecasters try to predict what the stock markets will do, what the economy will do, what numbers to pick in the lottery, who will win sporting events, and almost anything one might name. Regardless of who does it, forecasting is done to identify what is likely to happen in the future so as to be able to benefit most from the events.

QUALITATIVE FORECASTING MODELS

Qualitative forecasting models have often proven to be most effective for short-term projections. In this method of forecasting, which works best when the scope is limited, experts in the appropriate fields are asked to agree on a common forecast. Two methods are used frequently.

Delphi Method. This method involves asking various experts what they anticipate will happen in the future relative to the subject under consideration. Experts in the automotive industry, for example, might be asked to forecast likely innovative enhancements for cars five years from now. They are not expected to be precise, but rather to provide general opinions.

Market Research Method This method involves surveys and questionnaires about people's subjective reactions to changes. For example, a company might develop a new way to launder clothes; after people have had an opportunity to try the new method, they would be asked for feedback about how to improve the processes or how it might be made more appealing for the general public. This method is difficult because it is hard to identify an appropriate sample that is representative of the larger audience for whom the product is intended.

QUANTITATIVE FORECASTING MODELS

Three quantitative methods are in common use.

Time-Series Methods. This forecasting model uses historical data to try to predict future events. For example, assume that an investor is interested in knowing how long a recession will last. The investor might look at all past recessions and the events leading up to and surrounding them and then, from that data, try to predict how long the current recession will last.

A specific variable in the time series is identified by the series name and date. If gross domestic product (GDP) is the variable, it might be identified as GDP2000.1 for the first-quarter statistics for the year 2000. This is just one example, and different groups might use different methods to identify variables in a time period.

Many government agencies prepare and release time-series data. The Federal Reserve, for example, collects data on monetary policy and financial institutions and publishes that data in the *Federal Reserve Bulletin*. These data become the foundation for making decisions about regulating the growth of the economy.

Time-series models provide accurate forecasts when the changes that occur in the variable's environment are slow and consistent. When large-degree changes occur, the forecasts are not reliable for the long term. Since time-series forecasts are relatively easy and inexpensive to construct, they are used quite extensively.

The Indicator Approach. The U.S. government is a primary user of the indicator approach of forecasting. The government uses such indicators as the Composite Index of Leading, Lagging, and Coincident Indicators, often referred to as Composite Indexes. The indexes predict by assuming that past trends and relationships will continue into the future. The government indexes are made by averaging the behavior of the different indicator series that make up each composite series.

The timing and strength of each indicator series relationship with general business activity, reflected in the business cycle, change over time. This relationship makes forecasting changes in the business cycle difficult.

Econometric Models. Econometric models are causal models that statistically identify the relationships between variables and how changes in one or more variables cause changes in another variable. Econometric models then use the identified relationship to predict the future. Econometric models are also called regression models.

There are two types of data used in regression analysis. Economic forecasting models predominantly use time-series data, where the values of the variables change over time. Additionally, cross-section data, which capture the relationship between variables at a single point in time, are used. A lending institution, for example, might want to determine what influences the sale of homes. It might gather data on home prices, interest rates, and statistics on the homes being sold, such as size and location. This is the cross-section data that might be used with time-series data to try to determine such things as what size home will sell best in which location.

An econometric model is a way of determining the strength and statistical significance of a hypothesized relationship. These models are used extensively in economics to prove, disprove, or validate the existence of a casual relationship between two or more variables. It is obvious that this model is highly mathematical, using different statistical equations.

For the sake of simplicity, mathematical analysis is not addressed here. Just as there are these qualitative and quantitative forecasting models, there are others equally as sophisticated; however, the discussion here should provide a general sense of the nature of forecasting models.

THE FORECASTING PROCESS

When beginning the forecasting process, there are typical steps that must be followed. These steps follow an acceptable decision-making process that includes the following elements:

1. *Identification of the problem.* Forecasters must identify what is going to be forecasted, or what is of primary concern. There must be a timeline attached to the forecasting period. This will help the forecasters to determine the methods to be used later.

2. *Theoretical considerations.* It is necessary to determine what forecasting has been done in the past using the same variables and how relevant these data are to the problem that is currently under consideration. It must also be determined what economic theory has to say about the variables that might influence the forecast.

3. *Data concerns.* How easy will it be to collect the data needed to be able to make the forecasts is a significant issue.

4. *Determination of the assumption set.* The forecaster must identify the assumptions that will be made about the data and the process.

5. *Modeling methodology.* After careful examination of the problem, the types of models most appropriate for the problem must be determined.

6. *Preparation of the forecast.* This is the analysis part of the process. After the model to be used is determined, the analysis can begin and the forecast can be prepared.

7. *Forecast verification.* Once the forecasts have been made, the analyst must determine whether they are reasonable and how they can be compared against the actual behavior of the data.

Each of the seven steps has substages. The steps presented are the major concerns to the forecaster.

FORECASTING CONCERNS

Forecasting does present some problems. Even though very detailed and sophisticated mathematical models might be used, they do not always predict correctly. There are some who would argue that the future cannot be predicted at all—period!

Some of the concerns about forecasting the future are that (1) predictions are made using historical data, (2) they fail to account for unique events, and (3) they ignore coevolution (developments created by individual actions). Additionally, there are psychological challenges implicit in forecasting. An example of a psychological challenge is when plans based on forecasts that use historical data become so confining as to prohibit management freedom. It is also a concern that many decision makers feel that because they have the forecasting data in hand they have control over the future.

Regardless of the opponents to forecasting, the U.S. government, investment analysts, business managers, economists, and numerous others will continue to use forecasting techniques to predict the future. It is imperative for the users of the forecasts to understand the information and use the results as they are intended.

SEE ALSO *Budgets and Budgeting; Financial Forecasts and Projections; Research in Business*

BIBLIOGRAPHY

Fulmer, William E. (2000). *Shaping the Adaptive Organization.* New York: AMACOM.

Moore, Geoffrey H. (1983). *Business Cycles, Inflation, and Forecasting.* Cambridge, MA: Ballinger.

Sherman, Howard J., and Kolk, David X. (1996). *Business Cycles and Forecasting.* New York: HarperCollins.

Stock, James H., and Watson, Mark W., eds. (1993). *Business Cycles, Indicators, and Forecasting.* Chicago: University of Chicago Press.

Roger L. Luft

FOREIGN CORRUPT PRACTICES ACT OF 1977

The Foreign Corrupt Practices Act of 1977 (FCPA) evolved from investigations by the Office of the Special Prosecutor that provided evidence of illegal acts perpetrated by U.S. firms in foreign lands. More than 400 U.S. companies admitted to making questionable payments to various foreign governments and political parties as part of an amnesty program (U.S. Department of Justice, http://www.usdoj.gov). Given the environment of the 1970s and the proliferation of white-collar crimes (e.g., insider trading, bribery, false financial statements, etc.), particularly the payments made to foreign officials by corporations, Congress felt obligated to introduce legislation that led to the act. Congress's objective was to restore confidence in the manner U.S. companies transacted business.

THE ACT

The FCPA is unique. Throughout history, governments have had laws making it illegal for governmental officials to take a bribe. One basic provision of the FCPA is that it prohibits U.S. partnerships, companies, and organizations from not only giving payments but also offering or authorizing payments to foreign officials or political parties with the objective of encouraging or assuring business relationships.

There are two types of bribery provisions. The first prohibits any bribes made directly by the U.S. company. The second prohibits any organization from knowingly arranging for a bribe through an intermediary. Many thought that the FCPA would place U.S. companies at a disadvantage in the international marketplace because they could no longer influence foreign governments, officials, political parties, or candidates through gifts or payments. There has been no conclusive evidence that this has actually happened.

The FCPA includes record-keeping provisions for companies not involved in criminal conduct. These provisions were an amendment to the Securities and Exchange Act of 1934. The FCPA amendment requires all firms under the jurisdiction of the Securities and Exchange Commission (SEC) to maintain an adequate system of internal control whether or not they have foreign operations. This provision of the act applies to issuers of registered securities and issuers required to file periodic reports with the SEC.

ACCOUNTING PROVISIONS

The accounting provisions require companies to "keep books and records, and accounts, which, in reasonable detail, accurately and fairly reflect the transactions and dispositions of assets." The purpose of this accounting provision is to make it difficult for organizations to "cook the books" or use slush funds to hide any corrupt payments. Representative means for transfer of corrupt payments included:

- Overpayments
- Missing records (no receipt)
- Unrecorded transactions
- Misclassification of costs (bribes recorded as consulting fees or commissions)
- Retranscription of records

The accounting provisions include a requirement that companies design and maintain adequate systems of internal accounting controls that provide reasonable assurance that:

- Transactions are executed in accordance with management's authorization
- Transactions are recorded as necessary
- Access to assets is permitted only in accordance with management's authorization

Any internal document that misrepresents the actual nature of a financial transaction could be used as the basis for a charge that the "books and records" section of the FCPA has been violated.

ENFORCEMENT

Enforcement of the act is shared. Civil and criminal enforcement of the bribery provisions for those not required to file with the SEC rests with the Department of Justice. Responsibility for civil enforcement of the bribery provisions for those who have SEC filing requirements rests with the SEC.

In 1988 the FCPA was amended to allow for "facilitating payments" for expediting routine governmental action. These payments are distinguishable from corrupt payments in that these "grease payments" are for facilitating the performance of officials who are obligated to perform said duties. Questions regarding this amendment, affirmative defenses, or other provisions of the FCPA should be directed to counsel, or companies may wish to use the Department of Justice's Foreign Corrupt Practices Act Opinion Procedure. Under this procedure, upon receiving a question from a company or individual, the attorney general has thirty days to issue an opinion regard-

ing the inquiry. The objective is to alleviate uncertainty regarding acts covered by the FCPA.

PENALTIES

The FCPA provides penalties for violations. Criminal penalties for bribery violations include fines of up to $2 million for firms; fines of up to $100,000 and imprisonment of up to five years for officers, directors, and stockholders; and fines of up to $100,000 for employees and agents (fines imposed on individuals cannot be paid by companies). The SEC or attorney general may also bring actions that lead to civil penalties. Also, the act's penalties do not supersede penalties or fines levied under the provisions of other statutes. A violation of the bribery provisions of the FCPA may give rise to a private cause of action for treble damages under RICO (Racketeer Influenced and Corrupt Organizations Act).

The penalties can have long-term ramifications for companies. For example, a company found guilty of violating the FCPA may be barred from doing any business with the federal government. A company indicted for an FCPA violation may not be eligible to obtain various export licenses.

COMPLIANCE

Clearly, large multinational corporations cannot monitor every transaction of every dollar amount by every employee. However, companies do have a due-diligence obligation to implement adequate systems with sufficient internal controls. Key ways to avoid violation and liability include establishing policies and procedures that provide reasonable assurance that the business is adhering to the act's provisions. Suggested due-diligence steps for compliance with the FCPA include the following:

- Utilizing the compliance program under the Corporate Sentencing Guidelines Act
- Performing a risk evaluation of locations known for unethical business practices
- Performing risk evaluation of employees/agents who operate out of the home country
- Assuring that personnel who work out of the home country are knowledgeable regarding the provisions of the FCPA
- Assessing internal controls to be assured they are sufficient
- Monitoring internal controls, including reviews by auditors
- Reviewing critical transactions, such as those related to consulting services

- Establishing a procedure requiring that critical employees, vendors, and contractors provide written statements that they are in compliance with the requirements of the FCPA

SUBSEQUENT DEVELOPMENTS

On November 1, 1991, the Corporate Sentencing Guidelines Act was enacted. The guidelines appear to be a direct descendent of the FCPA. The guidelines for organizations "are designed so that the sanctions imposed upon organizations and their agents will, taken together, provide just punishment, adequate deterrence, and incentives for organizations to maintain internal mechanisms for preventing, detecting, and reporting criminal conduct" (U.S. Sentencing Guidelines, chapter 8, intro. comm., appendix p. A1).

In most corporations, accountants and auditors have responsibility to prevent, detect, and report errors and irregularities. The Corporate Sentencing Guidelines are legislation to deter white-collar crime. The guidelines' major objective is requiring organizations to monitor business activities to detect criminal conduct within their own ranks.

The guidelines allow organizations to use mitigating factors to reduce their exposure to fines. One mitigating factor is maintaining a corporate compliance program. The corporate compliance program is to be the responsibility of an officer or high-level employee. Elements of the compliance program include:

- Established standards and procedures
- Communication of the standards to employees
- Systems designed to detect criminal conduct
- A reporting system in place whereby individuals may report criminal conduct
- Disciplinary mechanisms that are consistently enforced

FURTHER GUIDANCE

Information regarding the FCPA or the Foreign Corrupt Practices Act Opinion Procedure may be obtained from the U.S. Department of Justice, 950 Pennsylvania Avenue NW, Washington, DC 20530-001, (202)514-2000.

SEE ALSO *Fraudulent Financial Reporting; International Trade*

Charles H. Calhoun

FOREIGN EXCHANGE

SEE *Currency Exchange*

FORENSIC ACCOUNTING

Forensic accounting, sometimes referred to as fraud examination accounting, is an emerging area of specialization within the accounting discipline. *Webster's Dictionary* defines *forensic* as "belonging to, used in, or suitable to courts of judicature or public discussion and debate." Forensic accounting can, therefore, be defined as accounting that is used in a court of law, including, but not limited to, the application of accounting theory, principles, and calculations to actual or to hypothetical issues in legal proceedings. The term is broad enough to include the many procedures that an accountant or auditor applies in a fraud investigation.

Job titles commonly used in this field include forensic accountant, investigative accountant, fraud examiner, and fraud auditor. These terms are essentially interchangeable. Forensic accountants draw their expertise from many areas, including accounting, auditing, cost accounting, taxation, and information technology. Forensic accounting is more than accounting—more than detective work—it is a multifaceted activity that requires the use of knowledge from a number of disciplines.

Detecting fraud or white-collar crime used to be thought of as part of the accounting function. Fraud was assumed to occur infrequently because of the presence of internal and external auditors, who would likely identify the presence of fraud in the financial statements. The problem of fraud, however, has become to be perceived as serious, and at times, occurring more than infrequently. Such awareness is the motivation for this new specialization in the accounting field.

Forensic accounting has been subdivided into two categories, (1) litigation support and (2) investigation and dispute resolution. Some practitioners choose to specialize in one of the categories. Other practitioners provide both types of services.

LITIGATION SUPPORT

Litigation support involves the presentation and interpretation of various issues related to assisting existing or pending litigation. In this area of expertise, the forensic accountant may be asked to assign an estimated value for damages sustained by parties involved in legal disputes and to assist in resolving disputes, even before they reach the courtroom.

For example, this area of litigation support provided to the legal profession might include such assignments as assisting in obtaining documentary evidence to support or rebut a claim, reviewing relevant supporting documents to form an initial assessment of the situation and identify possible areas of loss, assisting with suggesting and designing questions to be asked during the gathering of both the financial and nonfinancial evidence, attending the initial disclosure phase (called the discovery phase) of the trial proceedings to review various testimonies and assisting with the understanding of the financial issues, reviewing opposing damage reports and reporting on both the strengths and weaknesses of the positions taken, and assisting with the settlement discussions and negotiations.

INVESTIGATION AND DISPUTE RESOLUTION

The second category of forensic accounting is investigation and dispute resolution. It is part of the process to determine whether criminal matters, such as employee theft, securities fraud (including falsification of financial statements), identity theft, and insurance fraud, have occurred. Some of the work of the forensic accountant may include recommending actions that can be taken to minimize future damages and risk of loss.

Investigation may occur in civil matters, such as the forensic accountant searching for hidden assets in a divorce case. Another typical example would be the forensic accountant being engaged to investigate employee theft. Not only are forensic accountants often engaged to review the facts of a given situation and provide suggestions regarding possible courses of action, but they are also involved with assisting in the many other ways to protect and recover assets.

EXPERT CONSULTANT VERSUS EXPERT WITNESS

Because of the expertise forensic accountants possess, they are often engaged as expert consultants and/or expert witnesses. As expert consultants, the forensic accountants (investigators) are engaged by attorneys to develop evidence used by the attorneys in a variety of ways. Even if litigation is intended, the expert consultants may not be expected to testify; therefore, the various documents the consultants prepare may be protected by the attorney/client privilege or attorney work-product privilege. This means that the documents may not have to be provided to the opposing side in any litigation. If the expert consultants do not testify, their role may end when the fraud has been established, an estimated range of loss established, and a suspect identified. Additionally, expert consultants may be engaged to assist attorneys by identi-

fying and recommending expert witnesses, helping attorneys to prepare for testimony, and reviewing various documents.

Forensic accountants are in high demand to provide expert witness services. An expert witness is a person who can offer opinions about the situation based on insight developed through education, experience, and training. In the process of a court proceeding, the judge rules on whether an expert witness is qualified to provide evidence on the matter before the court. The need for an expert witness who is a forensic accountant generally arises when there is a dispute involving some area of accounting expertise. When investigators (forensic accountants) are engaged as expert witnesses, litigation is intended, and the investigators will often have to provide deposition and courtroom testimony. They can testify about the facts of the case and can also give opinions. Regardless of how educated, experienced, and trained forensic accountants may be, their credibility is weakened if they are unprepared or not familiar with the facts of the case.

CIVIL VERSUS CRIMINAL TRIALS

When an adequate level of evidence is obtained by the forensic accountant, a decision is made whether to pursue the case in court. As noted previously, forensic accountants often play an important role in civil and criminal action. *Civil* refers to private rights and remedies sought by civil actions, where the individual has been harmed, for which he or she can claim compensation. Civil fraud trials are typically started by the party suffering the loss and may result in a judgment for reimbursement for actual losses and attorneys' fees. Civil trials do not result in imprisonment.

Criminal fraud involves violation of a law (known as a statute) enacted by the state or federal legislation. Criminal fraud is prosecuted by the state and may result in punishment, such as fines, restitution, and/or prison time.

One of the major differences between civil and criminal fraud is the extent, or burden, of proof required for conviction. In a civil case, the burden of proof is to the extent of a "preponderance of the evidence" (which is usually interpreted to mean more than 50 percent), and the verdict may not be unanimous. In a criminal fraud case, the burden of proof is "beyond a reasonable doubt," and the verdict must usually be unanimous. Thus, it is more difficult to obtain a conviction for criminal fraud than one for civil fraud. The forensic accountant is well versed in the quality and type of documented evidence required for each court.

THE NEED FOR FORENSIC ACCOUNTANTS AND FRAUD EXAMINERS

Between 2001 and 2005, a number of top business stories disclosed financial statement fraud and its impact on the accounting profession, businesses, consumers, and investors. In response to several large businesses seeking bankruptcy, the federal government enacted very specific accounting and business laws, including the Sarbanes-Oxley Act of 2002. This act, among other regulations, states that chief executive officers and chief financial officers are directly responsible for the accuracy of financial statements, with significant fines and extensive prison terms for violators. The act also defines prohibited activities that are outside the normal scope of external auditors. Many businesspeople found the act to be the most sweeping legislation to affect the accounting profession since the Securities Act of 1933 and the Securities Exchange Act of 1934.

Many professional organizations, including the American Institute of Certified Public Accountants and the Association of Certified Fraud Examiners (ACFE), emphasize the need for education in the prevention, detection, and prosecution of accounting fraud. As a result, the field of forensic accounting and fraud examination has emerged in the effort to combat financial abuse.

According to the ACFE *Report to the Nation* in 2005, organizations lose an estimated $670 billion per year (approximately 6 percent of all small businesses' annual gross revenue in 2004) to fraud and abuse. It is no wonder forensic accounting and fraud examination is one of the fastest-growing sectors, not just within the accounting profession, but within all fields of employment.

According to *Accounting Today,* nearly 40 percent of the top 100 accounting firms in the United States have expanded, or were planning to expand, their forensic-related services. *U.S. News & World Report* (February 8, 2002) called forensic accounting one of the "20 hot job tracks of the future" and in 2002 designated the forensic accounting profession as one of the eight most secure career tracks in America. *SmartMoney Magazine* also in 2002 (Accounting Web US May 16, 2002) stated that this profession is one of the "ten hottest jobs" for the next decade with a salary potential of over $100,000. In addition, a national study conducted by Kessler International (August 2, 2001), a forensic accounting firm headquartered in New York City, revealed that two-thirds of the companies that responded to a national study stated that they have either used the services of a forensic accountant already or have considered doing so. The *Cincinnati Business Courier* in February 2003 stated that the major scandals at the beginning of the twenty-first century had prompted business owners to turn to forensic accountants and fraud examiners for proactive fraud checkups.

Other organizations and companies are also asking forensic accountants to search for wrongdoings. The Federal Bureau of Investigation (FBI), the Internal Revenue Service, and the U.S. Bureau of Alcohol, Tobacco and Firearms have forensic accountants who investigate situations from money laundering and identity-theft-related fraud to arson for profit and tax evasion. Law firms use forensic accountants to help divorcing clients uncover assets hidden by their spouses, and in the first decade of the twenty-first century, forensic accountants have uncovered instances of companies misstating their financial statements to inflate company profits or minimize losses.

Forensic accountants work in most major accounting firms and are needed for investigating mergers and acquisitions; they are also employed in tax investigations, economic crime investigations, all kinds of civil litigation support, specialized audits, and even in terrorist investigations. Forensic accountants work throughout the business world, in public accounting, corporations, and in all branches of government (from the FBI and Central Intelligence Agency to the offices of the local authorities). Forensic accounting firms are everywhere.

A GROWING TREND IN HIGHER EDUCATION

Since 2002 some colleges and universities have developed degree programs in forensic accounting and fraud examination, both at the undergraduate and graduate level. Additionally, many academic institutions have developed and are offering stand-alone courses in this field. Many other academic and professional organizations are developing seminars and training modules to handle the demand for training in this area.

SEE ALSO *Association of Certified Fraud Examiners; Fraudulent Financial Reporting*

BIBLIOGRAPHY

Albrecht, W., Albrecht, S., and Albrecht, C. C. (2006). *Fraud examination* (2nd ed.). Mason, OH: Thomson South-Western.

Association of Certified Fraud Examiners (2004). *Report to the Nation.* Available from http://www.acfe.com/fraud/report.asp.

Forensic Accounting. (2002). Forensic accounting demystified. http://www.forensicaccounting.com/home.html. Retrieved January 3, 2006.

PPC's guide to fraud detection (5th ed.). (2002). (Vols. 1–2). Fort Worth, TX: Thomson-Practitioners.

Wells, J. T. (2005). *Principles of fraud examination.* Hoboken, NJ: Wiley.

Richard O. Hanson

FRANCHISING

Franchising is an arrangement whereby a supplier, or franchiser, grants a dealer, or franchisee, the right to sell products or services in exchange for some type of consideration. It is a business arrangement involving a contract between a manufacturer or another supplier and a dealer that specifies the methods to be used in marketing a good or service. The franchiser may receive some percentage of total sales in exchange for furnishing equipment, buildings, management know-how, and market research. The franchisee supplies labor and capital, operates the franchised business, and agrees to abide by the provisions of the franchise agreement.

Historically, franchising was a grant by a king to allow a citizen an exclusive right to sell a product or render a service. For this right, the sovereign protected the exclusivity and the subject paid the government an appropriate tribute in service, food, goods, or money. Franchising in the United States started shortly after the Civil War (1861–1865), when the Singer Company began to set up sewing-machine franchises. The concept became increasingly popular after 1900 in the automobile industry. Because of this, other automotive franchises developed for gasoline, oil, and tires. In the 1950s, food operations made a dramatic entrance into franchising with the development of McDonald's, currently one of the world's largest franchise organizations.

Franchising operations account for billions of dollars in annual sales, with more than 500 outlets employing millions of people. A new franchise opens somewhere in the United States every six minutes. Franchising accounts for approximately 40 percent of all U.S. retail sales. Because of changes in the international marketplace, shifting employment options in the United States, the expanding U.S. economy, and corporate interest in more joint-venture activity, franchising will continue to increase rapidly.

Franchising represents the small entrepreneur's best chance to compete with the giant companies that dominate the marketplace. Without franchising, thousands of businesspeople would never have had the opportunity to own their own businesses.

The largest percentages of franchise operations are in the recreation, entertainment, and travel fields, followed closely by business services, nonfood retailing, and automotive products and services. Popular franchises include Subway, McDonald's, Wendy's International, Jackson Hewitt Tax Service, KFC, UPS Store, TCBY Treats, Taco Bell, and Jani-King.

Taco Bell is one of the leading fast food franchisers in the United States. **PHOTOGRAPH BY KELLY A. QUIN. THE GALE GROUP.**

TYPES OF FRANCHISE AGREEMENTS

Retail franchise agreements fall into three general categories. In one type of arrangement, a manufacturer authorizes a number of retail stores to sell a certain brand-name item. This franchise arrangement, one of the oldest, is common in the sales of cars and trucks, farm equipment, shoes, paint, earthmoving equipment, and gasoline. About 90 percent of all gasoline is sold through franchised independent service stations, and franchised dealers handle virtually all sales of new cars and trucks.

In the second type of retail franchise, a producer licenses distributors to sell a given product to retailers. This arrangement is common in the soft-drink industry. Most national manufacturers of soft drinks—such as Coca-Cola, Dr. Pepper, and PepsiCo—grant franchises to bottlers, which then service retailers.

In the third type of retail franchise, a franchiser supplies brand names, techniques, or other services, instead of complete products. The franchiser may provide certain production and distribution services, but its primary role in the arrangement is careful development and control of marketing strategies. This approach to franchising, very common in the early twenty-first century, is used by such organizations as Holiday Inn, AAMCO, McDonald's, Dairy Queen, KFC, and H&R Block.

A good franchise system can offer the prospective franchisee a diversified array of business savvy. In most instances, the franchisee enjoys the benefit of a nationally recognized trade name, national recognition, and the instant collective goodwill of the franchise. Standard quality and uniformity of a product or service coupled with an existing—and successful—system of marketing and accounting are other benefits. In addition, expert advice on location, design, capitalization, and operational issues is provided by the franchiser. Specialization on a national level is done in order to maintain the necessary research and market analysis that will enable the franchisee to remain competitive in an ever-changing marketplace. In other words, a business framework is supplied that reduces the number of risks that may arise when starting a new business. Most often these risks are associated with the financial investment involved. The franchise agreement, however, often offers a cost savings by sharing a centralized purchasing system, and in some instances, direct financial assistance.

ADVANTAGES AND DISADVANTAGES OF FRANCHISING

Franchising offers several advantages to both the franchisee and the franchiser. It enables a franchisee to start a business with limited capital and to benefit from the business experience of others. Moreover, nationally advertised franchises, such as ServiceMaster Clean and Burger King, are often assured of customers as soon as they open. If business problems arise, the franchisee can obtain guidance and advice from the franchiser at little or not cost. Franchised outlets are generally more successful than independently owned businesses. Fewer than 10 percent of franchised retail businesses fail during the first two years of operation, whereas approximately half of independent retail businesses fail during that period. The franchisee also receives material to use in local advertising and can benefit from national promotional campaigns sponsored by the franchiser. At the start of the twenty-first century, Taco Bell franchisees profited from a national advertising campaign featuring a Chihuahua demanding "Yo quiero Taco Bell" ("I want some Taco Bell"). The ads helped boost same-store sales at Taco Bell by 3 percent in an otherwise flat industry. The talking dog was especially popular among teenagers, who spend more than $12 billion per year at fast-food restaurants.

The franchiser gains fast and selective product distribution through franchise arrangements without incurring the high cost of constructing and operating its own outlets, thus giving it more capital for expanding production and advertising. It can also ensure, through the franchise agreement, that outlets are maintained and operated according to its own standards. The franchiser benefits because the franchisee, being a sole proprietor in most cases, is likely to be very highly motivated to succeed. Success of the franchise means more sales, which translate into higher income for the franchiser.

Despite these numerous advantages, franchise arrangements also have drawbacks for both parties. The franchiser can dictate many aspects of the business: decor, design of employees' uniforms, types of signs, and numerous other details of business operations. In addition, franchisees must pay to use the franchiser's name, products, and assistance. Usually franchisees must pay a one-time franchise fee as well as continuing royalty and advertising fees, often collected as a percentage of sales. For example, Subway requires franchisees to come up with $70,000 to $220,000 in start-up costs. Franchisees often must work very hard, putting in twelve-hour days, six or seven days a week. In some cases, franchise agreements are not uniform; one franchisee may pay more than another for the same services. The franchiser also gives up a certain amount of control when entering into a franchise agreement. Consequently, individual establishments may not be operated exactly the way the franchiser would like.

MONEY AND TIME COMMITMENTS

When entering into a franchise agreement, franchisees must be prepared to make major commitments of both money and time. They must be prepared to invest a substantial amount of money, both in the initial franchising fee and in start-up costs and carrying funds to provide a cash flow sufficient to operate the business during the beginning months or, if necessary, years. Most franchisees average a net profit of approximately $30,000 the first year of the contractual agreement with increase in residual profits annually the second year forward.

The second commitment is that of time; in the beginning, the proprietor will be obliged to devote long hours to the details of the business operation. Experience has shown that this commitment is the common denominator to many successful franchise operations. Franchisees must rely to a large extent upon their own aptitude and drive in order to learn the business. They must also rely upon the product, services, and business skills of the franchiser.

KEY CONSIDERATIONS

In deciding whether or not to enter into a franchise agreement, there are several key points that need to be considered. The first consideration is price and costs. What is the total cost? What are the initial fees? What are the ongoing costs? Are there any hidden extras? Are franchisees restricted in their right to purchase other goods?

The second consideration is the location. Where will the franchise be located? What is the territory that it will serve? What are the protections and limitations? Who will the competition be?

The third issue involves control and support. What controls will be in place? What policies and regulations govern the franchise agreement? What training and ongoing support will be supplied?

Advertising is the fourth consideration. The franchisee needs to determine what national and regional advertising will be supplied, as well as what the franchisee pays for and what the franchiser finances.

The last area of concern involves profits and losses, transfer and death, and duration and termination. Potential franchisees need to determine not only what protection they will receive for their earnings if they are successful, but also what obligations they will be responsible for if the franchise fails. In addition, they need to find out whether, in the event of their death, the franchise agreement can be transferred to their heirs or automatically reverts to the franchiser. Finally, they need to determine what stipulations, penalties, and other responsibilities are involved in terminating the contract with the franchiser should they no longer wish to continue in the business.

THE FRANCHISING SECTOR

A franchise is like any other business property in that it is the buyers' responsibility to know what they are buying. Poorly financed or poorly managed franchise systems are no better than poorly financed or poorly managed non-franchise businesses. It is important to remember that there are trends in franchises, just as in other types of businesses. Popular areas for franchising include auto rental, fast-food, haircutting, health and fitness, and real estate businesses.

The growth of the franchised fast-food industry has been truly spectacular. These franchise operations are second only to automobile dealerships and gasoline stations in gross volume of sales. Most often located at key intersections or on busy highways, fast-food enterprises enjoy a high visibility.

In this segment of the franchise industry, the majority of franchise operators have already owned other businesses before entering into a fast-food franchise. Many

successful operators are college graduates, but the significant number of successful franchisees with only a high school education suggests that education alone is not a determining factor. A fast-food franchise is the type of venture in which both husband and wife can contribute to the success of the business.

Most fast-food franchisers consider geographic location to be an important factor in the success of the operation. And, like franchisers in other fields, they cite the importance of adequate capitalization, the efficient operation of the franchise system, good customer relations, quality employees, and the contributions of the franchisees, such as their management skills and especially their hard work.

According to Cassano's Pizza and Subs, a franchiser with twelve outlets in four states, the successful franchise operator must have several traits:

- an excellent attitude toward customer service and customer relations

- an entrepreneurial ability and spirit combined with good business techniques

- a willingness to take a hands-on attitude toward the business

Newcomers to the Cassano's franchised fast-food business must have prior retail management experience and previous food-service experience. All new franchisees are trained at the home office in Dayton, Ohio, for one month. After that, the franchise provides ongoing training and managerial assistance.

GLOBAL FRANCHISING

Franchising is growing rapidly abroad, with hundreds of franchise companies operating in thousands of outlets overseas. Canada is the largest of these markets, followed by Japan, Europe, Australia, and the United Kingdom. In 1995 Subway signed a deal with Japanese financiers to open 1,000 franchise outlets in Japan. Subway tailored its products to fit the local tastes—for example, offering the Japanese market fried pork sandwiches.

Franchising can be a workable way for small firms to enter foreign markets, especially markets where there are few competitors. For example, Automation Paper Company, a small New Jersey-based supplier of high-technology paper products, used franchising to gain exclusive representation in target markets. The franchisees received rights to the company's trademark, as well as training for local staffs and the benefit of the firm's experience, credit lines, and advertising budget.

The problems facing franchise companies in international transactions are relatively less formidable than those facing other service sectors. Franchisers must comply with the same local requirements as other businesses, and the franchise agreements must comply with local contract law, antitrust law, and trademark and licensing laws. Aside from language and cultural differences, many of the problems of conducting business in foreign countries are the same as those involved in the United States. The success or failure of foreign franchising will depend in large measure on the soundness of the franchiser's domestic market position and on the franchiser's ability to provide the necessary expertise to others in another part of the world.

Some franchises popular in the United States actually started in another country. For example, Molly Maid started in Canada in 1980 and came to the United States four years later.

FRANCHISING TRENDS

All trends indicate that franchising will continue to expand both domestically and internationally, creating great opportunities for existing and new businesses; developing new entrepreneurs, new jobs, new products, new services; and providing export opportunities. Rising personal income, stable prices, high levels of consumer optimism, and increased competition for market share are turning many companies, both small and large, to franchising. Education will play an important role in the future of franchising, as both high schools and colleges increase the number of courses that are taught in marketing, business management, and entrepreneurship. In addition, changing patterns in American demographics, coupled with the increased number of women in the workforce, are influencing the number of new franchises each year.

Furthermore, shifting demographic patterns and the use of new technology have intensified competition among franchise companies. These factors have increased the number of mergers and acquisitions in the franchising system, and it was expected that this merger/acquisition trend would persist for several years. Creativity and imagination in the treatment of goods and services are the focus of most business ventures today. Education, computers, and the ability to work with and manage people will be profitably used by emerging businesses. All these developments suggest that franchising will be one of the leading methods of doing business as the first decade of the twenty-first century progresses, even in an environment of mixed signals in the economy. These signals include the economic trend of consumer demand for service-sponsored arrangements, which are currently the fastest growing type of franchise. Examples include Snelling and Snelling Inc. (employment service) and H&R Block (tax services).

ECONOMIC IMPACT OF FRANCHISING

In 2005, the total number of franchise establishments in the United States totaled 767,483. This means that nearly 3.2 percent of all US businesses operate as a francise. These franchises are also responsible for providing more than 9.7 million jobs in the economy, with an annual estimated payroll that totaled close to $230 billion. According to the International Franchise Association, franchised businesses provided more jobs than durable-goods manufacturers. These include franchises in industrial equipment/machinery; communications; lighting and other electrical equipment; trucks, cars, planes and other transportation equipment; lumber and wood products; furniture/fixtures; and computers.

SEE ALSO *Marketing*

BIBLIOGRAPHY

Blair, Roger D., and Lafontaine, Francine (2005). *The economics of franchising.* New York: Cambridge University Press.

Hoy, Frank, and Stanworth, John (Eds.) (2003). *Franchising: An international perspective.* New York: Routledge.

Kaufman, D. (2004, August). New study reveals an extraordinary economic reach. *New York Law Journal,* p. 3.

Kotler, Philip, and Armstrong, Gary (2006). *Principles of marketing* (11th ed.). Upper Saddle River, NJ: Pearson Prentice Hall.

Moore, Lisa (1991, June 10). The flight to franchising. *U.S. News & World Report,* pp. 78–81.

Pride, William M., and Ferrell, O. C. (2006). *Marketing concepts and strategies* (Rev. ed.). Boston: Houghton Mifflin.

U.S. Bureau of the Census. (2006). *Statistical abstract of the United States.* Washington, DC: Author.

Patricia A. Spirou

FRAUDULENT FINANCIAL REPORTING

The equity and credit markets (capital markets) in the United States have long been considered to be among the most efficient in the economically developed world. One reason for the efficient operation of these markets has been the public availability of creditable financial statements by those using them as a basis for their investment and credit decisions. A potential significant threat to the efficient functioning of these markets is the incidence of fraudulent financial reporting.

Fraudulent financial reporting is intentional or reckless conduct, acts, or omissions that result in materially misleading financial statements. Confidence in the operation of capital markets is compromised when the system of public disclosure is eroded by reported instances of fraudulent reporting.

In the mid-1980s the failure of a number of financial institutions led various groups to identify possible causes, including the extent of fraudulent financial reporting involved in the failures. In August 1986 Congressman John Dingell and other members of the Subcommittee on Oversight and Investigations of the U.S. House of Representatives' Committee on Energy and Commerce proposed legislation to amend the Securities Exchange Act of 1934 to require independent public accountants (auditors) to include procedures for material financial fraud detection, reporting on internal control systems, and reporting of fraudulent activities to appropriate enforcement and regulatory authorities. These legislative proposals were not accepted. The belief that the accounting profession could respond successfully without further intervention by the legislative branch of the federal government persisted.

A private-sector response to these legislative proposals was led by the Committee of Sponsoring Organizations (COSO) of the Treadway Commission. COSO oversaw the National Commission on Fraudulent Financial Reporting (the Treadway Commission). This commission, jointly sponsored and funded by the American Institute of Certified Public Accountants (AICPA), the American Accounting Association, Financial Executives International, the Institute of Internal Auditors, and the National Association of Accountants (now the Institute of Management Accountants), was formed to identify factors contributing to fraudulent financial reporting and to develop recommendations to reduce its future occurrence. The Treadway Commission issued its report in October 1987.

TREADWAY COMMISSION REPORT

The Treadway Commission concluded that the responsibility for fraudulent financial reporting was not vested in one group. While the commission conceded that financial statements are the responsibility of a company's management, it issued a series of recommendations for the public company, the independent public accountant, the Securities and Exchange Commission (SEC), and the educational community.

The report identified a number of factors that might contribute to fraudulent financial reporting, including a number of environmental, institutional, and individual personal incentives. Environmental considerations included professionalism, codes of corporate conduct, and corporate pressures. Institutional incentives include falsely improving financial appearances in financial statements for the purpose of maintaining market stock prices or to meet investor expectations, as well as delaying the report-

ing of financial difficulties in order to avoid failure to comply with covenants in debt agreements. Individual incentives include falsely reporting results in order to achieve targeted results for bonus or incentive compensation purposes, as well as to avoid penalties for poor performance in achieving targeted profit objectives.

The Treadway Commission indicated that the oversight bodies that establish auditing standards and those which monitor compliance have a continuing responsibility to uphold the integrity of the public disclosure system. The commission also concluded that many of the SEC's fraudulent financial reporting cases against auditors were for alleged failures to conduct the audits in accordance with generally accepted auditing standards.

RESPONSE OF THE AUDITING STANDARDS BOARD

In response to the Treadway Commission report and to other influences, the Auditing Standards Board (ASB) of the AICPA issued ten new auditing standards in 1988. These ten Statements on Auditing Standards included requirements affecting the auditor's responsibility to detect and report errors and irregularities, consideration of internal control structure in a financial statement audit, and communication with a company's audit committee.

CONTINUING ATTENTION TO THE PROBLEMS IN THE 1990S

Continuing attempts were made to gain an understanding of fraudulent financial reporting in the 1990s. The influence of the Treadway Commission report persisted. Several reports received serious consideration throughout the reporting environment. Nevertheless, in this decade no changes related to auditor responsibility for reporting about internal controls if fraud was to be deterred were considered critical. Internal controls continued to be evaluated in the context of planning an audit of financial statements, but the results of the assessment of internal controls and their effectiveness were not reported publicly.

INTERNAL CONTROL

In 1992 COSO issued *Internal Control—An Integrated Framework* for companies, their managements, and their auditors. The framework is a conceptual paradigm that provides subjective concepts of effective internal control. COSO defined internal control as a process designed by a company's management to provide reasonable assurance that the company achieve its objectives in the following areas:

- Reliability of financial reporting
- Compliance with applicable laws and regulations

- Effectiveness and efficiency of operations

The COSO framework identified five interrelated components of internal control:

1. The control environment that sets the tone of an organization

2. Risk assessment that identifies and analyzes potential risks

3. Control activities that are policies and procedures to ensure that management objectives are carried out

4. Information and communication that identify and process information which enable people to carry out responsibilities

5. Monitoring that assesses compliance with control procedures

The framework provides only reasonable assurance because there are inherent limitations in any system of internal control.

STUDY OF SEC ACCOUNTING AND ENFORCEMENT RELEASES

In 1999 COSO issued the results of a study of SEC accounting and enforcement releases between 1987 and 1997. This study attempted to gain an understanding of the participants and the extent and duration of fraudulent behavior. Because of the limitations of the study, the usefulness of the findings were at best tentative and primarily suggestive of the nature of the behavior of auditors and company officials.

BLUE RIBBON COMMITTEE REPORT

At the request of the SEC chairman, the New York Stock Exchange (NYSE) and the National Association of Securities Dealers (NASD) formed the Blue Ribbon Committee, which was charged with recommending ways to enhance the effectiveness of audit committees. The Blue Ribbon Committee, in its 1999 report, *Report and Recommendations of the Blue Ribbon Committee on Improving the Effectiveness of Corporate Audit Committees,* which was addressed to the heads of the two sponsoring organizations—NYSE and NASD—recommended stronger audit committee oversight responsibilities relating to financial reporting. Among the recommendations were the clarification of the relationship of the external auditor with management and the audit committee, improvement in oversights of the financial reporting process, and enhancing communications about accounting reporting processes between the external auditor and the audit committee.

CORPORATE SCANDALS AND THE SARBANES-OXLEY ACT

A series of business failures and financial scandals that began with Enron's disclosures of fraudulent behavior in second half of 2001 caused a serious decline in investor confidence in the capital markets. In an attempt to restore public investor confidence, the federal government passed the Sarbanes-Oxley Act of 2002, which amended the Securities Exchange Act of 1934 and expanded rules concerning corporate governance. Sarbanes-Oxley improved the oversight of external auditors and focused the attention of companies and auditors on internal control; it also increased penalties for noncompliance. The intent of these elements of Sarbanes-Oxley is to reduce the likelihood that material fraud will go undetected.

The Sarbanes-Oxley Act includes the following major provisions affecting both management and external auditors:

- The creation of the Public Companies Accounting Oversight Board (PCAOB)

- Rules designed to increase auditor independence

- New responsibilities for corporate directors, chief executive officers, and chief financial officers

- Enhanced financial disclosures

The PCAOB is a five-member board of financially literate members. The board has the authority to establish auditing standards, quality control standards, and independence standards for audits of public companies. In addition, the PCAOB has the authority to inspect the work of public company auditors. The PCAOB's deliberations result in the adoption of rules that are submitted to the SEC for approval. Prior to Sarbanes-Oxley, the AICPA's ASB was responsible for many of these functions on a self-regulatory basis.

The Sarbanes-Oxley Act strengthened auditor independence by making it unlawful for an auditor to perform audit services for a public company and to also perform nonattest services such as bookkeeping and other consultative services for the same audit client.

The Sarbanes-Oxley Act increased penalties imposed on the managements of public companies found to be responsible for false and misleading financial statements. Included in the act is a provision requiring a public company's chief executive officer and chief financial officer to certify the appropriateness of the financial statements and disclosures contained in the company's annual report.

Section 404 of the Sarbanes-Oxley Act and Auditing Standard No. 2 issued by the PCAOB require corporate management and the company's independent auditor to issue two reports that must be included in the company's annual report filed with the SEC. These two reports require management and the independent auditor of public companies to assess and report on the effectiveness of the company's internal control over financial reporting. Management must state in its report its responsibility for maintaining adequate internal control over financial reporting and give its assessment of whether or not internal control over financial reporting is effective or not.

The independent auditor must evaluate and report on the fairness of management's assessment. The auditor will also perform an independent audit of internal control over financial reporting and will issue an opinion on whether internal control is operating as of the assessment date. If one or more material weaknesses exist at the company's fiscal year-end, the auditor cannot conclude that internal control over financial reporting is effective.

The purpose of these reporting requirements is to increase the likelihood that material weaknesses in internal control over financial reporting will be identified and remediated.

Despite these requirements, it is still possible for fraudulent financial reporting to occur. Although the intended results of internal control reporting is to reduce the likelihood that material fraud will go undetected, no system of internal control provides absolute assurance that manipulation, collusion, or management override will not occur.

SEE ALSO *Auditing; Forensic Accounting*

BIBLIOGRAPHY

Blue Ribbon Committee. (1999). *Improving the effectiveness of corporate audit committees: Report and recommendations of the Blue Ribbon Committee on improving the effectiveness of corporate audit committees.* New York: New York Stock Exchange; Washington, DC: National Association of Securities Dealers.

Committee of Sponsoring Organizations of the Treadway Commission. (1992). *Internal control—Integrated framework.* New York: Author.

Committee of Sponsoring Organizations of the Treadway Commission. (1999). *Fraudulent financial reporting: 1987–1997: An analysis of U.S. public companies.* Retrieved January 13, 2006, from http://www.coso.org/Publications.htm

National Commission on Fraudulent Financial Reporting. (1987). *Report of the National Commission on Fraudulent Financial Reporting.* Washington, DC: Author.

Public Company Accounting Oversight Board. (2004, June 17). *Auditing Standard No. 2: An audit of internal control over financial reporting performed in conjunction with an audit of financial statements.* Retrieved January 13, 2006, from http://www.pcaobus.org/Standards/Standards_and_Related_Rules/Auditing_Standard_No.2.asp

Whittington, Ray, and Pany, Kurt (2006). *Principles of auditing and other assurance services* (15th ed.). Boston: McGraw-Hill/Irwin.

Gerard A. Lange

FREE ENTERPRISE

SEE *Economic Systems*

FUND ACCOUNTING

SEE *Government Accounting; Not-For-Profit Accounting*

FUTURE BUSINESS LEADERS OF AMERICA

Future Business Leaders of American (FBLA) is one of ten nationally recognized vocational student organizations in the United States (Gordon, 2003). The organization is a nonprofit educational association for students who are preparing for careers in business and business-related fields. The organization is composed of four divisions:

- FBLA for middle school students

- FBLA for high school students

- Phi Beta Lambda (PBL) for post-secondary students

- A professional division composed of businesspeople, educators, and other individuals who uphold the goals of the organization ("Frequently Asked Questions," 1999)

FBLA has been in existence since 1937. Dr. Hamden I. Forkner of Teachers College of Columbia University developed the first chapter in New York City (Vaughn et al., 1987). In 1940 the National Council for Business Education recognized and sponsored FBLA. The first high school chapter was chartered in Johnson City, Tennessee, on February 3, 1942. Currently, more than 25,000 active members participate in the organization.

Students participating in FBLA have the opportunity to develop leadership skills; enter a variety of competitions at local, state, and national levels; establish occupational goals; and learn from business and professional individuals in their communities. The goals of FBLA (and PBL) are:

- To promote competent, aggressive business leadership

- To understand American business enterprise

- To establish career goals

- To encourage scholarship

- To promote sound financial management

- To develop character and self-confidence

- To facilitate transition from school to work ("Frequently Asked Questions," 1999)

Conferences, seminars, awards, publications, and scholarships are services provided for members of the organization. By providing practical hands-on activities for students in the business arena, FBLA continues to prepare young men and women to become successful leaders in our ever-changing society. More information is available from FBLA or PBL at FBLA/PBL Inc., 1912 Association Drive, Reston, Virginia 22091-1591, (800)FBLA-WIN, or http://www.fbla-pbl.org/.

SEE ALSO *Business Professionals of America; DECA; SkillsUSA*

BIBLIOGRAPHY

"Frequently Asked Questions", Retrieved October 2, 2005, from http://www.fbla-pbl.org/.

Gordon, Howard R. D. (2003). *The History and Growth of Vocational Education in America* (2nd ed.). Prospect Heights, IL: Waveland Press.

Vaughn, P. R., Vaughn, R. C., and Vaughn, D. L. (1987). *Handbook for Advisors of Vocational Student Organizations.* Athens, GA: American Association for Vocational Instructional Materials.

Jill T. White

G

GATT

SEE *Trading Blocs*

GDP

SEE *Gross Domestic Product (GDP)*

GENERAL ACCOUNTING OFFICE (GAO)

SEE *United States Government Accountability Office*

GENERALLY ACCEPTED ACCOUNTING PRINCIPLES

Most individuals who understand the basics of financial reporting are familiar with the phrase *generally accepted accounting principles* (GAAP) and will readily identify the Financial Accounting Standards Board (FASB) as the standard-setting body in the United States responsible for establishing accounting principles for nongovernmental entities. However, some may not be aware that there is no single reference source for GAAP because these principles are derived from a variety of sources. For example, although the FASB is responsible for issuing FASB State-

ments of Financial Accounting Standards, Interpretations, and Technical Bulletins, the American Institute of Certified Public Accountants (AICPA) issues Statements of Position, Audit and Accounting Guides, and Practice Bulletins, and the FASB Emerging Issues Task Force (EITF) issues EITF Abstracts.

It may seem that accounting principles could be generally accepted because of popular vote or consensus of opinion. However, generally accepted accounting principles is a technical accounting phrase defined in Accounting Principles Board (APB) Statement No. 4, *Basic Concepts and Accounting Principles Underlying Financial Statement of Business Enterprises*, as "the conventions, rules, and procedures that define accepted accounting practice at a particular time." GAAP includes not only broad guidelines of general application but also detailed practices and procedures that provide a standard by which to measure financial presentations. For the most part, in financial reporting, generally accepted implies substantial authoritative support.

THE GAAP HIERARCHY

Although there is no single reference source for GAAP, there is a hierarchy established by the AICPA in Statement on Auditing Standards No. 69, *The Meaning of "Present Fairly in Conformity With Generally Accepted Accounting Principles" in the Independent Auditor's Report* (SAS 69). At the foundation of that hierarchy are the principles established by the FASB and its predecessors, the APB and the AICPA Committee on Accounting Procedure. From that foundation, the hierarchy formulates a pecking order for all the rules and procedures that are incorporated in the preparation of financial statements and that have come to be known as GAAP.

The GAAP hierarchy includes four successive categories (A to D), each of which establishes a different level of authority. Generally speaking, if there is a conflict between accounting principles relevant to the circumstances from one or more sources in Categories A, B, C, or D, the treatment specified by the source in the higher category is then followed. In other words, Categories A through D of the hierarchy descend in authority. Therefore, Category A takes precedence over all others, Category B takes precedence over Categories C and D, and Category C takes precedence over Category D. If a situation is not covered by guidelines in Categories A through D, other accounting literature should be considered. However, that literature should be consulted only when guidelines in higher categories are not applicable.

Category A. Category A consists of the following officially established accounting principles: (1) FASB Statements of Financial Accounting Standards, (2) FASB Interpretations, (3) APB Opinions, and (4) AICPA Accounting Research Bulletins. All of those accounting principles are included in Volumes I and II of *Original Pronouncements*, which is updated annually and published by the FASB. In addition, FASB Statements and Interpretations are available individually from the FASB as published.

The accounting principles included in Category A are often referred to as "Rule 203 pronouncements" because the bodies responsible for establishing those principles have been so designated by the AICPA Council, pursuant to Rule 203 of the AICPA Code of Professional Conduct. Specifically, from September 1939 to August 1959 the AICPA committees on terminology and on accounting procedure were responsible for issuing fifty-one Accounting Research Bulletins (ARBs). In 1953, the first forty-two of those were revised, restated, or withdrawn and now appear as ARB No. 43, *Restatement and Revision of Accounting Research Bulletins*. On September 1, 1959, the AICPA committees were superseded by the APB, which issued thirty-one Opinions until it ceased operations in June 1973. At that time, the FASB took over the responsibilities of standard setting from the APB and as of March 31, 2000, had issued 137 Statements of Financial Accounting Standards and forty-four Interpretations.

Category B. Category B consists of (1) FASB Technical Bulletins and, if cleared by the FASB, (2) AICPA Statements of Position and (3) AICPA Industry Audit and Accounting Guides. Technical Bulletins are available individually from the FASB as published and are also included collectively in Volume II of *Original Pronouncements*. Statements of Position and Audit and Accounting Guides

are available individually from the AICPA as published. In addition, Statements of Position are included collectively in *AICPA Technical Practice Aids*.

FASB Technical Bulletins provide timely guidance for applying Category A accounting principles and resolving accounting issues not directly addressed in those principles. The following kinds of guidance may be provided in a Technical Bulletin:

• Guidance that clarifies, explains, or elaborates on an underlying standard.

• Guidance for a particular situation (usually a specific industry) that differs from the general application required by the standard in an ARB, APB Opinion, or FASB Statement or Interpretation. For example, the guidance in a Bulletin may specify that the standard does not apply to enterprises in a particular industry or may provide for deferral of the effective date of a standard for that industry.

• Guidance that addresses areas not directly covered by existing standards.

The AICPA's Accounting Standards Executive Committee (AcSEC), which works closely with the FASB and its staff, is the senior technical committee of the AICPA authorized to set accounting standards and to speak for the AICPA on accounting matters. AcSEC's standard-setting activities are often industry-specific or narrow in scope, whereas the FASB's activities result in standards that are more general and broader in scope. AcSEC issues AICPA Statements of Position, which present conclusions with respect to an emerging problem or diversity in practice. In addition, AcSEC issues AICPA Audit and Accounting Guides, which either interpret GAAP as applicable to a specific industry or, in some cases, establish industry-specific GAAP. For example, Guides have been published for agricultural producers and cooperatives, airlines, casinos, construction contractors, and health care organizations.

Category C. Category C consists of (1) AcSEC Practice Bulletins that have been cleared by the FASB and (2) consensus positions of the FASB Emerging Issues Task Force (EITF). AcSEC Practice Bulletins are available individually from the AICPA as published and are also included collectively in *AICPA Technical Practice Aids*. Consensus positions of the EITF are available individually from the FASB as published and are included collectively in *EITF Abstracts*, which is published by the FASB.

The EITF was established by the FASB in 1984 to assist in the early identification of emerging issues affecting financial reporting and of problems in implementing authoritative pronouncements. Each EITF Abstract summarizes the accounting issue involved and the results of the EITF discussion, including any consensus reached on the issue. Each Abstract also reports, in its "status" section, subsequent developments on that issue, such as issuance of a relevant Securities and Exchange Commission Staff Accounting Bulletin or an FASB Technical Bulletin. If the EITF can reach consensus on an issue, usually that is taken as an indication that no action is needed by the FASB or AcSEC. Alternatively, if no consensus is possible, it may be an indication that action by one of those bodies is necessary.

AcSEC Practice Bulletins are used to disseminate AcSEC's views for the purpose of providing practitioners and preparers with guidance on narrow financial accounting and reporting issues. The issues covered by Practice Bulletins are limited to those that have not been and are not being considered by the FASB. Therefore, AcSEC Practice Bulletins, which are reviewed by the FASB, are only issued after the FASB has informed AcSEC that it has no current plans to consider the issue.

Category D. Category D includes (1) AICPA Accounting Interpretations, (2) FASB staff implementation guides, and (3) practices that are widely recognized and prevalent either generally or in an industry.

AICPA Accounting Interpretations (not to be confused with FASB Interpretations, which are included in Category A) were issued from March 1971 through November 1973. The purpose of the interpretations was to provide timely guidance for applying APB Opinions without the formal procedures required for an APB Opinion. In addition, they were used to clarify points on which past practice may have varied and been considered generally accepted. The interpretations, prepared by AICPA staff and reviewed by members of the accounting profession, are not considered to be official pronouncements of the APB. Although most of the interpretations have been superseded by other accounting standards, Volume II of *Original Pronouncements* includes those that continue in effect as well as reference pages for those that have been superseded.

Implementation guides, which appear in a question-and-answer format, are issued as aids to understanding and implementing various FASB Statements. Typically, those guides are issued when an unusually high number of inquiries are received and the accounting required by a given FASB Statement is particularly complex. The positions and opinions expressed in those guides are those of the FASB staff and do not represent official positions of the FASB. Staff implementation guides are available individually from the FASB as published and also are included collectively in *FASB Staff Implementation Guides*.

OTHER ACCOUNTING LITERATURE

Occasionally new transactions or events for which there are no established accounting principles must be reported. In those instances, it is sometimes possible to identify an analogous transaction or event for which there is an established principle and report the new transaction or event similarly. In the absence of a pronouncement in one of the four categories above or an analogous transaction or event, other accounting literature should be considered. Examples of other literature include FASB Concepts Statements; APB Statements; AICPA (AcSEC) Issues Papers; pronouncements of other accounting standard-setting bodies, professional associations, or regulatory agencies; technical information service inquiries; and accounting textbooks, handbooks, and articles.

SUMMARY

Generally accepted accounting principles are not a set of specific circumscribed standards that can be easily found in one convenient set of rules. Rather, they are an amalgam arising from various sources and with an established hierarchy. Generally accepted accounting principles range from official standards established by the FASB, through literature from the AICPA, to, in some situations, articles. Yet the system seems to work reasonably well. Financial statements prepared pursuant to GAAP are highly regarded in the United States for the quality and comparability of the information they provide. Thus, investors and other users have been well served by our system of financial reporting, which results in the fair presentation of financial information prepared in conformity with generally accepted accounting principles.

SEE ALSO *Accounting*

BIBLIOGRAPHY
Financial Accounting Standards Board (1999). *Accounting Standards: Vol. I. General Standards; Topical Index; Vol. II: Industry Standards; Topical Index/Appendixes.* New York: Wiley.

Edmund L. Jenkins
Cheri Reither Mazza

GLOBAL ECONOMY

Global economy is the exchange of goods and services integrated into a huge single global market. It is virtually a world without borders, inhabited by marketing individuals and/or companies who have joined the geographical world with the intent of conducting research and development and making sales.

International trade permits countries to specialize in the resources they have. Countries benefit by producing goods and services they can provide most cheaply and by buying the goods and services other countries can provide most cheaply. International trade makes it possible for more goods to be produced and for more human wants to be satisfied than if every country tries by itself to produce everything it needs.

U.S. FOREIGN TRADE

The United States is one of the world's leading trading nations. The exports and imports of the United States thrive so mightily that the profits of many large businesses, the jobs and incomes of many workers, and the incomes of many farmers are dependent upon them.

In such a market, companies may source from the United States, conduct research and development in another country, take orders in a third country, and sell wherever there exists demand, regardless of the customer's nationality.

CAUSES OF INCREASING GLOBALIZATION

In the days of Scottish economist Adam Smith (1723–1790), if a merchant wanted to trade a lot of wool for a case of port wine, the communication of that intent would require weeks. Sending a message to someone in India took months. Such circumstances lent themselves to fragmented and individualized markets run by family members or close friends. These industry managers were trusted to make decisions in the best interests of the company because no rapid means of communicating existed. The opportunity to closely coordinate the act of several foreign operations simply did not exist.

In the early twenty-first century, communication between most parts of the world is instantaneous. A manager in Berlin, Germany, can phone or e-mail a manager in Rio de Janeiro, Brazil, to discuss the latest news regarding the orange crop. These new capabilities allow vast amounts of business data to be transferred globally almost instantaneously at a reasonable cost. The world truly has become a smaller place in terms of communication.

Technological advances have increased the potential for the transportation of goods and individuals globally. This reality encourages a global market approach to business as companies attempt to reach the largest number of consumers at the lowest possible prices.

Another factor leading to a more globalized marketplace is the historical decrease in tariff and nontariff barriers. In 1930 the United States raised tariffs under the Hawley-Smoot Tariff Act. Other countries followed suit, and international trade slowed considerably. In 1947 sev-

eral leading trading nations created the General Agreement on Tariffs and Trade to serve as a forum for bringing down trade barriers. Between 1947 and 1994, trading countries around the world participated in eight rounds of negotiating in an effort to reduce tariffs.

Another agreement, the North American Free Trade Agreement, was implemented by Canada, Mexico, and the United States in 1994. This agreement reduced tariffs over a fifteen-year period, lifted many investment restrictions, allowed for easier movement of white-collar workers, opened up government procurement over a ten-year period, and created a mechanism for dispute resolution. As a result, retailers such as Wal-Mart and 7-Eleven have expanded operations into Mexico and many Mexican and Canadian firms have been enjoying the benefits of participating in the world's largest consumer market, the United States.

Multinational corporations search the globe for the lowest possible labor costs and weakest environmental safeguards. It is not unusual for them to get help from undemocratic governments that compete in the global marketplace by refusing to protect their citizens from environmental degradation and workplace abuse—ranging from below-survival wages to physical attacks.

OTHER FACTORS AFFECTING THE GLOBAL ECONOMY

Closely related to the liberalization of trade, technological advantages, and the convergence of consumer preferences are a set of competitive factors centered around the ideas of economies of scale (larger production volumes generating lower per-unit production costs) and locational advantages.

Another factor affecting the global economy has been the shifting of production among various plants located outside of the United States. This has occurred most significantly with the People's Republic of China. China is able to produce a wide variety of goods and services at much lower costs than is possible in the United States.

Overall, the future for the global economy is positive. Many challenges lie ahead, but the overall opportunity is very exciting and carries with it many unknown adventures in international trade in ways not yet known.

SEE ALSO *International Business; International Marketing; International Trade*

BIBLIOGRAPHY

Adonis, A. (1994, September 17). Lines open for the global village. *Financial Times*, p. 8.

Braithwaite, John, and Drahos, Peter (2000). *Global business regulation.* New York: Cambridge University Press.

Czinkota, Michael R., Ronkainen, Ilkka A., and Donath, Bob (2004). *Mastering global markets: Strategies for today's trade globalist.* Mason, OH: Thomson/Southwestern.

Global economic integration. (n.d.). Retrieved February 22, 2006, from About.com Web site: http://economics.about.com/od/useconomichistory/a/global.htm

Hill, Charles W. L. (2006). *Global business today* (4th ed.). Boston: McGraw-Hill/Irwin.

What is global economy? Retrieved February 7, 2006, from PR Resource Center Web site: http://www.ailins.com/agency/PR/unions/global_economy.html

G. W. Maxwell

GOALS AND OBJECTIVES

SEE *Management: Authority and Responsibility*

GOODS AND SERVICES

Goods and services are the outputs offered by businesses to satisfy the demands of consumer and industrial markets. They are differentiated on the basis of four characteristics:

1. *Tangibility:* Goods are tangible products such as cars, clothing, and machinery. They have shape and can be seen and touched. Services are intangible. Hair styling, pest control, and equipment repair, for example, do not have a physical presence.

2. *Perishability:* All goods have some degree of durability beyond the time of purchase. Services do not; they perish as they are delivered.

3. *Separability:* Goods can be stored for later use. Thus, production and consumption are typically separate. Because the production and consumption of services are simultaneous, services and the service provider cannot be separated.

4. *Standardization:* The quality of goods can be controlled through standardization and grading in the production process. The quality of services, however, is different each time they are delivered.

For the purpose of developing marketing strategies, particularly product planning and promotion, goods and services are categorized in two ways. One is to designate their position on a goods and services continuum. The second is to place them into a classification system.

The goods and services continuum enables marketers to see the relative goods/services composition of total products. A product's position on the continuum, in turn, enables marketers to spot opportunities. At the pure goods end of the continuum, goods that have no related services are positioned. At the pure services end are services that are not associated with physical products. Products that are a combination of goods and services fall between the two ends. For example, goods such as furnaces, which require accompanying services such as delivery and installation, are situated toward the pure goods end. Products that involve the sale of both goods and services, such as auto repair, are near the center. And products that are primarily services but rely on physical equipment, such as taxis, are located toward the pure services end.

The second approach to categorizing products is to classify them on the basis of their uses. This organization facilitates the identification of prospective users and the design of strategies to reach them. The major distinction in this system is between consumer and industrial products. Consumer goods and services are those that are purchased for personal, family, or household use. Industrial goods and services are products that companies buy to make the products they sell.

Two major changes have affected the marketing and production of goods and services since about 1950. The first was a shift in marketing philosophy from the belief that consumers could be convinced to buy whatever was produced to the marketing concept, in which consumer expectations became the driving force in determining what was to be produced and marketed. This change in orientation has resulted in increases in both lines of products and choices within the lines.

The second change was an increased demand for services. The growth in demand for services—and resulting production—continues to increase at a faster rate than the demand for manufactured goods.

SEE ALSO *Marketing*

BIBLIOGRAPHY

Bearden, William O., Ingram, Thomas N., and LaForge, Raymond W. (2007). *Marketing, Principles and Perspectives.* Boston: McGraw-Hill/Irwin.

Evans, Joel R., and Berman, Barry (2002). *Marketing: Marketing in the 21st Century* (8th ed.). Cincinnati, OH: Atomicdog-Publishing.Com.

Earl C. Meyer
Matthew F. Hazzard

GOVERNMENT ACCOUNTING

Government accounting has been viewed historically as a key element in the movement from absolute power, (i.e., the government or a king or emperor) to relative power (i.e., a shared model of government). Under the shared model of government, government accounting was used by a parliament to limit the king's power to (1) spend public money, (2) raise taxes to cover the expenditures, and (3) determine the purpose of the expenditure. The use of governmental accounting remained unchanged during the evolution into modern democratic systems.

Thus government accounting requires the executive to (1) state the amount, nature, and purpose of the planned expenditure and the taxes needed to fund it, (2) ask for and obtain approval from the legislature, and (3) comply with the expenditure authority—appropriation—granted by the legislature and demonstrate such compliance. Under government accounting, the legislature is allowed to steer and control the behavior of the government.

The basic foundation of governmental financial accounting and reporting in the United States was established by the Governmental Accounting Standards Boards (GASB) in its "Objectives of Financial Reporting," which stated that the purpose of financial reporting is to provide information to facilitate decision making by various groups (GASB, 1987). The groups were defined as (1) citizens of the governmental entity, (2) direct representatives of the citizens, such as legislatures and oversight bodies, and (3) investors, creditors, and others who are involved in the lending process. Although not specifically identified, intergovernmental agencies and other users have informational needs similar to the three primary user groups. While the three user groups have overlapping membership with corporate financial information users, citizens and legislative users are unique to governments. The use of governmental accounting information centers on political, social, and economic decisions in addition to determining the government's accountability.

Accountability (GASB, 1987, 56-58) was identified as the paramount objective of governmental financial reporting because it is based on the transfer of responsibility for resources or actions from the citizens to some other party, such as the management of the governmental entity. The assessment of accountability is fulfilled when financial reporting enables financial data users to determine to what extent current-period costs are financed by current-period revenues. Two basic types of budgets are used by governments and are the same as those used by corporate entities—an annual operating budget and a capital budget. Governmental annual operating budgets include estimated revenues and appropriations for expenditure for a specific fiscal year. Capital budgets control the expenditures for construction projects and fixed asset acquisitions. Operating or capital budgets are recorded in the accounting system as a means of control or compliance.

Many governmental entities are required by law to maintain a balanced budget in that revenues must equal or exceed appropriations; the latter situation results in a budgetary surplus. If a budgetary deficit occurs in a governmental entity with a balanced-budget requirement, additional appropriations must be enacted by the legislative process.

Governmental accounting uses a fund accounting structure as a means of controlling resources. That is, each type of financial activity is segregated into a separate set of self-balancing asset, liability, and net asset accounts. GASB codification identifies three fund groups—governmental, proprietary, and fiduciary (GASB, 1999, Sections 1100.103 and 1100.105). Governmental funds are used to account for financial resources used in the day-to-day operations of the government. Proprietary funds are those used to account for the government's business-type activities where fees are charged for the services rendered, for example, utility services. Fiduciary funds are those used to account for funds held by the government in trust for others that cannot be used to support the government's programs, for example, an employee pension fund.

State and local governments report dual-perspective financial information with both full accrual information and fund-based modified accrual information in accordance with GASB Standard No. 34, *Basic Financial Statements—and Management Discussion and Analysis—for Statement and Local Governments* (GASB, 1999).

The management's discussion and analysis (MD&A) is required supplementary information presented before the financial statements that is subjected to limited auditor review and presents an overview of the government's financial activities for the part year. This narrative description of the financial performance is much like the management discussion required of corporations by the Securities and Exchange Commission (SEC). The MD&A provides an objective and easily readable analysis of the government's financial activities based on currently known facts, decisions, or conditions. The discussion compares the government's current-year results with the previous year and may include charts, graphs, or tables to illustrate the discussion. The discussion is general rather than specific so that the most relevant information is provided. At a minimum, fourteen prescribed elements are a part of the MD&A discussion. These elements explain the relationship among the financial statements and any significant differences in the information provided in the financial statement.

The full accrual information reports the full cost of providing government services, with details on how much of the cost is borne by taxpayers and by specific users of the government's service. The full accrual reports are similar to those of profit-seeking corporations. The government's equity is displayed as net assets rather than stockholders' equity. The full accrual results of the government's financial activity are displayed in two government-wide reports—(1) the statement of net assets and (2) the statement of activities.

The statement of net assets displays information about the government as a whole, reports all financial and capital resources, and assists the financial statement user in assessing the medium- and long-term operational accountability of the government. Separate columns are used to distinguish between the financial data for the governmental activities and the business-type activities that comprise the total primary government. As the term *statement of net assets* implies, the statement format presents the assets minus liabilities that equal the total net assets, that is, equity. Assets and liabilities are presented in their order of liquidity. That is, assets are presented in the order to their nearness to producing cash, and liabilities are presented in the order to their nearness to consuming cash. Assets and liabilities may be displayed in a classified, current, and noncurrent format if desired. The government's net assets are presented in three components: (1) capital assets net of related accumulated depreciation and debt, (2) restricted net assets with constraints imposed on their use by parties outside the government, and (3) unrestricted net assets.

The statement of activities reports the net expense over revenue of each individual function or program operated by the government. The net expense over revenue format reports the relative financial burden of each of the programs on the government's resource provides—taxpayers. The format highlights the extent to which each program directly consumes the government's revenues or is financed by fees, contributions, or other revenues.

In addition to the government-wide full accrual information, state and local governments present financial statements on the fund-based modified accrual basis. In the modified accrual basis of accounting, revenues are recognized only when they become both measurable and available to finance expenditures for the fiscal period. Expenditures are recognized when the related liabilities are incurred, if measurable, except for unmatured interest on long-term debt, which is recognized when legally due.

Fund-based financial statements assist in assessing the government's short-term fiscal accountability. Most funds are established by governments to show restrictions on the planned use of resources or to measure, in the short-term, the revenues and expenditures of a particular activity.

Fund activity displayed in the fund-based financial statements is grouped by governmental, proprietary, and fiduciary categories as identified by the GASB codification. The equity component of modified accrual fund-based financial statements is reported as fund balance rather than net assets, which is used in the full accrual statement.

A balance sheet and a statement of revenues, expenditures, and change in fund balance are required for each of the three fund groups. Because the fund financial statements are prepared using the modified accrual basis, a required reconciliation is prepared that explains the differences between the net change in fund balances and the change in net assets in the government-wide statement of activities. The proprietary funds also present a statement of cash flows. Unlike corporate cash flow statements, the governmental cash flow statement is prepared using the direct method and has four categories—operating, noncapital financing, capital financing, and investing activities.

Although some similarities exist between accounting for state and local governments and accounting for the federal government, there are selected areas specific to each. For example, federal agencies account for quarterly apportionments to procure goods and services, a process that is generally ignored by state and local governments. The head of each agency in the executive branch of the federal government has the responsibility for establishing and maintaining accounting and control systems in conformity with principles, standards, and requirements established by the Federal Accounting Standards Advisory Board and the Federal Financial Management Improvement Act of 1996.

Federal accounting provides the information needed for financial management as well as the information needed to demonstrate compliance with budgetary and other legal requirements. Thus, federal accounting is based on a two-track system. One track is a self-balancing set of proprietary accounts intended to provide information for management. The other track is a set of self-balancing budgetary accounts that assure that available budgetary resources and authorities are not overexpended or overobligated and assist in budgetary reporting requirements.

Like its state and local government counterpart, the federal financial statements include an MD&A that provides a clear and concise description of the reporting entity and its mission, activities, program and financial results, and financial condition (OMB, 1996). Federal financial statements are less prescriptive than state and local financial statements because federal agencies are permitted significant latitude on the level of aggregation presented. The six statements in the federal financial report include a (1) balance sheet, (2) statement of net cost, (3) statement of changes in net position, (4) statement of budgetary resources, (5) statement of financing, and (6) statement of custodial activity.

SEE ALSO *Government Auditing Standards; Government Financial Reporting; Governmental Accounting Standards Board; Not-for-Profit Accounting*

BIBLIOGRAPHY

Federal Financial Management Improvement Act (1996). Public Law 104-208.

Governmental Accounting Standards Board (GASB) (1987). *Objectives of Financial Reporting.* (Concept Statement No. 1). Norwalk, CT: GASB of the Financial Accounting Foundation.

Governmental Accounting Standards Board (GASB) (1999). *Basic Financial Statements—and Management's Discussion and Analysis—for State and Local Governments* (Statement of Governmental Accounting Standard No. 34). Norwalk, CT: GASB of the Financial Accounting Foundation.

Governmental Accounting Standards Board (GASB) (2005). *Codification of Government Accounting and Financial Reporting Standards.* Norwalk, CT: GASB of the Financial Accounting Foundation.

Office of Management and Budget (OMB) (1996). *Bulletin 97-1,* Form and Content of Agency Financial Statements. U.S. Government, Washington. DC.

Mary L. Fischer

GOVERNMENT AUDITING STANDARDS

Government Auditing Standards, often referred to as the *Yellow Book,* is the publication that presents generally accepted government auditing standards (GAGAS) promulgated under the leadership of the comptroller general of the United States, who heads the U.S. Government Accountability Office. (At the time of the 2003 revision of the standards, the name of this office was the U.S. General Accounting Office.)

THE AUTHORITY OF GOVERNMENT AUDITING STANDARDS

The *Yellow Book* includes standards to guide all audits of governmental units, irrespective of the level of the unit, as well as guidance for reviews and agreed-upon procedures. The comptroller general noted:

> These standards are broad statements of auditors' responsibilities. They provide an overall framework for ensuring that auditors have the compe-

tence, integrity, ... objectivity, and independence in planning, conducting, and reporting on their work. (*Yellow Book,* p. 1)

RELATIONSHIP BETWEEN GAGAS AND OTHER PROFESSIONAL STANDARDS

The *Yellow Book* recognizes the value of other professional standards. Incorporated in this volume are the fieldwork and reporting standards and related statements on auditing standards for financial audits as declared by the Auditing Standards Board of the American Institute of Certified Public Accountants (AICPA), unless specifically excluded in the guidance in the *Yellow Book.* The AICPA general standard on criteria, and the fieldwork and reporting standards and related statements for attestation engagements, are also included, unless excluded specifically (p. 8).

LIMITATION OF THE *YELLOW BOOK*

The title, *Government Auditing Standards,* is somewhat misleading, because the guidance extends to engagements that are not audits. The June 2003 edition, considered a revision of the edition issued in June 1994, is, however, markedly different. In addition to audits, the 2003 edition includes guidance for engagements.

In the 2003 edition, even though nonaudit engagements are included, the same statement is required in reports of all engagements, which is "that the engagement was made in accordance with GAGAS." Yet, engagements that are reviews or agreed-upon procedures have different requirements, which do not include the rigorous standards of audits. The statement "in accordance with GAGAS" is not sufficiently specific since strategies and procedures differ markedly among audits (or examinations), reviews and agreed-upon procedures. The reader should be provided with more identifying information.

The Auditing Standards Board of the AICPA, on the other hand, provides guidance for reporting that requires reports to state explicitly the type of engagement completed and the guidance followed. A basic requirement for any report provided by a public accountant is that the report must not be any way be misleading or incomplete as to its nature, scope, and level of assurance.

THE GUIDANCE FOR AUDITS AND EXAMINATIONS

Financial audits, attestation examinations (considered an equivalent term to audits), and performance audits are guided by GAGAS.

Financial audits. These audits are completed primarily to provide reasonable assurance about whether financial statements are presented fairly in all material respects in conformity with generally accepted accounting principles (GAAP), or with a comprehensive basis of accounting, other than GAAP. Additionally, auditing compliance with regulations is included in this category.

Attestation examination. As noted in the guidance, "attestation engagements can cover a broad range of financial or nonfinancial subjects and can be a part of a financial audit or performance audit."

Performance audits. Such audits include systematic examination of relevant evidence to provide an independent assessment of the performance of a government organization, program, activity, or function.

Engagements that are combinations. A government audit may be a combination of the foregoing types. For example, external auditors conduct audits of government contracts and grants with private-sector organizations where financial, attestation, and performance objectives are audited. Furthermore, an audit engagement may be extended to include nonaudit activities for which the assurance is not equivalent to that provided as a result of an audit.

GENERAL STANDARDS FOR ALL ENGAGEMENTS

The introduction to Chapter 3 on general standards states: "These general standards concern the fundamental requirements for ensuring the credibility auditors' work.... These general standards provide the underlying framework that is critical in effectively applying the field work and reporting standards" (p. 27).

General standards require that the audit entity be organizationally independent and that the individual auditors assigned to an engagement maintain independence in attitude and in appearance and use professional judgment in both planning and performing audits. Staff assigned to perform an audit should collectively possess adequate professional competence for tasks assigned. Moreover, the audit organization must have an appropriate internal quality control system that is evaluated by external peer reviewers.

FIELD STANDARDS FOR FINANCIAL AUDITS

The field standards of GAGAS incorporate the three field standards as established by the AICPA's Auditing Standards Board, which relate to planning, understanding internal control, and obtaining sufficient evidential matter. Additional standards of GAGAS relate to the following: auditor communication, consideration of previous audits' results, detection of material misstatements, development of elements of a finding, and audit documentation.

REPORTING STANDARDS

Reporting standards incorporate the four reporting statements of the Auditing Standards Board. Those statements require that:

1. Financial statements are presented in accordance with generally accepted accounting principles

2. Any change in consistency is reported, even if auditor approved of such change

3. Disclosures are informative and are reasonably adequate

4. There is an expression of opinion

Additionally, these standards also require reporting:

- Auditors' compliance with GAGAS

- Internal control and compliance with laws, regulations, and provisions of contracts or grant agreements

- Deficiencies in internal control, fraud, illegal acts, violations of provisions of contracts or grant agreements, and abuse

- Views of responsible officials

- Privileged and confidential information

- Issuance and distribution details

GENERAL, FIELD, AND REPORTING STANDARDS FOR ATTESTATION EXAMINATIONS

In addition to the general standards for all engagements, the *Yellow Book*'s attestation standards accept the AICPA's general standard for attestation examinations that relates to criteria which must be available for the completion of such an engagement. Additionally, there are the following:

Field standards. The AICPA's attestation field standards related to examinations that require planning and obtaining sufficient evidence are accepted as field standards for GAGAS. The subjects of GAGAS field standards are: auditor communication; consideration of results of previous audits and attestation engagements; internal control; detection of fraud, illegal acts, violations of contracts and grant agreements and abuse; development elements of findings; and documentation of planning, evidence, and conclusions.

Reporting standards. The AICPA's reporting standards for all levels of reporting under attestation engagements are accepted for GAGAS. These are:

1. Subject matter or assertion and the character of the engagement are to be identified

2. Conclusions in relation the criteria are presented

3. Reservations that are significant, if any, are stated

4. If use of the report is restricted (specific circumstances are provided in the guidance)

GAGAS also prescribes the following standards that report:

- Auditors' compliance with GAGAS

- Deficiencies in internal control, fraud, illegal acts, violations of provisions of contracts or grants, and abuse

- Views of responsible officials

- Privileged and confidential information

- Issuance and distribution details

FIELD AND REPORTING STANDARDS FOR PERFORMANCE AUDITS

Field and reporting standards for performance audits overlap to some extent with those for financial audits. Field standards are related to (1) planning; (2) supervision; (3) design of the audit when laws, regulations, and other compliance requirements are significant to the audit objective; (4) understanding of management controls when relevant to the audit; and (5) sufficient, competent, relevant evidence.

Reporting standards are related to (1) preparation of written reports that communicate results; (2) appropriate issuance; (3) reporting audit objectives as well as scope and methodology; (4) the need for a complete, accurate, objective, convincing, and clear and concise report; and (5) report distribution.

THE IMPACT OF THE PUBLIC COMPANY ACCOUNTABILITY OVERSIGHT BOARD

With the passage of the Sarbanes-Oxley Act of 2002 and the subsequent establishment of the Public Company Accountability Oversight Board (PCAOB), a process of evaluating current auditing guidance and developing new guidance began. The comptroller general of the United

States noted: "As the PCAOB promulgates auditing standards for audits of these entities, GAO will continue to closely monitor the actions of both standard setting bodies [AICPA and PCAOB] and will issue clarifying guidance as necessary on the incorporation of future standards by either standard setting body" (*Yellow Book,* pp. 3, 4).

In mid-2005, for example, GAO provided guidance that allowed auditors to prepare GAGAS reports on internal control based on the definition of "material weakness" contained in PCAOB's Auditing Standard No. 2—Audit of Internal Control over Financial Reporting Performed in Conjunction with an Audit of Financial Statements.

SEE ALSO *Government Accounting; United States Government Accountability Office*

BIBLIOGRAPHY

U.S. Government Accounting Office. http://www.gao.gov

U.S. Government Accounting Office. Comptroller General of the United States. (2001, June). *Federal Information Systems controls audit manual: Vol. 1. Financial statements audits AIMD-12.19.s.* Retrieved November 14, 2005, from http://www.gao.gov/special.pubs/afm.html

U.S. Government Accounting Office. Comptroller General of the United States. (2004). *GAO/PCIE [President's Council on Integrity and Efficiency] financial audit manual (including July 2004 updates).* Retrieved November 14, 2005, from http://www.gao.gov/special.pubs/gaopcie

U.S. Government Accountability Office. Comptroller General of the United States. (2003, June). *Government auditing standards (The yellow book).* Washington, DC: GAO.

Bernard H. Newman
Mary Ellen Oliverio

GOVERNMENT FINANCIAL REPORTING

Government financial reporting is the process whereby governments report their financial position and activities to the public at large. These reports are the standard that citizens, oversight bodies, and other stakeholders use to judge their government's efficiency, effectiveness, and overall financial condition. This article examines government financial reporting from a historical perspective and will discuss this contemporary issue at the federal level.

HISTORY

Government financial reporting at the state and local levels evolved throughout of the twentieth century. The National Committee on Municipal Accounting (NCMA) was established in 1934 by the Government Finance Offi-

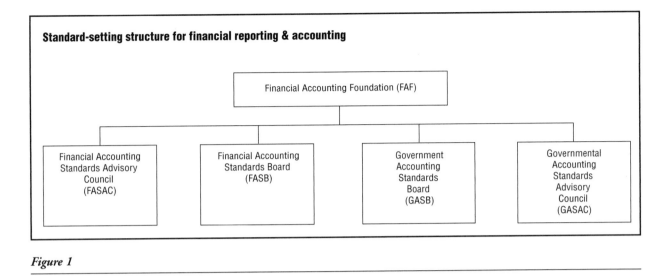

Standard-setting structure for financial reporting & accounting

Financial Accounting Foundation (FAF)

Financial Accounting Standards Advisory Council (FASAC)

Financial Accounting Standards Board (FASB)

Government Accounting Standards Board (GASB)

Governmental Accounting Standards Advisory Council (GASAC)

Figure 1

cers Association and began to promulgate formal standards. It issued the first "blue book" in 1936, Bulletin No. 6, *Municipal Accounting Statements*. From that point, government financial reporting, along with government accounting and auditing, began to develop into what it is in the early twenty-first century.

The National Council on Governmental Accounting (NCGA), which succeeded the NCMA, initiated the basic format of the current blue book, which was later officially titled *Governmental Accounting, Auditing and Financial Reporting* (*GAAFR*). In 1968 generally accepted accounting principles (GAAP) for government were established in *GAAFR*. Government accountants and financial managers use the blue book to this day as a reference for current standards and practices in government financial reporting.

In the past, some confusion existed concerning who set the standards that constituted GAAP for governments. This issue became prominent when the American Institute of Certified Public Accountants (AICPA) issued an industry audit guide in 1974 that, while endorsing most, modified principles set forth by the NCGA. The AICPA later recognized NCGA Statement No. 1, *Governmental Accounting and Financial Reporting Principles*. Even after this statement was recognized, questions still arose. Conflicts with the standards set by the NCGA generally were associated with pronouncements issued by the Financial Accounting Standards Board. These conflicts were not resolved until the Governmental Accounting Standards Board (GASB) was established in 1984. From then on, the GASB was clearly established as the primary authority for setting government standards.

The GASB was created as a five-member board under the Financial Accounting Foundation (FAF). In addition to the GASB, the FAF also established the Governmental Accounting Standards Advisory Council (GASAC) to

advise the GASB of its members' views and the views of the organizations they represent. The GASAC assists the FAF in approving appointments of GASB members. Figure 1 illustrates the relationships among these bodies.

FINANCIAL REPORTING AT PRESENT

Generally, government financial reporting is the process of communicating information concerning a government's financial position and activities. Government financial reports have several practical uses: They can be used to compare actual financial results against the legally adopted budget; assess financial condition and results of operations; assist in determining compliance with finance-related laws, rules, and regulations; and assist in evaluating efficiency and effectiveness. Although government financial reports cannot meet the needs of every user, they can be used in many ways to assess accountability and to make effective decisions.

At the federal level, the Office of Management and Budget (OMB) promulgates reporting standards. The office responsible for this function within the OMB is the Office of Federal Financial Management. Pursuant to the Chief Financial Officers Act of 1990, a deputy director for management was established within the OMB to coordinate financial management functions with the various federal agencies. Moreover, each agency of the federal government is required to specify a chief financial officer who is responsible for financial reporting, as well as all other financial management functions.

Each executive agency is required to prepare and submit audited financial statements to OMB after each fiscal year. One such report is a combined Performance and Accountability Report, which is designed to obtain a more accurate picture of agency performance in terms of both operational performance and financial information. Once the reports are submitted by the agencies, the U.S. Department of the Treasury, in consultation with the OMB, issues the *Financial Report of the United States Government.*

At the state and local levels, GASB has the responsibility to establish and improve financial reporting standards. Three primary user categories of government financial reports exist: citizens, legislative and oversight bodies, and investors and creditors. The executive branch and subordinate bureaus/agencies are not identified as primary users because they possess the ability to obtain this information from other sources.

Although various internal and supplemental financial reports exist, the most common is the comprehensive annual financial report (CAFR). The GASB's 1987 *Codification of Governmental Accounting and Financial Reporting Standards* stated, "every government should prepare and publish as a matter of public record, a comprehensive annual financial report." A trend toward fiscal discipline in government has generated a demand for better information on which to base decisions. Consequently, state and local governments changed their financial reporting from basic stewardship reports on the various government funds to a more corporate-style report that offers analysis of the long-term impact of financial management decisions. Specifically, as a result of GASB Statement 34, financial reports now include comprehensive information about the cost of providing government services and show all of a government's liabilities and assets, including infrastructure. GASB Statement 34 called for government-wide reporting, enhanced fund reporting, and a management discussion and analysis.

The concept of government-wide reporting was the most dramatic change. Until this significant change, government followed only the modified-accrual basis of accounting. The change is important to potential lenders and taxpayers because of the need to capitalize and depreciate general capital assets or infrastructure. Information concerning infrastructure will include the cost and the anticipated service life of roads, bridges, sewer and water systems and other capital assets. Since state and local governments invest $1 out of every $10 ($140 billion to $150 billion annually) in the construction, improvement, and rehabilitation of capital assets, that information should be valuable to all stakeholders.

The elements of fund reporting have not changed much over the years. Fund categories continue to apply their current measurement focus and basis of accounting; nevertheless, reporting fund types (such as special revenue and capital projects) is no longer required for governmental funds in the basic financial statements according to GASB Statement 34. This approach established two new fund types, permanent funds (governmental) and private-purpose trust funds (fiduciary). Governments must also provide a reconciliation to the government-wide financial statements at the bottom of fund statements or in a separate schedule.

A CONTEMPORARY FEDERAL ISSUE: OMB CIRCULAR A-123

In response to the Sarbanes-Oxley Act of 2002, requirements of which increased internal control responsibilities for management and auditors of publicly traded companies, the OMB announced a rewrite of OMB Circular A-123 on December 21, 2004. The official title of this circular is *Management's Responsibility for Internal Control,* but it is dubbed by many government financial mangers as "Sarbanes-Oxley for Government." It contains sweeping changes to many aspects of federal financial reporting. The revision of this document is an effort by the OMB to help ensure that federal agencies' fiduciary responsibilities for public funds are fulfilled by strengthening requirements related to evaluation, documentation, and reporting on internal controls.

The specific objectives of internal controls, as defined by OMB Circular A-123, are threefold: effective and efficient operations, reliable financial reporting, and compliance with applicable laws and regulations. As such, the changes announced in the circular were in keeping with the objectives. Effective in fiscal year 2006, federal agencies must:

- Assess and document their internal controls over financial reporting

- Document their assessment of the effectiveness and reliability of those internal controls

- Provide a separate assurance statement as part of the annual Federal Managers Financial Integrity Act Section 2 (assurances asserting whether the internal controls over financial reporting are effective)

SUMMARY

Citizens and other stakeholders use government financial reports to assess a government's performance and overall financial position in order to hold a government accountable for its actions. At the federal level, the OMB promulgates reporting standards and reviews audited financial statements from each agency. In turn, the Department of the Treasury, in consultation with the OMB, issues the *Financial Report of the United States Government* each fiscal year. In response to the Sarbanes-Oxley Act, the OMB announced a rewrite of OMB Circular A-123, which contains sweeping changes to many aspects of federal financial reporting, effective in fiscal year 2006.

At the state and local levels, the process of government financial reporting evolved during the twentieth century. The blue book, or *GAAFR,* was established and continues as the primary reference for government financial reporting standards. The GASB was established in 1984 and is the authority for setting those standards. The most common type of government financial report is the CAFR. These reports are not merely stewardship reports, but also include capital assets and a management discussion and analysis.

SEE ALSO *Government Accounting; Not-for-Profit Accounting*

BIBLIOGRAPHY

Berkowitz, S. J. (2005). Assessing and documenting internal controls over financial reporting. *The Journal of Government Financial Management, 54*(3), 42–48.

Government Finance Officers Association. (2005). *Governmental accounting, auditing and financial reporting.* Chicago: Author.

Governmental Accounting Standards Board. (1999). GASB overhauls reporting model. *Journal of Accountancy, 188*(2), 4.

Hawkins, K. W., and Hardwick, K. (2005). Revised OMB Circular A-123: SOX for federal agencies. *The Journal of Government Financial Management, 54*(3), 54–61.

Robert J. Muretta, Jr.

GOVERNMENT ROLE IN BUSINESS

Government regulation at the federal and state levels has a major impact on how businesses operate in the United States. In order to manage business activities in a complex society and to help respond to changing societal needs, governments at all levels have created numerous agencies and regulatory acts. Although the duties and functions of each agency vary, all influence the day-to-day business activities that take place within the United States.

Businesses that take a proactive stance toward understanding and complying with federal agencies and regulatory acts will minimize their chance of fines, prosecution, or other action. Therefore, it is in the best interest of businesses to maintain healthy relationships with regulatory agencies at all levels of government. Among the business activities regulated by government are competitive practices, industry-specific activities, Internet activities, general issues of concern, and monetary regulations.

COMPETITIVE PRACTICES

A number of laws have been passed to protect competitive practices. Among these laws are the Sherman Antitrust

Act of 1890, the Federal Trade Commission Act of 1914, and the Wheeler-Lea Act of 1938.

Sherman Antitrust Act of 1890. One of the earliest pieces of legislation that had a critical effect on the business sector was the Sherman Antitrust Act of 1890. The Sherman Antitrust Act was enacted in response to public outrage over a few large companies that were forcing their smaller competitors out of business and becoming monopolies. Since there was no competition, consumers were left with higher prices and usually a lower-quality product.

The act had two main sections and attempted to prevent the formation of monopolies. Specifically, section one maintained that forming a trust or a conspiracy resulting in the restraint of trade was illegal. Section two provided that persons monopolizing or attempting to monopolize trade were guilty of a misdemeanor. The federal government was (and is) looking for companies engaging in price fixing, in dividing up the market share among different companies to control the market, or in other business practices that may create a monopoly.

The U.S. Department of Justice is the federal agency responsible for enforcing the act. By prosecuting individuals and companies violating provisions of the law, imposing fines and jail time, or calling for injunctions, the Justice Department prevents monopolies from forming. The act also allows injured parties, usually other businesses, to file suit and get relief from the federal courts for infractions of the law. The Justice Department also reviews almost every large merger or acquisition that affects the U.S. marketplace. If the Justice Department opposes a proposed merger, companies involved in the transaction can try to work out an agreement to allay the government's concerns or oppose the Justice Department in federal court, asking a judge to rule on the merits of the case.

Most companies planning a merger or takeover normally have their legal departments conduct exhaustive research in order to answer potential questions from the Justice Department. The primary reason for this research is to avoid a long legal fight with the government that is expensive and can cause significant delays in the proposed merger or takeover. For more information regarding the Justice Department visit its Web site (http://www.usdoj.gov).

Federal Trade Commission Act of 1914. The Federal Trade Commission Act of 1914 created the Federal Trade Commission (FTC), which consists of five members with staggered terms of seven years each. Board members are nominated by the president and confirmed or rejected by the Senate. No more than three members of the FTC can be from the same political party. One person serves as the chairperson of the commission and guides the agency's daily operations.

The FTC was originally created to enforce the provisions of the Sherman Antitrust and Clayton Acts. The FTC has the power to investigate unfair competitive practices on its own. Firms may also petition the FTC to investigate alleged unfair competitive practices of which it might otherwise be unaware. The agency can hold public hearings to investigate the alleged infractions, and it may also issue cease-and-desist orders when it believes unfair competitive business practices are being used. Since the enforcement powers of the FTC and Department of Justice overlap, the two agencies often work together to solve problems.

Wheeler-Lea Act of 1938. The U.S. Congress responded to public complaints about improper and deceptive advertising by passing the Wheeler-Lea Act of 1938, which empowered the FTC to investigate businesses that engage in deceptive business activities or companies that use misleading or less than truthful advertising to entice consumers into their stores. A common deceptive practice that some companies have used is called bait and switch. This practice refers to advertising a product at an extremely low price to draw customers into a store but in reality having very little or none of the product available. Store employees then attempt to sell customers a more expensive product. This is but one example of what the FTC may investigate.

INDUSTRY-SPECIFIC FEDERAL AGENCIES

Federal legislation has created agencies to monitor and regulate particular industries because of concern over industry-specific practices, among them the Interstate Commerce Commission, the Federal Communications Commission, and the U.S. Food and Drug Administration.

Interstate Commerce Commission. In 1887 Congress passed legislation creating the Interstate Commerce Commission (ICC). Originally, only railroads were regulated, but as modern transportation methods developed, other transportation modes were added to its list of responsibilities. The primary purpose of the ICC was to monitor such items as the prices charged by railroad companies, which may have had a monopoly in some parts of the country. The commission could take corrective action, such as price modification, if it found that a railroad or other interstate business was engaging in monopolistic business activities and charging high prices for its services. Since this act applied to a limited number of industries, Congress later passed the Sherman Antitrust Act of 1890

to provide a much broader coverage of monopolies regardless of industry. The ICC was disbanded at the end of 1995.

Federal Communications Commission. The Federal Communications Commission (FCC) monitors and regulates citizens band radio, radio, telegraph, telephone, and television operations. It has broad powers to set acceptable standards for television regarding language, nudity, violence, or other material that may be perceived as inappropriate by the general public. For example, television shows that are adult-oriented or contain violence are typically on later in the evening so that children are less likely to see them. In addition, television shows often warn viewers about their content through a rating system; since the rating is displayed on the screen, viewers can make an informed decision before watching a particular program.

The FCC also has the power to fine broadcast companies that use inappropriate language in their programming. Since most television and radio stations know what are considered acceptable standards, fines are rarely issued. When fines are issued, however, a television or radio station may take the FTC to federal court to appeal the decision. Broadcast companies that fight the FCC over a show's content normally argue that the First Amendment gives them the right to broadcast the contested material. For more information regarding the FCC, visit its Web site (http://www.fcc.gov).

Food and Drug Administration. The Food and Drug Administration (FDA) is responsible for ensuring the safety of cosmetics, drugs, and food. One of the most important functions of the agency is new drug approval. The FDA requires pharmaceutical companies to provide detailed scientific data regarding new drugs prior to approval. Specifically, the FDA will review the potential benefits and negative side effects of all proposed drugs. The agency reviews the information submitted by the pharmaceutical company and may also conduct its own tests if additional study is deemed necessary.

The FDA is extremely important to the business community because if it rejects a new drug, the pharmaceutical company developing it cannot sell it. FDA regulators must balance the interests of the general public with those of the pharmaceutical company. The FDA does not endorse new drugs; rather, it approves them, stating that they are thought to be safe.

INTERNET ACTIVITIES

As business via the Internet increases, so too have the regulations that govern its practice. One such regulation is the Anticybersquatting Consumer Protection Act.

Anticybersquatting Consumer Protection Act. The Anticybersquatting Consumer Protection Act (ACPA) was signed by President Bill Clinton on November 29, 1999. The purpose of the ACPA was to protect businesses from individuals attempting to profit using an identical or similar name to that of an established business. Prior to enacting the ACPA businesses had virtually no recourse against individuals who registered the names of businesses as Internet domain names. Even after this act became law, businesses still have the burden of showing that individuals acted in bad faith when registering business names as domain names.

GENERAL FEDERAL REGULATORY AGENCIES

Federal legislation has also created agencies addressing a broad range of issues, including the Equal Employment Opportunity Commission, the Occupational Safety and Health Administration, the Environmental Protection Agency, and the Consumer Product Safety Commission.

Equal Employment Opportunity Commission. The Civil Rights Act of 1964 prohibits discrimination on the basis of race, color, creed, sex, or national origin. This law applies to almost every private company, nonprofit organization, and government employer, although some exceptions were granted to religious corporations, American Indian tribes, and private-membership clubs. The Civil Rights Act also created the Equal Employment Opportunity Commission (EEOC).

The original purpose of the EEOC was to monitor and enforce the provisions of the Civil Rights Act. Its powers were enhanced in 1972 with passage of the Equal Employment Act, which gave the EEOC the power to file civil lawsuits in federal court and to represent a person filing a grievance. Prior to filing the suit in federal court, the EEOC must first try to settle the case out of court with the alleged offending company—an attempt to promote a more conciliatory approach to solving discrimination problems and to reduce the number of court cases. The company could agree, for example, to settle the complaint by paying a fine, ordering remedial steps to prevent further discrimination, and/or working out the problem for the original complainant. In large cases the EEOC may work with the Civil Rights Division of the Department of Justice in order to settle the problem. More information regarding the EEOC may be found at its Web site (http://www.eeoc.gov).

Occupational Safety and Health Administration. Enacted in 1970, the Occupational Safety and Health Administration (OSHA), was designed to ensure safe and healthy working conditions in nearly every environment.

OSHA's basic premise is that employers must provide a work environment that is safe and free from hazards that may cause harm or death to their employees. In addition, employers are obligated to follow occupational safety and health standards that are ordered by the secretary of labor (OSHA falls under this department). Employers are given written guidelines so they know specific OSHA rules and regulations.

In order to verify that organizations are complying with these regulations, OSHA can conduct surprise inspections. Technically, employers can ask OSHA to show a search warrant before the search is executed, but this is not normally done because OSHA can get a warrant relatively quickly. OSHA investigators may inspect the building, but an employer has the right to have a representative accompany the regulators during the tour. The investigators review accident records and other documents to verify that compliance has been maintained. OSHA investigators also observe employees to verify that guidelines set by the agency are followed (e.g., wearing eye protection).

If OSHA investigators believe that violations have occurred, they can issue citations against the employer. If the employer agrees to pay a fine, OSHA will normally inspect the building at a later date to ensure compliance. If an employer believes that the fine or other sanction is inappropriate, a court order can be sought seeking relief from the fine or sanction. In rare instances, the secretary of labor may ask for an injunction against an employer. Injunctions are sought only in the most serious cases, such as those in which there is imminent danger to employees.

Environmental Protection Agency. One of the most pressing issues in the United States is protecting the environment. A combination of pressure from consumer groups, news media, and voters encouraged Congress to pass legislation creating the Environmental Protection Agency (EPA) in 1972. Prior to the creation of the EPA, no single federal agency had control over environmental issues, resulting in fragmented enforcement and confusing or conflicting codes. The EPA was created to act as the focal point regarding all pollution issues (e.g., air, noise, and water).

Congress has passed several laws addressing a host of environmental issues (e.g., noise, pesticide, radiation, and water pollution). When Congress passes a new law regarding the environment, it is the EPA's job to enforce its provisions with the powers contained in the legislation. One example of the EPA's power is that it can set acceptable air-quality standards for a state. If air-quality standards are not met within a specified frame of time, fines or other punitive measures may be imposed on the offending state.

Consumer Product Safety Commission. Another powerful federal agency was created in 1972 under the Consumer Product Safety Act. The law created the Consumer Product Safety Commission (CPSC), which was intended to protect consumers from defective and dangerous products. In addition, Congress also wanted to unify the majority of laws regarding product safety (except food, automobiles, and other products already regulated by federal agencies) so that they would be effective and clear. The CPSC is very powerful; it can ban products without a court hearing if they are deemed dangerous and can order recalls, product redesigns, and the inspection of production plants. In more severe cases, the CPSC may also charge officers, managers, and/or supervisors with criminal offenses. The CPSC also maintains a Web site (http://www.cpsc.gov).

FEDERAL MONETARY REGULATORY AGENCIES

Several federal agencies have been established to monitor monetary practices in the United States, including the Securities and Exchange Commission, the Federal Reserve Board, and the Federal Deposit Insurance Corporation.

Securities and Exchange Commission. The Securities and Exchange Commission (SEC) was established to regulate the securities industries in the United States. A quasi-regulatory and judicial agency, the SEC regulates publicly traded stock-offering companies by requiring them to issue annual and other financial reports. In addition, the SEC regulates the stock market, brokers who sell securities, and large investment firms. The SEC also looks for insider trading, such as trading on secret knowledge about a company, other white-collar crime that may affect a company's stock price, and securities fraud by stockbrokers.

The agency can initiate civil or criminal action against individuals or firms charged with securities violations. Depending on the circumstances, the penalties levied by the SEC can be severe, with large fines and long jail terms being the norm. The SEC normally works closely with the Department of Justice when criminal prosecution is involved. The SEC's actions can be appealed to the federal courts if the individual or firm believes the charges are inaccurate or unjust.

Federal Reserve Board. As the United States grew, the nation's banking system became more complex and subject to greater fluctuations without government regulation. The United States experienced an acute money panic in 1907 that put a severe strain on the banking system. As a result of the financial panic, the National Monetary Commission was established by Congress to study how

the United States could protect the banking system and, in turn, the money supply. National Monetary Commission recommendations were implemented by Congress in 1913 when the Federal Reserve Act was passed and the Federal Reserve Board was established. The primary purpose of the Federal Reserve Board is to function as a semi-independent board designed to protect the banking system in the United States.

Federal Reserve Board activities are guided by a board of governors. The board has seven members, all of whom are nominated by the president and confirmed or rejected by the Senate. Each member is appointed to a fourteen-year term, with vacancies occurring about every two years. To be nominated to the Federal Reserve Board, an individual must possess excellent academic credentials, be an established leader in the financial world, and have achieved an impeccable business reputation. In order to separate the board from political influences and to ensure that all decisions are based on economic rather than political issues, board members are appointed and will likely serve through several presidential administrations. The board is headed by the chairperson, who is considered to be the most powerful banker in the world. As such, the chairperson directs the overall mission of the board and consults regularly with the president, secretary of the treasury, banking executives, stock market representatives, and top banking regulators from other countries to coordinate financial policy.

Federal Deposit Insurance Corporation (FDIC). Created after the Great Depression of the 1930s, the Federal Deposit Insurance Corporation (FDIC) insures each account up to $100,000 in the event of a bank failure. In return for this protection, participating banks, credit unions, and other financial institutions must pay premiums, which the FDIC uses to build up funds for any future bailouts. More information about the FDIC and its activities may be found at its Web site (http://www.fdic.gov).

SUMMARY

Government regulations and agencies at all levels of government have had a major impact on how businesses operate. In order to manage business activities in a complex, ever-changing society, governments at all levels have created numerous regulatory agencies through the legislative process. Although the duties and function of agencies vary, all influence day-to-day business practices. Frequently regulated business activities include competitive practices, industry specific activities, Internet activities, general issues of concern, and monetary transactions.

SEE ALSO *Antitrust Legistlation; Deregulation; Environmental Protection Agency; Occupational Safety and Health Administration (OSHA); Securities and Exchange Commission*

BIBLIOGRAPHY

Anticybersquatting Consumer Protection Act. http://www.gigalaw.com/library/anticybersquattingact-1999-11-29-p1.html

Boone, L. E., and Kurtz, D. L. (2002). *Contemporary business* (10th ed.). New York: Harcourt College.

Boone, L. E., and Kurtz, D. L. (2004). *Contemporary marketing* (11th ed.). Mason, OH: Thomson South-Western.

Churchill, G., and Peter, J. P. (1998). *Marketing: Creating value for customers* (2nd ed.). Boston: Irwin/McGraw Hill.

Dickson, P. R. (1998). *Marketing management* (2nd ed.). New York: Dryden Press/Harcourt Brace College.

Kotler, P., and Armstrong, G. (2006). *Principles of marketing* (11th ed.). Upper Saddle River, NJ: Pearson Prentice-Hall.

McConnell, C. R., and Brue, S. L. (2002). *Economics: Principles, problems, and policies* (15th ed.). New York: McGraw-Hill/Irwin.

Allen D. Truell
Michael Milbier

GOVERNMENTAL ACCOUNTING STANDARDS BOARD

The Governmental Accounting Standards Board (GASB) was organized in 1984 under the auspices of the Financial Accounting Foundation to establish financial accounting and reporting standards for state and local government entities. These standards are important because external financial reporting can demonstrate financial accountability to the public. They are the basis for many legislative and regulatory decisions, as well as investment and credit policies. The foundation is responsible for selecting the seven members of GASB and its Advisory Council, funding their activities, and exercising general oversight. Except for the chairperson of GASB, all members are part time.

GASB's mission is to establish and improve standards of state and local governmental accounting and financial reporting that will (1) result in useful information for users of financial reports and (2) guide and educate the public, including issuers, auditors, and users of those financial reports. To accomplish its mission, GASB acts to:

1. Issue standards that improve the usefulness of financial reports based on (a) the needs of financial report users, (b) the primary characteristics of understandability, relevance, and reliability, and (c) the qualities of comparability and consistency

2. Keep standards current to reflect changes in the governmental environment

3. Provide guidance on implementation of standards

4. Consider significant areas of accounting and financial reporting that can be improved through the standard-setting process

5. Improve the common understanding of the nature and purposes of information contained in financial reports

GASB formulates and uses concepts to guide them in the development of their standards. These concepts provide a frame of reference for resolving accounting and financial reporting issues. This framework helps to establish reasonable bounds for judgment in preparing and using financial reports; it also helps the public understand the nature and limitations of financial reporting. GASB actively solicits and considers the views of its various constituencies on all accounting and financial reporting issues. GASB's activities are open to public participation and observation under due process procedures. These procedures are designed to permit timely, thorough, and open study of accounting and financial reporting issues. Consequently, broad public participation is encouraged in the accounting standard-setting process, which permits communication of all points of view and expressions of opinion at all stages of the process. Use of these procedures recognizes that general acceptance of the GASB conclusions is enhanced by demonstrating that the comments received during due process are considered carefully.

GUIDING PRINCIPLES

In establishing concepts and standards, the GASB exercises its judgment after research, due process, and careful deliberation. Some of the principles used by GASB are:

1. To *be objective and neutral in its decision making.* This principle ensures, as much as possible, that the information resulting from its standards is a faithful representation of the effects of state and local government activities. Objective and neutral means freedom from bias, precluding GASB from placing any particular interest above the interests of the many who rely on the information contained in financial reports.

2. To *weigh carefully the views of its constituents in developing concepts and standards.* This permits

GASB to (a) meet the accountability and decision-making needs of the users of government financial reports and (b) gain general acceptance among state and local government preparers and auditors of financial reports.

3. To *establish standards only when the expected benefits exceed the perceived costs.* GASB strives to determine that proposed standards (including disclosure requirements) fill a significant need and that the costs they impose, compared with possible alternatives, are justified when compared to the overall public benefit.

4. To *consider the applicability of its standards* to the separately issued general-purpose financial statements of governmentally owned special entities. GASB specifically evaluates similarities of special entities and of their activities and transactions in both the public and private sectors, and the need, in certain instances, for comparability with the private sector.

5. To *bring about needed changes in ways that minimize disruption of the accounting and financial reporting processes.* Reasonable effective dates and transition provisions are established when new standards are introduced. GASB considers it desirable that change should be evolutionary to the extent that can be accommodated by the need for understandability, relevance, reliability, comparability, and consistency.

6. To *review the effects of past decisions for appropriateness.* This permits continual interpretation, amendment, or replacement of standards, when deemed necessary.

PUBLICATIONS

As of December 31, 1998, more than thirty financial accounting and reporting standards had been issued since GASB's inception. A standard pertaining to a new financial reporting model for state and local governments has been exposed and is expected to be issued in 1999 with an effective date in 2001. Copies of these standards, along with other GASB publications, can be obtained from the GASB offices at 401 Merritt 7, P.O. Box 5116, Norwalk, Connecticut 06856-5116, (203) 847-0700, or http://www.gasb.org. GASB's Web site is a subpart of the FASB (Financial Accounting Standards Board) Web site.

OTHER FINANCIAL ACCOUNTING AND REPORTING STANDARD-SETTING BODIES

Additional standard-setting bodies for the public sector are:

1. The Federal Accounting Standards Advisory Board (FASAB) was established in 1990 by three U.S. government principals: the Comptroller General, the Director of the Office of Management and Budget, and the Treasurer. FASAB's primary function is to make recommendations to the principals for financial accounting and reporting standards to be adopted for the U.S. federal government. More information is available from FASAB at 441 G Street NW, Suite 6814, Washington, D.C. 20548, (202) 512-7350, or http://www.fasab.gov.

2. The Public Sector Committee of the International Federation of Accountants (IFAC-PSC) assumed responsibility in 1998 for developing a set of financial reporting standards to be adopted worldwide by public sector entities. More information is available from IFAC-PSC at 545 Fifth Ave., 14th floor, New York, NY, (212) 286-9344, or http://www.ifac.org. Standard-setting bodies for the private sector are:

1. The Financial Accounting Standards Board (FASB) also falls under the auspices of the Financial Accounting Foundation. Its responsibilities are to set the financial accounting and reporting standards to be applied by U.S. businesses. FASB is co-located with GASB in Connecticut and their Web site is http://www.fasb.org.

2. Financial accounting and reporting standards recommended for use by businesses throughout the world are established by the International Accounting Standards Board (IASB). More information is available from IASB at Cannon Street, London EC4M 6XH, United Kingdom; +44 20 7246 6410, or http://www.iasplus.com.

SEE ALSO *Government Accounting; Government Financial Reporting*

BIBLIOGRAPHY

Codification of Governmental Accounting and Financial Reporting Standards as of June 30, 1998 (1998). Norwalk, CT: Governmental Accounting Standards Board of the Financial Accounting Foundation.

Freeman, Robert J., Shoulders, Craig D., and Allison, Gregory S. (1996). *Governmental and Nonprofit Accounting: Theory and Practice* (8th ed.) Upper Saddle River, NJ: Pearson Education Inc.

Wilson, Earl R., and Kattelus, Susan C. (2004). *Accounting for Governmental and Nonprofit Entities.* New York: Irwin/McGraw-Hill.

Jesse W. Hughes

GREEN MARKETING

Green marketing is the production, promotion, pricing, and distribution of products and services that are environmental friendly. The concept of green marketing has its roots in the three distinct environmental movements that have occurred since the 1960s. These various environmental movements have become known as environmentalism. Environmentalism is the action of government agencies, for-profit businesses, nonprofit organizations, and others seeking to both protect and improve the environment.

The first movement occurred during the 1960s and 1970s when citizens and environmental groups became concerned with ecosystem damage such as clear-cut logging and human health problems resulting from polluted air and water. The second movement occurred during the 1970s and 1980s when environmentalism was driven by federal, state, and local governments that passed various laws and regulations designed to reduce the negative impact on the environment from business practices, products, and services.

The third movement of environmentalism is driven by businesses. During this stage, business has accepted responsibility for not causing harm to the environment. This acceptance of responsibility is known as environmental sustainability. Businesses practicing environmental sustainability seek to do no harm to the environment while at the same time remaining profitable through the products and services they sell. One strategy that businesses use to remain profitable is green marketing.

Examples of environmental sustainability and green marketing abound as more and more businesses continue to adopt environmentally sustainable practices. Dell, for example, understands that its responsibility for the computers it produces does not end when they leave the factory. As such, Dell has created the Dell Recycle program in which it attempts to lessen the impact of obsolete computers, keyboards, mice, monitors, and printers that might otherwise end up in landfills. By recycling obsolete computers, Dell is able to keep toxic chemicals out of landfills and to reuse useful materials.

Another example of environmental sustainability and green marketing are the forest management practices adopted by International Paper. International Paper practices sustainable forest management by administering and conserving all forest resources for current and future generations. As such, International Paper's environmental sustainability and green marketing encompasses the complete forest environment: air, plants, soils, trees, and wildlife. International Paper also partners with academic institutions, environmental groups, and government agencies to develop new ways of promoting responsible forest resource management. As such, International Paper's sustainable forest practices demonstrate that the planting,

BP p.l.c. has a world wide green marketing campaign. **IMAGE COURTESY OF THE ADVERTISING ARCHIVES.**

growing, and harvesting of trees and a healthy forest ecosystem can go hand in hand.

Further, the concept of environmental sustainability and green marketing has been extended by retailers of forest-based products. For example, Home Depot established a wood purchasing policy in 1999 that gives preference to the purchasing of wood products originating from certified well-managed forests, when practical, and to eliminating the purchase of wood products from endangered regions such as the Amazon. In addition, Home Depot practices and promotes the efficient and responsible use of wood products and the development and use of alternative environmental-friendly products as wood replacements.

SEE ALSO *Environmental Protection Agency; Marketing*

BIBLIOGRAPHY

Boone, Louis E., and Kurtz, David L. (2005). *Contemporary marketing 2006.* Eagan, MN: Thomson South-Western.

Kotler, Philip, and Armstrong, Gary (2006). *Principles of market-ing* (11th ed.). Upper Saddle River, NJ: Pearson Prentice-Hall.

Ottman, Jacquelyn A. (1998). *Green marketing* (2nd ed.). Lincolnwood, IL: NCT Business Books.

Pride, William M., and Ferrell, O. C. (2006). *Marketing concepts and strategies.* Boston: Houghton Mifflin.

Allen D. Truell

GROSS DOMESTIC PRODUCT (GDP)

Led by the auto industry, the United States economy grew rapidly in the 1920s, generating more jobs, more income, and more free time that the American consumer had in order to spend. As long as people were employed, paying for goods and services, there was really no need to measure how the economy was doing. However, in the 1930s, the American economy went bust and a frustrated Congress asked if there was any way to measure the depth of the Great Depression.

On January 4, 1934, economist Simon Kuznets (1901–1985), professor at the University of Pennsylvania, sent to the Senate a report entitled "National Income: 1929–1932," the first accounting of U.S. productivity, essentially the gross national product (GNP). More than 4,500 copies of this report were sold in just eight months. The basic concept that Kuznet had was to limit this accounting measurement to the marketplace, and thus to the amount that consumers paid for goods and services. Until 1992, the term GNP was used to refer to the total dollar value of all finished goods and services produced for consumption in society during a particular period of time (usually one year). In 1992 the Commerce Department began to compute gross domestic product (GDP) instead of GNP. The differences between the two are slight and involve how to count earning of assets owned by foreigners. GNP counts the earnings in the homeland of the owner of the asset, while GDP counts the earnings of a manufacturer in the country in which the assets exists. For the United States, there is virtually no difference between the two measures.

There are three basic components that determine the U.S. GDP:

1. Consumption, the amount that consumers pay for goods (durable and nondurable).

2. Investment, the amount of money spent on new production facilities, that is, plants and facilities.

3. Services, the amount that consumers pay for the services they use.

Several things that were not included in GNP but were subsequently included in the GDP are:

• Work that is provided in an economy by nonmarket transactions such as homemakers and military personnel. These factors were too difficult for Kuznets and his team to measure.

• Illegal activities such as gambling and drug trafficking. These factors are also difficult to estimate but Kuznets excluded them from GNP because he deemed them a "disservice" to the economy.

• Goods and services that are bartered. These were excluded because they cannot be measured.

• Sale of intermediate goods (raw materials).

• Sale of used goods (used cars, furniture, etc.).

• Purely financial transactions such as sale of stocks and bonds.

• Imports (goods made outside the United States).

The GDP is the ultimate benchmark that measures the expansion and contraction of the U.S. multitrillion dollar national economy. It covers everything that is produced and sold in the marketplace. Bankers, investment brokers, and government officials use the GDP to determine such things as interest rates, investment opportunities, and tax rates. The GDP is not the only measure of output, however, as economists use the GDP because it is the most comprehensive of output measures. This measure is important because it helps societies understand both inflation and employment.

In the flow of payments in the economy, *where* does one measure? Consider, for example, an automobile. The mining operator receives income from the sale of iron ore, the mill owner receives income from the sale of finished steel, and the automobile manufacturer receives income from the sale of the finished car. In order to avoid the inaccuracy of counting the same money three times, Kuznets decided to use only final sales. Thus the amount paid to the dealer for the car is the only amount used in calculating GDP. The labor cost of the workers at all three locations is added to GDP. In essence, the price of the automobile includes the cost of the materials purchased from suppliers. The value added to manufacture the automobile can be found by deducting the cost of one product from the total cost of the automobile.

The more goods and services a country produces, the healthier that country's economy becomes. There is a major flaw in measuring economic success, however, in that when GDP (production) increases, negative external-

Product and prices

Goods	Year 1		Year 2	
	Output	Prices	Output	Prices
Balls	10 balls	$50 per ball	10 balls	$55 per ball
Bats	10 bats	$25 per bat	12 bats	$25 per bat
Gloves	10 gloves	$25 per glove	9 gloves	$30 per glove

Table 1

ities (air and water pollution) also increase. The environment becomes degraded and negatively affects the quality of life. The GDP measures goods and services traded, but the negative externalities are not included in this counting. However, these negative externalities increase the GDP. For example, when the automobile industry wants to produce more cars, the smoke that is emitted from the smokestacks includes carcinogens that may make people in the area sick. A person who gets sick from the emitted smoke may go to the doctor. The doctor may prescribe medication. The cost of the visit to the doctor and the cost of the medication are added to the total value of the GDP.

Table 1 contains output and price statistics for a simple economy that produces only three goods. In the first year, the value of output, or GDP, is $1,000; in the second year, the GDP is $1,120. These numbers are obtained by multiplying quantities by prices and then summing the resulting values. They give us current dollar or nominal GDP, that is, the value of output measured in prices that existed when the output was produced.

The GDP has risen 12 percent from the first year to the second, but this increase is only partially due to additional output ($1,120 – $1,000 = $120). Part of the increase is due to changes in prices. To get a measure that contains only the increase in output, we can multiply the outputs of the second year by the prices of the first year. When we add up these values, they total $1,025. This number implies that if only the quantities of output had changed and not the prices, GDP would have increased only from $1,000 to $1,025, a rise of only 2.5 percent. This $1,025 is real GDP.

SEE ALSO *Macroeconomics/Microeconomics*

BIBLIOGRAPHY

Eggert, James (1997). *What is Economics?* (4th ed.). Mountain View, CA: Mayfield Publishing Company.

Mansfield, Edwin, and Behravesh, Nariman (2005). *Economics U$A* (7th ed.). New York: W.W. Norton & Co.

Mings, Turley, and Marlin, Matthew (2000). *Study of Economics: Principles, Concepts, & Applications* (6th ed.). Guilford, CT: Dushkin/McGraw-Hill.

Wilson, J. Holton, and Clark, J. R. (1996). *Economics.* Cincinnati, OH: South Western Educational Pub.

Gregory P. Valentine

H

HARDWARE

The concept of inventing hardware to assist in commercial productivity is not a modern concept. For example, thousands of years ago the Chinese sought greater efficiency in calculating numbers and invented the abacus, a handheld mechanical device. Another hardware milestone was reached when Charles Babbage (1791–1871) proposed a machine in 1822 that would calculate mathematical tables, and much of his design was used in later computers. Later, Herman Hollerith (1860–1929) designed a method to store numbers onto punched cards, which was used to calculate the 1890 census, and the company he founded eventually became IBM Corporation. The first decade of the twenty-first century revealed hardware devices that may be easily carried in a pocket and are embedded with wireless links to people or data around the world. This significantly extends the arena of the workplace to cars, airplanes, and homes.

THE COMPUTER ERA BEGINS

The first electronic computer, the ENIAC, was developed at the University of Pennsylvania in 1946. It used vacuum tubes and weighed 30 tons. Remington Rand Corporation produced the first commercial computer, the UNIVAC, in 1951. Transistors, which replaced vacuum tubes, were far smaller and took less power than tubes. Transistors were shortly thereafter replaced by integrated circuits, which further minimized size and lessened power requirements. The availability of integrated circuits made the first personal computer possible in 1977 when Steve Jobs (1955–) and Steve Wozniak (1950–) introduced the Apple II. IBM offered their first microcomputer in 1981, and Apple's Macintosh was introduced in 1984. The Macintosh was the first popular computer with a graphical user interface (GUI), and it also had a laser printer that could combine text and pictures. A GUI operating system receives input from both the keyboard and a pointing device (mouse). In the early twenty-first century all personal computers use a mouse or trackball for point and click ease of operation.

CLASSIFICATIONS AND DEFINITIONS OF COMPUTERS

There are four main classifications of computers: mainframe, minicomputer, microcomputer, and handheld. The major categories can be used only as general guidelines because of the huge variety in product lines. Cell phones include a microprocessor, and along with personal digital assistants (PDAs), are considered handheld computers. Computer servers have also been included in this discussion because of their important role in networking and Internet applications.

A mainframe computer is any large computer system such as that used by the Internal Revenue Service. Another example of mainframe use is by airlines, with thousands of users of the ticketing system connected simultaneously to one computer. The next smaller-sized computer is termed a minicomputer. It is of medium-scale and might serve up to several hundred users. Commonly known as personal computers (PCs), microcomputers are small-sized computers, including desktops and laptops. Handheld computers, including cell phones, have considerable storage for their size and include the capability of communications from virtually any place.

Apple President John Sculley, flanked by Apple co-founders, Steve Jobs and Steve Wozniak, unveiled the innovative briefcase-size Apple IIc at San Francisco's Moscone Center April 24, 1984.
© **BETTMANN/CORBIS**

Additionally, computers that are "servers" have taken on increased importance as the Internet has become so integral to commerce. A server can either connect a cluster of computers, or be used to store Web pages that can be retrieved by users. Most such computers are classified as minicomputers and can process many connections. They typically use the UNIX operating system.

COMPUTER COMPONENTS

Central processing unit (CPU): The CPU is at the heart of all computers. All data pass through it. The CPU is "the computing part of the computer. Also called the processor.… A complete computer system requires the addition of control units, input, output, and storage devices and an operating system" (*CMP Net Online Encyclopedia*). Microcomputers/personal computers commonly run at 2 gigahertz per second. Mainframe computers measure their speed in millions of instructions per second.

Random access memory (RAM): RAM consists of microchips that allow for the temporary storage of data.

RAM functions as the work place for the CPU. It is common for a computer to have 500 megabytes of RAM.

Input devices: Computers receive information from a variety of sources. The most common input devices are a keyboard along with a mouse. Desktop or laptop computers are the center of a workplace, with input links from digital cameras, handheld computers, scanners, microphones, and voice commands. Some devices, such as handheld computers, function as both input and output devices.

Output devices: An important output device is the computer monitor, which is increasingly lighter in weight and flat because of new liquid crystal display units that also enable laptop computers, cell phones, and PDAs to have color screens. It is also common for a screen on a cell phones or a PDA to be both an input and output device.

Computer projectors are commonly used to display data or information onto a large screen for group viewing, training, or showing Web sites. Many businesspeople travel with both a portable computer and a computer projector to visually display information for training or to aid in sales at remote sites.

The GUI and general popularity of computers have also promoted significant changes in the hardware options for printing. The earliest printers were essentially automatic typewriters and had little flexibility. Currently, there are a wide variety of printers (including ink-jet and laser) available and capable of color and black and white. The output has improved to near-professional quality prints. While many people have talked about paperless offices for decades, the popularity of printing devices and variety of papers attests to current uses.

Connection devices: Because of the increasing popularity and use of the Internet, all desktop and laptop units contain built-in network interface capability. Most newer laptops also come with the ability to use wireless communications. The network interface normally uses an Ethernet protocol, and these devices offer both input and output capability. Wireless technology allows users continual connectivity while out of the office. This has revolutionized everything from allowing the police to immediately trace stolen vehicles to an on-site roofing salesperson checking stock on particular colors of roofing.

Multimedia: Computers can reproduce both sound and video. Material can come from standard audio compact disks but increasingly more of it is from the Internet. Users can also view and/or edit both still and digital pictures or video.

Storage Devices: All computers use a hard drive to store programs and files. The size of an average hard drive is about 100 gigabytes. That size would have been considered enormous as recently as 2000. Further, changes have made the floppy disk obsolete; new computers do not come with a floppy disk drive. The newest storage device is the flash drive, which is smaller than a package of gum but can hold 1 gigabyte of storage. The hardware allowing for flash drives is also used on such devices as Sony's Memory Stick and other units that are designed to be supplemental storage for PDAs, iPods, cameras, telephones, MP3 players, and other mobile devices.

LOOK TO THE FUTURE

Computers are an increasingly critical component of the workplace, home, and school. New generations of hardware are supporting and even creating new avenues of interpersonal and data communications never possible previously. Hardware that used to fill rooms now is tucked into one's pocket. Cyberculture chronicler Howard Rheingold in an interview with Jesse Walker described the various new ways of connectivity (cell phones, pagers, handheld computers, etc.) as producing new forms of social interaction. Additionally, computing power is becoming more pervasive around the globe. For example, Rheingold stated his belief that mobile communication devices played roles in elections in South Korea, Kenya, and the United States at the start of the twenty-first century. Text messaging allows communication globally very quickly and simply.

Based on the history of hardware development, some trends emerge. Computer hardware will probably continue to become even smaller, lighter weight, more portable, and less expensive. Keyboards may even become obsolete as voice activation equipment becomes more sophisticated. Connectivity within and between systems on a global basis, as well as from home to work to school will accelerate to the point where, Rheingold predicted, more objects will be communicating via the Internet than people. Futurist Lane Jennings noted that handheld wireless phones, linked to the Internet (transmitting images and text) may radically transform how individuals and groups operate. Yet, cyberterrorism and/or hackers accessing hardware may leave computer users vulnerable.

Elementary and secondary schools increasingly emphasize the use of technology to access information and are changing the way students learn. New generations of students will be entering the workforce with more-sophisticated computer skills, and perhaps will be less fearful of "new hardware" and change in general than previous workforces. The foreseeable future holds the promise of more and more integration of work, home, and computers, with digital devices as companions and collaborators that exhibit uncanny understanding.

SEE ALSO *Information Processing: Historical Perspectives; Information Technology*

BIBLIOGRAPHY

CMP Net Online Encyclopedia. http://www.techweb.com/encyclopedia

Forcier, R. (1996). *The computer as a productivity tool in education.* Boston: Merrill.

Hutchinson, S., and Sawyer, S. (1998). *Computers, communications, and information.* Boston: Irwin/McGraw-Hill.

Jennings, Lane (2003, May/June). From virtual communities to smart mobs. *The Futurist, 37*(3).

Long, L., and Long, N. (1999). *Computers.* Upper Saddle River, NJ: Prentice-Hall.

Walker, Jesse (2003, April). Is that a computer in your pants? [an interview with Howard Rheingold]. *Reason Magazine.* Retrieved December 3, 2005, from http://www.reason.com/0304/fe.jw.is.shtml

Armand Seguin
Cynthia Shelton (Anast) Seguin

HAWTHORNE STUDIES

SEE *Motivation*

HEALTH ISSUES IN BUSINESS

Health issues in business are as critical in the early twenty-first century as they were in the mid-twentieth century. Many of the injuries and illnesses have changed but their impact is no less dramatic. The increased use of computers and job specialization have contributed to a new generation of occupational hazards, especially repetitive motion injuries, also known as cumulative trauma disorders. These are injuries caused by repetitive hand, arm, or finger motions that cause tendons to swell and become progressively more painful. In advanced cases, workers lose the strength in their thumb and fingers and eventually become unable to complete simple tasks, such as lifting a baby or tying their shoes. Cumulative trauma disorders were the most common type of illness reported in 1997, accounting for 64 percent of the 430,000 cases of illness reported.

FEDERAL AGENCIES

Two federal agencies are designed to operate in the occupational health and safety arena: the Occupational Safety and Health Administration (OSHA) and the National Institute for Occupational Safety and Health (NIOSH). Both were created by the same act of the U.S. Congress in 1970; each, however, has a very distinct purpose. OSHA, which is part of the U.S. Department of Labor, is respon-

---

The national occupational research agenda

Category	Priority research areas
Disease and Injury	Allergic and Irritant Dermatitis
	Asthma and Chronic Obstructive Pulmonary Disease
	Fertility and Pregnancy Abnormalities
	Hearing Loss
	Infectious Diseases
	Low Back Disorders
	Musculoskeletal Disorders of the Upper Extremities
	Traumatic Injuries
Work Environment and Workforce	Emerging Technologies
	Indoor Environment
	Mixed Exposures
	Organization of Work
	Special Populations at Risk
Research Tools and Approaches	Cancer Research Methods
	Control Technology and Personal Protective Equipment
	Exposure Assessment Methods
	Health Services Research
	Intervention Effectiveness Research
	Risk Assessment Methods
	Social and Economic Consequences of Workplace Illness and Injury
	Surveillance Research Methods

Table 1

---

sible for developing and enforcing rules and regulations in regard to workplace health and safety. NIOSH, which is part of the U.S. Department of Health and Human Services, is a research agency, identifying the causes of work-related disability and injury as well as potential hazards of new technology and practices.

Historically, OSHA agents have been compensated for the number of violations they have found at job sites. This has created an environment in which citations are given for all violations regardless of how small, causing employers to fear OSHA rather than seek its help with health and safety issues. Formerly, OSHA did not promote partnerships with companies to solve health- and safety-related issues in the workplace. OSHA now offers companies a choice between a partnership or a traditional enforcement relationship.

Companies that choose to go into partnership with OSHA work with the agency to develop health and safety programs. OSHA recognizes the companies that truly commit to the new partnership by reducing or eliminating workplace hazards through a more lenient inspection policy, priority assistance, and reductions in penalties up to 100 percent. By involving both the companies and the workers, a more collaborative relationship has developed that has initiated better workplace practices and solutions to health and safety issues.

NIOSH, whose primary role is research, has developed the National Occupational Research Agenda, which

identifies the top twenty-one health and safety research areas on which to focus its work through 2009 (see Table 1). The agenda was developed in collaboration with numerous stakeholders, including employers, employees, and labor organizations. Research areas were chosen based on the greatest needs and the areas most likely to produce the greatest overall gains to workers and industry as a whole. NIOSH is not able to tackle all of these alone. It must be a collaborative effort with the entire health and safety community.

LEGISLATION

Two acts passed in the 1990s have had a significant impact on people who are disabled or who have experienced serious illness. The first is the Americans with Disabilities Act, passed in July 1990. This act, which applies to employers with more than fifteen employees, prohibits discrimination against people with disabilities. Under this act, an employee is entitled to certain rights regarding employment upon returning from disability leave and proving the ability to perform the essential functions of the job. The employer is required to provide "reasonable accommodation" when necessary, that is, to change work schedules, adjust equipment, or modify tasks to enable the employee to continue to perform the job held prior to taking the disability leave. Reasonable accommodation is required except when the employer can prove that it would cause undue hardship on its part. Another option is to transfer the worker to another position within the company.

The second act is the Family and Medical Leave Act (FMLA), which was enacted in August 1993 and applies to employers with fifty or more employees. Employees who have worked for employers in this category for longer than one year are entitled to take up to twelve weeks of unpaid leave annually for certain medical or family situations, including suffering from a serious health condition themselves. The FMLA requires employers to guarantee employees who take a leave the right to return to an equivalent job—that is, the pay, benefits, and other terms and conditions of employment must be equivalent. This provides employees who are temporarily disabled with job security.

THE ROLE OF WORKERS' COMPENSATION LAWS

The original purpose of workers' compensation laws was to protect employers as well as employees in cases of occupational injury or illness. Employers were protected from lawsuits initiated by employees seeking restitution for workplace illness or injury, and employees were compensated for the cost of medical care in addition to lost wages. Currently, most private employers are required to have workers' compensation insurance, with the exception of employers in New Jersey, South Carolina, and Texas.

Workers' compensation insurance is no-fault. In other words, regardless of who is at fault (the worker, employer, or neither), the employer is responsible for compensating the worker for health care and lost wages. The employee's responsibility is to notify the employer as soon as an injury or illness occurs. Workers' compensation issues have become extremely complex because what is considered a compensable illness or injury (warranting restitution by the employer) varies considerably from state to state. The most liberal state is California, where any disease alleged to be aggravated by work-related stress could be compensable. This approach can distort statistical data and it also makes it extremely difficult to control the costs of workers' compensation insurance.

PREVENTION

Employers play a vital role in the prevention of workplace injuries and illnesses. They are responsible for evaluating workplace injuries to discover possible causes and for developing prevention strategies for those injuries. Other employer responsibilities include safety and hazard training, drug testing, workstation evaluations, and enforcement of the use of protective equipment. Employers have an array of resources from which to draw when analyzing workplace hazards and developing health and safety pro-

grams. These include industrial hygienists, certified safety professionals, federal and state OSHA programs, and NIOSH.

Ergonomics. Ergonomics also plays a significant role in the prevention of workplace injuries and illness. Ergonomics is the science of designing and arranging tools and equipment to fit workers. The overall goal is to prevent workplace illness and injuries that result from poor workstation design or improperly designed equipment.

Workstation evaluations are an example of an ergonomic program that many large companies employ. During this evaluation, a health and safety professional evaluates workers performing daily tasks at their workstations. The health and safety professional observes the workers in order to evaluate the "fit" of the workspace, furniture, and equipment to the workers.

In the case of a worker who spends the majority of the day at a computer, the professional would look at several factors to determine the degree to which the workstation fits. These factors include the height and position of the computer screen and keyboard in reference to the worker's body posture, the height and position of the worker's chair, and the types of movements the worker makes while performing tasks. From this evaluation, changes may be made to alleviate discomfort and prevent harmful injuries. These changes may include the repositioning of furniture, or in some cases, the purchase of more appropriate equipment and furniture. For example, a worker may be using a chair that does not provide the type of support the worker needs for sitting at the computer most of the day. "Standing" workstations are sometimes provided for workers who cannot sit comfortably all day, but are able to stand without discomfort.

Adding a screen shield is another example of a simple change that could drastically cut down on the amount of eye strain due to glare that a worker experiences at the computer. In addition to the evaluation, the health and safety professional gives the worker advice on how to sit, how to position hands on the keyboard, and how often to take breaks.

Early intervention is the key to preventing repetitive motion disorders such as carpal tunnel syndrome. Carpal tunnel syndrome is a condition that affects the median nerve in the wrist. Left unchecked it can cause pain, numbness, and tingling in the hand and wrist. Carpal tunnel syndrome accounts for 10 to 17 percent of repetitive motion injuries.

There are no comprehensive ergonomic standards in force in the United States as of 2006. In February 1999, OSHA proposed its first draft of ergonomics standards. Proponents believe it will help control the large numbers of musculoskeletal disorders (disorders involving both muscle and skeleton, such as back pain and neck strain). These disorders account for 34 percent of all lost workday injuries and illnesses and cost $15 billion to $20 billion annually in workers' compensation costs, according to the Bureau of Labor Statistics.

Business groups object to the federally imposed standards, saying that the standards will be a "blank check" for OSHA inspectors and will require all American businesses to become full-time experts in ergonomics. In addition, the U.S. Chamber of Commerce points out that there are currently (1) no scientifically established standards for what is "overuse" and (2) no existing studies that demonstrate the connection between ergonomic adjustments and injury prevention. While the connection does seem to make sense, it must be admitted that more studies need to be done before meaningful standards can be established.

WELLNESS AND OTHER PROGRAMS.

Another way employers are helping to prevent workplace injuries and illnesses is to maintain workplace wellness programs for employees. Wellness programs may include a variety of health and fitness programs for their employees. Research has shown that in addition to health benefits for employees, wellness programs also provide financial benefits for the employer. Wellness programs help employees stay healthy by providing fitness programs, weight management classes, counseling services, and informational resources on health issues. Keeping employees healthy is one means to a profitable business. Many corporations include wellness programs as part of their overall organizational strategy.

A final critical element in the prevention of workplace injuries and illnesses is the development of health and safety programs designed to train and educate workers on workplace hazards. OSHA recommends the following elements for a comprehensive health and safety program:

- Management leadership and commitment
- Meaningful employee participation
- Systematic hazard identification and control
- Employee and supervisor training
- Medical management and program evaluation

CONCLUSION

The field of occupational safety and health is extremely broad and complex. The prevention of occupational injuries and illnesses has to be a collaborative effort involving employers, employees, federal and state agencies, and health and safety professionals.

SEE ALSO *Americans with Disabilities Act of 1990; Ergonomics; Workers' Compensation*

BIBLIOGRAPHY

Carpal tunnel syndrome (CTS). (n.d.). Retrieved November 17, 2005, from http://www.slais.ubc.ca/courses/libr500/02-03-wt1/www/A_Davis/cts.htm

Herington, Thomas N., and Morse, Linda H. (Eds.). (1995). *Occupational injuries.* St. Louis, MO: Mosby-Year Book.

National Occupational Research Agenda. http://www.cdc.gov/niosh/images/table1.gif

Rosenstock, Linda, and Cullen, Mark R. (1994). *Textbook of clinical occupational and environmental medicine.* Philadelphia: Saunders.

Sims, Miriam (1997, March 28). Wellness programs are worth every dollar you spend. *St. Louis Business Journal.* Retrieved November 17, 2005, from http://stlouis.bizjournals.com/stlouis/stories/1997/03/31/focus5.html

U.S. Department of Health and Human Services. National Institute for Occupational Safety and Health. http://www.cdc.gov/niosh/homepage.html

U.S. Department of Labor. Bureau of Labor Statistics. http://stats.bls.gov

U.S. Department of Labor. Occupational Safety and Health Administration. http://www.osha.gov

Brenda J. Reinsborough

HUMAN RELATIONS

Owners and managers of profit and nonprofit organizations define human relations as fitting people into work situations so as to motivate them to work together harmoniously. The process of fitting together should achieve higher levels of productivity for the organization, while also bringing employees economic, psychological, and social satisfaction. Human relations covers all types of interactions among people—their conflicts, cooperative efforts, and group relationships. It is the study of why our beliefs, attitudes and behaviors sometimes cause interpersonal conflict in our personal lives and in work-related situations.

One of the most significant developments in recent years has been the increased importance of interpersonal skills in almost every type of work setting. For many employers, interpersonal skills represent an important category of transferable skills a worker is expected to bring to the job. Technical ability only is usually not enough to achieve career success. Studies indicate that many people who have difficulty in obtaining or holding a job possess the needed technical competence but lack interpersonal competence.

HUMAN RELATIONS MOVEMENT

Problems in human relations are not new—cooperative efforts carry the potential for conflicts among people. It is only within the past few decades that management has recognized that human relations can have considerable impact on organizational productivity. During this period, the human relations movement has matured into a distinct and important field of study.

Although it is difficult to pinpoint exactly when the human relations movement began, most researchers agree that the earliest developments emerged in the mid-1800s. In the beginning, the focus was mainly on improving efficiency, motivation, and productivity. But over time, this research became more involved with redefining the nature of work and perceiving workers as complex human beings.

Prior to the Industrial Revolution, most work was performed by individual craftworkers. Generally, each worker saw a project through from start to finish. Skills such as tailoring, carpentry, or shoemaking took a long time to perfect and were often a source of pride to an individual. Under this system, however, output was limited.

The Industrial Revolution had a profound impact on the nature of work and the role of the worker. Previously, an individual tailor could make only a few items of clothing in a certain time period; factories could make hundreds. Employers began to think of labor as another item in the manufacturing equation, along with raw materials and capital.

Employers at that time did not realize how workers' needs affected productivity. As a result, few owners or managers gave much thought to working conditions, safety precautions, or worker motivation. Hours were long and pay was low.

Around the turn of the century, Frederick Taylor (1856–1915) and other researchers interested in industrial problems introduced the concept of scientific management. They believed that productivity could be improved by breaking down a job into isolated, specialized tasks and assigning each of those tasks to specific workers. The development of scientific management coincided with the revolutionary concept of mass production. Eventually it paved the way for the assembly line.

Taylor's work was sharply criticized by those who believed it exploited workers. Employees were treated as a commodity, as interchangeable as the parts they produced. Taylor thought that by increasing production, the company would end up with a larger financial pie for everyone to share. Management would earn higher bonuses; workers would take home more pay. He did not foresee that his theories would be applied in ways that dehumanized the workplace.

In the late 1920s, Elton Mayo (1880–1949) and other researchers from Harvard University initiated what have become known as the Hawthorne Studies at the Hawthorne plant of Western Electric Company near Chicago. The purpose of the investigation was to explore the relationship between changes in physical working conditions and employee productivity. Specifically, Mayo was interested in the effect of different intensities of light on employee output. In one experiment, ample light was provided to a group of six female workers. Later, the amount of light was significantly reduced, but instead of productivity decreasing, as was expected, it actually increased.

The researchers attributed the phenomenon to what has since become known as the Hawthorne effect—employees who participate in scientific studies may become more productive because of the attention they receive from the researchers. This discovery became important in the human relations movement because it has been interpreted to mean that when employees feel important and recognized, they exhibit greater motivation to excel in their work activities.

HUMAN RELATIONS AS A FIELD OF STUDY

Human relations is an interdisciplinary field because the study of human behavior in organizational settings draws on the fields of communications, management, psychology, and sociology. It is an important field of study because all workers engage in human relations activities. Several trends have given new importance to human relations due to the changing workplace.

The labor market has become a place of constant change due to the heavy volume of mergers, buyouts, a labor shortage, closings, and changing markets. These changes have been accompanied by layoffs and the elimination of product lines. Even those industries noted for job security have recently engaged in layoffs. As the United States attempts to cope with rapid technological change and new competition from international companies, there is every reason to believe that there will be more volatility in the labor force. Interpersonal skills will be even more critical in the future.

Organizations are developing an increasing orientation toward service to clients. Relationships are becoming more important than physical products. Restaurants, hospitals, banks, public utilities, colleges, airlines, and retail stores all must now gain and retain patronage. In any service firm, there are thousands of critical incidents in which customers come into contact with the organization and form their impressions of its quality and service. Employees must not only be able to get along with customers, they must also project a favorable image of the organization they represent.

Most organizations recognize improved quality is the key to survival. The notion of quality as a competitive tool has been around for many years, but in the 2000s, it is receiving much more attention. In a period of fierce competition, a consumer may not tolerate poor quality. Human beings are at the heart of the quality movement because workers are given the power and responsibility to improve quality.

Companies are organizing their workers into teams in which each employee plays an important role. If team members cannot work together, the goals of the organization will suffer. In some cases, workers are cross-trained so they can do the work of others, if necessary.

The demographics of the workplace are also changing. Diversity is increasingly typical. In the years ahead, a large majority of those entering the work force will be women and minorities. Passage of the American with Disabilities Act in 1990 opened the employment door to more people with physical or mental impairments. In the future, there will be increased employment of the population over age sixty-five. Within this heterogeneous work force, a variety of values and work habits will be found. Supervisors will need to become skilled at managing diversity.

The leaders of the work force in the twenty-first century need different skills to be successful. Workers are better educated and better informed, and have higher expectations. They seek jobs that give not only a sense of accomplishment but also a sense of purpose. They want jobs that provide meaningful work. Managers must therefore shift from manager as order-giver to manager as facilitator. They must also learn how to assume the roles of teacher, mentor, and resource person.

Few lines of work will be immune from these trends. Employees must be flexible and adaptable in order to achieve success within a climate of change. It is important for everyone to develop those interpersonal skills that are valued by all employers.

UNDERSTANDING HUMAN BEHAVIOR

Mental perceptions are influenced by everything that has passed through an individual's mind. That includes all of a person's experiences, knowledge, biases, emotions, values, and attitudes. No two people have identical perceptions because no two people have precisely the same experiences.

Mental perceptions may sometimes lead to conflict. Each person has formed mental perceptions relating to a number of controversial issues. For example, most workers have an opinion on abortion and capital punishment, among other issues. When proponents and opponents clash in voicing mental perceptions of controversial issues, conflict occurs. If the issue is one pertinent to the workplace, such as affirmative action, human values have the potential to lead to problems.

Ethics also play a role in interpersonal conflict. Ethics refer to moral rules or values governing the conduct of a person or group. Perhaps more than anything else, an individual's adherence to values related to what is morally right determines the respect that others hold for that person. Lack of respect for one individual by another is likely to lead to poor human relations between the two.

The social dimension of behavior is determined by a person's personality, attitudes, needs, and wants. An individual's personality is the totality of complex characteristics, including behavior and emotional tendencies, personal and social traits, self-concept, and social skills. The objective of many training sessions for employees and supervisors is to improve a person's ability to get along with others. A person's personality has a major impact on human relations skills.

People reveal their attitudes through their personality. An attitude is a mental position one possesses with regard to a fact, issue, or belief. Attitudes that often present problems in the workplace are those that concern biased and prejudiced viewpoints. Generally, employees who possess positive attitudes and who are open-minded are judged to have more desirable personalities than those with negative attitudes who hold biased viewpoints.

COMMUNICATION

Perhaps the single most important aspect of designing any work environment is the plan that links all workers and supervisors with multiple channels of communication. Good communication may be cited as the most important component of sound human relations. Despite the recognition of the importance of communication, it presents one of the most difficult and perplexing problems faced in modern organizations.

Even in small organizations, where only a few people are involved, sound communication is difficult to establish. When an organization expands in numbers, as well as in diversity among its members, the establishment of communication channels becomes even more difficult. Good communication is essential for the smooth functioning of any organization. Managers need clear lines of communication to transmit orders and policies, build cooperation, and unify groups. Employees must be able to convey their concerns or suggestions and feel that management has heard them. Clear communication among co-workers is vital to good teamwork, problem solving, and conflict management. In short, effective human relations is founded on good communication.

When people in organizations want to send messages, conduct meetings, or communicate person to person, they have many options. With increased use of voice mail, e-mail, fax machines, and videoconferencing, it is a wonder people have time to read all the incoming information, let alone interpret and respond to it.

Costly communication breakdowns are a prime factor in organizational problems ranging from high employee turnover to low productivity. Poor communication also takes a toll in employee injuries and deaths, particularly in industries where workers operate heavy equipment or handle hazardous materials.

Although some communication breakdowns are inevitable, many can be avoided. Employees who are treated with respect, are empowered to think for themselves, and feel a sense of loyalty are more apt to communicate openly with other workers and leaders throughout the organization.

TYPES OF RELATIONSHIPS

Human relations occurs on several levels. Individuals interact in a variety of settings—as peers, subordinates, and supervisors. No matter what the setting, relationships are built. All types of groups exist in an organization. Formal groups are officially designated, while informal groups are formed unofficially by the members themselves. Some would argue the informal groups have more power. In either situation, important human relationships are taking place.

Employees relate to their work group, other formal groups, and informal groups. The norms set by a group can greatly influence a person's behavior. Dress and language are two examples. Considering the number of groups in the complex organizations of the twenty-first century, the influence is unlimited.

The organization provides an opportunity for individual satisfaction. To achieve such satisfaction, and to continue as a successful member in the organization, the individual must comply with organizational policies, procedures, and rules. The organization requires certain behaviors from its employees. The rewards for such behaviors are demonstrated in the form of raises, promotions, and continued employment. When the organization promotes an employee, it is relating to the individual.

Complex organizations depend on dividing the work among many formalized groups. Informal groups will also emerge, either positively or negatively affecting organizational outcomes. The relationship between organizations and groups must also be considered when quotas or standards are established. The acceptance or rejection of such standards illustrates the interaction between the organization and the group.

One also has a relationship to one's self. Are you happy with yourself? Are you happy with your relationships with others? With the organization? With your future? If not, perhaps you should analyze your relationship with yourself.

Managers and supervisors achieve results through people. Therefore, the complex organizations of the 2000s require managers and supervisors to display a concern for people. The successful leader creates an effective balance between people and productivity, and recognizes human relations as the key ingredient transforming organizational plans into organizational results. Although it is often misunderstood, effective human relations will lead to success.

Human relations is not limited to supervisors. It also applies to every employee in an organization. Statistics indicate that successful people competently practice interpersonal skills, while the incompetent are left behind. Fortunately, these skills can be developed. Good relationships must be built among individuals and within groups of an organization. Although this is not an easy task, success without good human relations in not possible. Every individual must be prepared to meet the challenge.

SEE ALSO *Management/Leadership Styles*

BIBLIOGRAPHY

Wray, Ralph, Luft, Roger L., and Highland, Patrick J. (1996). *Fundamentals of Human Relations: Applications for Life and Work.* Cincinnati, OH: Southwestern Publishing.

Patrick J. Highland

HUMAN RESOURCE MANAGEMENT

Humans are an organization's greatest assets; without them, everyday business functions such as managing cash flow, making business transactions, communicating through all forms of media, and dealing with customers could not be completed. Humans and the potential they possess drive an organization. Organizations are continuously changing. Organizational change impacts not only the business but also its employees. In order to maximize organizational effectiveness, human potential—individuals' capabilities, time, and talents—must be managed. Human resource management works to ensure that employees are able to meet the organization's goals.

"Human resource management is responsible for how people are treated in organizations. It is responsible for bringing people into the organization, helping them perform their work, compensating them for their labors, and solving problems that arise" (Cherrington, 1995, p. 5). There are seven management functions of a human resources (HR) department that will be specifically addressed: staffing, performance appraisals, compensation and benefits, training and development, employee and labor relations, safety and health, and human resource research.

Generally, in small organizations with fewer than a hundred employees there may not be an HR department, and so a line manager will be responsible for the functions of HR management (HRM). In large organizations with a hundred employees or more, a human resources manager will coordinate the HRM duties and report directly to the chief executive officer (CEO). HRM staff in larger organizations may include human resource generalists and human resource specialists. As the name implies, an HR generalist is routinely involved with all seven HRM functions, while the HR specialist focuses attention on only one of the seven responsibilities.

An understanding of the job analysis is necessary to understand the seven functions. An essential component of any HR unit, no matter the size, is the job analysis, which is completed to determine activities, skills, and knowledge required of an employee for a specific job. Job analyses are "performed on three occasions: (1) when the organization is first started, (2) when a new job is created, and (3) when a job is changed as a result of new methods, new procedures, or new technology" (Cherrington, 1995).

Jobs can be analyzed through the use of questionnaires, observations, interviews, employee recordings, or a combination of any of these methods. Two important tools used in defining the job are (1) a job description, which identifies the job, provides a list of responsibilities and duties unique to the job, gives performance standards, and specifies necessary machines and equipment; and (2) the job specification, which states the minimum amount of education and experience needed for performing the job (Mondy, Noe, and Gowan, 2005).

STAFFING

Both the job description and the job specification are useful tools for the staffing process, the first of the seven HR functions to be discussed. Someone (e.g., a department manager) or some event (e.g., an employee's leaving) within the organization usually determines a need to hire a new employee. In large organizations, an employee requisition must be submitted to the HR department that specifies the job title, the department, and the date the employee is needed. From there, the job description can be referenced for specific job-related qualifications to provide more detail when advertising the position—either internally, externally, or both (Mondy, Noe, and Gowan, 2005).

Not only must the HR department attract qualified applicants through job postings or other forms of advertising, but it also assists in screening candidates' resumes and bringing those with the proper qualifications in for an interview. The final say in selecting the candidate will probably be the line manager's, assuming all Equal Employment Opportunity Commission (EEOC) requirements are met. Other ongoing staffing responsibilities involve planning for new or changing positions and reviewing current job analyses and job descriptions to make sure they accurately reflect the current position.

PERFORMANCE APPRAISALS

Once a talented individual is brought into an organization, another function of HRM comes into play—creating an environment that will motivate and reward exemplary performance. One way to assess performance is through a formal review on a periodic basis, generally annually, known as a performance appraisal or performance evaluation. Because line managers are in daily contact with the employees and can best measure performance, they are usually the ones who conduct the appraisals. Other evaluators of the employee's performance can include subordinates, peers, group, and self, or a combination of one or more (Mondy, Noe, and Gowan, 2005).

Just as there can be different performance evaluators, depending on the job, several appraisal systems can be used. Some of the popular appraisal methods include (1) ranking of all employees in a group; (2) using rating scales to define above-average, average, and below-average performance; (3) recording favorable and unfavorable performance, known as critical incidents; and (4) managing by objectives, or MBO (Mondy, Noe, and Gowan, 2005).

Cherrington (1995) illustrates how performance appraisals serve several purposes, including: (1) guiding human resource actions such as hiring, firing, and promoting; (2) rewarding employees through bonuses, promotions, and so on; (3) providing feedback and noting areas of improvement; (4) identifying training and development needs in order to improve the individual's performance on the job; and (5) providing job-related data useful in human resource planning.

COMPENSATION AND BENEFITS

Compensation (payment in the form of hourly wages or annual salaries) and benefits (insurance, pensions, vacation, modified workweek, sick days, stock options, etc.) can be a catch-22 because an employee's performance can be influenced by compensation and benefits, and vice versa. In the ideal situation, employees feel they are paid what they are worth, are rewarded with sufficient benefits, and receive some intrinsic satisfaction (good work environment, interesting work, etc.). Compensation should be legal and ethical, adequate, motivating, fair and equitable, cost-effective, and able to provide employment security (Cherrington, 1995).

TRAINING AND DEVELOPMENT

Performance appraisals not only assist in determining compensation and benefits, but they are also instrumental in identifying ways to help individuals improve their current positions and prepare for future opportunities. As the structure of organizations continues to change through downsizing or expansion, the need for training and development programs continues to grow. Improving or obtaining new skills is part of another area of HRM, known as training and development.

"*Training* focuses on learning the skills, knowledge, and attitudes required to initially perform a job or task or to improve upon the performance of a current job or task, while *development* activities are not job related, but concentrate on broadening the employee's horizons" (Nadler and Wiggs, 1986, p. 5). Education, which focuses on learning new skills, knowledge, and attitudes to be used in future work, also deserves mention (Nadler and Wiggs, 1986).

Because the focus is on the current job, only training and development will be discussed. Training can be used in a variety of ways, including (1) orienting and informing employees, (2) developing desired skills, (3) preventing accidents through safety training, (4) supplying professional and technical education, and (5) providing supervisory training and executive education (Cherrington, 1995).

Each of these training methods has benefits to the individual as well as to the organization. Some of the benefits are reducing the learning time for new hires, teaching employees how to use new or updated technology, decreasing the number and cost of accidents because employees know how to operate a machine properly, providing better customer service, improving quality and quantity of productivity, and obtaining management involvement in the training process (Cherrington, 1995). When managers go through the training, they are showing others that they are taking the goals of training seriously and are committed to the importance of human resource development.

The type of training depends on the material to be learned, the length of time learners have, and the financial resources available. One type is instructor-led training, which generally allows participants to see a demonstration and to work with the product first-hand. On-the-job training and apprenticeships let participants acquire new skills as they continue to perform various aspects of the job. Computer-based training (CBT) provides learners at various geographic locations access to material to be learned at convenient times and locations. Simulation exercises give participants a chance to learn outcomes of choices in a nonthreatening environment before applying the concept to real situations.

Training focuses on the current job, while development concentrates on providing activities to help employees expand their current knowledge and to allow for growth. Types of development opportunities include mentoring, career counseling, management and supervisory development, and job training (Cherrington, 1995).

EMPLOYEE AND LABOR RELATIONS

Just as human resource developers make sure employees have proper training, there are groups of employees organized as unions to address and resolve employment-related issues. Unions have been around since the time of the American Revolution (Mondy, Noe, and Gowan, 2005). Those who join unions usually do so for one or both of two reasons—to increase wages and/or to eliminate unfair conditions. Some of the outcomes of union involvement include better medical plans, extended vacation time, and increased wages (Cherrington, 1995).

In the early twenty-first century, unions remain a controversial topic. Under the provisions of the Taft-Hartley Act, the closed-shop arrangement states employees (outside the construction industry) are not required to join a union when they are hired. Union-shop arrangements permit employers to hire nonunion workers contingent upon their joining the union once they are hired. The Taft-Hartley Act gives employers the right to file unfair labor practice complaints against the union and to express their views concerning unions (Cherrington, 1995).

Not only do HR managers deal with union organizations, but they are also responsible for resolving collective bargaining issues—namely, the contract. The contract defines employment-related issues such as compensation and benefits, working conditions, job security, discipline procedures, individuals' rights, management's rights, and contract length. Collective bargaining involves management and the union trying to resolve any issues peacefully—before the union finds it necessary to strike or picket and/or management decides to institute a lockout (Cherrington, 1995).

SAFETY AND HEALTH

Not only must an organization see to it that employees' rights are not violated, but it must also provide a safe and healthy working environment. Mondy, Noe, and Gowan (2005) define safety as "protecting employees from injuries caused by work-related accidents" and health as keeping "employees free from physical or emotional illness" (p. 432). In order to prevent injury or illness, the Occupational Safety and Health Administration (OSHA) was created in 1970. Through workplace inspections, citations and penalties, and on-site consultations, OSHA seeks to enhance safety and health and to decrease accidents, which lead to decreased productivity and increased operating costs (Cherrington, 1995).

Health problems recognized in the workplace can include the effects of smoking, alcohol and drug/substance abuse, AIDS, stress, and burnout. Through employee assistance programs (EAPs), employees with emotional difficulties are given "the same consideration and assistance" as those employees with physical illnesses (Mondy, Noe, and Gowan, 2005, p. 455).

HUMAN RESOURCE RESEARCH

In addition to recognizing workplace hazards, organizations are responsible for tracking safety- and health-related issues and reporting those statistics to the appropriate sources. The human resources department seems to be the storehouse for maintaining the history of the organization—everything from studying a department's high turnover or knowing the number of people presently employed, to generating statistics on the percentages of women, minorities, and other demographic characteristics. Data for the research can be gathered from a number of sources, including surveys/questionnaires, observations, interviews, and case studies (Cherrington, 1995). This research better enables organizations to predict cyclical trends and to properly recruit and select employees.

CONCLUSION

Research is part of all the other six functions of human resource management. With the number of organizations participating in some form of international business, the need for HRM research will only continue to grow. Therefore, it is important for human resource professionals to be up to date on the latest trends in staffing, performance appraisals, compensation and benefits, training and development, employee and labor relations, and safety and health issues, both in the United States and in the global market.

One professional organization that provides statistics to human resource managers is the Society for Human Resource Management (SHRM), the largest professional organization for human resource management professionals. Much of the research conducted within organizations is sent to SHRM to be used for compiling international statistics.

SEE ALSO *Management*

BIBLIOGRAPHY

Cherrington, David J. (1995). *The Management of Human Resources*. Englewood Cliffs, NJ: Prentice-Hall.

Mondy, R. Wayne, Noe, Robert M., and Gowan, Mary (2005). *Human Resource Management*. Upper Saddle River, NJ: Prentice-Hall.

Nadler, Leonard, and Wiggs, Garland D. (1986). *Managing Human Resource Development*. San Francisco: Jossey-Bass.

Christine Jahn

I

IDENTITY THEFT

Identity theft refers to stealing and illegally using another person's identity information, including name, date of birth, Social Security number (SSN), address, telephone number, and bank and credit card numbers. Identity theft has become the fastest-growing financial crime in the United States and around the world. As Assistant U.S. Attorney Sean B. Hoar reported, in the United States, 94 percent of financial-crime arrests in 1996 and 1997 involved identity theft, and actual losses to individuals and financial institutions totaled $450 million in 1996 and $745 million in 1997. Over the same period, Master-Card stated that losses because of identity theft represented about 96 percent of its member banks' overall fraud losses ($407 million in 1997).

METHODS OF IDENTITY THEFT

There are many methods of identity theft, but the two most common ones are the physical theft of identification documents and information and computer-based, cyberspace theft. In addition, there are organized crime schemes aimed at stealing personal information.

Physical thefts might include pickpockets stealing purses or wallets for credit cards, driver's licenses, passports, and checkbooks. At automated teller machine (ATM) stations, thieves can peek over people's shoulders when they use credit or debit cards in an attempt to learn the personal identification number associated with the card. Thieves steal mail, garbage, and recycling looking for bank statements, credit card receipts, and other sources of personal information. Even family members have been

known to assume the identity of another family member in order to commit financial fraud.

Poster unveiled at a news conference in Portland, Maine, January 5, 2004, where officials announced a nationwide campaign to educate the public about identity theft. **AP IMAGES**

Contact information for three credit bureaus

Credit bureau	Website	Credit report	Fraud unit
Experian	www.experian.com	888-397-3742	888-397-3742
Equifax	www.equifax.com	800-685-1111	888-766-0008
TransUnion	www.transunion.com	800-888-4213	800-680-7289

Table 1

On the Internet, thieves use high-tech skills to obtain people's usernames, passwords, credit card numbers, and other valuable information. At businesses and hospitals, employees may access their company networks to steal database files of customer and personnel records for criminal use. Organized crime schemes involve hiring hackers or bribing employees to steal valuable information from corporate databases.

PREVENTING IDENTITY THEFT

To avoid being the victim of identity theft, the following proactive measures should be taken:

- Do not give out personal information except when absolutely necessary

- Avoid having a SSN printed on a driver's license, a personal check, or membership cards

- Refuse to give a SSN over the phone, in an e-mail, or as identification for store purchase and refund

- Exercise caution when using credit or debit cards at ATM stations, stores, restaurants, and online stores; do not let others get access to such information

- Carefully review monthly statements from credit card companies and banks for accuracy; report any problem to them immediately

- Keep personal, financial, and medical records in secure places; shred old documents and mail such as preapproved credit card solicitations, credit card receipts, and bank statements before throwing them away

- Do not place outgoing mail in unlocked mailboxes because a red flag up on the mailbox could attract thieves; promptly remove delivered mail from unlocked mailboxes

STEPS FOR VICTIMS TO TAKE

Victims of identity theft should take the following countermeasures:

1. Immediately report the identity theft to the local police, and keep a copy of the police report as evidence

2. Immediately call each of the three credit bureaus (see Table 1) and request credit reviews and a 90-Day Initial Security Alert or a 7-Year Fraud Victim Alert to prevent further damages

3. Work cooperatively with any creditors of accounts where fraud occurred

SEE ALSO *Crime and Fraud; Cyber Crime*

BIBLIOGRAPHY

Experian. http://www.experian.com

Hoar, Sean B. (2001, March). Identity theft: The crime of the new millennium. *United States Attorneys' USA Bulletin, 49*(2). Retrieved November 17, 2005, from http://www.usdoj.gov/criminal/cybercrime/usamarch2001_3.htm

TransUnion. http://www.transunion.com

Jensen J. Zhao

IIA

SEE *Institute of Internal Auditors*

IMPORTS

SEE *Global Economy; International Investment; International Trade; Trading Blocs*

IMPULSE ITEMS

SEE *Consumer Behavior; Marketing Mix; Shopping*

INCOME

By working and being productive, households earn an income and businesses make a profit. The total amount that households and businesses receive *before* taxes and other expenses are deducted is called aggregate income. The amount of money that is left *after* taxes and other expenses have been deducted from one's pay is called disposable income. Discretionary income is what consumers (households) have to pay for the goods and services they desire. This article will focus only on households and how they consume their income. Households spend most of their discretionary income on consumption. Some consumers spend even more than their current discretionary income on consumption by borrowing. Consumption consists of almost everything that consumers purchase, from durable to nondurable goods as well as all types of services. The only exception to this rule is the purchase of a new home: It is counted as an investment because homes tend to appreciate in value.

Households (individuals) cannot spend all their earnings on consumer goods and services. Part of the income each household receives must be used to pay different kinds of taxes, such as income taxes to federal, state, and local governments. Most state and local governments also impose sales taxes. In addition to paying income and sales taxes, households may also have to pay property taxes to local governments. After paying taxes and spending income on consumables, some households put aside money as savings to be used for consumption at a later time.

Earnings differ among individuals and households because of several factors: (1) inborn differences, (2) human-capital differences, (3) work and job performance, (4) discrimination, (5) age, (6) labor mobility, (7) government programs and policies, and (8) luck.

Inborn differences are those characteristics that one is blessed with, such as strength, energy, stamina, mental capacity, natural ability, and motivation.

Human-capital differences reflect how people invest various amounts of both their physical and mental capacities toward the achievement of specific goals.

Work and job performance indicates how individuals differ in their preferences regarding the trade-off between work and leisure. Those who wish to work more usually receive a higher income; others prefer more leisure at the cost of earning a lower income. People also prefer different types of jobs. These specific job choices will affect the distribution of income.

Discrimination is treating people differently solely on the basis of factors unrelated to productivity.

Age affects earnings significantly. Most individuals earn little before the age of eighteen. Earnings tend to increase as workers gain experience and their productivity increases.

Labor mobility, which is the willingness to go where the jobs are or to move wherever the company has a need, enhances an individual's income potential. Immobility limits workers' response to changes in wage rates and can contribute to an unequal distribution of income.

Government policies and programs, such as benefit programs and the progressive income tax, reduce income inequality. The minimum wage may also increase income inequality.

Luck plays a role in determining the distribution of income, but choices are perhaps the most important factor.

BIBLIOGRAPHY

Mings, Turley (2000). *The Study of Economics: Principles, Concepts, and Applications* (6th ed.). Guilford, CT: Dushkin Publishing Group.

Gregory P. Valentine

INCOME TAX: HISTORICAL PERSPECTIVES

A tax consists of a rate and a base. Because income is the base for the income tax, a central question is: What constitutes income? Different theoretical concepts of income exist in economics, accounting, and taxation. The base of income to which the federal income tax rate structure applies is taxable income as constitutionally and statutorily defined. Thus, the concept of taxable income is grounded in theory and modified by political dynamics and administrative concerns.

From its modern introduction in 1913, the rate structure for the individual income tax has been progressive, meaning that tax rates graduate upward as the base of taxable income increases. Different tax rates apply to ranges of income, called brackets. Over time, the number of brackets and tax rates that apply to them have varied greatly. The tax rate applied to the last dollar of taxable income earned by a taxpayer is called the marginal tax rate. Total income tax as a percentage of total taxable income is the average tax rate, whereas total income tax as a percentage of total economic income is the effective tax rate.

ADOPTION AND EARLY IMPLEMENTATION OF FEDERAL INCOME TAX

Until the Civil War, federal revenues came from relatively low tariff rates imposed on a broad base of imported goods and from excise taxes. However, tariffs and excise taxes could not support escalations in government spending caused by the Civil War. Drawing on the example of the British Parliament's adoption of an income tax in

Income tax documents being manually sorted March 14, 1944. © **BETTMANN/CORBIS**

1799 to help finance the Napoleonic Wars, the U.S. Congress adopted the first federal income tax in 1861 to help finance the Civil War. Legislators regarded the war-motivated income tax as an indirect tax because neither real nor personal properties were taxed directly. The constitutionality of the tax was not challenged, and it expired in 1872.

During the post-Civil War years, high tariffs, often established to protect selected industries from foreign competition, and excise taxes were the major sources of revenues. By the early 1890s, tax structure was a political issue, with debate centering on the equity of the tax burden. In 1894, with strong Democratic support, a modest income tax was adopted. The first $4,000 of income was exempt from taxation, and the initial tax rate was 2 percent. The prevailing view was that this tax would apply to high-income taxpayers and corporations without extending to the wages and salaries of working people.

In 1895, the U.S. Supreme Court declared the income tax unconstitutional in the case of *Pollock v. Farmers' Loan and Trust Co.* on the basis that it was a direct tax. Article I, Section 9 of the U.S. Constitution provided that "No capitation, or other direct tax shall be laid, unless in proportion to the census." After the income tax was declared unconstitutional, Democrats began to introduce constitutional amendments to permit it. By the early 1900s, political support had broadened to include progressive Republicans. The Sixteenth Amendment, which legalized an income tax, was submitted to the states in 1909 and ratified in 1913. At this time, roughly 2 percent of American households paid the new tax.

MODIFICATIONS TO FEDERAL INCOME TAX OVER TIME

Various aspects of the federal income tax have changed since its inception.

World War I and Depression Years. During World War I, the Democrats altered the tax by adopting highly progressive rates and structuring the base to consist of the incomes of corporations and upper-income individuals. Additionally, an excess profits tax was imposed. This was a progressive tax on above-normal profits, and it generated most of the new tax revenue raised during World War I. Together the income tax and excess profits tax became an explicit means for the redistribution of income. To administer these taxes, the Bureau of Internal Revenue reorganized along functional lines, expanded in size, and employed such experts as accountants, lawyers, and economists. In 1916, "reporting at the source" was adopted, which required corporations to report salaries, dividends, and wages to the Treasury Department.

When the Republicans took control of the presidency and Congress in 1921, taxes on corporations and upper-income taxpayers were reduced, the excess profits tax was repealed, and the tax rate structure was adjusted to be less progressive. Many preferences were incorporated into tax law in the form of deductions, and the preferential taxation of capital gains was adopted. A capital gain is a gain that results from the sale of a capital asset, such as shares of stock in a corporation. In 1932 under President Hoover, and in 1935 and 1937 under President Roosevelt, tax rates increased and the tax base expanded. However, the income tax was not a dominant policy focus during the 1930s, partially because the federal government relied heavily on excise taxes and debt to obtain funds to support government activities.

World War II. The most significant impact of World War II on the individual income tax was to transform it to a mass tax that was broadly based and progressive. In 1941, changes were made to both rates and base. Higher tax rates were adopted and lower exemptions were allowed, thus expanding the base. Higher tax rates were adopted again in 1942. With the inclusion of a surtax, tax rates ranged from 13 percent on the first $2,000 of taxable income to 82 percent on taxable income in excess of $200,000. The number of taxpayers increased from 3.9 million in 1939 to 42.6 million in 1945. At the end of the war, 60 percent of households paid the income tax. The efficiency of collection was enhanced by the adoption of payroll withholding in 1943. By 1944, the individual income tax generated about 40 percent of federal revenues.

For corporations, progressive tax rates, also called graduated tax rates, were introduced in 1935, repealed in 1938, so corporations paid a flat tax during World War II. However, wartime corporations were subject to a graduated tax on excess profits, with the maximum rate of 50 percent after an allowance for a substantial credit.

During the World War II years, there was a major shift in the taxing power of the federal government relative to state and local governments. Federal revenues, as a percent of total taxes collected by all levels of government, increased from 16 percent in 1940 to 51 percent in 1950.

With some modifications, the basic structure of the income tax remained in place during the post–World War II years and continued in the early twenty-first century. Individual tax rates were reduced from wartime highs, and the tax base began to narrow with the adoption of exemptions, deductions, and credits. Inflation in the 1960s and 1970s created a condition called bracket creep. Taxpayers whose monetary incomes were increasing because of inflation, but with no equivalent increase in purchasing power, were pushed into higher tax brackets and thus subject to higher marginal tax rates. Because the corporate rate structure was not progressive, bracket creep did not apply to corporations. Although the corporate and individual income taxes had generated roughly the same revenue in 1950, by 1980, partially as a result of bracket creep, the individual income tax generated four times the revenue of the corporate tax.

After World War II. During the post–World War II years, the tax system was used increasingly as a means of financing. A government may deliver services by direct payment or indirectly by subsidy through a reduction in tax. For example, the deduction for home mortgage interest provides a tax subsidy for investing in housing. The term tax expenditure is used to describe subsidies for various purposes achieved by use of exemptions, deductions, and credits. Exempt income is not subject to tax. A deduction reduces the amount of income that is subject to tax, and a credit represents a direct reduction in the amount of tax liability. From 1967 to 1982, tax expenditure increased from 38 percent to 73.5 percent of tax receipts. Tax expenditure provisions complicate the determination of taxable income, the base for the income tax.

The sophisticated study of tax policy, which continued into the twenty-first century, began on a widespread basis during the post–World War II period. Central questions concerned the impact of tax policy on the amount of investment, the movement of capital, and labor-force participation.

From 1980 to 2000. The 1980s began with the adoption of the Economic Recovery Tax Act (ERTA) during President Reagan's term. A key provision of this act was the indexing of tax rates for inflation to eliminate bracket creep. ERTA provided for significant reductions in tax rates and began to reduce the role of the income tax in the nation's revenue system. During the 1980s, interest in tax reform grew, culminating in the passage of the Tax

Reform Act of 1986. The goal of this act was to be revenue-neutral, neither increasing nor decreasing revenues. It provided a reduction in tax rates by expanding the tax base through the elimination of some tax expenditures.

After passage of the 1986 Tax Reform Act, attention shifted to the taxation of capital gains and replacement of the income tax. Beginning in 1987, capital gains and ordinary income were taxed in the same manner. Then preferential treatment was reintroduced for capital gains. Commonly proposed alternatives to the income tax include the value-added tax and national sales taxes, two taxes for which the tax base would be consumption rather than income. Another alternative is the flat tax on income. In theory, with one single tax rate—a flat tax—all taxpayers would pay the same proportion of taxable income in taxes. If the base of taxable income were defined as earned income, taxpayers receiving only interest and dividends would be excluded from the payment of taxes. Currently interest and dividends are subject to a double tax. Corporations pay income tax on the earnings from which dividends and interest are paid, and individuals pay income tax on dividend and interest income that they receive. Most flat tax proposals eliminate double taxation.

ADMINISTRATION OF FEDERAL INCOME TAX

The Internal Revenue Service (IRS), which administers the income tax, is part of the U.S. Department of the Treasury. Adapting to changes in technology to achieve the most efficient processing of information is a major challenge for the IRS. For many years the IRS was organized on a geographical basis, but in 1998 it was reorganized into four functional divisions differentiated by type of taxpayer.

For corporate and individual taxpayers that report on a calendar-year basis, annual tax returns are due on or before March 15 and April 15, respectively, following the close of the calendar year. Providing that the tax due is paid, time extensions for filing returns may be obtained. Although the closing dates for the quarters differ, both individuals and corporations are subject to payment of estimated tax in quarterly installments. Taxpayers who fail to file tax returns or fail to pay taxes are subject to monetary penalties, fines, and possible prison sentences.

EXTENSION OF INCOME TAX TO THE STATE LEVEL

Wisconsin was the first state to adopt an income tax in 1911. Massachusetts and New York soon followed by adopting income taxes when faced with problems related to World War I. Most other states adopted the income tax

as a response to revenue crises created by the Great Depression. At the state level, definitions of taxable income differ from the federal definition and differ among states. Exemptions, deductions, and rates of taxation vary among states. As of January 2005, Nevada, South Dakota, Washington, and Wyoming did not impose individual or corporate income taxes; Alaska, Florida, and Texas did not impose an individual income tax. Formulas are used to allocate the income of multistate corporations among the states in which they operate.

SEE ALSO *Taxation*

BIBLIOGRAPHY

Brownlee, W. Elliot (2004). *Federal Taxation in America: A Short History*. Washington, D.C.: Woodrow Wilson Center Press.

Federation of Tax Administrators website. http://www.taxadmin.org. Accessed December 1, 2005.

Witte, John F. (1985). *The Politics and Development of the Federal Income Tax*. Madison: University of Wisconsin Press.

Jean E. Harris

INDUSTRIAL MARKETING

SEE *Business Marketing*

INFLATION

SEE *Business Cycle*

INFORMATION PROCESSING

Information processing is the manipulation of data to produce useful information; it involves the capture of information in a format that is retrievable and analyzable. Processing information involves taking raw information and making it more useful by putting it into context. In general, information processing means processing new data, which includes a number of steps: acquiring, inputting, validating, manipulating, storing, outputting, communicating, retrieving, and disposing. The future accessing and updating of files involves one or more of these steps. Information processing provides individuals with basic skills to use the computer to process many types of information effectively and efficiently. The term

Mainframe Computer Processing Room, 2000-2003. © WES THOMPSON/CORBIS

has often been associated specifically with computer-based operations.

IMPACT OF INFORMATION PROCESSING

Information processing has had an enormous impact on modern society. The marketplace has become increasingly complex with the escalating availability of data and information. Individuals need a sound understanding of how to create, access, use, and manage information, which is essential in the work environment. People need to understand the interrelationship among individuals, the business world nationally and internationally, and government to constructively participate as both consumers and producers. These general competencies must be coupled with those that lead to employment in business as well as advanced business studies.

According to market intelligence provider IDC, offices around the world were on track to produce 4.5 trillion pages of hard-copy information by 2007. Three vital factors to consider in the management of documents are (1) managing the documents more effectively, (2) controlling the costs associated with the documents processed,

and (3) using available resources more efficiently. Every organization, whether small or large, has a vested interest in information processing technology. Smarter document management in office environments is essential. Businesses are adding intelligence and structure to digital and paper documents in order to streamline business processes and to aid integration within the structured data systems. The emphasis is not on eliminating paper, but on handling the information embedded in the documents more efficiently. The focus has shifted to tailoring and managing technology to best meet needs.

EFFECTS OF INFORMATION PROCESSING

Information generates ideas and drives decisions. Documents are driven by regulatory compliance, plus the need to communicate with customers, suppliers, and employees—while dealing with multimedia, business process solutions, and related investments. Questions that should be considered include the following:

1. What techniques, procedures, and methods are used to share useful information?

2. What are the capabilities and limitations of hardware and software?

3. How can speed of operation, functionality, and capacity be increased?

4. What ways will an organization and individual use the information; for example, will the information be used to support strategic, tactical, or operational decisions, and to inform, persuade, educate, or entertain users?

5. What techniques are used for representing the design of solutions and output, including input-process-output charts, hierarchy charts, screen/hard-copy layout mock-ups, flow charts, or storyboards; what techniques—such as hyperlinks, buttons, icons, table of contents, index, or page numbering—are used for navigating complex documents?

In many businesses, office files are littered with paper documents. Time consuming and costly, this situation frustrates both customers and employees, often resulting in service delays. By automating paper-intensive processes, organizations can realize significant productivity gains.

The explosion in information and content has created business challenges, including:

- The inability of users to locate information needed

- The lack of clear organization to simplify navigation through repositories and on Web sites

- Manual tagging processes that take too much time

- The inability to personalize content for individual users and customers

MANAGEMENT OF INFORMATION PROCESSING

Businesses in the twenty-first century are complex, fluid, and customer-centric, therefore they need to establish and apply appropriate file-management procedures and techniques to store, communicate, and dispose of data and information efficiently and effectively. By automating routines to capture, process, manage and deliver business documents, organizations can safeguard data integrity and protect data from alteration.

The introduction of digital technologies enabled offices to start changes in the use of paper. In the early 1990s, a Xerox research study indicated that offices were not tending to use less paper rather keep less paper. Many office workers maintain paper for reading, annotating, and sharing information for discussion purposes; many businesses still rely on paper for such form-based documents as invoices, contracts, and customer correspon-

dence. Paper copies and/or microfilm are also archived for legal reasons by many businesses and organizations.

Businesses need to examine carefully the document work-flow process. This includes four stages/steps: capture, manage, store, and deliver. Each step supports the transfer of paper document content to electronic format, to route and use for specific applications. Richard V. Heiman and Anthony C. Picardi (2005) have stated that "information life-cycle management has now become possible. Intelligent documents have a life cycle built into them and travel on the backbone of enterprise transaction systems. Content comprehension, digital rights, and integration continues to evolve and will be built into an increasing array of smart applications."

Many business documents are governed by regulations such as the Sarbanes-Oxley Act of 2002 and the Health Insurance Portability and Accountability Act of 1996. These acts are meant to protect information security, accuracy, and confidentiality and dictate how organizations receive, process, use, store, protect, and share business information.

Business requires that information be accessible in real time. Real time is associated with speed—real-time information management is getting information where it needs to be when it needs to be there, whether that is microseconds, minutes, or days. Information has impact when it is connected to context, to other information, and to people. Context enhances the value of stored information. Business leaders need information that is readily accessible. They want to have real-time views in their businesses so that decisions are made when they need to be without tracking data and generating reports.

Traditionally in most businesses, organizations, and corporations, information has been isolated within a specific department on an individual employee's personal computer, in an individual database, or in a file cabinet. Businesses, however, have implemented multiple solutions to store various data and yet questions persist on how to consolidate and use storehouses of information to deliver better products and services while maintaining profit margins.

Capturing all information onto one true enterprise system is essential. Enterprise resource management (ERM) has arrived. The implementation of ERM in the business sector has helped businesses to manage people and workloads and to control of the processes of the business. Processes and communication systems that extend globally and respond instantaneously require flexibility. The processes as well as the systems must be integrated so that measurable results are delivered. ERM serves as a vehicle to manage information. It organizes data to be more useful to individual departments—enabling them to operate more efficiently, as well as creating streamlined processes to cut costs.

Changing internal processes can be difficult within an organization. Businesses must abandon old ways of preserving and protecting data. Data need to be shared within an organization on a rules- and roles-based system; reporting functions need to be streamlined, limiting decision making to a select few. Open lines of communication and collaboration within the organization, as well as with partners, suppliers, and customers, helps the organization achieve greater operational efficiency.

Constantly evolving business requirements mean that the work-flow processes have to be updated as needs change. Customization may be required. Businesses need to define and modify work-flow functions. Solutions that bridge the gap between back- and front-office worlds enable organizations to exchange information.

In the current work environment, businesses use the Internet on a daily basis. The Internet is no longer a tool just for electronic mail, research, and electronic commerce. It has become a tool for globalizing a business; it is a tool that enables an organization to tie together employees, suppliers, and customers. Free flow of information is generated across the country and internationally.

CHALLENGES OF INFORMATION PROCESSING

Businesses still face challenges as they attempt to revise internal processes, open communications to outside sources, and integrate disparate technology functions. Information should not be isolated in specific departments; it should be housed is such a way as to benefit the entire organization.

In the modern office, information processing encompasses a wide field. It ranges from textual information to digital information, qualitative analysis to quantitative analysis, as well as globally from the Internet to a single personal computer.

Computer documents may require a combination of software packages to be used; for example, placing a spreadsheet into a word-processing document or a spreadsheet graph in a presentation file. A variety of manipulations is involved in the processing of textual information. A document can be rearranged by the cutting and pasting of text, and graphics can be imported into a text document. Using image analysis software, images can be manipulated. The digital processing of numerical data can be accomplished through spreadsheet programs. Using spreadsheet programs, data can be queried in a "what if" statement, and statistical analysis and graphical representation of the data can be illustrated.

Integrating software applications is a powerful aspect of using software designed to be used in the Windows environment. Integration refers to the sharing of information among applications—word processing, spreadsheet, and database applications. Computer software not only shares common features but also is very often compatible; thus, information that is created in one software package can be shared in another.

The proliferation of computer software has dramatically changed the way end users create documents. As computer software became more sophisticated over the years, the software programs began to share common features. Modern offices use a combination of software packages to produce useful information. The field of information processing has had and continues to make a significant impact on society.

SEE ALSO *Careers in Information Processing; Desktop Publishing; Ethics in Information Processing; Information Processing: Historical Perspectives; Information Systems; Information Technology*

BIBLIOGRAPHY

Heiman, Richard V. & Picardi, Anthony C. (2005). *Worldwide Software 2005-2009 Forecast Summary.* Framingham, MA: IDC.

Information and communication in the 2004–2010 MTPDP (2004, November 13). *Manila Bulletin.*

O'Leary, Timothy J., and O'Leary, Linda I. (1996). *Microsoft Office integration.* New York: McGraw-Hill.

Oliverio, Mary Ellen, Pasewark, William, and White, Bonnie (2003). *The Office: Procedures and technology* (4th ed.). Mason, OH: Thomson South-Western.

Shelly, Gary B., Cashman, Thomas J., and Vermaat, Misty E. (2003). *Discovering computers 2004: A gateway to information.* Boston: Course Technology.

Mary Nemesh

INFORMATION PROCESSING: HISTORICAL PERSPECTIVES

Since the beginning of time, humans have attempted to derive methods to compute and to process data more efficiently. One of the earliest computing devices was the abacus developed in ancient Egypt during the thirteenth century. The abacus is a frame comprised of beads strung on wires used to add, subtract, divide, and multiply. Although this primitive device preceded pencil and paper, it is still used in the twenty-first century.

THE FIRST CALCULATING MACHINES

To increase the speed and accuracy of computing, John Napier, who was a mathematician, invented logarithms, which greatly assisted arithmetic calculations. He also invented "Napier's bones" in the early 1600s. This tool was a table made from wood or bones that included multiplication inscriptions. In 1642 Frenchman Blaise Pascal (1623–1662) invented the first adding machine, called the Arithmetic Machine. Gottfried Leibniz (1646–1716) expanded on Pascal's ideas and in 1671 developed the "step reckoner," which could perform addition, subtraction, multiplication, and division, as well as evaluate square roots.

In 1834 Charles Babbage (1791–1871) designed the forerunner of the computer, the mechanical Analytical Engine. It was designed to perform complicated calculations such as multiplication, division, addition, and subtraction. The Analytical Engine failed to be produced because of its mechanical nature. The mechanical parts were extremely slow and were subject to routine breakdowns. Although this machine was never actually produced, it influenced the design of modern computers. It included the four components of modern computing: input, storage, processing, and output. The machine allowed data input and it included a storage location to hold data for processing. It also had a processor to calculate numbers and to direct tasks to be performed, as well as an output device to print out information.

In 1884 Herman Hollerith (1860–1929) used electric components to devise a computer that the U.S. government used to help tabulate data for the 1890 U.S. census. This machine received hand-fed punched cards and allowed metal pins to pass through the holes into cups filled with mercury, completing an electric circuit. Hollerith later improved the design and started the Tabulating Machine Company in 1896. Later the company became International Business Machines (IBM) Corporation.

THE FIRST MODERN-DAY COMPUTERS

Howard Aiken (1900–1973), a Harvard professor, is credited with building the first digital computer, called the Mark I. This machine was similar to Babbage's Analytical Engine and was constructed out of switches and relays (metal bars surrounded by coils of wire). This 5-ton machine took five years to build, which rendered it obsolete before it was even completed.

At Iowa State University, John V. Atanasoff (1903–1995) and his graduate assistant, Clifford Berry (1918–1963), designed the first electronic digital special-purpose computer in the 1930s. The Atanasoff-Berry Computer used vacuum tubes for storage and arithmetic

Herman Hollerith (1860–1929). *Hollerith, inventor of the punch card system, also developed tabulating machines for the United States Bureau of the Census.* © **BETTMANN/CORBIS**

functions. Improving on this design, John Mauchly (1907–1980) and John Presper Eckert, Jr. (1919–1995) of the University of Pennsylvania designed the first large-scale electronic digital computer used for general purposes in 1945. Built by IBM, the electronic numerical integrator and computer, or ENIAC, weighed 30 tons and spanned 1,500 square feet. This huge machine used 18,000 vacuum tubes for storage and arithmetic calculations.

Eckert and Mauchly started their own company, which was later known as Remington Rand Corporation, and designed the Universal Automatic Computer (UNIVAC) in 1951. The UNIVAC became the first commercial computer made available to business and industry. This machine used magnetic tape to store input and output instead of the punched cards used in previous machines. IBM capitalized on the concept of commercial applications and developed the IBM 701 and the IBM 752 computer systems. Because of their smaller size relative to the UNIVAC I, the IBM models cornered over 70 percent of the industrial computer market.

Transistors replaced vacuum tubes and sparked the evolution of second-generation computers. Transistors,

Hollerith tabulator and sorter ca. 1900. © **HULTON-DEUTSCH COLLECTION/CORBIS**

invented in 1947, were less expensive than vacuum tubes, generated less heat, and produced more reliable computers. Computers made with transistors yielded greater demand as a result of their small size, lower cost, and better reliability.

As the demand for computers increased, computer programmers were becoming consumed with the tedious process of programming the computers to function. Computer programmers used machine language to give instruction to the computer. Machine language is binary code (comprised of 0s and 1s) that a computer understands directly. Each different computer model had a unique programming language. For example, UNIVAC had different machine language than that used with the IBM 752. To ease the task of programming computers, machine language was replaced with assembly language. Programmers used assemblers to convert or translate English-like code, developed using assembly language, into machine language. This low-level language improved the speed at which programs could be written.

The use of integrated circuits improved computer development, which resulted in third-generation computers. Integrated circuits, developed in 1958, used miniature-size transistors that were mounted on small chips of silicon about a quarter of an inch long on each side. These microchips allowed scientists to develop even smaller, faster, and reliable computers. IBM used microchips to develop the 360 series of computers. Instead of punched cards, users interacted with their computers using keyboards, monitors, and operating systems.

During the third-generation era, high-level programming languages were introduced. While third-generation computers were performing more complex data manipulation, communicating with the computers also became more complicated. Programming languages such as COBOL and FORTRAN were developed in the 1950s to make programming the computer easier. These high-level languages used compilers or interpreters to convert the English-like code into machine language.

FOURTH-GENERATION COMPUTERS

Fourth-generation computers were led by the development of the microprocessor. Called a semiconductor, this processor was produced in 1971 by a company called Intel. The semiconductor was a large-scale integrated circuit that contained thousands of transistors on a single chip. The development of this chip led to the invention of the first personal computer. With this invention, the use of computers spread from large businesses and the military to small businesses and homes.

IBM introduced its first home computer in 1981 and Apple developed the Macintosh home computer in 1984. The Intel 4004 chip fit all the components of a computer into one tiny chip. This innovation eventually led to the development of handheld devices. Handheld devices are portable computers that have many of the capabilities of a desktop computer. One popular handheld device is the personal digital assistant that allows a user to schedule and organize information.

THE INTERNET AND WORLD WIDE WEB

The powerful capability of microprocessors allowed small computers to link together to form networks or the Internet. The Internet, conceptualized in the late 1960s by researchers from the Advanced Research Projects Agency of the U.S. Department of Defense, is a network of computer networks that enable communication among computer users. The Internet facilitated the use of electronic mail, which is a commonly used form of communication.

The Internet has been enhanced by the World Wide Web (WWW), which enables computer users to search, view, and disseminate information on a plethora of subjects from Web sites. The WWW was developed in 1990 by Tim Berners-Lee (1955–). The Internet, coupled with the WWW, has changed profoundly the way industrialized nations communicate, disseminate, and process information.

FIFTH-GENERATION COMPUTERS

Fifth-generation computing devices are currently under development. The focus of this generation involves making computers behave like humans. This phenomenon was called artificial intelligence by John McCarthy (1927–) at the Massachusetts Institute of Technology in 1957. The area of artificial intelligence includes gaming, expert systems, natural languages, neural networks, and robotics. Gaming involves creating games that allow users to play against the computer. Expert systems are computer applications that perform the tasks of a human expert, such as diagnosing an illness. Natural languages allow computers to understand natural human languages such as English or Chinese. Neural networks attempt to function like the brain of a human or animal. Robotics includes creating computers that can use human senses such as seeing and hearing.

Although scientists are having a great deal of difficulty in making computers behave and think like humans, there have been some advances in this field. In the area of gaming, programmers have developed computer games that can "outthink" humans. In the area of natural languages, voice recognition software has been developed to convert spoken words to written words. It allows users to speak to the computer and in return the computer dictates what the user says into the form of words of the screen.

Information processing or data processing has become synonymous with computers. The development of the computer, the Internet and the WWW has vastly improved the way that information can be processed. These tools have provided society with more information processing capability than ever before. As the ever-changing world continues to evolve, one can be certain that more information-processing innovations are soon to follow.

SEE ALSO *Hardware; Information Processing; Office Technology*

BIBLIOGRAPHY

The five generations of computers. (n.d.). Retrieved November 17, 2005, from http://www.webopedia.com/DidYouKnow/Hardware_Software/2002/FiveGenerations.asp

History of computers. (n.d.). Retrieved November 17, 2005, from http://www.hitmill.com/computers/history/index.html

A history of computers. (n.d.). Retrieved November 17, 2005, from http://www.maxmon.com/history.htm

Introduction to computers. (n.d.). Retrieved November 17, 2005, from http://www97.intel.com/discover/Journey Inside/TJI_Intro/default.aspx

Schneider, David I. (2003). *An introduction to programming using Visual Basic .NET* (5th ed.). Upper Saddle River, NJ: Prentice Hall.

Ronda B. Henderson

INFORMATION SYSTEMS

Information systems refers to technology designed to handle the data that institutions receive, process, generate, save, backup, disseminate, and use to make decisions. Designs for such systems vary according to the missions, goals, objectives, and global market conditions of the institutions investing in the technology.

DATA, INFORMATION, AND KNOWLEDGE

Information should not be confused with the related concepts of data and knowledge. Data are simply characteristics or descriptions of relevant objects or events that influence business decisions. Common examples include inventory, sales, receipts, and payments of transactional activities frequently stored and retrieved in databases.

Information is an extension of data by adding organization in ways that add value and relevance to the data. Institutional users are then able derive interpretation that leads to conclusions and implications. When data become more valuable than simple retrieval, information has been produced.

Knowledge exists when users understand how existing information can be applied in higher-order tasks such as explaining phenomena, predicting happenings, or projecting trends. These abilities allow users to become experts rather than simply perform operations.

THE SYSTEMS CONCEPT

A system consists of elements that have either been designed into particular configurations or evolved into configurations over time. For example, a computer system for one user may be just one element, a computer, and related peripheral elements, devices. A system for multiple users may have many computers and peripheral devices. The main point of such a system, however, is that the elements allow users to use the system in some concerted manner to achieve personal or institutional missions, goals, and objectives.

THE INFORMATION SYSTEM

An information system is a melding of the concept of information with a system of technology to best facilitate organizational needs. An information system requires designers and users capable of systems thinking to keep the system dynamic within an environment of constantly changing variables over time.

CLASSIFICATION OF INFORMATION SYSTEMS

The need for information systems creates various classifications. The areas of need reflected in these classifications are organizational levels, functional areas, support areas, and the information system architecture.

Organizational Level Classification. Many organizations are so complex that their technological systems are organized in a hierarchical structure representative of their organizational charts. For example, information systems may be classified by departments, divisions, and/or work units. A major point, however, is that organizational information systems must be interconnected.

Functional Area Classification. An information system can be classified by the major functions of the organization that cross organizational structure. Typical functional information systems are developed for accounting, finance, manufacturing, marketing, and human resource management.

Support Area Classification. Information systems all have a support role in facilitating the meeting of institutional missions, goals, and objectives. Examples of support classification information systems are transaction processing systems, management information systems, knowledge management systems, office automation systems, decision support systems, group support systems, and intelligent support systems.

Transaction processing system: A transaction processing system (TPS) performs the routine functions of an organization, such as payroll, customer orders, billing, and expenses. A TPS provides support to the monitoring, collection, storage, processing, and dissemination need for these routine business processes.

Management information system: A management information system (MIS) supports activities to make sure that business strategies are being efficiently employed. Those support activities include planning, monitoring,

A typical personal computer system may include a tower, keyboard, monitor, mouse, and speakers. **PHOTOGRAPH BY KELLY A. QUIN. THE GALE GROUP.**

and control. Specific technology activities might include providing periodic reports on operational efficiency, effectiveness, and productivity.

Data and reports from MISs are used in making decisions, such as projecting inventory and sales levels. Typical information from a MIS includes statistical summaries, exception reports, periodic as well as on-demand reports, comparative analysis, projections, early detection, routine reports, and communications. Human relations issues, such as projecting employee retirement liability, are important to long-term employment policy.

Knowledge management system: Knowledge management is a collaborative organizational system wherein knowledge is shared and dispensed. Functions of a knowledge management system (KMS) include support for assisting organizations to identify, select, organize, dissem-

inate, and transfer information that represents expertise. For example, some individuals know so much about their organizations that continuing to operate without them, as in the case of employees accepting employment elsewhere, dying, or experiencing diminished capacity, is difficult. Knowledge management as a technological information system allows organizations to pull together the collective knowledge of its employees. That collective knowledge is then available to all of the institution's employees for decision making.

Examples of KMS mechanisms include electronic bulletin boards for posting information needs, threaded discussion groups for sharing on a particular topic over electronic mail (e-mail), knowledge tracking, and creating space on an organization's Web site for information about the organization and for descriptions of the projects of its employees.

Office automation systems: One of the earliest information systems to emerge was the office automation system (OAS). Functions of the office such as document processing, imaging, photocopying, data transfer, data storage, and communications have been forged into single software systems.

The effects of OAS have had a tremendous impact on who does the work. In much of the business environment, positions such being a secretary to an individual or being in a pool of clerical office workers have changed. Most employees in organizations do much of their own clerical work on their own desktops. Employees who were formerly isolated in offices and pools now have a much richer array of job duties and responsibilities.

Decision support systems: Decision support depends on how structured a particular problem that needs solving is. For example, some problems are unstructured in that similar problems have not occurred before and no ready routine exists for problem solving. Other problems have occurred routinely and a decision process exists for the problem.

Decision support systems (DSS) contain decision-modeling routines, such as what-if analysis, whereby users can try particular decisions in simulations before actual implementation. Problems needing decisions can be developed into scenarios where users enter what they know about the problem, enter possible decision designs, make choices among the designs, implement decisions, and observe effects. Once the effects are within the level of tolerance set by management, the decision is made.

Group support systems: Group support systems (GSS), sometimes called groupware, are interactive computer-based systems that allow groups of people throughout an institution to work on the same projects. The software contains routines for generation of ideas, resolution of conflicts, and freedom of expression.

A major problem encountered in group work is the development of negative behaviors, such as destructive miscommunication. Another problem is groupthink, a condition in which group work emerges as unimaginative and the members resist taking responsibility for the work. GSS contain functions that make information instantaneous and build consensus to make sure that members remain excited about the project. GSS also provide for early and continuous voting.

Intelligent support systems: Intelligent support systems (ISS), sometimes referred to as expert systems, are one of the more advanced forms of information systems. The premise of such systems is that they can apply reasoning—sometimes called artificial intelligence—to a particular area of problems and generate advice, recommendations, and solutions.

Problem areas for which ISS has been applied include early detection of conditions, patterns to identify fraud in accounting, voice recognition, computer security and password encryption, health diagnosis and prognosis, and disaster planning.

SYSTEM ARCHITECTURE CLASSIFICATION

Information architecture is the conceptualization of the information requirements of a core business of an organization as well as the ways in which those requirements are met. Information architecture can be centralized, such as for communications architecture, data architecture, and business architecture. Other strategic, managerial, and operational architectures may be decentralized.

System architecture is the specific technologies—such as computers, networks, databases, and communication devices—that anchor the information system. For example, an insurance company or an inventory company may have a system architecture that anchors the remainder of the institution's information system.

A frequent way of classifying information systems by system architecture is by focusing on the device structure where the actual computing or calculating happens. For example, the anchor technology may be a mainframe computer, strategically located stand-alone computers, or a distributed or networked system of desktop computers.

Mainframe Computers. A mainframe computer contains the computing power of the system. Computer terminals that have no computing power contend for access to the mainframe computer for computing that is then sent back to the respective computer terminal. Information systems using a mainframe are referred to as distributed because computing results must be distributed to users at various locations. Mainframe architecture is frequently used where the applications place heavy mathematical demands on the computer's brain, the central processing unit (CPU).

Stand-Alone Desktop Computers. Desktop computers, also known as personal computers, have the CPU in the unit on the users' workspace. The desktop stand-alone may come with devices on board such as compact disks, digital video devices, and digital video recorders, in addition to input and output devices such as keyboards, storage devices, monitors, and printers. Since a stand-alone with such devices represents multiple elements, it is also an information system.

Networked Desktop Computers. Desktop computers can be wired together in various ways to produce a network, sometimes called a local area network. In a network, devices and information can be shared by desktop users. A main desktop computer, called a server, maintains traffic over the writing schemes to make sure that documents, e-mail, and other communications arrive at the designated destination computer intact. A system of servers can be used for added capacity or for distinct purposes, such as e-mail and printing.

The information systems described here are all technological mechanisms tailored to meet both enterprise-wide and specific-need missions, goals, and objectives.

SEE ALSO *Information Processing; Software*

BIBLIOGRAPHY

Jones, Gareth, and George, Jennifer (2004). *Essentials of contemporary management.* New York: McGraw-Hill/Irwin.

Stair, Ralph M., and Reynolds, George W. (2003). *Principles of information systems* (6th ed.). Boston: Thomson/Course Technology.

Stair, Ralph M., and Reynolds, George W. (2006). *Fundamentals of information systems* (3rd ed.). Boston: Thomson/Course Technology.

Turban, Efraim, McLean, Ephraim, Wetherbe, James, et al. (2002). *Information technology for management: Transforming business in the digital economy* (3rd ed.). New York: Wiley.

Douglas C. Smith

INFORMATION TECHNOLOGY

Information technology (IT) turns arduous chores into efficient tasks and corporate activities into achievable accomplishments. Online banking, electronic mail (e-mail) communications, ATM transactions, and Internet-based research are possible because of IT. IT has evolved into an essential component of everyday life.

The Information Technology Association of America (ITAA) provides a concise definition of IT as, "the collection of products and services that turn data into useful, meaningful, accessible information." Tony Gunton provides a more comprehensive definition of IT as "electronic technologies for collecting, storing, processing, and communicating information … separated into two main categories (1) those which process information, such as computer systems, and (2) those which disseminate information, such as telecommunication systems" (1993, p. 150). Specific equipment (computers) and software are needed to process data so that information can be

acquired. IT is reliant upon items to electronically input, output, process, store, and retrieve data. Data may include, but are not limited to, text, graphics, sound, and video. Although IT is a complex entity, it makes daily tasks easier and more efficient.

Computers, networks, satellites, robotics, videotext, television, e-mail, electronic games, and automated office equipment are some of the many tools used in IT. The IT industry uses hardware and equipment such as computers, telephones, World Wide Web sites, transaction machines, and office equipment to transfer information. Specific software and services are used to ensure rapid processing of information that is reliable and secure.

HISTORY OF INFORMATION TECHNOLOGY

Although the term *information technology* first appeared in the 1970s, the basic concept can be traced to much earlier times, when the abacus (c. 1400), the movable press (1450s), and slide rule (1600s) were considered the first "computers." Although these tools may seem primitive, these "analog" computers provided valuable information for their users.

IT then took a huge leap as military and business industries combined their efforts in the early 1900s. Together they were a major force in IT research and development. Punched cards and electrical pulses quickly gave way to vacuum tubes and electronic digital computers.

The first electronic digital computer was designed at the University of Pennsylvania by John Presper Eckert, Jr. (1919–1995) and John W. Mauchly (1907–1980) in 1945. The electronic numerical integrator and computer, or ENIAC, was designed to discover, monitor, and predict flight paths of weapons. ENIAC was designed using 18,000 vacuum tubes that provided a week's worth of information in one hour, but was laden with maintenance problems.

The first commercial computer was the Universal Automatic Computer (UNIVAC), developed by Eckert and Mauchly in 1951. The UNIVAC I was used by the Census Bureau to predict the outcome of the 1952 presidential election. The development of ENIAC and UNIVAC I prompted an increase in IT research and development that continues into the twenty-first century. Computers are designed for a variety of purposes and are divided into four categories: supercomputer, mainframe computer, microcomputer, and minicomputer. The categories are defined by size, cost, and processing ability.

Supercomputers are developed for use in science and engineering, for designing aircraft and nuclear reactors, and for predicting worldwide weather patterns. These computers are of significant size and cost millions of dol-

Computing in 1951. *U.S. Air Force technicians evaluate the UNIVAC computer system which took up 352 square feet of floor space and ran at a then-astronomical rate of 2.25 megahertz.* **U.S. AIR FORCE/GETTY IMAGES**

lars. Information is processed quickly using multiple processors. Few supercomputers exist because of their cost.

Mainframe computers are large general-purpose computers requiring special attention and controlled atmospheres. They are used in large corporations to calculate and manipulate large amounts of information stored in databases. Mainframe computers are high-speed, multipurpose machines that cost millions.

Microcomputers were introduced in 1975 by the Massachusetts Institute of Technology (MIT). These desktop computers were designed using a single-chip microprocessor as its processing element. Tandy Corporation quickly followed MIT by offering Radio Shack's first microcomputer in 1976. The Apple microcomputer was introduced in 1977. IBM introduced the first personal computer (PC) in the fall of 1981, causing a dramatic increase in the microcomputer market. The microcomputer is generally known as a PC. The cost for PCs ranges from $500 to $2,000. Because of dramatic improvements in computer components and manufacturing, personal computers do more than the largest computers of the mid-1960s at a fraction of the cost.

Minicomputers came on to the scene in the early 1980s in small businesses, manufacturing plants, and factories. Minicomputers are multitasking machines that connect many terminals to each other and a mainframe computer. As such, they are able to process large amounts of data. Minicomputer systems (desktop, network, laptop, and handheld devices) range in price from $15,000 to $150,000.

Since the 1950s, four generations of computers have evolved. Each generation reflected a decrease in hardware size but an increase in computer operation capabilities. The first generation used vacuum tubes, the second used transistors, the third used integrated circuits, and the fourth used integrated circuits on a single computer chip. Advances in artificial intelligence that will minimize the need for complex programming characterize the fifth generation of computers, still in the experimental stage.

INFORMATION TECHNOLOGY PHASES

Information processing involves five phases: input, process, output, storage, and retrieval. Each of these phases and the devices associated with each are discussed below.

Input. Input refers to information or stimulus that enters a system. Input can include commands entered from the keyboard to data from another computer. Input devices include the keyboard, pointing devices (such as mouses), scanners and reading devices, digital cameras, audio and video input devices, and input devices for physically challenged users. Input devices are used to capture data at the earliest possible point in the workflow, so that the data are accurate and readily available for processing.

Processing. Processing occurs after data have been entered into the computer. When data are processed, they are transformed from raw facts into meaningful information. A variety of processes may be performed on the data, such as adding, subtracting, dividing, multiplying, sorting, organizing, formatting, comparing, graphing, and summarizing. Data processing includes the input, verification, organization, storage, retrieval, transformation, and extraction of information from data. Processing can also include the execution of a program.

Output. Output is information that comes out of a computer. Four common types of output are text, graphics, audio, and video. After the information has been processed, it can be listened to through speakers or a headset, printed onto paper, or displayed on a monitor. An output device is any computer component capable of conveying information to a user. Commonly used output devices include display devices, printers, speakers, headsets, data projectors, fax machines, and multifunction devices. A multifunction device is a single piece of equipment that looks like a copy machine but provides the functionality of a printer, scanner, copy machine, and perhaps a fax machine.

Storage. Storage refers to a variety of techniques and devices that retain data. Storage devices preserve items such as data, instructions, and information for retrieval and future use. Storage is measured in a hierarchy of bytes.

- *Bit:* single unit of data coded in binary form (0 or 1)

- *Byte:* most commonly comprised of 8 bits (combinations of 0s and 1s)
- *Kilobyte:* 1,024 bytes
- *Megabyte:* 1,024 kilobytes or 1 million bytes
- *Gigabyte:* 1,024 megabytes or 1 billion bytes
- *Terabyte:* 1,024 gigabytes or 1 trillion bytes

Devices used to store data include floppy disks, hard disks, compact disks (both read-only and disk-recordable), tapes, PC cards, smart cards, microfilm, and microfiche. Portable drives (flash drive/jump drive) can also serve as storage devices.

Retrieval. Retrieval is the ability to search for and locate information that has been stored. The information can be text, sound, images, or data. Information retrieved may include documents, information within documents, and information within a stand-alone database or hyperlinked database such as the Internet or intranets.

IT drives the educational, business, medical, and military worlds. As such, it is imperative that the relationship between and among the phases of IT work seamlessly to input, process, display (output), store, and retrieve data. Continuous research and development is needed to meet the future needs of the world.

THE FUTURE OF INFORMATION TECHNOLOGY

The future of IT is promising. People use computers in new ways every day. Computers are increasingly affordable, more powerful, and easier to use. Communication needs will continue to grow; the functions of e-mail, instant messaging, Weblogs, and wireless communications will improve as the demands of informational society increase. Daily tasks will continue to be enhanced as more people use Web-based technologies.

Potential problems concerning IT center on its delicate infrastructure. Educational, business, and military systems are mindful of the underlying foundation necessary to support its respective communities. In fact, researchers are already hard at work exploring possible solutions to the infrastructure concerns. One solution offered is the creation of a "mobile Internet." Another possible solution is the automation of data integration.

What will the future hold for IT? While questions exist, one thing is certain: IT will continue to grow and adapt making life more enjoyable and efficient.

SEE ALSO *Hardware; Information Processing; Information Technology; Office Technology*

BIBLIOGRAPHY

Fryman, Harriet (2004, March 1). The future of IT is automation. Retrieved September 21, 2005, from http://www.cioupdate.com/reports/article.php/3319601

Gunton, Tony (1993). *A Dictionary of information technology and computer science* (2nd ed.). Manchester, England: NCC Blackwell.

Information Technology Association of America. (n.d.). The U.S. information technology industry: A brief overview. Retrieved September 20, 2005, from http://www.itaa.org/eweb/DynamicPage.aspx?webcode=LTII &wps_key=86291cb4-0e13-41c7-89f0-e0767fcf4eb6

National Coordination Office for Information Technology Research and Development. (2001, February). *Using information technology to transform the way we learn. Report to the president.* Arlington, VA. (ERIC Document No. 462 969)

Reiser, R. A., and Dempsey, J. V. (2002). *Trends and issues in instructional design and technology.* Upper Saddle River, NJ: Prentice-Hall.

Reynolds, P. (2005). A vision of the Internet in 2010. In Les Lloyd (Ed.), *Best technology practices in higher education* (pp. 193–200). Medford, NJ: Information Today.

Smaldino, Sharon E., et al. (2005). *Instructional technology and media for learning* (8th ed.). Upper Saddle River, NJ: Pearson/Merrill/Prentice Hall.

Charlotte J. Boling

INPUT

SEE *Operations Management*

INSTANT MESSAGING

SEE *Communications Channels*

INSTITUTE OF INTERNAL AUDITORS

The Institute of Internal Auditors (IIA) was founded in 1941 by a small group of dedicated practitioners in the field they identified as "internal auditing." Few individuals at the time were aiding the heads of companies in maintaining sufficient controls for effective operations and for monitoring the quality of financial information processed and reported. The initial group's goal was to encourage competent individuals to consider the emerging field through the provision of educational activities and guidance for the practice of internal auditing. By the beginning of 2006, the IIA had more than 110,000 members.

In 1944 the IIA began publishing *Internal Auditor,* the magazine that would become one of the profession's leading publications. In 1947 the Statement of Responsibilities of Internal Auditing was issued and became the foundation for development of internal audit standards. The official motto, Progress through Sharing, was adopted in 1955 and continues to guide the IIA's efforts. IIA members approved the Code of Ethics in 1968; and in 1972 adopted a Common Body of Knowledge, which identified the content for the certified internal auditor (CIA) examination offered for the first time in 1973. In 2005 the IIA reached the milestone of 50,000 professionals having received the designation during the CIA's thirty-two-year history.

The IIA Research Foundation, founded in 1976, sponsors research on trends and issues in internal auditing. A tax-exempt 501(c)(3) corporation, it provides and expands research and education for the benefit of the internal audit profession, the business and government communities, and the general public.

In 1978 the International Standards for the Professional Practice of Internal Auditing were approved. Awareness of the importance of university preparation for the profession motivated a pilot program in internal auditing at Louisiana State University. The success of this initial program effort led to establishment of programs in other colleges and universities. By 1999 more than thirty-five colleges and universities throughout the globe were participants in the IIA's Endorsed Internal Audit Program.

Noteworthy developments in the 1980s included: the introduction of the IIA's first computer software product, audit Masterplan; the establishment of the Quality Assurance Review Service; the mandate of continuing professional development for CIAs; and the granting of consultative status to the IIA by the United Nations. The 1990s introduced the Global Auditing Information Network, which compiles and disseminates benchmarking information; the creation of the IIA's official Web site; and the development of specialty groups, services, and products to support membership needs. These include the Control Self-Assessment Center, Certification in Control Self-Assessment, Certified Governmental Auditor Program, Board of Environmental Auditors Certification, and the Chief Audit Executive Services Program.

In 1999 the IIA's board of directors approved a new professional practices framework (PPF). The board also approved a new definition of *internal auditing* as "an independent, objective assurance and consulting activity designed to add value and improve an organization's operations." The internal audit function is to ensure that an organization meets its objectives through a systematic, disciplined approach to evaluating and improving the effectiveness of risk management, control, and governance processes. The PPF comprises the International Standards for the Professional Practice of Internal Auditing, the Code of Ethics, Practice Advisories, and development and practice aids.

In 2002 the IIA added the financial services auditor group and the certified financial services auditor designations.

The IIA's mission is to provide dynamic leadership for the global profession of internal auditing. Activities in support of this mission include, but are not limited to:

- Advocating and promoting the value that internal audit professionals add to their organizations

- Providing comprehensive professional educational and development opportunities; standards and other professional practice guidance; and certification programs

- Researching, disseminating, and promoting to practitioners and stakeholders knowledge concerning internal auditing and its appropriate role in control, risk management, and governance

- Educating practitioners and other relevant audiences on best practices in internal auditingBringing together internal auditors from all countries to share information and experiences

The IIA is organized as a nonprofit association governed by a volunteer board elected by its membership. In 2006 the institute had 246 affiliates that served IIA members at the local level, with members in 160 countries and chapters or institutes in more than 90 countries. Volunteer committees support the local chapters, national institutes, and the international board.

In addition to offering a variety of membership options, certification programs, and standards and other guidance, the IIA provides professional development, promotes academic relations, publishes periodicals, offers an employment referral service, generates benchmarking information, provides audit services, and maintains partnerships with other professional organizations.

Additional information is available from the IIA at 247 Maitland Avenue, Altamonte Springs, FL 32701-4201; 407-937-1100 (phone); 407-937-1101 (fax); or, http://www.theiia.org.

SEE ALSO *Auditing*

Trish W. Harris

INSTITUTE OF MANAGEMENT ACCOUNTANTS

The Institute of Management Accountants (IMA) is the largest educational, nonprofit association in the world devoted exclusively to management accounting, finance, and information management. It was founded in 1919 in Buffalo, New York, as the National Association of Cost Accountants by a group of businesspeople to expand the knowledge and professionalism of people specifically interested in cost accounting.

Subsequently its name was changed to the National Association of Accountants and then in 1991 to the current name. These changes were made to reflect its broadened mission to disseminate the latest knowledge in accounting and finance to all those professionals employed in public and private companies as well as governmental and educational organizations. In its statement of mission, the IMA states that it will "provide to members personal and professional development opportunities through education, association with business professionals, and certification in management accounting and financial management skills and ensure that IMA is globally recognized by the financial community as a respected institution influencing the concepts and ethical practices of management accounting and financial management."

As an international educational organization, the IMA sponsors two certification programs: certified management accountant (CMA) and certified in financial management (CFM). These certification programs are administered by an affiliate, the Institute of Certified Management Accountants, which was established in 1972.

The flagship publication of the Institute is a monthly magazine, *Strategic Finance*. The IMA also publishes *Management Accounting Quarterly* four times per year and a quarterly newsletter, *Focus*, which goes to all members. Through another affiliate, the IMA Foundation for Applied Research (FAR), it conducts research and publishes field-based research and analysis. It also publishes, in conjunction with other organizations, a series of guides called *Statements on Management Accounting*. As part of its professional responsibilities, the IMA contributes to and comments on the accounting rule-making process through a senior-level committee.

The IMA offers its 65,000 members an opportunity to join three member interest groups—the Controllers Council, Cost Management Group, and Small-Business Council. Each group publishes a newsletter ten times per year featuring information on industry trends and practices, emerging technologies, and financial and management reporting issues. Members' surveys are conducted to keep members apprised of how their colleagues in other industries and organizations are handling key issues. In addition, members can join Internet-based groups that enable them to network and exchange information online dealing with their particular industry or special interests.

The IMA requires certified members to obtain a certain number of Continuing Professional Education credits every year. It offers a number of methods to achieve this objective, including an annual conference, chapter/council education programs, Regional Education Assistance Programs, self-study courses (including online offerings), a monthly video-subscription program, and national seminars. It also offers in-house education programs for companies, focusing on current trends, industry-specific developments, and continuing skills enhancement.

The IMA is governed by a volunteer president, executive committee, and board of directors. A salaried, full-time executive director directs the day-to-day operations of the Institute based on policy guidelines promulgated by the executive committee and board of directors. Activities also are conducted by approximately three hundred local chapters and twenty-four regional councils, which hold regular technical meetings and other functions. The IMA's headquarters is located at 10 Paragon Drive, Montvale, New Jersey, 07645-1718, (201) 474-1600; www.imanet. org; www.strategicfinancemag.com.

SEE ALSO *Accounting; Certified Management Accountant (CMA)/Certified in Financial Management (CFM)*

Kathy Williams
Robert F. Randall

INSURANCE

Insurance is vital to a free enterprise economy. Insurance is the process of spreading risk of economic loss among as many people or entities as possible who are subject to the same kind of risk; it is based on the laws of probability (chance of a given outcome happening) and large numbers (which enables the laws of probability to work). Society faces many perils (causes of loss)—some natural (e.g., earthquakes, hurricanes, tornados, flood, drought), some human (e.g., arson, theft, fraud, vandalism, contamination, pollution, terrorism), and some economic (e.g., expropriation, inflation, obsolescence, depressions/recessions).

Availability of insurance allows individuals and businesses to purchase policies that provide protection from financial loss attributable to death, accidents, sicknesses, damage to property, and injury caused to others. The person or organization seeking to transfer risk—the insured (policyholder) pays a relatively small amount (the premium) to an insurance company (the insurer), which issues an insurance policy in which the insurer agrees to reimburse the insured for any losses covered by the policy. Insurers are able to provide coverage for virtually any predictable loss.

EARLY HISTORY

The concept of insurance was introduced thousands of years ago and has evolved over many centuries. The Chinese, for example, divided their cargoes among many boats to reduce the severity of loss from the perils of the seas, while the biblical story of Joseph and the famine in Egypt illustrates the storing of grain during the seven good years to relieve shortages during the seven years of famine. Marine insurance emerged in London when ships sailed for the New World. Fire insurance arose from the great fire of London in 1666, in which 14,000 buildings were destroyed. In 1752 Benjamin Franklin (1706–1790) founded the first mutual fire insurance company in the United States, the Philadelphia Contributorship for the Insurance of Houses from Loss by Fire.

U.S. INSURANCE INDUSTRY

The U.S. insurance industry is made up of approximately 5,000 companies that provide insurance coverage of various types, with combined annual revenue of about $1 trillion. The industry is highly concentrated with the fifty largest companies holding more than 60 percent of the market. Within product segments, concentration is even higher.

The three broad categories of insurance are property and casualty, which generates about 60 percent of annual industry revenue; health, generating about 12 percent; and life, which generates 10 percent. Within the property and casualty segment, commercial insurance accounts for 60 percent of revenue. Because of the very different insurance issues involved in each, many agencies handle only one type of insurance. Agencies may also specialize in selling to individuals, businesses, or groups.

Insurance is sold either directly by insurers (direct insurers) or through the independent agency system, exclusive agencies, and brokers. There are about 130,000 insurance agency offices, with the largest insurance agencies holding only 20 percent of the total market. The industry is highly fragmented.

An insurance agent works on the insurance company's behalf, while an insurance broker represents the customer's interests. Many agencies, especially on the commercial side, function as brokers.

**Top ten U.S. life/health insurance groups
and companies by revenues, 2004**

Rank	Group/Company	Revenue (in millions)
1	MetLife	$39,535
2	Prudential Financial	28,343
3	New York Life Insurance	27,176
4	TIAA-CREF	23,411
5	MassMutual Life Insurance	23,159
6	Northwestern Mutual	17,806
7	AFLAC	13,281
8	UnumProvident	10,611
9	Guardian Life of America	8,893
10	Principal Financial	8,756

SOURCE: Insurance Information Institute (www.iii.org)

Table 1

The insurance industry employed about 2.3 million wage and salary workers in 2004. Insurance carriers accounted for 62 percent of jobs, while insurance agencies, brokerages, and providers of other insurance-related services accounted for 38 percent of jobs. In addition, about 151,000 workers in the industry were self-employed in 2004, mostly as insurance sales agents.

LIFE/HEALTH INSURANCE

Many insurance companies provide a variety of both life and health insurance policies. The two types, however, will be briefly discussed separately here.

Life Insurance. Life insurance is purchased to protect dependents against financial hardship when the insured person, the policyholder, dies. Many life insurance policies provide for the accumulation of savings that can be used in time of financial hardship. The Survey of Consumer Finances by the Federal Reserve Board revealed that 69 percent of American families owned some type of life insurance in 2001. Americans purchased $3.1 trillion of new life insurance coverage in 2004, which was 5 percent more than in 2003. By the end of 2004, total life insurance coverage in the United States reached $17.5 trillion, which was an increase of 3 percent from 2003.

Health Insurance. The majority of people in the United States, 245.3 million (84.3 percent of the population) had some health insurance coverage in 2004. There were 45.8 million (15.7 percent) of the population without health coverage. These figures from a U.S. Census Bureau report were based on a broad classification of health insurance coverage defined operationally as:

Private health insurance is coverage by a plan provided through an employer or union or purchased by an individual from a private company. Government health insurance includes the federal programs Medicare, Medicaid, and military health care; the State Children's Health Insurance Program (SCHIP); and individual state health plans. People were considered "insured" if they were covered by any type of health insurance for part or all of the previous year, and everyone else was considered uninsured. (DeNavas-Walt, Proctor, and Lee, 2005, p. 16)

Most insured people (59.8 percent) were covered by a health insurance plan related to employment for some or all of 2004. This proportion was lower than in 2003 (60.4 percent). The percentage of people covered by health insurance provided by the government increased between 2003 and 2004 from 26.6 to 27.2 percent; government insurance includes Medicare, Medicaid, and military health care. Medicaid coverage rose by 0.5 percent in 2004, while the percentage of people covered by Medicare remained unchanged, at 13.7 percent.

The top ten U.S. private life/health companies, ranked by revenues, are shown in Table 1.

PROPERTY/CASUALTY INSURANCE

A wide range of types of property and casualty insurance are provided by U.S. companies. The American Insurance Association (AIA) is the leading trade association for this segment of the insurance industry. There are 435 insurers in the AIA who write more than $120 billion in premiums each year. Member companies provide all types of property-casualty insurance, including personal and commercial auto insurance, commercial property and liability coverage for small businesses, workers' compensation, homeowners' insurance, medical malpractice coverage, and product liability insurance.

The property insurance marketplace faces many significant challenges, including skyrocketing water-damage claims and manmade catastrophes (terrorist attacks), in addition to the more traditional challenges associated with catastrophic natural disasters. The AIA's Web site (http://www.aiadc.org) lists current issues, as the association describes itself as active in "shaping public policies affecting an increasingly complex insurance marketplace." This association, however, while providing publications for purchase, has limited information for the inquiring citizen. The top ten U.S. property and casualty insurers by revenue are shown in Table 2.

ORGANIZATION OF COMPANIES

Insurers primarily operate as stock (owned by stockholders) or mutual (owned by policyholders) companies,

Top ten U.S. property/casualty companies by revenue, 2004		
Rank	Company/Group	Revenue (in millions)
1	American International Group	$98,610
2	Berkshire Hathaway	74,382
3	State Farm Insurance Cos.	58,819
4	Allstate	33,936
5	St. Paul Travelers Cos.	22,934
6	Hartford Financial Services	22,693
7	Nationwide	20,558
8	Liberty Mutual Insurance Group	19,754
9	Loews (CNA)	14,584
10	Progressive	13,782

SOURCE: Insurance Information Institute (www.iii.org)

Table 2

mutual meaning that they are legally owned by policyholders and consequently do not issue stock. Other forms of structure are pools and associations (groups of insurers), risk retention groups, purchasing groups, and fraternal organizations (primarily life and health insurance). An insurer within a given state is classified domestic, if formed under that state; foreign, if incorporated in another state; or alien, if incorporated in another country.

FUNCTIONS

The key functions of an insurer are marketing, underwriting (issuing policies), claims (investigation and payment of legitimate claims as well as defending against illegitimate claims), loss control, reinsurance, actuarial, collection of premiums, drafting of insurance contracts to conform with statutory law, and the investing of funds. Underwriters are expert in identifying, understanding, evaluating, and selecting risks. Actuaries play a unique and critical role in the insurance process: They price the product (the premium) and establish the reserves.

The primary goal of an insurer is to underwrite profitably. Disciplined underwriting combined with sound investing and asset/liability management enables an insurer to meet its obligations to both policyholders and stockholders. Underwriting combines many skills—investigative, accounting, financial, and psychological. While some lines of business (e.g., homeowners and auto insurance) are underwritten manually or class rated, many large commercial property and casualty risks are judgment rated, relying on the underwriter's skill, experience, and intuition.

PRODUCT AND RATINGS

An insurance policy varies among states and classes of business; nevertheless, there are features common to all policies.

- *Declaration page:* Names the policyholder, describes the property or liability to be insured, type of coverage, and policy limits

- *Insuring agreement:* Describes parties' responsibilities during the policy term

- *Conditions of the policy:* Details coverage and requirements in event of a loss

- *The exclusions:* Describes types of property and losses not covered; the states and insurers continually work together to make the policy more readable

Rating organizations include: A. M. Best, Moody's, and Standard & Poor's. Each of these rating organizations provides information about specific companies.

ROLE OF GOVERNMENT

Federal and state governments play important roles, as noted earlier, in relation to health insurance and in managing large social insurance programs, such as Social Security, unemployment compensation, federal deposit insurance, and pension benefit guaranty. In these areas, the government acts either as a partner or competitor to the insurance industry, or as an exclusive provider. Federal and state governments also manage property and casualty programs, such as "all-risk" crop, crime, flood, and workers' compensation.

REINSURANCE

Reinsurance is critical to the insurance process; it brings capacity, stability, and financial strength to insurers. The purpose of reinsurance is to spread large risks and catastrophes over as large a base as possible. It is the assumption by one insurance company (the reinsurer) of all or part of a risk undertaken by another insurance company (the cedent). It enables an insured with a sizable risk exposure to deal with and receive coverage from one insurer, rather than dealing with a number of insurers.

Reinsurance has made possible greater face amounts of life insurance coverage, even though the total number of policies fell in the early years of the twenty-first century. An applicant who is an unusual risk and is seeking a policy can be accommodated by being granted a policy with the insurer who can in turn transfer part of the risk to a reinsurer. Reinsurance can limit the investment risk inherent in high asset concentration from single products, such as annuities. As noted in *Life Insurers Fact Book:*

In 2005, 85 percent of life insurers with life premiums ceded at least some of those premiums as reinsurance. Among insurers with accident and health premium, 82 percent ceded accident and health premium; ... only 40 percent of insurers doing annuity business ... ceded annuity considerations. (American Council of Life Insurers, 2005, Chapter 6)

REGULATION

Insurance companies are overseen by state insurance regulators, whose authority is comprehensive. Insurance companies must meet risk-based capital standards, adhere to investment guidelines, and undergo regular on-site financial examinations. Companies must provide such information as changes in officers and directors, as well as quarterly and annual financial statements that are signed and attested to by company officers. Company financial policies are reviewed on actuarial and accounting standards.

Each state determines the company and licensing requirements, product filing rules, market conduct exams, and laws and regulations to ensure solvency and protection of consumers.

State insurance departments work with the National Association of Insurance Commissioners (NAIC) to develop and promote laws and regulations that serve as model laws, and with the state legislatures, which pass the laws and set the budgets. NAIC is the organization of insurance regulators—from the fifty U.S. states, the District of Columbia, and the four U.S. territories—that has as its mission the protection of public interest, the promotion of competitive markets, the facilitation of fair and equitable treatment of insurance consumers, and the improvement of state regulation of insurance.

State insurance departments also work with the courts, which interpret insurance regulations and policy wording; the U.S. Congress and the U.S. Government Accountability Office, which periodically evaluate state insurance regulation; and professional, trade, and consumer groups.

COMPETITION

Because the insurance market has many sellers and buyers, little product differentiation, and freedom of entry and exit, it is highly competitive. This is especially true in the property and casualty segment. While demand for insurance grows steadily over time, with the increase in exposures and legal requirements, the supply of insurance, because it is financial and flexible, can be easily shifted in and out of the market. This attracts capital during periods of high interest and stock market strength because of high profit expectations from investing underwriting cash flows.

CHALLENGES FACED BY THE PROPERTY/CASUALTY SEGMENT

Property/casualty firms have faced additionally significant challenges since Hurricane Katrina in 2005, including a daunting claims-adjusting environment and litigation. The AIA has endeavored to aid companies addressing the challenges and issues surrounding natural disasters on the Gulf Coast. One outcome from the Katrina disaster was renewed attention to improving building codes and building code enforcement.

GLOBALIZATION

Globalization is reshaping much of the business world, including the insurance world. The NAIC is one group that has increasingly been involved in insurance regulation in the international arena. NAIC has provided leadership in the International Association of Insurance Supervisors and in the International Accounting Standards Board. NAIC hosted an international symposium on the topic "State Insurance Regulators: Meeting Tomorrow's Global Challenges Today," in February 2006. The symposium addressed financial services markets and key regulatory developments in Europe, Latin America, China, and India. Leading regulators from several countries participated in the program, which aimed to advance the setting of global standards and to reduce differences in insurance supervision.

SOURCES FOR INFORMATION

A number of insurance-related organizations provide information for persons interested in learning more about insurance. These organizations include, in addition to the NAIC, some of the following:

American Council of Life Insurers: The American Council of Life Insurers is a Washington, D.C., trade association that has as members companies that offer life insurance, long-term care insurance, disability income insurance, reinsurance, annuities, pensions, and other retirement and financial protection products. Its annual *Life Insurers Fact Book* is an especially useful reference.

America's Health Insurance Plans: America's Health Insurance Plans is a national association representing approximately 1,300 members, who provide health benefits to more than 200 million Americans. The primary purpose of this association is to represent the interests of its members on legislative and regulatory issues at both federal and state levels.

AIA: The AIA is an advocate group for the companies that sell property/casualty insurance. As noted earlier, its free information is limited, but some current insurance issues receive particular attention from the association's leadership and committees.

SEE ALSO *Investments; Personal Financial Planning*

BIBLIOGRAPHY

Aizcorbe, Ana M., Kennickell, Arthur B., and Moore, Kevin B. (2003, January). Recent changes in U.S. family finances: Evidence from the 1998 and 2001 Survey of Consumer Finances. *Federal Reserve, 89,* 1–32.

American Council of Life Insurers. http://www.acli.org

American Council of Life Insurers. (2005). *Life insurers fact book* [Annual]. Washington, DC: Author.

America's Health Insurance Plans. http://www.ahip.org

Baldwin, Ben G. (2002). *The new life insurance investment advisor* (2nd ed.). New York: McGraw-Hill.

DeNavas-Walt, C., Proctor, B. D., and Lee, C. H. (2005, August). *Income, poverty, and health insurance coverage in the United States.* Current Population Reports P60-229. U.S. Department of Census. Washington, DC: Government Printing Office.

First Research. (n.d.). *Industry profiles* [Excerpts]. Retrieved February 23, 2006, from http://www.firstresearch.com/industry-analysis.asp

Insurance Information Institute. http://www.iii.org

Insurance Information Institute. (2004). Top twenty U.S. life/health insurance groups and companies by revenues. Retrieved February 23, 2006, from http://www.iii.org/media/facts/statsbyissue/industry

Insurance Information Institute. (2004). Top twenty U.S. property/casualty companies by revenues. Retrieved February 23, 2006, from http://www.iii.org/media/facts/statsbyissue/industry

National Association of Insurance Commissioners. http://www.naic.org

U.S. Department of Labor. (2005). *Occupational outlook handbook: 2006–07.* Washington, DC: Author.

Vaughan, Emmett J., and Vaughan, Therese M. (2003). *Fundamentals of risk and insurance* (9th ed.). New York: Wiley.

Anand Shetty
Edward J. Keller Jr.

INTEGRATED SOFTWARE

SEE *Information Systems; Software*

INTELLECTUAL CAPITAL

Intellectual capital is the term used to describe the intangible assets provided to an entity by its employees' efforts and also knowledge assets such as patents, trademarks, copyrights, and other results of human innovation and thought. Intellectual capital is often disaggregated into four categories:

1. Legally recognized intangible assets such as patents, copyrights, and franchises that are purchased

2. Legally salable and protected intangible assets such as trademarks, brands, customer lists, and customer orders

3. Structural intangible assets such as the systems and databases used within the company; examples of these systems are the information system, accounting system, purchasing system, and sales system

4. Human capital intangible assets such as what is in the minds of the individuals who work for the company; an example is the knowledge that researchers in a pharmaceutical company might have in their minds of past experiments and their results

SIGNIFICANCE IN CONTEMPORARY BUSINESS ORGANIZATIONS

The nature of business activity in the United States changed dramatically during the second half of the twentieth century. Jobs in service-producing industries increased greatly. At the same time, manufacturing, farming, construction, and other goods-producing jobs fell. The U.S. economy underwent a basic change in the ways the labor force is employed. While earlier the most significant businesses were industrial enterprises, with the largest segment of the labor force involved in the production of goods, in the twenty-first century U.S. economy, employment in service businesses exceeds that of employment in the production of goods.

In service businesses, and even in industrial and retail enterprises, there is general recognition that astute knowledge management leads to innovation and value creation, and therefore company success. Within the workforce of a company reside the individuals who have the knowledge that represents intellectual capital.

INADEQUACY OF GENERALLY ACCEPTED ACCOUNTING PRINCIPLES

Generally accepted accounting principles (GAAP), which establish what is recorded and reported in an entity's financial statements, ignore an entity's workforce as an asset and also ignore most of the other intangible assets possessed. The stock market analysts, on the other hand, appear to recognize such assets in determining a company's worth, as well as a company's future profit prospects. Companies in which knowledge is important, such as successful companies in the information processing and pharmaceutical fields, sell many times over book value, when purchased by other companies. Even successful industrial companies sell appreciably above book value, though not typically at the levels of companies where knowledge is critical.

The theoretical argument against current accounting is that the current model for reporting does not adequately measure and value the skills, information, and technological capabilities of the individuals in organizations, yet these factors are valuable to the progress of a company. Because of the significance of the unmeasured intellectual capital assets to the future of the entity, and therefore its market capitalization, current financial reporting lacks important informational content, sometimes even to the level of being misleading. Companies have been able to show accounting profits based on their tangible assets following GAAP, while their intellectual capital assets were losing value. Ultimately such companies did very poorly—their profits vanished. Good financial reporting should guide capital to the most promising investments.

An example of the inadequacy of GAAP in relation to recording intellectual capital is in the area of research and development costs of companies. That research improves the knowledge awareness of employees is a prevailing assumption. Intellectual capital would be considered to have been increased because of the learning and understanding gained by means of engaging in research and development. It would then be expected that future revenue would be greater for firms that had significant research and development costs. In some instances research and development results in valuable patents and copyrights. There is evidence that research is strongly associated with earnings, stock prices, and returns.

GAAP, however, mandates the expensing of research and development at the time of the expenditure. (A few exceptions allow for capitalizing some of such expenditures.) Such a ruling reflects the belief that there is no relationship between research and development costs and the future benefits to the firm or that the relationship cannot be established. Another belief is evident: Allowing the capitalization of research and development expenditures introduces the possibility of the manipulation of earnings by companies since establishing objectivity of reasons for amortizing or writing off capitalized costs is difficult to determine.

CURRENT REPORTING STANDARDS

Accounting guidance views intellectual capital as intangible assets and specifies exactly what the term means for accounting recognition. Traditionally such accounts as patents, copyrights, franchises, and goodwill appeared under the intangible assets balance sheet caption, in the instances where the company purchased such assets from other entities. Since internally developed intangible assets, such as patents and copyrights, are generally expensed under current research and development accounting principle, only minimal expenditures, such as the cost of securing a patent may be recorded as an intangible asset. Externally acquired patents and copyrights, however, are recorded at purchase price. Franchises are normally externally acquired and recorded at cost as intangible assets.

The GAAP rules for a purchased subsidiary state goodwill is the excess of the cost of an acquired subsidiary over the sum of the fair values of all identifiable assets that are acquired, less liabilities assumed, that are acquired. Besides tangible assets, identifiable assets include any assets that are intangible assets and meet criteria that make them separable from goodwill such as they can be sold, transferred, licensed, rented, or exchanged or there is a legal-contractual relationship. Examples of identifiable intangible assets separable from goodwill are customer lists, customer orders, brands, and trademarks. If these components of intellectual capital are internally created, there is no means under current GAAP to place their value on the balance sheet. Research and development costs of the acquired subsidiary must be expensed. Goodwill, then, is a residual amount, frequently described as the value of the human capital acquired.

Under current reporting standards the parent company and subsidiary company are required to be reported in the financial statements as if they are a single entity. Therefore, the consolidated financial statements are extremely difficult to understand with the parent's goodwill ignored while the subsidiary's goodwill is shown.

Finally, GAAP does not amortize goodwill because it is considered to have an indefinite useful economic life. Goodwill, however, must be considered annually for impairment. The implied fair value of the reporting unit is compared to its assets including the residual goodwill asset, less liabilities. If the implied current fair value of goodwill is determined to be less than the recorded goodwill, the recorded goodwill must be reduced or entirely eliminated. Because of business economic cycles there are sometimes very large write-offs of goodwill when there is a downturn in the economy and the stock market. It would appear that human capital would not suddenly disappear because of a downturn in the economy.

EFFORTS TO RECOGNIZE AND DISCLOSE INTELLECTUAL CAPITAL INFORMATION

Financial reporting limitations have led to efforts to measure intellectual capital indirectly outside the financial statements. Such measures sometimes accompany the financial statements in reports to stockholders. These nonfinancial measures include information on such items as revenue percentage per employee, employees who have contact with customers, satisfied customers, research and development costs, continuing education and training per employee, employee turnover, and employee satisfaction. One of the best known of the performance measurement strategies that imply the existence of intellectual capital is called the balanced scorecard. It creates measures in the financial, customer, internal business process, and learning and growth areas.

Those who wish to have a more comprehensive, realistic reporting of what provides value to businesses will continue to pay attention to intangible assets.

SEE ALSO *Copyrights; Franchising; Human Resources; Patents; Trademarks*

BIBLIOGRAPHY

Andriassen, D. (2004). *Making sense of intellectual capital: Designing a method for the valuation of intangibles.* Burlington, MA: Elsevier Butterworth-Heinemann.

Financial Accounting Standards Board (2001). *Statement of financial accounting standards no. 141: Business combinations.* Norwalk, CT: Author.

Financial Accounting Standards Board (2001). *Statement of financial accounting standards no. 142: Goodwill and other intangible assets.* Norwalk, CT: Author.

Kaplan, Robert S., and Norton, David P. (1996). *The balanced scorecard.* Cambridge, MA: Harvard Business School Press.

Lev, B. (1997, Spring). The intangibles research project. *Journal of Financial Statement Analysis, 2,* 34–36.

Bernard H. Newman

INTERACTIVE TECHNOLOGY

Interactive is a new buzzword, but its sense is ancient, a lot more ancient than that of the telephone or telegraph. The interesting scientific question now is: How long have people been using words and sentences to communicate with each other? Humans are not passive animals; they are very communicative.

The only 100 percent interactive (audio) technology remains today as it was at its beginning in 1875: the telephone—if interactive means truly equal two-way or multiple-way communication. Telegraphy, however, offers even more parallels with today's world than the telephone. It prefigured a major nonaudio trend in our current interactivity: computer nets which range from those used in local libraries and college classrooms to the worldwide Internet. All these, like the telegraph, use digital coding, not analog words.

The interactivity of e-mail and electronic bulletin boards has contributed greatly to the popularity of the Internet. Mail or telephone communications are fine for a one-on-one discussion, but they are pretty expensive if one is trying to communicate with a group. It costs nearly a dollar to print and mail a letter and, on average, that much for a long-distance phone call. To make such a call, one has to know the number and to have coordinated a time to talk. So it takes considerable time and effort to contact even a modest-size group. On an electronic bulletin board, all one has to do is type a message once and it is available to all readers.

LINEAR VERSUS NONLINEAR TECHNOLOGY

One way to understand the benefits brought about by interactive technology is to compare linear and nonlinear multimedia. An example of linear multimedia is the typical presentation that combines video and sound, but without choices. You watch it from beginning to end. Users are reacting to, not reacting with, what they see.

Nonlinear, interactive multimedia combine the same technologies as linear ones, but with a twist. The viewer is hands-on, controlling what is viewed. Nonlinear multimedia are more complex to produce, because cogent vignettes must be worked through and likely viewer choices must be logically mapped out before the presentation. Distribution is also then limited to technology that can be dynamic in the presentation. For this category, one must pay greater attention to the interface methodology used that will let the viewer control the experience.

USES OF INTERACTIVE TECHNOLOGY

The uses of interactive technology are varied. They are utilized in such varied circumstances as education, training, marketing, and information gathering.

Education and Training. Computers with social interfaces present information in such a way that it is customized for the particular user. Different learning rates are accommodated, because computers are able to pay individual attention to independent learners. Regardless of ability or disability, each user will be able to work at an individual pace.

The interactive network allows learners to quiz themselves anytime in a risk-free environment. A self-administered quiz is a form of self-exploration. A mistake will not call forth a reprimand; it will trigger the system to

Marshall McLuhan (1911–1980). Writer, educator and pioneering communications therorist, Marshall McLuhan coined the phrase "The medium is the message." © BETTMANN/CORBIS

help the student overcome a particular misunderstanding. As a result, students should be less apprehensive about formal tests, and such tests should contain fewer surprises, because ongoing self-quizzing gives a better sense of where we stand.

Interactivity is the key to successful online learning. Yet a survey of online instructional materials reveals a surprising deficiency in educational interactive programs, for three reasons: (1) cyber-courses are largely a combination of conventional classroom and textbook material, neither of which are conducive to interactivity; (2) instructors tend to think of interactivity primarily as a means of assessment, instead of learning; (3) the concept itself is extended to cover everything from navigational buttons to chatrooms to online games.

Marketing. Interactive technology has two distinct advantages over traditional means of gathering consumer data. First, it allows the information to be gathered in real time, and therefore the response to the customer can be more timely than with traditional media. The more one orders

from Amazon.com, for example, the more information about that consumer's reading tastes is acquired. This information is used immediately to update that buyer's "Recommended Reading List." This is critical; many sales are lost due to the lag time between the request for information and its provision.

Second, the information gathered is more specific, since the branching of questions can be as detailed as the marketer wishes. For example, if an initial set of questions asks the viewer to input his or her age and number of children, the next set of questions derives from the answer to the first, and so on. When this information is used to enhance a marketing database, marketers are able to respond to the individual needs of viewers, taking one-to-one marketing to its limits.

Gathering information. Interactive documents add value to traditional methods. Surveys that attempt to gauge satisfaction with expectations of, and responses to, new products can be more effective when done with interactive multimedia. In the previous example, Amazon.com would have more reliable information about a consumer's selections than it would have from any paper survey it might ask the public to complete. These surveys may gather more information by being more interesting than the paper alternatives. Once you get used to this sort of system, you find that being able to look at information in different ways makes the information more valuable. The flexibility invites exploration, and the exploration is rewarded with discovery.

INTERACTIVITY IS COOL

Using Marshall McLuhan's classic distinction between "hot" and "cool" media can make both the prospects and problems of interactivity clearer. In *Understanding the Media*, McLuhan (1964) explained that "a hot medium is one that extends one single sense in 'high definition.' High definition is the state of being well-filled with data" (p. 22). A cool medium, by contrast, is one in which "little is given and so much has to be filled in" (p. 23). McLuhan was primarily interested in the media themselves, and had little to say about that process of "filling in"—what today is called interactivity.

Learning is "cool" as a measure of the individual's involvement in the medium. One can easily recognize the difference between "hot" mindlessness of channel surfing and the "cool" absorption and involvement of learning. The challenge, then, is not only to produce a "cool" digital medium in which learning can take place, but to do so despite use of a screen that may remind us of television and the uninvolved behavior patterns it induces. The key to success in this challenge is interactivity—the activity of "filling in" the knowledge presented in the medium. Strategies for interactivity can be divided into three parts: passive, hyperlinked, and interpersonal.

PASSIVE INTERACTIVITY

Synchronous learning involves the simultaneous interaction of instructor and student. The traditional classroom is the traditional example of synchronous interaction where the instructor and students are in the same place at the same time. Distance learning, where the instructor and students are at different locations at the same time, frequently involves audio/visual connections and "chat rooms." Asynchronous learning, on the other hand, involves the interaction of instructor and student at different times.

"Passive interactivity" need not be a contradiction in terms, because one of the problems with digital instruction is the loss of context—both physical and psychological—that a classroom setting provides. To compensate for this, online training needs to create a visual "focus" for the lesson at hand—a referential map of where the student has been, and where he or she is headed, to provide a context for where he or she is now. Such a context allows a student to relate the subject matter of an individual lesson to the larger scope of the course. Passive interactive page designs are thus "interactive" because the visual mapping succeeds in making the student actively aware of its importance by providing a broader context for the current lesson.

HYPERLINKED INTERACTIVITY

The key to asynchronous learning is "hyperlinked interactivity," a feature of HTML, which makes possible the creation of multiple-choice questions, expert systems, and other such branching-informational models. Branching models approximate the way people actually work through problems. Individuals take different paths, ask different questions, and need different information. While books can utilize limited branching schemes in a clumsy way, only computers have complex and speedy branching capabilities. Complete interaction, combined with accessibility at our convenience, exact repeatability, and uniform quality gives asynchronous online learning the potential, in suitable situations, of not merely replacing the traditional learning experience, but surpassing it.

INTERPERSONAL INTERACTIVITY

Even asynchronous projects benefit from the variety of communication options now available on the Internet, including e-mail, listservs, and electronic bulletin boards. Such communication, which can be roughly grouped under the heading of "interpersonal interactivity," helps to reproduce online some of the advantages of collaborative peer learning. When utilized effectively, such communication can give people more direct and more convenient access to others and can make individual contributions more formal, thoughtful, and precise.

SUMMARY

All learning is a function of interaction. In taking training onto the Internet, instructors have an opportunity to script levels of interactivity in ways previously unavailable. To do so, however, requires rethinking online activities—not merely as means of assessment, but as the primary way to involve us and make learning "cool."

SEE ALSO *Artificial Intelligence; Information Processing*

BIBLIOGRAPHY

Gates, William H., III. (1999). *Business @ the Speed of Thought.* New York: Warner Books.

McLuhan, Marshall. (1964). *Understanding the Media.* Cambridge, MA: MIT Press.

Shapiro, Carl, and Varian, Hal. (1998). *Information Rules: A Strategic Guide to the Network Economy.* Campbridge, MA: Harvard Business School Press.

Varian, Hal R., Farrell, Joseph & Shapiro, Carl (2004). *The economics of information technology: an introduction.* Cambridge & New York: Cambridge University Press.

Philip D. Taylor

INTEREST RATES

An interest rate is a standardized measure of either: (1) the cost of borrowing money or (2) the return for lending money for a specified period of time (usually one year), such as 12% annual percentage rate (APR).

First consider the term "interest" from the perspective of a borrower. In this case, "interest" is the difference between the amount of money borrowed and the amount of money repaid. Interest expense is incurred as a result of borrowing money. On the other hand, interest revenue is earned by lending money.

For example, the amount of interest expense, as a result of borrowing $1000 on January 1, 20XX, and repaying $1,120 on December 31, 20XX is $120 ($1,120 – $1,000). The lender, on the other hand, received $1,120 on December 31, 20XX in exchange for lending $1,000 on January 1, 20XX, or a total of $120 in interest revenue. Thus, with regard to any particular lending event, interest revenue equals interest expense.

Effect of changing interest rates on the amount of monthly payments			
Borrow $100,000 for home purchase		Borrow $20,000 for auto purchase	
Interest rate	30-Year mortgage payment	Interest rate	4-Year auto loan
6%	$599.55	7%	$478.93
8%	$733.76	10%	$507.25

Table 1

Effect of changing interest rates on the value of an investment in debt, holding *n* constant			
$20,000 maturity value bonds paying 8% (stated) annual interest, due in 25 years		$20,000 in treasury bills paying 0% interest due in 90 days	
Market interest rate	Market value of the bonds	Market interest rate	Market value of the treasury bills
6%	$25,113	6%	$19,711
8%	$20,000	8%	$19,619
10%	$16,369	10%	$19,529

Table 2

The formula used to calculate the amount of interest is:

$$\text{interest} = \text{principal} \times \text{interest rate} \times \text{time} \quad [1]$$

where:

principal = amount of money borrowed

interest rate = percent paid or earned per year

time = number of years

Equation [1] can be rewritten as:

$$\text{interest rate} = \text{interest} \div \text{principal} \quad [2]$$

where:

time = one year

The principal is also known as the *present value*. The interest rate in equation [2] is called the annual percentage rate or *APR*. APR is the most useful measure of interest rate. (In the remainder of this discussion, the term "interest rate" refers to the APR.)

Equations [1] and [2] are useful in situations that involve only one cash flow (a single-payment scenario). Many economic transactions, however, involve multiple cash flows. For instance, a consumer acquires a good or service and in exchange promises to make a series of payments to the supplier. This type of transaction describes an annuity. An *annuity* is a series of equally spaced payments of equal amount. The annuity formula is:

$$\text{present value of annuity} = \text{annuity payment} \times \text{annuity factor}_{i,n} \quad [3]$$

where:

present value of annuity = value of the good or service received today (when the exchange transaction is finalized)

annuity payment = amount of the payment that is made each period

annuity factor = a number obtained from an ordinary annuity table that is determined by the interest rate (*i*) and the number of annuity payments (*n*).

An analysis of the effect of changes in interest rates requires controlling (or holding constant) two of the other three variables in equation [3].

The term "future cash flow(s)" describes cash that will be received in the future. Holding the number of payments and the amount of each payment constant, the present value of future cash flows is inversely related to the interest rate. Holding the number of payments and present value of the future cash flows constant, the amount of each payment is directly related to the interest rate. Holding the present value of the future cash flows and the amount of each payment constant, the number of payments is directly related to the interest rate. In summary, everything else held constant, increases in the interest rate (1) increase the amount of each payment, or (2) increase the number of payments required, or (3) decrease the present value of the future cash flows.

In order to understand the effect of changes in interest rates from a consumer's perspective, we first examine borrowing transactions in which the present value of the future cash flows and the number of payments are fixed. Consider, for instance, a thirty-year mortgage or a four-year auto loan. In each case, the effect of an increase in interest rates is an increase in the amount of the home or auto payment. This is shown in Table 1.

Well-known lending interest rates include the prime rate, the discount rate, and consumer rates for automobiles or mortgages. The *discount rate* is the rate that the Federal Reserve bank charges to banks and other financial institutions. This rate influences the rates these financial institutions then charge to their customers. The *prime rate* is the rate banks and large commercial institutions charge to lend money to their best customers. While the prime rate is not usually available to consumers, some consumer loans (such as mortgage lines of credit) are priced at "prime + 2 percent"; that is, a consumer will pay 2 percent over the prime rate to borrow money. When the Federal Reserve raises the discount rate, typically banks raise the prime rate and consumers pay higher interest rates.

Individuals lend money by investing in debt instruments, such as Treasury bills and bonds. In this scenario, the investor receives periodic payments (annuity payments) and a lump sum when the debt instrument matures. This stream of cash flows is valued as follows:

$$\text{market value} = \text{annuity payment} \times$$
$$\text{annuity factor}_{i,n} + \text{maturity value} \times$$
$$\text{present value factor}_{i,n} \ [4]$$

where:

market value = value of the debt instrument

annuity payment = amount of the payment that is made each period; it is equal to the interest rate stated on the debt instrument multiplied by the face value of the debt instrument

annuity factor = a number obtained from an ordinary annuity table that is determined by the interest rate (i) and the number of annuity payments (n)

maturity value = amount received by the investor when the instrument matures, also known as the face value of the debt instrument

present value factor = a number obtained from a present value table that is determined by the interest rate (i) and the number periods until maturity (n).

When an investor purchases a debt instrument, the following factors are "fixed": (1) the amount of each annuity payment, (2) the amount of the maturity value, and (3) the number of periods until maturity (this is also the number of annuity payments that will be received in the future). As interest rates increase, the market value of the investment will decrease; that is, the price of debt securities is inversely related to the market rate of interest. This is shown in Table 2.

The investors who keep the investment until the debt instrument matures will receive the market rate of interest on their investment from the date of purchase. The investor who sells their investment prior to maturity will receive the market rate of interest on the investment until it is sold. At that time, this investor will also receive either a gain or a loss due to changes in the market value of this investment. If market interest rates decrease, the investor

will receive a gain. If market interest rates increase, the investor will receive a loss on the value of the investment.

SEE ALSO *Finance; Investments*

Henry H. Davis

INTERNAL CONTROL SYSTEMS

Internal control can be described as any action taken by an organization to help enhance the likelihood that the objectives of the organization will be achieved. The definition of internal control has evolved as different internal control models have been developed. This article will describe these models, present the definitions of internal control they provide, and indicate the components of internal control. Various parties responsible for and affected by internal control will also be discussed.

THE COSO MODEL

In the United States many organizations have adopted the internal control concepts presented in the report of the Committee of Sponsoring Organizations of the Treadway Commission (COSO). Published in 1992, the COSO report defines internal control as:

> a process, effected by an entity's board of directors, management and other personnel, designed to provide reasonable assurance regarding the achievement of objectives in the following categories:

- effectiveness and efficiency of operations
- reliability of financial reporting
- compliance with applicable laws and regulations

COSO describes internal control as consisting of five essential components. These components, which are subdivided into seventeen factors, include:

1. The control environment
2. Risk assessment
3. Control activities
4. Information and communication
5. Monitoring

The COSO model is depicted as a pyramid, with the control environment forming a base for control activities, risk assessment, and monitoring. Information and communication link the different levels of the pyramid. As the base of the pyramid, the control environment is arguably the most important component because it sets the tone for the organization. Factors of the control environment include employees' integrity, the organization's commitment to competence, management's philosophy and operating style, and the attention and direction of the board of directors and its audit committee. The control environment provides discipline and structure for the other components.

Risk assessment refers to the identification, analysis, and management of uncertainty facing the organization. Risk assessment focuses on the uncertainties in meeting the organization's financial, compliance, and operational objectives. Changes in personnel, new product lines, or rapid expansion could affect an organization's risks.

Control activities include the policies and procedures maintained by an organization to address risk-prone areas. An example of a control activity is a policy requiring approval by the board of directors for all purchases exceeding a predetermined amount. Control activities were once thought to be the most important element of internal control, but COSO suggests that the control environment is more critical since the control environment fosters the best actions, while control activities provide safeguards to prevent wrong actions from occurring.

Information and communication encompasses the identification, capture, and exchange of financial, operational, and compliance information in a timely manner. People within an organization who have timely, reliable information are better able to conduct, manage, and control the organization's operations.

Monitoring refers to the assessment of the quality of internal control. Monitoring activities provide information about potential and actual breakdowns in a control system that could make it difficult for an organization to accomplish its goals. Informal monitoring activities might include management's checking with subordinates to see if objectives are being met. A more formal monitoring activity would be an assessment of the internal control system by the organization's internal auditors.

OTHER CONTROL MODELS

Some users of the COSO report have found it difficult to read and understand. A model that some believe overcomes this difficulty is found in a report from the Canadian Institute of Chartered Accountants, which was issued in 1995. The report, *Guidance on Control,* presents a control model referred to as Criteria of Control (CoCo). The CoCo model, which builds on COSO, is thought to be more concrete and user-friendly. CoCo describes internal control as actions that foster the best result for an organi-

zation. These actions, which contribute to the achievement of the organization's objectives, center around:

- Effectiveness and efficiency of operations
- Reliability of internal and external reporting
- Compliance with applicable laws and regulations and internal policies

CoCo indicates that control comprises:

those elements of an organization (including its resources, systems, processes, culture, structure and tasks) that, taken together, support people in the achievement of the organization's objectives.

CoCo model recognizes four interrelated elements of internal control, including purpose, capability, commitment, and monitoring and learning. An organization that performs a task is guided by an understanding of the purpose (the objective to be achieved) of the task and supported by capability (information, resources, supplies, and skills). To perform the task well over time, the organization needs a sense of commitment. Finally, the organization must monitor task performance to improve the task process. These elements of control, which include twenty specific control criteria, are seen as the steps an organization takes to foster the right action.

In addition to the COSO and CoCo models, two other reports provide internal control models. One is the Institute of Internal Auditors Research Foundation's Systems Auditability and Control (SAC), which was issued in 1991 and revised in 1994. The other is the Information Systems Audit and Control Foundation's COBIT (Control Objectives for Information and Related Technology), which was issued in 1996.

The Institute of Internal Auditors issued SAC to provide guidance to internal auditors on internal controls related to information systems and information technology (IT). The definition of internal control included in SAC is:

a set of processes, functions, activities, sub-systems, and people who are grouped together or consciously segregated to ensure the effective achievement of objective and goals.

COBIT focuses primarily on efficiently and effectively monitoring information systems. The report emphasizes the role and impact of IT control as it relates to business processes. This control model can be used by management to develop clear policy and good practice for control of IT. The following COBIT definition of internal control was adapted from COSO:

The policies, procedures, practices, and organizational structures are designed to provide reasonable assurance that business objectives will be achieved and that undesired events will be prevented or detected and corrected.

While the specific definition of internal control differs across the various models, a number of concepts are very similar across these models. In particular, the models emphasize that internal control is not only policies and procedures to help an organization accomplish its objectives but also a process or system affected by people. In these models, people are perceived to be central to adequate internal control.

These models also stress the concept of reasonable assurance as it relates to internal control. Internal control systems cannot guarantee that an organization will meet its objectives. Instead, internal control can only be expected to provide reasonable assurance that a company's objectives will be met. The effectiveness of internal controls depends on the competency and dependability of the organization's people. Limitations of internal control include faulty human judgment, misunderstanding of instructions, errors, management override of controls, and collusion. Further, because of cost-benefit considerations, not all possible controls will be implemented. Because of these inherent limitations, internal controls cannot guarantee that an organization will meet its objectives.

PARTIES RESPONSIBLE FOR AND AFFECTED BY INTERNAL CONTROL

While all of an organization's people are an integral part of internal control, certain parties merit special mention. These include management, the board of directors (including the audit committee), internal auditors, and external auditors.

The primary responsibility for the development and maintenance of internal control rests with an organization's management. With increased significance placed on the control environment, the focus of internal control has changed from policies and procedures to an overriding philosophy and operating style within the organization. Emphasis on these intangible aspects highlights the importance of top management's involvement in the internal control system. If internal control is not a priority for management, then it will not be one for people within the organization either.

As an indication of management's responsibility, top management at a publicly owned organization will include in the organization's annual financial report to the shareholders a statement indicating that management has established a system of internal control that management

believes is effective. The statement may also provide specific details about the organization's internal control system.

Internal control must be evaluated in order to provide management with some assurance regarding its effectiveness. Internal control evaluation involves everything management does to control the organization in the effort to achieve its objectives. Internal control would be judged as effective if its components are present and function effectively for operations, financial reporting, and compliance. The board of directors and its audit committee have responsibility for making sure the internal control system within the organization is adequate. This responsibility includes determining the extent to which internal controls are evaluated. Two parties involved in the evaluation of internal control are the organization's internal auditors and their external auditors.

Internal auditors' responsibilities typically include ensuring the adequacy of the system of internal control, the reliability of data, and the efficient use of the organization's resources. Internal auditors identify control problems and develop solutions for improving and strengthening internal controls. Internal auditors are concerned with the entire range of an organization's internal controls, including operational, financial, and compliance controls.

Internal control will also be evaluated by the external auditors. External auditors assess the effectiveness of internal control within an organization to plan the financial statement audit. In contrast to internal auditors, external auditors focus primarily on controls that affect financial reporting. External auditors have a responsibility to report internal control weaknesses (as well as reportable conditions about internal control) to the audit committee of the board of directors.

SEE ALSO *Accounting; Auditing*

BIBLIOGRAPHY
Bishop, W. G., III (1991, June). "Internal Control—What's That?" *Internal Auditor*, 117-123.

Canadian Institute of Chartered Accountants (1995). *Guidance on Control*. Toronto, Ontario, Canada.

Colbert, J. L., and Bowen, P. L. (1996). "A Comparison of Internal Controls: COBIT, SAC, COSO and SAS 55/78." *IS Audit and Control Journal*, 4, 26-35.

Committee of Sponsoring Organizations of the Treadway Committee (COSO) (1992). *Internal Control—Integrated Framework, Executive Summary*. www.coso.org.

Galloway, D. J. (1994, December). "Control Models in Perspective." *Internal Auditor*, 46-52.

Improving Audit Committee Performance: What Works Best (1993). Altamonte Springs, FL: Institute of Internal Auditors, Research Foundation.

Information Systems Audit and Control Foundation (1995). CoBIT: *Control Objectives and Information Related Technology.* Rolling Meadows, IL.

Institute of Internal Auditors Research Foundation (1994). *Control Objectives and Information Related Technology.* Altamonte Springs, FL.

Roth, J. (1997). *Control Model Implementation: Best Practices.* Altamonte Springs, FL: Institute of Internal Auditors, Research Foundation.

Simmons, M. R. (1997, December). "COSO Based Auditing." *Internal Auditor,* 68-73.

Audrey A. Gramling

INTERNATIONAL ACCOUNTING STANDARDS

Comparable, transparent and reliable financial information is fundamental for the smooth functioning of capital markets. In the global arena, the need for comparable standards of financial reporting has become paramount because of a dramatic growth in the number, reach, and size of multinational corporations; foreign direct investments; cross-border purchases; sales of securities; and the number of foreign securities listings on the stock exchanges. Nevertheless, because of the social, economic, legal, and cultural differences among the countries, the accounting standards and practices in different countries vary.

To improve the comparability of financial statements, harmonization of accounting standards is advocated. Harmonization strives to increase the harmony between accounting principles by setting limits on the alternatives allowed for similar transactions. Harmonization differs from standardization in that the latter allows no room for alternatives even in cases where economic realities differ.

The international accounting standards (IASs) resulting from the harmonization efforts hold important benefits. Investors and analysts benefit from enhanced comparability of financial statements. Multinational corporations benefit from not having to prepare different reports for the different countries in which they operate. Stock exchanges benefit from the growth in the listings and volume of securities transactions. The international standards also benefit developing countries and other countries that do not have a national standard-setting body or do not want to spend scarce resources to undertake the full process of preparing accounting standards.

THE ROLE OF THE INTERNATIONAL ACCOUNTING STANDARDS BOARD

The most important driving force in the development of IASs is the International Accounting Standards Board (IASB), an independent, privately funded accounting standard-setter based in London, United Kingdom. The IASB, established in 2001, is committed to developing a single set of high-quality, understandable and enforceable global accounting standards that require transparent and comparable information in general-purpose financial statements. Standards issued by the IASB are designated International Financial Reporting Standards (IFRSs). Standards issued by its predecessor, the International Accounting Standards Committee (IASC), from 1973 to 2001, continue to be designated IASs. Many published sources use the term *IFRSs* to encompass IFRSs, IASs and interpretations issued by the International Financial Reporting Interpretations Committee (IFRIC).

MEMBERSHIP

The IASB, consisting of fourteen members (12 full time and 2 part time), follows due process of setting accounting standards, which allows for a great deal of consultation and discussion and ensures that all interested parties can express their views at several points in the standard-setting process. The final standard requires approval by at least eight members. The IASB uses a principle-based approach rather than a rules-based approach in issuing accounting standards. IFRSs thus provide guidance for applying the general principles to typical transactions and encourage professional judgment in applying them to transactions specific to an entity or industry.

The IASB members are selected by the trustees of the IASC Foundation. In addition to reviewing broad strategic issues affecting accounting standards, the trustees raise funds for the IASB and also appoint members to two other committees, IFRIC and the Standards Advisory Council (SAC). IFRIC interprets the application of IFRSs and provides guidance on financial reporting issues not specifically addressed by the IFRSs. The SAC has forty-nine members with diverse geographic and functional backgrounds who provide advice to the IASB and the trustees of the IASC Foundation. The chair of the IASB is also the chair of the SAC.

STANDARDS ISSUED

As of December 31, 2005, forty-one IASs and five IFRSs had been issued. They cover a wide range of topics such as inventories, depreciation, research and development costs, income taxes, segment reporting, leases, business combinations, investments, earnings per share, interim financial reporting, intangible assets, employee benefits, impairment of assets, contingent liabilities, financial instruments, investment property, and agriculture. Of the forty-one IASs, only thirty-one were already in force, the remaining being withdrawn or replaced by later standards. The IASB also added to its agenda a project to jointly develop with the Financial Accounting Standards Board of the United States a single conceptual framework that converges and improves upon the existing frameworks of both boards.

RELATIONSHIPS WITH OTHER STANDARD-SETTERS

In addition to issuing accounting standards, the IASB cooperates with national accounting standard-setters to achieve convergence in accounting standards around the world. Seven of the full-time members of the IASB have formal liaison responsibilities with leading national accounting standard-setters (in Australia, Canada, Germany, France, Japan, the United Kingdom, and the United States) and are resident in their jurisdiction.

IFRSs are not mandatory. Their acceptability, however, has been on the rise—more than ninety countries claimed that they would be following IFRSs by 2005. Many stock exchanges accept IFRSs for cross-border listing purposes. The International Organization of Securities Commissions (IOSCO), an organization comprising of securities regulators from over 100 countries, has recommended that all its members allow multinational issuers to use IFRSs, as supplemented by reconciliation, disclosure, and interpretation where necessary to address outstanding substantive issues at a national or regional level. Notably, some countries that do not permit the use of IFRSs without a reconciliation to domestic generally accepted accounting principles (GAAP) are Canada, Japan, and the United States. In September 2004 the chief accountant of the U.S. Securities and Exchange Commission (SEC) stated at an IASB meeting that the SEC was considering the steps needed to eliminate the reconciliation from IFRSs to U.S. GAAP.

OTHER ORGANIZATIONS PARTICIPATING IN INTERNATIONAL STANDARDS

Many other organizations have also played an important role in the march toward IASs. Among the more important are:

International Federation of Accountants. The International Federation of Accountants (IFAC) is a worldwide association formed in 1977 to develop the accounting profession, harmonize the auditing practices, and reduce differences in the requirements to qualify as professional accountants in its member countries. In 2005 it had a membership of 163 national professional organizations in 120 countries, representing over 2.5 million accountants. The IFAC issues international standards on auditing and assurance services, education, public-sector accounting, quality-control standards, and ethics. In June 1999 the IFAC launched the International Forum on Accountancy Development to promote transparent financial reporting.

United Nations. Several organizations within United Nations have been involved in the IASs. Its Group of Experts published in 1976 a four-part report titled "International Standards of Accounting and Reporting for Transnational Corporations," which listed financial and nonfinancial items that should be disclosed by multinational corporations to host governments. Since then, it has worked to promote the harmonization of accounting standards by discussing and supporting best practices in a variety of areas, including environmental disclosures.

Organization for Economic Cooperation and Development. The Organization for Economic Cooperation and Development (OECD), which was formed in 1960, had thirty of the world's developed, industrialized countries as its members in 2005. A valuable contribution of the OECD is its surveys of accounting practices in member countries and its assessment of the diversity or conformity of such practices. Its Working Group on Accounting Standards supports efforts by regional, national, and international bodies promoting accounting harmonization. In 2004 OECD revised its Principles of Corporate Governance, which support the development of high-quality, internationally recognized standards to improve the comparability of information between countries.

European Union. The European Union (EU), a powerful regional alliance of twenty-five nations, aims to bring about a common market that allows free mobility of people, capital, and goods between member countries. To promote the cross-country economic integration, the EU has made significant progress in the harmonization of laws and regulations. Its commission establishes standardization and harmonization of corporate and accounting rules through the issuance of directives.

Directives incorporate uniform rules (to be implemented exactly in all member states), minimum rules (that may be strengthened by individual governments), and alternative rules (from which members can choose). Directives are mandatory in that each member country has the obligation to incorporate them into its respective national laws. Each country, however, is free to choose the form and method of implementation and also to add or delete options. During the 1990s it was decided not to issue any more accounting-related directives. Instead, beginning in 2005 the EU adopted a regulation that required all publicly listed companies to prepare consolidated financial statements using IFRSs.

North American Free Trade Agreement. The North American Free Trade Agreement (NAFTA) was formed in 1993 between Canada, Mexico, and the United States to create a common market. It phased out duties on most goods and services and promotes free movement of professionals, including accountants, within the three countries. Projects were under way to analyze the similarities and differences between financial reporting and accounting standards of the member countries of NAFTA.

Other Organizations. Some regional organizations—such as the Association of Southeast Asian Nations, Community of Sovereign States, Economic Cooperation Organization, Baltic Council, Asia Pacific Economic Cooperation, Confederation of Asian and Pacific Accountants, and Nordic Federation of Accountants—have made efforts toward harmonizing accounting and disclosure standards. G4—a group of standard-setting bodies in Australia, Canada, the United Kingdom, and the United States—has also started playing an important role in the harmonization of IASs.

PROGRESS FOR INTERNATIONAL STANDARDS

The process of harmonized IASs has come a long way on a rough path. While some critics doubt the feasibility of such standards, it is becoming increasingly clear that the question is not whether but when the IASs will gain worldwide acceptance. The likely endorsement by the IOSCO and the SEC will bring that time closer.

SEE ALSO *Accounting; International Federation of Accountants*

BIBLIOGRAPHY

Doupnik, Timothy S., and Perera, Hector (2005). *International accounting*. New York: McGraw-Hill/Irwin.

International Accounting Standards Board. http://www.iasb.org

McGregor, Warren (1999, June). An insider's view of the current state and future direction of international accounting standard setting. *Accounting Horizons, 13,* 159–168.

Pactor, Paul (1998, July). International accounting standards: The world's standards by 2002. *The CPA Journal*, pp. 14–21.

Zeff, Stephen A. (1998, Fall). The IASC's core standards: What will the SEC do? *Journal of Financial Statement Analysis*, pp. 67–78.

Zeff, Stephen A. (2002). Political lobbying on proposed standards: A challenge to the IASB. *Accounting Horizons, 1,* 43–54.

Mahendra Gujarathi

INTERNATIONAL ASSOCIATION OF ADMINISTRATIVE PROFESSIONALS

The International Association of Administrative Professionals (IAAP) is a nonprofit administrative support organization for office professionals, with over 40,000 members internationally. Membership is usually organized by chapters. IAAP seeks to support administrative professional excellence by providing professional development opportunities through a wide variety of activities. IAAP places high value on integrity, encouragement, leadership, loyalty, professionalism, relevance, pride, connection, and individual importance.

IAAP (then known as the National Secretaries Association [NSA]) was founded in Kansas City, Missouri, in 1942, by a group of secretaries who wanted the role of the secretary to take on a more professional image. In 1951 NSA introduced an examination known as the Certified Professional Secretaries Examination (which became the Certified Administration Professionals Examination) that provided members with the opportunity to demonstrate excellence in office skills and earn the designation "certified professional secretary."

In 1952 National Secretaries Day was introduced to recognize the hard work of women office workers. The tradition continues, and the fourth week of April is set aside as Administrative Professionals Week, recognizing all office workers.

IAAP offers online publications and other publications for purchase as well as a bimonthly journal called the *Office Pro*. An annual international convention is held as well as several regional conventions.

WHAT IS AN ADMINISTRATIVE PROFESSIONAL?

IAAP defines the term *administrative professional* as "an individual who is responsible for completing administrative tasks and coordinating and supporting information and individuals in an office environment" (http://www.iaap-hq.org/about.htm). The tasks performed by an administrative professional require outstanding skills in the areas of communication, technology, and management.

IAAP continues to be an outstanding and unique resource in meeting the needs of administrative professionals by providing diversified opportunities limited only by the individual member's motivation and quest for excellence in the profession.

The IAAP may be contacted at 10502 NW Ambassador Drive, PO Box 20404, Kansas City, MO 64195-0404; or http://www.iaap-hq.org.

SEE ALSO *Careers in Management*

Dorothy A. Maxwell

INTERNATIONAL BUSINESS

International business consists of transactions that are developed and carried out across two or more international borders to satisfy the business objectives of individuals and organizations. Technology has created opportunities for business internationally in ways that make boundaries of countries seamless in transacting business at the click of a computer.

MAJOR FACTORS AFFECTING THE GROWTH OF INTERNATIONAL BUSINESS

International business has experienced an unusually strong growth pattern since 2004. Several major factors are involved in this growth. One major factor deals with the surge in oil prices, a commodity in great demand by many nations.

Another major factor affecting the growth of international business has been the expansion of technology. Computers and all their applications have deeply penetrated international business, and using the Internet as an integral tool of communication has been paramount in promoting diversified international business opportunities.

A third major factor has been the decline in the value of the U.S. dollar. When prices are lower for U.S. goods, other nations rush to take advantage of the bargain prices.

EXPORTING AND IMPORTING

The primary activities that take place in international business transactions are exporting and importing. Exporting is the act of an individual or business in one country selling goods and services to a buyer in another country. Importing is the act of a buyer in one country buying goods and services from an exporting organization in another country.

For example, when an individual organization in Country A sells goods to a buyer in Country B, the Country A seller would receive the proceeds from the sale to Company B, just as in a domestic sale between two companies within the same borders.

The amount of the proceeds from the sale would be the amount agreed upon by the two companies, less any expenses incurred by Country A, the exporter. To calculate the annual income, however, it is necessary to calculate the balance of payments for a stipulated time, such as a month or years. The balance of payments may include gold, merchandise costs, services costs, interest and dividend payments, travelers' expenditures, and loan repayments.

Usually, trade between two countries does not involve ownership interest in the other nation's business firm. Occasionally, however, one of the trading nations makes a foreign direct investment in the other nation's trading firm with whom they are doing business.

A list of the items typically imported by the United States would include machinery, transport equipment, manufactured articles, crude materials, chemicals, food and live animals, minerals and lubricants, beverages, and tobacco.

In addition, almost all countries appear to have a need for engaging in international business. The major reason lies in the need to acquire sufficient quantities of needed commodities in order to have a healthy balance of needed items available. Virtually no country can produce enough of every kind of material it needs by itself. So, if Country A has plenty of a certain kind of raw material, it can trade it to Country B in exchange for Country B's manufacturing capacity and know-how, which Country B can trade to Country A, sometimes at lower prices.

Shortly after the 2004 U.S. presidential election, the value of the U.S. dollar went down. The reduced value, however, made U.S. prices abroad more attractive to buyers throughout the world. The United States began experiencing a serious trade deficit. It is worthy of taking note that capital-intensive products (such as cars, trucks, construction equipment, and industrial machinery) are manufactured by countries with a strong industrial base.

Labor-intensive products (such as shoes and clothing) are made in countries with low labor costs and relatively modern productive plants, often found in Asian countries.

General Motors plant sign in front of the General Motors plant in Silao, Mexico, March 12, 1996. © **DANNY LEHMAN/CORBIS**

GOVERNMENTAL INTERNATIONAL TRADE POLICIES

Domestic sales are those made where both seller and buyer are conducting business within the same borders. Domestic business organizations of all types—such as retail, wholesale, manufacturing, and agriculture—look to their government to protect them against firms from other nations taking away their customers and their sales.

A tariff is an example the kind of protective legislation used by governments that seek to provide this kind of protection. Suppose, for example, that $500 is the typical price of an item imported by Country A. When the residents of Country A learn they can buy the item from within the bounds of Country A from a foreign source for $500, they will tend to buy the lower-cost item, even if the item must be purchased from a foreign source. Imposition of a tariff by Country A would have the effect of a tax on the items. It would raise the real cost to a figure higher than the domestic cost.

Sometimes a country suffering from a protective tariff will enact a tariff of its own on a product. In 1930, for example, the U.S. Congress passed the Hawley-Smoot Tariff Act. This placed protective tariffs on some of imports. The legislation was popular among U.S. voters. The legislative analysts determined it was a large mistake. To correct the error, Congress reduced the price of affected products by 50 percent.

CULTURAL DIFFERENCES

With most foreign countries, there are cultural differences about which it is essential to question and to learn:

- Do men and women shake hands with each other?

- In business meetings, do participants "get right down to business" or would that be considered impolite?

- Should the American visitors' clothing be approximately the same as the foreign hosts?

- If the Americans bring their families, are there any special rules about associating with the children in that country?

- What sort of medical facilities are available for Americans?

- What languages are used?

- What holidays are observed in the country?

- What special rules about traffic accidents exist?

- What is the situation regarding religious observances?

INTERNATIONAL TRADE COMMISSION

The International Trade Commission is not technically a part of the U.S. government but rather an independent agency. Its principal task is to determine whether imports are injuring any domestic industry. The commission analyzes the manner in which the domestic industry relates to the international industry. It also investigates and reports on tariff and foreign trade matters. Upon request, it reports to Congress and/or the president.

It studies the methods by which the international laws operate. It investigates claims that are submitted regarding conflicts of opinions within the dependent trade's areas.

The commission was organized in 1916. Its original title was the U.S. Tariff Commission; it received its current title in 1975. The commission is headed by six commissioners who are appointed by the president with the approval of the U.S. Senate.

SEE ALSO *International Investment; International Marketing; International Trade*

BIBLIOGRAPHY

Ball, Donald A. et al. (2006). *International Business: the challenge of global competition* (10th ed.). Boston: McGraw-Hill/Irwin.

Hill, Charles W. L. (2007). *International Business: Competing in the Global Marketplace* (6th ed.). Boston: McGraw-Hill/Irwin.

Morrison, Janet (2006). *The International Business Environment: global and local marketplaces in a changing world* (2nd ed.). New York: Palgrave Macmillan.

Dorothy A. Maxwell

INTERNATIONAL FEDERATION OF ACCOUNTANTS

The International Federation of Accountants (IFAC) was officially constituted in October 1977 at the World Congress of Accountants in Munich. Its constitution was signed by sixty-three accountancy bodies in forty-nine countries. Its original terms of reference emphasized (1) the promotion of harmonized accounting standards, that is, measurement and disclosure standards, and (2) the development of harmonized professional standards, such as auditing, education, and ethical standards. This duality of purpose placed IFAC in potential conflict with the International Accounting Standards Committee (IASC), whose mission also embraced accounting harmonization. To minimize duplication of effort, both organizations agreed in 1982 to have a uniform membership in which IASC would concentrate on promoting harmonized accounting standards while IFAC would focus on promoting harmonized professional standards.

MEMBERSHIP

Support for IFAC's quest to develop a truly international and cohesive accountancy profession is reflected in its expanded membership of one hundred twenty-three professional accountancy bodies in eighty-seven countries. As of 1999, IFAC recognizes three types of members:

1. Full membership is open to national accountancy organizations that have a professional standard-setting role and that possess rigorous credentialing standards.

2. Associate membership is confined to national accountancy organizations that do not meet full membership criteria.

3. Affiliate membership is open to international organizations that have an interest in the accountancy profession.

ORGANIZATION

IFAC's governance structure is made up of the following components:

1. An *Assembly* comprised of representative from each member accountancy organization. Meeting every two and half years, it is responsible for electing *Council* and approving changes to IFAC's constitution.

2. A *Council* consisting of elected representatives from eighteen countries serving two-and-a-half-year terms. It establishes broad policies, appoints various technical committees and task forces, and oversees IFAC's operations through an Executive Committee.

3. An *Executive Committee* comprised of a president, deputy president, director general, and three other members of Council. It is responsible for the implementation of Council's established policies.

4. A *Secretariat*, headquartered in New York City, that provides overall direction and administration.

5. *Technical Committees and Task Forces* that carry on the work of IFAC. Each issues professional guidelines and relevant documents.

COMMITTEE ACTIVITIES

Six standing committees make up the backbone of the IFAC:

1. *Education Committee*: issues guidelines on entry-level and continuing professional education requirements, including prequalification, formal education, tests of professional competence, practical experience requirements and continuing education.

2. *Ethics Committee*: promotes a current code of ethics for accountants.

3. *Financial and Management Accounting Committee*: works to increase financial and management accountants' awareness of their professional responsibilities via publications, sponsored research, and forums for the exchange of ideas.

4. *Public Sector Committee*: produces guidelines and studies of international applicability to national, regional, and local governments and related agencies.

5. *Information Technology Committee*: assesses and relates the impact of information technology on accountant's roles and responsibilities.

6. *Membership Committee*: strives to increase IFAC's membership and maintain stringent membership criteria.

IFAC's Council occasionally appoints special task forces to address important issues. Task forces from the recent past include those on Anti-Corruption; Legal Liability; Quality Assurance; and Rebuilding Public Confidence in Financial Reporting.

IFAC has close ties with other international organizations such as IASC and the International Organization for Securities Commissions (IOSCO). The financial statements of an increasing number of companies are being audited in conformity with IFAC's International Standards on Auditing.

Further information on IFAC, its membership, activities, pronouncements and publications can be secured from the IFAC Web site, http://www.ifac.org.

SEE ALSO *Accounting; International Accounting Standards*

BIBLIOGRAPHY

Choi, Frederick D. S., Frost, Carol Ann, and Meek, Gary K. (2002). *International Accounting* (4th ed.). Upper Saddle River, NJ: Prentice-Hall.

Gruner, John W., and Salter, Stephen (2003). "Building a Cohesive Accountancy Profession." In Frederick D.S. Choi (ed.), *International Accounting and Finance Handbook* (3rd ed.). New York: John Wiley and Sons.

Frederick D. S. Choi

INTERNATIONAL INVESTMENT

International business is not a new phenomenon; it extends back into history beyond the Phoenicians around 1200 B.C.E.. Products have been traded across borders throughout recorded civilization, extending back beyond the Silk Road that once connected East with West from Xian to Rome. The Silk Road was probably the most influential international trade route of the last two millennia, literally shaping the world as it is known today. For example, pasta, cheese, and ice cream, as well as the compass and explosives, were brought to the Western world from China via the Silk Road.

What is relatively new—beginning first with large U.S. companies in the 1950s and 1960s, second with European and Japanese companies in the 1970s and 1980s, and third with companies from emerging economies in Asia and Latin America in particular—is the large number of companies engaged in international investment with interrelated production and sales operations located around the world. At no other time in economic history have countries been more economically interdependent than they are today.

Although the second half of the twentieth century saw the highest sustained growth rates of gross domestic product (GDP) in history, the growth in the international flow of goods and services has consistently surpassed the growth rate of the world economy. Simultaneously, the growth in international financial flow—including foreign direct investment, portfolio investment, and trading in currencies—has achieved a life of its own. Daily international financial flows exceed well over $1 trillion in the early twenty-first century.

Thanks to trade liberalization, heralded by the General Agreement on Tariffs and Trade and its successor, the World Trade Organization, the barriers to international trade and financial flows keep getting lower in an era of globalization. The emergence of competitive European and Japanese multinational companies, followed by emerging-economy multinational companies, has given the notion of global competition a touch of extra urgency and significance that is seen almost daily in print media such as the *New York Times, Financial Times,* and *Nikkei Shimbun,* as well as television media such as the BBC, NBC, and CNN.

The drive for globalization is being promoted through more free trade; more international investment; more Internet commerce; more networking of business, schools and communities; and more advanced technologies than ever before. The Asian financial crisis in 1997, followed by the terrorist attacks on the United States in 2001 and Argentina's financial crisis that worsened in 2002, sent the world economy into a global slowdown. On the other hand, the consistent demand in the United States and Europe as well as in many emerging economies, and some recovery in Asia have somewhat attenuated the forces of those crises. Since 2003 the world economy has been on the road to recovery, thanks primarily to increased investment in many parts of the world, particularly led by a surge of investment in China.

Although the severe slump in various parts of the world points up the vulnerabilities in the global marketplace, the long-term trends of increasing trade and investment and rising world incomes continue. As a consequence, even a firm that is operating in only one domestic market is not immune to the influence of economic activities external to that market. The net result of these factors has been the increased interdependence of countries and economies, increased competitiveness, and the concomitant need for firms to keep a constant watch on the international economic environment.

INTERTWINED WORLD ECONOMY

Human, natural, and capital resources shape the nature of international business. A country's relative endowments in those resources shape its competitiveness. Although wholesale generalizations should not be made, the role of human resources, among other resources, has become increasingly important as a primary determinant of industry and country competitiveness. As evidenced in the World Economic Forum's global competitiveness index of 2004 (see Table 1), all the top-ten-ranked countries, with the exception of the United States, have scarce natural resources. As a result, the increased portion of international trade and investment has become human- and capital-resources driven.

The importance of international trade and investment cannot be overemphasized for any country. In general, the larger the country's domestic economy, the less dependent it tends to be on exports and imports relative to its GDP. For the United States (GDP = $10.9 trillion in 2003), international trade in goods and services (including exports and imports) rose from 10 percent in

National competitiveness ranking

Country	Score	Rank
United States	65.7	1
Canada	64.1	2
Netherlands	63.5	3
Denmark	61.7	4
Belgium	60.5	5
Sweden	58.9	6
Finland	58.3	7
United Kingdom	57.6	8
France	57.3	9
Hong Kong	57.3	10

SOURCE: World Economic Forum, *Global Competitiveness Report 2004–2005,* http://www.weforum.org/site/homepublic.nsf/Content/Global+Competitiveness+Programme%5CGlobal+Competitiveness+Report, accessed September 30, 2005.

Table 1

1970 to about 23 percent in 2003. For Japan (GDP = $4.3 trillion), international trade accounted for a little less than 22 percent in 2003. For Germany (GDP = $2.4 trillion), trade formed about 67 percent of the GDP. For the Netherlands (GDP = $511 billion), trade value exceeded GDP, for as high as 107 percent of GDP (due to reexport); and for Singapore (GDP = $91 billion), trade was more than 350 percent of its GDP.

These trade statistics are relative to each country's GDP. In absolute dollar terms, however, a small relative trade percentage of a large economy still translates into large volumes of trade (see Table 2). As shown in the last column for both exports and imports in Table 2, the per capita amount of exports and imports is another important statistic for marketing purposes, since it represents, on average, how much each individual is involved in or dependent on international trade. For instance, individuals (consumers and companies) in the United States and Japan tend to be able to find domestic sources for their needs because their economies are diversified and extremely large. The U.S. per capita values of exports were $3,440 and imports were $5,208. The numbers for Japan were very similar to those of the United States, with $4,271 in exports and $3,886 in imports.

On the other hand, individuals in rich but smaller economies tend to rely more heavily on international trade—as illustrated by the Netherlands, with per capita exports of $22,338 and per capita imports of $20,481, and by Belgium with exports at a whopping $29,770 and imports at $27,690. Although China's per capita exports and imports are much smaller than the developed economies, its per capita exports value increased to $373, and imports to $360, in 2003—a 60 percent increase since 2001. One implication of these figures is that the

Leading exporters and importers in world trade in merchandise and services, 2003

Rank	Exporters	Value (in $ billions)	Value per capita	Rank	Importers	Value (in $ billions)	Value per capita
1	United States	1011.5	3,440	1	United States	1531.2	5,208
2	Germany	863.9	10,472	2	Germany	772.5	9,364
3	Japan	542.4	4,271	3	United Kingdom	509.1	8,542
4	France	485.6	8,093	4	Japan	493.5	3,886
5	China (excl. Hong Kong)	484.3	373	5	France	474.2	7,903
6	United Kingdom	448.0	7,517	6	China (excl. Hong Kong)	468.0	360
7	Italy	364.8	6,311	7	Italy	364.8	6,311
8	Netherlands	357.4	22,338	8	Netherlands	327.7	20,481
9	Canada	314.6	10,148	9	Canada	295.0	9,516
10	Belgium	297.7	29,770	10	Belgium	276.9	27,690

SOURCE: Computed from trade statistics in *International Trade Statistics 2004*, http://www.wto.org/english/res_e/statis_e/its2004_e.pdf, accessed September 30, 2005.

Table 2

higher the per capita trade, the more closely intertwined is that country's economy with the rest of the world. Intertwining of economies by the process of specialization due to international trade leads to job creation in both the exporting country and the importing country.

Nevertheless, beyond the simple figure of trade as a rising percentage of a nation's GDP lies the more interesting question of what rising trade does to the economy of a nation. A nation that is a successful trader—that is, it makes goods and services that other nations buy and it buys goods and services from other nations—displays a natural inclination to be competitive in the world market. The threat of a possible foreign competitor is a powerful incentive for firms and nations to invest in technology and markets in order to remain competitive. Also, apart from trade flows, foreign direct investment, portfolio investment, and daily financial flows in the international money markets profoundly influence the economies of countries that may be seemingly completely separate.

FOREIGN DIRECT INVESTMENT

Foreign direct investment (FDI)—which means investment in manufacturing and service facilities in a foreign country—is another facet of the increasing integration of national economies. Since the 1980s, the overall world inflow of FDI increased twenty-five-fold and in 2000 the inflow of FDI reached a record high of $1.39 trillion. In 2000, developed countries represented more than three-quarters of world FDI inflow, while developing countries reached only $249 billion in the same year. In 2003, however, global inflows of FDI declined for the third year in a row, which was prompted again by a fall in FDI inflows to developed countries. In particular, the FDI inflows to the United States fell by 53 percent to $30 billion from 2000

to 2003, which is the lowest level since 1993. It was only developing countries, most of which are from Asia, Africa, and the Pacific Rim, that witnessed an increase. The United States—once the world's largest FDI recipient country in the world—was outperformed by China, whose FDI inflow reached $53 billion in 2003.

In the past, FDI was considered to be an alternative to exports in order to avoid tariff barriers. Today, however, FDI and international trade have become complementary. For example, Dell Computer uses a factory in Ireland to supply personal computers in Europe instead of exporting from Austin, Texas. Similarly, Honda, a Japanese automaker with a major factory in Marysville, Ohio, is the largest exporter of automobiles from the United States. As firms invest in manufacturing and distribution facilities outside their home countries to expand into new markets around the world, they have added to the stock of FDI.

The increase in FDI is also promoted by the efforts of many national governments to attract multinationals and by the leverage that the governments of large potential markets, such as China and India, have in granting access to multinationals. Sometimes trade friction can also promote FDI. Investment in the United States by Japanese companies is, to some extent, a function of the trade imbalances between the two nations and of the U.S. government's consequent pressure on Japan to do something to reduce the bilateral trade deficit. Since most of the U.S. trade deficit with Japan is attributed to Japanese cars exported from Japan, Japanese automakers, such as Honda, Toyota, Nissan, and Mitsubishi, have expanded their local production by setting up production facilities in the United States. This localization strategy reduces Japanese automakers' vulnerability to retaliation by the

United States under the Super 301 laws of the Omnibus Trade and Competitiveness Act of 1988.

PORTFOLIO INVESTMENT

The increasing integration of economies also derives from portfolio investment (or indirect investment) in foreign countries and from money flows in the international financial markets. Portfolio investment refers to investments in foreign countries that are withdrawable at short notice, such as investment in foreign stocks and bonds.

In the international financial markets, the borders between nations have, for all practical purposes, disappeared. The enormous quantities of money that are traded on a daily basis have assumed a life of their own. When trading in foreign currencies began, it was as an adjunct to the international trade transaction in goods and services—banks and firms bought and sold currencies to complete the export or import transaction or to hedge the exposure to fluctuations in the exchange rates in the currencies of interest in the trade transaction.

In today's international financial markets, however, traders usually trade currencies without an underlying trade transaction. They trade on the accounts of the banks and financial institutions they work for, mostly on the basis of daily news on inflation rates, interest rates, political events, stock and bond market movements, commodity supplies and demand, and so on. The weekly volume of international trade in currencies exceeds the annual value of the trade in goods and services.

The effect of this trend is that all nations with even partially convertible currencies are exposed to the fluctuations in the currency markets. A rise in the value of the local currency due to these daily flows vis-à-vis other currencies makes exports more expensive (at least in the short run) and can add to the trade deficit or reduce the trade surplus. A rising currency value will also deter foreign investment in the country and encourage outflow of investment.

It may also encourage a decrease in the interest rates in the country if the central bank of that country wants to maintain the currency exchange rate and a decrease in the interest rate would spur local investment. An interesting example is the Mexican meltdown in early 1995 and the massive devaluation of the peso, which was exacerbated by the withdrawal of money by foreign investors. The massive depreciation of many Asian currencies in the 1997 to 1999 period, known as the Asian financial crisis, is also an instance of the influence of these short-term movements of money. Today, the influence of these short-term money flows is a far more powerful determinant of exchange rates than an investment by a Japanese or German automaker.

Despite its economic size, the United States continues to be relatively more insulated from the global economy than other nations. Most of what Americans consume is produced in the United States—which implies that, in the absence of a chain reaction from abroad, the United States is relatively more insulated from external shocks than, say, Germany and China.

The dominant feature of the global economy, however, is the rapid change in the relative status of various countries' economic output. In 1830 China and India alone accounted for about 60 percent of the manufactured output of the world. Nevertheless, the share of the world manufacturing output produced by the twenty or so countries that today are known as the rich industrial economies increased from about 30 percent in 1830 to almost 80 percent by 1913.

In the 1980s, the U.S. economy was characterized as "floundering" or even "declining," and many pundits predicted that Asia, led by Japan, would become the leading regional economy in the twenty-first century. Then the Asian financial crisis of the late 1990s changed the economic milieu of the world; by the early twenty-first century, the U.S. economy was growing at a faster rate than that of any other developed country. The United States and Western European economies have become the twin engines of the world economy, driven by increased trade and investment as a result of continued deregulation, improved technology, and transatlantic mergers, among other things. Obviously, a decade is a long time in the ever-changing world economy; and indeed, no single country has sustained its economic performance continuously.

SEE ALSO *Capital Investments; International Business; Investments*

BIBLIOGRAPHY

United Nations Conference on Trade and Development. (2005). *World investment report 2004.* Geneva: UNCTAD.

U.S. Census Bureau. (2005). *Statistical abstract of the United States.* Washington, DC: U.S. Government Printing Office.

World Trade Organization. (2004, October 25). 2004 trade growth to exceed 2003 despite higher oil prices (Press release). Retrieved November 18, 2005, from http://www.wto.org/english/news_e/pres04_e/pr386_e.htm

Masaaki Kotabe

INTERNATIONAL MARKETING

The American Marketing Association defines marketing as the process of planning and executing the conception, pricing, promotion, and distribution of ideas, goods, and services to create exchanges that satisfy individual and

Pepsi sign in Moscow shows the logo in both English and Russian. © **PETER TURNLEY/CORBIS**

organizational goals. A firm is considered an international organization when it engages in cultivating exchange relationships with individuals or organizations beyond its national boundaries. The decision to do business overseas is usually influenced either by the domestic or global economy.

Companies might be pushed into international marketing by the general lack of opportunity in the domestic markets. Organizations might be pulled into global markets, without necessarily abandoning their domestic markets, by growing opportunities for their products or services in other countries. Firms attempting to compete on a global basis should be aware that nations differ greatly in their political, legal, economic, and cultural environments. Complexity of the international marketing environment necessitates a careful consideration of whether to market aboard, where to market, and what objectives to pursue.

ASSESSING FOREIGN MARKETS

In general, in considering global marketing, an organization faces five major types of decisions. First, before expanding the firm's operations overseas, is to determine whether the firm's resources are compatible with the foreign market opportunities. If the response to this first determination is affirmative, the second consideration is the market-selection decision, that is, which foreign market or markets to enter. The third decision concerns the mode of entry and operational consideration in the attractive markets. The fourth, the marketing mix decision, considers the appropriate product, promotion, price, and distribution programs for the selected markets. Finally, the marketing organization decision determines the best way for the firm to achieve and maintain control over its international business operations.

Once a firm has prepared a list of promising markets to enter, the difficult task is to collect data related to the market potential and environmental forces of each country. Conducting research in the international market is difficult because of language diversity, general distrust of outsiders, high illiteracy rates in some countries, and the prevailing local customs.

ENTRY MODES

In general, companies select markets that rank high on market attractiveness. Among factors influencing market attractiveness are: high market growth potential, low political risk, favorable attitudes to foreign investment, and favorable competitive environment. Once a final decision is made about a country to enter, companies have several entry options. The entry modes are classified into export, contractual, and investment entry modes.

Exporting. The export entry mode is either indirect or direct. With indirect exporting a company may use domestic or international intermediaries, such as domestic-based export merchants or agents, trading companies, brokers, local wholesalers, and retailers. Indirect exporting is perhaps the lowest risk type of international marketing. The main drawback of indirect marketing, especially through domestic-based export merchants, is that the company relinquishes most of its international marketing activities to the merchants. Companies eventually may decide to handle their own export activities.

With direct exporting a company also has several options. For example, it may establish a domestic-based export department or division to handle export activities. The company may also establish an overseas sales branch. Finally, the company may use foreign-based distributors who buy and sell the goods on behalf of the company. In direct exporting, the investment level and risk factors are somewhat greater, but so is the potential return.

Contractual Entry. Contractual entry modes include licensing, turnkey construction contracts, and management contracts. Foreign licensing is a simple way of getting involved in international marketing. In licensing arrangements, a firm offers the right to use its intangible assets (manufacturing process, trade secrets, patents, company name, trademarks, or other items of value) to a licensee in exchange for royalties or some other form of payment. The licensor gains entry at little risk; the licensee gains production expertise or a well-known product or brand name. The major drawbacks of licensing are: (1) it is less flexible than exporting; (2) the firm has less control over a licensee than over its own exporting or manufacturing abroad; and (3) if sales are higher than expected, the licensor's profits are limited by the licensing agreement.

A turnkey construction contract is a mode of entry that requires that the contractor make the project operational before releasing it to the owner. Management contracts give a company the right to manage the day-to-day operations of a local company. Here the domestic firm supplies the management know-how to a foreign company that supplies the capital.

Investment Entry. Investment entry modes include sole ownership and joint ventures. Sole ownership investment

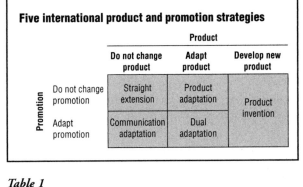

Table 1

entry strategy involves setting up a production subsidiary in a foreign country. Joint ventures involve a joint-ownership arrangement between a U.S. company, for example, and one in the host country to produce and market goods in a foreign market.

The ultimate form of international involvement is direct ownership of foreign-based assembly or manufacturing facilities. If a company wants full control (and profits), it may choose this mode of entry. Companies new to international operations would be well advised to avoid this scale of participation because direct investment entails the highest risk. Among potential risks a firm may face are currency devaluation, worsening markets, or expropriation.

ADAPTATION STRATEGIES

Once a decision for a market entry mode has been made, a firm must decide how much, if any, to adapt its marketing mix—product, promotion, price, and distribution—to a foreign market. Warren J. Keegan (1995) distinguished five adaptation strategies of product and communication to a foreign market (see Table 1). These strategies are discussed briefly below.

Straight Extension. In straight extension the same product is marketed to all countries (a "world" product), except for labeling and language used in the product manuals. The assumption behind this strategy is that consumer needs are essentially the same across national boundaries. Straight extension can be successful when products are not culture sensitive and economies of scale are present. The Philip Morris USA tobacco company used this strategy successfully with its Marlboro brand cigarette. The strategy has also been successful with cameras, consumer electronics, and many machine tools.

Product Modification. A product modification strategy keeps the physical product essentially the same; modifications, however, are made to meet local conditions or preference in package sizes or colors. Manufacturers of computers, copiers, cars, and calculators have been successful in using this strategy. Companies may develop a country-specific product. If this strategy is employed, the product is substantially altered or new products are produced across countries. For example, hand-powered washing machines have been successfully marketed in Latin America.

Communication Adaptation. It is extremely difficult to standardize advertising across countries because of variations in economic, social, and political environments. Companies, however, can use one message everywhere, varying only the language or color. Marlboro and Camel cigarettes, for example, essentially use the same message in their international promotion programs. Transferability of an advertising message is still a difficult problem even when the primary benefits of the product remain intact across national boundaries. Some promotional blunders are well known to marketing students. Coors's slogan "Turn it loose" in Spanish was read by some as "suffer from diarrhea"; in Spain, Chevrolet's Nova translated as "it doesn't go"; and a laundry soap ad claiming to wash "really dirty parts" was translated in French-speaking Quebec to read "a soap for washing private parts."

Dual Adaptation. The fourth strategy, dual adaptation, involves altering both the product and the communications. The classic example comes from National Cash Register, which manufactured a crank-operated cash register and promoted it to businesses in less-developed countries.

Product Invention. When products cannot be sold as they are, product invention strategy may be used. Ford and other automakers have sold completely different makes of cars in Europe than the ones they sell in the United States. Brewing companies have sold alcohol-free beer in countries where sales of alcoholic beverages are prohibited.

PRICE

Multinational companies find it difficult to adopt a standardized pricing strategy across countries because they have to deal with fluctuating exchange rates, differences among countries in transportation costs, governmental tax policies, and controls (such as dumping and price callings). Keegan proposed three global pricing alternatives. The first policy is called extension/ethnocentric. Under this policy, the firm sets the same price throughout the world and the customers absorb all freight and import duties. The main advantage of this policy is its simplicity, but its weakness is its failure to take into account local markets' demand and competitive conditions.

The second alternative is called adaptive/polycentric. Under this policy, local management establishes whatever price it deems appropriate at any particular time. This policy is sensitive to local conditions; nevertheless, it may favor product arbitrage where differences in price between markets exceed the freight and duty cost separating the markets.

The last alternative is called invention/geocentric pricing. This policy is an intermediary position. It neither sets a single worldwide price nor relinquishes total control over prices to local management. This policy recognizes both the importance of local factors (including costs) and the firm's market objectives.

CHANNELS OF DISTRIBUTION

Two major types of international alternatives are available to a domestic producer. The first is the use of domestic middlemen who provide marketing services from their domestic base. If this arrangement is chosen, there are several domestic middlemen available from which the companies may choose. Export management companies, manufacturers' export agents, trading companies, and complementary marketers are possible alternatives.

If a company is unwilling to deal with domestic middlemen, it may decide to deal directly with middlemen in foreign countries. This alternative shortens the channel of distribution, thereby bringing the manufacturer closer to the market. The main drawback of this alternative is that foreign middlemen are some distance away and, therefore, more difficult to control than domestic ones.

SUMMARY

International marketing has become increasingly important to U.S. firms. At the same time, global markets are becoming riskier because of fluctuating exchange rates, unstable governments, high product-communication adaptation costs, and several other factors. Therefore, the first step in considering expanding to the overseas markets is to understand the international marketing environment. Second, the firm should clearly define its objective for international operations. Third, in considering which foreign markets to target, a firm must analyze each country's physical, legal, economic, political, cultural, and competitive environments. Once the target market or markets are selected, the firm has to decide how to enter the target market. Companies must next decide on the extent to which their product, price, promotion, and distribution should be adapted to each country. Finally, the firm must develop an effective organization for pursuing international marketing.

SEE ALSO *International Business; International Trade; Marketing*

BIBLIOGRAPHY

American Marketing Association. (1995). *Dictionary of marketing terms* (2nd ed.; Peter D. Bennett, Ed.). Lincolnwood, IL: NTC Business Books.

Bennett, Roger, and Blythe, Jim (2002). *International marketing: Strategy planning, market entry and implementation* (3rd ed.). London: Kogan Page.

Cateora, Philip R., and Graham, John L. (2005). *International marketing* (12th ed.). Boston: McGraw-Hill/Irwin.

Coughlan, Anne T., et al. (2006). *Marketing channels* (7th ed.). Upper Saddle River, NJ: Pearson/Prentice Hall.

Czinkota, Michael R., and Ronkainen, Ilkka A. (2004). *International marketing* (7th ed.). Mason, OH: Thomson/South-Western.

Doole, Isobel, and Lowe, Robin (2004). *International marketing strategy: Analysis, development and implementation* (4th ed.). Stamford, CT: Thomson Learning.

Joshi, Rakesh Mohan (2005). *International marketing*. New York: Oxford University Press.

Keegan, Warren J. (1995). *Multinational marketing management* (5th ed.). Upper Saddle River, NJ: Prentice Hall.

Keegan, Warren J., and Green, Mark C. (2005). *Global marketing* (4th ed.). Upper Saddle River, NJ: Pearson/Prentice Hall.

Kotler, Philip, and Keller, Kevin (2006). *Marketing management: Analysis, planning, implementation, and control* (12th ed.). Upper Saddle River, NJ: Pearson Prentice Hall.

Lascu, Dana-Nicoleta (2005). *International marketing* (2nd ed.). Cincinnati: Atomic Dog.

Terpstra, Vern, and Sarathy, Ravi (2000). *International marketing* (8th ed.). Fort Worth, TX: Dryden.

Shaheen Borna

INTERNATIONAL MONETARY FUND

The International Monetary Fund was established to foster international trade and currency conversion, which it does through consultation and loan activities. When it was created in 1946, the IMF had thirty-nine member countries. By November 1999 membership in the IMF had grown to 182 member countries and by the mid-2000s membership included every major country, the former communist countries, and numerous small countries. The only exception were Cuba and North Korea.

To join the IMF, a country must deposit a sum of money called a quota subscription, the amount of which is based on the wealth of the country's economy. Quotas are reconsidered every five years and can be increased or decreased based on IMF needs and the prosperity of the member country. In 2005, the United States contributed the largest percentage of the annual contributions—18 percent—because it had the largest, richest economy in the world. Voting rights are allocated in proportion to the quota subscription.

HISTORICAL DEVELOPMENT

The Depression in the 1930s devastated international trade and monetary exchange, creating a great loss of confidence on the part of those engaged in international business and finance. Because international traders lost confidence in the paper money used in international trade, there was an intense demand to convert paper money into gold—a demand beyond what the treasuries of countries could supply. Nations that defined the value of their currency in terms of a given amount of gold were unable to meet the conversion demand and had to abandon the gold standard. Valuing currencies in terms of given amounts of gold, however, had given currencies stable values that made international trade flow smoothly.

The relationship between money and the value of products became confused. Some nations hoarded gold to make their currency more valuable so that their producers could buy raw materials at lower prices. Other countries, desperate for foreign sales of their goods, engaged in competitive devaluations of their currencies. World trade became difficult. Countries restricted the exchange of currency, and even encouraged barter. In the early 1940s Harry Dexter White (1892–1948) of the United States and John Maynard Keynes (1883–1946) of the United Kingdom proposed the establishment of a permanent international organization to bring about the cooperation of all nations in order to achieve clear currency valuation and currency convertibility as well as to eliminate practices that undermine the world monetary system.

Finally, at an international meeting in Bretton Woods, New Hampshire, in July 1944, it was decided to create a new international monetary system and a permanent international organization to monitor it. Forty-four countries agreed to cooperate to solve international trade and investment problems, setting the following goals, for the new permanent, international organization:

- Unrestricted conversion of currencies
- Establishment of a value for each currency in relation to others
- Removal of restrictive trade practices

CREATION OF THE INTERNATIONAL MONETARY FUND

In 1946 in Washington, D.C., the international organization to monitor the new international monetary system came into existence—the International Monetary Fund (IMF). The purposes of the IMF are as follows:

Economists and IMF founders John Maynard Keynes (left) and Harry D. White (right) March 1, 1946. **THOMAS D. MCAVOY/TIME LIFE PICTURES/GETTY IMAGES**

To promote international monetary consultation, cooperation, and collaboration

To facilitate the expansion and balanced growth of international trade

To promote exchange stability

To assist in the establishment of a multilateral system of payments

To make its general resources temporarily available to its members experiencing balance of payments difficulties under adequate safeguards

To shorten the duration and lessen the degree of disequilibrium in the international balances of payments of members

The Bretton Woods agreement created fixed exchange rates between countries based on the value of each country's currency in relation to gold or indirectly in relation to gold by relating their currency to the U.S. dollar. The United States in turn guaranteed that the dollar could be exchanged for gold at a fixed exchange rate. The United States, however, ultimately could not maintain the dollar's promised convertibility, ending it in 1971, in large part because of inflation and a subsequent run on the U.S. gold reserve. The fixed-exchange-rate system collapsed. This led to a managed flexible-exchange-rate system with agreement among major countries that they would try to coordinate exchange rates based on price indexes. However, without operational criteria for managing currency relationships, exchange rates have been increasingly determined by volatile international capital movements rather than by trade relationships.

ORGANIZATIONAL STRUCTURE

The organization of the IMF has at its top a board of governors and alternate governors, who are usually the ministers of finance and heads of central banks of each member country. Because of their positions, they are able to speak authoritatively for their countries. The entire board of governors and alternate governors meets once a year in Washington, D.C., to formally determine IMF policies. During the rest of the year, a twenty-four-member executive board, composed of representatives or the total board of governors, meets a number of times each week to supervise the implementation of the policies adopted by the board of governors. The IMF staff is headed by its managing director, who is appointed by the executive board. The managing director chairs meetings of the executive board after appointment. Most staff members work at IMF headquarters in Washington, D.C. A small number of staff members are assigned to offices in Geneva, Paris, and Tokyo and at the United Nations.

SURVEILLANCE AND CONSULTATIONS

At least annually, a team of IMF staff members visits each member country for two weeks. The team of four or five meets with government officials, makes inquiries, engages in discussions, and gathers information about the country's economic policies and their effectiveness. If there are currency exchange restrictions, the consultation includes inquiry as to progress toward the elimination of such restrictions. Statistics are also collected on such matters as exports and imports, tax revenues, and budgetary expenditures. The team reports the results of the visit to the IMF executive board. A summary of the discussion is transmitted to the country's government, and for countries agreeing to the release of the summary, to the public.

FINANCIAL ASSISTANCE

The IMF endeavors to stabilize the international monetary system by temporarily lending resources in the form of foreign currencies and gold to countries experiencing international payment difficulties. There are a number of reasons why a country may need such assistance. One possibility is that the country has a trade deficit, which is often offset by lending, capital investment, and possibly aid from richer countries. However, confidence in the country's economic system and its ability to repay its debts becomes diminished in such a situation. The IMF requires that the borrowing country provide a plan for reform that will ultimately result in resolving the payments problems. Reforms such as tighter fiscal and monetary policies, good government control of expenditures, elimination of corruption, and provision for greater disclosure are required.

The most immediate assistance to a member country with payments difficulty is permission to withdraw 25 percent of the quota subscription that was initially paid in the form of gold or convertible currency. If the country still cannot meet its payments obligations it can, ultimately, borrow up to three times its original quota payment. The borrowing country must produce a plan of reform that will overcome the payments problem.

The IMF has a number of additional lending plans to meet various problems experienced by its members as well as emergency lending programs. There are Stand-By Arrangements disbursed over one to two years for temporary deficits, the Compensatory and Contingency Financing Facility for sudden drops in export earnings, Emergency Assistance for natural disasters, Extended Fund Facility to correct structural problems with maturities of greater length, the Supplemental Reserve Facility to provide loans to countries experiencing short-term payments problems due to a sudden loss of market confidence in the country's currency, and the Systemic Transformation Facility for the former communist countries in Eastern Europe and Russia.

SPECIAL DRAWING RIGHTS (SDRS)

In the 1960s, during an expansion of the world economy while gold and the U.S. dollar were the reserve currencies, it appeared that reserves were insufficient to provide for international trade needs. The IMF was empowered to create a new reserve asset, called the special drawing right (SDR), which it could lend to member countries. The value assigned to the SDR is the average of the world's major currencies. Countries with strong currencies agreed to buy SDRs when needed by a country because of payment problems, and in turn sell other currencies. However, at present SDRs are used mostly for repayment of IMF loans. Creation of SDRs is limited by the IMF constitution to times when there is a long-term global reserve shortage. The board of governors and alternate governors is empowered to make such a determination.

LOANS TO POOR, INDEBTED COUNTRIES

The IMF has created various loan facilities such as the Trust Fund to provide loans to its poorest member countries. In addition, the IMF works cooperatively with the World Bank, other international organizations, individual countries, and private lenders to assist poor, debt-ridden countries. It encourages such countries to restructure their economies to create better economic conditions and better balance of payment conditions.

There have been critics of the IMF's effectiveness. Such critics have noted, for example, instances of massive corruption on the part of recipient governments that resulted in IMF funds being stolen and/or wasted. Also, there have been a number of instances in which IMF efforts have been assessed as unsuccessful. Recommended restrictive fiscal policies have been seen as causing troublesome conditions, such as food shortages and citizen unrest. Nobel-prize-winning economist Robert Mundell, for example, has taken the position that current IMF policy options are insufficient to achieve stable international currency exchange and thereby foster international trade. He recommends that a global currency and world central bank be created to establish a stable international currency.

SEE ALSO *Global Economy; International Investment; International Trade*

BIBLIOGRAPHY

Ethier, Wilfred J. (1998, September). *Essays in International Finance*, No. 210. "The International Commercial System." Princeton, NJ: International Finance Section, Department of Economics, Princeton University.

Fischer, Stanley, Cooper, Richard, et al. (1998, May). *Essays in International Finance*, No. 207. "Should the IMF Pursue Capital Account Convertibility?" Princeton, NJ: International Finance Section, Department of Economics, Princeton University.

Gotherstrom, Maria (1998). "Development and Financial Structure of the International Monetary Fund." *Economic Review—Sveriges Riksbank*, previously *Quarterly Review—Sveriges Riksbank* (Stockholm) 4, 60-74.

International Monetary Fund (2005). "The IMF at a Glance." Retrieved October 26, 2005, from http://www.imf.org/external/np/exr/facts/glance.htm

Kenen, Peter B., ed. (1996, October). *Essays in International Finance*, No. 200. "From Halifax to Lyons: What Has Been Done About Crisis Management?" Princeton, NJ: International Finance Section, Department of Economics, Princeton University.

The Operations of the Department of the Treasury's Financial Crimes Enforcement Network: Hearing before the Subcommittee on General Oversight and Investigations of the Committee on Banking and Financial Services, U.S. House of Representatives. 1998, 105-55. Washington, DC: U.S. Government Printing Office.

"What Is the International Monetary Fund?" (2004). Retrieved October 26, 2005, from http://www.imf.org/external/pubs/ft/exrp/what.htm.

Williamson, John, and Mahar, Mary (1998, November). *Essays in International Finance*, No. 211. "A Survey of Financial Liberalization." Princeton, NJ: International Finance Section, Department of Economics, Princeton University.

Bernard H. Newman

INTERNATIONAL TRADE

The world has a long, rich history of international trade that can be traced back to early Assyrian, Babylonian, Egyptian, and Phoenician civilizations. These and other early civilizations recognized that trade can be tied directly to an improved quality of life for the citizens of all the partners. Today, the practice of trade among nations is growing by leaps and bounds. There is hardly a person on earth who has not been influenced in some way by the growing trade among nations.

WHY INTERNATIONAL TRADE?

Modern countries engage in international trade for numerous reasons. Some countries are deficient in critical raw materials, such as lumber or oil. To make up for these various deficiencies, countries must engage in international trade to obtain the resources necessary to produce the goods and/or services desired by their citizens. In addition to trading for raw materials, nations also exchange a wide variety of processed foods and finished products. Each country has its own specialties that are based on its economy and the skills of its citizens. Three common specialty classifications are capital, labor, and land.

Capital-intensive products, such as cars and trucks, heavy construction equipment, and industrial machinery, are produced by nations that have a highly developed industrial base. Japan is an example of a highly developed industrial nation that produces large quantities of high-quality cars for export around the world. Another reason Japan has adapted to producing capital-intensive products is that it is an island nation; little land is available for land-intensive product production.

Labor-intensive commodities, such as clothing, shoes, or other consumer goods, are produced in countries that have relatively low labor costs and relatively modern production facilities. China, Indonesia, and the Philippines are examples of countries that produce many labor-intensive products. Products that require large tracts of land, such as cattle production and wheat farming, are examples of land-intensive commodities. Countries that do not have large tracts of land normally purchase land-intensive products from countries that do have vast amounts of suitable land. The United States, for example, is one of the leading exporters of wheat. The combination of advanced farming technology, skilled farmers, and large tracts of suitable farmland in the Midwest and the Great Plains makes the mass production of wheat possible.

Over time a nation's workforce will change, and thus the goods and services that a nation produces and exports will change. Nations that train their workers for future roles can minimize the difficulty of making a transition to a new, dominant market. The United States, for example, was the dominant world manufacturer from the end of World War II (1939–1945) until the early 1970s. But, beginning in the 1970s, other countries started to produce finished products more cheaply and efficiently than the United States, causing U.S. manufacturing output and exports to drop significantly. Rapid growth in computer technology, however, began to provide a major export for the United States. Practically speaking, the United States has been slowly transformed from a manufacturing-based economy into a new information age-based economy that relies on exporting cutting-edge technology, as high-tech software and computer companies proliferate.

POLITICAL ENVIRONMENT

Each country varies regarding international trade and relocation of foreign plants on its native soil. Some countries openly court foreign companies and encourage them to invest in their country by offering reduced taxes or some other investment incentives. Other countries impose strict regulations that can cause large companies to leave and open a plant in a country that provides more favorable operating conditions. When a company decides to conduct business in another country, it should also consider the political stability of the host country's government. Unstable leadership can create significant problems in recouping profits if the government of the host country falls or changes its policy toward foreign trade and investment. Political instability is often caused by severe economic conditions that result in civil unrest.

Another key aspect of international trade is paying for a product in a foreign currency. This practice can create potential problems for a company, since any currency is subject to price fluctuation. A company could lose money if the value of the foreign currency is reduced before it can be exchanged into the desired currency. Another issue regarding currency is that some nations do not have the necessary cash. Instead, they engage in countertrade, which involves the direct or indirect exchange of goods for other goods instead of for cash. Countertrade follows the same principles as bartering, a practice that stretches back into prehistory. A car company might trade new cars to a foreign government in exchange for high-quality steel that would be more costly to buy on the open market. The company can then use the steel to produce new cars for sale.

In a more extreme case, some countries do not want to engage in free trade with other nations, a choice known as self-sufficiency. There are many reasons for this choice, but the most important is the existence of strong political beliefs. For example, the Soviet Union and its communist allies traded only with each other because the Soviet Union feared that Western countries would attempt to

control their governments through trade. Self-sufficiency allowed the Soviet Union and its allies to avoid that possibility. These self-imposed trade restrictions, however, created a shortage of products that could not be produced among the group, making the overall quality of life within the Soviet bloc substantially lower than in the West since consumer demand could not be met. When the Berlin Wall came down, trade with the West was resumed, and the shortage of products was reduced or eliminated.

ECONOMIC ENVIRONMENT

An important factor influencing international trade is taxes. Of the different taxes that can be applied to imported goods, the most common is a tariff, which is generally defined as an excise tax imposed on imported goods. A country can have several reasons for imposing a tariff. For example, a revenue tariff may be applied to an imported product that is also produced domestically. The primary reason for this type of tariff is to generate revenue that can be used later by the government for a variety of purposes. This tariff is normally set at a low level and is not usually considered a threat to international trade. When domestic manufacturers in a particular industry are at a disadvantage, vis-à-vis imports, the government can impose what is called a protective tariff. This type of tariff is designed to make foreign products more expensive than domestic products and, as a result, protect domestic companies. A protective tariff is normally very popular with the affected domestic companies and their workers because they benefit the most directly from it.

In retaliation, a country that is affected by a protective tariff will frequently enact a tariff of its own on a product from the original tariff-enacting country. In 1930, for example, the U.S. Congress passed the Hawley-Smoot Tariff Act, which provided the means for placing protective tariffs on imports. The United States imposed this protective tariff on a wide variety of products in an attempt to help protect domestic producers from foreign competition. This legislation was very popular in the United States, because the Great Depression had just begun, and the tariff was seen as helping U.S. workers. The tariff, however, caused immediate retaliation by other countries, which imposed protective tariffs of their own on U.S. products. As a result of these protective tariffs, world trade was severely reduced for nearly all countries, causing the wealth of each affected nation to drop, and increasing unemployment in most countries.

Realizing that the 1930 tariffs were a mistake, Congress took corrective action by passing the Reciprocal Trade Agreements Act of 1934, which empowered the president to reduce tariffs by 50 percent on goods from any other country that would agree to similar tariff reductions. The goal was to promote more international trade and help establish more cooperation among exporting countries.

Another form of a trade barrier that a country can employ to protect domestic companies is an import quota, which strictly limits the amount of a particular product that a foreign country can export to the quota-enacting country. For example, the United States once threatened to limit the number of cars imported from Japan. Japan, however, agreed to voluntary export quotas, formally known as "voluntary export restrictions," to avoid U.S.-imposed import quotas. The power of import quotas has diminished because foreign manufacturers—to avoid such regulations—started building plants in the countries to which they had previously exported.

A government can also use a nontariff barrier to help protect domestic companies. A nontariff barrier usually refers to government requirements for licenses, permits, or significant amounts of paperwork in order to allow imports into its country. This tactic often increases the price of the imported product, slows down delivery, and creates frustration for the exporting country. The end goal is that many foreign companies will not bother to export their products to those markets because of the added cost and aggravation. Japan and several European countries have frequently used this strategy to limit the number of imported products.

CULTURAL ENVIRONMENT

Before a corporation begins exporting products, it must first examine the norms, taboos, and values of the countries in which it wants to sell its products. This information can be critical to the successful introduction of a product into a particular country and will influence how it is sold and/or marketed. Such information can prevent cultural blunders, such as the one General Motors committed when trying to sell its Chevy Nova in Spanish-speaking countries. *Nova* in Spanish means "doesn't go"—and few people would purchase a car named "doesn't go." This marketing error—resulting simply from ignorance of the Spanish language—cost General Motors millions in initial sales, as well as considerable embarrassment.

Business professionals also need to be aware of foreign customs regarding standard business practices. For example, people from some countries like to sit or stand very close when conducting business. In contrast, people from other countries prefer to maintain a spatial distance between themselves and the people with whom they are conducting business. Thus, before businesspeople travel overseas, they must be given training on how to conduct business in the country to which they are traveling.

Business professionals also run into another practice that occurs in some countries—bribery. The practice of bribery is common in several countries and is considered a normal business practice. If the bribe is not paid to a businessperson from a country where bribery is expected, a transaction is unlikely to occur. Laws in some countries prohibit businesspeople from paying or accepting bribes. As a result, navigating this legal and cultural thicket must be done very carefully in order to maintain full compliance with the law.

PHYSICAL ENVIRONMENT

Other factors that influence international trading activities are related to the physical environment. Natural physical features, such as mountains and rivers, and human-made structures, such as bridges and roads, can have an impact on international trading activities. For example, a large number of potential customers may live in a country where natural physical barriers make getting the product to market nearly impossible.

WORLD TRADE ORGANIZATIONS AND AGREEMENTS

After World War II, the world's leading nations wanted to create a permanent organization that would help foster world trade. Such an organization came into being in 1947 when representatives from the United States and twenty-three other nations signed the document creating the General Agreement on Tariffs and Trade (GATT), which now includes more than 100 countries as signatories. The threefold purpose of GATT was to:

1. foster equal, nondiscriminatory treatment for all member nations;

2. promote the reduction of tariffs by multilateral negotiations; and

3. foster the elimination of import quotas.

GATT nations meet periodically to review progress toward established objectives and to set new goals that member countries want to achieve. The goals and objectives of GATT vary and change over time as trade issues based on domestic and world economies evolve.

Likewise, representatives from Belgium, Denmark, France, Germany, Greece, Ireland, Italy, Luxembourg, the Netherlands, Portugal, Spain, and the United Kingdom came together to form the European Economic Community (EEC), sometimes called the Common Market, in 1958. The purpose of the EEC was to create equal and fair tariffs for all of the nations in the organization so that trade could flourish in Europe.

The United States and Canada signed the Canada-U.S. Free Trade Agreement in 1989, which provided for the removal of all trade barriers—such as tariffs, quotas, and other trade restrictions—between the two countries within a ten-year period. This act helped promote even more trade between the two countries, thus further strengthening an already strong trade relationship.

The United States, Canada, and Mexico signed the North American Free Trade Agreement (NAFTA) in 1994 in order to create a free-trade zone among the three countries. Leaders of these three countries realized that a large North American free-trade zone could compete effectively against the EEC and other trading blocs that might develop in the future. This competitive factor was a driving force in the nations' signing of the agreement, each believing that, over the long run, all three would benefit from the agreement.

In addition to feeling the impact of trade agreements and trade organizations per se, international trade is affected more indirectly by the financial stability and general economic well-being of all countries in the increasingly interconnected world. Thus two other international organizations ultimately affect the health of world trade.

To further promote trade among countries, the Allied nations of World War II met in 1944 in Bretton Woods, New Hampshire, to help set postwar global financial policies and thereby avoid future financial crises. The International Monetary Fund (IMF) was created as a result of that conference, its mission being to provide loans to countries that are in financial trouble. The IMF dictates the terms of the loans, which may include cutting domestic subsidies, privatizing government industries, and moderating trade policies. To fund these loans, IMF members make annual contributions, with each country's contribution determined by its size, national income, population, and volume of trade. Larger contributing countries, such as the United Kingdom and the United States, have more say as to what countries get loans and the terms of the loan.

The World Bank, with approximately 184 members, is another international organization to which the United States is a major contributor. The World Bank's mission is to help less-developed countries achieve economic growth through improved trade. It does so by providing loans and guaranteeing or insuring private loans to nations in need of financial assistance. The World Bank has been characterized as a last-resort lender, a facilitator of development projects so as to encourage the inflow of private banking funds, and a provider of technical assistance for fostering long-term economic growth.

SUMMARY

The world has a long history of international trade—trading among nations can be traced back to the earliest civilizations. Trading activities are directly related to an improved quality of life for the citizens of nations involved in international trade. It is safe to say that nearly every person on earth has benefited from international trading activities.

WEB SITES OF INTEREST

For further information about tariffs, the Hawley-Smoot Tariff Act, and the Reciprocal Trade Agreements Act of 1934: http://economics.about.com/cs/taxpolicy/a/tariffs.htm, http://www.state.gov/r/pa/ho/time/id/17606.htm, and http://www.itds.treas.gov/tradelaws.html

For more information regarding import quotas: http://internationalecon.com/v1.0/ch10/10c060.html

For more information regarding nontariff trade barriers: http://www.dti.gov.ph/contentment/9/62/127/585.jsp

For more information regarding bribery: http://www.berrymoorman.com/articles/1199rmwbribery.html

For more information about the GATT: http://www.ciesin.org/TG/PI/TRADE/gatt.html

For more information regarding the EEC: http://www.infoplease.com/ce6/history/A0817889.html

For more information on the Canada-U.S. Free Trade Agreement of 1989: http://www.agr.gc.ca/itpd-dpci/english/trade_agr/fta.htm

For information regarding the World Bank: http://www.worldbank.org

SEE ALSO *International Business; International Marketing; Marketing*

BIBLIOGRAPHY

Bhagwati, Jagdish (2002). *Free trade today.* Princeton, NJ: Princeton University Press.

Boone, Louis E., and Kurtz, David L. (2005). *Contemporary marketing 2006.* Eagan, MN: Thomson South-Western.

Braithwaite, John, and Drahos, Peter (2000). *Global business regulation.* New York: Cambridge University Press.

Churchill, Gilbert A., Jr., and Peter, Paul J. (1998). *Marketing: Creating value for customers* (2nd ed.). New York: Irwin McGraw-Hill.

Czinkota, Michael R., and Ronkainen, Ilkka A. (2004). *International marketing* (7th ed.). Mason, OH: Thomson/South-Western.

Czinkota, Michael R., Ronkainen, Ilkka A., and Donath, Bob (2004). *Mastering global markets: Strategies for today's trade globalist.* Mason, OH: Thomson/Southwestern.

Kotler, Philip, and Armstrong, Gary (2006). *Principles of marketing* (11th ed.). Upper Saddle River, NJ: Pearson Prentice-Hall.

McConnell, Campbell R., and Brue, Stanley L. (2005). *Economics: Principles, problems, and policies* (16th ed.). Boston: McGraw-Hill/Irwin.

Moon, Bruce E. (2000). *Dilemmas of international trade: Dilemmas in world politics* (2nd ed.). Boulder, CO: Westview.

Nelson, Carl A. (2000). *Import/export: How to get started in international trade* (3rd ed.). New York: McGraw-Hill.

Weiss, Kenneth D. (2002). *Building an import/export business* (3rd ed.). New York: Wiley.

Allen D. Truell
Michael Milbier

Tim Berners-Lee (1955–). Inventor of the World Wide Web and Director of the World Wide Web Consortium in Cambridge, Massachusetts, September 29, 2004. AP IMAGES

INTERNET

An internet is a collection of interconnected computers that use networking hardware and software to send and receive data. The Internet is the global network of interconnected computers and servers available to the public. The World Wide Web is the collection of graphically intensive Web pages that have enabled the Internet to become a societal phenomenon.

THE ORIGINAL INTERNET

In the 1950s researchers and scientists across the country linked their mainframe computers via telephone connections operating at very slow speeds. This first network supported communication of basic text-based computer data. In the beginning, only federal agencies and a few research universities were linked. The system was funded by the Advanced Research Project Agency, a technology and research group in the U.S. Department of Defense. The system was referred to as ARPANET.

The first four universities connected to ARPANET were Stanford University, the University of California-Los Angeles, the University of California-Santa Barbara, and the University of Utah. Communications research in the 1960s led to decentralized networks, queuing theory, and packet switching. These technologies allowed different types of computers to send and receive data. Computers transmitted information in a standardized protocol called packets. The addressing information in these packets told each computer in the system where the packet was supposed to go.

In 1972 the first electronic mail (e-mail) program was developed. It used file transfer protocol (FTP) to upload messages to a server that would then route the message to the intended computer terminal. This text-based communication tool greatly affected the rate at which collaborative work could be conducted between researchers at participating universities. This collaboration led to the development of the transmission control protocol (TCP), which breaks large amounts of data into packets of a fixed size, transmits the packets over the Internet using the Internet protocol (IP), and sequentially numbers them to allow reassembly at the recipient's end. The combination of TCP and IP is still the model used to move data over the Internet.

In 1984 the Pentagon, the leadership of the U.S. military, decided the growing academic and community-based Internet was far too open and lacked the security required for a military network. They transferred control of the original ARPANET to the National Science Foundation (NSF) and created a separate and secure network called MILNET. The NSF added a network backbone, renamed it NSFNet and made it available to a much larger number of colleges and universities.

With more universities connected and participating in the Internet, more programs and communication applications were created. A program called Telnet allowed remote users to run programs and computers from other sites. Gopher, developed at the University of Minnesota and named after the university's mascot, allowed menu-driven access to data resources on the Internet. Search engines such as Archie and Wide Area Index Search gave users the ability to search the Internet's numerous libraries and indexes. By the mid-1980s users at universities, research laboratories, private companies, and libraries were empowered by the new networking revolution. More than 30,000 host computers and modems were actively using the Internet.

THE INTERNET AND THE WORLD WIDE WEB

In August 1991, Dr. Tim Berners-Lee (1955–) of CERN (the European Organization for Nuclear Research) in Switzerland envisioned the concept of a graphical, page-based Internet—the World Wide Web. Although many people use the terms *Internet* and *World Wide Web* interchangeably, they refer to two separate, yet related, technologies. The Web is supported by hypertext markup language (HTML), a programming language used to create graphical Web pages, and hypertext transfer protocol (HTTP), the routing technology used to identify uniform resource locators (URLs) or Web page addresses.

Web pages are retrieved via Internet protocols and resources; the Web, however, is merely one of many Internet applications such as FTP, Telnet, and Gopher. Berners-Lee developed the Web as a way to simplify reading the location of documents by assigning standard names or file paths. In 1992 the first Web browsers, Viola and Mosaic, were developed. The ease of use and graphic capabilities (prior Internet data exchanges were primarily text-based) made Web browsers popular outside the academic community, and soon the general public found access to the Internet and World Wide Web to be useful.

The Internet and the World Wide Web continue to grow. The U.S. Census Bureau reported that in 2003, 61.8 percent of U.S. households had a computer and 54.7 percent had Internet access. Home use, however, does not reflect the number of people who use computers and the Internet at work, in libraries, at schools, and in community organizations. The Census Bureau found that nearly 60 percent of American adults used the Internet. Over 165 countries are connected to the Internet. Yet, no one nation or group operates or controls the Internet. Although there are entities that oversee the system, "no one is in charge." This allows for a free transfer and flow of information throughout the world. Search engines such as Google and Yahoo index the Web to help in the organization and retrieval of information.

USING THE INTERNET AND WORLD WIDE WEB

Accessing the Internet requires an Internet-capable computer and a modem to modulate/demodulate outgoing and incoming data packets. Modems connect computers to the Internet across telephone lines (dial-up) or by optical or wire cable (broadband or digital subscriber line, also known as DSL). The connection is provided by an Internet service provider (ISP), such as America Online, Comcast, or RoadRunner. For a monthly fee, these companies provide access to the Internet, e-mail, a certain amount of storage, and search utilities. These Internet providers will often offer portal sites that provide a Web browser, a chat service (Internet relay chat—IRC), instant messaging (IM), bulletin boards, newsgroups, and forums.

Each application requires a specific software program. Many computers are sold with these applications preloaded, such as Microsoft's Internet Explorer, the most popular Web browser. E-mail applications such as Eudora are purchased separately; many e-mail programs, however, are now Web-based. This means that users can access their Web-based e-mail program from any computer that is connected to the Internet. A specific software application is no longer required because the application runs from the server rather than from the computer itself.

All ISPs require a username and password, which establishes the user's identity and gives authorization to use the Internet service. The Internet service provider has its own higher-order identity on the Internet, known as a domain. For example, in the following e-mail address:

jones@abc.com

the first part of the address, "jones" identifies the user; this is the username. The "@" (pronounced "at") separates the username from the domain. In this example, "abc" is the domain name, and ".com" is the extension that identifies the entity as a commercial provider. Other extensions include .net for network, .edu for education, .mil for military, .gov for government, and .org for organization.

Affect on Business and Industry. The World Wide Web has created a new industry segment called electronic commerce (e-commerce). Businesses sell to other businesses (B2B) and to consumers (B2C) on the Internet using secure Web sites. The "dot.com" frenzy came to a head in the late 1990s when the number of online companies exceeded demand. Although online commerce declined slightly, it has remained stable since then. Strong e-commerce providers are either "pure-play" (having only an Internet presence, such as eBay and Amazon.com) or "brick-and-click" (having both a physical store as well as an online store, such as Wal-Mart, Sears, and most other major retail outlets).

Internet technology has also had an impact on business and industry by supporting telecommuting. Rather than commuting to work, employees work from home via telecommunications (e.g., e-mail, video streaming, and online portals). Overhead costs are lowered if office space and equipment can be reduced, and the flexibility for the employee can be a benefit.

Changing Education. Additionally, Internet use has changed the face of education. Nearly every school in the United States has computer technology and Internet access. Students use Web browsers to search for information, teachers use online databases to access lesson plans and learning resources, and schools build Web sites that provide homework information, school calendars, and other important information for parents, faculty, and students.

Distance learning or online education has also made great strides. High schools, colleges, universities, and for-profit providers are supplementing their face-to-face classes with Web-based learning environments, such as Blackboard, WebCT, and e-College. Students can download activities, participate in synchronous chat groups or asynchronous discussion forums, work collaboratively with other students on group projects, take tests, and post their homework for evaluation. Some courses are offered totally online without any face-to-face interaction between the student and instructor.

Changes in Information Transfer and Communication. The Internet is one of the most innovative and productive technologies in history. The Internet can send information from virtually any place on the globe to any other place in seconds. This communication tool has dramatically changed the concept of the "speed of business." In effect, the Internet has created a sense of time compression. No longer do large documents need to be mailed by expensive overnight carriers. Electronic files are sent as e-mail attachments in seconds or documents can be posted to Web sites where they can be downloaded by thousands of recipients. Distribution has also been affected. Rather than mailing 1,000 newsletters to an organization's membership, Listservs enable the message to be sent to one address. The message is sent to the Listserv address (e.g., "listserv@abc.com"), and anyone who has signed up or been added to the Listserv instantly receives the information.

A very popular new Web-based communication tool is the Weblog (or "blog"). Used by both companies and individuals, blogs are diaries posted to a host site that can be accessed by anyone. Some commercial blogs are designed for customer use. They offer free product advice, technical assistance, drivers and downloads, and product data to attract new customers. Microsoft's product developers use blogs to encourage interest in their work. In some cases, readers can post comments to forums, which the blogger monitors.

The ease of use and instantaneous communication of the Internet are generally seen as significant enhancements to society, but there are some negative aspects. The term *CyberEthics* refers to the ethical use of the Internet. For example, music or movie files are easily copied from compact disks or downloaded from file-sharing and peer-to-peer sites such as BearShare, e-donkey, Napster, and Kazaa. The Recording Industry Association of America (RIAA) attempts to combat piracy—the illegal duplication and distribution of any recording—via lawsuits and fines. The RIAA reported that worldwide, the industry was losing $4.2 billion to piracy each year.

CONCLUSION

The personal computer will continue to evolve, but experts predict other Internet-smart appliances would become standard. Wristwatches will provide Internet access and support computer applications such as Word. Televisions will anticipate viewers' program preferences and record shows it thinks they may like. Kitchen appliances will be programmed by Internet-based command centers that will download recipes, inventory current ingredients (how much milk is left?), and print shopping lists. Like the explorers who discovered new continents, Internet users are just beginning to discover the full impact of the medium on information, space, and time.

SEE ALSO *Electronic Commerce; Electronic Mail; Intranet/Extranet*

BIBLIOGRAPHY
Recording Industry Association of America. http://www.riaa.org

Lisa E. Gueldenzoph
Mark J. Snyder

INTERPERSONAL RELATIONS

SEE *Human Relations*

INTERSTATE COMMERCE

Interstate commerce is the transportation of products and services from one state to geographic points in other states. This involves the transportation of goods and serv-

A Wal-Mart truck on the side of the highway May 15, 2005 near Springer, New Mexico. **CHRIS HONDROS/GETTY IMAGES**

ices across state lines, creating a dependency on transportation modes and making the process subject to state laws regarding the transportation of goods.

RURAL ORIGINS

Transportation plays an important role in determining the profitability of operating both farm and nonfarm businesses in rural areas. Farms, businesses, and industries in rural areas rely on transportation services to achieve necessary production outputs and to deliver commodities and products to market.

Interstate commerce has its roots in farming. During most of the first decade after the Civil War (1861–1865), farmers in seven midwestern states were responsible for approximately one-half of the nation's output of corn, wheat, and oats. Illinois farms were the leaders in the production of each of these grains; farmers to the north provided large amounts of the hard varieties of wheat, while those to the south and east produced most of the corn. Based on the presence of abundant feed, these producers established locations for fattening livestock and producing meat products. Given this state of affairs, farmers were in the market for transport services to carry livestock and crops to major produce exchanges located in other states.

Chicago and St. Louis were established as collection centers, but these centers were not the sites of final consumption. By 1870 there were well-established lines of supply between states. The Great Lakes steamers and schooners provided most of the service between Chicago and the northern portions of the Great Lakes area, and the

four major railroads provided ground transportation. The two railroads with independent and complete service were the New York Central system and the Pennsylvania system.

Between 1874 and 1919, many laws were enacted that imposed economic regulation on the dominant means of interstate commerce in the United States: the railroad. Federal transportation regulations, however, were not of a sufficient magnitude to justify forming a cabinet-level department solely for matters of interstate commerce.

Economic conditions between 1874 and 1919 vacillated. Agricultural depression was extensive during the 1870s and 1880s and constituted a factor that ultimately resulted in the economic regulation of interstate railroads in 1887. Furthermore, an international depression occurred in 1893 that sent seventy-four railroad companies into financial distress. Between 1901 and 1919, U.S. society experienced relative prosperity; it was during this period that 145,000 miles of track were constructed to carry goods between states.

Executive and legislative agencies related to transportation functions proliferated between 1874 and 1919; it was during this same period that highway transportation began to increase in importance. Financing and planning of highway development within state lines was primarily the responsibility of each individual state. Nevertheless, the Bureau of Public Roads began to play a significant role. In addition, the airline industry had its beginnings during the early part of the twentieth century.

INTERSTATE COMMERCE COMMISSION ESTABLISHED

The Interstate Commerce Commission (ICC), an independent U.S. government agency established in 1887, was responsible for the economic regulation of services of specified carriers engaged in transportation between states. The first regulatory agency formed within the federal government, it was established in response to mounting public indignation against railroad malpractices and abuses. The ICC's effectiveness, however, was limited by the U.S. Congress's failure to give it enforcement power, by the U.S. Supreme Court's narrow interpretation of its powers, and by the vague language of its enabling act.

Beginning with the Hepburn Act of 1906, the ICC's domain was gradually extended beyond railroads to all common carriers (except airplanes) by 1940. It was also given the task of consolidating railroad systems and managing labor disputes in interstate transport. In the 1950s and 1960s, the ICC enforced Supreme Court rulings that required the desegregation of passenger terminal facilities.

Part I of the Interstate Commerce Act grouped together a series of laws that were enacted in the late 1800s and early 1900s. The first of these laws required that railroad carriers publicize their rate schedules and forbade rate changes without due notice to the public. Subsequent acts increased regulation and extended the ICC's jurisdiction. Part II of the act extended federal authority to motor carriers engaged in interstate commerce. Part III gave the federal government authority to regulate common carriers operating in interstate commerce in the coastal, intercoastal, and inland waters of the United States. Part IV comprised regulations governing the operations of freight operators.

Subsequently, the ICC's jurisdiction expanded to included trucking, bus lines, water carriers, freight forwarders, pipelines (those not already regulated by other agencies), and express-delivery agencies. The ICC controlled rates and enforced federal and local laws against discrimination in these areas. The safety functions of its jurisdiction were transferred to the U.S. Department of Transportation in 1967, and the deregulation of the late 1970s and the 1980s further reduced the ICC's role. Most ICC control over interstate trucking was removed in 1994, and the agency was terminated at the end of 1995. Many of its remaining functions were transferred to the National Surface Transportation Board.

FEDERAL OVERSIGHT

Interstate commerce is supervised by several federal agencies. At one time, this included the Civil Aeronautics Board, created by the Civil Aeronautics Act of 1938 to oversee the airline industry. This act dealt with the airline industry's ability to provide efficient service at reasonable charges without unjust discrimination, undue preferences, or advantages or unfair or destructive competitive practices. Forty years later, President Jimmy Carter signed into law the Airline Deregulation Act of 1978, which phased out the Civil Aeronautics Board and let the airlines determine their own pricing and routes. It was thought that a lack of competition had made the industry unresponsive to consumers. As a result, the industry became deregulated and the pricing wars began.

Many other federal regulatory agencies and laws deal with interstate commerce. The Federal Trade Commission (FTC) was established in 1914 with investigatory powers to be used in preventing unfair methods of competition. The FTC enforces laws and guidelines regarding business practices and takes action to stop false and deceptive advertising, pricing, packaging, and labeling. It assists businesses in complying with both state and federal laws, and it evaluates new business methods each year. It holds conferences on electronic commerce (e-commerce), which is the newest form of interstate commerce. When general sets of guidelines are needed to assist businesses involved in interstate commerce, the FTC encourages firms within that industry to establish a set of trade practices voluntarily.

The Clayton Antitrust Act, passed in the same year that the FTC was created (1914), prohibits specific practices such as price discrimination, exclusive dealer arrangements, and stock acquisitions whose effect may notably lessen competition or tend to create a monopoly.

In addition, the Federal Communications Commission (FCC) has evolved as a crucial regulatory component in e-commerce development. The FCC regulates communication by wire, radio, and television in interstate and foreign commerce. This agency has been undergoing rapid changes as a result of the need for e-commerce regulation.

CURRENT INTERSTATE COMMERCE ENVIRONMENT

The transportation environment in the early twenty-first century is much different from that of the twentieth century. The shift from a rural to an urban economic base, policy changes, and technological and organizational innovations have changed the way in which products and services are distributed in the United States. Fewer than 10 percent of the people living in nonmetropolitan areas are employed in farming, forestry, fisheries, or mining. Farms in the 2000s tend to be larger and more capital intensive. Large tractor-trailer trucks are rapidly replacing smaller vehicles in the delivery of production inputs to farms and products to market.

Nonagricultural demands for interstate commerce increased dramatically in the last quarter of the twentieth century. Manufacturing employment in nonmetropolitan areas grew at a rate three times that in metropolitan areas. Approximately 20 percent of nonmetropolitan residents were employed by manufacturing firms at the turn of the twenty-first century.

As a result of these changes, the amount and type of interstate traffic has also changed dramatically. The larger, heavier vehicles on these roads require major investments in bridges and in surfaces of paved roads. A Department of Transportation survey suggested that more than 50 percent of the local road mileage in the United States was structurally inadequate. This problem is one of surface type and condition and even safety deficiencies, such as inadequate lane widths or lack of shoulders.

The increased financial responsibility of local governments for construction and maintenance of rural road systems is a special concern for those rural regions dependent on interstate commerce. Transportation deregulation is another major federal policy change likely to influence the cost and availability of transportation services and facilities needed for interstate commerce. Technological and organizational innovations have accompanied the new deregulated environment. Railroad mergers, for example, have resulted in reduced service on many routes, potentially affecting the relative competitiveness of regions as a location for business or industry. Developments of unit-train facilities and railroad contracts encourage consolidation and growth of processing firms.

Transportation improvements that result in lower operating costs for area enterprises aid rural communities in efforts to attract new business and industry and encourage the expansion of existing firms. Business surveys consistently find that firms rank transportation access, cost, and quality as high-priority considerations in choosing a business location. The availability of highway transportation is particularly important to a wide variety of rural businesses that depend on the ability to deliver their products to other states.

Freight carriers are dependent on the rural road systems, which are financed through a combination of local tax revenues. The shared state-highway user taxes and fees vary from state to state. A faltering local economy can severely limit a local government's ability to raise revenue for road system improvements, and the likely result of this is a cycle of decline in interstate commerce. Without additional revenues, local road systems will continue to deteriorate, thus further reducing the attractiveness of the area for business and industry and thus further eroding the area's tax base.

Interstate commerce involves the transportation of services as well as goods. Of particular importance is the transportation of people between states. Formerly, carriers were partially protected from competition in return for fulfilling public service obligations. Under this arrangement, common carriers were not free to choose customers, nor were they free to eliminate parts of their services without the consent of the public. This obligation placed liabilities for loss and damage with the interstate carriers who were responsible for transportation losses. In addition, common carriers had to serve all customers without discrimination and had to have their rate-change proposals reviewed by regulatory bodies to determine whether these changes were reasonable.

In return for fulfilling these public obligations, common carriers were protected from new competition. When a company proposed to expand service to another state, an existing transportation company could argue that it currently serviced the traffic adequately and could oppose entry of a new interstate carrier. Often, the opposition of existing carriers prevented the entry of new carriers.

In the early 1980s, however, Congress passed major legislation changing the government's role. Policy changes essentially replaced the common carrier system with a market-transaction system similar to that of any other private business. The new market approach allows shippers and carriers to actively negotiate for transport services rather than accept one of a few alternatives offered by carrier consortiums. Deregulation increased economic efficiency in the provision of transportation services because carriers had new flexibility in adjusting to demand.

Highways, railways, and airways are the arteries that enable shoppers and tourists to travel between states. Because of this, passenger transportation plays a key role in rural economic development. Many rural industries draw their workers from surrounding communities up to 50 miles (80.5 km) away. For these industries, the interstate transportation system is a critical link providing them access to the labor force. Policies and investments that reduce the cost of interstate commerce in rural regions are a potential catalyst for rural economic development.

The urgency of finding workable solutions to interstate commerce issues has prompted new ways of thinking. In 1982 the U.S. government appropriated $5 million to provide technical assistance to local agencies through the Rural Technical Assistance Program. The principal delivery system for the program was a network of Technology Transfer Centers. Under the Federal Highway Administration program, the Technology Transfer Centers were designed to provide training and other technology transfer products to local users. One of the primary objectives of the program is to serve as a communications link among the various sources of new technology and the state and local agencies that can apply the technology in daily operations. In 1983 there were ten

Technology Transfer Centers. In 2006 there were more than fifty across the United States.

E-Commerce. The FCC has recently come to the forefront because of its responsibility to regulate e-commerce. The FCC sought comment on two rule-making dockets in 2000: the Access Charge Reform rule-making docket and the Complete Detariffing for Competitive Access Providers and Competitive Local Exchange Carriers rule-making docket, which is involved with the regulatory or market-based approaches that would ensure that competitive local exchange carriers (CLEC) rates for interstate access are reasonable. Many proposals are being discussed at these proceedings, and the FCC invites all interested parties to comment on whether mandatory detariffing of CLEC interstate-access service rates would provide a market-based deterrent to excessive terminating access charges.

In addition, the FTC has been sponsoring workshops throughout the United States that are intended to educate people about how marketplaces work and to explore the anticompetitive scenarios. The FTC will be involved in scrutinizing virtual competition in e-marketplaces. In addition to challenges that e-marketing poses is the tension that exists between a state's authority to tax and the authority of Congress to regulate interstate commerce. For example, foreign businesses are often shocked to learn that while treaties may segregate them from the federal taxation, state taxation can still be imposed, thus putting a real damper on foreign investment.

SEE ALSO *Interstate Commerce Commission*

BIBLIOGRAPHY

Brierty, Edward, and Reeder, Robert (1991). *Industrial marketing, analysis planning and control.* Englewood Cliffs, NJ: Prentice Hall.

Brown, W. (2005, January). Outside counsel: Federal Arbitration Act. *New York Law Journal,* p. 4.

Gillis, William (1989). *Profitability and mobility in rural America.* University Park: Pennsylvania State University Press.

Miller, Sidney (1953). *Inland transportation.* New York: McGraw-Hill.

Patricia A. Spirou

INTERSTATE COMMERCE COMMISSION

President Grover Cleveland signed the Interstate Commerce Act of 1887 and created the Interstate Commerce Commission (ICC), the U.S. government's first regulatory agency. The initial purpose of the ICC was to control railroads and their unfair business practices. The U.S. government's assumption of the role of regulator resulted from the U.S. Supreme Court's 1886 ruling in the case of *Wabash Railroad v. Illinois,* which prohibited states from controlling interstate commerce.

Railroads presented some special problems because they were capital-intensive, had high maintenance costs, and had two types of rail lines. This situation led to unfair pricing practices. For major trunk lines, where there was competition, the railroads charged lower rates and even gave rebates. For spur lines, where there was a monopoly, the railroad charged higher rates for the same type of cargo.

Even with the federal government taking charge of regulating railroads, the ICC still began with a rocky start. In its first sixteen court actions, the ICC won only one case; and the Supreme Court made several power-limiting judgments against the ICC. Later legislation, however, provided strength for ICC rulings. The 1903 Elkins Act addressed unfair competitive methods. The 1906 Hepburn Act eliminated the mandated court order to make ICC rulings binding and gave the ICC control of gas and water pipelines. The milestone Transportation Act of 1920 resulted in the ICC's moving from approving to actually setting railroad rates, being empowered to organize mergers, and to determining appropriate profit levels.

The Motor Carrier Act of 1935 placed the emerging trucking industry under ICC jurisdiction. Typical ICC duties included holding hearings to investigate complaints, approving transportation mergers, and overseeing consumer-protection programs.

By the 1960s the ICC had grown into a massive bureaucracy, peaking at 2,400 employees. Shortly thereafter, the agency came under severe criticism. Some groups argued that, because of regulation, the country's transportation was inefficient and perhaps corrupt. The major criticism—that regulation created artificially high rates—led to pressure for deregulation and signaled the beginning of the demise of the ICC. First, the Railroad Revitalization and Regulatory Reform Act of 1976 curtailed the ICC power to regulate rates unless the railroad had a monopoly on certain routes. In 1977 air cargo deregulation and the reforms taking place in the trucking industry further eroded the power of the ICC. After the early rocky years of deregulation, the transportation industry had become more efficient thanks to innovative technology, thereby reducing costs. The final act of deregulation came in 1994, when the ICC lost most of its control over the trucking industry.

By this time the number of ICC employees had dropped to 300 and the ICC constrained by a severely reduced budget. The Republicans, who had wanted to eliminate the ICC for a number of years, took control of Congress in 1995. As a first step, the fiscal 1996 spending bill gave the ICC no budget. Then the House Transportation and Infrastructure Committee approved a bill to dismantle the ICC, and the debate began. The major objection from the Democratic side was centered on protection for railroad workers who might lose their jobs because of mergers. After ironing out their differences, Congress sent President Bill Clinton legislation to terminate the ICC. On December 29, 1995, the 108-year-old ICC was disbanded.

SEE ALSO *Interstate Commerce*

BIBLIOGRAPHY

End of the line for ICC. (1996). *Nation's Business, 84*(3), 32.

ICC elimination. (1995–1996). *Congress and the Nation, 9,* 381–383.

President signs bill terminating ICC. (1996, January 6). *Congressional Quarterly Weekly Report, 54*(1), 58.

R.I.P., ICC. (1996, May/June). *American Heritage, 47*(3), 22.

Stone, R. D. (1991). *Interstate Commerce Commission and the railroad industry: A history of regulatory policy.* New York: Praeger.

Mary Jean Lush
Val Hinton

INTRANET/EXTRANET

The first global electronic network was the Internet, which is actually not one network, but a collection of smaller networks. This collection of networks is available to everyone who is connected to the Internet. The term *intranet,* however, refers to the type of private connections that are authorized only to persons who work within a particular organization. An *extranet* refers to connections that combine an organization's private network with partners, suppliers, or other outside agencies. What the intranet and extranet have in common with the Internet is that they all use Internet protocols. This means that user-friendly browser software—such as Internet Explorer—is the front end which links to all of the resources and requires little specialized training to use. *Intranet* and *extranet* are classifications of networks and few end users would know these terms. The distinctions, however, may be important to organizations.

While the typical computer user at home would have access only to the Internet, at work that same person could be using all three types of networks. The structure is invisible to users who know just that they are connected to the Internet and go about doing their daily tasks on the computer. At a workplace, access to the different channels or systems is granted by a background script when users log on and supply a password.

DEFINITIONS AND RELATIONSHIPS

To aid in understanding the different network classifications, here is an example: Maria, who is an administrative assistant in a local Ford automobile dealership, uses the Internet to access expedia.com to make travel arrangements for the dealership's owner to attend an upcoming sales meeting in Detroit. On the computer screen, Maria can also see the dealer's vehicle inventory and number of tires on hand. This would be classified as using the intranet. When Maria checks with a Firestone tire distributor for availability and pricing, however, a source clearly outside of the dealership, she would be using an extranet type of connection. Thus, Maria makes daily and seamless use of all three electronic networks without necessarily being conscious of the structural differences. It should be noted that many connections are not both ways. That is, the Firestone distributor cannot see how many cars are on hand at the Ford dealership, and the dealer cannot see the distributor's price on tires. Further, within an organization, not everybody would have access to the same information. Typically, access is granted on an as-needed basis, with appropriate authorization.

Internet. Although the Internet was initiated in the 1960s, its use in business has increased enormously since the 1990s. The CMP Media *TechEncyclopedia* defined *Internet* as:

(1) (Lower case "i"nternet) A large network made up of a number of smaller networks.

(2) (Upper case "I"nternet) The largest network in the world. It is made up of more than 100 million computers in more than 100 countries covering commercial, academic and government endeavors. Originally developed for the U.S. military, the Internet became widely used for academic and commercial research. Users had access to unpublished data and journals on a variety of subjects. Today, the Internet (also known as the Net) has become commercialized into a worldwide information highway, providing data and commentary on every subject and product on earth.

Intranet. The same work defines *intranet* as "An inhouse Web site that serves the employees of the enterprise. Although intranet pages may link to the Internet, an intranet is not a site accessed by the general public." The encyclopedia adds additional clarification as "The term as originally coined in the preceding definition has become so popular that it is often used to refer to any inhouse LAN [local area network] and client/server system rather than an HTTP-based Web server infrastructure."

Note the important difference: The intranet contains information that is available only to those who are "inhouse" (but not necessarily physically "in-house," the organization could have offices on multiple continents) or some type of corporate partner. Some additional typical uses of an intranet include access to production schedules, inventory, meetings, and training. The earlier example of Maria working at a Ford dealership is meant to be typical of a smaller organization. An establishment with global locations, however, could have a very complex intranet.

INTRANET USES

An organization's intranet may be used in many different ways. Besides data, ordering, and other uses that may well have been used prior to using Internet standards, today's intranet is frequently used for training and videoconferencing.

Employee Training. The American Society for Training and Development noted that classroom training was rapidly changing to electronic learning (e-learning) as corporations strove to meet widely scattered training needs ("Online and Corporate Universities," 2003). E-learning spans the range from training to operate call centers all the way up to learning corporate leadership skills; intranets are often used for this purpose.

Videoconferencing. An article in *PC Magazine* in January 2004 reported that while business travel had decreased, videoconferencing (also called Web conferencing or Webcasts) was increasing by leaps and bounds. The author of the article, L. Erlanger, went on to state:

> Yet we live in a global economy, and people in far-flung locations still need to meet. Increasingly, they are doing so via Web conferencing services, which lets both small and large groups of people share presentations and documents in real time over the Web. The services also deliver handy tools for collaboration, including chat rooms, whiteboards, document annotation, application sharing, Web polls, and Web tours.

This type of use would not be practical or cost effective without using the commonly available Internet standards on a firm's intranet.

EXTRANET

The CMP Media *TechEncyclopedia* defined *extranet* as:

> A Web site for customers rather than the general public. It can provide access to research, current inventories and internal databases, virtually any information that is private and not published for everyone. An extranet uses the public Internet as its transmission system, but requires passwords to gain entrance. Access to the site may be free or require payment for some or all of the services offered.

While companies may allow public access via the Internet to their Web site, this does not include links to sensitive information, but an intranet connection may allow access to much, but not all private data. According to Sanna Kallioranta and Richard Vlosky (2004), "An extranet serves as a bridge between the public Internet and the private intranet."

As an example, Company A manufactures computer monitors using liquid crystal displays (LCDs) made by Company B. Company A no doubt keeps an exact inventory of how many it has in stock; and it is possible that Company B is asked to monitor these numbers so that it can automatically ship LCDs to Company A when needed. As noted previously, Company B would not be granted access to other online data belonging to Company A. In another industry, construction, it is common for large construction projects to share information between contractors, architects, and engineers on schedules, progress, and drawings over is be classified as an extranet. Kallioranta and Vlosky also pointed out that using Internet protocols with an extranet is considerably less expensive than any other method.

ACCESS

Individual employees access to the Internet, intranets, and extranets varies with their need and is commonly assigned when they log on to the network. A top-level supervisor may have access to all levels of all systems. A network specialist is the person who assigns the correct codes to each employee. Since virtually all of a company's information is available via computer, who has access to what is an important issue in any organization. Further, every computer system on a network is a possible target of either hackers or spies from competing corporations. A hacker could destroy sensitive data, and a rival company could steal corporate secrets. Thus, every intranet and extranet has multiple layers of firewalls to ensure that access is obtained only by authorized people. Nevertheless, security is an ongoing concern.

DIGITAL ECONOMY

The Net has become an indispensable tool for businesses small and large. In 2004 Professor D. T. Quah from the University of London noted that "digital goods" take on increased meaning in the global marketplaces. Companies must embrace the Net and take every advantage to grow their businesses and remain viable in the twenty-first century. "Embracing the Net" includes using all aspects: Internet, intranet, and extranet.

IMPLICATIONS AND IMPACT

Net access to information has already drastically altered the way organizations communicate and conduct business. An employee does not need to know if the connection is via the open Internet, the private intranet, or the shared extranet. Access by unauthorized individuals is, however, a continuing issue. Nevertheless, Robert Moon, chief information officer of Micros Systems, said, "In less than three years, we've gone from the Web being a novelty to a critical application. It's now our main focus" (Booker, 1999, p. 32). Indeed, the worldwide Net concept will continue to alter the way organizations function both internally and externally in the twenty-first century, and in ways that could not be imagined in the twentieth century.

SEE ALSO *Internet*

BIBLIOGRAPHY

Booker, E. (1999, March 15). ERP's next frontier. *Internet Week,* pp. 31–32.

CMP Media. (2005). *TechEncyclopedia.* Retrieved January 19, 2006, from http://www.techweb.com/encyclopedia

Erlanger, L. (2004, January). Web conferencing: Take a meeting online. *PC Magazine.* Retrieved October 10, 2005, from http://www.pcmag.com

Gibson, S. (1998, November 16). Extranets' moment has come. *PC Week 133,* pp. 31–32.

Kallioranta, Sanna M., and Vlosky, Richard P. (2004). A model of extranet implementation success effects on business performance. Retrieved January 19, 2006, from http://www.rnr.lsu.edu/lfpdc/publication/papers/wp66.pdf

Online and corporate universities: Take learning to the head of the class. (2003, September). Retrieved January 19, 2006, from the *T+D* Web site: http://www.findarticles.com/p/articles/mi_m0MNT/is_9_57/ai_107490423

Quah, D. T. (2004) Digital goods and the new economy. Retrieved October 10, 2005, from the University of London–Centre for Economic Policy Research Web site: http://papers.ssrn.com/sol3/papers.cfm?abstract_id=410604

Armand Seguin
Cynthia Shelton (Anast) Seguin

INVENTORY CONTROL

Inventory control is the implementation of management's inventory policies in a manner that assures that the goals of inventory management are met. Wise control of inventory is often a critical factor in the success of businesses in which inventories are significant. The goal of inventory control is to be sure that optimum levels of inventories are available, that there are minimal stockouts (i.e., running out of stock), and that inventory is maintained in a safe, secure place and is always readily accessible to the proper personnel.

Policies relate to what levels of inventories are to be maintained and which vendors will be supplying the inventory. How and when inventories will be replenished, how inventory records are created, managed, and analyzed, and what aspects of inventory management will be outsourced are also important components of proper inventory management.

IN THE BEGINNING

Prior to the eighteenth century, possessing inventory was considered a sign of wealth. Generally, the more inventory you had, the more prosperous you were. Inventory existed as stores of wheat, herds of cattle, and rooms full of pottery or other manufactured goods.

This phenomenon occurred for good reason. There were a number of concerns for businesspeople then. Communication was difficult and unreliable, easily interrupted, and often took long periods of time to complete. Stocks were difficult to obtain, and supply was uncertain, erratic, and subject to a wide variety of pitfalls. Quality was inconsistent. More often than not, receiving credit for a purchase was not an option and a person had to pay for merchandise before taking possession of it. The financial markets were not as complex or as willing to meet the needs of business as they are today. In addition, the pace of life was a lot slower. Because change occurred gradually, it was relatively easy to forecast market needs, trends, and desires. Businesses were able to maintain large quantities of goods without fear of sudden shifts in the market, and these inventories served as buffers in the supply line. Customers had a sense of security, knowing that there was a ready supply of merchandise in storage, and that comfort often helped to minimize hoarding.

In the eighteenth and early nineteenth centuries, markets were very specialized. There was often one supplier for each market in each area of business. Except for the basic necessities of life, there was much local specialization and distinct specialization by region. For example, although there might be more than one grist-mill in a community, there would often be only one general store. If customers were unhappy with their existing supplier,

A properly organized warehouse aids in inventory control. ©
BENJAMIN RONDEL/CORBIS

they had to suffer some inconvenience to find an alternate source because of the monopolies that existed. This made it easier for businesses to market their products and allowed them to maintain large stocks if they had the capital to do so.

Inventory management was a concern then, as it is in the early twenty-first century. Inventories had to be monitored for accuracy and quality. They had to be protected from the elements, from theft, from spoiling, and from changes in the local economy. Tax laws could have an enormous impact on inventory levels.

THE EARLY TWENTY-FIRST CENTURY

The business world of the early twenty-first century shares few similarities with that of earlier times. Communication is quick, easy, reliable, and available through a host of media. Supply is certain and regular in most environments of merchandising and manufacturing. Tax laws are generally consistent and reliable. However, market changes can be abrupt and difficult to forecast. Global competition exists everywhere for almost everything. Products are available from anywhere in the world, with

delivery possible within in one day in many cases. Competition is driving the price of most products down to minimum profit levels. Inventories are managed for minimum stocking levels and maximum turnover. In the twenty-first century, high inventory is a sign of either mismanagement or a troubled economy. It is expensive and wasteful to hold and maintain high inventory levels. Proper utilization of space is also a critical component in today's business world, whether one is a retailer, wholesaler, or a manufacturer.

Modern retailers and manufacturers are equipped with an array of tools and support mechanisms to enable them to manage inventory. Technology is used in almost every area of inventory management to help control, monitor, and analyze inventory. Computers, especially, play an enormous role in modern inventory management.

INVENTORY MANAGEMENT SYSTEMS

Ongoing analyses of both inventory management and manufacturing processes have led to innovative management systems, such as just-in-time inventory or the economic-order quantity decision model.

Just-in-time inventory is a process developed by the Japanese based on a process invented by Henry Ford. David Wren (1999) describes how the process started:

> Henry Ford managed to cut his inventory by forty million dollars by changing how he obtained materials to produce automobiles. Through a process called vertical integration, Ford purchased mines and smelting operations to better control the source and supply of material to produce cars. In this way, he was able to reduce his standing inventory and increase turnover. In the 1950's, Taiichi Ohno, a mechanical engineer working for Toyota Motorcar Company, refined this process into what we know today as Just-in-Time inventory (p. 1).

Just-in-time inventory usually requires a dominant face—a major partner that has the resources to start the process and keep it organized and controlled—that organizes the flow and communication so that all the parties in the supply process know exactly how many parts are needed to complete a cycle and how much time is needed in between cycles. By having and sharing this information, companies are able to deliver just the right amount of product or inventory at a given time. This requires a close working relationship between all the parties involved and greatly minimizes the amount of standing or idle inventory.

In the economic-order quantity decision model, an analysis is made to determine the optimum quantity of product needed to minimize total manufacturing or production costs. In other words, through a complex analysis, management attempts to determine the minimum amount of product needed to do the job and still keep the cost of inventory as low as possible. This analysis considers the amount of time needed to generate an order; to process, manufacture, organize, and ship each product; to receive, inventory, store, and consume each product; and to process the paperwork upon receipt through the final payment process. This is a more independent process than just-in-time inventory; by allowing for a variety of suppliers to participate, it ensures competitiveness. Many companies today employ a mixture of both processes in order to maintain independence yet still have a close relationship with suppliers. Retailers, for example, work closely with suppliers to maintain the lowest possible inventories but still have enough products to satisfy customer demand. Often, companies have access to information about each other's inventory levels, allowing management to further analyze inventories to ensure that each is carrying the correct amount of stock to satisfy market needs and maintain minimum levels.

THE INVENTORY PROCESS

Inventory is generally ordered by computer, through a modem, directly from a supplier or manufacturer. The persons ordering the product have an inventory sales or usage history, which enables them to properly forecast short-term needs and also to know which products are not being sold or consumed. The computer helps management with control by tying in with the sales or manufacturing department. Whenever a sale is made or units of a product are consumed in the manufacturing process, the product is deleted from inventory and made part of a history file that can be reviewed manually or automatically, depending on how management wishes to organize that department. The supplier and the buyer often have a close working relationship; the buyer will keep the supplier informed about product changes and developments in the industry in order to maintain proper stock levels, and the supplier will often dedicate equipment and personnel to assist the buyer.

Even though small companies may work closely with larger suppliers, it is still very important that these small companies manage their inventory properly. Goods need to be stored in a suitable warehouse that meets the needs of the products. Some products require refrigeration, for example, while others require a warm and dry environment. Space is usually a critical factor in this ever-shrinking world since it is important to have enough space to meet the needs of customers and keep the warehouse from becoming overcrowded. Inventory needs to be monitored to prevent theft and inaccuracies. Taking physical inventory—physically checking each item against a list of items on hand—is a routine that should be performed a number of times a year. At the very least, inventories should always be checked each year just before the end of the fiscal year and compared against "book" or quantities listed as on hand in the computer or manual ledger. Adjustments can then be made to correct any inaccuracies. Taking inventory more than once a year, and thus looking at stocks over shorter periods of time, often results in discovering accounting or processing errors. It also serves as a notice to employees that management is watching the inventory closely, often deterring pilferage.

Alarm systems and closed-circuit television are just a few of the ways inventories can be monitored. Making sure that everyone allowed into inventory management systems has and uses his or her own password is critical to effective inventory control. By having redundant systems, management can also compare the two to make sure there is a balance. If they go too far out of balance, management is alerted.

IN THE END

Maintaining a clean, orderly, properly lighted, and secure warehouse or stockroom is the basic key to maintaining inventory control. Adding computer technology to aid in management and administration creates a system that is current and competitive. Properly training employees in modern techniques and standards results in a system that will be effective and profitable.

SEE ALSO *Costs*

BIBLIOGRAPHY

Burt, John (1992, February). "Controlling Inventory in Process Inventories: Integration is the Key." *Production & Inventory Management*, 12, 25, 29.

Christensen, David L. (1997, October). "Inventory Reviews—Inventory Control." *Internal Auditor*, 54, 50-53.

Malburg, Christopher R. (1994). *Controller's and Treasurer's Desk Reference*. New York: McGraw-Hill.

Thomas, Michael F., and Mackey, James T. (1994, April). "Activity-Based Cost Variances for Just-in-Times." *Management Accounting*, 75, 49-54.

Wren, Daniel A. (1999, September). "Just-in-Time Inventory." *Knowledge Management Magazine*.

Mark Lefebvre

INVESTMENTS

There was a time when many individuals thought that investing was for the rich and that very few people could afford to take on the risk that investments appeared to require. But, of course, times have changed; many Americans do invest. They realize that their long-term financial security does not look promising if it is based only on Social Security and company-provided pension plans. Both the numbers of people investing and the types of investments available have increased, especially since the early 1980s. The possibilities for investing funds are far more extensive than just stocks or bonds. In this entry, ten of the most popular investment instruments, from A (annuities) to Z (zero coupon bonds), will be discussed.

ANNUITIES

An annuity provides a means of reducing the risk of outliving one's investment income after retirement from full-time employment. Purchasing an annuity may be a possible solution to reducing this risk. An annuity may be considered the opposite of a traditional life insurance policy. An individual who buys insurance agrees to pay annual premiums to an insurance company. In return, the company will pay, according to instructions agreed upon at the time of purchase, the face value of the policy in a lump sum to beneficiaries when the purchaser dies.

By contrast, an individual who buys an annuity pays the insurance company a sum of money and, in return, will receive a monthly income for as long as the purchaser lives. Naturally, the longer one lives, the more money is received. The holder of an annuity never outlives the return, regardless of how long-lived the individual is. Life insurance protects one's beneficiaries against financial loss as a result of the purchaser's dying too soon, while annuities protect purchasers against financial loss as a result of living longer than their funds do.

Annuity income depends on life expectancy and is thus classified as life insurance. Understanding this is important because the classification allows the annuity's investment earnings to be treated as tax-deferred, with no tax on its accumulation until payments are received.

CERTIFICATE OF DEPOSIT

The concept of the certificate of deposit (CD) is simple. It is a savings instrument issued by a financial institution that pays the purchaser interest at a guaranteed rate for a specific term. When the CD reaches maturity, the investor receives the principal and interest earned. Unlike bond interest (paid periodically), the interest from a CD usually compounds, which means interest is earned on prior interest earned also. An investment in CDs, up to $100,000, is insured by the federal government.

CDs are appealing for safety, liquidity, and convenience. Less appealing is the lower yield when compared with other investments. CDs make sense as emergency funds, savings for short-term goals, a way to complete a long-term goal, and a place to "park" money while an investor seeks more profitable investments.

CORPORATE BONDS

A bond is a form of debt issued by a corporation in exchange for a sum of money lent by the buyer of the bond. The issuer of the bond promises to pay a specific amount of interest at stated intervals for a specific period. At the end of the repayment period (on the maturity date), the issuer repays the amount of money borrowed.

It is important to understand the differences between corporate bondholders and corporate stockholders. The holder of a corporate bond is a creditor of the corporation that issues the bond, not a part owner, as is a stockholder. Therefore, if the corporation's profits increase during the term of the bond, bondholders receive no benefit since the amount of interest they receive is fixed at the time the bond is purchased. On the other hand, the bondholders' investments are safer than those of the stockholders. Interest on bonds is paid out before dividends are distributed to stockholders. Furthermore, the claims of bondholders take precedence over those of the stockholders in the case of bankruptcy or liquidation.

When interest rates rise, bonds lose value; when interest rates fall, bonds become more attractive. Most bonds issued today are "callable," which means corporations can recall them if interest rates rise before the maturity dates.

GOLD

Some investors find gold an appealing investment. Gold has been used as money since biblical times. Several characteristics of gold have made it desirable as a medium of exchange and for investment. Gold is scarce. It is durable. More than 95 percent of all the gold ever mined during the past 5,000 years is still in circulation. It is inherently valuable because of its beauty and its usefulness in industrial and decorative applications.

Gold has been referred to as the "doomsday metal" because of its traditional role as a bulwark against economic, social, and political upheaval and the resulting loss of confidence in other investments, even those guaranteed by national governments.

As an investment, gold is not for the faint of heart or for people who desire a high level of predictability. Its value can fluctuate daily, owing to economic and political conditions. When interest rates in the United States fall, the dollar grows weaker in relation to other currencies. As a result, foreign businesspeople find U.S. investment less attractive, and some of them invest in gold instead. This forces the price of gold higher. When interest rates in the United States rise, the reverse occurs.

Investing in gold may be done in several ways: bullion, coins, shares and funds, and certificates. A number of companies specialize in the buying and selling of gold.

MONEY MARKET ACCOUNTS

Money market fund firms operate by combining many small investors' funds to accumulate the volume of money needed to buy money market instruments. Since the instruments purchased by the fund have differing maturities, the fund earns interest on a daily basis. Each investor receives a statement, usually monthly, of interest earned monthly. The amount earned on an investment varies continually as the current interest rates in the money market rise and fall.

A minimum deposit is required to open a money market account; $1,000 is typical. Additional funds may be added to one's investment at any time, and the funds are completely liquid—one can make withdrawals whenever one wishes.

Another important point about this type of investment: Because of the liquidity of a money market fund, it is an ideal way to invest idle cash that might otherwise find its way into a low-paying passbook savings account. For example, placing the proceeds from the sale of securities into a money market fund until one has decided upon one's next investment venture is a good way of earning continuous interest on one's money.

MUNICIPAL BONDS

Municipal bonds are issued by local and state governments to raise money to provide services and to build schools, roads, water and sewer facilities, and other public works. In order to meet these expenses, communities borrow money from citizens and institutions by issuing debt obligations known as municipal bonds (munis), which are tax-exempt.

Among the more popular varieties of municipal bonds available are the following:

1. *General obligation (GO) bonds.* These are backed by the full faith and credit of the issuing agency. Interest payments on GO bonds are supported by the taxing authority of the state or city government and are generally considered the safest form of municipal bond.

2. *Revenue bonds.* These are usually issued by a government agency or commission that has been charged with operating a self-supporting project, such as highway or bridge. The money raised through the sale of revenue bonds goes to finance the project, and the income realized from the completed project (tolls, for example) is used to pay the interest and principal on the bonds.

For the investor, the most important advantage of municipal bonds is that they earn interest income, which is tax-free at the federal level. If investors live in the state in which the bonds are issued, the bonds are usually free from state and local taxes as well. The downside of tax-free munis is high minimum investment requirements, lower yields, and the fact that the issuer can recall them before they mature.

MUTUAL FUNDS

Mutual funds are called mutual because a large number of investors' provided money to form a pool to be managed by knowledgeable investment professionals. The price of a share in the mutual fund is determined by the value of the fund's holdings. As the value of the stocks owned by the fund increases, the share price increases and the investors make a profit: If the value of the stocks decreases, the shares are worth less and investors suffer a loss. The price of a share in a mutual fund (determined by dividing the net value of the fund's assets by the number of shares outstanding) is usually announced once or twice a day. A mutual fund also earns dividends that may be paid directly to investors or reinvested to buy additional shares in the fund.

Therefore, mutual funds can make money for their investors in three distinct ways:

1. The shareholders receive dividends earned through the investment that the fund possesses.

2. If a security in the fund's portfolio is sold at a profit, a capital gains distribution will be made by the fund to its shareholders.

3. If the value of the fund's portfolio increases, the value of each share also increases.

Mutual funds offer an easy way to diversify money, control risk, and benefit from professional money management at a reasonable cost.

SAVINGS BONDS

The EE bond is a nonnegotiable security against the credit of the U.S. Treasury—nonnegotiable because once it is purchased, it cannot be resold to anyone else, but may be sold back only to the government at a fixed price. The bonds may, however, be transferred to someone else.

Series EE bonds are sold at half their face value and are available in denominations of $50, $100, $200, $500, $1,000, $5,000, and $10,000. Thus savings bonds are available for as little as $25, making them a practical choice for the investor with only a minimal amount of money to set aside. It is possible to purchase EE bonds online at TreasuryDirect (http://www.savingsbonds.

gov)—a government Web site that is run by the Bureau of the Public Debt, part of the U.S. Department of the Treasury—where the amount invested and what is paid differs from the paper EE bond just described.

Another type of savings bond is the I bond; it is sold at face value and will grow with inflation-indexed earnings for up to thirty years. The I bond can also be purchased online at TreasuryDirect.

There are advantages that both of these bonds possess:

- Competitive: Their rates of return are generally comparable to other forms of savings and accrue interest monthly and compound semiannually.

- Safe: They are backed by the full faith of the United States and are registered, which is helpful if bonds are lost, stolen or mutilated.

- Convenient: Bonds may be purchased at banks, online at TreasuryDirect, or where one works, if one's employer has such a deduction plan.

- Accessible: They are easily redeemable after six months.

- Tax benefits: The interest earned on savings bonds is exempt from all state and local income tax and is deferred for federal income tax until sale or maturity.

TREASURIES

Treasuries refers to a range of U.S. Treasury obligations. In a low-interest economy, many people switch to investments with higher yields, getting away from their traditional CDs. A safe and secure short-term investment that is an alternative for the CD is the Treasury bill (T-bill). Longer-term notes and bonds are also available.

Treasury obligations are tax-exempt at the state and local levels and are backed by "the full faith and credit" of the United States. The credit risk involved in this form of investment is considered practically nil. In comparison with similar obligations issued by corporations, Treasury obligations usually pay a yield, which is one or two percentage points lower. Many people, however, are willing to accept the slightly lower yield in exchange for the high level of safety.

There are four types of issues of Treasuries, which each require a minimum investment of $1,000. These are tax-free at state and local levels and can be bought through a broker, bank, or the Treasury. The T-bill is a thirteen- or twenty-six-week instrument that is issued at a discount but pays face value at maturity. Treasury notes earn and pay a fixed rate of interest every six months and are issued in terms of two, three, five, and ten years. Treasury bonds are sold at thirty-year maturities and pay interest every six

months. A fourth hybrid bond is a Treasury inflation-protected security, which provides protection against inflation based on the Consumer Price Index and is sold in terms of five, ten, and twenty years.

ZERO COUPON BONDS

Is there an instrument that lets an investor know exactly how much money will be available at a particular future date (whether it be for the education of one's child, retirement, etc.) and, if administered correctly, becomes tax deferred or even tax-exempt? Yes, the zero coupon bond meets these expectations.

Zero coupon bonds have some advantages over other types of long-term investments. They have become an excellent choice for individual retirement accounts, 401(k) plans, Keogh plans, and other pension funds, and most certainly for a child's college savings. They are therefore an ideal investment for investors who are more concerned about "outcome" rather than "income."

Bonds are debt obligations issued by a corporation or by a federal, state, or local government agency. When one buys a bond (usually at face value), one is buying a promise from the issuing institution to pay the amount of the face value of the bond at maturity.

Zero coupon bonds are sold at a price well below face value. Thus, these bonds are appealing to the small investor because they can be bought far more cheaply than ordinary debt obligations. The discount is usually from 50 to 75 percent.

SUMMARY

The variety of investments available provides varying advantages and disadvantages. A careful study of the different types in consideration of goals for investment and level of risk to be accepted is worthwhile. Such study provides the investor the basis for making decisions about the extent and nature of variability wanted in one's personal portfolio.

SEE ALSO *Bonds; Financial Literacy; Mutual Funds; Stocks*

BIBLIOGRAPHY

Graham, B., and Zweig, J. (2003). *The intelligent investor.* New York: HarperCollins.

Kiplinger's practical guide to your money (3rd ed.). (2005). Chicago: Dearborn.

Lange, J. (2006). *Retire secure.* Winchester, VA: Oakhill Press.

Tyson, Eric (2005). *Investment for dummies* (4th ed.). New York: Wiley.

Joel Lerner